Greek Lyric Poetry

Greek Lyric Poetry

A SELECTION
OF EARLY GREEK LYRIC
ELEGIAC AND IAMBIC
POETRY

by

DAVID A. CAMPBELL

Professor of Classics
University of Victoria
British Columbia, Canada

MACMILLAN

First edition 1967
Reprinted 1972

Published by
MACMILLAN EDUCATION LIMITED
Basingstoke and London
Macmillan Company of Australia Pty Ltd, Melbourne
Macmillan Company of Canada Ltd, Toronto
St Martin's Press Inc, New York
Companies and representatives
throughout the world

Library of Congress catalog card no. 67–17137

Printed in Great Britain by
ROBERT MACLEHOSE AND CO LTD
The University Press, Glasgow

TO CYNTHIA

οὐδέν, Κύρν', ἀγαθῆς γλυκερώτερόν ἐστι γυναικός.
μάρτυς ἐγώ . . .

Contents

Preface	*page* ix		
Introduction	xi		
Abbreviations	xxxi		
ARCHILOCHUS	1	*notes*	136
CALLINUS	8		161
TYRTAEUS	9		168
SEMONIDES	12		183
ALCMAN	18		192
MIMNERMUS	27		222
SOLON	29		231
STESICHORUS	38		253
SAPPHO	40		260
ALCAEUS	52		285
IBYCUS	63		305
ANACREON	67		313
XENOPHANES	74		331
PHOCYLIDES	77		342
DEMODOCUS	78		343
THEOGNIS	79		343
HIPPONAX	87		373
SIMONIDES	89		377

PRATINAS   *page* 100   *notes* 403

TIMOCREON   101   406

CORINNA   103   408

BACCHYLIDES   106   413

PRAXILLA   130   446

CARMINA POPULARIA   130   446

SCOLIA   132   449

Appendix on Metre   454
Index   461

Preface

BOTH as student and as lecturer I have bemoaned the lack of a suitably annotated text of the Greek lyric poets, and I hope that this volume will be found useful by others who have shared my plight. In writing it I have had the needs of sixth-formers and undergraduates in mind.

In a sense my book is a successor to Herbert Weir Smyth's *Greek Melic Poets*, published by Messrs. Macmillan & Co. in 1900 and now unhappily out of date, but it is not a revision of it: the commentary is on a less ample scale, and my selection of texts differs in that I include elegiac and iambic poetry and exclude poetry written after *c.* 450 B.C. There is no Pindar, because a poet of his importance deserves a volume of his own and would only be misrepresented by the selection of a few odes or fragments.

I have been fortunate in the timing of my work. Within recent years excellent texts of all the lyric poets have been published in *Poetarum Lesbiorum Fragmenta* (Edgar Lobel and Denys Page), *Poetae Melici Graeci* (Denys Page) and *Bacchylides* (Bruno Snell), and those who know these books will realise how much I am indebted to them. I have drawn heavily also on Professor Page's interpretative studies of Sappho and Alcaeus, Alcman and Corinna.

I have paid considerable attention to metrical matters in the hope that students will make an effort to master at least the easy metres. It is fairly certain that the rhythmical pattern of melody and words was identical; that is, the rhythm of the poem as sung was dictated solely by the longs and shorts of the words, not by the music, so that even if the melodies have disappeared beyond hope of recovery, we may at least enjoy and appreciate the rhythms.

I hope too that students will approach these poems in a critical spirit, prepared not to lump them together as a small package of the glory that was Greece, but to evaluate them separately and to be cautious in generalising. Criticism, however, will be valid only of poems which are or may be complete, and such poems are lamentably few; an image out of its context may be admired for the vividness or economy of its expression, but little else may be profitably said of it.

It is a pleasure to record my indebtedness to many friends: to the late Professor J. A. Davison for advice and encouragement in the early stages of the book and for the loan of material on Alcman and Stesichorus; to my colleagues Professors J. M. Cook, D. E. Eichholz and N. G. L. Hammond and to Mr. D. S. Raven for answering questions; to the librarian of the University of Bristol and his staff for obtaining rare books; to the *conseil* of the Fondation Hardt for a month's generous hospitality; to Miss M. Savery and Mr. S. E. Scully for help with the preparation of the manuscript; to Dr. A. B. Cottle for help with the proof-reading; and above all to Miss R. M. Harriott, who has read the work more than once, made many wise suggestions and corrected mistakes and inaccuracies. I am of course entirely to blame for errors which remain.

Introduction

ALL the poetry in this volume, with the exception of the work of Theognis, has survived not in regular manuscript tradition but through the haphazard discovery of papyrus scraps in Egypt or in quotation, usually fragmentary, in later writers who found the content, dialect, syntax, grammar or metre interesting. Such unity as the poems have may be found in two circumstances: they belong, roughly speaking, to the two centuries from 650 to 450; and they are short in comparison with epic poetry and drama.

To turn from Homer or even Hesiod to Archilochus is to enter a new world: we find the poet using an astonishing variety of metres with the greatest skill; and the material of his poetry is his own life — new surroundings, his love for a girl, the death of his brother-in-law, the treachery of a friend. If we move on to Alcman, our first writer of choral poetry, we find writing of great metrical complexity and baffling allusiveness: the singers, Spartan girls, at one moment relate a gloomy episode from Spartan mythology and at the next indulge in gay bantering of the choir-leaders.

The background of this poetry was the political, social and intellectual ferment of the Greek world in the seventh and sixth centuries, and much of the history of the period is reflected in, even reconstructed from, our poems. Political revolutions resulted in the almost complete disappearance of hereditary kingship and the rise of the tyrants: in the lyrics of Alcaeus we read the reactions of a man who took part in the struggle for power in Mytilene; his contemporary, Solon, used verse to record the aims of his legislation and to answer detractors in the years immediately before the establishment of tyranny in Athens; Theognis of Megara grumbles at the influx of peasants into the city, and exclaims against the new rich: πλοῦτος ἔμειξε γένος. The hardships of overseas settlers too are reflected in the poems: Archilochus left 'the figs and sea-faring life' of Paros for a new home and a dangerous life on Thasos. Trade flourished and men travelled abroad: Sappho's brother carried Lesbian wine to Egypt, and Alcaeus' brother fought in the army of Nebuchadrezzar: Hesiod's single sea-trip had been no further than from Aulis to Chalcis, and he can scarcely have enjoyed even that: δεινὸν δ' ἐστὶ θανεῖν μετὰ κύμασιν, he warns his brother.

Familiarity with other nations led to a reassessment of traditional ideas and values, and the Greeks began to think about man and his place in the universe. Thales, Anaximander and Anaximenes tried to understand the physical world and speculated about its origin. Xenophanes introduced relativism into religion by noting that the gods of the Ethiopians were snub-nosed and black, while Thracian gods were blue-eyed and red-haired, and he found fault with the gods as Homer and Hesiod portrayed them. Ethical questions were aired by Theognis and Simonides.

Little can be said with certainty about the development of music, but the ancients regarded the seventh century as a time of musical experiment; here too acquaintance with the instruments and theory of the East — Egypt, Babylon and Palestine — may have provided the impetus. Terpander, a musician and poet from Lesbos who worked in Sparta *c.* 650 B.C., is said to have given the lyre the seven strings which were standard for a century or more, and to have developed the cithara, a large concert-lyre. The potential of the aulos was explored by Clonas and other Peloponnesian musicians.

Writing was the most significant of all Greek borrowings, and it can hardly be by accident that our earliest surviving lyric poetry belongs to the years when our surviving examples of inscriptions suddenly become more numerous. Homer reveals that there was choral song and dance before Alcman, solo song before Archilochus; even without Homer's testimony we should have guessed as much. The earlier poetry was lost simply because it was neither written down nor transmitted like epic from one professional reciter to another. Archilochus was fortunate in that he or one of his companions decided that ἀσπίδι μὲν Σαΐων τις ἀγάλλεται or κήδεα μὲν στονόεντα or οὐ φιλέω μέγαν στρατηγόν was too good to be forgotten and had the skill and equipment with which to record it.

For the historical background A. R. Burn, *The Lyric Age of Greece* (London, 1960) is warmly recommended; for the philosophy G. S. Kirk and J. E. Raven, *The Presocratic Philosophers* (Cambridge, 1957), or W. K. C. Guthrie, *A History of Greek Philosophy* I (Cambridge, 1962); for the music Isobel Henderson, 'Ancient

Greek Music' in *The New Oxford History of Music*, vol. I, 336–403, or the article on Music in *The Oxford Classical Dictionary*; for writing and early poetry the contributions by Denys Page and K. J. Dover to Entretiens sur l'Antiquité Classique, tome X, *Archiloque* (Geneva, 1964).

The term 'lyric poetry' is used loosely to cover a wide variety of types, and it is important to remember the distinctions between them, so far as they are known and intelligible. The widest distinction is between poetry which was sung by a chorus and poetry which was performed by an individual; within the second of these types we distinguish between solo-song (monody), written in lyric metres and probably sung to lyre accompaniment, and elegiac and iambic poetry, not normally set to music but recited or at most intoned.

CHORAL POETRY

Three elements were united in this art-form, words, music and dance; and since nothing remains but the words, we can form only a faint idea of a performance. We surmise that the music was sung in unison, and that the accompanying instrument supplied the pitch, perhaps in a prelude, and then supported the melody in unison with the singers; but there is no hope of recovering the music of Alcman or even Pindar, and even if we did and could decipher it with confidence, we should not enjoy it. The dance was performed by the singers and was interpretative. Some idea of it may be obtained from vase-paintings and from accounts and allusions in ancient writers: for example, the geranos-dance, instituted on Delos by Theseus, represented his safe passage through the maze of the labyrinth. So far as we know, the poet was also the composer of the music, the chorus-master and the choreographer.

The three elements are clearly mentioned in the *Homeric Hymn to Apollo* (182 ff.): on Olympus the Muses sing of the joys of the gods and the sufferings of men, while the Graces and Hours dance with Harmonia, Hebe and Aphrodite, holding each other by the wrist; Artemis sings too, and Ares and Hermes sport among them; Apollo meanwhile plays his lyre and dances, καλὰ καὶ ὕψι βιβάς. A similar scene on earth was represented on Achilles' shield (*Il.* 18.590 ff.); it must have been typical of performances known to Homer himself, say *c.* 800 B.C. 'Youths and marriageable maidens were dancing on (the dancing-floor) with their hands on one another's wrists. . . . Here they ran lightly round, circling as smoothly on their accomplished feet as the wheel of a potter when he sits and works it with his hands to see if it will spin; and there they ran in lines to meet each other. A large crowd stood round enjoying the delightful dance, with a minstrel among them singing divinely to the lyre, while a couple of acrobats, keeping time with his music, threw cart-wheels in and out among the people' (tr. E. V. Rieu). Elsewhere on the shield Hephaestus had shown wedding processions in the streets, 'and the wedding-song rose loud, as boys danced whirling about and pipes and lyres kept up

their song' (491 ff.), and yet another scene had
music-makers — the vintage, where merry girls and
youths, carrying their grapes in baskets, danced round
a young boy who played the lyre and sang the lovely
Linus-song; 'and they beat out the rhythm and went
skipping along with song and shout' (567 ff.). A
scholiast on the passage gives a prose version of the
lament for the dead Linus, reconstructed by Bergk as
ὦ Λίνε πᾶσι θεοῖσι | τετιμένε, σοὶ γὰρ ἔδωκαν | πρώτῳ
μέλος ἀνθρώποισι | φωναῖς λιγυραῖς ἀεῖσαι· | Φοῖβος
δὲ κότῳ σ' ἀναιρεῖ, | Μοῦσαι δέ σε θρηνέουσιν (P.M.G.
880).

The germs of two other types of choral song appear
in the *Iliad* — the dirge and the paean. At Hector's
funeral professional singers begin the dirge (ἀοιδοὺς |
θρήνων ἐξάρχους), and the womenfolk take up the
keening; then Andromache, Hecuba and Helen
lament in turn, and each is followed by the keening of
the women (*Il.* 24.720 ff.: cf. *Od.* 24.58 ff.). The Greek
army twice sings a paean in the *Iliad*, when Apollo
puts an end to the pestilence (1. 472–4), and as a
triumphal song when Achilles kills Hector (22.391–2).
In *h. Ap.* 517–18 the ἰηπαιήων is sung by the musicians
of Crete.

In Homer, then, we find examples of songs of
celebration, of triumph, of thanksgiving and of
mourning. In none are the three elements of words,
song and dance united so closely as in later choral
poetry (cf. e.g. Pi. *P.* 1.1–4), but they are present in
various combinations and each is important. We
cannot say how developed the songs were, and it is
possible that the paean was little more than the cry

ἰὴ Παιάν, the wedding-song the simple Ὑμὴν ὦ Ὑμέναιε.

Our first examples of choral lyric belong to Sparta, where, as we have seen, Terpander and other pioneers of music-making lived and taught. Alcman is known to us as a writer of partheneia, songs for choruses of girls, but hymns and wedding-songs also were ascribed to him by ancient writers, and a small amount of his poetry seems to have been love-song for solo performance. If the Louvre Partheneion, our only large fragment, is typical of his work, he combined the narration of heroic story with gay allusions to his chorus-members and other figures of contemporary Sparta. The narrative deals with heroes of Spartan mythology, and we are left with an impression of a somewhat parochial composer whose work baffles not by the complexity of the writing but by its domestic allusions. We cannot say for certain whether he was the first to use triadic structure for choral poetry.

Our next choral composers, Stesichorus and Ibycus, belong to Sicily and Italy. Stesichorus wrote narrative songs in metres which were largely dactylic, and differs from Alcman in the catholicity of his choice of material: his myths were the tales of Troy, the Argonauts, Heracles, Thebes and Meleager — the myths treated in Epic poetry before him and by lyric poets and tragedians later. We are told that all his poetry was written in triadic structure, which implies choral performance, and the truth of this is not altered by the fact that some of his poetry was later performed as scolia in drinking-parties. The Sicilian fondness for choral poetry which we notice in the early fifth century may well have been created or fostered by Stesichorus. Ibycus wrote poetry so like that of Stesichorus that posterity sometimes had difficulty in distinguishing their work. He too took the great Greek myths as material for his narrative poetry. Unlike Stesichorus, he wrote love-poetry also, perhaps when he had left Italy for the circle of Polycrates of Samos to become the first court-poet of whom we hear after the Homeric bards. *P.M.G.* 282(a), the long papyrus fragment attributed to Ibycus or an imitator, provides an example of choral poetry used to flatter or at least commemorate the tyrant or his son. Anacreon, the other distinguished poet of the Samian court, was remembered especially for his amatory solo-songs, but we hear also of his partheneia.

Before Anacreon died the heyday of choral poetry had begun: Simonides was approximately his contemporary, and Pindar and Bacchylides belonged to the next generation. These three wrote choral songs of a bewildering variety of types, classified painstakingly but not always helpfully or even accurately by Alexandrian scholars. The life of Pindar in the Ambrosian MS. says that he wrote 17 books: Hymns, Paeans, Dithyrambs (2 books), Processional Songs (Προσόδια: 2 books), Partheneia (3 books), Dance-Songs ('Υπορχήματα: 2 books), Eulogies ('Εγκώμια), Dirges (Θρῆνοι) and Victory-odes ('Επινίκια: 4 books); most of these nine types of choral song were attributed to Simonides and Bacchylides also. We shall concern ourselves with five: paean, dithyramb, eulogy, victory-ode and dirge.

Paean

The two occasions on which a paean was sung by Homer's Greeks (*Il.* 1.473, 22.391 ἀείδοντες παιήονα) have already been noted; it seems likely that the song consisted only of the chanting of the formula ἰὴ Παιάν, 'Hail, Apollo.' Archilochus speaks of beginning the Lesbian paean to aulos accompaniment (76 αὐτὸς ἐξάρχων πρὸς αὐλὸν Λέσβιον παιήονα), and a fragment of Alcman shows that paeans were sung in the men's messes in seventh-century Sparta (98 θοίναις δὲ καὶ ἐν θιάσοισιν | ἀνδρείων παρὰ δαιτυμόνεσσι πρέπει παιᾶνα κατάρχην); but even these paeans need have been no more than the ritual chant. The early literary paean, sung by a choir and probably accompanied by the lyre, Apollo's instrument, was composed for religious occasions; Pindar's examples preserve the connexion with Apollo, although Sophocles addressed one to Asclepius, god of healing, and later we hear of paeans to Zeus, Poseidon, Dionysus and others. In Pindar's 5th *Paean* the refrain ἰήϊε Δάλι' Ἄπολλον occurs at the beginning of each five-line stanza, but in others there is no refrain at all.

Dithyramb

The word occurs first in Archilochus: ὡς Διωνύσοι' ἄνακτος καλὸν ἐξάρξαι μέλος | οἶδα διθύραμβον οἴνῳ συγκεραυνωθεὶς φρένας (77); the intoxication of the singer as he begins the melody makes it probable that this dithyramb was not a ceremonial choral hymn but a song sung like a paean at a party, perhaps of no artistic pretensions.

Herodotus (1.23) says that Arion of Lesbos wrote

and produced the first dithyrambs (in Corinth at the time of Periander, *c.* 600 B.C.), and we may believe that it was he who made the dithyramb an art-form. It seems to have been of two kinds: the song in Dionysus' honour, such as those Pindar composed for Athenians and Thebans or those sung at Delphi instead of the paean during Apollo's absence in the winter months; and the poem sung in competition at the Athenian festivals of the Dionysia and Thargelia by choirs of fifty men or boys. It was in these dithyrambs that Aristotle found the origin of tragedy, and they seem to have been regarded less as lyric poetry than as drama by Alexandrian scholars. The dithyramb had a strong narrative element, and in its early days had triadic structure; but changes were made in the early fifth century, and Bacchylides' *Theseus* is an example of unorthodoxy with its strophic construction and dramatic form. The proper instrument for dithyrambic accompaniment in our period was the aulos; *c.* 500 B.C. Pratinas protested against the growing importance of the instrumentalist at the expense of the chorus.

Eulogy (ἐγκώμιον)

By derivation the ἐγκώμιον μέλος is a song sung ἐν κώμῳ, at a revel, but the term came to be used of a song in honour of a distinguished man, perhaps originally the man whose dinner-party was followed by the κῶμος. Pindar uses the adjective ἐγκώμιος in contexts which indicate that it means roughly the same as ἐπινίκιος (e.g. *O.* 2.47: the victorious Theron deserves ἐγκωμίων . . . μελέων), and in Aristophanes (fr. 491 K.) and Plato (*Lg.* 822b) the ἐγκώμιον is clearly a victory-song. But when the Alexandrians classified lyric poetry, they distinguished between ἐπινίκια and ἐγκώμια, using the term ἐγκώμιον for any eulogy that was neither a dirge nor a victory-ode. So it is applied to the poems written by Pindar in honour of Thrasybulus of Acragas (see on Bacch. fr. 20B,) Hiero of Syracuse and others, and to Bacchylides' poem for Alexander (fr. 20B).

Victory-ode (ἐπινίκιον)

Thanks to the survival of the four books of Pindar we can speak with more confidence about this genre.

At the beginning of *Olympian* 9 Pindar contrasts his ode, performed when the victor had reached home, with the song of Archilochus which greeted the victor at the moment of his triumph at Olympia: καλλίνικος ὁ τριπλόος κεχλαδώς, he calls it, 'the triple καλλίνικος that rang out', and the scholiasts tell us that the song ran τήνελλα | ὦ καλλίνικε χαῖρ' ἄναξ Ἡράκλεες, | αὐτός τε καὶ Ἰόλαος, αἰχμητὰ δύο (fr. 120): cf. Ar. *Ach.* 1233-4 τήνελλα καλλίνικος ᾄδοντες, *Av.* 1764. It was addressed to Heracles as founder of the Olympic Games; τήνελλα is said to have been a representation of the sound of the lyre, and καλλίνικε must have been a refrain.

In *Nemean* 4, written for Timasarchus of Aegina, winner of the boys' wrestling-match, Pindar mentions that the boy's grand-father once celebrated a victory won by his uncle (89-90), and says that if the boy's father were still alive, he would be celebrating the present victory, singing to the cithara (13-16): we glimpse here an intimate family celebration, perhaps the forerunner of the epinician. The first epinician odes for choral presentation were probably written by Simonides, and the art-form was associated above all with him, his nephew Bacchylides and their rival Pindar.

We can say little with certainty about Simonides' methods, except that mythology sometimes occupied much of a poem. He wrote in honour of victors in a wide variety of events and from cities in Sicily, Italy and Thessaly as well as Carystus, Eretria and Aegina.

In the long formal odes of Pindar and Bacchylides three elements are usually found: mention of the victory, the victor, his family and his home town; the narration of a myth, usually connected with the victor's city or family; and some moralising, often of an austerity surprising in a festive poem. Pindar's odes, though not those of Bacchylides, are distinguished by the richness and boldness of their imagery. Pindar's were sung to the accompaniment of the lyre (e.g. *P.* 1.1 ff.) or the lyre and auloi together (e.g. *O.* 3.8–9); Bacchylides mentions auloi in the short poem for Argeius of Ceos (2.12) and auloi, perhaps mingling with lyres, in 10.54–5 (cf. 9.68).

Dirge (θρῆνος)

The lamentation at Hector's funeral (*Il.* 24.720 ff.) has already been mentioned. There the professional bards ἐθρήνεον, while the women ἐπὶ ... στενάχοντο and Andromache, Hecuba and Helen in turn led the γόος of the women, using words which expressed their personal loss. Perhaps the θρῆνος of the professionals embodied general material which they could apply to any bereavements, e.g. the thought that all men must die.

In the few remaining fragments of θρῆνοι Simonides speaks of the feebleness of man, the brevity of life and the inevitability of death, and this is the content of Cassandra's brief θρῆνος in A. *Ag.* 1322 ff. Pindar offers comfort in the idea that the soul is immortal. The grammarians tell us that the θρῆνος also included a eulogy of the dead man. It is unsafe to generalise from the extant scraps, but they suggest that the artistic θρῆνος was a song not of passionate lament but of quiet reflection and consolation.

For fuller accounts of choral lyric see the introduction to H. Weir Smyth, *Greek Melic Poets*, J. M. Edmonds, *Lyra Graeca* iii, 583–679, A. E. Harvey, 'The Classification of Greek Lyric Poetry', *C.Q.* n.s. 5 (1955), 157–75, A. W. Pickard-Cambridge, *Dithyramb, Tragedy and Comedy*[2] (1962).

MONODY

Monody or solo-song in lyric metres is represented only by the two great poets of Lesbos, Sappho and Alcaeus, by Ibycus and Anacreon and by the anonymous scolia.

Sappho's poetry, written for her own need or the pleasure of her friends, is concerned with her emotions — her loves, hates and jealousies — and with the activities of her family and friends. Hardly any of it was meant for a wide audience: she wrote some wedding-songs, and a little of her poetry is narrative;

her invocations of Aphrodite are private. Alcaeus, her contemporary, shows a man's wider interests: he wrote political poems, vituperative rather than reflective, and drinking-songs, together with love-poetry, now mostly lost, and hymns to deities and heroes. Both poets display great craftsmanship in the construction of their poems, and they speak directly and concisely with a notable lack of artifice. It is usually assumed that they sang their poetry to their own accompaniment on the barbitos, a lyre with longer strings and deeper register than the λύρα, but there is little firm evidence, and some of their poetry may have been spoken. They used the vernacular of the island almost exclusively, and wrote in a rich variety of metres.

The two finest surviving poems of Ibycus (286 and 287) can hardly have been other than solo-song; that he should write personal love-poetry is not surprising if Anacreon was his contemporary at Polycrates' court. Anacreon's extant poems are mostly witty pieces about love and wine; he wrote in gay, simple metres, and the architecture of his poems was masterly.

The Attic scolia or drinking-songs were probably improvisations, composed in the late sixth and fifth centuries at Athenian drinking-parties and preserved because of their high quality. Many were political, some were prayers to gods, others had a moral content.

ELEGIAC COUPLETS

The elegiac couplet was well described by W. R. Hardie, *Res Metrica* 49, as 'a variation upon the heroic hexameter, in the direction of lyric poetry'. Its first line is a heroic hexameter; its second line, misleadingly called the pentameter, begins with a hexameter-opening of the type μῆνιν ἄειδε, θεά, pauses and then repeats itself, so that the pattern of the whole couplet is an approximation to ab/aa. This rhythm seems to have commended itself for use in poems on a scale smaller than epic, although long narrative poems in elegiac couplets are not unknown: Semonides is said to have used the metre for his *History of Samos*, and Mimnermus used it for his *Smyrneis*. It was above all the vehicle for exhortation and for reflection on a wide variety of themes — warfare, politics, ethics, man's life in general. Its form helped the poet to marshal his ideas into brief, striking phrases, often made more memorable by the balance and even the internal rhyme of the pentameter.

The earliest surviving elegiacs were written in the middle of the seventh century by Archilochus, Callinus, Tyrtaeus and perhaps also Semonides. Which of these was the earliest is a question which exercised the ancients; it seems likely that none of them was the 'inventor' of the couplet, but that they were all working within a tradition of elegiac poetry, and that they owe their survival to the development of writing. Our earliest inscribed pentameter belongs to the second half of the seventh century: a kettle-rim of that date, found on Samos (the birthplace of Semonides), has the inscription με]γάλης ἀντὶ φιλημ[οσύνης (Friedländer 94).

The range of our first elegiac couplets is astonishing. Archilochus, Callinus and Tyrtaeus use them to exhort troops to battle; Tyrtaeus uses them also for

wider political purposes, probably to inspire the
Spartans with pride in the achievements and institu-
tions of their country. In Archilochus we find pithy
epigrams on military topics — the use of his spear, the
loss of his shield; a witty couplet (if it is authentic) on
the easily accessible girl whom they called Pasiphile;
two proud lines of autobiography; and a poem or
poems of consolation written after a shipwreck. If
Semonides is rightly included in the earliest group, we
can point also to his history of his birthplace, Samos,
and to a reflective poem, prompted by a line of
Homer, on the brevity of man's life.

This diversity of theme makes it unlikely that the
elegiac couplet had its origins in the θρῆνος as Horace
claimed: *versibus impariter iunctis querimonia primum,* /
mox etiam inclusa est voti sententia compos (*A.P.* 75–6). It
seems more likely that the couplet was used for epitaphs as for dedications because of its effectiveness for
brief statement. The epitaph in elegiac metre appears
first only *c.* 560 B.C. and was perfected by Simonides
at the time of the Persian Wars.

A close connexion between the elegiac couplet and
the aulos is usually regarded as proven: Bowra, for
example, writes, 'In practice the elegiac couplet
seems to have been a song sung to the accompaniment
of the flute, just as lyric poetry was sung to the lyre'
(*E.G.E.* 5–6). Archilochus' couplets 'were probably
improvised and sung in the intervals of fighting, when
someone had a flute and the poet was called upon for a
song' (8–9: cf. 42, 141). But the evidence, which
comes mainly from late historians, geographers and
lexicographers, is inconclusive: elegiacs may well have

been set to aulos accompaniment for festival performances, or, as in the case of Theognis, for convivial
occasions, but we need not imagine that all elegiacs
were sung to the aulos. Solon was said to have recited
his *Salamis* in the agora, and it may be prudent to
imagine the elegiacs of Tyrtaeus and the others as
recited rather than sung.

Another feature which would give some unity to the
corpus of early elegiac poetry was suggested by
Jaeger (*Paideia*, tr. Highet i. 86): 'Apart from the
elegiac metre itself ... there is only one constant
element in elegiac poetry. It is always *addressed to
someone*: either to one individual or to a collection of
people.' This generalisation is a useful reminder of the
didactic nature of much early elegiac, but it is not true
even of the few fragments we possess: Archilochus'
short epigrams have no addressee, frr. 1 and 17 of
Solon, almost certainly complete poems, are addressed
to no-one, and there is no mention of an addressee in
Mimnermus 1 and 2, although our text may be
complete. Even if Jaeger's generalisation were true,
it would not distinguish elegiac from, say, the iambic
fr. 1 of Semonides.

See J. M. Edmonds, *Elegy and Iambus* i. 1–38,
Friedländer, *Epigrammata* 65–145, David A. Campbell,
'Flutes and Elegiac Couplets', *J.H.S.* 84 (1964),
63–8.

IAMBIC AND TROCHAIC POETRY

Aristotle (*Poet.* 1449a.24) said that iambics were closer
than any other metre to the rhythms of conversation.

This may be why we find the metre used for proverbial sayings, such as παχεῖα γαστὴρ λέπτον οὐ τίκτει νόον, and for cult-ritual in the Anthesteria and the Eleusinian Mysteries; both uses are likely to have a long history. The trochaic rhythm too, often classed as iambic in ancient writers, appears as a vehicle for folk-lore: σῖτον ἐν πηλῷ φύτευε, τὴν δὲ κριθὴν ἐν κόνει.

The iambics and trochaics of Archilochus display the structural features which are standard in later writers. 'Plutarch', having no earlier examples, called Archilochus the inventor of both metres (de Mus. 28.1141a); inventor or not, he is likely to have left his mark on them. He uses iambics for an extended composition — P. Oxy. 2310 fr. 1, col. i has some fifty trimeters —, but no other long fragment survives. The extant pieces are concerned with a variety of subjects. Personal abuse, for which iambics were later regarded as the appropriate medium, belongs to the stanzas built of trimeter and dimeter. His trochaic tetrameters too cover a wide range of subjects, but they are most frequently used for solemn reflection. He sometimes mixes iambics and trochaics with dactylic lengths.

Semonides of Amorgos used simple iambic trimeters both for pessimistic comment on man's life and for frivolous satirical lines on women. Hipponax varied the trimeter by distorting the end of the line, and used this 'limping' iambic (σκάζων or χωλίαμβος) for harsh satirical verse often on squalid matters in what seems to have been a deliberate attempt to vulgarise poetry. Anacreon used a predominantly iambic rhythm for his virulent attack on Artemon

(388), graceful trochaics for his delicious πῶλε Θρηκίη (417).

In Athens, however, Solon had used both iambics and trochaics for a serious purpose, the defence of his political reforms. This is vigorous poetry, more lively and direct than the elegiac couplets in which most of his extant work is written, and it may have helped to pave the way for the iambics of drama.

There is little in our surviving poetry to substantiate Aristotle's suggestion that the trochaic metre was less dignified than the iambic (*Poet.* 1449a.22), but it would certainly be more monotonous in extended compositions. It may well have been the earlier of the two: see A. M. Dale, *C.Q.* n.s. 13 (1963), 47.

Abbreviations

THE following books have been referred to in abbreviated form or by the author's name:

C. M. Bowra, *Early Greek Elegists*, Cambridge, Mass., 1938 (*E.G.E.*); *Greek Lyric Poetry*², Oxford, 1961 (*G.L.P.*)

A. R. Burn, *The Lyric Age of Greece*, London, 1960

J. Carrière (ed.), *Théognis, poèmes élégiaques*, Paris, 1948 (Budé)

P. Chantraine, *Grammaire Homérique*, 2 vols., Paris, 1948, 1953 (*G.H.*)

Companion to Homer, ed. A. J. B. Wace and F. H. Stubbings, London, 1962

J. Defradas, *Les Élégiaques Grecs*, Paris, 1962

J. D. Denniston, *The Greek Particles*², Oxford, 1954 (*G.P.*)

H. Diels, *Die Fragmente der Vorsokratiker*, 3 vols., 6th ed. by W. Kranz, Berlin, 1951–2 (D.-K.)

J. M. Edmonds, *Elegy and Iambus*, 2 vols., London, 1931 (Loeb); *Lyra Graeca*, 3 vols., London, 1922–7 (Loeb)

H. Fränkel, *Dichtung und Philosophie des frühen Griechentums*², Munich, 1962

P. Friedländer (with H. B. Hoffleit), *Epigrammata*: Greek Inscriptions in Verse from the beginnings to the Persian Wars, Berkeley and Los Angeles, 1948

W. W. Goodwin, *Syntax of the Moods and Tenses of the Greek Verb*, London, 1929 (*M.T.*)

T. Hudson-Williams, *Early Greek Elegy*, London, 1926;
  The Elegies of Theognis, London, 1910

R. Kühner, *Ausführlich Grammatik der griechischen
  Sprache*: 3rd ed., part II, Syntaxe, by B. Gerth,
  1898–1904

R. Lattimore (tr.), *Greek Lyrics*[2], Chicago, 1960

B. Lavagnini, *Aglaia: Nuova Antologia della Lyrica
  Greca da Callino a Bacchilide*, Turin, 1937

E. Lobel and D. Page, *Poetarum Lesbiorum Fragmenta*,
  Oxford, 1955 (L.-P.)

D. Page, *Alcman: the Partheneion*, Oxford, 1951;
  Poetae Melici Graeci, Oxford, 1962 (*P.M.G.*);
  Sappho and Alcaeus, Oxford, 1955 (*S. & A.*); *Lyrica
  Graeca Selecta*, Oxford, 1968 (*L.G.S.*)

A. W. Pickard-Cambridge, *Dithyramb, Tragedy and
  Comedy*[2], rev. T. B. L. Webster, Oxford, 1962
  (*D.T.C.*)

J. U. Powell, *Collectanea Alexandrina*, Oxford, 1925

D. S. Raven, *Greek Metre*, London, 1962 (*G.M.*)

R. Reitzenstein, *Epigramm und Skolion*, Giessen, 1893

M. N. Tod, *A Selection of Greek Historical Inscriptions*[2],
  Oxford, 1946 (*G.H.I.*)

T. B. L. Webster, *Greek Art and Literature* 700–530 B.C.,
  London, 1959 (*G.A.L.*)

U. von Wilamowitz-Moellendorff, *Sappho und Simonides*, Berlin, 1913 (*S.S.*)

D. Young (ed.), *Theognis*, Leipzig, 1961 (Teubner)

Authors and periodicals are for the most part
referred to by the abbreviations used in Liddell and
Scott, *Greek-English Lexicon*, 9th ed., revised by H.
Stuart Jones (1925–40).

The numbering of the elegiac and iambic poets is that of E. Diehl, *Anthologia Lyrica Graeca*, rev. R. Beutler, Leipzig, 1949, 1952 (Teubner). For Sappho and Alcaeus I have used the marginal numbers of E. Lobel and D. Page, *Poetarum Lesbiorum Fragmenta*, for Bacchylides the numbers in the editions of Kenyon and Snell, for the other lyric poets the marginal numbers of D. Page, *Poetae Melici Graeci*.

Angular brackets ⟨ ⟩ indicate words or letters mistakenly omitted by a scribe.

Square brackets [ ] indicate a lacuna in the text.

Dots below letters indicate that the reading is uncertain. Dots within brackets represent the estimated number of letters lost, dots outside brackets mutilated or otherwise illegible letters.

Greek Lyric Poetry

ARCHILOCHUS

(1)

εἰμὶ δ' ἐγὼ θεράπων μὲν Ἐνυαλίοιο ἄνακτος
  καὶ Μουσέων ἐρατὸν δῶρον ἐπιστάμενος.

1 εἰμὶ δ' ἐγὼ Ath.   ἀμφότερον Plu., Them.   ἄνακτος Ath. θεοῖο
Plu., Them.   2 ἐρατᾶν Plu.

(2)

ἐν δορὶ μέν μοι μᾶζα μεμαγμένη, ἐν δορὶ δ' οἶνος
  Ἰσμαρικός, πίνω δ' ἐν δορὶ κεκλιμένος.

(3)

οὔ τοι πόλλ' ἐπὶ τόξα τανύσσεται οὐδὲ θαμειαί
  σφενδόναι, εὖτ' ἂν δὴ μῶλον Ἄρης συνάγῃ
ἐν πεδίῳ· ξιφέων δὲ πολύστονον ἔσσεται ἔργον·
  ταύτης γὰρ κεῖνοι δαίμονές εἰσι μάχης
δεσπόται Εὐβοίης δουρικλυτοί.   5

(5A)

ἀλλ' ἄγε σὺν κώθωνι θοῆς διὰ σέλματα νηός   6
  φοίτα καὶ κοίλων πώματ' ἄφελκε κάδων,
ἄγρει δ' οἶνον ἐρυθρὸν ἀπὸ τρυγός· οὐδὲ γὰρ ἡμεῖς
  νήφειν ἐν φυλακῇ τῇδε δυνησόμεθα.

(6)

ἀσπίδι μὲν Σαΐων τις ἀγάλλεται, ἣν παρὰ θάμνῳ
    ἔντος ἀμώμητον κάλλιπον οὐκ ἐθέλων,
αὐτὸν δ᾽ ἐξεσάωσα. τί μοι μέλει ἀσπὶς ἐκείνη;
    ἐρρέτω· ἐξαῦτις κτήσομαι οὐ κακίω.

3 αὐτόν μ᾽ Olymp., Elias ψυχὴν δ᾽ Ar. αὐτὸς δ᾽ ἐξέφυγον θανάτου
τέλος Sext.

(7)

κήδεα μὲν στονόεντα, Περίκλεες, οὔτε τις ἀστῶν
    μεμφόμενος θαλίῃς τέρψεται οὐδὲ πόλις·
τοίους γὰρ κατὰ κῦμα πολυφλοίσβοιο θαλάσσης
    ἔκλυσεν· οἰδαλέους δ᾽ ἀμφ᾽ ὀδύνῃς ἔχομεν
πνεύμονας. ἀλλὰ θεοὶ γὰρ ἀνηκέστοισι κακοῖσιν,   5
    ὦ φίλ᾽, ἐπὶ κρατερὴν τλημοσύνην ἔθεσαν
φάρμακον. ἄλλοτέ τ᾽ ἄλλος ἔχει τάδε· νῦν μὲν ἐς ἡμέας
    ἐτράπεθ᾽, αἱματόεν δ᾽ ἕλκος ἀναστένομεν,
ἐξαῦτις δ᾽ ἑτέρους ἐπαμείψεται. ἀλλὰ τάχιστα
    τλῆτε γυναικεῖον πένθος ἀπωσάμενοι.   10

2 μεμφόμενος: μυρόμενος ci. Meineke, alii alia   4 ὀδύνῃ ἴσχομεν
et sim. codd., em. Gaisford   7 τ᾽ et δ᾽ codd.

(18)

ἥδε δ᾽ ὥστ᾽ ὄνου ῥάχις
ἕστηκεν ὕλης ἀγρίης ἐπιστεφής.

οὐ γὰρ τι καλὸς χῶρος οὐδ᾽ ἐφίμερος
οὐδ᾽ ἐρατός, οἷος ἀμφὶ Σίριος ῥοάς.

(22)

‘οὔ μοι τὰ Γύγεω τοῦ πολυχρύσου μέλει
οὐδ᾽ εἷλέ πώ με ζῆλος οὐδ᾽ ἀγαίομαι

θεῶν ἔργα, μεγάλης δ' οὐκ ἐρέω τυραννίδος·
ἀπόπροθεν γάρ ἐστιν ὀφθαλμῶν ἐμῶν.

(25)

ἔχουσα θαλλὸν μυρσίνης ἐτέρπετο
ῥοδῆς τε καλὸν ἄνθος,
ἡ δέ οἱ κόμη
ὤμους κατεσκίαζε καὶ μετάφρενα.

(53)

ἔα Πάρον καὶ σῦκα κεῖνα καὶ θαλάσσιον βίον.

(54)

ὡς Πανελλήνων ὀϊζὺς ἐς Θάσον συνέδραμεν.

(55)

μηδ' ὁ Ταντάλου λίθος
τῆσδ' ὑπὲρ νήσου κρεμάσθω.

(56)

Γλαῦχ', ὅρα· βαθὺς γὰρ ἤδη κύμασιν ταράσσεται
πόντος, ἀμφὶ δ' ἄκρα Γυρέων ὀρθὸν ἵσταται νέφος,
σῆμα χειμῶνος· κιχάνει δ' ἐξ ἀελπτίης φόβος.

2 γύριον, γύρεον, γυρεῦον et sim. codd., em. Xylander

(58)

τοῖς θεοῖς †τ' εἰθεῖ' ἄπαντα†· πολλάκις μὲν ἐκ κακῶν
ἄνδρας ὀρθοῦσιν μελαίνῃ κειμένους ἐπὶ χθονί,

1 τίθει πάντα Trinc. τίθει τὰ πάντα Grotius (θεοῖσι) ῥεῖα πάντα
Wilamowitz τέλεια πάντα Hommel

πολλάκις δ' ἀνατρέπουσι καὶ μάλ' εὖ βεβηκότας
ὑπτίους κλίνουσ'· ἔπειτα πολλὰ γίγνεται κακά
καὶ βίου χρήμῃ πλανᾶται καὶ νόου παρήορος.   5

4 κινοῦσ' cod., em. Valckenaer

(60)

οὐ φιλέω μέγαν στρατηγὸν οὐδὲ διαπεπλιγμένον
οὐδὲ βοστρύχοισι γαῦρον οὐδ' ὑπεξυρημένον·
ἀλλά μοι σμικρός τις εἴη καὶ περὶ κνήμας ἰδεῖν
ῥοικός, ἀσφαλέως βεβηκὼς ποσσί, καρδίης πλέως.

1 διαπεπλεγμένον et διαπεπηγμένον codd., em. Hemsterhuys   3
περὶ κνήμας ἰδεῖν: κατὰ κνήμην ἰδεῖν schol. Theocr.   ἐπὶ κνήμαισιν
δασύς Dio   4 ῥοικός Galen, schol. Theocr.   ῥαιβός Dio, Pollux

(64)

οὔ τις αἰδοῖος μετ' ἀστῶν οὐδὲ περίφημος θανών
γίγνεται· χάριν δὲ μᾶλλον τοῦ ζοοῦ διώκομεν
οἱ ζοοί· κάκιστα δ' αἰεὶ τῷ θανόντι γίγνεται.

1 οὐδὲ: καὶ codd.   2 ζώου, ζωοῦ codd., em. Porson   3 ζώοι
κάκιστα δέει codd., em. iam in exemplari Grotiano

(65)

οὐ γὰρ ἐσθλὰ κατθανοῦσι κερτομεῖν ἐπ' ἀνδράσιν.

(66)

         ἓν δ' ἐπίσταμαι μέγα,
τὸν κακῶς μ' ἔρδοντα δέννοις ἀνταμείβεσθαι κακοῖς.

2 δρῶντα codd., με add. Hecker, em. Turyn, Pfeiffer   δεινοῖς codd.,
em. Herzog.

(67a)

θυμέ, θύμ' ἀμηχάνοισι κήδεσιν κυκώμενε,
†αναδευ†, δυσμενέων δ' ἀλέξευ προσβαλὼν ἐναντίον
στέρνον, †ἐν δοκοῖσιν ἐχθρῶν† πλησίον κατασταθείς
ἀσφαλέως· καὶ μήτε νικῶν ἀμφάδην ἀγάλλεο
μηδὲ νικηθεὶς ἐν οἴκῳ καταπεσὼν ὀδύρεο,   5
ἀλλὰ χαρτοῖσίν τε χαῖρε καὶ κακοῖσιν ἀσχάλα
μὴ λίην· γίγνωσκε δ' οἷος ῥυσμὸς ἀνθρώπους ἔχει.

2 ἀνάδυ ci. Bücheler ἄνα δέ Liebel ἄνα συ Pfeiffer   3 ἐνδόκοισιν
fort. scribend.

(71)

εἰ γὰρ ὣς ἐμοὶ γένοιτο χεῖρα Νευβούλης θιγεῖν.

(74)

'χρημάτων ἄελπτον οὐδέν ἐστιν οὐδ' ἀπώμοτον
οὐδὲ θαυμάσιον, ἐπειδὴ Ζεὺς πατὴρ Ὀλυμπίων
ἐκ μεσημβρίης ἔθηκε νύκτ' ἀποκρύψας φάος
ἡλίου λάμποντος, ὑγρὸν δ' ἦλθ' ἐπ' ἀνθρώπους δέος.
ἐκ δὲ τοῦ καὶ πιστὰ πάντα κἀπίελπτα γίγνεται   5
ἀνδράσιν. μηδεὶς ἔθ' ὑμέων εἰσορῶν θαυμαζέτω,
μηδ' ἐὰν δελφῖσι θῆρες ἀνταμείψωνται νομόν
ἐνάλιον καί σφιν θαλάσσης ἠχέεντα κύματα
φίλτερ' ἠπείρου γένηται, τοῖσι δ' ὑλήειν ὄρος
                  'Αρ]χηνακτίδης   10
             ]ητου πάις

4 λυγρὸν codd. ὑγρὸν Valckenaer   5 οὐκ ἄπιστα codd. καὶ πιστὰ
Liebel κἄπιστα Doederlein, Pfeiffer   7 μηδεινα codd., em.
Valckenaer   9 ἡδὺ ἦν Stob. ὑλήειν Bergk: potius]νειν quam
]ηειν pap.

]τύθη γάμω.[
]...γνε..
]νέειν
]   15
ἀν]δράσιν

(77)

ὡς Διωνύσοι᾽ ἄνακτος καλὸν ἐξάρξαι μέλος
οἶδα διθύραμβον οἴνῳ συγκεραυνωθεὶς φρένας.

(79a)

π. [   ]ν[...]....[
    κύμ[ασι] πλα[ζόμ]ενος
κἀν Σαλμυδ[ησσ]ῷ γυμνὸν εὐφρονέσ[τατα
    Θρήικες ἀκρό[κ]ομοι
λάβοιεν — ἔνθα [πό]λλ᾽ ἀναπλήσει κακά   5
    δούλιον ἄρτον ἔδων —
ῥίγει πεπηγότ᾽ αὐτόν, ἐκ δὲ τοῦ χνόου
    φυκία πόλλ᾽ ἐπέχοι,
κροτέοι δ᾽ ὀδόντας ὡς [κύ]ων ἐπὶ στόμα
    κείμενος ἀκρασίη   10
ἄκρον παρὰ ῥηγμῖνα κυμαντῷ [.].[.].ι.
    ταῦτ᾽ ἐθέλοιμ᾽ ἂν ἰδεῖν,
ὅς μ᾽ ἠδίκησε, λ[ὰ]ξ δ᾽ ἐπ᾽ ὁρκίοις ἔβη
    τὸ πρὶν ἑταῖρος [ἐ]ών.

5 ἐνθαναπλησει pap.]λλα .. πλισαι[..]κα schol.   7 χνου pap.,
em. Masson   8 επιχοι pap. επει | η ... νοι schol. ἐπέχοι ed. pr.
ἐπιχέοι Cantarella, Masson

(88)

πάτερ Λυκάμβα, ποῖον ἐφράσω τόδε;
    τίς σὰς παρήειρε φρένας,

ἧς τὸ πρὶν ἠρήρεισθα; νῦν δὲ δὴ πολύς
    ἀστοῖσι φαίνεαι γέλως.

(89)

    αἶνός τις ἀνθρώπων ὅδε,
ὡς ἄρ' ἀλώπηξ καἰετὸς ξυνωνίην
    ἔμειξαν.

(92a)

'ὁρᾷς ἵν' ἔστ' ἐκεῖνος ὑψηλὸς πάγος
    τρηχύς τε καὶ παλίγκοτος;
ἐν τῷ κάθηται σὴν ἐλαφρίζων μάχην.'

(94)

'ὦ Ζεῦ πάτερ Ζεῦ, σὸν μὲν οὐρανοῦ κράτος,
    σὺ δ' ἔργ' ἐπ' ἀνθρώπων ὁρᾷς
λεωργὰ καὶ θεμιστά, σοὶ δὲ θηρίων
    ὕβρις τε καὶ δίκη μέλει.'

3 καθέμι[σ]τας οἱ Stob. FP   καὶ ἃ θέμις Stob. L, Clem.   τε καὶ
ἀθέμιστα Euseb., em. Liebel

(103)

πόλλ' οἶδ' ἀλώπηξ, ἀλλ' ἐχῖνος ἓν μέγα.

(104)

    δύστηνος ἔγκειμαι πόθῳ
ἄψυχος, χαλεπῇσι θεῶν ὀδύνῃσιν ἕκητι
    πεπαρμένος δι' ὀστέων.

(112)

τοῖος γὰρ φιλότητος ἔρως ὑπὸ καρδίην ἐλυσθεὶς
    πολλὴν κατ' ἀχλὺν ὀμμάτων ἔχευεν
κλέψας ἐκ στηθέων ἀπαλὰς φρένας

(118)

ἀλλά μ' ὁ λυσιμελής, ὦ 'ταῖρε, δάμναται πόθος.

CALLINUS

(1)

μέχρις τεῦ κατάκεισθε; κότ' ἄλκιμον ἕξετε θυμόν,
    ὦ νέοι; οὐδ' αἰδεῖσθ' ἀμφιπερικτίονας
ὦδε λίην μεθιέντες; ἐν εἰρήνῃ δὲ δοκεῖτε
    ἧσθαι, ἀτὰρ πόλεμος γαῖαν ἅπασαν ἔχει.

    .   .   .   .   .   .

    καί τις ἀποθνήσκων ὕστατ' ἀκοντισάτω.   5
τιμῆέν τε γάρ ἐστι καὶ ἀγλαὸν ἀνδρὶ μάχεσθαι
    γῆς πέρι καὶ παίδων κουριδίης τ' ἀλόχου
δυσμενέσιν· θάνατος δὲ τότ' ἔσσεται, ὁππότε κεν δή
    Μοῖραι ἐπικλώσωσ'· ἀλλά τις ἰθὺς ἴτω
ἔγχος ἀνασχόμενος καὶ ὑπ' ἀσπίδος ἄλκιμον ἦτορ   10
    ἔλσας, τὸ πρῶτον μειγνυμένου πολέμου.
οὐ γάρ κως θάνατόν γε φυγεῖν εἱμαρμένον ἐστίν
    ἄνδρ', οὐδ' εἰ προγόνων ᾖ γένος ἀθανάτων.
πολλάκι δηιοτῆτα φυγὼν καὶ δοῦπον ἀκόντων
    ἔρχεται, ἐν δ' οἴκῳ μοῖρα κίχεν θανάτου.   15

4 non indicant lacunam codd.   8 τοτ' cod. unus ποτ' vulgo
15 ἔρχεται codd. ἔργεται Bergk

ἀλλ' ὃ μὲν οὐκ ἔμπης δήμῳ φίλος οὐδὲ ποθεινός,
τὸν δ' ὀλίγος στενάχει καὶ μέγας, ἤν τι πάθῃ·
λαῷ γὰρ σύμπαντι πόθος κρατερόφρονος ἀνδρός
θνήσκοντος, ζώων δ' ἄξιος ἡμιθέων·
ὥσπερ γάρ μιν πύργον ἐν ὀφθαλμοῖσιν ὁρῶσιν·   20
ἔρδει γὰρ πολλῶν ἄξια μοῦνος ἐών.

(3)

νῦν δ' ἐπὶ Κιμμερίων στρατὸς ἔρχεται ὀβριμοεργῶν.

TYRTAEUS

(8)

ἀλλ' — Ἡρακλῆος γὰρ ἀνικήτου γένος ἐστέ —
θαρσεῖτ'· οὔπω Ζεὺς αὐχένα λοξὸν ἔχει·
μηδ' ἀνδρῶν πληθὺν δειμαίνετε μηδὲ φοβεῖσθε,
ἰθὺς δ' ἐς προμάχους ἀσπίδ' ἀνὴρ ἐχέτω
ἐχθρὴν μὲν ψυχὴν θέμενος, θανάτου δὲ μελαίνας   5
κῆρας ὁμῶς αὐγαῖς ἠελίοιο φίλας.
ἴστε γὰρ ὡς Ἄρεος πολυδακρύου ἔργ' ἀίδηλα·
εὖ δ' ὀργὴν ἐδάητ' ἀργαλέου πολέμου
καὶ μετὰ φευγόντων τε διωκόντων τ' ἐγένεσθε,
ὦ νέοι, ἀμφοτέρων δ' ἐς κόρον ἠλάσατε.   10
οἳ μὲν γὰρ τολμῶσι παρ' ἀλλήλοισι μένοντες
ἔς τ' αὐτοσχεδίην καὶ προμάχους ἰέναι,
παυρότεροι θνήσκουσι, σαοῦσι δὲ λαὸν ὀπίσσω·
τρεσσάντων δ' ἀνδρῶν πᾶσ' ἀπόλωλ' ἀρετή.

6 ὁμῶς om. codd., suppl. Grotius ἴσως Diehl   7 ἀρίδηλα codd.
ἀίδηλα Frobenius, Gesner   9 ἄγεσθε, ἔγευσθε codd. ἐγένεσθε
Triclinius

οὐδεὶς ἂν ποτε ταῦτα λέγων ἀνύσειεν ἕκαστα,   15
    ὅσσ', ἢν αἰσχρὰ πάθῃ, γίγνεται ἀνδρὶ κακά·
ἁρπαλέον γὰρ ὄπισθε μετάφρενόν ἐστι δαΐζειν
    ἀνδρὸς φεύγοντος δηΐῳ ἐν πολέμῳ·
αἰσχρὸς δ' ἐστὶ νέκυς κακκείμενος ἐν κονίῃσι
    νῶτον ὄπισθ' αἰχμῇ δουρὸς ἐληλαμένος.   20
ἀλλά τις εὖ διαβὰς μενέτω ποσὶν ἀμφοτέροισιν
    στηριχθεὶς ἐπὶ γῆς, χεῖλος ὀδοῦσι δακών,
μηρούς τε κνήμας τε κάτω καὶ στέρνα καὶ ὤμους
    ἀσπίδος εὐρείης γαστρὶ καλυψάμενος·
δεξιτερῇ δ' ἐν χειρὶ τινασσέτω ὄβριμον ἔγχος,   25
    κινείτω δὲ λόφον δεινὸν ὑπὲρ κεφαλῆς·
ἔρδων δ' ὄβριμα ἔργα διδασκέσθω πολεμίζειν,
    μηδ' ἐκτὸς βελέων ἑστάτω ἀσπίδ' ἔχων,
ἀλλά τις ἐγγὺς ἰὼν αὐτοσχεδὸν ἔγχεϊ μακρῷ
    ἢ ξίφει οὐτάζων δήιον ἄνδρ' ἑλέτω·   30
καὶ πόδα πὰρ ποδὶ θεὶς καὶ ἐπ' ἀσπίδος ἀσπίδ' ἐρείσας,
    ἐν δὲ λόφον τε λόφῳ καὶ κυνέην κυνέῃ
καὶ στέρνον στέρνῳ πεπλημένος ἀνδρὶ μαχέσθω,
    ἢ ξίφεος κώπην ἢ δόρυ μακρὸν ἑλών.
ὑμεῖς δ', ὦ γυμνῆτες, ὑπ' ἀσπίδος ἄλλοθεν ἄλλος   35
    πτώσσοντες μεγάλοις βάλλετε χερμαδίοις
δούρασί τε ξεστοῖσιν ἀκοντίζοντες ἐς αὐτούς
    τοῖσι πανόπλοισι πλησίον ἱστάμενοι.

17 ἀργαλέον codd.   ἁρπαλέον Ahrens   33 πεπαλημένος codd.
πεπλήμενος Brunck   37–8 secludendi?

(9)

οὔτ' ἂν μνησαίμην οὔτ' ἐν λόγῳ ἄνδρα τιθείην
    οὔτε ποδῶν ἀρετῆς οὔτε παλαιμοσύνης,

1 τιθείην codd.   τιθείμην codd. Plat. bis   2 παλαιμ-, παλαισμ-
codd.

οὐδ' εἰ Κυκλώπων μὲν ἔχοι μέγεθός τε βίην τε,
   νικῴη δὲ θέων Θρηίκιον Βορέην,
οὐδ' εἰ Τιθωνοῖο φυὴν χαριέστερος εἴη,   5
   πλουτοίη δὲ Μίδεω καὶ Κινύρεω μάλιον,
οὐδ' εἰ Τανταλίδεω Πέλοπος βασιλεύτερος εἴη,
   γλῶσσαν δ' Ἀδρήστου μειλιχόγηρυν ἔχοι,
οὐδ' εἰ πᾶσαν ἔχοι δόξαν πλὴν θούριδος ἀλκῆς·
   οὐ γὰρ ἀνὴρ ἀγαθὸς γίγνεται ἐν πολέμῳ,   10
εἰ μὴ τετλαίη μὲν ὁρῶν φόνον αἱματόεντα
   καὶ δήων ὀρέγοιτ' ἐγγύθεν ἱστάμενος.
ἥδ' ἀρετή, τόδ' ἄεθλον ἐν ἀνθρώποισιν ἄριστον
   κάλλιστόν τε φέρειν γίγνεται ἀνδρὶ νέῳ.
ξυνὸν δ' ἐσθλὸν τοῦτο πόληΐ τε παντί τε δήμῳ,   15
   ὅστις ἀνὴρ διαβὰς ἐν προμάχοισι μένῃ
νωλεμέως, αἰσχρῆς δὲ φυγῆς ἐπὶ πάγχυ λάθηται
   ψυχὴν καὶ θυμὸν τλήμονα παρθέμενος,
θαρσύνῃ δ' ἔπεσιν τὸν πλησίον ἄνδρα παρεστώς·
   οὗτος ἀνὴρ ἀγαθὸς γίγνεται ἐν πολέμῳ.   20
αἶψα δὲ δυσμενέων ἀνδρῶν ἔτρεψε φάλαγγας
   τρηχείας, σπουδῇ δ' ἔσχεθε κῦμα μάχης.
ὃς δ' αὖτ' ἐν προμάχοισι πεσὼν φίλον ὤλεσε θυμὸν
   ἄστυ τε καὶ λαοὺς καὶ πατέρ' εὐκλεΐσας,
πολλὰ διὰ στέρνοιο καὶ ἀσπίδος ὀμφαλοέσσης   25
   καὶ διὰ θώρηκος πρόσθεν ἐληλαμένος,
τόνδ' ὀλοφύρονται μὲν ὁμῶς νέοι ἠδὲ γέροντες,
   ἀργαλέῳ τε πόθῳ πᾶσα κέκηδε πόλις,
καὶ τύμβος καὶ παῖδες ἐν ἀνθρώποις ἀρίσημοι
   καὶ παίδων παῖδες καὶ γένος ἐξοπίσω·   30
οὐδέ ποτε κλέος ἐσθλὸν ἀπόλλυται οὐδ' ὄνομ' αὐτοῦ,
   ἀλλ' ὑπὸ γῆς περ ἐὼν γίγνεται ἀθάνατος,

6 κινυρέοιο μᾶλλον codd., em. Schmidt   16 ἄνηρ codd. ἂν εὖ
Upton   23 αὐτὸς δ' codd. ὃς δ' αὖτ' Bergk. αὐτὰρ ὃς Defradas

ὅντιν' ἀριστεύοντα μένοντά τε μαρνάμενόν τε
   γῆς πέρι καὶ παίδων θοῦρος Ἄρης ὀλέσῃ.
εἰ δὲ φύγῃ μὲν κῆρα τανηλεγέος θανάτοιο,   35
   νικήσας δ' αἰχμῆς ἀγλαὸν εὖχος ἕλῃ,
πάντες μιν τιμῶσιν ὁμῶς νέοι ἠδὲ παλαιοί,
   πολλὰ δὲ τερπνὰ παθὼν ἔρχεται εἰς Ἀίδην·
γηράσκων ἀστοῖσι μεταπρέπει, οὐδέ τις αὐτόν
   βλάπτειν οὔτ' αἰδοῦς οὔτε δίκης ἐθέλει,   40
πάντες δ' ἐν θώκοισιν ὁμῶς νέοι οἵ τε κατ' αὐτόν
   εἴκουσ' ἐκ χώρης οἵ τε παλαιότεροι.
ταύτης νῦν τις ἀνὴρ ἀρετῆς εἰς ἄκρον ἱκέσθαι
   πειράσθω θυμῷ μὴ μεθιεὶς πολέμου.

39 γηράσκων δ' vulgo γηράσκων cod. unus   44 πόλεμον codd.
πολέμου Gesner

SEMONIDES

(1)

ὦ παῖ, τέλος μὲν Ζεὺς ἔχει βαρύκτυπος
πάντων ὅσ' ἐστὶ καὶ τίθησ' ὅκῃ θέλει.
νόος δ' οὐκ ἐπ' ἀνθρώποισιν· ἀλλ' ἐφήμεροι
ἃ δὴ βοτὰ ζώομεν οὐδὲν εἰδότες
ὅκως ἕκαστον ἐκτελευτήσει θεός.   5
ἐλπὶς δὲ πάντας κἀπιπειθείη τρέφει
ἄπρηκτον ὁρμαίνοντας· οἱ μὲν ἡμέρην
μένουσιν ἐλθεῖν, οἱ δ' ἐτέων περιτροπάς.
νέωτα δ' οὐδεὶς ὅστις οὐ δοκεῖ βροτῶν
πλούτῳ τε κἀγαθοῖσιν ἵξεσθαι φίλος.   10
φθάνει δὲ τὸν μὲν γῆρας ἄζηλον λαβόν,

4 δὴ βροτοὶ, αἴδη βοτὰ, ἄδηι βοτὰ codd., em. Ahrens

πρὶν τέρμ' ἵκηται· τοὺς δὲ δύστηνοι βροτῶν
φθείρουσι νοῦσοι· τοὺς δ' "Αρει δεδμημένους
πέμπει μελαίνης 'Αΐδης ὑπὸ χθονός.
οἱ δ' ἐν θαλάσσῃ λαίλαπι κλονεύμενοι   15
καὶ κύμασιν πολλοῖσι πορφυρῆς ἁλός
θνήσκουσιν, εὖτ' ἂν μὴ δυνήσωνται ζόειν.
οἱ δ' ἀγχόνην ἅψαντο δυστήνῳ μόρῳ
καὐτάγρετοι λείπουσιν ἡλίου φάος.
οὕτω κακῶν ἄπ' οὐδέν· ἀλλὰ μυρίαι   20
βροτοῖσι κῆρες κἀνεπίφραστοι δύαι
καὶ πήματ' ἐστίν. εἰ δ' ἐμοὶ πιθοίατο,
οὐκ ἂν κακῶν ἐρῷμεν οὐδ' ἐπ' ἄλγεσι
κακοῖς ἔχοντες θυμὸν αἰκιζοίμεθα.

12–13 νόσοι | φθείρουσι βροτῶν θνητῶν, νόσοι | φθείρουσι θνητῶν
codd., βροτῶν | φθείρουσι νοῦσοι Page 17 ζώειν codd., em. Porson

(2)

τοῦ μὲν θανόντος οὐκ ἂν ἐνθυμοίμεθα,
εἴ τι φρονοῖμεν, πλεῖον ἡμέρης μιῆς.

(6)

γυναικὸς οὐδὲν χρῆμ' ἀνὴρ ληίζεται
ἐσθλῆς ἄμεινον οὐδὲ ῥίγιον κακῆς.

(7)

χωρὶς γυναικὸς θεὸς ἐποίησεν νόον
τὰ πρῶτα. τὴν μὲν ἐξ ὑὸς τανύτριχος,
τῇ πάντ' ἀν' οἶκον βορβόρῳ πεφυρμένα
ἄκοσμα κεῖται καὶ κυλίνδεται χαμαί·
αὐτὴ δ' ἄλουτος ἀπλύτοις ἐν εἵμασιν   5
ἐν κοπρίῃσιν ἡμένη πιαίνεται.

5 ἄπλυτος codd. ἄπλουτος Trincavelli, em. Valckenaer

τὴν δ' ἐξ ἀλιτρῆς θεὸς ἔθηκ' ἀλώπεκος
γυναῖκα πάντων ἴδριν· οὐδέ μιν κακῶν
λέληθεν οὐδὲν οὐδὲ τῶν ἀμεινόνων·
τὸ μὲν γὰρ αὐτῶν εἶπε πολλάκις κακόν,   10
τὸ δ' ἐσθλόν· ὀργὴν δ' ἄλλοτ' ἀλλοίην ἔχει.

τὴν δ' ἐκ κυνὸς λιτουργόν, αὐτομήτορα,
ἣ πάντ' ἀκοῦσαι, πάντα δ' εἰδέναι θέλει,
πάντῃ δὲ παπταίνουσα καὶ πλανωμένη
λέληκεν, ἢν καὶ μηδέν' ἀνθρώπων ὁρᾷ.   15
παύσειε δ' ἄν μιν οὔτ' ἀπειλήσας ἀνήρ,
οὐδ' εἰ χολωθεὶς ἐξαράξειεν λίθῳ
ὀδόντας οὐδ' ἂν μειλίχως μυθεύμενος,
οὐδ' εἰ παρὰ ξείνοισιν ἡμένη τύχῃ·
ἀλλ' ἐμπέδως ἄπρηκτον αὐονὴν ἔχει.   20

τὴν δὲ πλάσαντες γηίνην Ὀλύμπιοι
ἔδωκαν ἀνδρὶ πηρόν· οὔτε γὰρ κακὸν
οὔτ' ἐσθλὸν οὐδὲν οἶδε τοιαύτη γυνή·
ἔργων δὲ μοῦνον ἐσθίειν ἐπίσταται.
κοὐδ' ἢν κακὸν χειμῶνα ποιήσῃ θεός,   25
ῥιγῶσα δίφρον ἆσσον ἕλκεται πυρός.

τὴν δ' ἐκ θαλάσσης, ἣ δύ' ἐν φρεσὶν νοεῖ·
τὴν μὲν γελᾷ τε καὶ γέγηθεν ἡμέρην·
ἐπαινέσει μιν ξεῖνος ἐν δόμοις ἰδών·
'οὐκ ἔστιν ἄλλη τῆσδε λωίων γυνή   30
ἐν πᾶσιν ἀνθρώποισιν οὐδὲ καλλίων·'
τὴν δ' οὐκ ἀνεκτὸς οὐδ' ἐν ὀφθαλμοῖς ἰδεῖν
οὔτ' ἆσσον ἐλθεῖν, ἀλλὰ μαίνεται τότε
ἄπλητον ὥσπερ ἀμφὶ τέκνοισιν κύων,
ἀμείλιχος δὲ πᾶσι κἀποθυμίη   35
ἐχθροῖσιν ἶσα καὶ φίλοισι γίγνεται·

12 λιτοργόν codd., em. Gesner   25. κοὔτ' ἄν, χ' οταν codd.
οὐδ' ἢν Schneidewin   29 μὲν codd. μιν Valckenaer

ὥσπερ θάλασσα πολλάκις μὲν ἀτρεμὴς
ἕστηκ᾽ ἀπήμων χάρμα ναύτῃσιν μέγα
θέρεος ἐν ὥρῃ, πολλάκις δὲ μαίνεται
βαρυκτύποισι κύμασιν φορευμένη·   40
ταύτῃ μάλιστ᾽ ἔοικε τοιαύτη γυνή
ὀργήν· φυὴν δὲ πόντος ἀλλοίην ἔχει.

    τὴν δ᾽ ἐκ †τεσποδιης† καὶ παλιντριβέος ὄνου,
ἣ σύν τ᾽ ἀνάγκῃ σύν τ᾽ ἐνιπῇσιν μόγις
ἔστερξεν ὧν ἅπαντα κἀπονήσατο   45
ἀρεστά. τόφρα δ᾽ ἐσθίει μὲν ἐν μυχῷ
προνύξ, προῆμαρ, ἐσθίει δ᾽ ἐπ᾽ ἐσχάρῃ.
ὁμῶς δὲ καὶ πρὸς ἔργον ἀφροδίσιον
ἐλθόντ᾽ ἑταῖρον ὁντινῶν ἐδέξατο.

    τὴν δ᾽ ἐκ γαλῆς δύστηνον οἰζυρὸν γένος·   50
κείνῃ γὰρ οὔ τι καλὸν οὐδ᾽ ἐπίμερον
πρόσεστιν οὐδὲ τερπνὸν οὐδ᾽ ἐράσμιον.
εὐνῆς δ᾽ ἀληνής ἐστιν ἀφροδισίης,
τὸν δ᾽ ἄνδρα τὸν παρεόντα ναυσίῃ διδοῖ.
κλέπτουσα δ᾽ ἔρδει πολλὰ γείτονας κακά,   55
ἄθυστα δ᾽ ἱρὰ πολλάκις κατεσθίει.

    τὴν δ᾽ ἵππος ἁβρὴ χαιτέεσσ᾽ ἐγείνατο,
ἣ δούλι᾽ ἔργα καὶ δύην περιτρέχει,
κοὔτ᾽ ἂν μύλης ψαύσειεν οὔτε κόσκινον
ἄρειεν οὔτε κόπρον ἐξ οἴκου βάλοι,   60
οὔτε πρὸς ἱπνὸν ἀσβόλην ἀλευμένη
ἵζοιτ᾽· ἀνάγκῃ δ᾽ ἄνδρα ποιεῖται φίλον.
λοῦται δὲ πάσης ἡμέρης ἄπο ῥύπον
δίς, ἄλλοτε τρίς, καὶ μύροις ἀλείφεται·
αἰεὶ δὲ χαίτην ἐκτενισμένην φορεῖ   65
βαθεῖαν ἀνθέμοισιν ἐσκιασμένην.

45 ἔερξεν, ἔερξεν, ἔστερξεν codd.   58 περιτρέπει codd. -τρέχει
Lattimore -τρέμει L.S.J.

καλὸν μὲν ὦν θέημα τοιαύτη γυνή
ἄλλοισι, τῷ δ' ἔχοντι γίγνεται κακόν,
ἢν μή τις ἢ τύραννος ἢ σκηπτοῦχος ᾖ,
ὅστις τοιούτοις θυμὸν ἀγλαΐζεται.   70

    τὴν δ' ἐκ πιθήκου· τοῦτο δὴ διακριδόν
Ζεὺς ἀνδράσιν μέγιστον ὤπασεν κακόν.
αἴσχιστα μὲν πρόσωπα· τοιαύτη γυνή
εἶσιν δι' ἄστεος πᾶσιν ἀνθρώποις γέλως·
ἐπ' αὐχένα βραχεῖα κινεῖται μόγις,   75
ἄπυγος, αὐτόκωλος. ἆ τάλας ἀνήρ,
ὅστις κακὸν τοιοῦτον ἀγκαλίζεται.
δήνεα δὲ πάντα καὶ τρόπους ἐπίσταται
ὥσπερ πίθηκος· οὐδέ οἱ γέλως μέλει·
οὐδ' ἄν τιν' εὖ ἔρξειεν, ἀλλὰ τοῦτ' ὁρᾷ   80
καὶ τοῦτο πᾶσαν ἡμέρην βουλεύεται,
ὅκως τιν' ὡς μέγιστον ἔρξειεν κακόν.

    τὴν δ' ἐκ μελίσσης· τήν τις εὐτυχεῖ λαβών·
κείνη γὰρ οἴη μῶμος οὐ προσιζάνει,
θάλλει δ' ὑπ' αὐτῆς κἀπαέξεται βίος.   85
φίλη δὲ σὺμ φιλεῦντι γηράσκει πόσι
τεκοῦσα καλὸν κοὐνομάκλυτον γένος.
κἀριπρεπὴς μὲν ἐν γυναιξὶ γίγνεται
πάσῃσι, θείη δ' ἀμφιδέδρομεν χάρις.
οὐδ' ἐν γυναιξὶν ἥδεται καθημένη,   90
ὅκου λέγουσιν ἀφροδισίους λόγους.
τοίας γυναῖκας ἀνδράσιν χαρίζεται
Ζεὺς τὰς ἀρίστας καὶ πολυφραδεστάτας.

    τὰ δ' ἄλλα φῦλα ταῦτα μηχανῇ Διός
ἔστιν τε πάντα καὶ παρ' ἀνδράσιν μένει.   95
Ζεὺς γὰρ μέγιστον τοῦτ' ἐποίησεν κακόν,
γυναῖκας. ἤν τι καὶ δοκέωσιν ὠφελεῖν,

82 τι χ' ὡς, στίχ' ὡς codd. τιν' ὡς Meineke

ἔχοντί τοι μάλιστα γίγνεται κακόν·
οὐ γάρ κοτ' εὔφρων ἡμέρην διέρχεται
ἅπασαν, ὅστις σὺν γυναικὶ †πέλεται†,   100
οὐδ' αἶψα λιμὸν οἰκίης ἀπώσεται,
ἐχθρὸν συνοικητῆρα, δυσμενέα θεόν.
ἀνὴρ δ' ὅταν μάλιστα θυμηδεῖν δοκῇ
κατ' οἶκον ἢ θεοῦ μοῖραν ἢ ἀνθρώπου χάριν,
εὑροῦσα μῶμον ἐς μάχην κορύσσεται.   105
ὅκου γυνὴ γάρ ἐστιν, οὐδ' ἐς οἰκίην
ξεῖνον μολόντα προφρόνως δεχοίατο.
ἥτις δέ τοι μάλιστα σωφρονεῖν δοκεῖ,
αὕτη μέγιστα τυγχάνει λωβωμένη·
κεχηνότος γὰρ ἀνδρὸς — οἱ δὲ γείτονες   110
χαίρουσ' ὁρῶντες καὶ τόν, ὡς ἁμαρτάνει.
τὴν ἣν δ' ἕκαστος αἰνέσει μεμνημένος
γυναῖκα, τὴν δὲ τοὐτέρου μωμήσεται·
ἴσην δ' ἔχοντες μοῖραν οὐ γιγνώσκομεν.
Ζεὺς γὰρ μέγιστον τοῦτ' ἐποίησεν κακόν   115
καὶ δεσμὸν ἀμφέθηκεν ἄρρηκτον πέδης,
ἐξ οὗ τε τοὺς μὲν Ἀίδης ἐδέξατο
γυναικὸς εἵνεκ' ἀμφιδηριωμένους.

98 τω, τωι codd. τοι Winterton   100 πέλεται codd. γίγνεται
Bergk, alia alii   116 πέδη, πέδηι codd. πέδης Meineke

(29)

ἓν δὲ τὸ κάλλιστον Χῖος ἔειπεν ἀνήρ·
'οἵη περ φύλλων γενεή, τοίη δὲ καὶ ἀνδρῶν.'
παῦροι μὴν θνητῶν οὔασι δεξάμενοι
στέρνοις ἐγκατέθεντο· πάρεστι γὰρ ἐλπὶς ἑκάστῳ
ἀνδρῶν, ἥ τε νέων στήθεσιν ἐμφύεται.   5

3 μιν cod. μὴν Meineke

θνητῶν δ' ὄφρα τις ἄνθος ἔχῃ πολυήρατον ἥβης,
  κοῦφον ἔχων θυμὸν πόλλ' ἀτέλεστα νοεῖ·
οὔτε γὰρ ἐλπίδ' ἔχει γηρασέμεν οὔτε θανεῖσθαι
  οὐδ', ὑγιὴς ὅταν ᾖ, φροντίδ' ἔχει καμάτου.
νήπιοι, οἷς ταύτῃ κεῖται νόος, οὐδὲ ἴσασιν   10
  ὡς χρόνος ἔσθ' ἥβης καὶ βιότου ὀλίγος
θνητοῖς. ἀλλὰ σὺ ταῦτα μαθὼν βιότου ποτὶ τέρμα
  ψυχῇ τῶν ἀγαθῶν τλῆθι χαριζόμενος.

ALCMAN

(I)

```
– ∪ – ᴗ | – ∪ –                              1, 3, 5, 7
ᴗ ⋮ – ∪ ∪ – ⋮ ∪ – –                          2, 4, 6, 8
– ∪ – ᴗ | – ∪ – ᴗ | – ∪ – ᴗ                   9, 10
– ∪ – ᴗ | – ∪ –                               11, 12
– ◡◡ – ∪ ∪ – ∪ ∪ – ∪ ∪                        13
– ◡◡ – ∪ ∪ – ∪ ∪ –                            14
or  – ◡◡ ⋮ – ∪ ∪ – ⋮ ∪ – –
```

                    ]Πωλυδεύκης

prototypes ⟨ οὐ μόνο]ν Λύκαισον ἐν καμοῦσιν ἀλέγω
of ⟨
strophes ⟨ ἀλλ' Ἔνα]ρσφόρον τε καὶ Σέβρον ποδώκη   ⟩ *strophe*
antistroph⟨ Ἀλκιμό]ν τε τὸν βιατὰν   ⟩
         Ἱππόθω]ν τε τὸν κορυστὰν   5
         Εὐτείχη] τε Ϝάνακτά τ' Ἀρήιον   ⟩ *antis*
            ]ά τ' ἔξοχον ἡμισίων·

2 e schol. suppl.   3 suppl. Bergk   4, 5, 9 supplementa
audacius admisi   6 suppl. ex Anec. Ox. Cramer i. 158. 31

καὶ   ]ν τὸν ἀγρόταν
Σκαῖον] μέγαν Εὔρυτόν τε
"Αρεος ἂν] πώρω κλόνον   10
"Αλκωνά] τε τὼς ἀρίστως
οὐδ' ἀμῶς] παρήσομες
κράτησε γ]ὰρ Αἶσα παντῶν
καὶ Πόρος] γεραιτάτοι
σιῶν· ἀπ]έδιλος ἀλκά   15
μή τις ἀνθ]ρώπων ἐς ὠρανὸν ποτήσθω
μηδὲ πη]ρήτω γαμῆν τὰν 'Αφροδίταν
Κυπρίαν Ϝ]άν[α]σσαν ἤ τιν'
     ] ἢ παίδα Πόρκω
εἰναλίω· Χά]ριτες δὲ Διὸς δόμον   20
ἀμφιέπου]σιν ἐρογλεφάροι·

      ]τάτοι
      ]τα δαίμων
      ]ι φίλοις
   ἔδ]ωκε δῶρα   25
      ]γαρέον
      ]ώλεσ' ἤβα
      ]ρονον
   μ]αταίας
      ]έβα· τῶν δ' ἄλλος ἰῷ   30
      ]μαρμάρῳ μυλάκρῳ
     ] . εν 'Αΐδας
      ]αυτοι
      ]'πον· ἄλαστα δὲ
Ϝέργα πάσον κακὰ μησάμενοι.   35

10–11 suppl. Bergk   12–18 suppl. Blass   20 suppl. Crusius,
Blass   21 suppl. exempli gratia Page   25 ἔδωκε vel δέδωκε
28 θρόνον vel χρόνον   35 εργα pap.

ἔστι τις σιῶν τίσις·
ὁ δ' ὄλβιος, ὅστις εὔφρων
ἀμέραν [δι]απλέκει
ἄκλαυτος· ἐγὼν δ' ἀείδω
'Αγιδῶς τὸ φῶς· ὁρῶ   40
F' ὥτ' ἄλιον, ὅνπερ ἇμιν
'Αγιδὼ μαρτύρεται
φαίνην· ἐμὲ δ' οὔτ' ἐπαινῆν
οὔτε μωμήσθαι νιν ἁ κλεννὰ χοραγὸς
οὐδ' ἀμῶς ἐῇ· δοκεῖ γὰρ ἤμεν αὕτα   45
ἐκπρεπὴς τὼς ὥπερ αἴτις
ἐν βοτοῖς στάσειεν ἵππον
παγὸν ἀεθλοφόρον καναχάποδα
τῶν ὑποπετριδίων ὀνείρων.

ἦ οὐχ ὁρῆς; ὁ μὲν κέλης   50
'Ενητικός· ἁ δὲ χαίτα
τᾶς ἐμᾶς ἀνεψιᾶς
'Αγησιχόρας ἐπανθεῖ
χρυσὸς [ὡ]ς ἀκήρατος·
τό τ' ἀργύριον πρόσωπον,   55
διαφάδαν τί τοι λέγω;
'Αγησιχόρα μὲν αὕτα·
ἁ δὲ δευτέρα πεδ' 'Αγιδὼ τὸ Γεῖδος
ἵππος 'Ιβηνῷ Κολαξαῖος δραμήται·
ταὶ Πεληάδες γὰρ ἇμιν   60
'Ορθρίᾳ φᾶρος φεροίσαις

39 ἄκλαυτος pap., corr. Wilamowitz   41 F' Diels: scriba quid
voluerit incertum   43 φαίνεν, επαινὲν pap.   44 μωμέσθαι
pap.   45 δοκεει pap. εἵμεν, η suprascr., pap.   46 ωιπερ pap.
51 ενετικος, ⊣⊢ suprascr., pap.: corr. Diels   58 ἀγὶδὼι ἁ ειδος
pap.   59 ειβηνωι, δραμείται pap.   60 πελειάδες pap.   61
ορθρίαι pap. 'Ορθίᾳ e schol. Diels

νύκτα δι' ἀμβροσίαν ἅτε σήριον
ἄστρον ἀυηρομέναι μάχονται.

* replace digamma*

οὔτε γάρ τι πορφύρας
τόσσος κόρος ὥστ' ἀμύναι,   65
οὔτε ποικίλος δράκων
παγχρύσιος. οὐδὲ μίτρα
Λυδία, νεανίδων
ἰανογ[λ]εφάρων ἄγαλμα,
οὐδὲ ταὶ Ναννῶς κόμαι,   70
ἀλλ' οὐ[δ'] Ἀρέτα σιειδής,
οὐδὲ Σύλακίς τε καὶ Κλεησισήρα,
οὐδ' ἐς Αἰνησιμβρ[ό]τας ἐνθοῖσα φασεῖς·
Ἀσταφίς [τ]έ μοι γένοιτο
καὶ ποτιγλέποι Φίλυλλα   75
Δαμαρ[έ]τα τ' ἐρατά τε Ϝιανθεμίς·
ἀλλ' Ἀγησιχόρα με τηρεῖ.

οὐ γὰρ ἁ κ[α]λλίσφυρος
Ἀγησιχ[ό]ρ[α] πάρ' αὐτεῖ,
Ἀγιδοῖ [δ' ἴκτ]αρ μένει   80
θωστήρ[ιά τ'] ἄμ' ἐπαινεῖ;
ἀλλὰ τᾶν [εὐχάς], σιοί,
δέξασθε· [σι]ῶν γὰρ ἄνα
καὶ τέλος· [χο]ροστάτις,
Ϝείποιμί κ', [ἐ]γὼν μὲν αὐτὰ   85
παρσένος μάταν ἀπὸ θράνω λέλακα
γλαύξ· ἐγὼ[ν] δὲ τᾷ μὲν Ἀώτι μάλιστα
Ϝανδάνην ἐρῶ· πόνων γὰρ

62 σιριον, σειριον suprascr. ut videtur   63 αυειρ- pap.   76
ιανθ- pap.   80 fortasse [δὲ π]αρμένει   82 suppl. Blass   85
ειποιμι pap.   88 ἀνδ- pap.

ἇμιν ἰάτωρ ἔγεντο·
ἐξ 'Αγησιχόρ[ας] δὲ νεάνιδες   90
ἰρ]ήνας ἐρατ[ᾶ]ς ἐπέβαν.

τῷ] τε γὰρ σηραφόρῳ
αὐ]τῶς εδ[
τ[ῷ] κυβερνάτᾳ δὲ χρὴ
κ[ἠ]ν ναῒ μάλιστ' ἀκούην·   95
ἁ δὲ τᾶν Σηρην[ί]δων
ἀοιδοτέρα μ[ὲν οὐχί,
σιαὶ γάρ, ἀντ[ὶ δ' ἕνδεκα
παίδων δεκ[ὰς ἅδ' ἀείδ]ει·
φθέγγεται δ' [ἄρ'] ὥ[τ' ἐπὶ] Ξάνθω ῥοαῖσι   100
κύκνος· ἁ δ' ἐπιμέρῳ ξανθᾷ κομίσκᾳ

desunt iv versus

91 suppl. Page   93 suppl. Blass   97 suppl. Weil   98 e
schol. suppl.   99 suppl. Wilamowitz, Blass   100 suppl.
Blass   105 in marg. coronis

(3)

```
‒ ᴗ ᴗ ‒ ᴗ ᴗ ‒ ᴗ ᴗ ‒ ᴗ ᴗ
‒ ᴗ ‒ ᴗ | ‒ ᴗ ‒ ᴗ̮
‒ ᴗ ‒ ‒ | ‒ ᴗ ‒ ᴗ̮
‒ ᴗ ‒ ᴗ | ‒ ᴗ ‒
‒ ‒ ᴗ ᴗ ‒ ᴗ ‒ ⦙ ᴗ̮ ‒ ᴗ ‒          5
‒ [?] ᴗ ‒
‒ ᴗ ᴗ ‒ ‾‾ ‒ ᴗ ᴗ ‒ ᴗ ᴗ
‒ ‾‾ ‒ ᴗ ᴗ ‒ ‾‾ ‒ ᴗ ᴗ
‒ ᴗ ᴗ ‒ ᴗ ᴗ ‒ ⦙ ᴗ̮ ‒ ᴗ ‒ ‒
```

'Ολ]υμπιάδες περί με φρένας
]ς ἀοιδας

]ω δ' ἀκούσαι
]ας ὀπός
] . . ρα καλὸν ὑμνιοισᾶν μέλος   5
] . οι
ὕπνον ἀ]πὸ γλεφάρων σκεδ[α]σεῖ γλυκύν
]ς δέ μ' ἄγει πεδ' ἀγῶν' ἴμεν
ᾶχι μά]λιστα κόμ[αν ξ]ανθὰν τινάξω.

] . σχ[ἀπ]αλοὶ πόδες   10

λυσιμελεῖ τε πόσῳ, τακερώτερα   61
δ' ὕπνω καὶ σανάτω ποτιδέρκεται·
οὐδέ τι μαψιδίως γλυκ[ῆα κ]ήνα·

Ἀ[σ]τυμέλοισα δέ μ' οὐδὲν ἀμείβεται
ἀλλὰ τὸ]ν πυλεῶν' ἔχοισα   65
[ὥ] τις αἰγλά[ε]ντος ἀστήρ
ὠρανῶ διαιπετής
ἢ χρύσιον ἔρνος ἢ ἁπαλὸ[ν ψίλ]ον
.᾿.]ν
    ]. διέβα ταναοῖς πο[σί·]   70
-κ]ομος νοτία Κινύρα χ[άρ]ις
ἐπὶ π]αρσενικᾶν χαίταισιν ἴσδει·

Ἀ]στυμέλοισα κατὰ στρατόν
]μέλημα δάμῳ

(14a)

−∪∪−∪∪−∪∪−∪∪
−∪∪−∪∪−
∪−∪−|∪−∪−|∪−−

Μῶσ' ἄγε Μῶσα λίγηα πολυμμελὲς
αἰὲν ἀοιδὲ μέλος
νεοχμὸν ἄρχε παρσένοις ἀείδην.

(16)

```
– – ◡ – | – – ◡ –
– – ◡ – | ◡ ◡ ◡ ◡ –
◡ – ◡ – | ◡ – ◡ –
◡ ◡ ◡ – ◡ | – ◡ – –
– ◡ – ◡ | – ◡ – –
```

οὐκ ἦς ἀνὴρ ἀγρεῖος οὐ-
δὲ σκαιὸς οὐδὲ †παρὰ σοφοῖ-
σιν† οὐδὲ Θεσσαλὸς γένος,
Ἐρυσιχαῖος οὐδὲ ποιμήν,
ἀλλὰ Σαρδίων ἀπ' ἀκρᾶν.

1 ἦς Chrysippus   εἰς Stephanus   ἄγριος Stephanus, P. Oxy.
2389 fr. 9 i 14 ante corr. ἀγροῖκος Chrysippus   4 οὐδ' Ἐ. οὐδὲ
codd., οὐδ' del. Hartung   5 ἄκραν, ἄκρας codd.

(20)

```
– – ◡ – | ◡ – ◡ –
```

ὥρας δ' ἔσηκε τρεῖς, θέρος
καὶ χεῖμα κὠπώραν τρίταν
καὶ τέτρατον τὸ Ϝῆρ, ὄκα
σάλλει μέν, ἐσθίην δ' ἄδαν
οὐκ ἔστι.

2 χειμάχωι· παραν cod., corr. anon.   3–4 τοηροκας ἀλλ' εἰ μὲν
ἐσθειεν cod.

(26)

‒ ∪ ∪ ‒ ∪ ∪ ‒ ∪ ∪ ‒ ∪ ∪ ‒ ∪ ∪ ‒ ‒

οὔ μ' ἔτι, παρσενικαὶ μελιγάρυες ἱαρόφωνοι,
γυῖα φέρην δύναται· βάλε δὴ βάλε κηρύλος εἴην,
ὅς τ' ἐπὶ κύματος ἄνθος ἅμ' ἀλκυόνεσσι ποτήται
νηδεὲς ἦτορ ἔχων, ἁλιπόρφυρος ἱαρὸς ὄρνις.

1 οὐ μέν τι Antigonus   4 νηλεὲς Antigonus ἀδεὲς Photius, em.
Boissonade εἴαρος codd., em. Hecker

(27)

‒ ‒‒ ‒ ∪ ∪ ‒ ∪ ∪ ‒ ∪ ∪

Μῶσ' ἄγε Καλλιόπα θύγατερ Διὸς
ἄρχ' ἐρατῶν Ϝεπέων, ἐπὶ δ' ἵμερον
ὕμνῳ καὶ χαρίεντα τίθη χορόν.

2–3 ἱερὸν ὕμνον Syrianus

(41)

‒ ‒ ∪ ‒ | ∪ ‒ ∪ ‒ | ‒ ∪ ∪ ‒ ∪ ∪ ‒ ‒

ἔρπει γὰρ ἄντα τῶ σιδάρω τὸ καλῶς κιθαρίσδην

ἔρπει: ῥέπει ci. Scaliger

(56)

‒ ∪ ∪ ‒ ∪ ∪ ‒ ∪ ∪ ‒ ∪ ∪ ‒ ‒‒   1-5
‒ ∪ ∪ ‒ ‒ ∪ ∪ ‒ ∪ ∪ ‒ ‒ ‒ ‒   6

πολλάκι δ' ἐν κορυφαῖς ὀρέων, ὅκα
σιοῖσι Ϝάδη πολύφανος ἑορτά,
χρύσιον ἄγγος ἔχοισα, μέγαν σκύφον,

οἷά τε ποιμένες ἄνδρες ἔχοισιν,
χερσὶ λεόντεον ἐν γάλα θεῖσα   5
τυρὸν ἐτύρησας μέγαν ἄτρυφον ᾿Αργειφόντᾳ.

5 ἐπαλαθεῖσα Athenaeus, corr. Hermann   6 ἀργειοφόνται
Athenaeus ἀργιφόντᾳ gramm. anon.

(58)

_ ◡ _ _ ◡ _ _ ◡ _ _ ◡ _ _ ◡ _ _ _

᾿Αφροδίτα μὲν οὐκ ἔστι, μάργος δ᾿ ῎Ερως οἷα ⟨παῖς⟩
        παίσδει,
ἄκρ᾿ ἐπ᾿ ἄνθη καβαίνων, ἃ μή μοι θίγῃς, τῶ κυπαιρίσκω.

1 παῖς suppl. Bentley

(59a)

◡ _ ◡ _ | ◡̲ _ ◡ _ | ◡ _ _

῎Ερως με δηὖτε Κύπριδος Ϝέκατι
γλυκὺς κατείβων καρδίαν ἰαίνει.

(89)

_ ⦙ _ ◡ ◡ _ ◡ ◡ _ ⦙ ◡ _ ◡ _ _
_ ◡ _ ◡ | _ ◡ _ _
_ ◡ _ ◡ ◡ _ ◡ _ ⦙ ◡ _ ◡ _ _
_ _ ◡ _ _ _ ⦙ _ ◡ _ ◡ _
_ _ ◡ _ | _ _ ◡ _ | ◡ _ ◡ _   5
_ _ ◡ _ _ _ _ ◡ ◡ _ ◡ _

εὕδουσι δ᾿ ὀρέων κορυφαί τε καὶ φάραγγες
πρώονές τε καὶ χαράδραι

1 φάλαγγες cod., em. de Villoison   2 πρώτονέστέ cod., em.
Welcker

φῦλά τ' ἑρπέτ' ὅσα τρέφει μέλαινα γαῖα
θῆρές τ' ὀρεσκῷοι καὶ γένος μελισσᾶν
καὶ κνώδαλ' ἐν βένθεσσι πορφυρέας ἁλός·   5
εὕδουσι δ' οἰωνῶν φῦλα τανυπτερύγων.

3 τε ἑρπετά θ' ὅσα cod.: alii alia

MIMNERMUS

(1)

τίς δὲ βίος, τί δὲ τερπνὸν ἄτερ χρυσῆς Ἀφροδίτης;
    τεθναίην, ὅτε μοι μηκέτι ταῦτα μέλοι,
κρυπταδίη φιλότης καὶ μείλιχα δῶρα καὶ εὐνή,
    οἷ' ἥβης ἄνθεα γίγνεται ἁρπαλέα
ἀνδράσιν ἠδὲ γυναιξίν· ἐπεὶ δ' ὀδυνηρὸν ἐπέλθῃ   5
    γῆρας, ὅ τ' αἰσχρὸν ὁμῶς καὶ κακὸν ἄνδρα τιθεῖ,
αἰεί μιν φρένας ἀμφὶ κακαὶ τείρουσι μέριμναι,
    οὐδ' αὐγὰς προσορῶν τέρπεται ἠελίου,
ἀλλ' ἐχθρὸς μὲν παισίν, ἀτίμαστος δὲ γυναιξίν·
    οὕτως ἀργαλέον γῆρας ἔθηκε θεός.   10

4 οἱ, εἰ codd.   οἷ' Bergk οἱ' Ahrens   6 καλὸν codd.   κακὸν
Hermann   7 μὲν codd., em. Bergk

(2)

ἡμεῖς δ' οἷά τε φύλλα φύει πολυάνθεμος ὥρη
    ἔαρος, ὅτ' αἶψ' αὐγῇς αὔξεται ἠελίου,
τοῖς ἴκελοι πήχυιον ἐπὶ χρόνον ἄνθεσιν ἥβης
    τερπόμεθα, πρὸς θεῶν εἰδότες οὔτε κακόν

1 -άνθεμος, -άνθεος codd.   2 αὐγῇ codd., em. Schneidewin

οὔτ' ἀγαθόν· Κῆρες δὲ παρεστήκασι μέλαιναι, 5
    ἢ μὲν ἔχουσα τέλος γήραος ἀργαλέου,
ἡ δ' ἑτέρη θανάτοιο· μίνυνθα δὲ γίγνεται ἥβης
    καρπός, ὅσον τ' ἐπὶ γῆν κίδναται ἠέλιος.
αὐτὰρ ἐπὴν δὴ τοῦτο τέλος παραμείψεται ὥρης,
    αὐτίκα δὴ τεθνάναι βέλτιον ἢ βίοτος· 10
πολλὰ γὰρ ἐν θυμῷ κακὰ γίγνεται· ἄλλοτε οἶκος
    τρυχοῦται, πενίης δ' ἔργ' ὀδυνηρὰ πέλει·
ἄλλος δ' αὖ παίδων ἐπιδεύεται, ὧν τε μάλιστα
    ἱμείρων κατὰ γῆς ἔρχεται εἰς Ἀίδην·
ἄλλος νοῦσον ἔχει θυμοφθόρον· οὐδέ τίς ἐστιν 15
    ἀνθρώπων, ᾧ Ζεὺς μὴ κακὰ πολλὰ διδοῖ.

(5)

ἀλλ' ὀλιγοχρόνιον γίγνεται ὥσπερ ὄναρ
ἥβη τιμήεσσα· τὸ δ' ἀργαλέον καὶ ἄμορφον
    γῆρας ὑπὲρ κεφαλῆς αὐτίχ' ὑπερκρέμαται,
ἐχθρὸν ὁμῶς καὶ ἄτιμον, ὅ τ' ἄγνωστον τιθεῖ ἄνδρα,
    βλάπτει δ' ὀφθαλμοὺς καὶ νόον ἀμφιχυθέν. 5

2 ἀργαλέον Stobaeus οὐλόμενον Theognis   3 αὐτίχ' ὑπὲρ κεφαλῆς
γῆρας ὑπερκρέμαται Theognis

(10)

ἠέλιος μὲν γὰρ πόνον ἔλλαχεν ἤματα πάντα,
    οὐδέ κοτ' ἄμπαυσις γίγνεται οὐδεμία
ἵπποισίν τε καὶ αὐτῷ, ἐπεὶ ῥοδοδάκτυλος Ἠώς
    Ὠκεανὸν προλιποῦσ' οὐρανὸν εἰσαναβῇ·
τὸν μὲν γὰρ διὰ κῦμα φέρει πολυήρατος εὐνή 5
    κοίλη Ἡφαίστου χερσὶν ἐληλαμένη

1 ἔλαχεν πόνον codd. πόνον ἔλλαχεν Hermann   6 κοίλη codd.,
em. Meineke

χρυσοῦ τιμήεντος, ὑπόπτερος, ἄκρον ἐφ' ὕδωρ
    εὕδονθ' ἁρπαλέως χώρου ἀφ' Ἑσπερίδων
γαῖαν ἐς Αἰθιόπων, ἵνα δὴ θοὸν ἅρμα καὶ ἵπποι
    ἑστᾶσ', ὄφρ' Ἠὼς ἠριγένεια μόλῃ.   10
ἔνθ' ἐπεβήσεθ' ἑῶν ὀχέων Ὑπερίονος υἱός.

9 ἵν' ἀλήθοον, ἵνα οἱ θοὸν codd., em. Meineke   11 ἐπέβη ἑτέρων
codd., em. Schneidewin

(13)

οὐ μὲν δὴ κείνου γε μένος καὶ ἀγήνορα θυμόν
    τοῖον ἐμεῦ προτέρων πεύθομαι, οἵ μιν ἴδον
Λυδῶν ἱππομάχων πυκινὰς κλονέοντα φάλαγγας
    Ἕρμιον ἂμ πεδίον, φῶτα φερεμμελίην·
τοῦ μὲν ἄρ' οὔκοτε πάμπαν ἐμέμψατο Παλλὰς Ἀθήνη   5
    δριμὺ μένος κραδίης, εὖθ' ὅ γ' ἀνὰ προμάχους
σεύαιθ' αἱματόεντος ἐν ὑσμίνῃ πολέμοιο
    πικρὰ βιαζόμενος δυσμενέων βέλεα·
οὐ γάρ τις κείνου ληῶν ἔτ' ἀμεινότερος φώς
    ἔσκεν ἐποίχεσθαι φυλόπιδος κρατερῆς   10
ἔργον, ὅτ' αὐγῇσιν φέρετ' εἴκελος ἠελίοιο.

6 εὖθ' ὅτ', ἔσθ' ὅτ', ὁππότ' codd. εὖθ' ὅ γ' Schneidewin   7 σεύηθ',
σεῦ' ἦθ' codd., em. Schneidewin αἱματόεν ὑσμίνῃ codd., suppl.
Gesner   9 δηίων ἔτ' codd. ληῶν ἔτ' Wilamowitz δηίων ἔπ' Bergk
11 ὠκέος codd., εἴκελος Meineke

SOLON

(1)

Μνημοσύνης καὶ Ζηνὸς Ὀλυμπίου ἀγλαὰ τέκνα,
    Μοῦσαι Πιερίδες, κλῦτέ μοι εὐχομένῳ·

ὄλβον μοι πρὸς θεῶν μακάρων δότε καὶ πρὸς ἁπάντων
   ἀνθρώπων αἰεὶ δόξαν ἔχειν ἀγαθήν·
εἶναι δὲ γλυκὺν ὧδε φίλοις, ἐχθροῖσι δὲ πικρόν,   5
   τοῖσι μὲν αἰδοῖον, τοῖσι δὲ δεινὸν ἰδεῖν.
χρήματα δ' ἱμείρω μὲν ἔχειν, ἀδίκως δὲ πεπᾶσθαι
   οὐκ ἐθέλω· πάντως ὕστερον ἦλθε δίκη.
πλοῦτον δ' ὃν μὲν δῶσι θεοί, παραγίγνεται ἀνδρί
   ἔμπεδος ἐκ νεάτου πυθμένος ἐς κορυφήν·   10
ὃν δ' ἄνδρες μετίωσιν ὑφ' ὕβριος, οὐ κατὰ κόσμον
   ἔρχεται, ἀλλ' ἀδίκοις ἔργμασι πειθόμενος
οὐκ ἐθέλων ἕπεται, ταχέως δ' ἀναμίσγεται ἄτη·
   ἀρχὴ δ' ἐξ ὀλίγου γίγνεται ὥστε πυρός
φλαύρη μὲν τὸ πρῶτον, ἀνιηρὴ δὲ τελευτᾷ·   15
   οὐ γὰρ δὴν θνητοῖς ὕβριος ἔργα πέλει.
ἀλλὰ Ζεὺς πάντων ἐφορᾷ τέλος, ἐξαπίνης δέ
   ὥστ' ἄνεμος νεφέλας αἶψα διεσκέδασεν
ἠρινός, ὃς πόντου πολυκύμονος ἀτρυγέτοιο
   πυθμένα κινήσας, γῆν κατὰ πυροφόρον   20
δηώσας καλὰ ἔργα θεῶν ἕδος αἰπὺν ἱκάνει
   οὐρανόν, αἰθρίην δ' αὖτις ἔθηκεν ἰδεῖν·
λάμπει δ' ἠελίοιο μένος κατὰ πίονα γαῖαν
   καλόν, ἀτὰρ νεφέων οὐδὲν ἔτ' ἔστιν ἰδεῖν—
τοιαύτη Ζηνὸς πέλεται τίσις, οὐδ' ἐφ' ἑκάστῳ   25
   ὥσπερ θνητὸς ἀνὴρ γίγνεται ὀξύχολος,
αἰεὶ δ' οὔ ἑ λέληθε διαμπερές, ὅστις ἀλιτρόν
   θυμὸν ἔχει, πάντως δ' ἐς τέλος ἐξεφάνη·
ἀλλ' ὃ μὲν αὐτίκ' ἔτεισεν, ὃ δ' ὕστερον· οἱ δὲ φύγωσιν
   αὐτοί, μηδὲ θεῶν μοῖρ' ἐπιοῦσα κίχῃ,   30
ἤλυθε πάντως αὖτις· ἀναίτιοι ἔργα τίνουσιν

11 τιμῶσιν codd. μετίωσιν Ahrens, alii alia   13 ἄτῃ, ἄτη codd.
16 δὴ codd. δὴν Gesner   27 οὔτε codd. οὔ ἑ Hermann   31
αὐτίκ' codd., em. Wyttenbach, Brunck

ἢ παῖδες τούτων ἢ γένος ἐξοπίσω.
θνητοὶ δ' ὧδε νοεῦμεν ὁμῶς ἀγαθός τε κακός τε·
    εὐθηνεῖν αὐτὸς δόξαν ἕκαστος ἔχει,
πρίν τι παθεῖν· τότε δ' αὖτις ὀδύρεται· ἄχρι δὲ τούτου   35
    χάσκοντες κούφαις ἐλπίσι τερπόμεθα.
χὥστις μὲν νούσοισιν ὑπ' ἀργαλέῃσι πιεσθῇ,
    ὡς ὑγιὴς ἔσται, τοῦτο κατεφράσατο·
ἄλλος δειλὸς ἐὼν ἀγαθὸς δοκεῖ ἔμμεναι ἀνήρ
    καὶ καλὸς μορφὴν οὐ χαρίεσσαν ἔχων·   40
εἰ δέ τις ἀχρήμων, πενίης δέ μιν ἔργα βιᾶται,
    κτήσεσθαι πάντως χρήματα πολλὰ δοκεῖ.
σπεύδει δ' ἄλλοθεν ἄλλος· ὁ μὲν κατὰ πόντον ἀλᾶται
    ἐν νηυσὶν χρῄζων οἴκαδε κέρδος ἄγειν
ἰχθυόεντ' ἀνέμοισι φορεύμενος ἀργαλέοισιν,   45
    φειδωλὴν ψυχῆς οὐδεμίαν θέμενος·
ἄλλος γῆν τέμνων πολυδένδρεον εἰς ἐνιαυτὸν
    λατρεύει, τοῖσιν καμπύλ' ἄροτρα μέλει·
ἄλλος Ἀθηναίης τε καὶ Ἡφαίστου πολυτέχνεω
    ἔργα δαεὶς χειροῖν ξυλλέγεται βίοτον,   50
ἄλλος Ὀλυμπιάδων Μουσέων πάρα δῶρα διδαχθείς,
    ἱμερτῆς σοφίης μέτρον ἐπιστάμενος·
ἄλλον μάντιν ἔθηκεν ἄναξ ἑκάεργος Ἀπόλλων,
    ἔγνω δ' ἀνδρὶ κακὸν τηλόθεν ἐρχόμενον,
ᾧ συνομαρτήσωσι θεοί· τὰ δὲ μόρσιμα πάντως   55
    οὔτε τις οἰωνὸς ῥύσεται οὔθ' ἱερά·
ἄλλοι Παιῶνος πολυφαρμάκου ἔργον ἔχοντες
    ἰητροί, καὶ τοῖς οὐδὲν ἔπεστι τέλος·
πολλάκι δ' ἐξ ὀλίγης ὀδύνης μέγα γίγνεται ἄλγος,
    κοὐκ ἄν τις λύσαιτ' ἤπια φάρμακα δούς·   60

32 ἡγεμόνων ὀπίσω codd., em. Stob. B²   34 ἐν δηνην codd.
εὐθηνεῖν Ahrens   εὖ δεινὴν Bücheler, alii alia   42 κτήσασθαι
codd., em. Bergk   πάντων codd., em. Gesner

C

τὸν δὲ κακαῖς νούσοισι κυκώμενον ἀργαλέαις τε
  ἁψάμενος χειροῖν αἶψα τίθησ᾿ ὑγιῆ.
Μοῖρα δέ τοι θνητοῖσι κακὸν φέρει ἠδὲ καὶ ἐσθλόν,
  δῶρα δ᾿ ἄφυκτα θεῶν γίγνεται ἀθανάτων.
πᾶσι δέ τοι κίνδυνος ἔπ᾿ ἔργμασιν, οὐδέ τις οἶδεν   65
  ᾗ μέλλει σχήσειν χρήματος ἀρχομένου·
ἀλλ᾿ ὃ μὲν εὖ ἔρδειν πειρώμενος οὐ προνοήσας
  ἐς μεγάλην ἄτην καὶ χαλεπὴν ἔπεσεν,
τῷ δὲ κακῶς ἔρδοντι θεὸς περὶ πάντα δίδωσιν
  συντυχίην ἀγαθήν, ἔκλυσιν ἀφροσύνης.   70
πλούτου δ᾿ οὐδὲν τέρμα πεφασμένον ἀνδράσι κεῖται·
  οἳ γὰρ νῦν ἡμέων πλεῖστον ἔχουσι βίον,
διπλασίως σπεύδουσι· τίς ἂν κορέσειεν ἅπαντας;
  κέρδεά τοι θνητοῖς ὤπασαν ἀθάνατοι,
ἄτη δ᾿ ἐξ αὐτῶν ἀναφαίνεται, ἣν ὁπόταν Ζεύς   75
  πέμψῃ τεισομένην, ἄλλοτε ἄλλος ἔχει.

75 ὁπόταν Stobaeus ὁπότε Theognis   76 ἄλλοτε τ᾿ ἄλλος Stob.,
Theogn. AO, τ᾿ om. Theogn. cett.

(3)

ἡμετέρα δὲ πόλις κατὰ μὲν Διὸς οὔποτ᾿ ὀλεῖται
  αἶσαν καὶ μακάρων θεῶν φρένας ἀθανάτων·
τοίη γὰρ μεγάθυμος ἐπίσκοπος ὀβριμοπάτρη
  Παλλὰς ᾿Αθηναίη χεῖρας ὕπερθεν ἔχει.
αὐτοὶ δὲ φθείρειν μεγάλην πόλιν ἀφραδίῃσιν   5
  ἀστοὶ βούλονται χρήμασι πειθόμενοι,
δήμου θ᾿ ἡγεμόνων ἄδικος νόος, οἷσιν ἑτοῖμον
  ὕβριος ἐκ μεγάλης ἄλγεα πολλὰ παθεῖν·
οὐ γὰρ ἐπίστανται κατέχειν κόρον οὐδὲ παρούσας
  εὐφροσύνας κοσμεῖν δαιτὸς ἐν ἡσυχίῃ.   10

πλουτοῦσιν δ' ἀδίκοις ἔργμασι πειθόμενοι

οὔθ' ἱερῶν κτεάνων οὔτε τι δημοσίων
φειδόμενοι κλέπτουσιν ἐφ' ἁρπαγῇ ἄλλοθεν ἄλλος,
   οὐδὲ φυλάσσονται σεμνὰ Δίκης θέμεθλα,
ἣ σιγῶσα σύνοιδε τὰ γιγνόμενα πρό τ' ἐόντα,   15
   τῷ δὲ χρόνῳ πάντως ἦλθ' ἀποτεισομένη·
τοῦτ' ἤδη πάσῃ πόλει ἔρχεται ἕλκος ἄφυκτον,
   ἐς δὲ κακὴν ταχέως ἤλυθε δουλοσύνην,
ἣ στάσιν ἔμφυλον πόλεμόν θ' εὕδοντ' ἐπεγείρει,
   ὃς πολλῶν ἐρατὴν ὤλεσεν ἡλικίην·   20
ἐκ γὰρ δυσμενέων ταχέως πολυήρατον ἄστυ
   τρύχεται ἐν συνόδοις τοῖς ἀδικοῦσι φίλαις.
ταῦτα μὲν ἐν δήμῳ στρέφεται κακά· τῶν δὲ πενιχρῶν
   ἱκνοῦνται πολλοὶ γαῖαν ἐς ἀλλοδαπήν
πραθέντες δεσμοῖσί τ' ἀεικελίοισι δεθέντες.   25

οὕτω δημόσιον κακὸν ἔρχεται οἴκαδ' ἑκάστῳ·
   αὔλειοι δ' ἔτ' ἔχειν οὐκ ἐθέλουσι θύραι,
ὑψηλὸν δ' ὑπὲρ ἕρκος ὑπέρθορεν, ηὗρε δὲ πάντως,
   εἰ καί τις φεύγων ἐν μυχῷ ἦ θαλάμου.
ταῦτα διδάξαι θυμὸς Ἀθηναίους με κελεύει,   30
   ὡς κακὰ πλεῖστα πόλει Δυσνομίη παρέχει,
Εὐνομίη δ' εὔκοσμα καὶ ἄρτια πάντ' ἀποφαίνει
   καὶ θαμὰ τοῖς ἀδίκοις ἀμφιτίθησι πέδας·
τραχέα λειαίνει, παύει κόρον, ὕβριν ἀμαυροῖ,
   αὐαίνει δ' ἄτης ἄνθεα φυόμενα,   35

13 ἐφ' ἁρπαγῇ, ἀφαρπαγῇ codd.   16 ἀποτισομένη Dem. cod. B
(corr.) ἀποτισαμένη cett.   19 ἐπεγείρει, ἐπεγείρειν, ἐπαγείρειν
codd. ἐπέγειρεν ci. Schneidewin   22 φίλοις codd. φίλαις Bergk
post 25 παίκακα δουλοσύνης ζυγὰ φέρουσι κακά cod. un.   28
πάντων, πάντας, πάντως codd.   29 εἴ γέ τις codd., em. anon. ἦ
θαλάμῳ codd., em. Schneidewin, Bergk

εὐθύνει δὲ δίκας σκολιὰς ὑπερήφανά τ' ἔργα
  πραΰνει, παύει δ' ἔργα διχοστασίης,
παύει δ' ἀργαλέης ἔριδος χόλον, ἔστι δ' ὑπ' αὐτῆς
  πάντα κατ' ἀνθρώπους ἄρτια καὶ πινυτά.

(5)

δήμῳ μὲν γὰρ ἔδωκα τόσον γέρας ὅσσον ἀπαρκεῖ,
  τιμῆς οὔτ' ἀφελὼν οὔτ' ἐπορεξάμενος·
οἳ δ' εἶχον δύναμιν καὶ χρήμασιν ἦσαν ἀγητοί,
  καὶ τοῖς ἐφρασάμην μηδὲν ἀεικὲς ἔχειν·
ἔστην δ' ἀμφιβαλὼν κρατερὸν σάκος ἀμφοτέροισι,   5
  νικᾶν δ' οὐκ εἴασ' οὐδετέρους ἀδίκως.

δῆμος δ' ὧδ' ἂν ἄριστα σὺν ἡγεμόνεσσιν ἔποιτο,
  μήτε λίαν ἀνεθεὶς μήτε βιαζόμενος·
τίκτει γὰρ κόρος ὕβριν, ὅταν πολὺς ὄλβος ἔπηται
  ἀνθρώποισιν ὅσοις μὴ νόος ἄρτιος ᾖ.   10

ἔργμασιν ἐν μεγάλοις πᾶσιν ἀδεῖν χαλεπόν.

1 γέρας Arist. κράτος Plu. ἀπαρκεῖ Arist. ἐπ- Plu.   2 ἐπορεξάμενος Plu. ἀπ- Arist.   8 βιαζόμενος Arist. πιεζόμενος Plu.

(10)

ἐκ νεφέλης πέλεται χιόνος μένος ἠδὲ χαλάζης,
  βροντὴ δ' ἐκ λαμπρᾶς γίγνεται ἀστεροπῆς·
ἀνδρῶν δ' ἐκ μεγάλων πόλις ὄλλυται, ἐς δὲ μονάρχου
  δῆμος ἀιδρείῃ δουλοσύνην ἔπεσεν·
λίην δ' ἐξάραντ' οὐ ῥᾴδιόν ἐστι κατασχεῖν   5
  ὕστερον, ἀλλ' ἤδη χρὴ τάδε πάντα νοεῖν.

5 λίης δ' ἐξέραντα ῥαίδιον, em. Schneidewin, Bergk   6 τάδε
suppl. Passow περὶ Dindorf, om. codd.

(13)

ὄλβιος, ᾧ παῖδές τε φίλοι καὶ μώνυχες ἵπποι
  καὶ κύνες ἀγρευταὶ καὶ ξένος ἀλλοδαπός.

(19)

παῖς μὲν ἄνηβος ἐὼν ἔτι νήπιος ἕρκος ὀδόντων
  φύσας ἐκβάλλει πρῶτον ἐν ἕπτ' ἔτεσιν.
τοὺς δ' ἑτέρους ὅτε δὴ τελέσῃ θεὸς ἕπτ' ἐνιαυτούς,
  ἥβης ἐκφαίνει σήματα γιγνομένης.
τῇ τριτάτῃ δὲ γένειον ἀεξομένων ἔτι γυίων   5
  λαχνοῦται, χροιῆς ἄνθος ἀμειβομένης.
τῇ δὲ τετάρτῃ πᾶς τις ἐν ἑβδομάδι μέγ' ἄριστος
  ἰσχύν, ἥν τ' ἄνδρες σήματ' ἔχουσ' ἀρετῆς.
πέμπτῃ δ' ὥριον ἄνδρα γάμου μεμνημένον εἶναι
  καὶ παίδων ζητεῖν εἰσοπίσω γενεήν.   10
τῇ δ' ἕκτῃ περὶ πάντα καταρτύεται νόος ἀνδρός
  οὐδ' ἔρδειν ἔθ' ὁμῶς ἔργ' ἀπάλαμνα θέλει.
ἑπτὰ δὲ νοῦν καὶ γλῶσσαν ἐν ἑβδομάσιν μέγ' ἄριστος
  ὀκτώ τ'· ἀμφοτέρων τέσσαρα καὶ δέκ' ἔτη.
τῇ δ' ἐνάτῃ ἔτι μὲν δύναται, μαλακώτερα δ' αὐτοῦ 15
  πρὸς μεγάλην ἀρετὴν γλῶσσά τε καὶ σοφίη.
τῇ δεκάτῃ δ' εἴ τις τελέσας κατὰ μέτρον ἵκοιτο,
  οὐκ ἂν ἄωρος ἐὼν μοῖραν ἔχοι θανάτου.

5 ἐπὶ codd. ἔτι Emperius   8 ἣν Clem. ἢ, οἳ Philo ἢ Anecd.
Par. ἤ Anatolius ἥν Sylburg.

(22)

ἀλλ' εἴ μοι κἂν νῦν ἔτι πείσεαι, ἔξελε τοῦτον,
  μηδὲ μέγαιρ', ὅτι σεῦ λῷον ἐπεφρασάμην,
καὶ μεταποίησον, Λιγυαστάδη, ὧδε δ' ἄειδε
  'ὀγδωκονταέτη μοῖρα κίχοι θανάτου.'

μηδέ μοι ἄκλαυστος θάνατος μόλοι, ἀλλὰ φίλοισι   5
  καλλείποιμι θανὼν ἄλγεα καὶ στοναχάς.

γηράσκω δ' αἰεὶ πολλὰ διδασκόμενος.

2 τοῖον codd. λῷον Bergk   3 ναιγιασταδη, αγιασταδὶ (αιγ-) codd.,
em. Bergk, Diels   6 καλλείποιμι Stobaeus ποιήσαιμι Plutarch

(23)

'οὐκ ἔφυ Σόλων βαθύφρων οὐδὲ βουλήεις ἀνήρ·
ἐσθλὰ γὰρ θεοῦ διδόντος αὐτὸς οὐκ ἐδέξατο.
περιβαλὼν δ' ἄγραν ἀγασθεὶς οὐκ ἐπέσπασεν μέγα
δίκτυον, θυμοῦ θ' ἁμαρτῆ καὶ φρενῶν ἀποσφαλείς·
ἤθελεν γάρ κεν κρατήσας, πλοῦτον ἄφθονον λαβὼν   5
καὶ τυραννεύσας Ἀθηνῶν μοῦνον ἡμέραν μίαν,
ἀσκὸς ὕστερον δεδάρθαι καὶ ἐπιτετρίφθαι γένος.'

                         εἰ δὲ γῆς ἐφεισάμην
πατρίδος, τυραννίδος δὲ καὶ βίης ἀμειλίχου
οὐ καθηψάμην μιάνας καὶ καταισχύνας κλέος,   10
οὐδὲν αἰδεῦμαι· πλέον γὰρ ὧδε νικήσειν δοκέω
πάντας ἀνθρώπους.

(24)

ἐγὼ δὲ τῶν μὲν οὕνεκα ξυνήγαγον
δῆμον, τί τούτων πρὶν τυχεῖν ἐπαυσάμην;
συμμαρτυροίη ταῦτ' ἂν ἐν δίκῃ χρόνου
μήτηρ μεγίστη δαιμόνων Ὀλυμπίων
ἄριστα, Γῆ μέλαινα, τῆς ἐγώ ποτε   5
ὅρους ἀνεῖλον πολλαχῇ πεπηγότας·
πρόσθεν δὲ δουλεύουσα, νῦν ἐλευθέρα.
πολλοὺς δ' Ἀθήνας πατρίδ' ἐς θεόκτιτον
ἀνήγαγον πραθέντας, ἄλλον ἐκδίκως,
ἄλλον δικαίως, τοὺς δ' ἀναγκαίης ὑπό   10
χρειοῦς φυγόντας γλῶσσαν οὐκέτ' Ἀττικήν
ἱέντας, ὡς ἂν πολλαχῇ πλανωμένους,
τοὺς δ' ἐνθάδ' αὐτοῦ δουλίην ἀεικέα
ἔχοντας ἤθη δεσποτῶν τρομευμένους
ἐλευθέρους ἔθηκα.   ταῦτα μὲν κράτει   15
ὁμοῦ βίην τε καὶ δίκην συναρμόσας
ἔρεξα καὶ διῆλθον ὡς ὑπεσχόμην.
θεσμοὺς δ' ὁμοίως τῷ κακῷ τε κἀγαθῷ
εὐθεῖαν εἰς ἕκαστον ἁρμόσας δίκην
ἔγραψα.   κέντρον δ' ἄλλος ὡς ἐγὼ λαβών,   20
κακοφραδής τε καὶ φιλοκτήμων ἀνήρ,
οὐκ ἂν κατέσχε δῆμον· εἰ γὰρ ἤθελον
ἃ τοῖς ἐναντίοισιν ἥνδανεν τότε,
αὖθις δ' ἃ τοῖσιν οὕτεροι φρασαίατο,
πολλῶν ἂν ἀνδρῶν ἥδ' ἐχηρώθη πόλις.   25
τῶν οὕνεκ' ἀλκὴν πάντοθεν ποιεύμενος
ὡς ἐν κυσὶν πολλῇσιν ἐστράφην λύκος.

15-16 κρατηομου Arist. pap. Berol. κρατει[-η] ομου Aristides ὁμοῦ
Plutarch κρατεει νομου Arist. pap. Lond.

STESICHORUS

(185)

```
 _ _∪∪_∪∪ _∪∪ _∪∪ _ _
  _∪∪ _∪∪ _∪∪ _∪∪ _ _
∪∪ _∪∪ _∪∪ _∪∪ _∪∪ _ _
∪∪ _∪∪ _∪∪ _∪∪ _ _ _∪∪_
∪∪ _∪∪ _ _ _∪∪ _∪∪
∪∪ _∪∪
```

ἆμος δ᾽ Ὑπεριονίδας δέπας ἐσκατέβαινε
χρύσεον, ὄφρα δι᾽ ὠκεανοῖο περάσας
ἀφίκοιθ᾽ ἱαρᾶς ποτὶ βένθεα νυκτὸς ἐρεμνᾶς,
ποτὶ ματέρα κουριδίαν τ᾽ ἄλοχον παίδας τε φίλους·
ὁ δ᾽ ἐς ἄλσος ἔβα δάφναισι κατάσκιον   5
ποσὶ παῖς Διός.

3 ἀφίκηθ᾽ Ath., em. Blomfield   6 ποσὶν παῖς Ath.   ποσὶ παῖς
Suchfort

(187)

```
_∪_∪ ⫶ _∪∪_∪∪_ _ ⫶ _∪∪_∪∪_∪
_∪∪_∪∪_∪
_∪∪_∪∪_∪ ⫶ _∪∪_∪∪_ _
```

πολλὰ μὲν Κυδώνια μᾶλα ποτερρίπτουν ποτὶ δίφρον
    ἄνακτι,
πολλὰ δὲ μύρσινα φύλλα
καὶ ῥοδίνους στεφάνους ἴων τε κορωνίδας οὔλας.

(192)

```
– – ∪ ∪ – ∪ ∪ – ∪
– ∪ – – | – ∪ – – | –
– – ∪ ∪ – ∪ ∪ – –
```

οὐκ ἔστ' ἔτυμος λόγος οὗτος·
οὐδ' ἔβας ἐν νηυσὶν εὐσέλμοις
οὐδ' ἵκεο πέργαμα Τροίας.

2 ἐυσσέλμοις ci. Blomfield

(219)

```
– ∪ ∪ ⋮ – ∪ ∪ – ∪ ∪ – ∪ ⋮ – ∪ ∪ – ∪ ∪ – ∪
    – ∪ ∪ – ∪ ∪ – ⋮ – ∪ ∪ – ∪ ∪ –
```

τᾷ δὲ δράκων ἐδόκησε μολεῖν κάρα βεβροτωμένος ἄκρον,
ἐκ δ' ἄρα τοῦ βασιλεὺς Πλεισθενίδας ἐφάνη.

(223)

```
            – ∪ ∪ – ∪ ∪ –
– ⋮ – ∪ ∪ – ∪ ∪ – ∪ ⋮ – ∪ ∪ – ∪ ∪ – –
– ∪ – – | – ∪ – ∪ | – ∪ –
∪ ⋮ – ∪ ∪ – ∪ ∪ – ∪ ⋮ – ∪ ∪ – ∪ ∪
– ∪ ∪ – ∪ ∪                                    5
```

οὕνεκα Τυνδάρεος
ῥέζων ποτὲ πᾶσι θεοῖς μόνας λάθετ' ἠπιοδώρου
Κύπριδος· κείνα δὲ Τυνδαρέου κόραις
χολωσαμένα διγάμους τε καὶ τριγάμους τίθησι
καὶ λιπεσάνορας.   5

1 οὕνεκά ποτε codd.: ποτέ post ῥέζων Suchfort   2 μόνας A μιᾶς
MTB

SAPPHO

(1)

‒ ∪ ‒ ⏓ ⁝ ‒ ∪ ∪ ‒ ⁝ ∪ ‒ ‒   1, 2, 3

‒ ∪ ∪ ‒ ‒   4

ποικιλόθρον᾽ ἀθανάτ᾽ ᾽Αφρόδιτα,
παῖ Δίος δολόπλοκε, λίσσομαί σε,
μή μ᾽ ἄσαισι μηδ᾽ ὀνίαισι δάμνα,
πότνια, θῦμον,

ἀλλὰ τυίδ᾽ ἔλθ᾽, αἴ ποτα κἀτέρωτα   5
τὰς ἔμας αὔδας ἀίοισα πήλοι
ἔκλυες, πάτρος δὲ δόμον λίποισα
χρύσιον ἦλθες

ἄρμ᾽ ὑπασδεύξαισα· κάλοι δέ σ᾽ ἆγον
ὤκεες στροῦθοι περὶ γᾶς μελαίνας   10
πύκνα δίννεντες πτέρ᾽ ἀπ᾽ ὠράνωἴθε-
ρος διὰ μέσσω,

αἶψα δ᾽ ἐξίκοντο· σὺ δ᾽, ὦ μάκαιρα,
μειδιαίσαισ᾽ ἀθανάτῳ προσώπῳ
ἤρε᾽ ὄττι δηῦτε πέπονθα κὤττι   15
δηῦτε κάλημμι,

κὤττι μοι μάλιστα θέλω γένεσθαι
μαινόλᾳ θύμῳ· τίνα δηῦτε πείθω
ἄψ σ᾽ ἄγην ἐς Fὰν φιλότατα; τίς σ᾽, ὦ
Ψάπφ᾽, ἀδικήει;   20

1 ποικιλόθρον᾽, ποικιλόφρον (vel sim.) codd.]ικιλοθρο[pap.   19
.]ψ σ. ἄγην[pap. μαισαγηνεσσαν vel και- codd. Fὰν Edmonds

καὶ γὰρ αἰ φεύγει, ταχέως διώξει·
αἰ δὲ δῶρα μὴ δέκετ', ἀλλὰ δώσει·
αἰ δὲ μὴ φίλει, ταχέως φιλήσει
κωὐκ ἐθέλοισα.

ἔλθε μοι καὶ νῦν, χαλέπαν δὲ λῦσον   25
ἐκ μερίμναν, ὄσσα δέ μοι τέλεσσαι
θῦμος ἰμέρρει, τέλεσον· σὺ δ' αὔτα
σύμμαχος ἔσσο.

24 κωϋκεθέλουσα, κ' ὤυκ' ἐθέλοις, κῶ εἰ καὶ θέλεις codd.

(2)

δεῦρύ μ' ἐκ Κρήτας ἐπ[ὶ τόνδ]ε ναῦον
ἄγνον, ὄππ[ᾳ τοι] χάριεν μὲν ἄλσος
μαλί[αν], βῶμοι δὲ τεθυμιάμε-
νοι [λι]βανώτῳ·

ἐν δ' ὔδωρ ψῦχρον κελάδει δι' ὔσδων   5
μαλίνων, βρόδοισι δὲ παῖς ὀ χῶρος
ἐσκίαστ', αἰθυσσομένων δὲ φύλλων
κῶμα καταίρει·

ἐν δὲ λείμων ἰππόβοτος τέθαλεν
ἠρίνοισιν ἄνθεσιν, αἰ δ' ἄηται   10
μέλλιχα πνέοισιν [
[   ]

1 δευρυμμεκρητας π[   ]. ναυγον ostr., interp. et suppl. L.-P.   2
suppl. Page   3 δεμιθυμ- ostr. δὲ τεθυμ- ci. Norsa   5 υσχων
vel. υζων ostr.   8 καταγριον vel καταιριον ostr. καταρρεῖ
Hermog. καταίρει Page   10 post τεθαλε τωτιτονριννοισ ostr.
ἠρίνοισιν Vogliano, Schubart αιααιηται ostr. αἰ δ' ἄηται L.-P.

ἔνθα δὴ σὺ . . . . ἔλοισα Κύπρι
χρυσίαισιν ἐν κυλίκεσσιν ἄβρως
ὀμμεμείχμενον θαλίαισι νέκταρ   15
οἰνοχόαισον

13 συσ . . μελοισα vel συσ . . ανελοισα ostr.   14 ακρως ostr.
ἀβροῖς Ath.   15 ὀμμεμείχμενον L.-P. . . μειχμενον ostr.
συνμεμίγμενον Ath.

(5)

Κύπρι καὶ] Νηρήϊδες, ἀβλάβη[ν μοι
τὸν κασί]γνητον δ[ό]τε τυίδ᾽ ἴκεσθα[ι
κὤσσα F]οι θύμῳ κε θέλῃ γένεσθαι
πάντα τε]λέσθην,

ὄσσα δὲ πρ]όσθ᾽ ἄμβροτε πάντα λῦσα[ι   5
καὶ φίλοισ]ι Ϝοῖσι χάραν γένεσθαι
κὠνίαν ἔ]χθροισι, γένοιτο δ᾽ ἄμμι
πῆμ᾽ ἔτι μ]ηδ᾽ εἶς·

τὰν κασιγ]νήταν δὲ θέλοι πόησθαι
ἔμμορον] τίμας, [ὀν]ίαν δὲ λύγραν   10
      ]οτοισι π[ά]ροιθ᾽ ἀχεύων
      ].να

suppl. e.p. (Grenfell, Hunt, Blass) praeter 1 Κύπρι καὶ Earle, 1 μοι,
2 τὸν Diels, Wilamowitz, 4 πάντα Jurenka, 5 λῦσαι Diels, 6 καὶ
Diels, 7 Blass, 8 Page, 9 τὰν Diels, Wilamowitz, 10 ἔμμορον
Wilamowitz

(15b)

Κύ]πρι, κα[ί σ]ε πι[κροτάτ]αν ἐπεύρ[οι,
μη]δὲ καυχάσ[α]ιτο τόδ᾽ ἐννέ[ποισα   10

suppl. e.p. (Grenfell, Hunt, Wilamowitz) praeter 9 ἐπεύροι,
10 Lobel

Δ]ωρίχα, τὸ δεύ[τ]ερον ὡς πόθε[ννον
εἰς] ἔρον ἦλθε.

(16)

ο]ἰ μὲν ἰππήων στρότον οἰ δὲ πέσδων
οἰ δὲ νάων φαῖσ' ἐπ[ὶ] γᾶν μέλαι[ν]αν
ἔ]μμεναι κάλλιστον, ἔγω δὲ κῆν' ὄττω τις ἔραται·

πά]γχυ δ' εὔμαρες σύνετον πόησαι   5
π]άντι τ[ο]ῦτ', ἀ γὰρ πόλυ περσκέθοισα
κάλλος [ἀνθ]ρώπων Ἐλένα [τὸ]ν ἄνδρα
τὸν [πανάρ]ιστον

καλλ[ίποι]σ' ἔβα 'ς Τροΐαν πλέοι[σα
κωὐδ[ὲ πα]ῖδος οὐδὲ φίλων το[κ]ήων   10
πά[μπαν] ἐμνάσθη, ἀλλὰ παράγαγ' αὔταν
      ]σαν

      ]αμπτον γὰρ [
      ] . . . κούφως τ[   ]οησ[.]ν
. .]με νῦν Ἀνακτορί[ας ὀ]νέμναι-   15
σ' οὐ] παρεοίσας·

τᾶ]ς κε βολλοίμαν ἐρατόν τε βᾶμα
κἀμάρυχμα λάμπρον ἴδην προσώπω
ἢ τὰ Λύδων ἄρματα κἀν ὄπλοισι
πεσδομ]άχεντας.   20

1–7 suppl. e.p. (Grenfell, Hunt, Wilamowitz)   8 πανάριστον
ci. L.-P.   9 suppl. L.-P.,   10 L.-P. et e.p.,   11 Theander
15 κἄμε ci. L.-P. rel. suppl. e.p.   17 τε βολλ. pap., em. e.p.
20 suppl. Page

(31)

φαίνεταί μοι κῆνος ἴσος θέοισιν
ἔμμεν' ὤνηρ, ὄττις ἐνάντιός τοι
ἰσδάνει καὶ πλάσιον ἆδυ φωνείσας ὑπακούει

καὶ γελαίσας ἰμέροεν, τό μ' ἦ μὰν   5
καρδίαν ἐν στήθεσιν ἐπτόαισεν·
ὡς γὰρ ἔς σ' ἴδω βρόχε', ὤς με φώναι-
σ' οὐδ' ἒν ἔτ' εἴκει,

ἀλλ' ἄκαν μὲν γλῶσσα †ἔαγε†, λέπτον
δ' αὔτικα χρῷ πῦρ ὑπαδεδρόμηκεν,   10
ὀππάτεσσι δ' οὐδ' ἒν ὄρημμ', ἐπιρρόμβεισι δ' ἄκουαι,

κὰδ δέ μ' ἴδρως ψῦχρος ἔχει, τρόμος δὲ
παῖσαν ἄγρει, χλωροτέρα δὲ ποίας
ἔμμι, τεθνάκην δ' ὀλίγω 'πιδεύης   15
φαίνομ' ἔμ' αὔτ[ᾳ.

ἀλλὰ πὰν τόλματον, ἐπεὶ †καὶ πένητα†

5 μὴ ἐμὰν Long. cod. P, em. Lobel   7 ὡς γὰρ σῖδω P, em. Lobel
βρόχεώς P, distinxit Tollius φωνὰς P, em. Danielsson   9 ἀλλάκᾰν
P, distinx. L.-P. ἀλλὰ κᾰμ apogg.   13 ἔκαδε μ' ἴδρῶς ψυχρός
κακχέεται P ἆδεμ' ἴδρὼς κακὸς χέεται An. Ox. i. 208 Cramer κὰδ
δέ μ' ἴδρως ψῦχρος ἔχει Page   15 πιδεύσην P 'πιδεύης ci.
Hermann 'πιδεύην Ahrens   16 vid. Dai Papiri della Società Itali-
ana (Firenze, 1965), 16–17 (Manfredo Manfredi)

(34)

ἄστερες μὲν ἀμφὶ κάλαν σελάνναν
ἂψ ἀπυκρύπτοισι φάεννον εἶδος
ὅπποτα πλήθοισα μάλιστα λάμπῃ
γᾶν

3 ὁπότ' ἂν Eust. ὁπόταν An. Par.   λάμπῃ Eust. λάμπει An. Par.
4 ⟨ἐπὶ παῖσαν⟩ suppl. Neue

(44)

⏑ ⏑ ⋮ – ⏑ ⏑ – ⏑ ⏑ – ⏑ ⏑ – ⋮ ⏑ –

Κυπρο. [   ]ας·
κάρυξ ἦλθε θε[   ]ελε[. . .] . θεις
Ἴδαος ταδεκα . . . φ[. .] . ις τάχυς ἄγγελος
         deest unus versus
τάς τ' ἄλλας Ἀσίας . [.]δε.αν κλέος ἄφθιτον·
Ἔκτωρ καὶ συνέταιρ[ο]ι ἄγοισ' ἐλικώπιδα   5
Θήβας ἐξ ἱέρας Πλακίας τ' ἀ[π' ἀι]ν‹ν›άω
ἄβραν Ἀνδρομάχαν ἐνὶ ναῦσιν ἐπ' ἄλμυρον
πόντον· πόλλα δ' [ἐλί]γματα χρύσια κάμματα
πορφύρ[α] καταύτ[. .]να, ποίκιλ' ἀθύρματα,
ἀργύρα τ' ἀνάριθμα ποτήρια κἀλέφαις.   10
ὢς εἶπ'· ὀτραλέως δ' ἀνόρουσε πάτ[η]ρ φίλος·
φάμα δ' ἦλθε κατὰ πτόλιν εὐρύχορον φίλοις·
αὔτικ' Ἰλίαδαι σατίναι[ς] ὐπ' ἐυτρόχοις
ἆγον αἰμιόνοις, ἐπ[έ]βαινε δὲ παῖς ὄχλος
γυναίκων τ' ἄμα παρθενίκα[ν] τ . . [. .]ροσφύρων,   15
χῶρις δ' αὖ Περάμοιο θύγ[α]τρες[
ἴππ[οις] δ' ἄνδρες ὔπαγον ὐπ' ἀρ[ματ-
π[   ]ες ἠίθεοι μεγάλω[σ]τι δ[

omnia suppl. e.p. (Grenfell, Hunt, Wilamowitz) praeter

δ[   ]. ἀνίοχοι φ[. . . . .] . [
π[']ξα.ο[20

desunt aliquot versus

ἴ]κελοι θέοι[ς
]ἄγνον ἀολ[λε-

ὄρμαται[   ]νον ἐς Ἴλιο[ν,
αὖλος δ᾽ ἀδυ[μ]έλης [κίθαρίς] τ᾽ ὀνεμίγνυ[το
καὶ ψ[ό]φο[ς κ]ροτάλ[ων, λιγέ]ως δ᾽ ἄρα πάρ[θενοι   25
ἄειδον μέλος ἄγν[ον, ἴκα]νε δ᾽ ἐς αἴθ[ερα
ἄχω θεσπεσία γελ[
πάντα δ᾽ ἦς κὰτ ὄδο[ις
κράτηρες φίαλαί τ᾽ ὀ[. . .]υεδε[. .] . . εακ[.] . [
μύρρα καὶ κασία λίβανός τ᾽ ὀνεμείχνυτο·   30
γύναικες δ᾽ ἐλέλυσδον ὅσαι προγενέστερα[ι,
πάντες δ᾽ ἄνδρες ἐπήρατον ἴαχον ὄρθιον
Πάον᾽ ὀνκαλέοντες ἐκάβολον εὐλύραν,
ὕμνην δ᾽ Ἔκτορα κ᾽Ἀνδρομάχαν θεοεικέλο[ις.

24–26 init. (Hunt), 24 κίθαρίς vel μάγαδίς, 25 λιγέως, 26 ἴκανε,
αἴθερα (L.-P.), 28 ὄδοις (Hunt) ὄδον (L.-P.).   2 ἔλεγε στάθεις ci.
Jurenka   31 ε]λελυσδ[ο]ν superscr. ξα P.Oxy. 1232 ολολυζο[ν]
P.Oxy. 2076

(47)

Ἔρος δ᾽ ἐτίναξέ μοι
φρένας, ὡς ἄνεμος κὰτ ὄρος δρύσιν ἐμπέτων.

(49)

ἠράμαν μὲν ἔγω σέθεν Ἄτθι πάλαι ποτά· . . .
σμίκρα μοι πάις ἔμμεν᾽ ἐφαίνεο κἄχαρις.

1 ἄτοι, ἄτε codd. Ἄτθι Bentley   2 ἔμμεναι, ἔτι codd. φαίνεο,
φαίνεαι codd., em. Bergk

(55)

‒ ⌣̣ : ‒ ⌣ ⌣ ‒ : ‒ ⌣ ⌣ ‒ : ‒ ⌣ ⌣ ‒ : ⌣ ‒

κατθάνοισα δὲ κείσῃ οὐδέ ποτα μναμοσύνα σέθεν
ἔσσετ' οὐδὲ πόθα εἰς ὕστερον· οὐ γὰρ πεδέχῃς βρόδων
τῶν ἐκ Πιερίας, ἀλλ' ἀφάνης κἀν 'Αίδα δόμῳ
φοιτάσῃς πεδ' ἀμαύρων νεκύων ἐκπεποταμένα.

2 οὐδέποκ' codd. οὐδὲ πόθα εἰς Wilamowitz οὐδ' ἴα τοῖς Page

(81b)

⌣̣ : ‒ ⌣ ⌣ ‒ : ‒ ⌣ ⌣ ‒ : ‒ ⌣ ⌣ ‒ : ⌣ ‒ ‒

σὺ δὲ στεφάνοις, ὦ Δίκα, πέρθεσθ' ἐράτοις φόβαισιν
ὄρπακας ἀνήτω συναέρραισ' ἀπάλαισι χέρσιν·
εὐάνθεα γὰρ †πέλεται† καὶ Χάριτες μάκαιραι
μᾶλλον ποτόρην, ἀστεφανώτοισι δ' ἀπυστρέφονται.

1 παρθεσθ Ath. cod. A, em. Bentley ἐράταις A, em. Fick   2
συνερραις A, em. Hunt ἀπαλλαγιση A, em. Casaubon   3 μακαιρα
A, em. Wilamowitz   4 προτερην A ποτόρην Seidl, Diehl
προφέρην Lobel

(94)

⌣̣ ⌣̣ : ‒ ⌣ ⌣ ‒ : ⌣ ‒   1, 2
‒ ⌣̣ : ‒ ⌣ ⌣ ‒ ⌣ ⌣ ‒ : ⌣ ‒   3

τεθνάκην δ' ἀδόλως θέλω·
ἄ με ψισδομένα κατελίμπανεν

πόλλα καὶ τόδ' ἔειπέ [μοι·
'ὤμ' ὡς δεῖνα πεπ[όνθ]αμεν·
Ψάπφ', ἦ μάν σ' ἀέκοισ' ἀπυλιμπάνω.'   5

3 suppl. Blass

τὰν δ' ἔγω τάδ' ἀμειβόμαν·
'χαίροισ' ἔρχεο κἄμεθεν
μέμναισ', οἶσθα γὰρ ὥς σε πεδήπομεν·

αἰ δὲ μή, ἀλλά σ' ἔγω θέλω
ὄμναισαι [. . . .] . [. . .] . . αι   10
. . [   ] καὶ κάλ' ἐπάσχομεν.

πό[λλοις γὰρ στεφάν]οις ἴων
καὶ βρ[όδων κρο]κίων τ' ὔμοι
κα . . [   ] πὰρ ἔμοι περεθήκαο,

καὶ πό[λλαις ὐπα]θύμιδας   15
πλέκ[ταις ἀμφ' ἀ]πάλᾳ δέρᾳ
ἀνθέων ἔ[βαλες] πεποημμέναις,

καὶ πόλλῳ [   ]. μύρῳ
βρενθείῳ . [   ]ρυ[. .]ν
ἐξαλείψαο κα[ὶ βασ]ιληίῳ,   20

καὶ στρώμν[αν ἐ]πὶ μολθάκαν
ἀπάλαν πα . [   ] . . . ων
ἐξίης πόθο[ν   ] . νίδων

κωὔτε τις[οὔ]τε τι
ἶρον οὔδυ[   ]   25
ἔπλετ' ὄππ[οθεν ἄμ]μες ἀπέσκομεν

8 ωσε em. Schubart   12 suppl. Page   13 βρόδων suppl.
Schubart κροκίων ci. Page   15–16 suppl. ex Ath. 15. 674d
17 suppl. Theander   18 πόλλῳ ci. Page   20 suppl. Schubart
ex Ath. 15. 690e   21 suppl. Schubart   24 οὔτε τι ci. Page
26 suppl. Lobel, Wilamowitz

οὐκ ἄλσος . [χ]όρος
                        ]ψοφος
                        ] . . . οιδιαι

         .   .   .   .   .

27 χόρος ci. L.-P.

(96)

```
– ∪ – ⁞ ∪ ∪ – ∪ ∪ – ∪ –
          ∪ ∪ – ∪ ∪ – ∪ –
          ∪ ∪ – ∪ ∪ – ∪ – ⁞ ∪ – –
```

         .   .   .   .   .

         ]Σαρδ . [. .]
         πόλ]λακι τυίδε [ν]ῶν ἔχοισα

ὠσπ . [. . .] . ὤομεν, . [. . .] . . χ[. .]-
σε θέᾳ σ' ἰκέλαν ἀρι-
γνώτᾳ, σᾷ δὲ μάλιστ' ἔχαιρε μόλπᾳ.   5

νῦν δὲ Λύδαισιν ἐμπρέπεται γυναί-
κεσσιν ὥς ποτ' ἀελίω
δύντος ἀ βροδοδάκτυλος σελάννα

πάντα περρέχοισ' ἄστρα· φάος δ' ἐπί-
σχει θάλασσαν ἐπ' ἀλμύραν   10
ἴσως καὶ πολυανθέμοις ἀρούραις·

ἀ δ' ἐέρσα κάλα κέχυται, τεθάλαισι δὲ βρόδα κἄπαλ' ἄν-
θρυσκα καὶ μελίλωτος ἀνθεμώδης·

4–5 σεθεασικελαναρι-γνωτασεδε cod., em. Solmsen, Lobel   8
μήνα cod. σελάννα ci. Schubart

πόλλα δὲ ζαφοίταισ’, ἀγάνας ἐπι-   15
μνάσθεισ’ Ἄτθιδος ἰμέρῳ
λέπταν ποι φρένα κ[ᾶ]ρ[ι σᾷ] βόρηται·

  .   .   .   .   .

17 κ[ᾶ]ρι σᾶ⟨ι⟩ ci. Page

(102)

◡ – ◡ – ◡ – – ┊ ◡ ◡ – ◡ – ◡ – –

γλύκηα μᾶτερ, οὔτοι δύναμαι κρέκην τὸν ἴστον,
πόθῳ δάμεισα παῖδος βραδίναν δι’ Ἀφροδίταν.

(104a)

Ἔσπερε πάντα φέρων ὄσα φαίνολις ἐσκέδασ’ αὔως,
†φέρεις ὄιν, φέρεις† αἶγα, φέρεις ἄπυ μάτερι παῖδα.

1 φέρεις Demetr. cod. P φέρων cett.   2 φέρεις οἶνον φέρεις αἶγα
φέρεις ματέρι παῖδα Demetr. cod. P φέρεις οἶον φέρεις οἶνον φέρεις
αἶγα φέρεις ἄποιον μητέρι παῖδα Et. Gen. B p. 129 Miller ὄιν
Manuzio οἶν Bentivoglio φέρεις ἄπυ μάτερι ci. Bergk

(105a)

οἶον τὸ γλυκύμαλον ἐρεύθεται ἄκρῳ ἐπ’ ὔσδῳ,
ἄκρον ἐπ’ ἀκροτάτῳ, λελάθοντο δὲ μαλοδρόπηες·
οὐ μὰν ἐκλελάθοντ’, ἀλλ’ οὐκ ἐδύναντ’ ἐπίκεσθαι.

(105c)

οἴαν τὰν ὐάκινθον ἐν ὤρεσι ποίμενες ἄνδρες
πόσσι καταστείβοισι, χάμαι δέ τε πόρφυρον ἄνθος . . .

(110a)

⏑⏑⏑ : – ⏑⏑ – ⏑⏑ – : –

θυρώρῳ πόδες ἐπτορόγυιοι,
τὰ δὲ σάμβαλα πεμπεβόηα,
πίσσυγγοι δὲ δέκ' ἐξεπόναισαν.

(111)

– – : – ⏑⏑ – : –   1
⏑ : – ⏑⏑ – ⏑⏑ – : –   3, 6

ἴψοι δὴ τὸ μέλαθρον —
ὑμήναον —
ἀέρρετε τέκτονες ἄνδρες·
ὑμήναον.
γάμβρος †εἰσέρχεται ἴσος† Ἄρευι,   5
ἄνδρος μεγάλω πόλυ μέζων.

2 et 4 om. Demetr. cod. P.   5 εἰσέρχεται ἴσος Demetr. cod. P
ἔρχεται ἴσος Hephaest. εἰσ' ἴσ' Lobel

(115)

⏑ – : – ⏑⏑ – ⏑⏑ – ⏑⏑ – : –

τίῳ σ', ὦ φίλε γάμβρε, κάλως ἐικάσδω;
ὄρπακι βραδίνῳ σε μάλιστ' ἐικάσδω.

(130)

⏑⏑⏑ : – ⏑⏑ – ⏑⏑ – : ⏑ –

Ἔρος δηὖτέ μ' ὁ λυσιμέλης δόνει,
γλυκύπικρον ἀμάχανον ὄρπετον.

(132)

–⏑–⏑|–⏑–|–⏑–⏑|–⏑–⏑
–⏑–⏑|–⏑–|–⏑⏑–⏑––
–⏑–⏑|–⏑–⏑|––⏑–|⏑––

ἔστι μοι κάλα πάις χρυσίοισιν ἀνθέμοισιν
ἐμφέρην ἔχοισα μόρφαν Κλέις ἀγαπάτα,
ἀντὶ τᾶς ἔγωὐδὲ Λυδίαν παῖσαν οὐδ' ἐράνναν . . .

Fr. Adesp. 976 (*P.M.G.*)

⏓⋮–⏑⏑–⋮⏑––

δέδυκε μὲν ἀ σελάννα
καὶ Πληΐαδες, μέσαι δὲ
νύκτες, παρὰ δ' ἔρχετ' ὤρα,
ἔγω δὲ μόνα κατεύδω.

1 σελάνα codd. et schol. ν sup. ν scr. Hephaist. cod. A   2 μέσαι, σ
sup. σ scr., I μέσσαι M

ALCAEUS

(6)

⏓–⏑–⏓⋮–⏑⏑–⋮⏑–   1, 2
⏓–⏑–⏓⋮–⏑––   3
–⏑⏑–⏑⏑–⋮⏑––   4

τόδ' αὖτε κῦμα τὼ προτέρω †νέμω
στείχει, παρέξει δ' ἄμμι πόνον πόλυν

1 νέμω Heracl. ABG Ald. νόμω O

ἄντλην, ἐπεί κε νᾶος ἔμβᾳ
          ] .όμεθ᾽ ε[

          ] . . [. .] · [5
[   ]
φαρξώμεθ᾽ ὡς ὤκιστα [τοίχοις,
ἐς δ᾽ ἔχυρον λίμενα δρό[μωμεν·

καὶ μή τιν᾽ ὄκνος μόλθ[ακος ἀμμέων
λάβη· πρόδηλον γὰρ μέγ᾽ [ἀέθλιον·   10
μνάσθητε τὼ πάροιθα μ[όχθω·
νῦν τις ἄνηρ δόκιμος γε[νέσθω.

καὶ μὴ καταισχύνωμεν [ἀνανδρίᾳ
ἔσλοις τόκηας γᾶς ὕπα κε[ιμένοις·

                .   .   .   .   .

3 ἐμβαίνει codd. ἔμβᾳ Seidler ἐμβαί—νηι ci. Page   8, 9, 12,
14 suppl. Grenfell, Hunt   10 λαχηι superscr. β pap. suppl.
Wilamowitz   11, 13 suppl. Diehl

                        (34a)

−∪−⏑ ⋮ −∪∪−⋮∪−−   1, 2, 3
−∪∪−−   4

δεῦτέ μοι νᾶ]σον Πέλοπος λίποντε[ς,
παῖδες ἴφθ]ιμοι Δ[ίος] ἠδὲ Λήδας,
εὐνόῳ] θύ[μ]ῳ προ[φά]νητε, Κάστορ
καὶ Πολύδε[υ]κες·

οἳ κὰτ εὔρηαν χ[θόνα] καὶ θάλασσαν   5
παῖσαν ἔρχεσθ᾽ ὠ[κυπό]δων ἐπ᾽ ἵππων,

suppl. Grenfell, Hunt, Wilamowitz praeter 1 δεῦτέ μοι Page νᾶ-
Lobel, 3 εὐνόῳ Diehl

ῥήα δ' ἀνθρώποι[ς] θα[ν]άτω ῥύεσθε
ζακρυόεντος,

εὐσδ[ύγ]ων θρώσκοντ[ες ἐπ'] ἄκρα νάων
π]ήλοθεν λάμπροι πρό[τον' ὀν]τρ[έχο]ντες   10
ἀργαλέα δ' ἐν νύκτι φ[άος φέ]ροντες
ναῒ μ[ε]λαίνᾳ·   .   .   .   .   .

9 εὐσδύγων Edmonds, 10 πρότον' ὀντρέχοντες Bowra

(38A)

◡◡⋮ – ◡◡ – ◡◡ – ◡◡ – ⋮ ◡ –

πῶνε [καὶ μέθυ' ὦ] Μελάνιππ' ἄμ' ἔμοι· τί [φαῖς
†ὄταμε[. . . .]διννάεντ'† Ἀχέροντα μεγ[

ζάβαι[ς ἀ]ελίω κόθαρον φάος [ἄψερον
ὄψεσθ'; ἀλλ' ἄγι μὴ μεγάλων ἐπ[ιβάλλεο·

καὶ γὰρ Σίσυφος Αἰολίδαις βασίλευς [ἔφα   5
ἀνδρῶν πλεῖστα νοησάμενος [θανάτω κρέτην·

ἀλλὰ καὶ πολύιδρις ἔων ὑπὰ κᾶρι [δὶς
διννάεντ' Ἀχέροντ' ἐπέραισε, μ[

αὔτῳ μόχθον ἔχην Κρονίδαις βα[σίλευς κάτω
μελαίνας χθόνος· ἀλλ' ἄγι μὴ τά[δ' ἐπέλπεο·   10

θᾶς] τ' ἀβάσομεν αἴ ποτα κἄλλοτα . [
. . .]ην ὄττινα τῶνδε πάθην τά[χα δῷ θέος.

. . . . ἄνε]μος βορίαις ἐπι . [

suppl. 1 καὶ μέθυ' ὦ, 3 ἄψερον, 12 Diehl   1 φαῖς Schmidt,
3 ζάβαις ἀελίω, 10, 13 Grenfell, Hunt, Wilamowitz, 4–5, 7, 10
Wilamowitz, 6, 9 Page.   11 θᾶς τ' ci. Page.

(42)

ὡς λόγος, κάκων ἄ[χος ἔννεκ' ἔργων
Περράμῳ καὶ παῖσ[ί ποτ', Ὤλεν', ἦλθεν
ἐκ σέθεν πίκρον, π[ύρι δ' ὤλεσε Ζεῦς
Ἴλιον ἴραν.

οὐ τεαύταν Αἰακίδαι[ς ἄγανος   5
πάντας ἐς γάμον μάκ[αρας καλέσσαις
ἄγετ' ἐκ Νή[ρ]ηος ἔλων [μελάθρων
πάρθενον ἄβραν

ἐς δόμον Χέρρωνος· ἔλ[υσε δ' ἄγνας
ζῶμα παρθένω· φιλό[τας δ' ἔβαλε   10
Πήλεος καὶ Νηρεΐδων ἀρίστ[ας,
ἐς δ' ἐνίαυτον

παῖδα γέννατ' αἰμιθέων [φέριστον
ὄλβιον ξάνθαν ἐλάτη[ρα πώλων·
οἱ δ' ἀπώλοντ' ἀμφ' Ἐ[λένᾳ Φρύγες τε   15
καὶ πόλις αὔτων.

suppl. 1–3, 5, 10 Page, 13 Diehl, cetera e.p. (Grenfell, Hunt, Wilamowitz)

(45)

Ἔβρε, κ[άλ]λιστος ποτάμων πὰρ Ἆ[ἶνον
ἐξί[ησθ' ἐς] πορφυρίαν θάλασσαν
Θρᾳκ[ίας ἐρ]ευγόμενος ζὰ γαίας
.]ιππ[.] . [. .]ι·

καί σε πόλλαι παρθένικαι 'πέπ[οισιν   5
. . . .]λων μήρων ἀπάλαισι χέρ[σι
. . . .]α· θέλγονται τὸ [σ]ὸν ὡς ἄλει[ππα
θή[ἵο]ν ὕδωρ
                        .   .   .   .

1–3, 5, 7, 8 suppl. Lobel   1 Ἆ[ἶνον Lobel vel Ἆ[ἶνῳ Page
3 Θρᾳκ[ίας vel Θρᾳῖκ[ων Lobel   6 suppl. Grenfell, Hunt,
Wilamowitz

(129)

] . ρά . α τόδε Λέσβιοι
. . .] . . . . εὔδειλον τέμενος μέγα
ξῦνον κά[τε]σσαν, ἐν δὲ βώμοις
ἀθανάτων μακάρων ἔθηκαν,

κἀπωνύμασσαν ἀντίαον Δία,   5
σὲ δ' Αἰολήαν [κ]υδαλίμαν θέον
πάντων γενέθλαν, τὸν δὲ τέρτον
τόνδε κεμήλιον ὠνύμασσ[α]ν

Ζόννυσσον ὠμήσταν. ἄ[γι]τ' εὔνοον
θῦμον σκέθοντες ἀμμετέρα[ς] ἄρας   10
ἀκούσατ', ἐκ δὲ τῶν[δ]ε μόχθων
ἀργαλέας τε φύγας ῥ[ύεσθε,

omnia suppl. Lobel

τὸν "Υρραον δὲ πα[ῖδ]α πεδελθέτω
κήνων 'Ε[ρίννυ]ς ὤς ποτ' ἀπώμνυμεν
τόμοντες ἄ . . [΄ . .]ν . .   15
μηδάμα μηδένα τῶν ἑταίρων

ἀλλ' ἢ θάνοντες γᾶν ἐπιέμμενοι
κείσεσθ' ὑπ' ἄνδρων οἳ τότ' ἐπικ . ΄ ην
ἤπειτα κακκτάνοντες αὔτοις
δᾶμον ὑπὲξ ἀχέων ῥύεσθαι.   20

κήνων ὁ φύσγων οὐ διελέξατο
πρὸς θῦμον, ἀλλὰ βραϊδίως πόσιν
ἔ]μβαις ἐπ' ὀρκίοισι δάπτει
τὰν πόλιν ἄμμι δέδ[.] . . [.] .ί.αις

οὐ κὰν νόμον [.]ον . . [   ] ΄ [ ]   25
γλαύκας ἀ[.] . . [.] . . [
γεγρά . [
Μύρσιλ[ο

desunt iv versus

(130)

⌣ ⌣ : – ⌣ ⌣ – : – ⌣ ⌣ – : ⌣ –   1, 2
⌣ ⌣ : – ⌣ ⌣ – : ⌣ – –   3
⌣ : – ⌣ ⌣ – : – ⌣ ⌣ – : ⌣ –   4

ἄγνοις . . ςβιότοις . . ις ὁ τάλαις ἔγω
ζώω μοῖραν ἔχων ἀγροϊκωτίκαν
ἰμέρρων ἀγόρας ἄκουσαι
καρυ[ζο]μένας ᾿Ωγεσιλαΐδα

omnia suppl. et corr. Lobel

καὶ β[ό]λλας· τὰ πάτηρ καὶ πάτερος πάτηρ   20
καγγ[ε]γήρασ' ἔχοντες πεδὰ τωνδέων
τὼν [ἀ]λλαλοκάκων πολίταν,
ἔγ[ωγ' ἀ]πὺ τούτων ἀπελήλαμαι

φεύγων ἐσχατίαισ', ὡς δ' 'Ονυμακλέης
ἔνθα[δ'] οἶος ἐοίκησα λυκαιμίαις   25
. [   ]ον [π]όλεμον· στάσιν γὰρ
πρὸς κρ . [. . . .] . οὐκ †ἄμεινον† ὀννέλην·

.] . [. . .] . [. .] . μακάρων ἐς τέμ[ε]νος θέων
ἔοι[. . . . .] με[λ]αίνας ἐπίβαις χθόνος·
χλι . [.] . [.] . [.]ν συνόδοισί μ' αὔταις   30
οἴκημμι κ[ά]κων ἔκτος ἔχων πόδας,

ὄππα Λ[εσβί]αδες κριννόμεναι φύαν
πώλεντ' ἐλκεσίπεπλοι, περὶ δὲ βρέμει
ἄχω θεσπεσία γυναίκων
ἴρα[ς ὀ]λολύγας ἐνιαυσίας   35

. . . . . .

(308b)

χαῖρε Κυλλάνας ὁ μέδεις, σὲ γάρ μοι
θῦμος ὕμνην, τὸν κορύφαισιν †αὐγαῖς
Μαῖα γέννατο Κρονίδᾳ μίγεισα
παμβασίληϊ.

2 αὐγαῖς, ἀγναῖς codd. αὔταις ci. Schulze ἄκραις Meineke ἄγνα
Bowra

(326)

ἀσυννέτημμι τῶν ἀνέμων στάσιν·
τὸ μὲν γὰρ ἔνθεν κῦμα κυλίνδεται,
τὸ δ' ἔνθεν, ἄμμες δ' ὂν τὸ μέσσον
νᾶϊ φορήμμεθα σὺν μελαίνᾳ,

χείμωνι μόχθεντες μεγάλῳ μάλα·   5
πὲρ μὲν γὰρ ἄντλος ἰστοπέδαν ἔχει,
λαῖφος δὲ πὰν ζάδηλον ἤδη,
καὶ λάκιδες μέγαλαι κὰτ αὖτο,

χόλαισι δ' ἄγκοννναι, τὰ δ' ὀή[ϊα
4—stays
         .   .   .   .   .

1 ἀσυννέτην νὴ et al. codd., em. Ahrens   9 ἄγκυραι codd.
ἄγκονναι Unger ὀήϊα ci. L.-P.

(332)

νῦν χρῆ μεθύσθην καί τινα πὲρ βίαν
πώνην, ἐπεὶ δὴ κάτθανε Μύρσιλος . . .

1 πρὸς βίαν Ath. cod. A, em. Lobel   2 πονεῖν A, em. Ahrens

(333)

οἶνος γὰρ ἀνθρώπω δίοπτρον.

ἀνθρώποις codd., em. Lobel

(335)

οὐ χρῆ κάκοισι θῦμον ἐπιτρέπην·
προκόψομεν γὰρ οὐδὲν ἀσάμενοι,

ὦ Βύκχι, φαρμάκων δ' ἄριστον
οἶνον ἐνεικαμένοις μεθύσθην.

3 φάρμακον Ath. cod. A, em. Lobel

(338)

ὔει μὲν ὁ Ζεῦς, ἐκ δ' ὀράνω μέγας
χείμων, πεπάγαισιν δ' ὑδάτων ῥόαι
‹   ἔνθεν   ›
‹   .   ›

κάββαλλε τὸν χείμων', ἐπὶ μὲν τίθεις   5
πῦρ, ἐν δὲ κέρναις οἶνον ἀφειδέως
μέλιχρον, αὐτὰρ ἀμφὶ κόρσᾳ
μόλθακον ἀμφι‹βάλων› γνόφαλλον.

8 ἀμφιγνόφαλλον Ath. codd. AC ἀμφιβάλων suppl. Grotefend

(346)

$- \underset{\cdot}{\cup} \mid - \cup \cup - \mid : - \cup \cup - \mid : - \cup \cup - \mid : \cup -$

πώνωμεν· τί τὰ λύχν' ὀμμένομεν; δάκτυλος ἀμέρα.
κὰδ δἄερρε κυλίχναις μεγάλαις †αιτα† ποικίλαις·

οἶνον γὰρ Σεμέλας καὶ Δίος υἶος λαθικάδεον
ἀνθρώποισιν ἔδωκ'. ἔγχεε κέρναις ἔνα καὶ δύο

πλήαις κὰκ κεφάλας, ‹ἀ› δ' ἀτέρα τὰν ἀτέραν κύλιξ   5
ὠθήτω . . .

1 τὸν λύχνον σβέννυμεν, τὸν λύχνον ἀμμένομεν codd., em. Porson
2 αιταποικιλλις, αιταποικιλα codd. αἶψ ἀπὺ πασσάλων Ahrens, Lobel
αἶ ‹πο›τα ποικίλαις ci. Page   3 -καδέα, -κηδέα codd., em. Lobel
5 suppl. Porson

(347)

τέγγε πλεύμονας οἴνῳ, τὸ γὰρ ἄστρον περιτέλλεται,
ἀ δ' ὤρα χαλέπα, πάντα δὲ δίψαισ' ὐπὰ καύματος,

ἄχει δ' ἐκ πετάλων · ἄδεα τέττιξ, πτερύγων δ' ὔπα
κακχέει λιγύραν ⟨πύκνον⟩ ἀοίδαν, ⟨θέρος⟩ ὄπποτα

φλόγιον †καθέταν ἐπιπτάμενον καταυδείη†   5
⟨   ⟩

ἄνθει δὲ σκόλυμος· νῦν δὲ γύναικες μιαρώταται,
λέπτοι δ' ἄνδρες, ἐπεὶ ⟨δὴ⟩ κεφάλαν καὶ γόνα Σείριος

ἄσδει . . .

1 τέγγε πνεύμονας (vel πλεύ-) οἴνῳ, οἴνῳ πνεύμονα τέγγε codd.
4 suppl. Bergk   5 πεπτάμενον ci. Hartung καταυλέῃ ci. Ahrens

(350)

⏑⏑⏑ : –⏑⏑– : –⏑⏑– : ⏑–

ἦλθες ἐκ περάτων γᾶς ἐλεφαντίναν
λάβαν τὼ ξίφεος χρυσοδέταν ἔχων
. . . τὸν ἀδελφὸν Ἀντιμενίδαν . . . φησὶν Ἀλκαῖος Βαβυλωνίοις συμμαχοῦντα τελέσαι
ἄεθλον μέγαν, εὐρύσαο δ' ἐκ πόνων,
κτένναις ἄνδρα μαχαίταν βασιλήιων   5
παλάσταν ἀπυλείποντα μόναν ἴαν
παχέων ἀπὺ πέμπων . . .

5 βασιλήων codd., em. Bergk   6 μόνον ἀνίαν codd., em. Ahrens

(357)

$$- \underline{\smile} - \smile \smile - \smile - \;\vdots\; \underline{\smile}\,\underline{\smile} - \smile \smile - \smile - \;\vdots\; \underline{\smile} - \smile -$$

[   ] ... [   ]

μαρμαίρει δὲ μέγας δόμος χάλκῳ, παῖσα δ' ἄρ' εὖ κεκόσμη-
    ται στέγα

λάμπραισιν κυνίαισι, κὰτ τᾶν λεῦκοι κατέπερθεν ἵππιοι
    λόφοι

νεύοισιν, κεφάλαισιν ἄνδρων ἀγάλματα· χάλκιαι δὲ πασ-
    σάλοις

κρύπτοισιν περικείμεναι λάμπραι κνάμιδες, ἔρκος ἰσχύρω
    βέλεος,   5

θόρρακές τε νέω λίνω κοῖλαί τε κὰτ ἄσπιδες βεβλήμεναι·

πὰρ δὲ Χαλκίδικαι σπάθαι, πὰρ δὲ ζώματα πόλλα καὶ
    κυπάσσιδες.

τῶν οὐκ ἔστι λάθεσθ' ἐπεὶ δὴ πρώτιστ' ὑπὰ τῶργον
    ἔσταμεν τόδε.

2 Ἄρη Ath. cod. A   π]αισαδᾶ[pap.   ἄρ' εὖ Page   5 ερκ[pap.
ἄρκος Ath. cod. A   8 πρώτισθ' ὑπὸ ἔργον codd., em. Lobel

(362)

ἀλλ' ἀνήτω μὲν περὶ ταῖς δέραισι
περθέτω πλέκταις ὑπαθύμιδάς τις,
κὰδ δὲ χευάτω μύρον ἆδυ κὰτ τὼ
στήθεος ἄμμι.

IBYCUS

(282a)

```
– ⌣⌣ – ⌣⌣ – ⌣⌣ – ⌣ ⌣                         str. 1, 2
– ⌣⌣ – ⌣⌣ –                                        3
⌣⌣ – ⌣ ⌣ ⦙ – ⌣ – –                                  4


⌣⌣ – ⌣⌣ – ⌣ ⌣ – –                            ep. 1, 2, 3
– ⌣ ⦙ – ⌣ ⌣ – ⌣ ⌣ – ⌣ ⌣ – ⦙ –                       4
– ⌣ ⌣ – ⦙ – ⌣ ⌣ – ⦙ ⌣ –                             5
```

οἳ κ]αὶ Δαρδανίδα Πριάμοιο μέ-
γ' ἄσ]τυ περικλεὲς ὄλβιον ἠνάρον
Ἄργ]οθεν ὀρνυμένοι
Ζη]νὸς μεγάλοιο βουλαῖς

ξα]νθᾶς Ἑλένας περὶ εἴδει   5
δῆ]ριν πολύυμνον ἔχ[ο]ντες
πό]λεμον κατὰ δακρ[υό]εντα,
Πέρ]γαμον δ' ἀνέ[β]α ταλαπείριο[ν ἄ]τα
χρυ]σοέθειραν δ[ι]ὰ Κύπριδα.

νῦ]ν δέ μοι οὔτε ξειναπάταν Π[άρι]ν   10
ἐστ'] ἐπιθύμιον οὔτε τανί[σφ]υρ[ον
ὑμ]νῆν Κασσάνδραν
Πρι]άμοιό τε παῖδας ἄλλου[ς

Τρο]ίας θ' ὑψιπύλοιο ἁλώσι[μο]ν
ἆμ]αρ ἀνώνυμον· οὐδ' ἐπ[ελεύσομαι   15

11 ἐστ'] suppl. Maas ἦν] Grenfell, Hunt ἦς] Wilamowitz   15
ἐπ[ελεύσομαι suppl. Wilamowitz ἐπ[ανέρχομαι Grenfell, Hunt

D

ἠρ]ώων ἀρετὰν
ὑπ]εράφανον οὕς τε κοίλα[ι

ναες] πολυγόμφοι ἐλεύσα[ν
Τροί]ᾳ κακόν, ἥρωας ἐσθ[λούς·
τῶν] μὲν κρείων Ἀγαμέ[μνων   20
ἆ]ρχε Πλεισθ[ενί]δας βασιλ[εὺ]ς ἀγὸς ἀνδρῶν
Ἀτρέος ἐσ[θλοῦ] πάις ἐκ π[ατρό]ς·

καὶ τὰ μὲ[ν ἂν] Μοίσαι σεσοφ[ισμ]έναι
εὖ Ἑλικωνίδ[ες] ἐμβαίεν λόγ[ῳ·
θνατὸς δ' οὔ κ[ε]ν ἀνὴρ   25
διερὸ[ς] τὰ ἕκαστα εἴποι

ναῶν ὡ[ς Μεν]έλαος ἀπ' Αὐλίδος
Αἰγαῖον δ[ιὰ πό]ντον ἀπ' Ἄργεος
ἠλύθο[ν ἐς Τροΐα]ν
ἱπποτρόφο[ν οἵ τ]ε φώτες   30

χ]αλκάσπ[ιδες υἷ]ες Ἀχα[ι]ῶν
τ]ῶν μὲν πρ[οφ]ερέστατος α[ἰ]χμᾷ
. . .] . πόδ[ας ὠ]κὺς Ἀχιλλεὺς
καὶ μέ]γας Τ[ελαμ]ώνιος ἄλκι[μος Αἴας
. . . . . .] . ατ[. . . . . . .]γυρος.   35

        Τυδέος υἱ]ὸς ἀπ' Ἄργεος
                ]ς ἐς Ἴλιον
                ]
                ] . [.] .

36 suppl. Lobel

καὶ Ζεύξιππος ὃν] ἀ χρυσεόστροφ[ος   40
Ὕλλις ἐγήνατο, τῷ δ᾽ [ἄ]ρα Τρωίλον
ὡσεὶ χρυσὸν ὀρει-
χάλκῳ τρὶς ἄπεφθο[ν] ἤδη

Τρῶες Δ[α]ναοί τ᾽ ἐρό[ε]σσαν
μορφὰν μάλ᾽ ἐίσκον ὅμοιον.   45
τοῖς μὲν πέδα κάλλεος αἰέν,
καὶ σύ, Πο⟨υ⟩λύκρατες, κλέος ἄφθιτον ἑξεῖς
ὡς κατ᾽ ἀοιδὰν καὶ ἐμὸν κλέος.

40 suppl. Barron   47 Πολύ- pap., prob. Page Πουλύ- Grenfell,
Hunt

(286)

− ∪ ∪ − ∪ ∪ − ∪ −	1, 2, 3
− ∪ ∪ − ∪ ∪ − ⌣ − ∪ ∪	4, 5, 6
− ∪ ∪ − ∪ ∪ − ∪ − −	7
− ∪ ∪ − ∪ ∪ − ∪ −	8, 9
− ∪ ∪ − ∪ ∪ − ∪ ∪ − ∪ ∪	10
− ∪ ∪ − ∪ ∪ − −	11
− ∪ ∪ − ∪ ∪ − ∪ − −	12
− ∪ ∪ − ∪ ∪	13

ἦρι μὲν αἵ τε Κυδώνιαι
μαλίδες ἀρδόμεναι ῥοᾶν
ἐκ ποταμῶν, ἵνα Παρθένων
κᾶπος ἀκήρατος, αἵ τ᾽ οἰνανθίδες
αὐξόμεναι σκιεροῖσιν ὑφ᾽ ἕρνεσιν   5
οἰναρέοις θαλέθοισιν, ἐμοὶ δ᾽ ἔρος
    οὐδεμίαν κατάκοιτος ὥραν·
ἀλλ᾽ ἅθ᾽ ὑπὸ στεροπᾶς φλέγων

8 τε ὑπό codd. ἀλλ᾽ ἅθ᾽ ὑπό Melhorn

Θρηίκιος βορέας ἀίσ-
σων παρὰ Κύπριδος ἀζαλέαις μανί-   10
αισιν ἐρεμνὸς ἀθαμβὴς
    ἐγκρατέως πεδόθεν τινάσσει
ἀμετέρας φρένας.

11–12 ἀθάμβησεν κραταιῶς codd., em. Schweighäuser, Hermann
παιδ' ὅθεν codd., em. Naeke φυλάσσει codd. τινάσσει Naeke φλάσεν
ci. Hermann

(287)

⌣̲ ⋮ – ⌣ ⌣ – ⌣ ⌣ – ⌣ ⌣ –   1–3
  ⌣ ⋮ – ⌣ ⌣ – ⌣ ⌣ – – –   4
  – ⋮ – ⌣ ⌣ – ⌣ ⌣ – ⌣ ⌣ –   5
– ⌣ ⌣ – ⌣ ⌣ – ⌣ ⌣ – ⌣ ⌣ – –   6
⌣ ⌣ ⋮ – ⌣ ⌣ – ⌣ ⌣ – ⌣ ⌣ – ⌣ ⌣ –   7

Ἔρος αὖτέ με κυανέοισιν ὑπὸ
βλεφάροις τακέρ' ὄμμασι δερκόμενος
κηλήμασι παντοδαποῖς ἐς ἄπειρα δίκτυα Κύπριδος ἐσβάλλει·
ἦ μὰν τρομέω νιν ἐπερχόμενον,   5
ὥστε φερέζυγος ἵππος ἀεθλοφόρος ποτὶ γήρᾳ
ἀέκων σὺν ὄχεσφι θοοῖς ἐς ἅμιλλαν ἔβα.

4 βάλλει codd. ἐσβάλλει Clemm (εἰσ-)

(288)

– ⌣ ⌣ – – – ⌣ ⌣ – – –   1
– ⌣ ⌣ – ⌣ ⌣ – ⌣ ⌣ – ⌣ ⌣   2
– ⌣ ⌣ – ⌣ ⌣ – –   3
– ⌣ ⌣ – ⌣ ⌣ – ⌣ ⌣ – –   4

Εὐρύαλε γλαυκέων Χαρίτων θάλος, ⟨Ὡρᾶν⟩
καλλικόμων μελέδημα, σὲ μὲν Κύπρις
ἅ τ' ἀγανοβλέφαρος Πει-
θὼ ῥοδέοισιν ἐν ἄνθεσι θρέψαν.

1 γλαυκέων codd. γλυκέων ci. Jacobs, Fiorillo   Ὡρᾶν suppl. Page

(317a)

```
– ⋮ – ∪ ∪ – ∪ ∪ – ∪ ∪ –
– ∪ – ∪ ⋮ – ∪ ∪ – ∪ ∪ – –
– ∪ ∪ – ∪ ∪ – ∪ ∪ – ∪ –
– ∪ ∪ – ∪ ∪ – ∪ –
```

τοῦ μὲν πετάλοισιν ἐπ' ἀκροτάτοις
ἱζάνόισι ποικίλαι αἰολόδειροι
πανέλοπες λαθιπορφυρίδες ⟨τε⟩ καὶ
ἀλκυόνες τανυσίπτεροι.

1–2 ἀκροτάτοισι ξανθοῖσι Ath. cod. A, em. Wilamowitz   2–3
ποικ. πανέλ. αἰολόδ. A, transpos. Hermann   3 τε suppl. Bergk

ANACREON

(348)

```
– – ⋮ – ∪ ∪ – ⋮ ∪ –          1, 2, 4–7
– – ⋮ – ∪ ∪ – ⋮ –            3, 8
```

γουνοῦμαί σ' ἐλαφηβόλε
ξανθὴ παῖ Διὸς ἀγρίων
    δέσποιν' Ἄρτεμι θηρῶν·
ἤ κου νῦν ἐπὶ Ληθαίου

4 ἴκου codd. plurimi   ἤκου dett. recc.   ἴκευ Wilamowitz, alii

δίνησι θρασυκαρδίων   5
ἀνδρῶν ἐσκατορᾷς πόλιν
χαίρουσ’, οὐ γὰρ ἀνημέρους
    ποιμαίνεις πολιήτας.

(356)

∪ ∪ – ∪ – ∪ – –
∪ ∪ – – ⋮ ∪ ∪ – –   (a) 5, (b) 5

(a) ἄγε δὴ φέρ’ ἡμὶν ὦ παῖ
    κελέβην, ὅκως ἄμυστιν
    προπίω, τὰ μὲν δέκ’ ἐγχέας
    ὕδατος, τὰ πέντε δ’ οἴνου
    κυάθους ὡς ἀνυβριστί   5
    ἀνὰ δηὖτε βασσαρήσω.

(b) ἄγε δηὖτε μηκέτ’ οὕτω
    πατάγῳ τε κἀλαλητῷ
    Σκυθικὴν πόσιν παρ’ οἴνῳ
    μελετῶμεν, ἀλλὰ καλοῖς
    ὑποπίνοντες ἐν ὕμνοις.   5

(a) 5–6 ὡς ἂν ὑβριστιῶσανα codd. ἀνυβριστὶ ci. Baxter ἀνυβρίστως
Pauw

(357)

– – ⋮ – ∪ ∪ – ⋮ ∪ –
– ◡ ⋮ – ∪ ∪ – ⋮ –   3, 8, 11

ὦναξ, ᾧ δαμάλης Ἔρως
καὶ Νύμφαι κυανώπιδες
    πορφυρῆ τ’ Ἀφροδίτη
συμπαίζουσιν, ἐπιστρέφεαι

δ' ὑψηλὰς ὀρέων κορυφάς·
γουνοῦμαί σε, σὺ δ' εὐμενὴς
ἔλθ' ἡμίν, κεχαρισμένης
    δ' εὐχωλῆς ἐπακούειν·
Κλεοβούλῳ δ' ἀγαθὸς γένεο
σύμβουλος, τὸν ἐμόν γ' ἔρω-
    τ', ὦ Δεόνυσε, δέχεσθαι.

5

10

5 ὑψηλῶν Dion. cod. U ὑψηλᾶς ... κορυφᾶς PW   7 ἔλθοις μοι
PW   8 ἐπακούων PW   10 δ' ἔρωτα B δὲ ἔρωτα UV δέ τ'
ἔρωτα PW γ' ἔρωτ' Kan

(358)

σφαίρῃ δηῦτέ με πορφυρῇ
βάλλων χρυσοκόμης Ἔρως
νήνι ποικιλοσαμβάλῳ
    συμπαίζειν προκαλεῖται·
ἡ δ', ἐστὶν γὰρ ἀπ' εὐκτίτου
Λέσβου, τὴν μὲν ἐμὴν κόμην,
λευκὴ γάρ, καταμέμφεται,
    πρὸς δ' ἄλλην τινὰ χάσκει.

5

1 πορφυρεν codd., em. Barnes (-έῃ)   3 ποικίλος λαμβάνω Ath.
ποικίλους (ω super ου script.) ἀμβάλω Et. Sorb. in adnot. Et. Mag.
448.29 Gaisford, em. Seidler   5 ἀπευκτικοῦ Ath., em. Barnes

(359)

Κλεοβούλου μὲν ἔγωγ' ἐρέω,
Κλεοβούλῳ δ' ἐπιμαίνομαι,
    Κλεόβουλον δὲ διοσκέω.

3 δὲ διοσκνέω, διὸς κνέων, δὲ διιδεῖν ἐπιποθῶ codd., em. Bergk

(360)

ὦ παῖ παρθένιον βλέπων
δίζημαί σε, σὺ δ' οὐ κοεῖς,
οὐκ εἰδὼς ὅτι τῆς ἐμῆς
    ψυχῆς ἡνιοχεύεις.

2 οὐ καιεις Ath. οὐκ ἀίεις epitom. οὐ κοεῖς Bergk οὐ κλύεις Erfurdt

(361)

ἐγὼ δ' οὔτ' ἂν 'Αμαλθίης
βουλοίμην κέρας οὔτ' ἔτεα
πεντήκοντά τε κἀκατὸν
    Ταρτησσοῦ βασιλεῦσαι.

τ' ἂν οὔτ' codd. δ' οὔτ' ἂν Casaubon ἔγωγ' οὔτ' ἂν Melhorn

(376)

```
-- ¦ - ∪ ∪ - ¦ ∪ -
-- ¦ - ∪ ∪ - ¦ - ∪ ∪ - ¦ - ∪ ∪ - ¦ ∪ - --
```

ἀρθεὶς δηῦτ' ἀπὸ Λευκάδος
πέτρης ἐς πολιὸν κῦμα κολυμβῶ μεθύων ἔρωτι.

(388)

```
- ∪ ∪ - ¦ - ∪ ∪ - ¦ ∪ - ∪ - ¦ ∪ - ∪ -          1, 2
or - ∪ ∪ - ¦ - ∪ ∪ - ¦ - ∪ ∪ - ¦ ∪ - ∪ -
∪ - ∪ - ¦ ∪ - ∪ -                                3
```

πρὶν μὲν ἔχων βερβέριον, καλύμματ' ἐσφηκωμένα,
καὶ ξυλίνους ἀστραγάλους ἐν ὠσὶ καὶ ψιλὸν περὶ
πλευρῆσι ⟨δέρμ' ἤει⟩ βοός,

3 suppl. Bergk

νήπλυτον εἴλυμα κακῆς ἀσπίδος, ἀρτοπώλισιν
κἀθελοπόρνοισιν ὁμιλέων ὁ πονηρὸς Ἀρτέμων, 5
κίβδηλον εὑρίσκων βίον,
πολλὰ μὲν ἐν δουρὶ τιθεὶς αὐχένα, πολλὰ δ' ἐν τροχῷ,
πολλὰ δὲ νῶτον σκυτίνη μάστιγι θωμιχθείς, κόμην
πώγωνά τ' ἐκτετιλμένος·
νῦν δ' ἐπιβαίνει σατινέων χρύσεα φορέων κατέρματα 10
†παῖς Κύκης† καὶ σκιαδίσκην ἐλεφαντίνην φορεῖ
γυναιξὶν αὔτως ‹ἐμφερής›.

4 νεόπλουτον Ath. A   νεόπλυτον E, em. Schoemann   11 παῖς ὁ
Κύκης ci. Hermann   12 suppl. Schoemann

(395)

∪ ∪ – ∪ – ∪ – –
∪ ∪ – – : ∪ ∪ – –   5, 11

πολιοὶ μὲν ἡμὶν ἤδη
κρόταφοι κάρη τε λευκόν,
χαρίεσσα δ' οὐκέτ' ἥβη
πάρα, γηραλέοι δ' ὀδόντες,
γλυκεροῦ δ' οὐκέτι πολλὸς   5
βιότου χρόνος λέλειπται·

διὰ ταῦτ' ἀνασταλύζω
θαμὰ Τάρταρον δεδοικώς·
Ἀίδεω γάρ ἐστι δεινὸς
μυχός, ἀργαλῆ δ' ἐς αὐτὸν   10
κάτοδος· καὶ γὰρ ἑτοῖμον
καταβάντι μὴ ἀναβῆναι.

2 δὲ Stob. codd. SA δὲν Trinc. τε Bergk

(396)

∪∪−∪−∪−− ⋮ ∪∪−∪−∪−−

φέρ' ὕδωρ φέρ' οἶνον ὦ παῖ φέρε ⟨δ'⟩ ἀνθεμόεντας ἡμὶν
στεφάνους· ἔνεικον, ὡς δὴ πρὸς Ἔρωτα πυκταλίζω.

1 δ' suppl. Casaubon   2 ὡς δὴ πρὸς Ἔρωτα Orion ὡς μὴ πρὸς
τὸν Ἔ. Ath., Eust. ὡς ἤδη πρὸς Ἔ. Et. Gen.

(398)

−⋮∪∪−∪−∪−−
   ∪∪−∪−∪−−

ἀστραγάλαι δ' Ἔρωτός εἰσιν
μανίαι τε καὶ κυδοιμοί.

(408)

∪∪−−⋮∪∪−−⋮∪∪−−
∪∪−∪−∪−−⋮∪∪−−
∪∪−−⋮∪∪−∪−∪−−

ἀγανῶς οἷά τε νεβρὸν νεοθηλέα
γαλαθηνὸν ὅς τ' ἐν ὕλῃ κεροέσσης
ἀπολειφθεὶς ἀπὸ μητρὸς ἐπτοήθη.

(413)

∪∪−−⋮∪∪−∪−∪−∪−−

μεγάλῳ δηὖτέ μ' Ἔρως ἔκοψεν ὥστε χαλκεὺς
πελέκει, χειμερίῃ δ' ἔλουσεν ἐν χαράδρῃ.

(417)

$$-\cup-\underline{\cup}\mid-\cup-\underline{\cup}\mid-\cup-\underline{\cup}\mid-\cup-\underline{\cup} \qquad 1, 3, 5$$
$$-\cup-\underline{\cup}\mid-\cup-\underline{\cup}\mid-\cup-\underline{\cup}\mid-\cup- \qquad 2, 4, 6$$

πῶλε Θρηκίη, τί δή με λοξὸν ὄμμασι βλέπουσα
νηλέως φεύγεις, δοκεῖς δέ μ' οὐδὲν εἰδέναι σοφόν;
ἴσθι τοι, καλῶς μὲν ἄν τοι τὸν χαλινὸν ἐμβάλοιμι,
ἡνίας δ' ἔχων στρέφοιμί σ' ἀμφὶ τέρματα δρόμου·
νῦν δὲ λειμῶνάς τε βόσκεαι κοῦφά τε σκιρτῶσα παίζεις·   5
δεξιὸν γὰρ ἱπποπείρην οὐκ ἔχεις ἐπεμβάτην.

4 στρέφοιμ' ἀμφὶ codd., em. Bergk

(419)

$$-\cup--\mid-\cup--\mid-\cup--\mid-\cup-$$

ἀλκίμων σ' ὦ 'ριστοκλείδη πρῶτον οἰκτίρω φίλων·
ὤλεσας δ' ἥβην ἀμύνων πατρίδος δουλητην.

(96D.)

οὐ φιλέω ὃς κρητῆρι παρὰ πλέῳ οἰνοποτάζων
    νείκεα καὶ πόλεμον δακρυόεντα λέγει,
ἀλλ' ὅστις Μουσέων τε καὶ ἀγλαὰ δῶρ' Ἀφροδίτης
    συμμίσγων ἐρατῆς μνήσκεται εὐφροσύνης.

1 φιλέω ὃς Ath. codd. CE φιλεος A

XENOPHANES

(1)

νῦν γὰρ δὴ ζάπεδον καθαρὸν καὶ χεῖρες ἁπάντων
    καὶ κύλικες· πλεκτοὺς δ' ἀμφιτιθεῖ στεφάνους,
ἄλλος δ' εὐῶδες μύρον ἐν φιάλη παρατείνει·
    κρατὴρ δ' ἕστηκεν μεστὸς εὐφροσύνης·
ἄλλος δ' οἶνος ἕτοῖμος, ὃς οὔποτέ φησι προδώσειν   5
    μείλιχος ἐν κεράμοις ἄνθεος ὀζόμενος·
ἐν δὲ μέσοις ἁγνὴν ὀδμὴν λιβανωτὸς ἵησι,
    ψυχρὸν δ' ἐστὶν ὕδωρ καὶ γλυκὺ καὶ καθαρόν·
πάρκεινται δ' ἄρτοι ξανθοὶ γεραρή τε τράπεζα
    τυροῦ καὶ μέλιτος πίονος ἀχθομένη·   10
βωμὸς δ' ἄνθεσιν ἂν τὸ μέσον πάντη πεπύκασται,
    μολπὴ δ' ἀμφὶς ἔχει δώματα καὶ θαλίη.
χρὴ δὲ πρῶτον μὲν θεὸν ὑμνεῖν εὔφρονας ἄνδρας
    εὐφήμοις μύθοις καὶ καθαροῖσι λόγοις·
σπείσαντάς τε καὶ εὐξαμένους τὰ δίκαια δύνασθαι   15
    πρήσσειν — ταῦτα γὰρ ὦν ἐστι προχειρότερον —
οὐχ ὕβρις πίνειν ὁπόσον κεν ἔχων ἀφίκοιο
    οἴκαδ' ἄνευ προπόλου μὴ πάνυ γηραλέος.
ἀνδρῶν δ' αἰνεῖν τοῦτον, ὃς ἐσθλὰ πιὼν ἀναφαίνει,
    ὥς οἱ μνημοσύνη καὶ τόνος ἀμφ' ἀρετῆς.   20
οὔ τι μάχας διέπει Τιτήνων οὐδὲ Γιγάντων
    οὐδέ ⟨τι⟩ Κενταύρων, πλάσματα τῶν προτέρων,

2 ἀμφιτιθεὶς Ath. A, em. Dindorf   5 οἶνος ἐστὶν ἕτοιμος AE,
em. Musurus   16 ὦν A ὢν Nestle   17 πίνειν δ' AE, em.
Bergk   20 ωση A ὡς ἡ E, em. Coraes, Schneidewin   τὸν ὃς
AE, interpr. Schneidewin, Diels   21 διέπειν A διέπει E   22
τι suppl. Meineke κε Kalinka τε Ludwich cum dett.   πλασμάτων
προτέρων AE, em. Schweighäuser

ἢ στάσιας σφεδανάς· τοῖς οὐδὲν χρηστὸν ἔνεστι·
  θεῶν <δὲ> προμηθείην αἰὲν ἔχειν ἀγαθόν.

23 φενδόνας A, em. Osann   24 suppl. Scaliger ἀγαθήν A ἀγαθόν
Hermann ·

(2)

ἀλλ' εἰ μὲν ταχυτῆτι ποδῶν νίκην τις ἄροιτο
  ἢ πενταθλεύων, ἔνθα Διὸς τέμενος
πὰρ Πίσαο ῥοῆς ἐν Ὀλυμπίῃ, εἴτε παλαίων
  ἢ καὶ πυκτοσύνην ἀλγινόεσσαν ἔχων,
εἴτε τι δεινὸν ἄεθλον, ὃ παγκράτιον καλέουσιν,   5
  ἀστοῖσίν κ' εἴη κυδρότερος προσορᾶν,
καί κε προεδρίην φανερὴν ἐν ἀγῶσιν ἄροιτο,
  καί κεν σῖτ' εἴη δημοσίων κτεάνων
ἐκ πόλιος καὶ δῶρον, ὅ οἱ κειμήλιον εἴη·
  εἴτε καὶ ἵπποισιν, ταῦτά κε πάντα λάχοι   10
οὐκ ἐὼν ἄξιος ὥσπερ ἐγώ· ῥώμης γὰρ ἀμείνων
  ἀνδρῶν ἠδ' ἵππων ἡμετέρη σοφίη.
ἀλλ' εἰκῇ μάλα τοῦτο νομίζεται, οὐδὲ δίκαιον
  προκρίνειν ῥώμην τῆς ἀγαθῆς σοφίης.
οὔτε γὰρ εἰ πύκτης ἀγαθὸς λαοῖσι μετείη   15
  οὔτ' εἰ πενταθλεῖν οὔτε παλαισμοσύνην
οὐδὲ μὲν εἰ ταχυτῆτι ποδῶν, τόπερ ἐστὶ πρότιμον
  ῥώμης ὅσσ' ἀνδρῶν ἔργ' ἐν ἀγῶνι πέλει,
τούνεκεν ἂν δὴ μᾶλλον ἐν εὐνομίῃ πόλις εἴη·
  σμικρὸν δ' ἄν τι πόλει χάρμα γένοιτ' ἐπὶ τῷ,   20
εἴ τις ἀεθλεύων νικῷ Πίσαο παρ' ὄχθας·
  οὐ γὰρ πιαίνει ταῦτα μυχοὺς πόλιος.

6 προσέραν A, em. Jacobs   10 κ' εἰ πάντα A, em. Schweighäuser
15 λαοῖσιν ἔτ' εἴη A, em. Stephanus

(3)

ἀβροσύνας δὲ μαθόντες ἀνωφελέας παρὰ Λυδῶν,
    ὄφρα τυραννίης ἦσαν ἄνευ στυγερῆς,
ἤεσαν εἰς ἀγορὴν παναλουργέα φάρε᾽ ἔχοντες,
    οὐ μείους ὥσπερ χίλιοι εἰς ἐπίπαν,
αὐχαλέοι, χαίτησιν ἀγαλλόμενοι εὐπρεπέεσσιν,   5
    ἀσκητοῖς ὀδμὴν χρίμασι δευόμενοι.

2 ησσανευ A, em. Dindorf   5 αγαλλομεν A, interpr. Diels

(6)

νῦν αὖτ᾽ ἄλλον ἔπειμι λόγον, δείξω δὲ κέλευθον

      .   .   .   .   .

καί ποτέ μιν στυφελιζομένου σκύλακος παριόντα
    φασὶν ἐποικτῖραι καὶ τόδε φάσθαι ἔπος·
'παῦσαι, μηδὲ ῥάπιζ᾽, ἐπεὶ ἦ φίλου ἀνέρος ἐστίν
    ψυχή, τὴν ἔγνων φθεγξαμένης ἀίων.'   5

1 οὖν τ᾽ codd. αὖτ᾽ Stephanus

(7)

ἤδη δ᾽ ἑπτά τ᾽ ἔασι καὶ ἑξήκοντ᾽ ἐνιαυτοί
    βληστρίζοντες ἐμὴν φροντίδ᾽ ἀν᾽ Ἑλλάδα γῆν·
ἐκ γενετῆς δὲ τότ᾽ ἦσαν ἐείκοσι πέντε τε πρὸς τοῖς,
    εἴπερ ἐγὼ περὶ τῶνδ᾽ οἶδα λέγειν ἐτύμως.

(10)

πάντα θεοῖς ἀνέθηκαν Ὅμηρός θ᾽ Ἡσίοδός τε
    ὅσσα παρ᾽ ἀνθρώποισιν ὀνείδεα καὶ ψόγος ἐστίν,
κλέπτειν μοιχεύειν τε καὶ ἀλλήλους ἀπατεύειν.

(13)

ἀλλ' εἰ χεῖρας ἔχον βόες ⟨ἵπποι τ'⟩ ἠὲ λέοντες
ἢ γράψαι χείρεσσι καὶ ἔργα τελεῖν ἅπερ ἄνδρες,
ἵπποι μέν θ' ἵπποισι, βόες δέ τε βουσὶν ὁμοίας
καί ⟨κε⟩ θεῶν ἰδέας ἔγραφον καὶ σώματ' ἐποίουν
τοιαῦθ' οἷόν περ καὐτοὶ δέμας εἶχον ἕκαστοι.   5

1 suppl. Diels   3 ὁμοίας Theodor. ὁμοῖοι Clem. ὅμοιοι Euseb.
4 suppl. Sylburg   5 ὁμοῖον, ὅμοιον codd. ἕκαστοι Herwerden,
Hiller

(18)

πὰρ πυρὶ χρὴ τοιαῦτα λέγειν χειμῶνος ἐν ὥρῃ
ἐν κλίνῃ μαλακῇ κατακείμενον, ἔμπλεον ὄντα,
πίνοντα γλυκὺν οἶνον, ὑποτρώγοντ' ἐρεβίνθους·
'τίς πόθεν εἶς ἀνδρῶν; πόσα τοι ἔτε' ἐστί, φέριστε;
πηλίκος ἦσθ', ὅθ' ὁ Μῆδος ἀφίκετο;' . . .   5

(28)

ἥν τ' Ἶριν καλέουσι, νέφος καὶ τοῦτο πέφυκε,
πορφύρεον καὶ φοινίκεον καὶ χλωρὸν ἰδέσθαι.

PHOCYLIDES

(1)

καὶ τόδε Φωκυλίδου· Λέριοι κακοί· οὐχ ὃ μέν, ὃς δ' οὔ·
πάντες, πλὴν Προκλέους· καὶ Προκλέης Λέριος.

(3)

καὶ τόδε Φωκυλίδου· τί πλέον, γένος εὐγενὲς εἶναι,
οἷς οὔτ' ἐν μύθοις ἔπεται χάρις οὔτ' ἐνὶ βουλῇ;

1 τὸ codd. τί Brunck

(4)

καὶ τόδε Φωκυλίδου· πόλις ἐν σκοπέλῳ κατὰ κόσμον
οἰκεῦσα σμικρὴ κρέσσων Νίνου ἀφραινούσης.

(8)

νυκτὸς βουλεύειν, νυκτὸς δέ τοι ὀξυτέρη φρὴν
ἀνδράσιν· ἡσυχίη δ' ἀρετὴν διζημένῳ ἐσθλή.

2 ἀρετὴ codd., em. Schneidewin

DEMODOCUS

(1)

<καὶ τόδε Δημοδόκου·> Μιλήσιοι ἀξύνετοι μέν
οὔκ εἰσι, δρῶσιν δ' οἱάπερ ἀξύνετοι.

1 suppl. Bergk

(4)

Καππαδόκην ποτ' ἔχιδνα κακὴ δάκεν· ἀλλὰ καὶ αὐτή
κάτθανε γευσαμένη αἵματος ἰοβόλου.

THEOGNIS

(19–26)

Κύρνε, σοφιζομένῳ μὲν ἐμοὶ σφρηγὶς ἐπικείσθω
    τοῖσδ' ἔπεσιν, λήσει δ' οὔποτε κλεπτόμενα,   20
οὐδέ τις ἀλλάξει κάκιον τοὐσθλοῦ παρεόντος·
    ὧδε δὲ πᾶς τις ἐρεῖ· 'Θεύγνιδός ἐστιν ἔπη
τοῦ Μεγαρέως· πάντας δὲ κατ' ἀνθρώπους ὀνομαστός.'
    ἀστοῖσιν δ' οὔπω πᾶσιν ἁδεῖν δύναμαι·
οὐδὲν θαυμαστόν, Πολυπαΐδη· οὐδὲ γὰρ ὁ Ζεύς   25
    οὔθ' ὕων πάντεσσ' ἁνδάνει οὔτ' ἀνέχων.

23 ὀνομαστός AO   ὀνομαστοῦ XUrI

(39–52)

Κύρνε, κύει πόλις ἥδε, δέδοικα δὲ μὴ τέκῃ ἄνδρα
    εὐθυντῆρα κακῆς ὕβριος ἡμετέρης.   40
ἀστοὶ μὲν γὰρ ἔθ' οἴδε σαόφρονες, ἡγεμόνες δέ
    τετράφαται πολλὴν εἰς κακότητα πεσεῖν.
οὐδεμίαν πω, Κύρν', ἀγαθοὶ πόλιν ὤλεσαν ἄνδρες,
    ἀλλ' ὅταν ὑβρίζειν τοῖσι κακοῖσιν ἅδῃ
δῆμόν τε φθείρουσι δίκας τ' ἀδίκοισι διδοῦσι   45
    οἰκείων κερδέων εἴνεκα καὶ κράτεος·
ἔλπεο μὴ δηρὸν κείνην πόλιν ἀτρεμέεσθαι,
    μηδ' εἰ νῦν κεῖται πολλῇ ἐν ἡσυχίῃ,
εὖτ' ἂν τοῖσι κακοῖσι φίλ' ἀνδράσι ταῦτα γένηται,
    κέρδεα δημοσίῳ σὺν κακῷ ἐρχόμενα.   50

45 φθείρουσι, διδοῦσι A φθείρωσι, διδῶσι rell.   47 ἀτρεμέ' εσθαι
A ἀτρεμέεσθαι OXUrI ἀτρεμεῖσθαι Bergk ἀτρέμ' ἔσεσθαι
Schömann ἀτρέμας ἧσθαι Hudson-Williams ἀτρεμέ' ἧσθαι Young

ἐκ τῶν γὰρ στάσιές τε καὶ ἔμφυλοι φόνοι ἀνδρῶν
    μούναρχοί θ'· ἃ πόλει μήποτε τῆδε ἅδοι.

52 μούναρχοι δὲ ΑΟ μούναρχος δὲ XUrI μούναρχοί θ'· ἃ Ahrens

(53–68)

Κύρνε, πόλις μὲν ἔθ' ἥδε πόλις, λαοὶ δὲ δὴ ἄλλοι,
    οἳ πρόσθ' οὔτε δίκας ᾔδεσαν οὔτε νόμους,
ἀλλ' ἀμφὶ πλευραῖσι δορὰς αἰγῶν κατέτριβον,   55
    ἔξω δ' ὥστ' ἔλαφοι τῆσδ' ἐνέμοντο πόλεος.
καὶ νῦν εἰσ' ἀγαθοί, Πολυπαΐδη· οἱ δὲ πρὶν ἐσθλοί
    νῦν δειλοί. τίς κεν ταῦτ' ἀνέχοιτ' ἐσορῶν;
ἀλλήλους δ' ἀπατῶσιν ἐπ' ἀλλήλοισι γελῶντες,
    οὔτε κακῶν γνώμας εἰδότες οὔτ' ἀγαθῶν.   60
μηδένα τῶνδε φίλον ποιεῦ, Πολυπαΐδη, ἀστῶν
    ἐκ θυμοῦ χρείης οὕνεκα μηδεμιῆς·
ἀλλὰ δόκει μὲν πᾶσιν ἀπὸ γλώσσης φίλος εἶναι,
    χρῆμα δὲ συμμείξῃς μηδενὶ μηδ' ὁτιοῦν
σπουδαῖον· γνώσῃ γὰρ ὀιζυρῶν φρένας ἀνδρῶν,   65
    ὥς σφιν ἐπ' ἔργοισιν πίστις ἔπ' οὐδεμία,
ἀλλὰ δόλους ἀπάτας τε πολυπλοκίας τ' ἐφίλησαν
    οὕτως ὡς ἄνδρες μηκέτι σωζόμενοι.

56 τῆσδ ... πόλεος A τήνδ' ... πόλιν OXUrI   62 οὕνεκα A
εἵνεκα OXUrI

(77–8)

πιστὸς ἀνὴρ χρυσοῦ τε καὶ ἀργύρου ἀντερύσασθαι
    ἄξιος ἐν χαλεπῇ, Κύρνε, διχοστασίῃ.

(87–92)

μή μ' ἔπεσιν μὲν στέργε, νόον δ' ἔχε καὶ φρένας ἄλλῃ,
    εἴ με φιλεῖς καί σοι πιστὸς ἔνεστι νόος.
ἤ με φίλει καθαρὸν θέμενος νόον, ἤ μ' ἀποειπών
    ἔχθαιρ' ἀμφαδίην νεῖκος ἀειράμενος.   90
ὃς δὲ μιῇ γλώσσῃ δίχ' ἔχει νόον, οὗτος ἑταῖρος
    δεινός, Κύρν', ἐχθρὸς βέλτερος ἢ φίλος ὤν.

(113–14)

μήποτε τὸν κακὸν ἄνδρα φίλον ποιεῖσθαι ἑταῖρον,
    ἀλλ' αἰεὶ φεύγειν ὥστε κακὸν λιμένα.

(155–8)

μήποτέ τοι πενίην θυμοφθόρον ἀνδρὶ χολωθείς
    μηδ' ἀχρημοσύνην οὐλομένην πρόφερε·
Ζεὺς γάρ τοι τὸ τάλαντον ἐπιρρέπει ἄλλοτε ἄλλῳ,
    ἄλλοτε μὲν πλουτεῖν, ἄλλοτε μηδὲν ἔχειν.

155 μοι . . . χαλεφθείς Stob.   156 οὐλομένην codd. Κύρνε κακὴν
Stob.   157 ἄλλως Stob. MA τ' ἄλλως Stob. S   158 μηδὲν
A, Stob.   δ' οὐδὲν OXUrI

(173–82)

ἄνδρ' ἀγαθὸν πενίη πάντων δάμνησι μάλιστα,
    καὶ γήρως πολιοῦ, Κύρνε, καὶ ἠπιάλου.
ἣν δὴ χρὴ φεύγοντα καὶ ἐς βαθυκήτεα πόντον   175
    ῥιπτεῖν καὶ πετρέων, Κύρνε, κατ' ἠλιβάτων.

175 ἣν δὴ χρὴ codd. χρὴ πενίην testes omnes   βαθυ- AO μεγα-
XUrI test. plurimi

καὶ γὰρ ἀνὴρ πενίῃ δεδμημένος οὔτε τι εἰπεῖν
  οὔθ' ἔρξαι δύναται, γλῶσσα δέ οἱ δέδεται.
χρὴ γὰρ ὁμῶς ἐπὶ γῆν τε καὶ εὐρέα νῶτα θαλάσσης
  δίζησθαι χαλεπῆς, Κύρνε, λύσιν πενίης.   180
τεθνάμεναι, φίλε Κύρνε, πενιχρῷ βέλτερον ἀνδρί
  ἢ ζώειν χαλεπῇ τειρόμενον πενίῃ.

177 καὶ codd. πᾶς test. omn.   179 χρὴ δ' ἀεὶ κατὰ γῆν Stob.
180 δίζησθαι Α δίζεσθαι rell., Stob.   181 τεθνάμεναι Α τεθνᾶναι
XUr τεθνάναι I

(183–92)

κριοὺς μὲν καὶ ὄνους διζήμεθα, Κύρνε, καὶ ἵππους
  εὐγενέας, καί τις βούλεται ἐξ ἀγαθῶν
βήσεσθαι· γῆμαι δὲ κακὴν κακοῦ οὐ μελεδαίνει   185
  ἐσθλὸς ἀνήρ, ἤν οἱ χρήματα πολλὰ διδῷ,
οὐδὲ γυνὴ κακοῦ ἀνδρὸς ἀναίνεται εἶναι ἄκοιτις
  πλουσίου, ἀλλ' ἀφνεὸν βούλεται ἀντ' ἀγαθοῦ.
χρήματα μὲν τιμῶσι· καὶ ἐκ κακοῦ ἐσθλὸς ἔγημε
  καὶ κακὸς ἐξ ἀγαθοῦ· πλοῦτος ἔμειξε γένος.   190
οὕτω μὴ θαύμαζε γένος, Πολυπαΐδη, ἀστῶν
  μαυροῦσθαι· σὺν γὰρ μίσγεται ἐσθλὰ κακοῖς.

183 κύνας μὲν δὴ νῶι διζήμεθα Stob.³ διζοίμεθα Stob.¹, ²   184
ἀγαθοῦ Stob.¹, ²   185 κτήσεσθαι Stob.² κτήσασθαι Stob.¹
186 οἱ: τις Stob.¹, ² διδῷ: φέρῃ Stob.³   189 μὲν: γὰρ Stob.¹, ²

(213–18)

θυμέ, φίλους κατὰ πάντας ἐπίστρεφε ποικίλον ἦθος,
  ὀργὴν συμμίσγων ἥντιν' ἕκαστος. ἔχει·
πουλύπου ὀργὴν ἴσχε πολυπλόκου, ὃς ποτὶ πέτρῃ,   215
  τῇ προσομιλήσῃ, τοῖος ἰδεῖν ἐφάνη.

213 θυμέ Α Κύρνε Ο dett.

νῦν μὲν τῇδ' ἐφέπου, τοτὲ δ' ἀλλοῖος χρόα γίνου.

κρέσσων τοι σοφίη γίνεται ἀτροπίης.

218 κραιπνόν OXUrI

(237–54)

σοὶ μὲν ἐγὼ πτέρ' ἔδωκα, σὺν οἷς ἐπ' ἀπείρονα πόντον

πωτήσῃ, κατὰ γῆν πᾶσαν ἀειρόμενος

ῥηϊδίως· θοίνῃς δὲ καὶ εἰλαπίνῃσι παρέσσῃ

ἐν πάσαις πολλῶν κείμενος ἐν στόμασιν,   240

καί σε σὺν αὐλίσκοισι λιγυφθόγγοις νέοι ἄνδρες

εὐκόσμως ἐρατοὶ καλά τε καὶ λιγέα

ᾄσονται. καὶ ὅταν δνοφερῆς ὑπὸ κεύθεσι γαίης

βῇς πολυκωκύτους εἰς Ἀΐδαο δόμους,

οὐδέποτ' οὐδὲ θανὼν ἀπολεῖς κλέος, ἀλλὰ μελήσεις 245

ἄφθιτον ἀνθρώποις αἰὲν ἔχων ὄνομα,

Κύρνε, καθ' Ἑλλάδα γῆν στρωφώμενος, ἠδ' ἀνὰ νήσους

ἰχθυόεντα περῶν πόντον ἐπ' ἀτρύγετον,

οὐχ ἵππων νώτοισιν ἐφήμενος· ἀλλά σε πέμψει

ἀγλαὰ Μουσάων δῶρα ἰοστεφάνων.   250

πᾶσι δ', ὅσοισι μέμηλε, καὶ ἐσσομένοισιν ἀοιδή

ἔσσῃ ὁμῶς, ὄφρ' ἂν γῆ τε καὶ ἠέλιος.

αὐτὰρ ἐγὼν ὀλίγης παρὰ σεῦ οὐ τυγχάνω αἰδοῦς,

ἀλλ' ὥσπερ μικρὸν παῖδα λόγοις μ' ἀπατᾷς.

238 πωτήσει AO   κατὰ: καὶ Bergk   ἀειράμενος O   251 πᾶσι διὸς οἶσι A   πᾶσιν οἶσι O   πᾶσι γὰρ οἶσι dett. interpr. Lachmann

(341–50)

ἀλλά, Ζεῦ, τέλεσόν μοι, Ὀλύμπιε, καίριον εὐχήν·

δὸς δέ μοι ἀντὶ κακῶν καί τι παθεῖν ἀγαθόν.

τεθναίην δ', εἰ μή τι κακῶν ἄμπαυμα μεριμνέων

εὑροίμην, δοίην δ' ἀντ' ἀνιῶν ἀνίας.

αἶσα γὰρ οὕτως ἐστί. τίσις δ' οὐ φαίνεται ἡμῖν   345
    ἀνδρῶν, οἳ τἀμὰ χρήματ' ἔχουσι βίῃ
συλήσαντες· ἐγὼ δὲ κύων ἐπέρησα χαράδρην
    χειμάρρῳ ποταμῷ πάντ' ἀποσεισάμενος.
τῶν εἴη μέλαν αἷμα πιεῖν· ἐπί τ' ἐσθλὸς ὄροιτο
    δαίμων, ὃς κατ' ἐμὸν νοῦν τελέσειε τάδε.   350

(351–4)

ἆ δειλὴ πενίη, τί μένεις προλιποῦσα παρ' ἄλλον
    ἄνδρ' ἰέναι; μὴ δήν μ' οὐκ ἐθέλοντα φίλει·
ἀλλ' ἴθι καὶ δόμον ἄλλον ἐποίχεο, μηδὲ μεθ' ἡμέων
    αἰεὶ δυστήνου τοῦδε βίου μέτεχε.

352 μ' ἦν δὴν A   τί δή μ' O   τί δε δή μ' XI   μὴ δήν μ' Hudson-Williams   μὴ δή μ' Bekker   μὴ ὦν δὴν Young

(425–8)

'πάντων μὲν μὴ φῦναι ἐπιχθονίοισιν ἄριστον'
    μηδ' ἐσιδεῖν αὐγὰς ὀξέος ἠελίου,
'φύντα δ' ὅπως ὤκιστα πύλας 'Αίδαο περῆσαι'
    καὶ κεῖσθαι πολλὴν γῆν ἐπαμησάμενον.

425 πάντων: ἀρχὴν test. plur.   428 γαῖαν ἐφεσσάμενον Sext. Emp.

(447–52)

εἴ μ' ἐθέλεις πλύνειν, κεφαλῆς ἀμίαντον ἀπ' ἄκρης
    αἰεὶ λευκὸν ὕδωρ ῥεύσεται ἡμετέρης,
εὑρήσεις δέ με πᾶσιν ἐπ' ἔργμασιν ὥσπερ ἄπεφθον
    χρυσὸν ἐρυθρὸν ἰδεῖν τριβόμενον βασάνῳ,   450
τοῦ χροιῆς καθύπερθε μέλας οὐχ ἅπτεται ἰός
    οὐδ' εὐρώς, αἰεὶ δ' ἄνθος ἔχει καθαρόν.

(503–10)

οἰνοβαρέω κεφαλήν, Ὀνομάκριτε, καί με βιᾶται
    οἶνος, ἀτὰρ γνώμης οὐκέτ' ἐγὼ ταμίης
ἡμετέρης, τὸ δὲ δῶμα περιτρέχει. ἀλλ' ἄγ' ἀναστάς   505
    πειρηθῶ μή πως καὶ πόδας οἶνος ἔχει
καὶ νόον ἐν στήθεσσι· δέδοικα δὲ μή τι μάταιον
    ἔρξω θωρηχθεὶς καὶ μέγ' ὄνειδος ἔχω.
οἶνος πινόμενος πουλὺς κακόν· ἢν δέ τις αὐτὸν
    πίνῃ ἐπισταμένως, οὐ κακόν, ἀλλ' ἀγαθόν.   510

503 βεβιᾶται A   505 ἀλλά γ' AOI

(531–4)

αἰεί μοι φίλον ἦτορ ἰαίνεται, ὁππότ' ἀκούσω
    αὐλῶν φθεγγομένων ἱμερόεσσαν ὄπα.
χαίρω δ' εὖ πίνων καὶ ὑπ' αὐλητῆρος ἀκούων,
    χαίρω δ' εὔφθογγον χερσὶ λύρην ὀχέων.

533 ἀκούων: Pierson ἀείδων ex 825

(567–70)

ἥβῃ τερπόμενος παίζω· δηρὸν γὰρ ἔνερθεν
    γῆς ὀλέσας ψυχὴν κείσομαι ὥστε λίθος
ἄφθογγος, λείψω δ' ἐρατὸν φάος ἠελίοιο·
    ἔμπης δ' ἐσθλὸς ἐὼν ὄψομαι οὐδὲν ἔτι.

(667–82)

εἰ μὲν χρήματ' ἔχοιμι, Σιμωνίδη, οἷά περ ἤδη
    οὐκ ἂν ἀνιῴμην τοῖς ἀγαθοῖσι συνών.

667 ᾔδειν OXI   668 ἀνοίμην A ἀνιῴμην OXI

νῦν δέ με γινώσκοντα παρέρχεται, εἰμὶ δ' ἄφωνος
    χρημοσύνη, πολλῶν γνοὺς ἄρ' ἄμεινον ἔτι   670
οὕνεκα νῦν φερόμεσθα καθ' ἱστία λευκὰ βαλόντες
    Μηλίου ἐκ πόντου νύκτα διὰ δνοφερήν·
ἀντλεῖν δ' οὐκ ἐθέλουσιν· ὑπερβάλλει δὲ θάλασσα
    ἀμφοτέρων τοίχων. ἦ μάλα τις χαλεπῶς
σῴζεται. οἱ δ' ἔρδουσι· κυβερνήτην μὲν ἔπαυσαν   675
    ἐσθλόν, ὅτις φυλακὴν εἶχεν ἐπισταμένως·
χρήματα δ' ἁρπάζουσι βίῃ, κόσμος δ' ἀπόλωλεν,
    δασμὸς δ' οὐκέτ' ἴσος γίνεται ἐς τὸ μέσον·
φορτηγοὶ δ' ἄρχουσι, κακοὶ δ' ἀγαθῶν καθύπερθεν.
    δειμαίνω, μή πως ναῦν κατὰ κῦμα πίῃ.   680
ταῦτά μοι ἠνίχθω κεκρυμμένα τοῖς ἀγαθοῖσιν·
    γινώσκοι δ' ἄν τις καὶ κακός, ἂν σοφὸς ᾖ.

670 γνοῦσαν A   γνοὺς ἂν XI   γνούς O   γνούς περ codd. al.   γνοὺς
ἄρ' Dover κακόν codd. κακός Brunck

(783–8)

ἦλθον μὲν γὰρ ἔγωγε καὶ εἰς Σικελήν ποτε γαῖαν,
    ἦλθον δ' Εὐβοίης ἀμπελόεν πεδίον
Σπάρτην δ' Εὐρώτα δονακοτρόφου ἀγλαὸν ἄστυ·   785
    καί μ' ἐφίλευν προφρόνως πάντες ἐπερχόμενον·
ἀλλ' οὔτις μοι τέρψις ἐπὶ φρένας ἦλθεν ἐκείνων.
    οὕτως οὐδὲν ἄρ' ἦν φίλτερον ἄλλο πάτρης.

785 δ' AO   τ' XI

(1069–70b)

ἄφρονες ἄνθρωποι καὶ νήπιοι, οἵτε θανόντας
    κλαίουσ', οὐδ' ἥβης ἄνθος ἀπολλύμενον.   1070
τέρπεό μοι, φίλε θυμέ· τάχ' αὖ τινες ἄλλοι ἔσονται
    ἄνδρες, ἐγὼ δὲ θανὼν γαῖα μέλαιν' ἔσομαι.

1070a αὖ: ἂν OXI   ἔσοιντο XI

(1101-4)

ὅστις σοι βούλευσεν ἐμεῦ πέρι, καί σ' ἐκέλευσεν
    οἴχεσθαι προλιπόνθ' ἡμετέρην φιλίην —
ὕβρις καὶ Μάγνητας ἀπώλεσε καὶ Κολοφῶνα
    καὶ Σμύρνην. πάντως, Κύρνε, καὶ ὔμμ' ἀπολεῖ.

(1197-1202)

ὄρνιθος φωνήν, Πολυπαΐδη, ὀξὺ βοώσης
    ἤκουσ', ἥτε βροτοῖς ἄγγελος ἦλθ' ἀρότου
ὡραίου· καί μοι κραδίην ἐπάταξε μέλαιναν,
    ὅττι μοι εὐανθεῖς ἄλλοι ἔχουσιν ἀγρούς,   1200
οὐδέ μοι ἡμίονοι κυφὸν ἕλκουσιν ἄροτρον
    τῆς †ἄλλης μνηστῆς† εἵνεκα ναυτιλίης.

1201 ἡνίοχοι A   κύφων' ... ἀρότρου XI

HIPPONAX

(24a)

Ἑρμῆ, φίλ' Ἑρμῆ, Μαιαδεῦ, Κυλλήνιε,
ἐπεύχομαί τοι· κάρτα γὰρ κακῶς ῥιγῶ.

. . . .

δὸς χλαῖναν Ἱππώνακτι καὶ κυπασσίσκον
καὶ σαμβαλίσκα κἀσκερίσκα καὶ χρυσοῦ
στατῆρας ἑξήκοντα τοὐτέρου τοίχου.   5

1 Μαιάδος, Μαιάδευσος, Μαιάδερος Tzetz. codd. Μαιαδεῦ Heliodorus

(24b)

δὸς χλαῖναν Ἱππώνακτι· κάρτα γὰρ ῥιγῶ
καὶ βαμβαλύζω.

2 βαμβακύζω codd. βαμβαλύζω Schneidewin

(25)

ἐμοὶ γὰρ οὐκ ἔδωκας οὔτε κω χλαῖναν
δασεῖαν ἐν χειμῶνι φάρμακον ῥίγευς,
οὔτ᾽ ἀσκέρῃσι τοὺς πόδας δασείῃσιν
ἔκρυψας, ὥς μοι μὴ χίμετλα ῥήγνυται.

1 χωλεύαν, χωδαῖνε, χλαῖναν, τὴν χλαῖναν codd. κω χλαῖναν Schneidewin 4 ῥίγνυται Tzetz. H γίγνηται APV

(29)

ἐμοὶ δὲ Πλοῦτος — ἔστι γὰρ λίην τυφλός —
ἐς τᾠκί᾽ ἐλθὼν οὐδάμ᾽ εἶπεν· ‘Ἱππῶναξ,
δίδωμί τοι μνᾶς ἀργύρου τριήκοντα
καὶ πόλλ᾽ ἔτ᾽ ἄλλα·’ δείλαιος γὰρ τὰς φρένας.

(70)

⏖ ⏑ – ⏓ | ⏖ ⏑ – ⏓ | – ⏑ – ⏑ | – – –

λάβετέ μευ ταἱμάτια, κόψω Βουπάλου τὸν ὀφθαλμόν.
ἀμφιδέξιος γάρ εἰμι κοὐκ ἁμαρτάνω κόπτων.

1 θοιμάτιον codd., em. Bergk

(77)

Μοῦσά μοι Εὐρυμεδοντιάδεα τὴν ποντοχάρυβδιν,
τὴν ἐγγαστριμάχαιραν, ὃς ἐσθίει οὐ κατὰ κόσμον,

[handwritten annotations: "by stoning or voting pebbles", "double entendre", "by vote of peeble"]

ἔννεφ', ὅπως ψηφῖδι ⟨κακὸς⟩ κακὸν οἶτον ὄληται
βουλῇ δημοσίῃ παρὰ θῖν' ἁλὸς ἀτρυγέτοιο.

3 suppl. Cobet

[81]

γάμος κράτιστός ἐστιν ἀνδρὶ σώφρονι,
τρόπον γυναικὸς χρηστὸν ἕδνον λαμβάνειν·
αὕτη γὰρ ἡ προὶξ οἰκίαν σῴζει μόνη.
ὅστις δὲ †τρυφῶς† τὴν γυναῖκ' ἄγει λαβών,
συνεργὸν οὗτος ἀντὶ δεσποίνης ἔχει   5
εὔνουν, βεβαίαν εἰς ἅπαντα τὸν βίον.

2 ἔνδον codd., em. Haupt

(Fr. Chol. Adesp. 1)

δύ' ἡμέραι γυναικός εἰσιν ἥδισται,
ὅταν γαμῇ τις κἀκφέρῃ τεθνηκυῖαν.

[handwritten: supply ησ]

SIMONIDES

(520)

```
– – – ∪ ∪ – –
– ∪ – – – ∪ ∪ – ∪ ∪ –
– ∪ – – – ∪ ∪ – ∪ ∪ –
∪ ∪ – ∪ ∪ – ∪ – ∪ ∪ – ∪ ∪ –
– – ∪ ∪ – ∪ – ∪ ∪ – ∪ ∪ –                           5
– – ∪ ∪ –
```

ἀνθρώπων ὀλίγον μὲν
κάρτος, ἄπρακτοι δὲ μεληδόνες, αἰ-

ὦνι δ' ἐν παύρῳ πόνος ἀμφὶ πόνῳ·
ὁ δ' ἄφυκτος ὁμῶς ἐπικρέμαται θάνατος·
κείνου γὰρ ἴσον λάχον μέρος οἵ τ' ἀγαθοὶ   5
ὅστις τε κακός.

3 δὲ codd. δ' ἐν Pflugk, Schneidewin

(521)

– ⋮ – ∪ ∪ – ⋮ – ∪ ∪ – ⋮ – ∪ ∪ – ∪ ∪ – ⋮ ∪ –
– ⋮ – ∪ ∪ – ⋮ – ∪ ∪ – ⋮ – ∪ ∪ – ⋮ ∪ –
– ⋮ – ∪ ∪ – ∪ ∪ – ∪ ∪ – ⋮ – –
– – – ∪ – ∪ –

ἄνθρωπος ἐὼν μή ποτε φάσῃς ὅ τι γίνεται αὔριον,
μηδ' ἄνδρα ἰδὼν ὄλβιον ὅσσον χρόνον ἔσσεται·
ὠκεῖα γὰρ οὐδὲ τανυπτερύγου μυίας
οὕτως ἁ μετάστασις.

1 φήσῃς, φήσῃ, φῇς, φῄς, εἴπῃς codd. φάσῃς Bergk   αὔριον om.
Stob. 9   2 ὄλβιον om. Stob. 9

(531)

– – ⋮ – ∪ ∪ – ⋮ ∪ – –
– ∪ – ∪ | – ∪ – ∪ | – ∪ – –
– – ∪ ∪ – ∪ ∪ – ⋮ – – ∪ ∪ – ∪ ∪ – –
– ∪ ∪ – ∪ ∪ – ⋮ ∪ – –
– ∪ – ∪ ∪ – ∪ – ⋮ – – ∪ –   5
– – ∪ ∪ – ∪ ∪ – ⋮ ∪ – ∪ – | – – ∪ –
– ∪ ∪ – ∪ ∪ – ⋮ ∪ – ∪ – | ∪ – ∪ –
– – ∪ ∪ – ∪ ∪ – ⋮ ∪ – –
– ∪ ⋮ – ∪ ∪ – ∪ ∪ –

τῶν ἐν Θερμοπύλαις θανόντων
εὐκλεὴς μὲν ἁ τύχα, καλὸς δ' ὁ πότμος,

1 Θερμοπύλαισι codd. dett.

βωμὸς δ' ὁ τάφος, πρὸ γόων δὲ μνᾶστις, ὁ δ' οἶκτος ἔπαινος·
ἐντάφιον δὲ τοιοῦτον εὑρὼς
οὔθ' ὁ πανδαμάτωρ ἀμαυρώσει χρόνος.   5
ἀνδρῶν ἀγαθῶν ὅδε σηκὸς οἰκέταν εὐδοξίαν
Ἑλλάδος εἵλετο· μαρτυρεῖ δὲ καὶ Λεωνίδας,
Σπάρτας βασιλεύς, ἀρετᾶς μέγαν λελοιπὼς
κόσμον ἀέναόν τε κλέος.

4 τοιοῦτον οὔτ' εὑρὼς codd., οὔτ' del. Bergk   7 καὶ Arsenius,
om. Diodorus   8 ὁ Σπάρτας codd., ὁ del. Bergk

(542)

```
_ ◡ ◡ _ ◡ ◡ _ ⋮ ◡ _ ◡ _ _
◡ ◡ _ _ ⋮ _ ◡ _ ◡ ◡ _ ◡ _
   _ ◡ _ ◡ _ _ ⋮ ◡ _ ◡ _
◡ ◡ _ ◡ _ ⋮ _ ◡ _ ◡ ◡ _ ◡ _
   _ ◡ _ ◡ _ ◡ _                                              5
◡ ◡ _ ⋮ _ ◡ _ ◡ ◡ _
_ _ ◡ _ ⋮ _ ◡ _ ◡ ◡ _
◡ _ _ | ◡ _ _
_ ◡ _ ◡ _ _
_ ◡ _ ◡ _ _                                                  10
```

ἄνδρ' ἀγαθὸν μὲν ἀλαθέως γενέσθαι
χαλεπὸν χερσίν τε καὶ ποσὶ καὶ νόῳ
    τετράγωνον ἄνευ ψόγου τετυγμένον·
        desunt vii versus

οὐδέ μοι ἐμμελέως τὸ Πιττάκειον
νέμεται, καίτοι σοφοῦ παρὰ φωτὸς εἰ-
    ρημένον· χαλεπὸν φάτ' ἐσθλὸν ἔμμεναι.
θεὸς ἂν μόνος τοῦτ' ἔχοι γέρας, ἄνδρα δ' οὐκ
    ἔστι μὴ οὐ κακὸν ἔμμεναι,   15

ὃν ἀμήχανος συμφορὰ καθέλῃ·
πράξας γὰρ εὖ πᾶς ἀνὴρ ἀγαθός,
κακὸς δ' εἰ κακῶς [
[ἐπὶ πλεῖστον δὲ καὶ ἄριστοί εἰσιν
[οὓς ἂν οἱ θεοὶ φιλῶσιν.]   20

τοὔνεκεν οὔ ποτ' ἐγὼ τὸ μὴ γενέσθαι
δυνατὸν διζήμενος κενεὰν ἐς ἄ-
    πρακτον ἐλπίδα μοῖραν αἰῶνος βαλέω,
πανάμωμον ἄνθρωπον, εὐρυεδέος ὅσοι
    καρπὸν αἰνύμεθα χθονός·   25
ἐπὶ δ' ὑμὶν εὑρὼν ἀπαγγελέω.
πάντας δ' ἐπαίνημι καὶ φιλέω,
ἑκὼν ὅστις ἔρδῃ
μηδὲν αἰσχρόν· ἀνάγκᾳ
δ' οὐδὲ θεοὶ μάχονται.   30

[
[
[οὐκ εἰμὶ φιλόψογος, ἐπεὶ ἔμοιγε ἐξαρκεῖ
ὃς ἂν μὴ κακὸς ᾖ] μηδ' ἄγαν ἀπάλαμνος εἰ-
    δώς γ' ὀνησίπολιν δίκαν,   35
ὑγιὴς ἀνήρ· οὐδὲ μή μιν ἐγὼ
μωμήσομαι· τῶν γὰρ ἠλιθίων
ἀπείρων γενέθλα.
πάντα τοι καλά, τοῖσίν
τ' αἰσχρὰ μὴ μέμεικται.   40

16 ὃν ἂν codd., ἂν del. Bergk   17 πράξας μὲν γὰρ codd., μὲν del.
Hermann   24 εὐρυεδοῦς Plat. codd. εὐρυοδοῦς vel -εδοῦς Plu.
codd.   26 ἔπειθ' ὑμῖν codd. bis ἐπὶ δ' ὕμμιν Bergk ἐπί τ' ὕμμιν
Schneidewin   36 οὐ μὴν ἐγὼ codd. οὔ μιν ἐγὼ Schleiermacher
οὐδὲ μή μιν ἐγὼ Bergk

(543)

⏑ ⏑ – ⏑ –

– – ⏑ ⏑ –

⏑ ⏑ – ⏑ – ⏑ –

– – ⋮ – ⏑ ⏑ – ⋮ – – ⏑ –

⏑ – ⏑ ⋮ – ⏑ ⏑ – ⋮ – ⏑ ⏑ – ⋮ –   5

– ⏑ ⏑ – ⏑ ⏑ – ⏑ ⏑ – ⏑ ⏑

– – ⋮ – ⏑ ⏑ – ⏑ ⏑ – ⋮ ⏑ –

⏑ ⏑ – ⋮ – ⏑ ⏑ – ⋮ –

– ⏑ – ⏑ – –

⏑ ⏑ – ⏑ ⏑ – ⏑ ⏑ – ⏑ ⏑ – –   10

– ⏑ – ⏑ – –

– ⏑ ⏑ – | ⏑ – ⏑ –

– – ⏑ – | ⏑ – ⏑ –

⏑ – ⋮ – ⏑ ⏑ – ⋮ –

– ⏑ ⏑ – ⏑ ⏑ – ⋮ – ⏑ ⏑ –   15

– – ⋮ – ⏑ ⏑ –

– ⏑ ⏑ – ⏑ ⏑ ⋮ – ⏑ – | – ⏑ –

– ⏑ – – ⋮ – ⏑ ⏑ – ⋮ ⏑ –

– ⏑ ⏑ – ⋮ – ⏑ –

– ⏑ ⏑ – ⋮ ⏑ – –   20

⏑ ⏑ – ⋮ – ⏑ ⏑ –

– ⏑ – ⏑ | – ⏑ – ⏑ | – ⏑ – | – ⏑ –

⏑ ⏑ – ⏑ – ⏑ – ⏑ – –

– ⏑ ⏑ – ⋮ ⏑ –

– ⏑ ⏑ – ⏑ ⏑ – ⏑ ⏑ – ⏑ –   25

– – ⏑ ⏑ –

– – ⏑ –

ὅτε λάρνακι

ἐν δαιδαλέᾳ
ἄνεμός τέ μιν πνέων
κινηθεῖσά τε λίμνα δείματι
ἔρειπεν, οὐκ ἀδιάντοισι παρειαῖς   5
ἀμφί τε Περσέι βάλλε φίλαν χέρα
εἶπέν τ'· 'ὦ τέκος, οἷον ἔχω πόνον·

σὺ δ' ἀωτεῖς, γαλαθηνῷ
δ' ἤθεϊ κνοώσσεις
ἐν ἀτερπέι δούρατι χαλκεογόμφῳ   10
<τῷ>δε νυκτιλαμπεῖ
κυανέῳ δνόφῳ ταθείς·
ἅλμαν δ' ὕπερθε τεᾶν κομᾶν
βαθεῖαν παριόντος
κύματος οὐκ ἀλέγεις, οὐδ' ἀνέμου   15
φθόγγον, πορφυρέᾳ
κείμενος ἐν χλανίδι, πρόσωπον καλόν.
εἰ δέ τοι δεινὸν τό γε δεινὸν ἦν,
καί κεν ἐμῶν ῥημάτων
λεπτὸν ὑπεῖχες οὖας.   20

κέλομαι δ', εὗδε βρέφος,
εὑδέτω δὲ πόντος, εὑδέτω δ' ἄμετρον κακόν·

3 τε μὴν PM τ' ἐμῆι V τέ μιν ci. Schneidewin τε μέμνε Page
(deinde δὲ λίμνα | δείμά τ' ἔρειπέ μιν)   4 δὲ codd. τε Brunck
δείματι V δεῖ ματι P δεῖμα M   5 ἔρειπεν MV ἔριπεν P   7
τέκος Ath. τέκνον Dion.   8–9 αυταις εγαλαθηνωδει θει PV αὐταῖς
ἀγαλαθηνώδει . . . . M αὖτε εἰς γαλαθηνῶι δ' ἤτορι Ath., em. Casaubon, Bergk   9 κνοώσσεις Dion. PV κνώσσεις Ath. Dion. M
10–11 -γόμφω δε codd., suppl. Page   12 ταδ' εις codd., em.
Schneidewin   13 αὐλέαν PV αὐλαίαν M ἅλμαν Bergk ἄχναν
Page   17 πρόσωπον καλόν MV πρόσωπον καλὸν πρόσωπον P

μεταβουλία δέ τις φανείη,
Ζεῦ πάτερ, ἐκ σέο·
ὅττι δὲ θαρσαλέον ἔπος εὔχομαι   25
ἢ νόσφι δίκας,
σύγγνωθί μοι.'

(567)

$- \cup \cup - \cup \cup -$
$- - - - \cup \cup - \cup \cup -$
$\cup \cup - \cup \cup - -$
$- \cup \cup - - \cup \cup -$
$\quad - \cup \cup - \cup \cup - -$

τοῦ καὶ ἀπειρέσιοι
πωτῶντ' ὄρνιθες ὑπὲρ κεφαλᾶς,
ἀνὰ δ' ἰχθύες ὀρθοὶ
κυανέου 'ξ ὕδατος ἄλ-
      λοντο καλᾷ σὺν ἀοιδᾷ.

(579)

$- \cup - \cup -$
$- \cup \cup - - - \cup - \cup - \cup \cup - -$
$\dagger \qquad \qquad \dagger - \cup - \cup - \cup -$
$- \cup - \vdots - \cup \cup - \vdots \cup - -$
$\cup - \cup - \vdots - \cup \cup - \vdots \cup - -$ 5
$- \cup - \cup -$
$- - \cup - \cup - - -$

ἐστί τις λόγος
τὰν 'Αρετὰν ναίειν δυσαμβάτοις ἐπὶ πέτραις,

2 δυσαμβάτοις Clem. δυσβάτοις Theod.

E

†νῦν δέ μιν θοαν† χῶρον ἁγνὸν ἀμφέπειν·
οὐδὲ πάντων βλεφάροισι θνατῶν
ἔσοπτος, ᾧ μὴ δακέθυμος ἱδρὼς   5
ἔνδοθεν μόλῃ,
ἵκῃ τ᾽ ἐς ἄκρον ἀνδρείας.

4 βλεφάροις codd., em. Ilgen   7 ἀνδρείᾳ ci. Wilamowitz

(581)

‒ ∪ ‒ ‒ ‒ ∪ ∪ ‒ ∪ ∪ ‒ ‒ ‒ ∪ ∪ ‒ ‒
‒ ∪ ∪ ‒ ∪ ∪ ‒ ‒ ∪ ∪ ‒ ∪ ∪ ‒
‒ ∪ ∪ ‒ ∪ ∪ ‒ ‒ ∪ ‒ ∪ ∪ ‒ ‒
‒ ∪ ‒ ‒ ‒ ∪ ‒ ‒ ‒ ∪ ∪ ‒ ‒ ‒
∪ ‒ ∪ ∪ ‒ ∪ ∪ ‒ ‒ ‒ ∪ ‒ ∪   5
‒ ∪ ∪ ‒ ∪ ∪ ‒ ‒ ‒ ∪ ‒ ‒
‒ ∪ ‒ ∪ ‒ ‒

τίς κεν αἰνήσειε νόῳ πίσυνος Λίνδου ναέταν Κλεόβουλον,
ἀενάοις ποταμοῖς ἄνθεσί τ᾽ εἰαρινοῖς
ἀελίου τε φλογὶ χρυσέας τε σελάνας
καὶ θαλασσαίαισι δίναις ἀντιθέντα μένος στάλας;
ἅπαντα γάρ ἐστι θεῶν ἥσσω· λίθον δὲ   5
καὶ βρότεοι παλάμαι θραύοντι· μωροῦ
φωτὸς ἅδε βούλα.

3 χρυσᾶς codd., em. Hermann   4 ἀντία θέντα ci. Bergk   6
βρότειοι codd., em. Hermann

(595)

‒ ∪ ∪ ‒ ∪ ∪ ‒ ∪ ∪ ‒ ‒
∪ ‒ ∪ ∪ ‒ ‒ ‒ ∪ ∪ ‒ ‒
‒ ∪ ∪ ‒ ∪ ∪ ‒ ∪ ∪ ‒
∪ ∪ ‒ ∪ ∪ ‒ ∪ ∪ ‒

οὐδὲ γὰρ ἐννοσίφυλλος ἀήτα
τότ᾽ ὦρτ᾽ ἀνέμων, ἅτις κ᾽ ἀπεκώλυε
κιδναμένα μελιαδέα γᾶρυν
ἀραρεῖν ἀκοαῖσι βροτῶν.

2 κατεκώλυε codd., em. Page   3 σκιδναμένα codd., em. Wyttenbach, Schneidewin

(76D.)

ἦ μέγ᾽ Ἀθηναίοισι φόως γένεθ᾽, ἡνίκ᾽ Ἀριστογείτων Ἵππαρχον κτεῖνε καὶ Ἁρμόδιος.

(83D.)

μνῆμα τόδε κλεινοῖο Μεγιστία, ὅν ποτε Μῆδοι
    Σπερχειὸν ποταμὸν κτεῖναν ἀμειψάμενοι,
μάντιος, ὃς τότε Κῆρας ἐπερχομένας σάφα εἰδώς
    οὐκ ἔτλη Σπάρτης ἡγεμόνας προλιπεῖν.

1 κλεινοῖο, κλειτοῖο codd.

(84D.)

σῆμα καταφθιμένοιο Μεγακλέος εὖτ᾽ ἂν ἴδωμαι,
    οἰκτίρω σέ, τάλαν Καλλία, οἷ᾽ ἔπαθες.

(85D.)

ἀνδρὸς ἀριστεύσαντος ἐν Ἑλλάδι τῶν ἐφ᾽ ἑαυτοῦ
    Ἱππίου Ἀρχεδίκην ἥδε κέκευθε κόνις·
ἣ πατρός τε καὶ ἀνδρὸς ἀδελφῶν τ᾽ οὖσα τυράννων
    παίδων τ᾽ οὐκ ἤρθη νοῦν ἐς ἀτασθαλίην.

(87D.)

Δίρφυος ἐδμήθημεν ὑπὸ πτυχί, σῆμα δ' ἐφ' ἡμῖν
  ἐγγύθεν Εὐρίπου δημοσίᾳ κέχυται
οὐκ ἀδίκως· ἐρατὴν γὰρ ἀπωλέσαμεν νεότητα
  τρηχεῖαν πολέμου δεξάμενοι νεφέλην.

(90D.)

ὦ ξεῖν', εὔυδρόν ποτ' ἐναίομεν ἄστυ Κορίνθου,
  νῦν δ' ἄμ' Αἴαντος νᾶσος ἔχει Σαλαμίς.

1 ξεῖν', ξένε codd.   2 δὲ ἀνάματος Plu.   μετ' Αἴαντος Fav.   δ'
ἄμ' Αἴαντος Bergk

(91D.)

μυριάσιν ποτὲ τῇδε τριακοσίαις ἐμάχοντο
  ἐκ Πελοποννάσου χιλιάδες τέτορες.

1 διηκοσίαις Diod.

(92D.)

ὦ ξεῖν', ἀγγέλλειν Λακεδαιμονίοις ὅτι τῇδε
  κείμεθα τοῖς κείνων ῥήμασι πειθόμενοι.

1 ἄγγειλον Lyc., Diod.   ὦ ξέν' ἀπάγγειλον Strabo   2 ῥήμασι
πειθόμενοι Herod., Anth. Pal., Suda   πειθόμενοι νομίμοις Lyc., Diod.,
Strabo

(97D.)

τούσδ' ἀπὸ Τυρρηνῶν ἀκροθίνια Φοίβῳ ἄγοντας
  ἓν πέλαγος, μία ναῦς, εἷς τάφος ἐκτέρισεν.

(99D.)

πολλὰ πιὼν καὶ πολλὰ φαγὼν καὶ πολλὰ κάκ᾽ εἰπών
  ἀνθρώπους κεῖμαι Τιμοκρέων Ῥόδιος.

(121D.)

ἄσβεστον κλέος οἵδε φίλῃ περὶ πατρίδι θέντες
  κυάνεον θανάτου ἀμφεβάλοντο νέφος·
οὐδὲ τεθνᾶσι θανόντες, ἐπεί σφ᾽ ἀρετὴ καθύπερθεν
  κυδαίνουσ᾽ ἀνάγει δώματος ἐξ Ἀΐδεω.

(122D.)

τῶνδε δι᾽ ἀνθρώπων ἀρετὰν οὐχ ἵκετο καπνός
  αἰθέρα δαιομένας εὐρυχόρου Τεγέας·
οἳ βούλοντο πόλιν μὲν ἐλευθερίᾳ τεθαλυῖαν
  παισὶ λιπεῖν, αὐτοὶ δ᾽ ἐν προμάχοισι θανεῖν.

(130D.)

αἰαῖ, νοῦσε βαρεῖα, τί δὴ ψυχαῖσι μεγαίρεις
  ἀνθρώπων ἐρατῇ πὰρ νεότητι μένειν;
ἣ καὶ Τίμαρχον γλυκερῆς αἰῶνος ἄμερσας
  ἠΐθεον, πρὶν ἰδεῖν κουριδίην ἄλοχον.

(135D.)

σῶμα μὲν ἀλλοδαπὴ κεύθει κόνις, ἐν δέ σε πόντῳ,
  Κλείσθενες, Εὐξείνῳ μοῖρ᾽ ἔκιχεν θανάτου
πλαζόμενον· γλυκεροῦ δὲ μελίφρονος οἴκαδε νόστου
  ἤμπλακες, οὐδ᾽ ἵκευ Χῖον ἐς ἀμφιρύτην.

(138D.)

Κρὴς γενεὰν Βρόταχος Γορτύνιος ἐνθάδε κεῖμαι
οὐ κατὰ τοῦτ' ἐλθών, ἀλλὰ κατ' ἐμπορίαν.

(142D.)

ἦ σεῦ καὶ φθιμένας λεύκ' ὀστέα τῷδ' ἐνὶ τύμβῳ
ἴσκω ἔτι τρομέειν θῆρας, ἄγρωσσα Λυκάς.
τὰν δ' ἀρετὰν οἶδεν μέγα Πήλιον ἅ τ' ἀρίδηλος
Ὄσσα Κιθαιρῶνός τ' οἰονόμοι σκοπιαί.

PRATINAS

(708)

⏑⏑⏑⏑|⏑⏑⏑⏑|⏑⏑⏑⏑|–⏑⏑
⏑⏑⏑⏑|⏑⏑⏑⏑|⏑⏑–|⏑⏑⏑⏑|⏑⏑⏑⏑|⏑⏑–
⏑⏑⏑⏑|⏑⏑⏑⏑|⏑⏑–|⏑⏑–|⏑⏑–|⏑⏑–
⏑⏑⏑⏑|⏑⏑–|⏑⏑–|⏑⏑–
–⏑⏑–⏑⏑–⋮⏑–⏑–|⏑–⏑–   5
–⏑–|–⏑–|–⏑–⏑⋮–⏑⏑–⏑⏑–⋮⏑
–⏑–⏑|–⏑–|–⏑–⏑|–⏑–
––⏑–|⏑–⏑–⋮⏑–⏑⏑–⋮⏑–⏑––
–⏑–⏑|–⏑–
–⏑–|–⏑–|–⏑––|–⏑–⏑   10
⏑⏑⏑ ⏑⏑⏑|⏑⏑⏑ ⏑⏑⏑
⏑⏑⏑ ⏑⏑⏑|⏑⏑⏑ ⏑⏑⏑|⏑–
⏑–⏑|⏑–⏑–|⏑–⏑–
–⏑–|–⏑–|–⏑–⏑|–⏑–⏑|–⏑–
⏑–⏑–|⏑–⏑–|⏑–⏑–   15
⏑–⏑–|⏑–⏑–|–⏑–⏑––

τίς ὁ θόρυβος ὅδε; τί τάδε τὰ χορεύματα;
τίς ὕβρις ἔμολεν ἐπὶ Διονυσιάδα πολυπάταγα θυμέλαν;
ἐμὸς ἐμὸς ὁ Βρόμιος, ἐμὲ δεῖ κελαδεῖν, ἐμὲ δεῖ παταγεῖν
ἀν' ὄρεα σύμενον μετὰ Ναϊάδων
οἷά τε κύκνον ἄγοντα ποικιλόπτερον μέλος.   5
τὰν ἀοιδὰν κατέστασε Πιερὶς βασίλειαν· ὁ δ' αὐλὸς
ὕστερον χορευέτω· καὶ γάρ ἐσθ' ὑπηρέτας.
κώμῳ μόνον θυραμάχοις τε πυγμαχίαισι νέων θέλοι
      παροίνων
ἔμμεναι στρατηλάτας.
παῖε τὸν φρυνεοῦ ποικίλαν πνοὰν ἔχοντα,   10
φλέγε τὸν ὀλεσισιαλοκάλαμον
λαλοβαρύοπα παραμελορυθμοβάταν
ὑπαὶ τρυπάνῳ δέμας πεπλασμένον.
ἢν ἰδού· ἅδε σοι δεξιᾶς καὶ ποδὸς διαρριφά·
θρίαμβε διθύραμβε κισσόχαιτ' ἄναξ,   15
⟨ἄκου'⟩ ἄκουε τὰν ἐμὰν Δώριον χορείαν.

6 κατεστα ἐπιερεις βασιλεια οὐδ' A   ὁ δ' pro οὐδ' (om. τὰν-βασιλ.)
E, em. Heringa, Bergk   8 κωμῶν μόνον A   κώμων μόνων E, em.
Bergk   θεαεί A   θέα E   θέλει Dobree   θέλοι Wilamowitz   10
φρυναιου A, em. Girard   13 θυπα A (om. E)   θ' ὑπαὶ Emperius
ὑπαὶ Page   14 δεξιὰ A (om. E), em. Bamberger   16 suppl.
Page

TIMOCREON

(727)

```
- - ᴜ ᴜ - ᴜ ᴜ - - - ᴜ - - - ᴜ - ᴜ
- ᴜ ᴜ - ᴜ ᴜ - ᴜ - ᴜ - ᴜ - - - ᴜ - -
- ᴜ ᴜ - ᴜ ᴜ - -
ᴜ - ᴜ ᴜ - ᴜ ᴜ - - - - - - -
or (12)  - - ᴜ - - - ᴜ - - - ᴜ - ᴜ - ᴜ - -
```

ἀλλ' εἰ τύ γε Παυσανίαν ἢ καὶ τύ γε Ξάνθιππον
    αἰνεῖς
ἢ τύ γε Λευτυχίδαν, ἐγὼ δ' 'Αριστείδαν ἐπαινέω
ἄνδρ' ἱερᾶν ἀπ' 'Αθανᾶν
ἐλθεῖν ἕνα λῷστον, ἐπεὶ Θεμιστοκλῆν ἤχθαρε Λατώ,

ψεύσταν ἄδικον προδόταν, ὃς Τιμοκρέοντα ξεῖνον
    ἐόντα   5
ἀργυρίοισι κοβαλικοῖσι πεισθεὶς οὐ κατᾶγεν
πατρίδ' 'Ιαλυσὸν εἴσ‹ω›,
λαβὼν δὲ τρί' ἀργυρίου τάλαντ' ἔβα πλέων εἰς ὄλεθρον,

τοὺς μὲν κατάγων ἀδίκως, τοὺς δ' ἐκδιώκων, τοὺς δὲ
    καίνων·
ἀργυρίων δ' ὑπόπλεως 'Ισθμοῖ γελοίως πανδόκευε   10
ψυχρὰ ‹τὰ› κρεῖα παρίσχων·
οἱ δ' ἤσθιον κηὔχοντο μὴ ὥραν Θεμιστοκλέος γενέσθαι.

4 ἐλθεῖν ἕνα λῷστον UMA   ὃς ἦλθε λεκτὸς S   Θεμιστοκλῆα UMA
-κλέα δὲ S   -κλῆν Wilamowitz   ἤχθαιρε S   6 σκυβαλ- UMAS
(marg.) κυμβαλ- S κοβαλ- Bergk   7 εἰς πατρίδ' 'Ιαλυσὸν codd.,
em. Page   10 ἀργυρίων ὑπόπλεως 'Ισθμοῖ (-οις M) δὲ πανδόκευε
γέλοιως UMA   ἀργυρίου δὲ ὑπόπλεως κτλ. S, em. Enger   11
ψυχρὰ κρέα παρέχων codd., em. Page

(731)

−∪−⏝| ⏝∪−⏝   1–5
−∪−−|−∪−   6

ὤφελέν σ' ὦ τυφλὲ Πλοῦτε
μήτε γῇ μήτ' ἐν θαλάσσῃ

1 ὤφελες ὦ codd. (ὄφ-, ὄφειλ- Suda), em. Ilgen   2 μήτ' ἐν γῇ
codd. (τῇ γῇ Sud. V), em. Brunck

μήτ' ἐν ἠπείρῳ φανῆμεν,
ἀλλὰ Τάρταρόν τε ναίειν
κ'Ἀχέροντα· διὰ σὲ γὰρ πάντ'   5
    αἰὲν ἀνθρώποις κακά.

3 ἠπείρῳ codd. οὐρανῷ ci. Schneidewin   φανήμεναι codd., em.
Bergk   5–6 πάντ' ἐν codd. πάντ' α⟨ἱ⟩εν Page πάντ' ⟨ἐστ'⟩ ἐν
Meineke

CORINNA

(654.i.12–34)

∪∪−− | ∪∪−−   1–5
∪∪−− ⋮ ∪∪−∪−−   6

    ]εν . [. . . . .]Κώρει-
τες ἔκρου]ψαν δάθιο[ν θι]ᾶς
βρέφο]ς ἄντροι, λαθρά[δα]ν ἀγ-
κο]υλομείταο Κρόνω, τα-   15
νίκα νιν κλέψε μάκηρα Ῥεία

μεγ]άλαν τ' [ἀ]θανάτων ἔσ-
s] ἔλε τιμάν.' τάδ' ἔμελψεμ·
μάκαρας δ' αὐτίκα Μώση
φ]ερέμεν ψᾶφον ἔ[τ]αττον   20
κρ]ουφίαν κάλπιδας ἐν χρου-
σοφαῖς· τὺ δ' ἄμα πάντε[ς] ὦρθεν·

πλίονας δ' εἷλε Κιθηρών·
τάχα δ' Ἑρμᾶς ἀνέφαν[έν

12]κώ . η pap.   κώρει | τες ci. Lobel

νι]ν ἀούσας ἐρατὰν ὡς   25
ἔ]λε νίκαν, στεφ[ά]νυσιν
. . .] . . ατώ . ανεκόσμιον
μάκα]ρες· τῶ δὲ νόος γεγάθι·

ὁ δὲ λο]ύπησι κά[θ]εκτος
χαλεπ]ῆσιν Ϝελι[κ]ὼν ἐ-   30
. . . . .] λιττάδα [π]έτραν
. . . . .]κεν δ᾽ ὄ[ρο]ς· ὑκτρῶς
. . . . .]ων οὐψ[ό]θεν εἴρι-
σέ νιν ἐ]μ μου[ρι]άδεσσι λάυς·

          .   .   .   .   .

27 δ᾽ ἐλατάων νιν ci. Bolling

                    (654.iii.12–51)

⏓ ⏑⏑ ⏑⏑ – ⏑ | – ⏑ ⏑ –   1–4
or ⏒ ⏒ : – ⏑ ⏑ – : ⏑ –
⏑⏑⏑⏑ ⏒ : – ⏑ ⏑ – : –   5

τᾶν δὲ πήδω[ν τρῖς μ]ὲν ἔχι
Δεὺς πατεὶ[ρ πάντω]ν βασιλεύς,
τρῖς δὲ πόντ[ω γᾶμε] μέδων
Π[οτιδάων, τ]ᾶν δὲ δουῖν   15
    Φῦβος λέκτ[ρα] κρατούνι,

τὰν δ᾽ ἴαν Μή[ας] ἀγαθὸς
πῆς ῾Ερμᾶς· οὔ[τ]ω γὰρ ῎Ερως
κὴ Κούπρις πιθέταν, τιὼς
ἐν δόμως βάντας κρουφάδαν
    κώρας ἐννί᾽ ἐλέσθη.   20

τή ποκ' εἰρώων γενέθλαν
ἐσγεννάσονθ' εἰμ[ιθί]ων
κάσσονθη π[ο]λου[σπ]ερίες
τ' ἀγείρω τ'· ἐς [μ]α[ντοσ]ούνω   25
    τρίποδος ὦτ[. . . . . .]

τόδε γέρας κ[. . . . .]ν
ἐς πεντείκο[ντα] κρατερῶν
ὁμήμων πέρ[οχο]ς προφά-
τας σεμνῶν [ἀδο]ύτων λαχὼν   30
    ἀψεύδιαν 'Ακ[ρη]φεῖν·

πράτοι [μὲν] γὰ[ρ Λατ]οΐδας
δῶκ' Εὐωνούμοι τριπόδων
ἐς ἱῶν [χρε]ισμὼς ἐνέπειν,
τὸν δ' ἐς γᾶς βαλὼν Οὐριεὺς   35
    τιμὰ[ν] δεύτερος ἴσχεν,

πῆς [Ποτ]ιδάωνος· ἔπι-
τ' 'Ωα[ρί]ων ἁμὸς γενέτωρ
γῆα[ν Ϝ]ὰν ἀππασάμενος·
χὼ μὲν ὠραν[ὸ]ν ἀμφέπι   40
    τιμὰν δ' [ἔλλαχο]ν οὔταν.

τώνεκ[. . . . . . .]ν ἐνέπω
τ' ἀτ[ρ]έκ[ιαν χρει]σμολόγον·
τοὺ δέ [νου Ϝικέ τ' ἀ]θανάτυς
κὴ λού[. . . . .] φρένας   45
    δημόν[εσσ' ἐκου]ρεύων.'

29 suppl. Lobel   41, 43 suppl. Wilamowitz   44 schol. ειχε

ὡς ἔφα [μάντις] π[ε]ραγείς·
τὸν δ᾽ Ἀ[σωπὸς ἀσ]πασίως
δεξιᾶς ἐ[φαψάμ]ενος
δάκρού τ᾽ [ὀκτάλ]λων προβαλ[ὼν   50
    ὧδ᾽ ἀμίψ[ατο φ]ωνῇ·

.   .   .   .   .

664 (a)

μέμφομη δὲ κὴ λιγουρὰν
Μουρτίδ᾽ ἰώνγ᾽ ὅτι βανὰ φοῦ-
σ᾽ ἔβα Πινδάροι πὸτ ἔριν.

BACCHYLIDES

(3)

str. ⏒ – ⏑ ⏖ | ⏑ ⏖ ⏑ – | ⏑ – –
      ⏒ ⦙ – ⏑ ⏑ – ⏑ ⏑ – ⦙ ⏑ – –
      ⏒ ⦙ – ⏑ ⏑ – ⏑ ⏑ – ⦙ ⏑ – –
         – ⏑ – ⏒ ⦙ – ⏑ ⏑ – ⦙ ⏑ – –

ep. ⏒ – ⏑ ⏑ – ⏑ ⏑ – –
        – ⏑ – ⏒ – ⏑ ⏑
     – ⏑ – ⏒ – ⏑ –
        – – ⏑ ⏑ – ⏑ –
     – ⏑ – ⏒ – ⏑ – ⏑ – ⏑ –
        – ⏑ – ⏒ – ⏑ –

ἀριστοκάρπου Σικελίας κρέουσαν
Δάματρα ἰοστέφανόν τε Κούραν
ὕμνει, γλυκύδωρε Κλεοῖ, θοάς τ᾽ Ὀ-
    λυμπιοδρόμους Ἱέρωνος ἵππους.

3 Κλειοῖ pap., em. Blass

σεύον]το γὰρ σὺν ὑπερόχῳ τε Νίκᾳ   5
σὺν ᾿Αγ]λαΐᾳ τε παρ᾽ εὐρυδίναν
᾿Αλφεόν, τόθι] Δεινομένεος ἔθηκαν
    ὄλβιον τ[έκος στεφάνω]ν κυρῆσαι·

θρόησε δὲ λ[αὸς
    ἃ τρισευδαίμ[ων ἀνήρ,   10
ὃς παρὰ Ζηνὸς λαχὼν
    πλείσταρχον Ἑλλάνων γέρας
οἶδε πυργωθέντα πλοῦτον μὴ μελαμ-
    φαρέϊ κρύπτειν σκότῳ.

βρύει μὲν ἱερὰ βουθύτοις ἑορταῖς,   15
βρύουσι φιλοξενίας ἀγυιαί·
λάμπει δ᾽ ὑπὸ μαρμαρυγαῖς ὁ χρυσός,
    ὑψιδαιδάλτων τριπόδων σταθέντων

πάροιθε ναοῦ, τόθι μέγιστον ἄλσος
Φοίβου παρὰ Κασταλίας ῥεέθροις   20
Δελφοὶ διέπουσι. θεὸν θ[εό]ν τις
    ἀγλαϊζέθω γὰρ ἄριστος ὄλβων·

ἐπεί ποτε καὶ δαμασίππου
    Λυδίας ἀρχαγέταν,
εὖτε τὰν πεπ[ρωμέναν   25
    Ζηνὸς τελέ[σσαντος κρί]σιν
Σάρδιες Περσᾶ[ν ἁλίσκοντο στρ]ατῷ,
    Κροῖσον ὁ χρυσά[ορος

φύλαξ᾽ ᾿Απόλλων. [ὁ δ᾽ ἐς] ἄελπτον ἆμαρ
μ[ο]λὼν πολυδ[άκρυο]ν οὐκ ἔμελλε   30

8 τέκος suppl. Edmonds   9 ἀπείρων suppl. Blass   ἀγασθείς
Schadewaldt   16 -ξενίαις Richards, alii   26 τελέσσαντος
suppl. Wackernagel   τελειοῦσαι Kenyon   κρίσιν Weil   κτίσιν
Kenyon

μίμνειν ἔτι δ[ουλοσύ]ναν, πυ[ρ]ὰν δὲ
    χαλκ[ο]τειχέος π[ροπάροι]θεν αὐ[λᾶς

ναῆσατ᾽, ἔνθα σὺ[ν ἀλόχῳ] τε κεδ[νᾷ
σὺν εὐπλοκάμοι[ς τ᾽] ἐπέβαιν᾽ ἄλα[στον
θ]υ[γ]ατράσι δυρομέναις· χέρας δ᾽ [ἐς   35
    αἰ]πὺν αἰθέρα σφετέρας ἀείρας

γέγω]νεν· ‘ὑπέρ[βι]ε δαῖμον,
    πο]ῦ θεῶν ἐστιν χάρις;
πο]ῦ δὲ Λατοίδας ἄναξ;
    ἔρρουσ]ιν ᾿Αλυά[τ]τα δόμοι   40
        ] μυρίων
        ]ν.

        ] ἄστυ,
ἐρεύθεται αἵματι χρυσο]δίνας
Πακτωλός, ἀεικελίως γυναῖκες   45
    ἐξ ἐϋκτίτων μεγάρων ἄγονται·

τὰ πρόσθεν [ἐχ]θρὰ φίλα· θανεῖν γλύκιστον.’
τόσ᾽ εἶπε, καὶ ἁβ[ρο]βάταν κ[έλε]υσεν
ἅπτειν ξύλινον δόμον. ἔκ[λα]γον δὲ
    παρθένοι, φίλας τ᾽ ἀνὰ ματρὶ χεῖρας   50

ἔβαλλον· ὁ γὰρ προφανὴς θνα-
    τοῖσιν ἔχθιστος φόνων·
ἀλλ᾽ ἐπεὶ δεινοῦ πυρὸς
    λαμπρὸν διάϊ[σσεν μέ]νος,
Ζεὺς ἐπιστάσας [μελαγκευ]θὲς νέφος   55
    σβέννυεν ξανθὰ[ν φλόγα.

44 suppl. Kenyon

ἄπιστον οὐδέν, ὅ τι θ[εῶν μέ]ριμνα
τεύχει· τότε Δαλογενὴ[ς Ἀπό]λλων
φέρων ἐς Ὑπερβορέο[υς γ]έροντα
   σὺν τανισφύροις κατ[έν]ασσε κούραις   60

δι' εὐσέβειαν, ὅτι μέ[γιστα] θνατῶν
ἐς ἀγαθέαν ⟨ἀν⟩έπεμψε Π[υθ]ώ.
ὅσο[ι] ⟨γε⟩ μὲν Ἑλλάδ' ἔχουσιν, [ο]ὔτι[ς,
   ὦ μεγαίνητε Ἱέρων, θελήσει

φάμ]εν σέο πλείονα χρυσὸν   65
   Λοξί]ᾳ πέμψαι βροτῶν.
εὖ λέ]γειν πάρεστιν, ὅσ-
   τις μ]ὴ φθόνῳ πιαίνεται
. . . . .]λη φίλιππον ἄνδρ' ἀρήϊον
  . . . .]ίου σκᾶπτρον Διός   70

ἰοπλό]κων τε μέρο[ς ἔχοντ]α Μουσᾶν·
. . . .]μαλέᾳ ποτ[ὲ . . . . . .]΄ ιων
. . . .]νος ἐφάμερον α[. . . . . .].
  . . . .]ᾳ σκοπεῖς· βραχ[ύς ἐστιν αἰών·

. . . .]΄ εσσα δ' ἐλπὶς ὑπ[75
ἐφαμ]ερίων· ὁ δ' ἄναξ [Ἀπόλλων
. . . . .]΄ λος εἶπε Φέρη[τος υἱ·
   'θνατὸν εὖντα χρὴ διδύμους ἀέξειν

62 ἀγαθέαν ἔπεμψε pap., em. Blass, alii   63 ὅσο[ι] μὲν pap.,
em. Blass, alii   68 ἰαίνεται pap.: π add. corrector alter   69
θεοφιλῆ suppl. Herwerden   70 ξεινίου suppl. Nairn τεθμίου vel
δαμίου Blass   75 αἰγλήεσσα suppl. Schadewaldt   77 ὁ βου-
κόλος suppl. Kenyon

γνώμας, ὅτι τ᾽ αὔριον ὄψεαι
    μοῦνον ἁλίου φάος,   80
χὤτι πεντήκοντ᾽ ἔτεα
    ζωὰν βαθύπλουτον τελεῖς.
ὅσια δρῶν εὔφραινε θυμόν· τοῦτο γὰρ
    κερδέων ὑπέρτατον.᾽

φρονέοντι συνετὰ γαρύω· βαθὺς μέν   85
αἰθὴρ ἀμίαντος· ὕδωρ δὲ πόντου
οὐ σάπεται· εὐφροσύνα δ᾽ ὁ χρυσός·
    ἀνδρὶ δ᾽ οὐ θέμις, πολιὸν π[αρ]έντα

γῆρας, θάλ[εια]ν αὖτις ἀγκομίσσαι
ἥβαν. ἀρετᾶ[ς γε μ]ὲν οὐ μινύθει   90
βροτῶν ἅμα σ[ώμ]ατι φέγγος, ἀλλὰ
    Μοῦσά νιν τρ[έφει.] Ἱέρων, σὺ δ᾽ ὄλβου

κάλλιστ᾽ ἐπεδ[είξ]αο θνατοῖς
    ἄνθεα· πράξα[ντι] δ᾽ εὖ
οὐ φέρει κόσμ[ον σι]ω-   95
    πά· σὺν δ᾽ ἀλαθ[είᾳ] καλῶν
καὶ μελιγλώσσου τις ὑμνήσει χάριν
    Κηΐας ἀηδόνος.

(5)

str. − − ∪ ∪ − ∪ ∪ −
      − ∪ − − − ∪ − −
      − − ∪ ∪ − ∪ ∪ −
      − − ∪ ∪ − ∪ ∪ − ⏟ − ∪ −
      − ∪ ∪ − ∪ ∪ −   5
      − − ∪ ∪ − ∪ ∪ −

```
   – ⏑ – – – ⏑ – –
   – ⏑ – ⏟ – ⏑ –
   – – ⏑ – ⏑ ⏑ – – – ⏑ – –
   – ⏑ – ⏑ – ⏑ –                        10
   – – ⏑ – – – – –
   – ⏑ – – – ⏑ –
   – – ⏑ – – – – –
   – ⏑ – – – ⏑ –
   – ⏑ – – – ⏑ –                        15

ep. – – ⏑ ⏑ – – ⏑ – – – ⏑ – ⏟
   – ⏑ – – – ⏑ –
   – – ⏑ ⏑ ⏑ – – ⏟ – ⏑ – –
   – ⏑ – – – ⏑ – –
   – ⏑ ⏑ – – ⏑ ⏑ –                      5
   – – ⏑ – – – ⏑ – ⏟ – ⏑ –
   – – ⏑ – ⏑ ⏑ ⏑ – ⏟
   – ⏑ – ⏟ – ⏑ – ⏟
   – ⏑ ⏑ – – ⏑ –
   – ⏑ – – – ⏑ – ⏟ – ⏑ – –              10
```

εὔμοιρε Συρακ[οσίω]ν
    ἱπποδινήτων στραταγέ,
γνώσῃ μὲν ἰοστεφάνων
    Μοισᾶν γλυκύδωρον ἄγαλμα, τῶν γε νῦν
αἴ τις ἐπιχθονίων,   5
    ὀρθῶς· φρένα δ' εὐθύδικ[ο]ν
ἀτρέμ' ἀμπαύσας μεριμνᾶν
    δεῦρ' ἄθρησον νόῳ·
ἦ σὺν Χαρίτεσσι βαθυζώνοις ὑφάνας
    ὕμνον ἀπὸ ζαθέας   10

6 -δικον vel -δικαν   8 ἐπάθρησον Richards ἐν νόῳ Pfeiffer, metri
causa   9 η pap. ἦ Platt, Jurenka ῇ, ἦ (ubi), εἰ, ἤ (= εἰ) alii

νάσου ξένος ὑμετέραν πέμ-
　　πει κλεεννὰν ἐς πόλιν,
χρυσάμπυκος Οὐρανίας κλει-
　　νὸς θεράπων· ἐθέλει δὲ
　　γᾶρυν ἐκ στηθέων χέων　　　　　　　15

αἰνεῖν Ἱέρωνα. βαθὺν
　　δ' αἰθέρα ξουθαῖσι τάμνων
ὑψοῦ πτερύγεσσι ταχεί-
　　αις αἰετὸς εὐρυάνακτος ἄγγελος
Ζηνὸς ἐρισφαράγου　　　　　　　　　　20
　　θαρσεῖ κρατερᾷ πίσυνος
ἰσχύϊ, πτάσσοντι δ' ὄρνι-
　　χες λιγύφθογγοι φόβῳ·
οὔ νιν κορυφαὶ μεγάλας ἴσχουσι γαίας,
　　οὐδ' ἁλὸς ἀκαμάτας　　　　　　　　25
δυσπαίπαλα κύματα· νωμᾶ-
　　ται δ' ἐν ἀτρύτῳ χάει
λεπτότριχα σὺν ζεφύρου πνοι-
　　αῖσιν ἔθειραν ἀρίγνω-
　　τος μετ' ἀνθρώποις ἰδεῖν·　　　　　30

τὼς νῦν καὶ <ἐ>μοὶ μυρία πάντᾳ κέλευθος
　　ὑμετέραν ἀρετάν
ὑμνεῖν, κυανοπλοκάμου θ' ἕκατι Νίκας
　　χαλκεοστέρνου τ' Ἄρηος,
Δεινομένευς ἀγέρω-　　　　　　　　　35
　　χοι παῖδες· εὖ ἔρδων δὲ μὴ κάμοι θεός.
ξανθότριχα μὲν Φερένικον
　　Ἀλφεὸν παρ' εὐρυδίναν

14 δέ secl. Walker, Maas　　　28 πνο- pap., em. Weil　　31 μοι
pap., em. Blass

πῶλον ἀελλοδρόμαν
    εἶδε νικάσαντα χρυσόπαχυς Ἀώς,   40

Πυθῶνί τ' ἐν ἀγαθέᾳ·
    γᾷ δ' ἐπισκήπτων πιφαύσκω·
οὔπω νιν ὑπὸ προτέ[ρω]ν
    ἵππων ἐν ἀγῶνι κατέχρανεν κόνις
πρὸς τέλος ὀρνύμενον·   45
    ῥιπᾷ γὰρ ἴσος Βορέα
ὃν κυβερνήταν φυλάσσων
    ἵεται νεόκροτον
νίκαν Ἱέρωνι φιλοξείνῳ τιτύσκων.
    ὄλβιος ᾧτινι θεός   50
μοῖράν τε καλῶν ἔπορεν
    σύν τ' ἐπιζήλῳ τύχᾳ
ἀφνεὸν βιοτὰν διάγειν· οὐ
    γάρ τις ἐπιχθονίων
πάντα γ' εὐδαίμων ἔφυ.   55

καὶ γάρ π]οτ' ἐρειψιπύλαν
    παῖδ' ἀνίκ]ατον λέγουσιν
δῦναι Διὸς] ἀργικεραύ-
    νου δώματα Φερσεφόνας τανισφύρου,
καρχαρόδοντα κύν' ἄ-   60
    ξοντ' ἐς φάος ἐξ Ἀΐδα,
υἱὸν ἀπλάτοι' Ἐχίδνας·
    ἔνθα δυστάνων βροτῶν
ψυχὰς ἐδάη παρὰ Κωκυτοῦ ῥεέθροις,
    οἷά τε φύλλ' ἄνεμος   65
Ἴδας ἀνὰ μηλοβότους

49 -ξενωι pap., em. Kenyon   56 καὶ γάρ suppl. Jurenka καί
τοί Blass   58 δῦναι Palmer

πρῶνας ἀργηστὰς δονεῖ.
ταῖσιν δὲ μετέπρεπεν εἴδωλον θρασυμέμνονος ἐγ-
χεσπάλου Πορθανίδα·   70

τὸν δ' ὡς ἴδεν Ἀλκμή‹ν›ιος θαυμαστὸς ἥρως
τεύχεσι λαμπόμενον,
νευρὰν ἐπέβασε λιγυκλαγγῆ κορώνας,
χαλκεόκρανον δ' ἔπειτ' ἔξ
εἵλετο ἰὸν ἀνα-   75
πτύξας φαρέτρας πῶμα· τῷ δ' ἐναντία
ψυχὰ προφάνη Μελεάγρου,
καί νιν εὖ εἰδὼς προσεῖπεν·
'υἱὲ Διὸς μεγάλου,
στᾶθί τ' ἐν χώρᾳ, γελανώσας τε θυμόν   80

μὴ ταύσιον προΐει
τραχὺν ἐκ χειρῶν ὀϊστόν
ψυχαῖσιν ἔπι φθιμένων·
οὔ τοι δέος.' ὡς φάτο· θάμβησεν δ' ἄναξ
Ἀμφιτρυωνιάδας,   85
εἶπέν τε· 'τίς ἀθανάτων
ἢ βροτῶν τοιοῦτον ἔρνος
θρέψεν ἐν ποίᾳ χθονί;
τίς δ' ἔκτανεν; ἦ τάχα καλλίζωνος Ἥρα
κεῖνον ἐφ' ἁμετέρᾳ   90
πέμψει κεφαλᾷ· τὰ δέ που
Παλλάδι ξανθᾷ μέλει.'
τὸν δὲ προσέφα Μελέαγρος
δακρυόεις· 'χαλεπὸν
θεῶν παρατρέψαι νόον   95

78 -εειπεν pap., em. Kenyon

ἄνδρεσσιν ἐπιχθονίοις.
   καὶ γὰρ ἂν πλάξιππος Οἰνεύς
παῦσεν καλυκοστεφάνου
   σεμνᾶς χόλον Ἀρτέμιδος λευκωλένου
λισσόμενος πολέων   100
   τ' αἰγῶν θυσίαισι πατήρ
καὶ βοῶν φοινικονώτων·
   ἀλλ' ἀνίκατον θεά
ἔσχεν χόλον· εὐρυβίαν δ' ἔσσευε κούρα
   κάπρον ἀναιδομάχαν   105
ἐς καλλίχορον Καλυδῶ-
   ν', ἔνθα πλημύρων σθένει
ὄρχους ἐπέκειρεν ὀδόντι,
   σφάζε τε μῆλα, βροτῶν
   θ' ὅστις εἰσάνταν μόλοι.   110

τῷ δὲ στυγερὰν δῆριν Ἑλλάνων ἄριστοι
   στασάμεθ' ἐνδυκέως
ἐξ ἄματα συνεχέως· ἐπεὶ δὲ δαίμων
   κάρτος Αἰτωλοῖς ὄρεξεν,
θάπτομεν οὓς κατέπε-   115
   φνεν σῦς ἐριβρύχας ἐπαΐσσων βίᾳ,
Ἀ[γκ]αῖον ἐμῶν τ' Ἀγέλαον
   φ[έρτ]ατον κεδνῶν ἀδελφεῶν,
οὓς τέ]κεν ἐν μεγάροις
   . . . . .]ς Ἀλθαία περικλειτοῖσιν Οἰνέος·   120

. . . . . ὤ]λεσε μοῖρ' ὀλοά
. . . . . .]ς· οὐ γάρ πω δαΐφρων

115 τους κατεπεφνε pap., em. Kenyon   118 φέρτατον vel
φίλτατον   120 πατρὸς suppl. Kenyon θοῦρις Schwartz παῖδας
Schadewaldt   121 σύν τ' vel σὺν δ' suppl. Edmonds   122
πλεῦνας suppl. Housman

παῦσεν] χόλον ἀγροτέρα
    Λατοῦς θυγάτηρ· περὶ δ' αἴθωνος δορᾶς
μαρνάμεθ' ἐνδυκέως   125
    Κουρῆσι μενεπτολέμοις·
ἔνθ' ἐγὼ πολλοῖς σὺν ἄλλοις
    Ἴφικλον κατέκτανον
ἐσθλόν τ' Ἀφάρητα, θοοὺς μάτρωας· οὐ γὰρ
    καρτερόθυμος Ἄρης   130
κρίνει φίλον ἐν πολέμῳ,
    τυφλὰ δ' ἐκ χειρῶν βέλη
ψυχαῖς ἔπι δυσμενέων φοι-
    τᾷ θάνατόν τε φέρει
    τοῖσιν ἂν δαίμων θέλῃ.   135

ταῦτ' οὐκ ἐπιλεξαμένα
    Θεστίου κούρα δαΐφρων
μάτηρ κακόποτμος ἐμοὶ
    βούλευσεν ὄλεθρον ἀτάρβακτος γυνά,
καῖέ τε δαιδαλέας   140
    ἐκ λάρνακος ὠκύμορον
φίτρον †ἐγκλαύσασα†· τὸν δὴ
    μοῖρ' ἐπέκλωσεν τότε
ζωᾶς ὅρον ἁμετέρας ἔμμεν. τύχον μὲν
    Δαϊπύλου Κλύμενον   145
παῖδ' ἄλκιμον ἐξεναρί-
    ζων ἀμώμητον δέμας,
πύργων προπάροιθε κιχήσας·

137 κορα pap., em. Kenyon   142 ἐγκλαύσασα pap., def. Blass,
Weir Smyth ἀγκλαύσασα Jebb ('wailing'), Brooks ('opening')
ἐγλαβοῦσα (=ἐκλ.) Schwartz ἐξαύσασα Wackernagel, Schulze
143 ποτὲ Kenyon

τοὶ δὲ πρὸς εὐκτιμέναν
φεῦγον ἀρχαίαν πόλιν   150

Πλευρῶνα· μίνυθεν δέ μοι ψυχὰ γλυκεῖα·
    γνῶν δ' ὀλιγοσθενέων,
αἰαῖ· πύματον δὲ πνέων δάκρυσα τλά[μων,
    ἀγλαὰν ἥβαν προλείπων.'
φασὶν ἀδεισιβόαν   155
    'Αμφιτρύωνος παῖδα μοῦνον δὴ τότε
τέγξαι βλέφαρον, ταλαπενθέος
    πότμον οἰκτίροντα φωτός·
καί νιν ἀμειβόμενος
    τᾶδ' ἔφα· 'θνατοῖσι μὴ φῦναι φέριστον   160

μηδ' ἀελίου προσιδεῖν
    φέγγος· ἀλλ' οὐ γάρ τίς ἐστιν
πρᾶξις τάδε μυρομένοις,
    χρὴ κεῖνο λέγειν ὅτι καὶ μέλλει τελεῖν.
ἦρά τις ἐν μεγάροις   165
    Οἰνῆος ἀρηϊφίλου
ἔστιν ἀδμήτα θυγάτρων,
    σοὶ φυὰν ἀλιγκία;
τάν κεν λιπαρὰν ἐθέλων θείμαν ἄκοιτιν.'
    τὸν δὲ μενεπτολέμου   170
ψυχὰ προσέφα Μελεά-
    γρου· 'λίπον χλωραύχενα
ἐν δώμασι Δαϊάνειραν,

151 μινυνθα pap. μινύνθᾱ def. Pfeiffer μίνυθεν Wilamowitz   160
τοιδ pap. τοδ vel ταδ corrector alter τᾶδ' Snell τᾷδ' Wilamowitz
τοῖ' Housman   161 μητ pap. μηδ' Stobaeus   169 θελων
pap., em. Kenyon

νῆϊν ἔτι χρυσέας
  Κύπριδος θελξιμβρότου.'   175

λευκώλενε Καλλιόπα,
  στᾶσον εὐποίητον ἅρμα
αὐτοῦ· Δία τε Κρονίδαν
  ὕμνησον 'Ολύμπιον ἀρχαγὸν θεῶν,
τόν τ' ἀκαμαντορόαν   180
  'Αλφεόν, Πέλοπός τε βίαν,
καὶ Πίσαν, ἔνθ' ὁ κλεεννὸς
  ποσσὶ νικάσας δρόμῳ
ἦλθ]εν Φερένικος <ἐς> εὐπύργους Συρακόσ-
  σας 'Ιέρωνι φέρων   185
εὐδ]αιμονίας πέταλον.
  χρὴ] δ' ἀλαθείας χάριν
αἰνεῖν, φθόνον ἀμφ[οτέραισιν
  χερσὶν ἀπωσάμενον,
  εἴ τις εὖ πράσσοι βροτῶν.   190

Βοιωτὸς ἀνὴρ τᾶδε φών[ησεν, γλυκειᾶν
  'Ησίοδος πρόπολος
Μουσᾶν, ὃν <ἂν> ἀθάνατοι τι[μῶσι, τούτῳ
  καὶ βροτῶν φήμαν ἔπ[εσθαι.
πείθομαι εὐμαρέως   195
  εὐκλέα κελεύθου γλῶσσαν οὐ̣[
πέμπειν 'Ιέρωνι· τόθεν γὰρ
  πυθμένες θάλλουσιν ἐσθλ[ῶν,

184 ἐς suppl. Blass, Housman   191 τᾶδε Snell τᾶδε Wilamowitz
γλυκειᾶν suppl. Bruhn λιγεῖαν Wilamowitz   193 ἂν suppl.
Housman, alii   τούτῳ suppl. Housman κείνῳ Wilamowitz   196
οὐκ ἐκτὸς προείς Jurenka οὐ πλανώμενος Bucherer οὐκ ἐκτὸς δίκας
Jebb

τοὺς ὁ μεγιστοπάτωρ
    Ζεὺς ἀκινήτους ἐν εἰρήν[ᾳ φυλάσσοι.   200

200 suppl. Palmer

(17)

```
str.  ∪ ∪ ∪ − ∪ − − ∪ − ∪ −
        − ∪ ∪ ∪ − ∪ − ∪ − ∪ − ∪
        − − ∪ − ∪ −
      − ∪ − − ∪ ∪ ∪ ⏑
      − − ∪ ∪ ∪ − − ∪ ∪                         5
        ∪ − ∪ − − ∪ − −
        ∪ − ∪ − ∪ ∪ ∪ − ∪ ∪ ∪ − −
      ∪ − ∪ − − ∪ ∪ ∪
        − ∪ − ∪ − ∪ −
      − ∪ ∪ − ∪ − ∪                             10
        − ∪ − ∪ ∪ − ∪ ∪ −
        ∪ − ∪ − ∪ − ∪ −
        ∪ − − ∪ − ∪ −
        ∪ − ∪ ∪ ∪ − ∪ − ∪
        − − ∪ − − ∪ ⏑                            15
      − ∪ ∪ ∪ − ∪ − −
        ∪ − ∪ − ∪ ⏑
      − − ∪ ∪ ∪ − ∪ −
        − ∪ ∪ ∪ − ∪ − ⏑
      − − ∪ ∪ ∪ − ∪ − ∪ −                        20
      ∪ ∪ ∪ − ∪ ∪ ∪ −
        ∪ − ∪ − − ∪ −
      − ∪ − ∪ ∪ ∪ − ∪ − − ∪ ⏑

ep.   ∪ − ∪ ∪ ∪ − ∪ − −
      ∪ − ∪ − ∪ −
      − ∪ ∪ ∪ − ∪ −
```

```
– ⏑ – ⏑ – ⏑ – – ⏑ – ⏑ – ⏒
⏑ – ⏑ ⏑ ⏑ – ⏑ –                              5
– ⏑ – – ⏑ ⏑ ⏑ – ⏑ –
– ⏑ ⏑ ⏑ – ⏑ – ⏑ – –
– – ⏑ – – ⏑ – ⏑ ⏑ ⏒
– ⏑ – ⏑ – ⏑ – ⏑ –
⏑ ⏑ ⏑ – ⏑ – ⏑ –                              10
– ⏑ – – ⏑ –
        ⏑ – ⏑ – – ⏑ – – – ⏑ ⏑
        ⏑ – ⏑ – – ⏑ –
        – ⏑ – ⏑ – ⏑ –
– ⏑ – ⏑ ⏑                                    15
        ⏑ – ⏑ – ⏑ – ⏑ – ⏑ – – ⏑ –
⏑ – ⏑ – – ⏑ ⏑ ⏑ – ⏑ ⏒
– ⏑ – – ⏑ – ⏑ –
        ⏑ ⏑ ⏑ – –
⏑ – ⏑ – – ⏑ – – ⏑ –                          20
```

κυανόπρωρα μὲν ναῦς μενέκτυ[πον
   Θησέα δὶς ἑπτά τ' ἀγλαοὺς ἄγουσα
   κούρους Ἰαόνων
Κρητικὸν τάμνε πέλαγος·
τηλαυγέϊ γὰρ ἐν φάρεϊ   5
   βορήϊαι πίτνον αὖραι
   κλυτᾶς ἕκατι π[ε]λεμαίγιδος Ἀθάνας·
κνίσεν τε Μίνωϊ κέαρ
   ἱμεράμπυκος θεᾶς
Κύπριδος [ἁ]γνὰ δῶρα·   10
   χεῖρα δ' οὐ[κέτι] παρθενικᾶς
   ἄτερθ' ἐράτυεν, θίγεν

7 πελεμ- Wackernagel, Housman πολεμ- Kenyon   10 ἁγνὰ
suppl. Blass αἰνὰ Kenyon

δὲ λευκᾶν παρηΐδων·
βόασέ τ᾽ Ἐρίβοια χαλκο-
θώρακα Πανδίονος   15
ἔκγονον· ἴδεν δὲ Θησεύς,
μέλαν δ᾽ ὑπ᾽ ὀφρύων
δίνασεν ὄμμα, καρδίαν τέ οἱ
σχέτλιον ἄμυξεν ἄλγος,
εἶρέν τε· Διὸς υἱὲ φερτάτου,   20
ὅσιον οὐκέτι τεᾶν
ἔσω κυβερνᾷς φρενῶν
θυμ[όν]· ἴσχε μεγαλοῦχον ἥρως βίαν.

ὅ τι μὲν ἐκ θεῶν μοῖρα παγκρατὴς
ἄμμι κατένευσε καὶ Δίκας ῥέπει τά-   25
λαντον, πεπρωμέναν
αἶσαν ἐκπλήσομεν, ὅταν
ἔλθῃ· [σ]ὺ δὲ βαρεῖαν κάτε-
χε μῆτιν. εἰ καί σε κεδνὰ
τέκεν λέχει Διὸς ὑπὸ κρόταφον Ἴδας   30
μιγεῖσα Φοίνικος ἐρα-
τώνυμος κόρα βροτῶν
φέρτατον, ἀλλὰ κἀμὲ
Πιτθέος θυγάτηρ ἀφνεοῦ
πλαθεῖσα ποντίῳ τέκεν   35
Ποσειδᾶνι, χρύσεον
τέ οἱ δόσαν ἰόπλοκοι κά-
λυμμα † Νηρηΐδες.
τῶ σε, πολέμαρχε Κνωσίων,
κέλομαι πολύστονον   40
ἐρύκεν ὕβριν· οὐ γὰρ ἂν θέλοι-
μ᾽ ἄμβροτον ἐραννὸν Ἀο[ῦς

42 αμβροτοι᾽ pap. -τον Snell -του Wackernagel, Wilamowitz

ἰδεῖν φάος, ἐπεί τιν' ἠϊθέ[ων
σὺ δαμάσειας ἀέκον-
    τα· πρόσθε χειρῶν βίαν   45
δείξομεν· τὰ δ' ἐπιόντα δα[ίμω]ν κρινεῖ.'

τόσ' εἶπεν ἀρέταιχμος ἥρως·
τάφον δὲ ναυβάται
φωτὸς ὑπεράφανον
θάρσος· Ἀλίου τε γαμβρῷ χόλωσεν ἦτορ,   50
ὕφαινέ τε ποταινίαν
μῆτιν, εἶπέν τε· 'μεγαλοσθενές
Ζεῦ πάτερ, ἄκουσον· εἴπερ με νύμ[φ]α
Φοίνισσα λευκώλενος σοὶ τέκεν,
νῦν πρόπεμπ' ἀπ' οὐρανοῦ θοάν   55
πυριέθειραν ἀστραπάν
σᾶμ' ἀρίγνωτον· εἰ
    δὲ καὶ σὲ Τροιζηνία σεισίχθονι
      φύτευσεν Αἴθρα Ποσει-
      δᾶνι, τόνδε χρύσεον   60
χειρὸς ἀγλαὸν
    ἔνεγκε κόσμον ἐκ βαθείας ἁλός,
δικὼν θράσει σῶμα πατρὸς ἐς δόμους.
εἴσεαι δ' αἴκ' ἐμᾶς κλύῃ
    Κρόνιος εὐχᾶς   65
ἀναξιβρέντας ὁ πάντω[ν με]δ[έω]ν.'

κλύε δ' ἄμεμπτον εὐχὰν μεγασθενὴς
    Ζεύς, ὑπέροχόν τε Μίνοϊ φύτευσε
      τιμὰν φίλῳ θέλων
παιδὶ πανδερκέα θέμεν,   70

68 νιν[O¹ μιν[O² μίνωι A *Μίνοϊ* Snell

ἄστραψέ θ'· ὁ δὲ θυμάρμενον
   ἰδὼν τέρας χέρα πέτασσε
   κλυτὰν ἐς αἰθέρα μενεπτόλεμος ἥρως
εἶρέν τε· 'Θησεῦ τάδ' ἐ<μὰ>
   μὲν βλέπεις σαφῆ Διὸς   75
δῶρα· σὺ δ' ὄρνυ' ἐς βα-
   ρύβρομον πέλαγος· Κρονίδας
   δέ τοι πατὴρ ἄναξ τελεῖ
   Ποσειδὰν ὑπέρτατον
   κλέος χθόνα κατ' ἠΰδενδρον.'   80
   ὣς εἶπε· τῷ δ' οὐ πάλιν
θυμὸς ἀνεκάμπτετ', ἀλλ' εὐ-
   πάκτων ἐπ' ἰκρίων
σταθεὶς ὄρουσε, πόντιόν τέ νιν
   δέξατο θελημὸν ἄλσος.   85
τάφεν δὲ Διὸς υἱὸς ἔνδοθεν
κέαρ, κέλευσέ τε κατ' οὖ-
   ρον ἴσχεν εὐδαίδαλον
νᾶα· μοῖρα δ' ἑτέραν ἐπόρσυν' ὁδόν.

ἴετο δ' ὠκύπομπον δόρυ· σόει   90
   νιν βορεὰς ἐξόπιν πνέουσ' ἄητα·
   τρέσσαν δ' Ἀθαναίων
ἠϊθέων <πᾶν> γένος, ἐπεὶ
ἥρως θόρεν πόντονδε, κα-
   τὰ λειρίων τ' ὀμμάτων δά-   95
κρυ χέον, βαρεῖαν ἐπιδέγμενοι ἀνάγκαν.

72 χειρας ΑΟ χειρα Ο¹ χέρα Richards   74 ταδε | Α ταδε[Ο
τάδ' ἐμὰ suppl. Platt   80 ευδενδρον pap., em. Kenyon   88
ισχειν pap., em. Kenyon   91 εξοπιθεν pap., em. Kenyon
92 αητᾱ pap. ἄητα Platt, Housman   93 suppl. Kenyon

φέρον δὲ δελφῖνες ἁλι-
  ναιέται μέγαν θοῶς
Θησέα πατρὸς ἱππί-
  ου δόμον· ἔμολέν τε θεῶν   100
  μέγαρον. τόθι κλυτὰς ἰδών
ἔδεισε⟨ν⟩ Νηρῆος ὀλ-
  βίου κόρας· ἀπὸ γὰρ ἀγλαῶν λάμπε γυίων σέλας
ὧτε πυρός, ἀμφὶ χαίταις   105
  δὲ χρυσεόπλοκοι
δίνηντο ταινίαι· χορῷ δ' ἔτερ-
  πον κέαρ ὑγροῖσι ποσσίν.
εἶδέν τε πατρὸς ἄλοχον φίλαν
σεμνὰν βοῶπιν ἐρατοῖ-   110
  σιν Ἀμφιτρίταν δόμοις·
ἅ νιν ἀμφέβαλεν ἀϊόνα πορφυρέαν,

κόμαισί τ' ἐπέθηκεν οὔλαις
ἀμεμφέα πλόκον,
τόν ποτέ οἱ ἐν γάμῳ   115
δῶκε δόλιος Ἀφροδίτα ῥόδοις ἐρεμνόν.
ἄπιστον ὅ τι δαίμονες
θέλωσιν οὐδὲν φρενοάραις βροτοῖς·
νᾶα πάρα λεπτόπρυμναν φάνη· φεῦ,
οἵαισιν ἐν φροντίσι Κνώσιον   120
ἔσχασεν στραταγέταν, ἐπεί
μόλ' ἀδίαντος ἐξ ἁλός
θαῦμα πάντεσσι, λάμ-

97 δελφῖνες ἐν ἁλὶ | ναιέται pap., ut vid.   102 ἔδεισε νηρεος pap.,
em. Kenyon   108 υγροισιν εν ποσιν pap., em. Kenyon   112
-βαλλεν pap., em. Kenyon   118 θελωσιν pap. θέωσιν Crusius
λῶσιν Palmer

πε δ' ἀμφὶ γυίοις θεῶν δῶρ', ἀγλαό-
θρονοί τε κοῦραι σὺν εὐ-   125
    θυμίᾳ νεοκτίτῳ
ὠλόλυξαν, ἔ-
    κλαγεν δὲ πόντος· ἤϊθεοι δ' ἐγγύθεν
νέοι παιάνιξαν ἐρατᾷ ὀπί.
Δάλιε, χοροῖσι Κηΐων   130
    φρένα ἰανθείς
ὄπαζε θεόπομπον ἐσθλῶν τύχαν.

(18)

∪ ∪ − − ∪ ∪ − ∪ − ⋮ −
    ⎼ − ∪ ∪ − ∪ − ⋮ ∪ − ⎵
∪ ∪ ∪ − ∪ ∪ − ∪ − ⋮ −
    − − ∪ ∪ − ∪ − ⋮ ∪ − −
⎵ ⎵ ⎵ − ∪ ∪ − ∪ −   5
    − ⎵ − ∪ ∪ − ∪ − ⋮ − −
    ⎵ − ∪ − ∪ −
− − − ∪ ∪ − ∪ ⎵
− ∪ − ∪ ∪ − ⋮ −
    − − ∪ ∪ − ∪ ⎵   10
− ⎵ − ∪ ∪ − ⋮ −
    ⎵ − ∪ ∪ − ∪ − ⋮ ∪ − ∪ −
− ⎵ − ∪ ∪ − ∪ −
    − ∪ − ∪ − ∪ −
− − − ∪ ∪ − ∪ − ⋮ ∪ − −   15

ΧΟ. βασιλεῦ τᾶν ἱερᾶν Ἀθανᾶν,
        τῶν ἁβροβίων ἄναξ Ἰώνων,
    τί νέον ἔκλαγε χαλκοκώδων
        σάλπιγξ πολεμηΐαν ἀοιδάν;
    ἦ τις ἁμετέρας χθονὸς   5
        δυσμενὴς ὅρι' ἀμφιβάλλει

στραταγέτας ἀνήρ;
ἢ λῃσταὶ κακομάχανοι
ποιμένων ἀέκατι μήλων
    σεύοντ᾽ ἀγέλας βίᾳ;   10
ἢ τί τοι κραδίαν ἀμύσσει;
    φθέγγευ· δοκέω γὰρ εἴ τινι βροτῶν
ἀλκίμων ἐπικουρίαν
    καὶ τὶν ἔμμεναι νέων,
ὦ Πανδίονος υἱὲ καὶ Κρεούσας.   15

ΑΙΓ. νέον ἦλθεν δολιχὰν ἀμείψας
    κᾶρυξ ποσὶν Ἰσθμίαν κέλευθον·
ἄφατα δ᾽ ἔργα λέγει κραταιοῦ
    φωτός· τὸν ὑπέρβιόν τ᾽ ἔπεφνεν
Σίνιν, ὃς ἰσχύϊ φέρτατος   20
    θνατῶν ἦν, Κρονίδα Λυταίου
    σεισίχθονος τέκος·
σὺν τ᾽ ἀνδροκτόνον ἐν νάπαις
Κρεμμυῶνος ἀτάσθαλόν τε
    Σκίρωνα κατέκτανεν·   25
τάν τε Κερκυόνος παλαίστραν
    ἔσχεν, Πολυπήμονός τε καρτερὰν
σφῦραν ἐξέβαλεν Προκό-
    πτας, ἀρείονος τυχών
φωτός. ταῦτα δέδοιχ᾽ ὅπᾳ τελεῖται.   30

ΧΟ. τίνα δ᾽ ἔμμεν πόθεν ἄνδρα τοῦτον
    λέγει, τίνα τε στολὰν ἔχοντα;
πότερα σὺν πολεμηΐοις ὅ-

9 δ᾽ εκατι pap., em. Palmer, van Branteghem   16 ηλθε pap.,
em. Kenyon   24 κρεμμυωνος pap., em. Kenyon   28 εξεβαλλεν
pap., em. Kenyon

πλοῖσι στρατιὰν ἄγοντα πολλάν;

ἦ μοῦνον σὺν ὀπάοσιν   35

στείχειν ἔμπορον οἷ' ἀλάταν

ἐπ' ἀλλοδαμίαν,

ἰσχυρόν τε καὶ ἄλκιμον

ὧδε καὶ θρασύν, ὃς τ⟨οσ⟩ούτων

ἀνδρῶν κρατερὸν σθένος   40

ἔσχεν; ἦ θεὸς αὐτὸν ὁρμᾷ,

δίκας ἀδίκοισιν ὄφρα μήσεται·

οὐ γὰρ ῥᾴδιον αἰὲν ἔρ-

δοντα μὴ 'ντυχεῖν κακῷ.

πάντ' ἐν τῷ δολιχῷ χρόνῳ τελεῖται.   45

ΑΙΓ. δύο οἱ φῶτε μόνους ἁμαρτεῖν

λέγει, περὶ φαιδίμοισι δ' ὤμοις

ξίφος ἔχειν ⟨   ⟩

ξεστοὺς δὲ δύ' ἐν χέρεσσ' ἄκοντας

κηΰτυκτον κυνέαν Λάκαι-   50

ναν κρατὸς πέρι πυρσοχαίτου·

χιτῶνα πορφύρεον

στέρνοις τ' ἀμφί, καὶ οὔλιον

Θεσσαλὰν χλαμύδ'· ὀμμάτων δὲ

στίλβειν ἄπο Λαμνίαν   55

φοίνισσαν φλόγα· παῖδα δ' ἔμμεν

πρώθηβον, ἀρηΐων δ' ἀθυρμάτων

μεμνᾶσθαι πολέμου τε καὶ

χαλκεοκτύπου μάχας·

δίζησθαι δὲ φιλαγλάους Ἀθάνας.   60

35 οπλοισιν pap., em. Goligher, alii   39 ος τουτων pap.   ὃς
τοσούτων Platt   ὃς τοιούτων Kenyon   48 ἐλεφαντόκωπον Des-
rousseaux   51 υπερ pap., em. Blass   56 εμεν pap., em.
Kenyon

F

(fr. 4)

⏑ ⏑ ⏑ ⏑ ⏑ ⏑
    ⏑ ⏑ ⏑ ⏑ ⏑ ⏑ ⏑
⏑ ⏑ ⏑ ⏑ ⏑ ⏑ ⏑   25
⏑ ⏑ ⏑ ⏑ ⏑ ⏑
⏑ ⏑ ⏑ ⏑ ⏑ ⏑ ⏑ ⏑
⏑ ⏑ ⏑ ⏑ ⏑
⏑ ⏑ ⏑ ⏑ ⏑
⏑ ⏑ ⏑ ⏑ ⏑   30
⏑ ⏑ ⏑ ⏑ ⏑ ⏑ ⏑ ⏑ ⏑
⏑ ⏑ ⏑
⏑ ⏑ ⏑ ⏑ ⏑
    ⏑ ⏑ ⏑ ⏑ ⏑
⏑ ⏑ ⏑ ⏑ ⏑ ⏑ ⏑   35
⏑ ⏑ ⏑ ⏑ ⏑ ⏑
⏑ ⏑ ⏑ ⏑ ⏑
⏑ ⏑ ⏑ ⏑ ⏑
⏑ ⏑ ⏑ ⏑ ⏑ ⏑ ⏑ ⏑
⏑ ⏑ ⏑ ⏑ ⏑   40

τίκτει δέ τε θνατοῖσιν εἰ-
    ρήνα μεγαλάνορα πλοῦτον
καὶ μελιγλώσσων ἀοιδᾶν ἄνθεα   25
δαιδαλέων τ᾽ ἐπὶ βωμῶν
θεοῖσιν αἴθεσθαι βοῶν ξανθᾷ φλογί
μηρί᾽ εὐτρίχων τε μήλων
γυμνασίων τε νέοις
αὐλῶν τε καὶ κώμων μέλειν.   30
ἐν δὲ σιδαροδέτοις πόρπαξιν αἰθᾶν

24]άνορα[pap.   εἰρήνη μεγάλα πλοῦτον Stob.   28 μηρίταν
εὐτρίχων τε Stob.   (pap.]χων τε[), em. Blass

ἀραχνᾶν ἱστοὶ πέλονται
ἔγχεά τε λογχωτὰ ξίφεα
  τ' ἀμφάκεα δάμναται εὐρώς.
χαλκεᾶν δ' οὐκ ἔστι σαλπίγγων κτύπος,   35
οὐδὲ συλᾶται μελίφρων
ὕπνος ἀπὸ βλεφάρων
ἀῷος ὃς θάλπει κέαρ.
συμποσίων δ' ἐρατῶν βρίθοντ' ἀγυιαί,
παιδικοί θ' ὕμνοι φλέγονται.   40

38 ἆμος Stob., em. Blass

(fr. 20B)

\- \- ◡ ◡ \- ◡ ◡ \- ◡ \- ◡ \- ◡
\- ◡ ◡ \- ◡ ◡ \- ◡ \- ◡ \- \-
\- ◡ ◡ \- ◡ ◡ \- ◡ \- ◡ \- \-
\- ◡ \- ◡ \- ◡ \- \- \- \- ◡ \-

ὦ βάρβιτε, μηκέτι πάσσαλον φυλάσ[σων
ἑπτάτονον λιγυρὰν κάππαυε γᾶρυν·
δεῦρ' ἐς ἐμὰς χέρας· ὁρμαίνω τι πέμπ[ειν
χρύσεον Μουσᾶν 'Αλεξάνδρῳ πτερόν

καὶ συμπος[ίαι]σιν ἄγαλμ' [ἐν] εἰκάδες[σιν,   5
εὖτε νέων ἁ[παλὸν] γλυκεῖ' ἀνάγκα
σευομενᾶν κυλίκων θάλπησι θυμόν,
Κύπριδός τ⟨ε⟩ ἐλπὶς αἰθύσσῃ φρένας,

ἀμμειγνυμένα Διονυσίοισι δώροις·
ἀνδράσι δ' ὑψοτάτω πέμπει μερίμνας·   10

5 συμποσίαισιν Maas, -οισιν Grenfell, Hunt   6 suppl. Maas
7 σευομένα Ath., em. Blass   8 Κύπριδος ἐλπὶς δ' αἰθύσσει Ath.
]ις αιθυσσηι φρε[pap.   τε suppl. Maas

αὐτίκα μὲν πολίων κράδεμνα λύει,
πᾶσι δ' ἀνθρώποις μοναρχήσειν δοκεῖ·

χρυσῷ δ' ἐλέφαντί τε μαρμαίρουσιν οἶκοι
πυροφόροι δὲ κατ' αἰγλάεντα πόντον
νᾶες ἄγουσιν ἀπ' Αἰγύπτου μέγιστον   15
πλοῦτον· ὡς πίνοντος ὁρμαίνει κέαρ.

. . . . . .

11 αὐτὰς, αὐτὴ Ath. codd., em. Kaibel   14 πόντον om. Ath.
]α πο[pap., iam suppl. Erfurdt

PRAXILLA

(747)

κάλλιστον μὲν ἐγὼ λείπω φάος ἠελίοιο,
δεύτερον ἄστρα φαεινὰ σεληναίης τε πρόσωπον
ἠδὲ καὶ ὡραίους σικύους καὶ μῆλα καὶ ὄγχνας.

3 ὄχνους cod., em. Schneidewin

CARMINA POPULARIA

(848)

⏖ ⋮ – ∪ ∪ – ⋮ –   1–10
– ∪ ∪ – –   11
– ∪ – – | – ∪ ∪ ∪ ∪ | – ∪ – ∪ | – ∪ –   12
⏒ – ∪ – | ⏒ – ∪ – | ⏖ – ∪ –   13–19

ἦλθ᾽ ἦλθε χελιδὼν
καλὰς ὥρας ἄγουσα,
καλοὺς ἐνιαυτούς,
ἐπὶ γαστέρα λευκά,
ἐπὶ νῶτα μέλαινα.   5
παλάθαν σὺ προκύκλει
ἐκ πίονος οἴκου
οἴνου τε δέπαστρον
τυροῦ τε κάννυστρον·
καὶ πύρνα χελιδὼν   10
καὶ λεκιθίταν
οὐκ ἀπωθεῖται· πότερ᾽ ἀπίωμες ἢ λαβώμεθα;
εἰ μέν τι δώσεις· εἰ δὲ μή, οὐκ ἐάσομες·
ἢ τὰν θύραν φέρωμες ἢ τὸ ὑπέρθυρον
ἢ τὰν γυναῖκα τὰν ἔσω καθημέναν·   15
μικρὰ μέν ἐστι, ῥᾳδίως νιν οἴσομες.
ἂν δὴ †φέρῃς τι, μέγα δή τι† φέροις·
ἄνοιγ᾽ ἄνοιγε τὰν θύραν χελιδόνι·
οὐ γὰρ γέροντές ἐσμεν, ἀλλὰ παιδία.

3 καὶ καλοὺς codd., em. Hermann   6 οὐ προκυκλεῖς codd., em.
Hermann   10 πυρῶν αχελιδὼν Ath. A   πυρῶν ἁ χελιδὼν C
πύρνα χελιδὼν Bergk

(853)

```
− ∪ − − | − ∪ − − | ∪ ∪ − −
− − ∪ − ⋮ − ∪ ∪ − ⋮ −
− ∪ − ∪ | ∪ ∪ ∪ − −
    − ∪ − | − ∪ −
− ∪ − − | − ∪ −                                      5
    ∪ − ∪ ∪ ∪ | − − ∪ −
```

ὢ τί πάσχεις; μὴ προδῷς ἄμμ᾽, ἱκετεύω·
πρὶν καὶ μολεῖν κεῖνον, ἀνίστω,

μὴ κακόν <σε> μέγα ποιήσῃ
 κἀμὲ τὰν δειλάκραν.
ἀμέρα καὶ ἤδη· τὸ φῶς   5
 διὰ τᾶς θυρίδος οὐκ εἰσορῇς;

3–4 κακὸν μέγα ποιήσῃς· καί με τὴν Ath. A, post Toupium em.
Bergk 5 καὶ δή ci. Bergk 6 ἐκορῃς A, em. Meineke

(869)

⏑ – ⏑ ⏑ –
– – – ⏑ ⏑ – (?) –
⏑ ⏑ ⦙ – ⏑ ⏑ – ⦙ – ⏑ ⏑ – ⦙ –

ἄλει μύλα ἄλει·
καὶ γὰρ Πιττακὸς ἄλει
μεγάλας Μυτιλήνας βασιλεύων.

SCOLIA
(884)

– ⌣ ⦙ – ⏑ ⏑ – ⦙ ⏑ – ⏑ – –   1, 2
⏑ ⏑ – ⏑ – ⦙ – ⏑ ⏑ –   3
– ⏑ ⏑ – ⏑ – ⦙ – ⏑ ⏑ – ⏑ –   4

Παλλὰς Τριτογένει' ἄνασσ' Ἀθηνᾶ,
ὄρθου τήνδε πόλιν τε καὶ πολίτας
ἄτερ ἀλγέων καὶ στάσεων
καὶ θανάτων ἀώρων, σύ τε καὶ πατήρ.

(887)

ὦ Πὰν 'Αρκαδίας μεδέων κλεεννᾶς,
ὀρχηστὰ βρομίαις ὀπαδὲ Νύμφαις,
γελάσειας ὦ Πὰν ἐπ' ἐμαῖς
εὐφροσύναις, ἀοιδαῖς κεχαρημένος.

1, 3 ἴω πὰν codd., em. Hermann   4 εὐφροσύναις ταῖσδ' ἀοιδαῖς
ἀοιδε (vel ἄειδε) κεχ. codd. εὐφροσύναις, ἀοιδαῖς κεχ. ci. Hermann
εὔφροσι ταῖσδ' ἀοιδαῖς κεχ. Wilamowitz

(889)

εἴθ' ἐξῆν ὁποῖός τις ἦν ἕκαστος
τὸ στῆθος διελόντ', ἔπειτα τὸν νοῦν
ἐσιδόντα, κλείσαντα πάλιν,
ἄνδρα φίλον νομίζειν ἀδόλῳ φρενί.

(890)

ὑγιαίνειν μὲν ἄριστον ἀνδρὶ θνητῷ,
δεύτερον δὲ καλὸν φυὰν γενέσθαι,
τὸ τρίτον δὲ πλουτεῖν ἀδόλως,
καὶ τὸ τέταρτον ἡβᾶν μετὰ τῶν φίλων.

(892)

⏑⏑ : – ⏑ ⏑ – : ⏑ –   1, 3, 4
– : – ⏑ ⏑ – : ⏑ –   2

ὁ δὲ καρκίνος ὧδ' ἔφα
χαλᾷ τὸν ὄφιν λαβών·
'εὐθὺν χρὴ τὸν ἑταῖρον ἔμμεν καὶ μὴ σκολιὰ φρονεῖν.'

1 δὲ om. Ath. codd. dett.

(893)

ἐν μύρτου κλαδὶ τὸ ξίφος φορήσω
ὥσπερ Ἁρμόδιος κ' Ἀριστογείτων
ὅτε τὸν τύραννον κτανέτην
ἰσονόμους τ' Ἀθήνας ἐποιησάτην.

(894)

φίλταθ' Ἁρμόδι', οὔ τί που τέθνηκας,
νήσοις δ' ἐν μακάρων σέ φασιν εἶναι,
ἵνα περ ποδώκης Ἀχιλεὺς
Τυδεΐδην τέ φασιν Διομήδεα.

1 ἁρμόδι' οὔ τι που scholl. Ar. ἁρμοδίου πω Ath.   που vel πω Aristid.
or. 1. 133   4 T. τέ φασι τὸν ἐσθλὸν Δ. Ath.   T. τέ φασιν Δ. ci.
Lowth   T. παρ' ἐσθλὸν Δ. Manzoni

(895)

ἐν μύρτου κλαδὶ τὸ ξίφος φορήσω
ὥσπερ Ἁρμόδιος κ' Ἀριστογείτων
ὅτ' Ἀθηναίης ἐν θυσίαις
ἄνδρα τύραννον Ἵππαρχον ἐκαινέτην.

(896)

αἰεὶ σφῶν κλέος ἔσσεται κατ' αἶαν,
φίλταθ' Ἁρμόδιε κ' Ἀριστόγειτον,
ὅτι τὸν τύραννον κτανέτην
ἰσονόμους τ' Ἀθήνας ἐποιησάτην.

(900)

$- \cup \cup - \cup - \cup - \vdots - \cup \cup - \cup -$
$- \cup \cup - - - \cup - \vdots - \cup \cup - \cup \cup - \cup -$

εἴθε λύρα καλὴ γενοίμην ἐλεφαντίνη
καί με καλοὶ παῖδες φέροιεν Διονύσιον ἐς χορόν.

(901)

εἴθ᾽ ἄπυρον καλὸν γενοίμην μέγα χρυσίον
καί με καλὴ γυνὴ φοροίη καθαρὸν θεμένη νόον.

(902)

$\underset{\smile}{\cup} \underset{\smile}{\cup} \vdots - \cup \cup - \vdots - \cup \cup - \vdots - \cup \cup - \vdots \cup -$

σύν μοι πῖνε συνήβα συνέρα συστεφανηφόρει,
σύν μοι μαινομένῳ μαίνεο, σὺν σώφρονι σωφρόνει.

(903)

ὑπὸ παντὶ λίθῳ σκορπίος ὦ ἑταῖρ᾽ ὑποδύεται.
φράζευ μή σε βάλῃ· τῷ δ᾽ ἀφανεῖ πᾶς ἕπεται δόλος.

(904)

ἁ ὗς τὰν βάλανον τὰν μὲν ἔχει, τὰν δ᾽ ἔραται λαβεῖν·
κἀγὼ παῖδα καλὴν τὴν μὲν ἔχω, τὴν δ᾽ ἔραμαι λαβεῖν.

(907)

αἰαῖ Λειψύδριον προδωσέταιρον,
οἵους ἄνδρας ἀπώλεσας, μάχεσθαι
ἀγαθούς τε καὶ εὐπατρίδας,
οἳ τότ᾽ ἔδειξαν οἵων πατέρων ἔσαν.

Notes

ARCHILOCHUS

Archilochus occupies a cardinal position in Greek literature as the earliest surviving poet to find the material for his poetry in his own emotions, and as a writer of great versatility and invention in his use and adaptation of metrical forms. The Alexandrian scholars excluded him from their canon of nine λυρικοί, since his iambics, trochaics and dactyls were not lyric metres by their definition, but the content of his poems justifies us in regarding him as the earliest lyric poet.

We know a considerable amount about his life from his own work and from later testimony in literature and inscriptions. He was born on the island of Paros, where his father Telesicles, son of Tellis, was a prominent citizen. Critias' statement (fr. 44 D–K) that his mother Enipo was a slave is probably a mistaken deduction from some passage in Archilochus' poetry. Telesicles was asked to lead a colony to Thasos, possibly *c.* 680, and Archilochus seems to have gone with a second wave of settlers a generation later, perhaps between 660 and 650. Our fragments suggest that he found life there no better than life on Paros with its 'figs and sea-faring' (53): he speaks of the steep wooded mountains he found on the unlovely island (18), of the miserable Greeks who went as his fellow-settlers (54), and of the troubles of the Thasians (19,129 Bergk) in their wars against the neighbouring Thracians (6), when the gold-mines of the region were probably at stake. Archaeology suggests that Archilochus' discontent had little to do with material circumstances, since his Paros was not a poor island nor his Thasos barbarian. There is little evidence for the commonly held view that he became a mercenary soldier, but fighting forms the background of several poems, and he died fighting, killed in one of the wars between Paros, to which he must have returned, and its neighbour Naxos. Archilochus' unhappy love-affair with Neobule is well-known. She was promised to him in marriage, but her father Lycambes changed his mind and may have selected another husband for her (see 74 introd.). Archilochus railed against him and his daughter or daughters to such effect that they hanged themselves — or so the story went some centuries later.

Jacoby's arguments (*C.Q.* 35 (1941), 97 ff.) for dating Archilochus from *c.* 680 to *c.* 640 are generally accepted. The crucial facts are the reference to Gyges (22.1), who was contemporary (Hdt. 1.12.2) and was king of Lydia from 687 to 652 (each date may be a few years too early); the reference to the eclipse of the sun (74.2–4), which was probably that of 6 April 648, less probably that of 27 June 660, and almost certainly not that of 14 March 711; and the report that Archilochus died fighting and was therefore not an old man at the time. The intriguing discovery in Thasos of the cenotaph of his friend Glaucus, son of Leptines, gives some confirmation of this dating, since the monument belongs to the end of the 7th or beginning of the 6th century and was presumably erected at no great interval after Glaucus' death.

A series of archaeological discoveries on Paros has added to our knowledge of Archilochus and tantalized by failing to provide complete poems and answer crucial questions. Two stones inscribed in the 1st century B.C., published in 1900–04, gave fragments of an account of Archilochus' life compiled by a local historian, Demeas, with quotations from Archilochus' poetry. These were supplemented by two further stones of the 3rd century B.C., published in 1954: one of these tells us that a certain Mnesiepes established a sanctuary of Archilochus ('Αρχιλόχειον) in accordance with Apollo's oracles; then follows the legend of Archilochus' meeting with the Muses: the young Archilochus was sent to town by his father to sell a cow, and met on his way a group of jolly women, who asked if the cow was for sale; when told that it was, they said they would give him a good price, whereupon they and the cow disappeared and Archilochus found a lyre before his feet. Soon after, his father was told by Apollo at Delphi that his son would be immortal and famous. Another column, unhappily much damaged, seems to give an account of Archilochus' introduction to Paros of a new form of Dionysiac worship: he was punished by his fellow-citizens for blasphemy but vindicated by an oracle of Apollo. The second stone speaks of Archilochus' services in the war against Naxos, and gives the line-beginnings of a poem in thirty trochaic tetrameters, in which Archilochus seems to appeal to his friend Erxies in Thasos to help the Parians against the Naxians. The texts of these stones, which were presumably erected in the Archilochium, are in the editions of Tarditi and Treu: they are variously referred to as the Monumentum Archilochium and the Monumentum Parium (fr. 51 Diehl).

Archilochus' memory may have been revered on Paros, but Pindar spoke harshly: ψογερὸν 'Αρχίλοχον βαρυλόγοις ἔχθεσιν | πιαινόμενον (P. 2. 100–1). It was the violence of his invective that most later writers recalled: *Archilochum proprio rabies armavit iambo* (Hor. *A.P.* 79). The young Horace compared his pugnacity with that of Archilochus and Hipponax: *cave, cave; namque in malos asperrimus | parata tollo cornua, | qualis Lycambae spretus infido gener | aut acer hostis Bupalo* (*Epod.* 6. 13–16). Later he claimed to have followed Archilochus in metre and spirit, but not in his subject-matter: *Parios ego primus iambos | ostendi Latio, numeros animosque secutus | Archilochi, non res et agentia verba Lycamben* (*Epist.* 1.19.23–5; cf. 30–1). Quintilian's pithy assessment is well-known: *summa in hoc vis elocutionis, cum validae tum breves vibrantesque sententiae, plurimum sanguinis atque nervorum, adeo ut videatur quibusdam, quod quoquam minor est, materiae esse, non ingenii vitium* (10.1.60).

The range of Archilochus would scarcely be guessed from these references; he did not always fatten himself on his heavy-worded hatreds: indeed, not even all his iambic and trochaic poetry was virulent invective. In his elegiacs we find neat epigrams, consolatory poems and a detailed prediction of battle; his trochaics include a cry for help in war, an address to his troubled soul and lines on the ideal commander; in his iambics we find an enchanting description of a girl and Charon the carpenter's rejection of tyranny.

An important feature of the poems is that their metres are 'neutral in respect of ethos' (Maas, *Greek Metre*, tr. Lloyd-Jones,

§ 73): not all the poems on war are in elegiacs, not all the invective is iambic; it is only in later writers that we find an insistence on the appropriateness of certain metres to certain topics. Archilochus' achievement was not the demarcation of the subject-matter of elegiacs, iambics and trochaics, but rather his sure handling of these metres — an indication that he did not invent them but inherited a tradition — and his inventiveness in combining rhythms. Of his lyrics only the tiniest snatches survive, apart from his hymn to Heracles which rang out at Olympia with its threefold καλλίνικε (120: cf. Pi. *O.* 9.1–2).

Much of the language of Archilochus' poetry belongs to the epic tradition, no matter the metre in which he was writing. Elegiac couplets, of course, offer a pre-fabricated home to Homeric formulas, but much of the vocabulary of the iambic and trochaic fragments also is epic. We must remember, however, that we know very little about the 7th century Ionic vernacular of Paros or Thasos, so that we cannot always say for certain if a given form is an epic borrowing, an everyday expression, or property common to epic and the vernacular. In any case there are several poems, iambic and trochaic, which owe little or nothing to epic, iambic lines such as 21 ψυχὰς ἔχοντες κυμάτων ἐν ἀγκάλαις, trochees such as frr. 60, 74; and even in the elegiacs we find phrases which are not borrowings from Homer, although the component words are epic, e.g. in fr. 7 θεοὶ ... τλημοσύνην ἔθεσαν | φάρμακον, αἱματόεν δ' ἕλκος (of the death of friends), γυναικεῖον πένθος. Page suggests (in *Archiloque* 119 ff) that those iambic and trochaic poems in which there is little or no traditional element were composed with the help of writing, whereas the elegiac pieces and others in which traditional language is predominant were oral compositions. This may be true, and it seems certain that Archilochus' poems, especially those which were appropriate to only a single occasion, survived simply because they were written down by Archilochus or a friend.

The poems of Archilochus are edited by Giovanni Tarditi with *testimonia*, *index verborum*, and Italian translation (Rome, 1968). There is a German edition by Max Treu (Munich, 1959) and a French edition by Lasserre and Bonnard in the Budé series

(1958). Entretiens sur l'Antiquité Classique, tome X, *Archiloque* (Fondation Hardt, Genève, 1964) contains the following papers: 'A. et Thasos: histoire et poesie' (J. Pouilloux), 'A. und Paros' (N.-M. Kontoleon), 'Die Sprache des A.' (Anton Scherer), 'A. and the Oral Tradition' (Denys Page), 'The Poetry of A.' (K. J. Dover), 'A. und Kallimachos' (Winfried Bühler), 'A. and Horace' (E. Wistrand).

ARCHILOCHUS 1

Quoted by Athenaeus 14.627b–c as evidence that the ancients thought courage the greatest of the civic virtues. The ancients may indeed have thought so, but there is nothing to prove it in Archilochus' couplet. The fact that he mentions his soldiering before his poetry is quite unimportant: his point is that he has combined the two activities. The couplet is quoted too in Plutarch *Phocion* 7.6 and Themistius *Or.* 15 p. 185b. It is not impossible that it forms a complete poem.

1. εἰμὶ δ' ἐγώ: a line-beginning (though not the beginning of a speech) at *Od.* 6.196. Plutarch has the Homeric ἀμφότερον for εἰμὶ δ' ἐγώ, but he was probably adapting Archilochus' couplet to suit his context.

It is usually said that a quotation-fragment which begins with δέ or ἀλλά cannot be the beginning of a poem, but there is room for doubt on the matter. There are several such quotations which look uncommonly like the beginnings of poems, notably Tyrtaeus 8 (ἀλλ' — Ἡρακλῆος γὰρ . . .), Mimnermus 1 (τίς δὲ βίος . . .) and 2 (ἡμεῖς δ' οἶά τε φύλλα . . .), Solon 3 (ἡμετέρα δὲ πόλις . . .), Xenophanes 2 (ἀλλ' εἰ μὲν ταχυτῆτι . . .), Timocreon 727 (ἀλλ' εἰ τύ γε Παυσανίαν . . .); see also Scol. 892, Archil. 74.1n. Many poems of Theognis begin with δέ, and ἀλλά occurs at the beginning of three poems (341, 583, 1055). There was a tendency for oracles to begin with δέ, ἀλλά or καί. In prose writers speeches may begin with δέ: cf. Hdt. 8.142.1 διαδεξάμενοι ἔλεγον οἱ ἀπὸ Σπάρτης ἄγγελοι· ἡμέας δὲ ἔπεμψαν Λακεδαιμόνιοι . . . , X. *Anab.* 5.5.13, where Xenophon begins a speech with ἡμεῖς δέ, ὦ ἄνδρες Σινωπεῖς, ἥκομεν. . . . He may be taken to imply, 'You have made

your position clear: now hear ours.' There are cases of δέ
at the beginning of a speech where no contrast is implied,
e.g. X. *Cyr.* 4.5.23, 7.1.21: 'the object is, no doubt, to give
a conversational turn to the opening ("Well"), and to
avoid formality' (Denniston *G.P.* 172). So a poet might
have used a particle to make an implicit contrast: if Solon
began with ἡμετέρα δὲ πόλις, he may have left his readers
or listeners to supply the μέν clause, 'other cities may
perish'; similarly Archilochus with εἰμὶ δ' ἐγὼ . . . ,
Tyrtaeus with ἀλλά. Mimnermus and Theognis may have
wished to give an air of informality to their short poems by
beginning with δέ.

θεράπων . . . Ἐνυαλίοιο: not in Homer, but cf. the common
θεράποντες Ἄρηος (e.g. *Il.* 2.110).

Ἐνυαλίοιο ἄνακτος: line-ending at Hes. *Sc.* 371.

2. καὶ Μουσέων: for καί after μέν cf. *Il.* 1.267 κάρτιστοι μὲν
ἔσαν καὶ καρτίστοις ἐμάχοντο, Tyrt. 9.11–12, and see
Denniston *G.P.* 374. Μουσέων is to be taken with θεράπων,
'I am the servant too of the Muses, acquainted with their
lovely gift': cf. Hes. *Th.* 99–100, *Margites* 1.1–2 ἀοιδός, |
Μουσάων θεράπων, *h.Hom.* 32.19–20, Thgn. 769, Archil.
51.IVB.10 (where Μουσάων θεράποντ' refers to Archilochus himself); for ἐπιστάμενος cf. Sol. 1.52. Μουσέων is
disyllabic: -εων in these gen. plurals nearly always under-
goes synizesis in Homer: see Chantraine *G.H.* i.201.
Archilochus has synizesis also at 7.7 ἡμέας, 22.1 Γύγεω,
22.3 θεῶν, ἐρέω, 53 ἔα, 56.2 Γυρέων, 60.1 φιλέω, 60.4
ἀσφαλέως, 67a.2 δυσμενέων, 67a.4 ἀσφαλέως, 74.6 ὑμέων,
79a.9 κροτέοι, 112.3 στηθέων.

ἐρατὸν δῶρον: cf. *Il.* 3.64 δῶρ' ἐρατά . . . Ἀφροδίτης. For the
gift of the Muses cf. Hes. *Th.* 103 δῶρα θεάων (sc. the
Muses), 93 Μουσάων ἱερὴ δόσις, Alcm. 59(b) 1–2 Μωσᾶν
δῶρον, Sol. 1.51 Μουσέων πάρα δῶρα διδαχθείς.

ARCHILOCHUS 2

Quoted by Athenaeus 1.30f: 'Archilochus compares the wine of
Naxos with nectar; elsewhere he says ἐν δορὶ . . . κεκλιμένος.'
Also in Synesius *Epist.* 129b, *Suda* s.v. ὑπνομαχῶ and (ἐν δορὶ δ'

οἶνος . . . κεκλιμένος) s.v. Ἰσμαρικὸς οἶνος. The couplet has an air of completeness.

1. ἐν δορί: I translate, 'In my spear is my kneaded barley-bread, in my spear is my Ismaric wine (i.e. my spear provides my bread and wine), on my spear I lean when I drink it.' Both uses of ἐν are unparalleled, but the use in l. 1 resembles its instrumental use (L.S.J. s.v. A.III). Archilochus speaks of the soldier's life as does Hybrias the Cretan in his scolion (ap. Ath. 15.695f, *P.M.G.* 909: probably 5th or 4th century B.C.) ἔστι μοι πλοῦτος μέγας δόρυ καὶ ξίφος. Alternatively we may suppose that the soldier's rations are in a knapsack slung from his spear in the Mycenean manner: see the vase-painting reproduced in H. L. Lorimer, *Homer and the Monuments*, pl. III, fig. 1b: the μᾶζα might be a dough to which water was added before it was eaten uncooked; and if the Ismaric wine was particularly strong and could be much diluted, both commodities would save space in the knapsack. Most recent interpretations take as their starting-point Bowra's view (*Anales de Filologia Clásica* 6 (1954), 37 ff) that ἐν δορί must have the same meaning in each clause: Bowra gives the words a local sense, 'at my spear'; Davison (*C.R.* 74 (1960), 1 ff) suggests 'equipped with my spear', i.e. on active service, and similar views are held by Webster (*G.A.L.* 30) and Ehrenberg (*Cl. Phil.* 57 (1962). 239–40), who compares the anonymous comic fragment ἀνὴρ ἄριστος τἆλλα πλὴν ἐν ἀσπίδι (451K); Davison offers also 'in my ship', which he prefers; Pocock suggests 'in or on a tree' (*C.R.* 75 (1961), 179–80). None of these explanations is wholly satisfactory. I do not see why the meaning of ἐν δορί need be so straitjacketed: Archilochus' couplet is neat enough even if his uses of ἐν δορί are not all alike and even if they are somewhat forced. Sappho's repeated ὄττι (1.15–17) is no less effective because we must translate it by 'what' twice and 'why' once.

μᾶζα μεμαγμένη: cf. Hdt. 1.200 μάζαν μαξάμενος, Aristophanes' pun at *Eq.* 55 μᾶζαν μεμαχότος, and the proverb

μᾶζαν ἑαυτῷ μεμαγμένην ξὺν πολλῷ τῷ πόνῳ (Theodorus
Metochita *Misc.* p. 559 Müller).

2. Ἰσμαρικός: it was a potent Ismaric wine which Odysseus
used to incapacitate the Cyclops: see *Od.* 9.196 ff, 345 ff.
But not all Ismaric wines were so strong that one part
required twenty parts of water, and Homer makes it plain
that Odysseus' wine, a gift from the priest of Apollo in
Ismarus, was *du premier cru*, a remarkable wine by Ismaric
standards (203–11). Ismarus was on the Thracian coast
not far from Thasos, and Ismaric wine may have been no
more than the *vin du pays* which Archilochus drank during
campaigns against Thracian tribes. Latin writers mention
Ismaric wine: cf. Virgil *Georg.* 2.37, Propertius 2.33b.32,
Ovid *Met.* 9.642.

κεκλιμένος: cf. fr. 33 πρὸς τοῖχον ἐκλίνθησαν, *Il.* 3.135 ἀσπίσι
κεκλιμένοι; for ἐγκλίνω cf. *Il.* 6.77–8 πόνος ὔμμι . . . ἐγκέκλιται.

ARCHILOCHUS 3

This passage, which may have been part of a harangue to
troops, is quoted by Plutarch *Theseus* 5 as an illustration of the
close combat of the Abantes.

1. ἐπὶ τόξα τανύσσεται: cf. *Il.* 4.112 τὸ μὲν (sc. τόξον) . . .
τανυσσάμενος, and for the tmesis 16.567 Ζεὺς δ' ἐπὶ νύκτ'
ὀλοὴν τάνυσε κρατερῇ ὑσμίνῃ.

θαμειαί: cf. *Il.* 11.552, 17.661 θαμέες . . . ἄκοντες, 12.44–5
θαμειὰς | αἰχμάς.

2. σφενδόναι: slings are used in Homer only by the Locrians:
Il. 13.716–17 τόξοισιν καὶ ἐϋστρεφεῖ οἰὸς ἀώτῳ | . . . πεποιθότες.
σφενδόνη occurs once only in Homer, at *Il.* 13.599–600
ἐϋστρεφεῖ οἰὸς ἀώτῳ, | σφενδόνῃ, where it is a bandage.

μῶλον Ἄρης συνάγῃ: cf. *Il.* 2.401 etc. μῶλον Ἄρηος, 2.381
ξυνάγωμεν Ἄρηα, 5.861 ἔριδα ξυνάγοντες Ἄρηος, 14.448
σύναγον κρατερὴν ὑσμίνην.

3. ξιφέων . . . πολύστονον . . . ἔργον: cf. *Il.* 11.73 Ἔρις . . .
πολύστονος, 15.451 πολύστονος . . . ἰός (arrow), Hes. *Op.*
145–6 Ἄρηος | ἔργ(α) . . . στονόεντα.

4. δαίμονες: only here in the sense of δαήμονες, 'skilled', with
gen. as at *Od.* 8.263 δαήμονες ὀρχηθμοῖο, *Il.* 13.811 μάχης

ἀδαήμονες. Cf. Hsch. δαίμων· δαήμων and Plato who says (*Crat.* 398b) that δαίμονες, gods, were so called ὅτι φρόνιμοι καὶ δαήμονες ἦσαν. The best MSS. of Plutarch have δαήμονες here, but the synizesis of αη is harsh and δαίμονες, the *difficilior lectio*, should be kept.

5. δεσπόται: the first instance of the word, though Homer has δέσποινα. 'The spear-famed lords of Euboea' are the Abantes, whom Homer mentions as a warlike race, ready to lunge at the enemy with their ashen spears (*Il.* 2.536 ff: cf. Str. 10.1.13, pp. 448–9); they had disappeared from history by classical times. The fighting which Archilochus predicts need not have been in Euboea, but if it was it formed no part of the Lelantine War which is dated some 50 years before Archilochus' fighting days.

δουρικλυτοί: unexpected epithet for sword-fighters. Page suggests ἄορι κλυτοί (*P.C.P.S.* 7 (1961), 68).

ARCHILOCHUS 5A

Lines 6–9 were quoted by Athenaeus 11.483d for the use of κώθων, 'cup'. The beginnings of 6–9 together with the scraps of 1–5 are in *P. Oxy.* 854: 3 begins ξεινοι[, 4 δεῖπνον δορυ[, 5 οὔτ' ἐμοὶ ὡς αι[

6. κώθωνι: a Spartan cup often used by soldiers (Critias ap. Ath. 11.483b).

θοῆς . . . νηός: cf. *Il.* 1.12 θοὰς . . . νῆας, *Od.* 1.260 θοῆς ἐπὶ νηός.

7. ἄφελκε: the verb, like ἄγρει (8), suggests violent activity.

8. οἶνον ἐρυθρόν: so *Od.* 5.165.

ἀπὸ τρυγός: i.e. drain the red wine to the dregs.

ARCHILOCHUS 6

The text is compiled from quotations in Aristophanes, the Neoplatonists Olympiodorus and Elias, and Plutarch. Lines 1–3 (to ἐξεσάωσα) are in Ar. *Pax* 1298 ff and (with αὐτὸς δ' ἐξέφυγον θανάτου τέλος in l.3) Sextus Empiricus, *Pyrrh. hyp.* 3.216. 1–2 are in Plutarch *Lac. inst.* 34 p. 239b, twice in Strabo (10.2.17 p. 457 and 12.3.20 p. 549, in connexion with the Saians) and in the *Vita Arati* p. 76s Maass. Lines 3–4 (to ἐρρέτω) are in Olympiodorus in

Plat. *Gorg.* p. 128 Norvin and Elias, *proleg. philos.* 8 p. 22 Busse.
Plutarch loc. cit. gives 3 (from ἀσπίς)–4. The poem is almost
certainly complete. Sextus quoted it after telling the story of the
Spartan mother who ordered her son to return from battle with
his shield or on it. Three other distinguished poets claimed to
have thrown away their shields on the battlefield: Alcaeus (428:
see Hdt. 5.94–5, Str. 13.600), Anacreon (381b: cf. 437), Horace
(*Od.* 2.7.9–10).

1. Σαΐων: a Thracian tribe from the mainland opposite Samo-
   thrace.

   ἀγάλλεται: cf. *Il.* 18.131–2 τὰ μὲν (sc. ἔντεα) . . . | αὐτὸς ἔχων
   ὤμοισιν ἀγάλλεται, 17.472–3.

2. ἔντος: in sing. only here and *P. Oxy.* 2313 fr. 5 l. 5 (fragmentary tetrameters by Archil.).

   ἀμώμητον: only once (*Il.* 12.109) in Homer, who prefers
   ἀμύμων: cf. *Il.* 15.463 ἐν ἀμύμονι τόξῳ.

   κάλλιπον = κατέλιπον by apocope as in Homer; κατέλιπον
   with its sequence of short syllables could not be used in
   epic or elegiac poetry.

   οὐκ ἐθέλων: also at *Il.* 4.300.

3. ἐξεσάωσα: cf. *Il.* 4.12, *Od.* 4.501 ἐξεσάωσε(ν). There may be
   a pun on Σαΐων. The version of this line in Sextus Empiricus
   is more conventional and less lively than the other and so
   more likely to have been a stopgap. Archilochus may well
   have written αὐτὸν δ' ἐξεσάωσα with its archaic reflexive
   pronoun.

4. ἐρρέτω: so at the beginning of a line in *Il.* 9.377, 20.349, *Od.*
   5.139; when Homer has ἔρρε and ἔρρετε, they occupy the
   same emphatic position.

ARCHILOCHUS 7

From Stobaeus 4.56 (παρηγορικά). 30. Philostratus, *Vita
Apollonii* 7.26, refers to the lines. To me they have the air of a
complete poem: l. 1 sounds like a beginning, and 9–10 sound like
an end, as well as echoing the central couplet (τλημοσύνην . . .
τλῆτε). The sense of the poem would be: 'mourning will not be
thought out of place, so fine were the men whom we lost: never-
theless the gods gave us endurance, and when our turn for

misfortune comes we must endure it.' But the lines are generally regarded as forming part of the elegiac poem which Archilochus wrote on the death of his sister's husband who perished in a shipwreck (fr. 10: Plutarch, *aud. poet.* 6. p. 23ab. The two lines quoted there by Plutarch have been identified as part of the tattered *P. Oxy.* 2356 which has fragments of 27 lines). If fr. 7 is part of the larger poem, it is perhaps surprising that Archilochus addresses Pericles rather than his own sister; and the tone of the lines is very different from that of 10.3–4, which Plutarch (ibid. 12.33ab) quotes as part of Archilochus' poem on his brother-in-law: οὔτε τι γὰρ κλαίων ἰήσομαι οὔτε κάκιον | θήσω τερπωλὰς καὶ θαλίας ἐφέπων. (Longinus) *de sublim.* 10 says that Archilochus in his poem on the shipwreck selected and united the most important points and inserted nothing frivolous, mean or trivial.

1. κήδεα . . . στονόεντα: so at *Od.* 9.12: cf. *Il.* 1.445 πολύστονα κήδεα.

   Περίκλεες: addressed also in fr. 8, and admonished for gate-crashing parties in fr. 78.

2. μεμφόμενος: 'finding fault with' mourning.

   θαλίης τέρψεται: cf. *Od.* 11.603 τέρπεται ἐν θαλίης, and for the simple dative *Il.* 11.643 μύθοισιν τέρποντο.

   οὐδέ following οὔτε gives the effect of climax in the second limb. See Denniston *G.P.* 193 and cf. *Od.* 13.207, Alcm. 1.67.

3. τοίους γάρ: cf. line-beginning at *Od.* 4.826 τοίη γάρ.

   κῦμα πολυφλοίσβοιο θαλάσσης: line-ending at *Il.* 2.209, 6.347, *h. Hom.* 6.4, *Cypr.* 7.8.

4. οἰδαλέους: only here in early poetry. Cf. *Il.* 9.646 ἀλλά μοι οἰδάνεται κραδίη χόλῳ.

   ἀμφ' ὀδύνης: for ἀμφί, 'in connexion with, over' cf. *Od.* 4.153–4 ὅσα κεῖνος ὀϊζύσας ἐμόγησεν | ἀμφ' ἐμοί.

5. πνεύμονας: possibly to be taken literally, but the lungs are the seat of love in S. fr. 855N².15 Διὸς τυραννεῖ πλευμόνων (sc. Κύπρις).

   ἀλλὰ . . . γάρ: used to contrast 1–5 with the more important pronouncement of 5–7: see Denniston *G.P.* 101.

   ἀνηκέστοισι κακοῖσιν: cf. Hes. *Th.* 612 ἀνήκεστον κακόν, *Il.* 5.394 ἀνήκεστον . . . ἄλγος.

6. ἐπὶ . . . ἔθεσαν: cf. *Il.* 4.190–1 of a doctor, ἐπιθήσει | φάρμακα.

τλημοσύνην: in h. Ap. 191; cf. Il. 24.49 τλητὸν γὰρ μοῖραι θυμὸν
θέσαν ἀνθρώποισιν. Archilochus gives advice of the same kind
in fr. 67.

7. τάδε: i.e. κακά. For the idea and the phrasing cf. Od. 4.236–7
ἀτὰρ θεὸς ἄλλοτε ἄλλῳ | Ζεὺς ἀγαθόν τε κακόν τε διδοῖ.
Archilochus expands the theme in fr. 58.

8. ἐτράπετο: aorist with perfect force.

8. ἐπαμείψεται: cf. Il. 6.339 νίκη δ᾽ ἐπαμείβεται ἄνδρας.

10. τλῆτε: the verb (which of course echoes τλημοσύνην, 6) is
plural: the advice is for Pericles and his fellow-mourners.
πένθος ἀπωσάμενοι: cf. Il. 12.276 νεῖκος ἀπωσαμένους.

ARCHILOCHUS 18

Plutarch, Exil. 12. p. 604bc gives 1–2: 'Archilochus, dis-
regarding the cornfields and vineyards of Thasos, denigrated the
island for its ruggedness and unevenness in these words' (ἥδε
. . . ἐπιστεφής). Athenaeus 12.523d gives 3–4: 'Archilochus
marvelled at the prosperity of the land of the Sirites: at any rate
he describes Thasos as inferior to it in these words' (οὐ . . . ῥοάς).

Metre: iambic trimeter; so in 22, 25.

1. ὄνου ῥάχις: cf. Il. 9.208 συὸς . . . ῥάχιν. Archil.'s comparison does not recur, but Hdt. 3.54.2 has ἐπὶ τῆς ῥάχιος τοῦ
ὄρεος: cf. 7.216.

2. ἐπιστεφής: cf. Il. 8.232, Od. 2.431 κρητῆρας ἐπιστεφέας
οἴνοιο, 'mixing-bowls full of wine', Od. 1.148 κρητῆρας
ἐπεστέψαντο ('they filled') ποτοῖο, Alcm. 19.1–2 τραπέσδαι |
μακωνιᾶν ἄρτων ἐπιστεφοίσαι.

3. Cf. Semon. 7.51 οὔ τι καλὸν οὐδ᾽ ἐπίμερον.

4. ἀμφὶ Σίριος ῥοάς: cf. Il. 11.732 ἀμφὶ ῥοὰς ποταμοῖο. Siris
was an Ionian colony on the gulf of Tarentum in South
Italy, in a fertile plain between two rivers, Siris and Aciris.
It cannot have been long-established if the story that it
was founded by Colophonians fleeing from Gyges is true.

It was destroyed c. 550–520 B.C. by its neighbours
Croton, Sybaris and Metapontum, and rebuilt nearby in
432 B.C. by Tarentum with the name of Heraclea (Pliny
N.H. 3.97, Str. 6.264). Archilochus' comparison suggests
that he had seen Siris for himself.

ARCHILOCHUS 22

Aristotle *Rhet.* 3.17, p. 1418b.28 says some things are better put in the mouth of another person in the manner of Archilochus' invective when he makes the father speak of the daughter in χρημάτων ... ἀπώμοτον (fr. 74) and Charon the carpenter speak in the poem which begins οὔ μοι τὰ Γύγεω. Plutarch *tranq. animi* 10, p. 470c with no mention of the author quotes l. 1 then 2–4: that the lines are in fact consecutive is suggested by imitations of the piece in *Anacreontea* 8 and Gregory of Nazianzus *ad anim. suam* 84 ff. The lines are mentioned and cited by several other writers: cf. Herodotus 1.12.2 Γύγης, τοῦ καὶ Ἀρχίλοχος ὁ Πάριος, κατὰ τὸν αὐτὸν χρόνον γενόμενος, ἐν ἰάμβῳ τριμέτρῳ ἐπεμνήσθη. Gyges was king of Lydia c. 687 to c. 652. We know nothing of Charon the carpenter.

1. οὔ μοι κτλ.: for the string of negatives cf. 60.1–2, where ἀλλά follows.

   τὰ Γύγεω: this idiom is not Homeric.

2. ἀγαίομαι: cf. *Od.* 20.16 ἀγαιομένου κακὰ ἔργα.

3. θεῶν ἔργα: cf. *Il.* 16.120 ἔργα θεῶν.

   οὐκ ἐρέω τυραννίδος: cf. Hdt. 1.96.2 ἐρασθεὶς τυραννίδος. The word τύραννος appears first in *h. Hom.* 8.5 (if that hymn is early) of Ares, ἀντιβίοισι τύραννε, 'master of the rebellious'. According to Hippias (*F.G.H.* 6F6) it was first used of monarchs in the time of Archilochus: the present passage gives our earliest example of τυραννίς; cf. also *P. Oxy.* 2310 fr. 1(a) col. i.20 κείνης ἄνασσε καὶ τ[υραν]νίην ἔχε. ἐρέω is Ionic for ἐράω.

ARCHILOCHUS 25

The main sources are the grammarian Ammonius p. 123 Val., who quotes ἔχουσα ... ἄνθος to show that ῥοδῆ means 'rose-bush', and Synesius *laudatio calvitii* 75bc, who gives the rest and says that Archilochus is praising a courtesan's hair. The fragments may well belong to the same poem and may even form three consecutive lines. If Synesius is correct, the poem is not about Archilochus' fiancée, Neobule.

2. ῥοδῆς τε καλὸν ἄνθος: cf. *Cypr.* 4.4 ῥόδου τ᾽ ἐνὶ ἄνθεϊ καλῷ.

4. ὤμους . . . καὶ μετάφρενα: cf. *Od.* 8.528 μετάφρενον ἠδὲ καὶ
   ὤμους, *Il.* 2.265 μετάφρενον ἠδὲ καὶ ὤμω.

κατεσκίαζε: cf. Hes. *Th.* 716–17 κατὰ δ᾽ ἐσκίασαν βελέεσσι |
   Τιτῆνας, Anacr. 347.1–2 καὶ κ[όμη]ς, ἥ τοι κατ᾽ ἁβρὸν |
   ἐσκία[ζ]εν αὐχένα. Homer has κατασκιάω (*Od.* 12.436).

ARCHILOCHUS 53

Athenaeus 3.76b: 'Archilochus mentions the figs in the island
of Paros in these words.' We may guess that he went on to contrast Thasos with the poverty-stricken Paros. He is said to have
left Paros through poverty and frustration (Critias ap. Aelian
V.H. 10.13 = D.-K. 44).

Metre: trochaic tetrameter catalectic; so 54–77.

   ἔα Πάρον: 'let Paros be': ἔα is monosyllabic; the same
   synizesis occurs at *Il.* 5.256 ἐᾷ if that is the correct reading
   (but see Chantraine *G.H.* i.305).

   σῦκα: figs were cheap: Archilochus seems to have used
   συκοτραγίδης, 'fig-eater', as an insulting term for a miser
   (fr. 194 Bergk).

ARCHILOCHUS 54

Quoted by Strabo 8.370 for Archilochus' use of Πανέλληνες.
P. Oxy. 2313 has]εςθα .[(fr. 18.2) and in the next line π]λουτ[ο-.
   Πανελλήνων: already in *Il.* 2.530, Hes. *Op.* 528, fr. 26Rz.

   ὀϊζύς: 'dregs, down-and-outs', lit. 'misery': cf. fr. 129 Bergk
   Θάσον δὲ τὴν τρισοιζύρην πόλιν.

ARCHILOCHUS 55

Quoted by the scholiast on Pindar *O.* 1.57 for the mention of
the stone of Tantalus, and by Plutarch *praec. reip.* 6 p. 803a.
Pausanias 10.31.12 refers to the passage in his account of Polygnotus' frescoes in the Lesche of the Cnidians at Delphi. Our
quotation has been spotted in *P. Mus. Brit.* 487B; its context
seems to have been warfare.

1. ὁ Ταντάλου λίθος: Tantalus was punished for stealing nectar
   and ambrosia, the food of the gods, who had admitted him
   to their company. According to *Od.* 11.582 ff and most
   authors his punishment was everlasting hunger and thirst:
   he was tantalized by fruit and water which disappeared

when he tried to consume them. The version of Archilochus and Pindar, found according to Pindar's scholiast in
Alcaeus and Alcman also, contained an equally refined
punishment — everlasting fear of a stone suspended over
his head, always on the point of falling. The painting of
Polygnotus combined the two versions.

2. τῆσδε ... νήσου: Thasos, at a guess.

ARCHILOCHUS 56

Heraclitus, *alleg. Hom.* 5: 'Archilochus, caught up in the
Thracian troubles, compares the war to the billows of the sea in
roughly the following words: Γλαῦχ' ... φόβος.' 1–3 (χειμῶνος)
are in Theophrastus *sign. tempest.* 3.8 and Plutarch *superstit.*
8 p. 169b, l. 1, also in Syrianus in Hermog. p. 73, 12 Rabe. The
allegory is not apparent in our three lines, but it may be prudent to
accept Heraclitus' statement: the situation is the same at Alcaeus
6 and 326. Diehl attached to our three lines *P. Mus. Brit.* 2652A,
eight tattered tetrameters on a storm at sea, but we cannot be
certain that they belong here.

1. Γλαῦκε: addressed in 68.1 Γλαῦκε, Λεπτίνεω πάι, and 13,
   teased in 59 for his elaborate curls, mentioned in the Parian
   Monument (51.IV A.6 ff) for his courage in battle in
   Thasos. His cenotaph has been discovered in Thasos with
   the inscription Γλαύκου εἰμὶ μνῆμα τοῦ Λεπτίνεω· ἔθεσαν δέ
   με οἱ Βρέντεω παῖδες.
   ταράσσεται: cf. *Od.* 5.291,304 ἐτάραξε δὲ πόντον.

2. ἄκρα Γυρέων: probably the cliffs in the south of Tenos: see
   F. H. Sandbach in *C.R.* 56 (1942), 63 ff. Cicero *Att.*
   5.12.1 seems to recall Archilochus' lines: *itaque erat in animo
   nihil festinare Delo nec me movere nisi omnia ἄκρα Γυρέων pura
   vidissem.* The Locrian Ajax was wrecked Γυρῇσι ...,
   | πέτρῃσιν μεγάλῃσι on his way home from Troy (*Od.*
   4.500–1: cf. 507 Γυραίην πέτρην).

3. ἐξ ἀελπτίης: Hesychius explains as ἐξ ἀνελπίστου. The meaning
   may be 'from the unexpected comes fear' rather than
   simply 'unexpectedly'. Pi. *P.* 12.31 has ἀελπτίᾳ.
   φόβος: 'fear', not 'flight' as in Homer.

ARCHILOCHUS 58

Quoted by Stobaeus 4.41 (ὅτι ἀβέβαιος ἡ τῶν ἀνθρώπων εὐπραξία μεταπιπτούσης ῥᾳδίως τῆς τύχης).24 under Archilochus' name.

1. The correct text is uncertain. The asyndeton shows that the sequel is explanatory, so that either 'ascribe all things to the gods' or 'all things are easy for the gods' (e.g. Wilamowitz τοῖς θεοῖσι ῥεῖα πάντα, if the adjectival use of ῥεῖα does not rule it out) would make sense. For the idea that man is at the mercy of the gods cf. fr. 8 πάντα Τύχη καὶ Μοῖρα, Περίκλεες, ἀνδρὶ δίδωσιν, and for the insecurity of man's condition 7.7–9, 67.7, 74.1–2.

2. μελαίνη . . . χθονί cf. Semon. 1.14 μελαίνης . . . χθονός, Alc. 38.10, 130.29, and the Homeric γαῖα μέλαινα. The epithet may refer to rich dark soil, but may also have had 'some deep religious association which was doubtless forgotten even by the time of Homer, but which continued to make the adjective a regular concomitant of the word γῆ' (A. E. Harvey, C.Q. n.s. 7 (1957), 216–17). With κειμένους ἐπὶ χθονί cf. Il. 20.483 ἐπὶ χθονὶ κεῖτο.

3. εὖ βεβηκότας: 'well established': cf. S. El. 979 τοῖσιν ἐχθροῖς εὖ βεβηκόσιν, Hdt. 7.164.1 τυραννίδα . . . εὖ βεβηκυῖαν.

4. ὑπτίους κλίνουσι: cf. Od. 9.371 ἀνακλινθεὶς πέσεν ὕπτιος, Il. 7.271–2 ὁ δ' ὕπτιος ἐξετανύσθη | ἀσπίδι ἐγχριμφθείς· τὸν δ' αἶψ' ὤρθωσεν Ἀπόλλων.

5. βίου χρήμῃ: 'in need of livelihood'. L.S.J. call χρήμη an Ionic form for χρεία, citing Vit. Hom. 13, 14, a doubtful supplement in Callimachus and a conjecture in Democritus 277 D.–K. For the sense cf. Tyrt. 6.5–8.

πλανᾶται: unless our text is misleading, there is a harsh change here from plural to singular.

παρήορος: 'unhinged', as at Il. 23.603. Cf. fr. 88.2 τίς σὰς παρήειρε φρένας;

ARCHILOCHUS 60

Dio Chrysostomus 33.17: 'Archilochus speaks thus about a general, οὐ φιλέω . . . ὑπεξυρημένον, ἀλλά μοι, φησίν, εἴη ῥαιβός,

ἀσφαλέως βεβηκὼς καὶ ἐπὶ κνήμαισιν δασύς. Galen in Hippocr. *artic.*
3 (*C.M.G.* 18.1. p. 537) gives 3–4 and (p. 604) 1, 3–4. Erotianus
fr. 43 Nachmanson has a version of 3–4 (ποσσί), Schol. Theocritus
4.49 a version of 3–4 (ῥοικός). The short, knock-kneed commander of Archilochus' choice cuts a very unhomeric figure:
Tydeus was small, but not knock-kneed (*Il.* 5.801 μικρὸς μὲν
ἔην δέμας, ἀλλὰ μαχητής); only the insubordinate ranker Thersites
is described in similar terms: cf. *Il.* 2.217 φολκὸς ἔην, χωλὸς δ'
ἕτερον πόδα etc. The στρατηγός may have been Glaucus: see 2n.

1. διαπεπλιγμένον: 'with long, straddling legs'. Cf. *Od.* 6.318
of Nausicaa's mules, εὖ μὲν τρώχων, εὖ δὲ πλίσσοντο
πόδεσσιν, where the Scholiast gives πλίξ, 'step'. Hesychius
has διαπεπλιχώς· διεστώς. κεχηνώς ('gaping').

2. βοστρύχοισι γαῦρον: cf. fr. 162 Bergk διαβεβοστρυχωμένον and
fr. 59 where τὸν κεροπλάστην ... Γλαῦκον is explained
as 'Glaucus with the elaborate hair-do'. γαῦρος is an uncommon word of which Euripides is fond: *Or.* 1532
ξανθοῖς ... βοστρύχοις γαυρούμενος echoes Archilochus.
ὑπεξυρημένον: 'part-shaven'; which part is not explained.

3. ῥοικός: 'knock-kneed' or 'bandy-legged'? Dio and Pollux
(2.193) vouch for ῥαιβός here, and Pollux elucidates:
ῥαιβοὺς δὲ καλοῦσιν, οἷς καμπύλα εἰς τὸ ἔνδον τὰ σκέλη,
βλαισοὺς δέ, οἷς τὸ ἀπὸ τῶν γονάτων εἰς τὸ ἔξω ἀπέστραπται·
καὶ τὸ μὲν Ἀρχίλοχος, τὸ δὲ Ξενοφῶν (*re equest.* 1.3) λέγει.

ARCHILOCHUS 64

From Stobaeus 4.58 (ὅτι τῶν πλείστων μετὰ θάνατον ἡ μνήμη
διαρρεῖ ταχέως).4.

1–2. Semon. 2 expresses the view that the dead are best forgotten; contrast the epigram on the physician Charon
(*S.P.A.W.* 1935 p. 702 = Friedländer, *Epigrammata* no. 86):
χαῖρε Χάρων, οὐδ[ε]ίς τυ κακῶς λέγει οὐδὲ θανόντα, | πολλοὺς
ἀνθρώπων λυσάμενος (sic) καμάτου. Plu. *Solon* 21 mentions
a law of Solon κωλύων ... τὸν τεθνηκότα κακῶς ἀγορεύειν.

ARCHILOCHUS 65

From Stobaeus 4.57 (ὅτι οὐ χρὴ παροινεῖν εἰς τοὺς τετελευτηκότας). 4, Clement of Alexandria *strom.* 6.5.10 and the Scholiast on *Od.* 22.412, a line which Archilochus may have had in mind: οὐχ ὁσίη κταμένοισιν ἐπ' ἀνδράσιν εὐχετάασθαι. Cf. too Chilon's τὸν τεθνηκότα μὴ κακολογεῖν.

ARCHILOCHUS 66

From Theophilus *ad Autolycum* 2.53, p. 176 Otto (ὅτι οἱ τὰ ἄδικα πράσσοντες μέλλουσιν κολάζεσθαι).

1. ἐν ... μέγα: cf. fr. 103 οἶδ(ε) ... ἐν μέγα, Semon. 29 ἐν δὲ τὸ κάλλιστον ... ἔειπεν.

2. δέννοις: Herzog's emendation for MSS. δεινοῖς may be correct: cf. *P. Oxy.* 2313 fr. 15.2 δ]έννος ὕβριν a.[. But the MSS. reading is more forceful and gains support from Aeschylus' echoes at *Cho.* 123 and *Sept.* 1049. For prayers for vengeance on one's enemies cf. Sol. 1.5n. Archilochus speaks in the same tone elsewhere: ἐπ]ίσταμαί τοι τὸν φιλ[έο]ν[τα] μὲν φ[ι]λέειν, | τὸ]ν ἐχθρὸν ἐχθαίρειν τε [κα]ὶ κακο[στομέειν (*P. Oxy.* 2310 fr. 1(a). 1. 14–15). Treu points out that only Antigone thought and acted otherwise in pre-Christian Greece.

ARCHILOCHUS 67a

From Stobaeus 3.20 (περὶ ὀργῆς). 28, under Archilochus' name. Dionysius of Halicarnassus, *comp. verb.* 17 gives l. 1 as an example of the trochaic rhythm. Apostolius 18.8a has 6–7. Aristotle *Pol.* 7.6, p. 1328a gives σὺ γὰρ δὴ παρὰ φίλων ἀπάγχεαι (67b) from a poem of Archilochus addressed to his θυμός (... διὸ καὶ Ἀρχίλοχος προσηκόντως τοῖς φίλοις ἐγκαλῶν διαλέγεται πρὸς τὸν θυμόν), but the words need not have formed part of our poem: Archilochus may well have communed with his 'heart' in more than one tetrameter poem, and in any case 67a has an air of completeness.

1. θυμέ: cf. Odysseus' words at *Od.* 20.18 ff τέτλαθι δή, κραδίη κτλ., and *Il.* 22.98–9 ὀχθήσας δ' ἄρα εἶπε πρὸς ὃν μεγαλήτορα θυμόν· ὤ μοι ἐγών κτλ.: also 122 ἀλλὰ τί ἦ μοι ταῦτα φίλος

διελέξατο θυμός; In later writers cf. Thgn. 695,877 and
especially 1029 τόλμα, θυμέ, κακοῖσιν (also, for the gist of
the poem, 355 ff), E. *Med.* 1056, Philetas 7.

2. The text of 2–3 is uncertain. ἀναδεν of MSS. is variously
emended to ἀνάδυ (Bücheler), which gives an unparalleled
imperative form from ἀνέδυν and an unacceptable anapaest at the beginning of the line, ἄνα δέ (Liebel), ἄνα συ
(Pfeiffer), neither very convincing. δυσμενέων is generally
taken as gen. plural with ἀλέξευ (an impossible construction) or with ἐναντίον, but it may be the participial
δυσμενέων of *Od.* 2.72.

3. ἐν δοκοῖσιν: Hesychius has ἔνδοκος· ἐνέδρα ('ambush'), so
that ἐνδόκοισιν may be correct; but the mention of am-
bushes (Jaeger suggests ἐν λόχοισιν, *C.R.* 60 (1946) 103) is
surprising.

4. ἀσφαλέως: 'steadfastly' as in *Il.* 17.436. *Od.* 17.235.
ἀμφάδην: Homer has ἀμφαδόν and ἀμφαδίην.

7. ῥυσμός: the Ionic form of ῥυθμός. Editors compare Thgn.
964 and Anacr. 416, where ῥυθμός means the 'tempera-
ment' of a man. Here the context suggests rather that
Archilochus is speaking of the variations ('rhythms',
perhaps)· in man's life, as at 7.7–9: so Lattimore translates
'All our life is up-and-down like this'. This sense seems
unparalleled except by Eupolis 356.2K μένει δὲ χρῆμ᾽
οὐδὲν ἐν ταὐτῷ ῥυθμῷ. See also W. Jaeger, *Paideia* i (Eng.
tr.) 123–4, R. Renehan, *Cl. Phil.* 58 (1963), 36–7.

ARCHILOCHUS 71

Plutarch *de E* 5, p. 386d: everyone who prays says εἰ γὰρ
ὤφελον ('if only I might'), and Archilochus says εἰ γὰρ ...
θιγεῖν. For θιγγάνω with accus. cf. Alcm. 58.2 ἃ μή μοι θίγῃς,
S. *Ant.* 546–7 with Jebb's note. Archil. may have wished to avoid
using two genitives, χειρός and Νευβούλης.

ARCHILOCHUS 74

1–9 are quoted by Stobaeus 4.46 (περὶ ἐλπίδος). 10 under
Archilochus' name. The ends of 5–16 are in *P. Oxy.* 2313. fr. 1a.
Cf. Aristotle *Rhet.* 3.17, p. 1418b.28: Archilochus' fault-finding is

put in the mouth of the father who speaks of his daughter in χρημάτων δ᾽ ἄελπτον ... ἀπώμοτον (cf. fr. 22 note). The view that the father and daughter are Lycambes and Neobule gains some support from the papyrus, where one Archenactides and marriage are mentioned: Treu suggests that Lycambes passed Archilochus over in favour of the wealthier Archenactides, and that Archenactides seduced and finally jilted the girl (*Archilochos* 162,223). This would explain Archilochus' invective and give good reason for his putting it in Lycambes' mouth. Lycambes would be saying, 'The eclipse shows that anything is possible; my daughter's behaviour confirms it.' Archenactides might, of course, be the father to whom Aristotle refers. But it would be prudent to make no identification at all: it is remarkable that Aristotle himself does not name the father, although he names Charon in connexion with fr. 22.

1. χρημάτων: the MSS. of Aristotle, who implies clearly that this is the beginning of the poem, give χρημάτων δ᾽; Stobaeus omits δ᾽. See Archil. 1. 1n.

   ἄελπτον: 'not to be expected'; so E. fr. 761N² ἄελπτον οὐδέν, πάντα δ᾽ ἐλπίζειν χρεών.

   ἀπώμοτον: 'which one may swear impossible'; so S. *Ant.* 388 βροτοῖσιν οὐδέν ἐστ᾽ ἀπώμοτον.

2 ff. The eclipse is probably that of April 6, 648 B.C., which was total at Paros. For the other possible dates and the difficulties raised by this one see Jacoby *C.Q.* 35 (1941) 97–8. Plu. *fac.* 931e tells us that eclipses are mentioned also by Mimnermus (fr. 20 Bergk), Cydias (*P.M.G.* 715), Stesichorus (*P.M.G.* 271) and Pindar (*Pae.* 9).

3. φάος: cf. *Il.* 1.605 *et al.* λαμπρὸν φάος ἠελίοιο.

4. ὑγρὸν ... δέος: presumably 'fear that turns men's limbs to water', but no close parallel is cited. MSS. λυγρὸν is disqualified on metrical grounds. See J. C. Kamerbeek, *Mnemosyne* 14 (1961), 6–7.

5. Tr. 'henceforth all things are credible and all things are to be expected by men'. With ἐπίελπτος, the opposite of ἄελπτος, cf. ἐπιέλπομαι at *Il.* 24.491, *Od.* 21.126. Treu notes Ovid *Trist.* 1.8.8 *et nihil est, de quo non sit habenda fides.*

6 ff. There are similar expressions of improbability at Hdt.
   5.92a, Hor. *Epod.* 16.34, *Od.* 1.2.7 ff.
8. θαλάσσης . . . κύματα: cf. *Od.* 13.88 θαλάσσης κύματ', *Il.*
   2.144.
   ἠχέεντα: cf. *Il.* 1.157 θάλασσά τε ἠχήεσσα.
9. ὑλήειν ὄρος: Lobel notes that η and ι are not ruled out as
   the letter before ειν, but that ν is most likely: which brings
   no salvation, since neither ᾗ δύνειν nor ἡδὺ νεῖν is
   satisfactory. The form ὑλήειν is attested by the grammarian Choeroboscus in Theod. 2.214 Hilgard: cf. *A.P.*
   6.217.8 ὑλῆεν . . . ὄρος.
10. Ἀρ]χηνακτίδης: the name Archenax is known in Thasos: cf.
    I.G. XII (8).280.17.

ARCHILOCHUS 77

From Athenaeus 14.628a: 'according to Philochorus the
ancients when pouring libations do not always sing dithyrambs
(διθυραμβοῦσιν): when they pour libations they sing of Dionysus
amid wine and drunkenness, but of Apollo in a quiet, orderly
manner. At any rate Archilochus says, ὡς Δ. . . . . φρένας.'

1. ὡς: probably the conjunction, 'since'.
   Διωνύσοιο: the Parian Monument (51.E¹.III) speaks of the
      innovations which Archilochus introduced to the worship
      of Dionysus in Paros.
   ἐξάρξαι, 'to begin' a song: the term is used also in fr. 76
      of the paean, αὐτὸς ἐξάρχων πρὸς αὐλὸν Λέσβιον παιήονα,
      and in the passage of Aristotle where he speaks of the
      origins of tragedy (*Poet.* 1449a.10) καὶ ἡ μὲν (sc. τραγῳδία)
      ἀπὸ τῶν ἐξαρχόντων τὸν διθύραμβον . . . κατὰ μικρὸν ηὐξήθη:
      cf. *Il.* 24.720–1 ἀοιδοὺς | θρήνων ἐξάρχους.
2. διθύραμβον: Archilochus' dithyramb may have been no
   more than an artless formula of praise: but the Parian
   Monument (loc. cit.) seems to give a four- or five-line
   stanza written by him in honour of Dionysus, and that or
   something similar may have been his dithyramb; in which
   case the statement of Herodotus (1.23) and Aristotle (in
   Proclus p. 320a.31) that Arion (half-a-century later)
   invented the dithyramb can hardly be explained by saying

that it was Arion who gave it literary form: see A. E. Harvey, *C.Q.* n.s. 5 (1955), 172–4, Treu *Archilochos* 224, Pickard-Cambridge *D.T.C.* 9–10.

οἴνῳ συγκεραυνωθείς: cf. Call. fr. 544 Pfeiffer: τοῦ ⟨◡⟩ μεθυπλῆγος φροίμιον Ἀρχιλόχου (where Ἀρχιλόχου is a correction of Ἀντιλόχου).

ARCHILOCHUS 79a

From a 2nd century A.D. papyrus in the library of the University of Strasbourg. Controversy over the authorship of the poem and its companion pieces 79b and 80 has raged since they were published by Reitzenstein in 1899: Reitzenstein attributed the poems to Archilochus, Blass in 1900 to Hipponax: the attribution remains uncertain. A reference to Ἱππωνα[in 80.3 (either Hipponax or Hipponactides may have been written) was taken as a sign that fr. 80 was by Hipponax, who frequently mentions himself by name; but the context of the reference tells against the authorship of Hipponax, since Ἱππωνα[appears in close relationship with such undesirable characters as Ariphantus, a thief with the stink of a billy-goat. Arguments from the vocabulary, orthography, syntax and metre of the pieces are inconclusive, as are arguments based on Horace *Epod.* 10, a prayer for the shipwreck of the stinking Mevius. Perhaps the splendour of the invective tips the scales in favour of Archilochus: Treu (p. 228) notes the skill with which the piece is constructed, so that the telling words come at the beginnings of the lines, except in the concluding couplet when ἠδίκησε and λάξ are emphasised by the caesura. The poem gains in intensity from its breathless sequence of optatives, interrupted only by the prediction in l.5, ἀναπλήσει, and abruptly concluded by the indicative mood in l.13.

See G. M. Kirkwood, *T.A.P.A.* 92 (1961), 267–82.

Metre: alternating iambic trimeter and hemiepes.

2. κύμασι πλαζόμενος: cf. *Od.* 5.388–9 κύματι πηγῷ | πλάζετο, *Il.* 21.268–9. For the 'Attic correption' (in which ι is short before the mute + liquid πλ) cf. 80.4 ἄριστα βροτῶν and e.g. *Od.* 6.119 αὖτε βροτῶν. In Archilochus as in Homer lengthening is the rule; indeed these two passages may be the only exceptions in Archilochus, since fr. 14 is probably

not genuine and the text is better emended at 28.2. Both exceptions occur in dactylic lines.

3. *Salmydessus*: a place on the Black Sea coast of Thrace, notorious for its dangerous shallows: cf. A. *Pr.* 726–7 τραχεῖα πόντου Σαλμυδησσία γνάθος, | ἐχθρόξενος ναύταισι, μητρυιὰ νεῶν, Hdt. 4.93, S. *Ant.* 969–70. Salmydessus had a well-organised wrecking industry, and the coastline was divided into allotments by boundary-marks (στῆλαι) to ensure fair play for rival wreckers (*X. An.* 7.5.12–13).

εὐφρονέστατα: ironic; cf. fr. 11 κρύπτωμεν ⟨δ'⟩ ἀνιηρὰ Ποσειδάωνος ἄνακτος | δῶρα, where Poseidon's gifts are probably corpses.

4. Θρήικες ἀκρόκομοι: a line-beginning at *Il.* 4.533. The hair-style may have been a top-knot, or the crown of the head may have been the only part left unshaven.

5. πόλλ' ἀναπλήσει κακά: cf. *Il.* 15.132 ἀναπλήσας κακὰ πολλά.

6. δούλιον ἄρτον: cf. Hippon. 39.6 δούλιον χόρτον, A. *Ag.* 1041 δουλίας μάζης.

7. αὐτόν: object of λάβοιεν (5): the wish has been roughly interrupted by the prediction of slavery.

ἐκ δὲ τοῦ χνόου κτλ.: 'after the scum may much seaweed cover him': at *Il.* 9.7 πολλὸν δὲ παρὲξ ἅλα φῦκος ἔχευεν the subject is κῦμα κελαινόν.

9. ἐπὶ στόμα: so at *Il.* 6.43.

ὡς κύων may refer both to the gnashing of teeth and (as at A. *Ag.* 3) to the prone position.

10. ἀκρασίη: i.e. powerless.

11. ἄκρον παρὰ ῥηγμῖνα: cf. *Il.* 20.229 ἄκρον ἐπὶ ῥηγμῖνος, where ῥηγμῖνα is suggested as an emendation.

13. ὅς μ' ἠδίκησε: the omission of the antecedent adds vigour to the sentence.

λὰξ δ' ἐπ' ὁρκίοις ἔβη: cf. *Il.* 4.157 κατὰ δ' ὅρκια πιστὰ πάτησαν, and the striking imitation in Alc. 129.22–3 βραϊδίως πόσιν | ἔμβαις ἐπ' ὀρκίοισι (Alcaeus spoke of ἑταίρων at l.16).

14. τὸ πρίν: so at *Il.* 5.54, ἑταῖρος ἐών at *Od.* 8.586. The paragraphus in the papyrus shows that the poem ended here.

ARCHILOCHUS 88

Quoted by the scholiast on the rhetor Hermogenes 7.820 Walz for the sake of the metre; the first two lines are in various grammarians and metricians. Archilochus' attack on Lycambes is referred to by Hor. *Epod.* 6.13, *Epist.* 1.19.23–5, 30–1. The lines are almost certainly the beginning of a poem in which Archilochus told the fable of the eagle and the fox to illustrate Lycambes' treachery: see reconstructions of the poem (Epode 1) by Lasserre, *Les Épodes d'Archiloque* 28–52, Adrados, *Emerita* 23 (1955) 12–24, Webster, *G.A.L.* 32, also Treu, 230–6. In the fable as retold some decades later by Aesop (*fab.* 1 Hausrath) an eagle and a fox vowed mutual friendship, but the eagle stole the fox's cubs to feed its young; retribution came when the eagle took a piece of burning meat from an altar: the nest caught fire and the young fell to the ground and were eaten by the fox. Frr. 89, 92a, 94 probably belong to the same poem, and two fragments have turned up in papyrus finds (*P. Oxy.* 2315 fr. 1 and 2316).

Metre: iambic trimeter alternating with dimeter.

2. παρήειρε φρένας: see 58.5n. and cf. *Il.* 16.341 παρηέρθη δὲ κάρη.
3. ἧς ... ἠρήρεισθα: (pluperf. of ἀραρίσκω): cf. *Od.* 10.553 οὔτε φρεσὶν ἧσιν ἀρηρώς, *Il.* 24.201–2 (Hecuba to Priam) ὤ μοι, πῇ δή τοι φρένες οἴχονθ᾽, ἧς τὸ πάρος περ | ἔκλεο ... ;
4. γέλως: cf. Semon. 7.74 εἶσιν δι᾽ ἄστεος πᾶσιν ἀνθρώποις γέλως, S. *O.C.* 902–3, Call. 195, 30 Pfeiffer.

ARCHILOCHUS 89

From the grammarian Ammonius p. 6 Valckenaer among others. For the fable see 88n.

Metre: as 88.

1. αἶνος: the term used by Hesiod of his 'fable', *Op.* 202.
2. ξυνωνίην: cf. Ar. *Av.* 651–3 ἐν Αἰσώπου λόγοις | ἐστὶν λεγό-μενον δή τι, τὴν ἀλώπεχ᾽, ὡς | φλαύρως ἐκοινώνησεν αἰετῷ ποτε.

ARCHILOCHUS 92a

Quoted by Atticus in Eusebius *praep. ev.* 15.795a. The words seem to have been spoken to the fox about the eagle by a third animal.

Metre: as 88.

G

2. παλίγκοτος: 'spiteful, malignant'. Treu compares Homer's λᾶας ἀναιδής (*Od.* 11.598) for the personification.

ARCHILOCHUS 94

From Stobaeus 1.3 (περὶ δίκης κτλ.), 34. There is a version of 1–3 (θεμιστά) in Clement of Alexandria *strom.* 5.127.1 and Eusebius *praep. ev.* 13.687. The fox, powerless to get his revenge on the eagle, prays to Zeus.

Metre: as 88.

2. ἐπ᾽ ... ὁρᾷς: 'thou overseest', an example of tmesis. Cf. *Od.* 13.214 ἀνθρώπους ἐφορᾷ (sc. Zeus).
3. λεωργά: like πανοῦργα, 'wicked' (cf. λέως 'wholly').
4. δίκη: Hes. *Op.* 276 ff on the other hand said that fish, animals and birds prey on each other ἐπεὶ οὐ δίκη ἐστὶ μετ᾽ αὐτοῖς.
   μέλει: cf. *Op.* 238 οἷς ὕβρις τε μέμηλε.

ARCHILOCHUS 103

Zenobius 5.68 quotes the proverb and continues: 'Archilochus mentions it in an epode; Homer has the line as does the tragedian Ion.' Archilochus is known to have attributed the *Margites* to Homer (fr. 153 Bergk), and the proverb may have been quoted there. It is not likely that we have part of a fable here as Bowra would suggest, *C.Q.* 34 (1940) 26 ff. Archilochus may simply be saying that his iambics are his only weapon, but deadly.

Metre: iambic trimeter.

Cf. 66.1 ἓν δ᾽ ἐπίσταμαι μέγα.

ARCHILOCHUS 104

From Stobaeus 4.20 (περὶ ᾽Αφροδίτης), 45, under Archilochus' name.

Metre: iambic dimeter alternating with dactylic hexameter.

1. πόθῳ: cf. 118 ἀλλά μ᾽ ὁ λυσιμελής, ὦ ᾽ταῖρε, δάμναται πόθος.
2. χαλεπῇσι ... ὀδύνησιν: cf. *h. Ap.* 358 ὀδύνησιν ... χαλεπῇσι.
   θεῶν ... ἕκητι: cf. *Od.* 20.42 Διός τε σέθεν (sc. Athena) τε ἕκητι, Alcm. 59(a).1.
3. πεπαρμένος: cf. *Il.* 5.399 ὀδύνῃσι πεπαρμένος.

ARCHILOCHUS 112

From Stobaeus 4.20.43, with Archilochus' name. The aorist tense suggests that he is recalling an old love, but it is hazardous to make it part of an attack on the aging Neobule.

Metre: 1, dactylic tetrameter + ithyphallic ($- \cup - \cup - \underline{\cup}$); 2, iambic trimeter catalectic. Horace uses the couplet in *Od.* 1.4.

1. ὑπὸ καρδίην ἐλυσθείς: cf. *Od.* 9.433 of Odysseus under the ram, ὑπὸ γαστέρ' ἐλυσθείς. Page notes the resemblance in spirit to *Il.* 14.315–16 and Hes. *Sc.* 41.

2. Cf. *Il.* 20.321 κατ' ὀφθαλμῶν χέεν ἀχλύν, 20.421 of Hector's anguish, κάρ ῥά οἱ ὀφθαλμῶν κέχυτ' ἀχλύς.

3. ἀπαλὰς φρένας: cf. *Il.* 11.115 ἀπαλόν τέ σφ' ἦτορ ἀπηύρα, 'robbed them of their tender life.'

ARCHILOCHUS 118

Quoted for the metre by Hephaestion 15.9, p. 50 Consbruch.
Metre: hemiepes + ia. dim.
λυσιμελής: of sleep in *Od.* 20.57, of love in Hes. *Th.* 120–2 Ἔρος . . . | λυσιμελής, πάντων δὲ θεῶν πάντων τ' ἀνθρώπων | δάμναται ἐν στήθεσσι νόον, Carm. Pop. 873.3–4 ὁ λυσιμελὴς | Ἔρως. Cf. *Od.* 18.212 of Penelope's effect on the suitors, τῶν δ' αὐτοῦ λύτο γούνατ', ἔρῳ δ' ἄρα θυμὸν ἔθελχθεν. With λυσιμελής . . . . πόθος cf. Alcm. 3.61 λυσιμελεῖ τε πόσῳ.

CALLINUS

Callinus lived in Ephesus in the middle of the 7th century. His chronology is linked with that of the Cimmerian invasions of Ionia: fr. 3 must have been written soon after the fall of Sardis, which is dated by the records of Asshur-bani-pal to 652.

CALLINUS 1

From Stobaeus 4.10 (ἔπαινος τόλμης). 12. This vigorous piece may have spurred on the Ephesians in the war against their neighbours, the Magnesians: cf. Str. 14.647: 'Callinus refers to the Magnesians as still prosperous and successful in the war against the Ephesians.' It may equally well belong to the time of the Cimmerian invasion.

The dependence of the early elegiac poets on Homer is clearly exemplified by this piece. All the vocabulary is Homeric with two exceptions: ἀμφιπερικτίονας (but Homer has περικτίονας and uses the double prefix ἀμφιπερι-) and ποθεινός (Homer has ποθέω and ποθή). Almost all the lines begin with words used by Homer at the beginning of his lines, and all the hexameters end with words or groups of words used by Homer as line-endings, except for ποθεινός (but Homer ends lines with ποθέοντε and ποθέοντες). The pentameter-endings are a good illustration of the methods of the elegiac writers: lines 7 and 9 have the beginnings of Homeric lines (κουριδίης ἀλόχου, ἀλλά τις αὐτὸς ἴτω) with slight alterations; lines 11, 15 and 17 have Homeric hexameter-endings (πολέμοιο, θανάτοιο, μή τι πάθῃσι) with alternative forms of the words; lines 4, 13 and 21 show Homeric hexameter-endings (ἔχουσι, ἀθανάτοισι, μοῦνον ἐόντα) with different parts of verbs, cases of nouns, etc.; and with the remaining lines 2, 5 and 19 we may compare Homer's line-endings περικτίονας ἀνθρώπους, ὕστατα τοξάσσαιτο, ἡμιθέων γένος ἀνδρῶν. The elegiac poets indeed formed their own stock of formulaic pentameter-endings: with Callinus' endings cf. Thgn. 1058 ἀμφιπερικτίοσιν, Tyrt. 6.6 κουριδίη τ' ἀλόχῳ, Tyrt. 5.5 μοῖρα κίχοι θανάτου (also used by Mimn. 6.2 and Sol. 22.4: cf. Thgn. 340 μοῖρα κίχη θανάτου, 820 μοῖρα λάβοι θανάτου, Sol. 19.18 μοῖραν ἔχοι θανάτου, Friedländer 77, from Eretria, 6th century B.C., θανάτου δὲ ἐνθάδε μοῖρ' ἔχιχε, sic).

The simile of the tower (20) is Homeric too, though not the vivid picture of the warrior who escapes death on the battlefield only to die at home (14–15). The image of 10–11, 'keeping a stout heart hidden behind his shield', is also more lively than Homeric parallels quoted by editors. The remarkable thing is that Callinus used so much that was Homer's and yet composed a poem of such freshness and power.

1. μέχρις τεῦ κατάκεισθε; 'how long do you mean to lie idle?' The construction with the present tense does not recur in Greek till Paulus Silentiarius resurrects it some twelve centuries after Callinus at the beginning of two poems in

elegiac couplets (*A.P.* 5.220, 225). Homer has the future: *Il.* 24.128–9 τέο μέχρις . . . σὴν ἔδεαι κραδίην; But the present tense is found in Latin with *quoad* and *quo usque*: cf. Ter. *Phorm.* 147–8 *senem | quoad exspectati' vostrum*? Cic. *Planc.* 31.75 *quo usque ita dicis*? For κατάκειμαι of culpable inactivity cf. Xen. *Anab.* 3.1.14 ὅπως δ' ἀμυνούμεθα οὐδεὶς παρασκευάζεται, ἀλλὰ κατακείμεθα ὥσπερ ἐξὸν ἡσυχίαν ἄγειν. κεῖμαι, κάθημαι and ἧμαι are found with the same meaning. We need not follow Reitzenstein and say with Bowra (*E.G.E.* 14) that the scene is convivial and that the men are 'lying idly at a feast'.

κότε: the Ionic form of πότε, not found in Homer but familiar from Herodotus; see κως (12).

2. νέοι: i.e. fighting men, as in *Il.* 11.503 νέων δ' ἀλάπαζε φάλαγγας and Tyrt. 8.10. They are married men with families (7). In Tyrt. 7.15 the νέοι are the younger soldiers, and are contrasted with τοὺς παλαιοτέρους (19). In X. *Mem.* 1.2.35 Charicles defines οἱ νέοι as the under-thirties.

αἰδεῖσθε: cf. *Od.* 2.65 ἄλλους τ' αἰδέσθητε περικτίονας ἀνθρώπους, *Il.* 6.442 αἰδέομαι Τρῶας. In these passages αἰδέομαι with accusative means 'feel a sense of shame before'; cf. too *Il.* 5.529–30 with its general resemblance to Callinus: ὦ φίλοι, ἀνέρες ἔστε καὶ ἄλκιμον ἦτορ ἔλεσθε, | ἀλλήλους τ' αἰδεῖσθε κατὰ κρατερὰς ὑσμίνας. More commonly the meaning is 'feel a sense of respect or regard for', e.g. the gods, suppliants, an oath.

ἀμφιπερικτίονας: Homer has this double prefix in *Il.* 8.348 (-στρώφα) and *Od.* 8.175 (-στρέφεται). The word ἀμφιπερικτίονας fills the second half of the pentameter; other examples from early elegists are Thgn. 1058 ἀμφιπερικτίοσιν, Tyrt. 3b.6 ἀνταπαμειβομένους. Hudson-Williams quotes examples from later elegists, and Catullus 68.112 has *Amphitryoniades* (cf. Bacchyl. 5.85). Mimn. 6.2 and Sol. 22.4 have ἑξηκονταέτη and ὀγδωκονταέτη as the first half of pentameters.

3. Callinus has enjambement between pentameter and hexameter thrice in this poem, most conspicuously after 7,

where the effect is strengthened by the pause after
δυσμενέσιν.

μεθιέντες: 'slacking'. Homer has this intransitive use, e.g.
Il. 6.523 ἀλλὰ ἑκὼν μεθιεῖς τε καὶ οὐκ ἐθέλεις.

4. After this pentameter the MSS. of Stobaeus continue with
   another pentameter. The gap in the text is probably small.

5. τις: 'every one of you', as in 9. Homer has this use in
   vigorous appeals to troops, e.g. *Il.* 2.382 εὖ μέν τις δόρυ
   θηξάσθω ('Sharpen all spears', Rieu); 17.227–8 τῷ τις νῦν
   ἰθὺς τετραμμένος ἢ ἀπολέσθω | ἠὲ σαωθήτω, as do Tyrtaeus
   8.21 (=7.31), 8.29 and Herodotus 6.9.3 νῦν τις ὑμέων εὖ
   ποιήσας φανήτω, 9.98: cf. also Thgn. 184.

6. τε generalises as in Homer, who uses it in relative clauses
   denoting habitual action, proverbs, maxims and similes,
   e.g. *Il.* 17.32 ῥεχθὲν δέ τε νήπιος ἔγνω, 'even a fool is wise
   after the event.' See Denniston, *G.P.* 520 ff, L. R. Palmer in
   Comp. Hom. 176–7. Denniston, who does not mention the
   Callinus passage, points out that the epic use is γάρ τε, not
   τε γάρ (536).

9. *Μοῖραι*: μοῖρα, originally 'part, portion' (cf. μείρομαι, 'get
   as one's share'), came to be used like μόρος and αἶσα of a
   man's portion in life: cf. 15 μοῖρα κίχεν θανάτου. In the
   Iliad Moira is a goddess of fate, death and evil generally;
   she is κραταίη, ὀλοή, κακή and δυσώνυμος. The personified
   plural is found only once in Homer, in *Il.* 24.49 τλητὸν γὰρ
   Μοῖραι θυμὸν θέσαν ἀνθρώποισιν. The three Fates, Κλωθώ,
   Λάχεσις and Ἄτροπος, occur first in Hesiod, *Theog.* 218,
   905.

   ἐπικλώσωσι: in the *Iliad* Moira spins a man's destiny for him
   at his birth: cf. 24.210–11 τῷ δ᾽ ὡς ποθι Μοῖρα κραταιὴ |
   γεινομένῳ ἐπένησε λίνῳ. Αἶσα does so in 20.127–8. In the
   Odyssey the verb ἐπικλώθω is common in this sense, but the
   spinner is not Moira (the personification is not found in the
   Odyssey), but Zeus (4.208), δαίμων (16.64) or the gods in
   general (1.17 etc.). In *Od.* 7.197–8 we find the Κλῶθες
   spinning: πείσεται ἅσσα οἱ Αἶσα κατὰ Κλῶθές τε βαρεῖαι |
   γεινομένῳ νήσαντο λίνῳ. With ἐπικλώσωσι here supply
   θάνατον.

11. ἔλσας: 'concentrating', from εἴλω. Cf. *Il.* 13.408 τῇ ὕπο (sc. τῇ ἀσπίδι) πᾶς ἐάλη. Homer uses the verb of armies 'crowded' against ships or walls.

μειγνυμένου πολέμου: Homer has αὐτοσχεδίῃ μεῖξαι χεῖράς τε μένος τε (*Il.* 15.510), Alcaeus μείξαντες ἀλλάλοισ᾽ Ἄρευα (330), Pindar βίαν μεῖξαν (*P.* 4.213). πόλεμος is 'battle', as frequently in the *Iliad*; after Homer it usually means 'war', as in 4 above.

12. εἱμαρμένον ἐστίν = εἵμαρται, 'it is fate's decree' (μείρομαι). The idea that a soldier must not shirk battle since the circumstances of his death, whether on the battlefield or elsewhere, are predestined is Homeric: before going into battle Hector says to Andromache, οὐ γάρ τίς μ᾽ ὑπὲρ αἶσαν ἀνὴρ Ἄιδι προϊάψει· | μοῖραν δ᾽ οὔ τινά φημι πεφυγμένον ἔμμεναι ἀνδρῶν, | οὐ κακόν, οὐδὲ μὲν ἐσθλόν, ἐπὴν τὰ πρῶτα γένηται (*Il.* 6.487 ff). *Il.* 23.322 ff adds the idea that the soldier who survives battle does not thereby escape old age or death, and it is this idea that Callinus elaborates here. Aeschylus has it too (fr. 362 N²): ἀλλ᾽ οὔτε πολλὰ τραύματ᾽ ἐν στέρνοις λαβὼν | θνήσκει τις, εἰ μὴ τέρμα συντρέχοι βίου, | οὔτ᾽ ἐν στέγῃ τις ἥμενος παρ᾽ ἑστίᾳ | φεύγει τι μᾶλλον τὸν πεπρωμένον μόρον. So does Euripides (fr. 10 N²): κατθανεῖν δ᾽ ὀφείλεται | καὶ τῷ κατ᾽ οἴκους ἐκτὸς ἡμένῳ πόνων. Cf. Simon. 524 ὁ δ᾽ αὖ θάνατος κίχε καὶ τὸν φυγόμαχον and Hor. *Od.* 3.2.14 *mors et fugacem persequitur virum.*

13. οὐδ᾽ εἰ ... ᾖ: in general conditions with the subjunctive mood Homer uses both the simple εἰ and εἰ with κε or ἄν. Callinus' practice varies even within this poem: cf. 17 ἤν τι πάθῃ. Tyrtaeus likewise has εἰ φύγῃ (9.35) and ἢν αἰσχρὰ πάθῃ (8.16), and Mimnermus, Solon and Theognis too exhibit both constructions. See Goodwin, *M.T.* 468, 470; Palmer in *Comp. Hom.* 166.

προγόνων ... γένος ἀθανάτων: γένος is probably 'child' (nom. case); the same construction is found in *Il.* 21.186 φῆσθα σὺ μὲν ποταμοῦ γένος ἔμμεναι εὐρὺ ῥέοντος. There is no need to explain γένος as adverbial accusative and take the genitive with the verb. γένος in expressions like ἡ δ᾽ ἄρ᾽ ἔην θεῖον γένος οὐδ᾽ ἀνθρώπων (*Il.* 6.180, of the Chimaera), δῖον γένος (9.538, of the Calydonian boar), σὸν γένος (19.124), seems to mean 'child'.

14. πολλάκι: note the asyndeton (i.e. absence of any connecting particle) at the beginning of this sentence: 14–15 amplify 12–13 by providing an example. Homer frequently has asyndeton when a sentence explains or amplifies the previous one, e.g. Od. 22.73–4 ἀλλὰ μνησώμεθα χάρμης· | φάσγανά τε σπάσσασθε καὶ ἀντίσχεσθε τραπέζας.

15. ἔρχεται, 'he comes home': the sense is made clear by the preceding line and by the words ἐν δ' οἴκῳ which follow at once. Hudson-Williams points out that ἔρχεσθαι is the regular word for the home-coming of Odysseus, quoting inter alia Od. 14.382 ff, where Eumaeus tells how a wandering Aetolian predicted Odysseus' home-coming: καὶ φάτ' ἐλεύσεσθαι ἢ ἐς θέρος ἢ ἐς ὀπώρην.

μοῖρα κίχεν θανάτου: see 9n. μοῖρα ... θανάτοιο is common in the Odyssey. For the stock pentameter-ending see the introduction to this poem. κίχεν is gnomic aorist: the augment is omitted as in Homer.

16. ἀλλ' ἔμπης: 'but in any case'.

17. τὸν δ', i.e. the warrior who dies in battle, ὁ μέν, the warrior who dies at home.

ὀλίγος καὶ μέγας: 'both great and small'. The two words do not seem to be used together elsewhere with reference to social standing, but μέγας commonly means 'mighty, impressive', and is contrasted with ὀλίγος in Homer, so that the phrase presents no difficulty. See A. C. Moorhouse, 'The meaning and use of μικρός and ὀλίγος in the Greek poetical vocabulary', C.Q. 41 (1947), 31–45, especially 37.

ἤν τι πάθῃ: the common Homeric euphemism, 'if anything (bad) happens to him.'

18. λαῷ: the Ionic form is ληός (Attic λεώς), but the elegists took over the Aeolian form λᾱός from Homer.

19. ζώων: participle of ζώω, which when contracted gives the Attic ζῶ.

ἄξιος ἡμιθέων: cf. Il. 8.234–5 νῦν δ' οὐδ' ἑνὸς ἄξιοί εἰμεν | Ἕκτορος. ἡμίθεοι appear only once in Homer, in Il. 12.23 ἡμιθέων γένος ἀνδρῶν, where they are the warriors who died at Troy. Some of the heroes of the Trojan war were 'half-gods' in that they had one divine parent, e.g. Achilles and Aeneas; but in Hesiod *Op.* 156 ff their half-divinity is their status between divinity and humanity (ἀνδρῶν ἡρώων θεῖον γένος, οἳ καλέονται | ἡμίθεοι, προτέρη γενεὴ — 'the race before ours' — κατ' ἀπείρονα γαῖαν). The word is frequently applied by later writers to the heroes of mythology: Hesiod's examples are the warriors killed at Thebes and Troy; Alcaeus 42.13 uses the word of Achilles, Pindar *P.* 4.184 of the Argonauts; cf. Cor. 654. iii. 22–3 εἰρώων . . . εἰμιθίων.

20. ὥσπερ πύργον: cf. *Od.* 11.556, where Odysseus says to the dead Ajax, τοῖος γάρ σφιν πύργος ἀπώλεο. The metaphor was common, especially in the dramatists, e.g. S. *Aj.* 159, *O.T.* 1201, E. *Alc.* 311, *Med.* 390. Alcaeus 112.10 has ἄνδρες γὰρ πόλιος πύργος ἀρεύιος.

21. ἔρδει . . . πολλῶν ἄξια: 'his actions are like an army's' (Lattimore).

CALLINUS 3

Quoted by Strabo in his account of Ephesus (14.647). Strabo tells us that Callinus mentioned the capture of Sardis in the poem.

ἐπὶ . . . ἔρχεται: an example of tmesis. Κιμμερίων: Homer (*Od.* 11.15 ff) sited the Cimmerians on the river Ocean at the extreme edge of the world, where like Tacitus' Britons they passed a sunless, fogbound existence. Shortly before 700 an invasion of the Scythians displaced them from their home in and near the Crimea, which bears their name. They moved east, then south across the Caucasus, won victories against the kingdoms in the north-west corner of the Assyrian empire, and settled for some thirty years in Cappadocia. The next generation marched west, conquered Phrygia and attacked Gyges' kingdom of Lydia. Aided by the Treres, a Thracian tribe mentioned by Callin. 4, they defeated Gyges, who was killed in battle, and took Sardis. The Ionian cities were the next target: Magnesia fell, but Ephesus resisted successfully. Pestilence finally forced the invaders to withdraw.

ὀβριμοεργῶν: ὄβριμος in the *Iliad* appears in formulaic line-endings, ὄβριμος Ἄρης, ὄβριμος Ἕκτωρ, ὄβριμον ἔγχος, with the sense 'strong': cf. ὀβριμοπάτρη of Athena. In the *Odyssey* it seems to show its alleged connexion with words connoting weight (e.g. βρίθω, βριθύς but note the ῑ): it is used of Polyphemus' great bundle of firewood (9.233 ὄβριμον ἄχθος) and of the stone with which he blocks his cave-entrance (9.241,305). In the *Iliad* ὀβριμοεργός is used, as here, of 'violent', 'savage' criminals (Heracles, 5.403; Achilles, 22.418).

TYRTAEUS

Tyrtaeus like Callinus was a war poet. Of his surviving verses a few deal with Sparta's history and constitution, but the four longest fragments are all poems of the battle-field. Fr. 1, a tattered papyrus of the third century B.C., forecasts the course of an imminent battle; fr. 6–7 (so numbered since it has been taken for two separate poems) is a cry for bravery in battle, given urgency by a vivid picture of the hardships to be expected by the defeated warrior; fr. 8, which must have been written after a set-back, encourages the Spartans and exhorts them to fight fear-lessly; fr. 9 praises courage as man's greatest excellence in war-time: dead or alive, the courageous man is honoured by his country.

The background of Tyrtaeus' poetry is the second Messenian war. Two generations earlier the Spartans had fought a bitter twenty-year war for possession of the rich plains of Messene to the west of Sparta (cf. Tyrt. 4.3 Μεσσήνην ἀγαθὸν μὲν ἀροῦν, ἀγαθὸν δὲ φυτεύειν and 4.4–8 ἀμφ' αὐτὴν δ' ἐμάχοντ' ἐννεακαίδεκ' ἔτη | . . . αἰχμηταὶ πατέρων ἡμετέρων πατέρες· | εἰκοστῷ δ' οἱ μὲν κατὰ πίονα ἔργα λιπόντες | φεῦγον Ἰθωμαίων ἐκ μεγάλων ὀρέων — i.e. the Messenians fled from their stronghold on Mount Ithome). After the Spartan victory the Messenians were reduced to serfdom, 'worn down by great burdens like asses' (5.1 ὥσπερ ὄνοι μεγάλοις ἄχθεσι τειρόμενοι), and after some fifty years of oppression they revolted with help from other Peloponnesian states. Another long grim war was fought before the Spartans, spurred on by Tyrtaeus' poetry, could re-establish supremacy. When they did so, they decided that they could maintain their position only by submitting to a rigorous military discipline, and life in Sparta became spartan. The crafts of vase-painters, ivory-carvers and poets, which had all flourished, now died.

The chronology of the wars, and so of Tyrtaeus, is difficult to establish. King Theopompus, under whose leadership the Spartans won the first Messenian war, belonged to the eighth generation before Leotychidas (Hdt. 8.131.2), who ruled from c. 491 to 469. A more precise date for the first war is given by the disappearance of Messenians from the lists of Olympic victors after 736: presumably the demands of the war caused this, so that we have an approximate date for its beginning. We know too that the Spartans founded Tarentum c. 706 as a result of the war, so that we have a period of thirty years in which to set the twenty-year war. The second war and with it Tyrtaeus' war poems might belong to any period from the sixties to the thirties of the next century. K. J. Dover argues convincingly (in *Archiloque* 190–4) that Tyrtaeus took two stylistic features, avoidance of the epic δέ τε and non-observance of digamma, from Ionian elegiac poets, and that accordingly he wrote later than Archilochus and Callinus. The *Suda* says he flourished (ἤκμαζε) in Ol.35 (640–637 B.C.).

The spirit of Tyrtaeus' poems suggests that he was a Lace-daemonian of some authority. According to Strabo 8.362 he said that he was a general in the war (φησὶν αὐτὸς στρατηγῆσαι τὸν πόλεμον τοῖς Λακεδαιμονίοις); Athenaeus too mentions his στρατηγία (14.630f; cf. Lycurgus, *Leocr.* 106), but whether he was literally a στρατηγός is uncertain. In 1.54 he identifies himself with the rank and file: μονίῃ πεισόμεθ' ἡγεμ[όνων, 'we shall trust in the steadfastness of the leaders', and Lattimore's comment is apt (*Greek Lyrics* 14): 'he probably was simply a poet writing in a semi-official capacity. I, at least, cannot imagine a general, even in the seventh century, instructing his troops to set their teeth and shake terribly the crests of their helmets.' Another account of him appears as early as Plato *Lg.* 629a: he was an Athenian by birth, but became a Spartan citizen. Pausanias

4.15.6 and a scholiast on the *Laws* embellish this: he was a lame schoolmaster from Athens, somewhat feeble-minded and altogether expendable, and when Sparta requested help from Athens in her war with Messene the Athenians handed him over. The story of his Athenian birth, now generally discredited, was probably due to a fourth-century Greek reluctance to believe that Sparta ever had a native-born poet and to Athenian readiness to claim him for her own. The origin of the story is suggested by Philochorus' remark (328F 215) that Tyrtaeus went from Aphidna in Attica to the help of the Spartans: he may in fact have belonged to the Laconian Aphidna. There was still another version, since the *Suda* makes him 'a Spartan or a Milesian' — 'Milesian' possibly because of the almost pure Ionic dialect of his poetry.

The *Suda* lists Tyrtaeus' works: 'he wrote *The Constitution* for the Spartans and *Good Advice* ('Ὑποθῆκαι) in elegiac couplets and songs of war, five books.' Pausanias 4.15.6 mentions his anapaestic verse, and a few lines in anapaests quoted by Dio Chrysostomus 2.59 and attributed to Tyrtaeus by a scholiast may be from the songs of war: ἄγετ', ὦ Σπάρτας εὐάνδρου | κοῦροι πατέρων πολιητᾶν, | λαιᾷ μὲν ἴτυν προβάλεσθε, | δόρυ δ' εὐτόλμως πάλλοντες | μὴ φειδόμενοι τᾶς ζωᾶς· | οὐ γὰρ πάτριον τᾷ Σπάρτᾳ (*P.M.G.* 856). We have references elsewhere to his elegiac poem *Eunomia*, 'Discipline', the term which was applied in later times (first in Hdt. 1.65.2) to the Spartan political and educational system: cf Ar. *Pol.* 5.6.2 and Str. 8.362, where four lines from the poem are quoted.

Tyrtaeus' vocabulary is almost exclusively Homeric: of the non-Homeric words half can be found in Hesiod and the Homeric hymns, a few are technical expressions and proper names, e.g. γυμνῆτες, πάνοπλοι, and others are only slight variants on Homer, e.g. μειλιχόγηρυς for Homer's μελίγηρυς. Only rarely does he allow features of Spartan vernacular: he has the future ἀλοιησεῦ[μεν] (1.55: Ionic ἀλοιήσομεν) and accusative plurals of the first declension in -ᾰς (1.14 χαίτας, 3a.5 δημότας, 5.4 δεσπότας: Ionic -ᾱς); the rest of his language is the Ionic Greek of Homer. Although he uses much material from the *Iliad*, he can strike memorable phrases of his own, e.g. 1.55 ἀλοιησεῦ[μεν] of

the Spartans in battle, 'we shall thrash them'; 4.3 Μεσσήνην
ἀγαθὸν μὲν ἀροῦν, ἀγαθὸν δὲ φυτεύειν, 5.1 ὥσπερ ὄνοι μεγάλοις
ἄχθεσι τειρόμενοι, 8.5–6 ἐχθρὴν μὲν ψυχὴν θέμενος κτλ., 8.22 (=7.32)
στηριχθεὶς ἐπὶ γῆς, χεῖλος ὀδοῦσι δακών, 9.22 ἔσχεθε κῦμα μάχης. His
poetry impressed later Greeks, Athenians and Cretans as well
as Spartans (Pl. *Lg.* 629a: cf. Lycurgus, *Leocr.* 107, Ath. 14.630 f).

Modern scholars have questioned the authenticity of the poems
which have come down to us under Tyrtaeus' name. When it was
established that much of Pausanias' account of the second
Messenian war was derived from the third-century romantic epic
poem of Rhianus, it was natural that Tyrtaeus too should come
under suspicion. E. Schwartz ('Tyrtaios', *Hermes* 34 (1899),
428 ff) maintained that 'Tyrtaeus' was written by a fifth-century
Athenian, and since then many scholars have dated some or all of
the poems to the fifth or fourth centuries. Fr. 9 has come under
gravest suspicion, since its form and content suggested the work
of fifth- and fourth-century sophists in Athens. Jaeger ('Tyrtaios
über die wahre ἀρετή', *Sitz. Berl. Akad.* 23 (1932), 537 ff=*Scripta
Minora* II.75 ff) argued for its authenticity by pointing out that it
was known to Solon and Pindar and imitated by Xenophanes 2,
but his conclusions are not accepted by all scholars: H. Fraenkel,
D.P., 384–6, regards it as a product of the late archaic period, *c.* 500
B.C. Archaeologists have cast doubt on parts of fr. 8: see 8.24n.

(See C. Prato, *Tyrtaeus*, 1968.)

TYRTAEUS 8

Quoted by Stobaeus 4.9 (περὶ πολέμου). 16 and attributed by
him to Tyrtaeus.

1. ἀλλά in commands and exhortations expresses 'a transition
   from arguments for action to a statement of the action
   required' (Denniston, *G.P.* 14); cf. 21, 29 below and
   Callin. 1.9. But it seems, like δέ, to have been used on
   occasion at the beginning of a poem: cf. Thgn. 341, 583,
   1055, Timocr. 727.1. See Archil. 1.1n.

   Ἡρακλῆος . . . γένος: i.e. Heraclidae (as Tyrtaeus calls them,
   2.2) or Dorians. Hyllus, eldest son of Heracles, was adopted
   by Aegimius, son of Dorus who gave his name to the
   Dorians. Since Heracles was a descendant of Perseus and
   so of the lords of Tiryns, this adoption bolstered the

Dorians' claim to be masters of the Peloponnese. Thanks to their connexion with Heracles the Spartans might also expect the favour of his father Zeus (2). On the case of γένος (here 'descendants') see Callin. 1.13n.

2. αὐχένα λοξὸν ἔχει: the meaning must be 'is displeased' or 'pays no attention'. The phrase recurs in a different context in Thgn. 535–6 οὔποτε δουλείη κεφαλὴ ἰθεῖα πέφυκεν, | ἀλλ' αἰεὶ σκολιὴ καὐχένα λοξὸν ἔχει: a slave never looks anyone straight in the eye: his head is always crooked and his neck at an angle. Tyrtaeus must mean that Zeus is still sympathetic and has not yet averted his eyes. Cf. Il. 13.3 where Zeus turns his shining eyes away from the Trojans.

4. ἰθὺς ... ἐς προμάχους, 'straight towards the front line.' Homer has ἰθὺς πρὸς τεῖχος (Il. 12.137). The πρόμαχοι must be the front rank of the hoplite phalanx; in Homer they are the warriors who range over the battle-field fighting in advance of the λαός, the main body.

ἀνήρ: 'everyone', as τις in Callinus 1.5 etc. and τις ἀνήρ in Tyrt. 9.43, Alc. 6.12.

5–6. The soldier must hate his life and count black death as dear as the sunlight. Tyrtaeus has the first example of the word φιλοψυχεῖν, 'to love one's life' and so 'to be cowardly' (7.18), but the present couplet is still more vivid and no apt parallel is quoted.

ὁμῶς was supplied by Grotius to fill the gap in the MSS. Cf. Il. 9.312 ἐχθρὸς γάρ μοι κεῖνος ὁμῶς Ἀΐδαο πύλῃσιν, 'I hate him as I hate the gates of Hades.' ἴσως (Diehl³) is non-Homeric and so less likely. Defradas points out that by a chiasmic construction the couplet is enclosed by the opposites ἐχθρήν and φίλας.

7. Ἄρεος πολυδακρύου: cf. Il. 3.132 πολύδακρυν Ἄρηα, Il. 17.192 μάχης πολυδακρύου.

ἀΐδηλα: lit. 'making unseen' (ἀ-, ἰδεῖν), so 'destructive'. It is applied to Ares in Il. 5.897, Od. 8.309.

10. νέοι: see Callin. 1.2n.

ἠλάσατε: the intransitive use is copied by Solon 4.6 οἱ πολλῶν ἀγαθῶν ἐς κόρον [ἠ]λάσατε, 'have reached satiety.' Homer has an intransitive use of the infin. ἐλάαν, in μάστιξεν δ' ἐλάαν.

12. αὐτοσχεδίην: Homer uses αὐτοσχεδίην and σχεδίην adverbially, 'at close quarters', like αὐτοσχεδόν, and the dative αὐτοσχεδίῃ (*Il.* 15.510) has the same meaning. Tyrtaeus uses the word here as if it were a true noun, 'the hand-to-hand fighting.'

13. σαοῦσι δὲ λαὸν ὀπίσσω: not 'these save the people afterward' (Edmonds), but 'they save the army behind them'. In the closest parallels in Homer, σαώσετε λαὸν Ἀχαιῶν (*Il.* 13.47) and ἐπὶ δ' ἴαχε λαὸς ὄπισθε(ν) (*Il.* 13.834, 17.723), λαός means 'the army'. The sing. λαός in Homer, especially in the *Iliad* (which Tyrtaeus as a war poet echoes more than the *Odyssey*), usually means 'soldiers'. In 9.24 Tyrtaeus uses the plural λαούς for 'citizens'.

14. τρεσσάντων ... ἀνδρῶν, 'men who have fled', the usual meaning in Homer, who has ἀνδρῶν τρεσσάντων in this sense (*Il.* 14.522). At Sparta ὁ τρέσας became a technical term for a runaway or coward: cf. Hdt. 7.231 ὄνειδός τε εἶχε ὁ τρέσας Ἀριστόδημος καλεόμενος, Plu. *Ages.* 30 οἱ ἐν τῇ μάχῃ καταδειλιάσαντες, οὓς αὐτοὶ τρέσαντας ὀνομάζουσι.

πᾶσ' ἀπόλωλ' ἀρετή: cf. *Od.* 17.322–3 ἥμισυ γάρ τ' ἀρετῆς ἀποαίνυται εὐρύοπα Ζεὺς | ἀνέρος, εὖτ' ἄν μιν κατὰ δούλιον ἦμαρ ἕλησιν, 'Zeus, the wide-thunderer, robs a man of half his areté when the day of slavery seizes him.' In neither of these passages does ἀρετή show the later sense of 'moral virtue': see introduction to Tyrt. 9. In the present passage Tyrtaeus probably means that when men turn tail and run, all the qualities that make a fine soldier are forgotten.

15. Asyndeton as in Callin. 1.14.

16. ἢν αἰσχρὰ πάθῃ: 'if he suffers disgrace', euphemistically for 'if he behaves disgracefully'.

17. ἁρπαλέον: MSS. ἀργαλέον gives the wrong sense. Ahrens' emendation is apt: 'it is attractive to pierce from behind the back of a fleeing man.' ἁρπαλέος, 'to be eagerly seized' (ἁρπάζω), is used by Theognis 1353 as the opposite of ἀπηνής. The verbal force remains in Mimnermus 1.4–5 οἷ' ἥβης ἄνθεα γίγνεται ἁρπαλέα | ἀνδράσιν ἠδὲ γυναιξίν. ἀεργηλόν (Allen, *C.Q.* 26 (1932), 87) is hardly suitable: the word means

'unworking, idle' and is attested only in Alexandrian poetry
and in an anonymous lyric line (*P.M.G.* 996).

ὄπισθε: cf. 20 νῶτον ὄπισθ' . . . ἐληλάμενος. The brave
soldier is wounded from the front, πρόσθεν ἐληλάμενος,
9.26.

18. δηίῳ ἐν πολέμῳ: the beginning of a line in *Il.* 5.117: cf. 26n.

19. κακκείμενος: for κατακείμενος by apocope; cf. the Homeric
formula, οἱ μὲν κακκείοντες ἔβαν οἰκόνδε ἕκαστος.

20. νῶτον: accus. retained with a passive participle.

21. τις: 'every man' as in 29: cf. Callin. 1.5n.

εὖ διαβάς, 'with feet set well apart': cf. *Il.* 12.458, where
Hector heaves a boulder at the gate of the Greek camp εὖ
διαβάς, ἵνα μὴ οἱ ἀφαυρότερον βέλος εἴη ('lest his missile
should lose any of its force').

22. στηριχθεὶς ἐπὶ γῆς, 'firmly planted on the ground': cf. *Il.*
21.241–2 οὐδὲ πόδεσσιν | εἶχε στηρίξασθαι.

χεῖλος ὀδοῦσι δακών: Homer uses ὀδὰξ ἐν χείλεσι φύντες
(*Od.* 1.381 etc.), 'planting their teeth in their lips', of the
suitors suppressing their fury. 21–2 are repeated in Tyrt.
7.31–2.

24. ἀσπίδος εὐρείης γαστρί: the expression is without parallel,
but it seems to describe the same type of shield as the
κοίλησ' ἀσπίσι of 1.50, and it is quite appropriate to the
hoplite type of shield. The difficulties in the passage are
caused by the remainder of the couplet — the shield is to
cover the soldier from shoulder to shin. H. L. Lorimer, 'The
Hoplite Phalanx', *A.B.S.A.* 42 (1947), 122 ff states the
anomaly: 'at one period, and one only, in the history of
Greek warfare was such a shield in use — . . . in the
fifteenth and sixteenth centuries' (122). 'It is . . . impossible
to attribute to any seventh-century poet the implied statement that the hoplite shield could cover simultaneously
thighs and shins below and breast and shoulders; the
exhortation, whatever its date, cannot have been a real
call to contemporary soldiers' (126). Arguing that the
nodding helmet-plume of the next couplet (26) is also
inappropriate to hoplite equipment and ἐκτὸς βελέων (28)
inappropriate to hoplite warfare, Miss Lorimer rejects

23–8 and with them 21–2 (=7.31–2) as *pastiche*, hardly earlier than the fifth or fourth century.

A better solution is suggested by N. G. L. Hammond, 'The Lycurgean Reform at Sparta', *J.H.S.* 70 (1950), 51, n. 50: 'one reason (for the perplexing nature of Tyrtaeus' evidence on weapons, armour and tactics) may be that the Messenian wars were not struggles between hoplite forces but partook more of guerilla tactics; and, as it takes two hoplite sides to make a hoplite battle, the Spartans may have been compelled by their enemy to modify their equipment and their tactics.' The missiles (28) and the activities of the light-armed soldiers (35–8) are best explained by the guerilla nature of the war. As for the helmet-plume (26), a bronze statuette from Selinos in eastern Laconia, dated 540–510, shows a warrior with plumed helmet (Winifred Lamb, *Greek and Roman Bronzes* 91 with Plate 28a), and similar 6th century bronzes, which may show Spartan influence, are known from Dodona. Alcaeus describes helmets with white horse-hair plumes (357.3). See too Anthony Snodgrass, *Early Greek Armour and Weapons* 181–2.

26. λόφον: cf. *Il.* 3.337 δεινὸν δὲ λόφος καθύπερθεν ἔνευεν. The words δεινὸν ὑπὲρ κεφαλῆς form the beginning of a hexameter in *Il.* 18.226.

27. The nobility of this line is not derivative, although the vocabulary is all Homeric.

διδασκέσθω: middle, as in Sol. 22.7 γηράσκω δ' αἰεὶ πολλὰ διδασκόμενος, S. *Ant.* 354–6 φθέγμα . . . ἐδιδάξατο.

30. ἑλέτω: 'kill', as often in Homer.

31–3: cf. *Il.* 13.130–3 φράξαντες δόρυ δουρί, σάκος σάκεϊ προθε-λύμνῳ· | ἀσπὶς ἄρ' ἀσπίδ' ἔρειδε, κόρυς κόρυν, ἀνέρα δ' ἀνήρ. | ψαῦον δ' ἱππόκομοι κόρυθες λαμπροῖσι φάλοισι | νευόντων· ὣς πυκνοὶ ἐφέστασαν ἀλλήλοισιν. *Il.* 13.131–3 =16.215–17. But the Homeric passages both refer to the advance of one side in close formation, whereas Tyrtaeus has manipulated the words to describe the clash of two sides in the hoplite style of fighting, as στέρνον στέρνῳ shows; cf. too 1.56 ἀνδράσιν αἰχμηταῖς ἐγγύθεν ἰσ[τάμενοι].

ἐν δέ: 'and also.' In Homer this adverbial use normally means 'and therein', 'and among them'; L.S.J. quote *Od.* 5.260 (ἐν δ' ὑπέρας τε κάλους τε πόδας τ' ἐνέδησεν ἐν αὐτῇ) as the only example of the meaning 'moreover' before Sophocles, but even there ἐν anticipates the words ἐνέδησεν ἐν αὐτῇ.

πεπλημένος: perfect passive participle of πελάζω: cf. *Od.* 12.108 σκοπέλῳ πεπλημένος. Here the participle has the retained accusative as well as the dative: 'having drawn near, crest to crest, helmet to helmet, chest to chest.'

35. γυμνῆτες: 'light-armed soldiers' (cf. ψιλοί), contrasted with οἱ πάνοπλοι (38). Both terms are found here for the first time. The light-armed troops hurl stones, the missiles of Agamemnon himself in *Il.* 11.265 (μεγάλοισί τε χερμαδίοισιν), and spears; but the shields behind which they hide are surely their own, not those of the πάνοπλοι (as Lattimore, *Greek Lyrics* 16).

37. δούρασί τε ξεστοῖσιν ἀκοντίζοντες: this last couplet is clumsily attached to the previous sentence and editors may be right in deleting it.

TYRTAEUS 9

Quoted by Stobaeus 4.10 (ἔπαινος τόλμης) in two parts, 1–14 and 15–44, the second attributed to Tyrtaeus only by Trincavelli in the *editio princeps* of Stobaeus (1535). Theognis 1003–6 has a version of 13–16 consecutively, thus linking the two parts. Plato *Lg.* 629a attributes the poem to Tyrtaeus, quotes the first line and summarises the first section: οὔτ' ἂν μνησαίμην οὔτ' ἐν λόγῳ ἄνδρα τιθείμην, οὔτ' εἴ τις πλουσιώτατος ἀνθρώπων εἴη, φησίν, οὔτ' εἰ πολλὰ ἀγαθὰ κεκτημένος, εἰπὼν σχεδὸν ἅπαντα, ὃς μὴ περὶ τὸν πόλεμον ἄριστος γίγνοιτ' ἀεί. Plato refers to the poem again in *Lg.* 660e–61a. There is every possibility that we are dealing with a complete poem.

Tyrtaeus has arranged his material symmetrically (20 + 2 + 20 + 2): at 20 we reach the end of a section (which itself falls into two equal parts, 20 echoing 10); 21–2 fill out the idea of 20. 23–42 form the other main section, and the final couplet contains the exhortation.

The poem contains Tyrtaeus' reflections on the quality that is needed in war — high physical courage. In fr. 6–7 and fr. 8 Tyrtaeus mingled reflection with exhortation and instruction: here it is not until the last couplet that he abandons generalisation for exhortation, as the following summary shows:

1–22. The prowess that matters in a man is not speed, strength, good looks, wealth, power or eloquence: all that matters is fierce courage. A man is no good in war without it; with it he is a blessing to the whole populace: such a man is good in war and routs the enemy.

23–42. If the courageous soldier dies in battle, he is mourned by the whole populace and remembered for ever; if he survives, he is honoured and respected for the rest of his life.

43–4. This is the prowess that every man should now aim at.

Deeper significance has been found in the poem, especially by Jaeger (loc. cit. and Paideia, tr. Highet, i.74 ff) and Bowra (E.G.E. 62 ff): in Bowra's view Tyrtaeus was trying 'to find out a coherent explanation of man's place in the world' (70) and to define the idea of the ἀνὴρ ἀγαθός and of his ἀρετή. For Tyrtaeus 'the "good man" is he who stands up to the enemy, and in this his excellence, his ἀρετή, lies' (ibid. 65). Jaeger holds that Tyrtaeus is trans-valuing the idea of areté: 'he has recast the Homeric ideal of the single champion's areté into the areté of the patriot' (Paideia 87); 'there is only one standard of true areté — the state. Whatever helps the state is good, whatever injures it is bad (ibid. 89).

This is to read too much into the poem. In lines 10 and 20, where the words ἀνὴρ ἀγαθός occur, their scope is shown on each occasion by the phrase ἐν πολέμῳ: 'a man is not good in war (in battle, perhaps) unless he can stand up to the enemy' and 'it is this man who is good in war'. Bowra's translation of 20 is mis-leading: 'So the good man is revealed in war.' His translation of 13, 'This is man's excellence and finest guerdon' is not the only possible one; and his translation of the last couplet, 'Let a man try to reach the height of prowess With his heart, and never slack in war', omits the emphatic ταύτης and the particularising νῦν. But ταύτης . . . ἀρετῆς must mean 'this excellence', 'this prowess', and it is likely that ἥδ' ἀρετή in 13 means the same thing: 'this excellence, this prize is the best among men.' θοῦρις ἀλκή is the excellence in question, not ποδῶν ἀρετή or the other ἀρεταί rejected in lines 2–9. In Tyrtaeus ἀρετή has not moved further towards its later meaning of 'moral virtue' than it had in Homer: in both writers it refers sometimes to particular forms of excellence (e.g. *Il.* 15.642 παντοίας ἀρετάς, ἠμὲν πόδας ἠδὲ μάχεσθαι: so in Tyrt. 9.2), sometimes to courage (*Il.* 13.277 ἐς λόχον, ἔνθα μάλιστ' ἀρετὴ διαείδεται ἀνδρῶν: so most probably in Tyrt. 11 πρὶν ἀρετῆς πελάσαι τέρμασιν ἢ θανάτου), sometimes to general, though not moral, excellence (*Il.* 9.498 of the gods, τῶν περ καὶ μείζων ἀρετὴ τιμή τε βίη τε: so in Tyrt. 8.14, an echo of *Od.* 17.322–3).

Jaeger's view that for Tyrtaeus 'there is only one standard of true areté — the state' is also misleading. What Tyrtaeus says is that the brave warrior is 'a blessing for all to share — for the city and the whole people' (15): his prowess, unlike that of the runner, the wrestler and the others, ensures the city's very survival.

1. τιθείην: so Stobaeus, but Plato has τιθείμην on both occasions of quoting the line, and in the similar expression ἐν τιμῇ τίθεσθαι (Hdt. 3.3.2) the middle is used. See L.S.J. τίθημι B.II.

2. ποδῶν ἀρετῆς: 'prowess in running': see the introduction to this poem. Homer has ποδῶν ἀρετὴν ἀναφαίνων (*Il.* 20.411). ἀρετῆς is a genitive of the type usually called causal, found with legal terms and verbs denoting emotions, e.g. ἑτάροιο χολωσάμενος (*Il.* 4.501), 'angry because of his friend'; εὐχωλῆς ἐπιμέμφεται (*Il.* 1.65), 'he finds fault with us because of a broken vow.' Tyrtaeus' device of listing rival qualities only to discard them is found also in Thgn. 699–718, Sapph. 16.1–3: cf. too Xenoph. 2.

3. Κυκλώπων: for their size and strength see *Od.* 9.
   μέγεθός τε βίην τε is a Homeric line-ending (*Il.* 7.288); indeed almost all the hexameter-endings in this poem have exact or approximate parallels in Homer and Hesiod.

4. θέων: participle of θέω.
   Θρηΐκιον Βορέην: so in Hes. *Op.* 553, Ibyc. 286.9. In *Il.* 9.5 both Boreas and Zephyrus blow from Thrace; for Boreas' speed cf. *Od.* 5.385 κραιπνὸν Βορέην, Hes. *Th.* 379 Βορέην . . . αἰψηροκέλευθον, Thgn. 715–16 in a passage similar to

this: 'not even if you were faster than the swift Harpies or the sons of Boreas.'

5. *Tithonus* was a Trojan youth (brother of Priam, *Il.* 20.237), with whom Eos, goddess of the dawn, fell in love. She secured from Zeus the promise that he should never die, but forgot to ask that he should not grow old either (*h. Hom.* 5.200–1, 218–38). He is more often cited for the decrepitude of his old age than for his youthful good looks: cf. Mimn. 4, Ar. *Ach.* 688, Callim. *Iamb.* 4.53, Hor. *Od.* 2.16.30, Lucian, *Dial. Mort.* 356.

6. *Midas*: the king of Phrygia whose touch turned everything to gold. The historical Midas belongs to the last decade of the 8th century if he is the Mita of Assyrian documents. Herodotus saw a throne at Delphi which was said to be that of Midas. The story of his touch of gold is told in Ovid, *Met.* 11.85 ff. *Cinyras* appears in *Il.* 11.20 ff as the king of Cyprus who sent Agamemnon a splendid bronze breastplate. In Pindar *P.* 2.15–17 he is 'the obedient priest of Aphrodite, dearly loved by gόlden-haired Apollo', and he is mentioned for his great wealth in *N.* 8.18. Other writers make him the son of Apollo and father of Adonis. Midas and Cinyras reappear together in an anonymous Alexandrian line: ὄλβιος ἦν ὁ Μίδας, τρὶς δ' ὄλβιος ἦν ὁ Κινύρας (J. E. Powell, *Coll. Alex.*, Lyr. Adesp. 37.32): see too Alcm. 3.71.

μάλιον: cf. Hsch. μάλιον· μᾶλλον. Note synizesis in Μίδεω, Κινύρεω and 7 Τανταλίδεω.

7. *Pelops*, son of Tantalus: in mythology the successful suitor of Hippodameia, princess of Pisa. He gave his name to the whole peninsula of the Peloponnese: cf. *Cypria* 11.3–4 νῆσον ... Τανταλίδου Πέλοπος. Of all the figures in Tyrtaeus' catalogue only Pelops and Adrastus have Peloponnesian connexions. The comparative βασιλεύτερος is Homeric (e.g. *Il.* 10.239 μηδ' εἰ βασιλεύτερός ἐστιν) and always occurs at this point in the line.

8. *Adrastus*: the king of Argos who led the expedition of the Seven against Thebes in an attempt to put his son-in-law Polynices on the throne. His story seems to have been told in the cyclic poem *Thebais*: in Homer he is mentioned only

in passing as ruler of Sicyon (*Il.* 2.572), as father-in-law of
Tydeus and so grandfather of Diomedes (*Il.* 14.121), and
as owner of the marvellous horse Arion (*Il.* 23.347); his
eloquence is not attested in Homer, but Plato *Phaedr.*
269a has μελίγηρυν Ἄδραστον, an echo of Tyrtaeus or
perhaps of the *Thebais*. μελίγηρυς is the Homeric form
of the epithet, e.g. in *Od.* 12.187 of the Sirens' song.

9. θούριδος ἀλκῆς: one of the commonest line-endings in the
Iliad. θοῦρις, 'furious', is a fem. form of the adjective
θοῦρος, which Homer uses in the *Iliad* as an epithet of
Ares: cf. 34 below.

11. τετλαίη: for the optative in the protasis after a present
indicative in the apodosis see Goodwin, *M.T.* 501(c); the
optative here despite the absence of ἄν or κε seems to have
potential force, 'unless he could bear to see . . .'

μέν is answered by καί (12), not δέ; see Archil. 1.2n.

12. δηίων: a spondee as in Thgn. 552. This conforms with Homeric
practice: δηι- followed by a long vowel is monosyllabic,
but in δήιον ἄνδρα (as Tyrt. 8.30) or δηίῳ ἐν πολέμῳ
(8.18) disyllabic.

ὀρέγοιτο: 'aim at', with genitive of the target; cf. *Il.* 6.466
οὗ παιδὸς ὀρέξατο φαίδιμος Ἕκτωρ, 'held out his hands to
his child.'

13. ἥδ' ἀρετή: see introduction to this poem. I translate, 'This
excellence, this prize is the best among men and the finest
for a youth to win.' The verb φέρειν is more appropriate
to the second noun, ἄεθλον, but that presents no difficulty.
ἥδ' ἀρετή, like ταύτης . . . ἀρετῆς (43), means 'this excellence', i.e. θοῦρις ἀλκή, not the excellences which Tyrtaeus
has just rejected in 2–9 — ποδῶν ἀρετή and the others.
13–16 appear in Theognis 1003–6 with σοφῷ for νέῳ.

16. ὅστις ἀνὴρ . . . μένῃ: the relative clause explains τοῦτο (15),
as if Tyrtaeus had written εἴ τις ἀνὴρ . . . μένῃ.

διαβάς: see 8.21n. Upton's emendation ὅστις ἂν εὖ preserves
the expression εὖ διαβάς as we find it in Homer, elsewhere
in Tyrtaeus and with reference to the present passage in
Plato, *Lg.* 630b, but the syntax is not in itself faulty: see
Callin. 1.13n.

17. νωλεμέως: Tyrtaeus has few examples of enjambement between his couplets; at 4.5 νωλεμέως αἰεί is less striking because of the caesura after αἰεί. Homer has the same enjambement at *Il*. 13.3. The tmesis in ἐπὶ πάγχυ λάθηται is also Homeric: cf. *Il*. 10.99 φυλακῆς ἐπὶ πάγχυ λάθωνται.

18. παρθέμενος: Homeric analogy suggests that we translate 'risking his life and steadfast spirit': cf. *Od*. 2.237 σφὰς . . . παρθέμενοι κεφαλάς, 3.74 ψυχὰς παρθέμενοι. Cf. too Tyrt. 6.14 ψυχέων μηκέτι φειδόμενοι. But the adjective τλήμονα tells against this translation, and 'displaying a steadfast heart and soul' or 'making heart and soul steadfast' is preferable.

21. ἔτρεψε: gnomic aorist; so ἔσχεθε (22).

22. τρηχείας: Homer uses the adjective only of rough, rugged places, e.g. Ithaca, and of a jagged stone. It does not seem to be used of savage people before Pindar, and in Tyrtaeus and Hesiod (*Sc*. 119 ὑσμίνη τρηχεῖα) τρηχύς may refer to the jagged appearance of the enemy spears: cf. *horrere* in Ennius, *hastis sparsis longis campus splendet et horret*. The metaphor κῦμα μάχης is, as far as we can tell, Tyrtaeus' own.

23. ὃς δ' αὖτ': Bergk's correction of MSS. αὐτὸς δ': the emphatic αὐτός has no point, whereas the relative pronoun, looking forward to τόνδ' (27), is exactly what we need. αὖτε = 'furthermore'. Defradas suggests αὐτὰρ ὅς which is also acceptable but is less likely to have puzzled a copyist.

25. ἀσπίδος ὀμφαλοέσσης: in Homer the epithet refers to the knob in the middle of the shield, but the hoplite shield had no such knob. The epithet might refer to the studs which fastened the rim of the hoplite shield to its backing; otherwise we must say that Tyrtaeus used the Homeric epithet without regard for or knowledge of its proper meaning. See H. L. Lorimer, 'The Hoplite Phalanx', *A.B.S.A.* 42 (1947), 122.

27. Tyrtaeus uses three ways of saying 'both young and old': cf. 37 and 41–2. Homer has ἠμὲν νέοι ἠδὲ γέροντες thrice in the *Iliad*, νέοι ἠδὲ παλαιοί twice in the *Odyssey*, all as line-endings. 'Though Tyrtaeus' variations may be slight, they

show some care for the technique of his craft: . . . he felt that he must do something to differentiate one line from another' (Bowra *E.G.E.* 51–2).

28. κέκηδε: perfect tense of κήδω, used with present significance.

29. τύμβος: in *Od.* 4.584 Menelaus says χεῦ' *Ἀγαμέμνονι τύμβον*, ἵν' ἄσβεστον κλέος εἴη, 'I heaped up a burial-mound for Agamemnon, that his fame might be imperishable.' With παῖδες ἐν ἀνθρώποις ἀρίσημοι cf. Hector's prayer in *Il.* 6.476 ff that his son should be as eminent among the Trojans as he.

30. A pentameter version of *Il.* 20.308 καὶ παίδων παῖδες, τοί κεν μετόπισθε γένωνται: cf. Sol. 1.32 ἢ παῖδες τούτων ἢ γένος ἐξοπίσω .

33. ἀριστεύοντα: *Il.* 6 again comes to mind: Glaucus' advice from his father was αἰὲν ἀριστεύειν καὶ ὑπείροχον ἔμμεναι ἄλλων (208).

μένοντα: 'holding his ground' as in *Il.* 11.317 μενέω καὶ τλήσομαι, 16.659. For ὅντιν' . . . ὀλέσῃ and εἰ δὲ φύγῃ (35) see Callin. 1.13n.

35. τανηλεγέος θανάτοιο: probably 'death that brings long sorrow' (τανα-, ἄλγος or ἀλεγεινός): cf. the other Homeric line-ending (*Il.* 20.154) δυσηλεγέος πολέμοιο, 'war that brings bitter sorrow.'

36. Literally, 'in victory he obtains his glorious spear-prayer.' The nearest Homeric parallel (*Il.* 7.203 δὸς νίκην Αἴαντι καὶ ἀγλαὸν εὖχος ἀρέσθαι) does not have αἰχμῆς, and in Pindar's κλέος ἄνθησεν αἰχμᾶς (*P.* 1.66) αἰχμᾶς can be explained as a straightforward possessive genitive, 'the glory of their spear burst into flower.' Tyrtaeus' genitive denotes in a more general way the sphere in which the prayer was made: see L. R. Palmer in *Comp. Hom.* 131–2 with his examples, πόλεμος Ἀχαιῶν, a war in which the Achaeans are concerned, an Achaeans-war; Τρώων πόνος, 'efforts with regard to the Trojans.'

38. εἰς Ἀίδην: Homer uses only the genitive, εἰς Ἀίδαο, εἰς Ἄϊδος, Ἀιδόσδε. *h. Merc.* 572 has εἰς Ἀίδην and Mimn. 2.14 uses the same half-line as Tyrtaeus.

39. Only an inferior MS. of Stobaeus omits δ' after γηράσκων, but

the asyndeton is correct, as 39–42 explain τιμῶσιν and πολλὰ ... τερπνὰ παθών. For the epexegetic use of asyndeton cf. Callin. 1.14n.

40. For βλάπτειν with genitive = 'cheat of' cf. *Od.* 1.195 ἀλλά νυ τόν γε θεοὶ βλάπτουσι κελεύθου, 'are keeping him from his journey.'

αἰδοῦς: 'respect.'

41. Cf. *Od.* 2.14 ἕζετο δ᾽ ἐν πατρὸς θώκῳ, εἶξαν δὲ γέροντες, 16.42 τῷ δ᾽ ἕδρης ἐπιόντι πατὴρ ὑπόειξεν Ὀδυσσεύς, both passages referring to Telemachus. For the young giving up their seats to their elders cf. Hdt. 2.80.1, where it appears as an Egyptian and Spartan custom, and Ar. *Nub.* 993, where the Just Reasoning recommends it as proper behaviour. A version of 37–42, abbreviated and otherwise altered, occurs at Thgn. 935–8.

43. τις ἀνήρ: 'every man': cf. Callin. 1.5n. for τις and Tyrt. 8.4 for ἀνήρ, both in the same sense. Alc. 6.12 has νῦν τις ἄνηρ δόκιμος γε[νέσθω.

ταύτης ... ἀρετῆς εἰς ἄκρον ἱκέσθαι is most probably an echo of Hes. *Op.* 289 ff. τῆς δ᾽ ἀρετῆς ἱδρῶτα θεοὶ προπάροιθεν ἔθηκαν | ἀθάνατοι· μακρὸς δὲ καὶ ὄρθιος οἶμος ἐς αὐτὴν | καὶ τρηχὺς τὸ πρῶτον· ἐπὴν δ᾽ εἰς ἄκρον ἵκηται, | ῥηιδίη δὴ ἔπειτα πέλει, χαλεπή περ ἐοῦσα.

44. θυμῷ: 'with all his heart', 'spiritedly', as in 6.13 θυμῷ γῆς περὶ τῆσδε μαχώμεθα.

μὴ μεθιεὶς πολέμου: 'not slacking in battle': cf. Callin. 1.3 ὧδε λίην μεθιέντες.

πολέμου, Gesner's emendation of MSS. πόλεμον, is confirmed by *Il.* 6.330 μεθιέντα ... στυγεροῦ πολέμοιο.

SEMONIDES OF AMORGOS

Little is known for certain about him. The entry in the *Suda* (Adler iv. p. 363) runs, 'Simonides, son of Crines, of Amorgos, iambic writer. He wrote elegiac poetry in two books and iambics.

He was born (or "flourished": γέγονε) 490 years after the Trojan War. He was the first to write iambics according to some.' Part of the entry under Simmias of Rhodes (Adler p. 360) seems to belong to Semonides: 'he was originally a Samian, but in the colonisation of Amorgos he was sent as leader by the Samians. He founded Amorgos in three cities, Minoa, Aegialus and Arcesime. He was born (or "flourished") 406 years after the Trojan War. According to some he was the first writer of iambics, and wrote various other things including a History of Samos.'

His name is almost invariably spelt Σιμωνίδης in our sources, but Choeroboscus upholds the spelling Σημ-, which is generally adopted as a useful means of distinguishing the iambic poet from the lyric poet, Simonides of Ceos. His date is uncertain: Clement of Alexandria made him a contemporary of Archilochus; Cyril gives the date 664–1; Proclus' dating ἐπ' Ἀνανίου τοῦ Μακεδόνος (Photius Bibl. 319b.30) affords no light. Literary considerations, probably more reliable than dates given by ancient writers, suggest that he belongs to the second half of the 7th century, since Semon. 7.51–2 is an unmistakable echo of Archil. 18.3–4, Semon. 7 is itself the precursor of Phoc. 2, and Semon. 1 may have influenced Sol. 1. He was probably a younger contemporary of Archilochus, and if the account of the colonisation of Amorgos is correct he had a political career not unlike Archilochus'.

Of his writings his iambics alone have survived, apart from the elegiac fr. 29 which is now generally accepted as his. A citation from Book 2 of the Iambics (Ath. 2.57d: fr. 28) suggests that it may have been the iambics and not the elegiacs that were in two books. Of the longer fragments, 1 and 29 are expressions of pessimism reminiscent of Mimnermus, and 7 is a tirade on women, often very amusing, occasionally naive and repetitive. His personal invective, attested by Lucian Pseudol. 2, has all but disappeared: frr. 2, 16 and 26 may be remnants. He writes Ionic Greek, with many echoes of Homer and Hesiod, particularly in the elegiac fragment. In language, prosody and subject-matter he follows Archilochus without ever displaying the same brilliance.

SEMONIDES I

From Stobaeus 4.34 (περὶ τοῦ βίου ὅτι βραχὺς κτλ.). 15, with the attribution Σιμωνίδου. Metre and content show that Semonides is the author. The piece, which probably is a whole poem, has clear affinities with Sol. 1 in its language, its expression of pessimism and its catalogue of men's frustrations.

Metre: iambic trimeter; so 2, 6, 7.

1. ὦ παῖ: there is a similar didactic tone in fr. 20 ⟨ἦ⟩ πολλὰ μὲν δὴ προεκπονέω, Τηλέμβροτε.

τέλος: cf. Archil. 84.2 καὶ τέλος αὐτὸς ἔχει (sc. Zeus) and see Sol. 1.58n. Euripides imitates the passage: *Or.* 1545–6 τέλος ἔχει δαίμων βροτοῖς, | τέλος ὅπᾳ θέλῃ.

βαρύκτυπος: of Zeus at h. *Cer.* 3, Hes. *Op.* 79, *Th.* 388; cf. 7.40n.

3. νόος: scanned as a monosyllable; Homer has the contracted form νοῦς at *Od.* 10.240. Semonides has synizesis at 1.8 ἐτέων, 7.1 θεὸς (but see note there), 39 θέρεος, 43 παλιντρι-βέος, 54 παρεόντα, 74 ἄστεος, 78 δήνεα, 97 δοκέωσιν, 102 δυσμενέα, 104 θεοῦ.

ἐπ': perhaps ἔπ' for ἔπεστι as *Od.* 2.58 οὐ γὰρ ἔπ' ἀνήρ: cf. 20 ἄπ'.

ἐφήμεροι: 'from day to day', 'one day at a time': cf. *Od.* 21.85 ἐφημέρια φρονέοντες (Rieu: 'who can't see further than their noses').

4. ἃ δή: 'with depreciatory or sceptical colour', Denniston *G.P.* 219, who compares X. *Cyr.* 8.2.14 εὐδαίμονα . . . ἧ δὴ προβάτων εὐδαιμονία. If ζώομεν is correct, we have a choriamb (– ∪ ∪ –) for two iambs in the second metron, a phenomenon not found elsewhere. Ahrens suggested ζώουσιν.

5. ἕκαστον: neuter, like πάντων (2).

6. ἐλπίς: cf. the story of Pandora's box in Hes. *Op.* 94 ff. and Sol. 1.36 κούφαις ἐλπίσι τερπόμεθα.

ἐπιπειθείη: cited elsewhere by L.S.J. only from the 3rd century A.D. Porphyrius.

7. μένουσιν ἐλθεῖν: cf. *Od.* 1.422 μένον δ' ἐπὶ ἕσπερον ἐλθεῖν.

8. ἐτέων περιτροπάς: cf. *Il.* 2.295 περιτροπέων ἐνιαυτός.

9. νέωτα: 'next year', elsewhere only with εἰς or ἐς, as in Zen. 2.43 ἀεὶ γεωργὸς εἰς νέωτα πλούσιος.

10. ἵξεσθαι φίλος: 'come as a friend to, turn out a friend of'
    Wealth and Blessings, if the text is correct: cf. διὰ φιλίας
    ἰέναι with dative (X. An. 3.2.8).

14. μελαίνης ... χθονός: see Archil. 58.2n.

15. λαίλαπι κλονεύμενοι: cf. Il. 11.306 λαίλαπι τύπτων (sc.
    Ζέφυρος).

16. πορφυρῆς ἁλός: cf. Il. 16.391 ἐς δ' ἅλα πορφυρέην. The
    adjective may refer to the heaving motion of the sea or to
    its bright colour.

17. 'they die, when they have not the strength to live' — because
    at the fated hour their vital force fails them, while suicides
    die αὐτάγρετοι. But the infin. ζόειν is suspect, and further
    emendation may be necessary.

18. ἄψαντο: gnomic aorist.

19. αὐτάγρετοι: the adjective means 'free to be chosen' at Od.
    16.148, h. Merc. 474, here 'freely choosing'. ἀγρέω is
    Aeolic for αἱρέω: cf. Attic αὐθαίρετος.
    λείπουσιν ἠλίου φάος: cf. Il. 18.11 λείψειν φάος ἠελίοιο.

20. For similar insistence on man's miseries cf. Hes. Op. 100–105,
    176–8, Mimn. 2.11–16, Sol. 1.43 ff.
    μυρίαι: so μυρία λυγρά at Hes. Op. 100.

21. κῆρες: 'deaths'. Mimn.'s use at 2.5 is wider: see note there.
    ἀνεπίφραστοι: only here: either 'undreamed of' or 'un-
    countable'.

23. Semonides' advice is not clear: possibly 'we should not love
    our misery, nor torture ourselves by letting our hearts dwell
    on evil sufferings'. This chimes in with the advice at the
    end of fr. 29, where the hedonism is explicit.

SEMONIDES 2

From Stobaeus 4.56 (παρηγορικά). 5; attributed there like fr. 1
to 'Simonides'. Semonides may have in mind the advice given by
Odysseus at Il. 19.228–9 ἀλλὰ χρὴ τὸν μὲν καταθαπτέμεν ὅς κε
θάνησιν, | νηλέα θυμὸν ἔχοντας, ἐπ' ἤματι δακρύσαντας. Reitzen-
stein suggested that frr. 1 and 2 belong to the same poem.

1. τοῦ μὲν θανόντος: the reference may be general, 'the dead',
   or (Edmonds) particular, 'if he were to die.'

SEMONIDES 6

From Clement of Alexandria, *Strom.* 6.13.1: 'Hesiod having said (*Op.* 702–3) οὐ μὲν γάρ τι γυναικὸς ἀνὴρ ληίζετ' ἄμεινον | τῆς ἀγαθῆς, τῆς δ' αὖτε κακῆς οὐ ῥίγιον ἄλλο, Simonides said γυναικὸς . . . κακῆς.' Also in Eusebius, *P.E.* 10.3.18: cf. *Anecdota* ed. Boissonade 1.22. Editors who believe fr. 7 to be incomplete suggest that these two lines belong to it. Semonides' version displays the neatness of the iambic metre.

SEMONIDES 7

From Stobaeus 4.22 (περὶ γάμου: ψόγος γυναικῶν). 193 (Σιμωνίδου). 56 is quoted by Ath. 5.179d, 57–70 by Ael. *Hist. Anim.* 16.24. Hes. *Th.* 590–602 has a tirade against women which shows a general resemblance with the concluding part of Semonides' poem (96 ff: see 96n.): according to Hesiod, Zeus' creation of woman was punishment for Prometheus' theft of fire: see also *Op.* 54 ff. Phoc. 2 is a brief and less pungent version of 1–93.

1. χωρίς: either 'differently' (i.e. from the mind of man), or more probably 'variously, in different ways'.

   θεός: we either have a dactyl -κὸς θεὸς or scan θεός as a monosyllable; so in 7. Cf. 39n.

2. ὑός: 'sow', since all the parents listed by Semon. are either feminine or common, presumed feminine: see also 12 αὐτομήτορα and 57 ἐγείνατο.

   τανύτριχος: 'bristly' or 'long-haired', in which case the species is unfamiliar. Hes. *Op.* 516 uses the epithet of a goat.

7. ἀλιτρῆς: the wickedness is apparent in 10–11.

10. τὸ μὲν γὰρ αὐτῶν κτλ.: 'for of these (i.e. κακῶν and ἀμεινόνων) she often calls the latter bad, the former good': she shows no sense of responsibility; or perhaps she is inconsistent, as in 11.

    εἶπε: gnomic aorist, as in 45, 49.

11. ἄλλοτ' ἀλλοίην: cf. Hes. *Op.* 483 ἄλλοτε δ' ἀλλοῖος Ζηνὸς νόος.

12. λιτουργόν: cf. Hsch. λιτουργόν· κακοῦργον. κύων in Homer often denotes shamelessness: Helen uses it of herself at *Il.* 6.344, 356.

αὐτομήτορα: 'the image of her mother', though no parallel is cited; cf. 57 τὴν δ' ἵππος . . . ἐγείνατο.

14. πάντη . . . παπταίνουσα: cf. Od. 12.233 πάντη παπταίνοντι.

15. λέληκεν: like Scylla: cf. Od. 12.85–7, Alcm. 1.86n. 'Verbs expressing sustained sounds, especially cries of animals, are usually in the Perfect: γέγωνε, 'shouts', βέβρυχε, 'roars', κεκληγώς, λεληκώς, μεμηκώς, μεμυκώς, τετριγώς, ἀμφιαχυῖα' (Monro, Grammar of the Homeric Dialect². 31).

17–18. Cf. Irus' threat to Odysseus, Od. 18.28–9 χαμαὶ δέ κε πάντας ὀδόντας | γναθμῶν ἐξελάσαιμι συὸς ὣς ληϊβοτείρης.

18. μειλίχως μυθεύμενος: cf. Il. 6.343 μύθοισι . . . μειλιχίοισι.

19. εἰ . . . τύχῃ: for the subjunctive cf. Callin. 1.13n.

20. ἄπρηκτον: 'unprofitable' or 'unmanageable': both senses are found in Homer.

21. πλάσαντες γηΐνην: cf. the creation of woman in Hes. Op. 60 ff, esp. 70 ἐκ γαίης πλάσσε κλυτὸς Ἀμφιγυήεις.

22. πηρόν: 'feeble-minded', either neuter or an unparalleled feminine form: for two-termination adjs. in -ρος see Kühner-Blass i. 535.

οὔτε γὰρ κακόν κτλ.: i.e. she is wholly ignorant. The meaning is different at Mimn. 2.4–5: see note there.

25. κακὸν χειμῶνα: cf. Hes. Op. 496 κακοῦ χειμῶνος.

26. δίφρον ἆσσον κτλ.: cf. Od. 19.506 ἀσσοτέρω πυρὸς ἕλκετο δίφρον Ὀδυσσεύς.

27. δύ' ἐν φρεσὶν νοεῖ: cf. Od. 3.26 ἄλλα . . . ἐνὶ φρεσὶ σῇσι νοήσεις.

28. γελᾷ: appropriate to both sea and woman: see Stanford, Greek Metaphor 114–16.

32. οὐκ ἀνεκτός: cf. Il. 10.118 οὐκέτ' ἀνεκτός.

ἐν ὀφθαλμοῖς ἰδεῖν: cf. Od. 10.385 ἐν ὀφθαλμοῖσιν ἰδέσθαι, Callin. 1. 20.

34. ἄπλητον: cf. Hes. Th. 315 ἄπλητον κοτέουσα.

ὥσπερ . . . κύων: cf. Homer's simile at Od. 20.14–15 ὡς δὲ κύων ἀμαλῇσι περὶ σκυλάκεσσι βεβῶσα | ἄνδρ' ἀγνοιήσασ' ὑλάει κτλ.

37–42. Here alone Semonides reverts to the woman's 'parent' and makes an explicit comparison. He may have liked the picture of the 'sea-woman': it is certainly one of his best, and he reaches an Aeschylean grandeur in 40: but 42 is feeble and editors who delete it may be correct.

38. ἀπήμων: cf. Hes. *Op.* 670 πόντος ἀπήμων.
χάρμα . . . μέγα: so *Il.* 24.706 μέγα χάρμα πόλει.

39. θέρεος: probably an iamb rather than a tribrach: cf. 1n. and 43 παλιντριβέος, 74 ἄστεος.

40. βαρυκτύποισι: of Poseidon at Hes. *Th.* 818: cf. 1.1n.

43. †τεσποδιης†: the adjective concealed here can hardly be the otiose 'dusty-grey' (Meineke's σποδείης or the unmetrical πολιῆς).

παλιντριβέος: presumably 'thumped again and again, obstinate'.

45. ἔστερξεν ὧν ἅπαντα: 'puts up with everything after all.' ὧν (for οὖν) is used to mark a contrast with the ass's reluctance expressed in 43–4. See Denniston *G.P.* 421–2.

47. προνύξ, προῆμαρ: both words here only. Homer has πανῆμαρ, *Od.* 13.31.

51–2. An amusing echo of Archilochus' description of Thasos, 18.3–4 οὐ γάρ τι καλὸς χῶρος οὐδ' ἐφίμερος | οὐδ' ἐρατός· οἰζυρόν too reminds us of Archilochus: cf. fr. 54n.

53. ἀληνής: Hsch. ἀληνής· μαινόμενος.

56. ἄθυστα δ' ἱρά: presumably she purloins sacrifices which await consecration on the altar.

57. χαιτέεσσα: so in Phoc.'s imitation, 2.3 ἵππου χαιτηέσσης.

58. περιτρέχει: MSS. περιτρέπει cannot mean 'turn away from' (L.S.J.). Either περιτρέμει (suggested in L.S.J.) or περιτρέχει (Lattimore) would suit a fastidious mare.

61. ἀσβόλην ἀλευμένη: 'since she avoids the soot': the negative οὔτε applies only to ἵζοιτο.

62. ἀνάγκη δ' ἄνδρα ποιεῖται φίλον: Lattimore's interpretation is best (*A. J. Phil.* 65 (1944) 172–3): 'she makes her husband intimate with hard times': Lattimore points to 69–70 which show that the mare-woman is a luxury, and compares 101–2 and Thgn. 351–2: he might have added Semon. 1.10.

65. ἐκτενισμένην: also in Archil. 165 Bergk. In 66 ἐσκιασμένην reminds us of Archil. 25.4.

66. βαθεῖαν: cf. Hes. *Th.* 977 βαθυχαίτης of Aristaeus.

68. τῷ δ' ἔχοντι: 'her husband': cf. 98 ἔχοντι and *Od.* 4.569 ἔχεις Ἑλένην, L.S.J. s.v. A4.

κακόν: so e.g. *Il.* 5.63 (νῆας . . .) αἳ πᾶσι κακὸν Τρώεσσι γένοντο.

69–70. Page (*C.R.* 68 (1954), 106) suspects the lines on the grounds that Semon. elsewhere scans τοῖοῦτος and elsewhere uses the dative -οισι, not -οις, except at 74 ἀνθρώποις. But I can find τοιοῦτος only in the repeated line-ending τοιαύτη γυνή (23,41,67); and since ἀνθρώποις (74) is a genuine exception we may as well admit a second exception nearby. The lines seem very much in character.

71. διακριδόν: cf. *Il.* 12.103 διακριδὸν . . . ἄριστοι.

74. γέλως: cf. Archil. 88.3–4 πολύς | ἀστοῖσι φαίνεαι γέλως.

75. ἐπ᾽ αὐχένα βραχεῖα: cf. ἐπὶ γαστέρα λευκά, ἐπὶ νῶτα μέλαινα in the swallow-song, *P.M.G.* 848.4–5.

76. αὐτόκωλος: hardly 'skin and bone' (L.S.J.), but 'all legs', which forms a coherent picture with ἄπυγος. Cf. 12 αὐτομήτορα, 'her mother all over.' Most editors adopt Bergk's emendation αὐόκωλος, 'with withered legs.'
ἆ τάλας ἀνήρ: cf. Homer's ἆ δειλέ.

78. δήνεα . . . ἐπίσταται: cf. *Il.* 4.361 ἤπια δήνεα οἶδε.

79. οὐδέ οἱ γέλως μέλει: 'nor does she mind being laughed at': cf. 74.

84. προσιζάνει: a word applicable to bees alighting; the choice of words in 85 may be due to the idea of flowers.

87. ὀνομάκλυτον γένος: cf. *h. Merc.* 59 γενεὴν ὀνομακλυτόν.

89. θείη . . . χάρις: cf. *Od.* 2.12 θεσπεσίην δ᾽ ἄρα τῷ γε χάριν κατέχευεν ᾿Αθήνη. For ἀμφιδέδρομεν cf. *Od.* 6.45 λευκὴ δ᾽ ἐπιδέδρομεν αἴγλη, Pi. *P.* 3.39–40 σέλας δ᾽ ἀμφέδραμεν . . . ᾿Αφαίστου.

94–5. These lines have been suspected, but they form the transition from the description of the exceptional bee-woman to the concluding passage, in which Semonides returns to his uncompromising misogyny. If 94–5 are omitted, the γάρ of 96 will introduce a recapitulation of the whole poem.

96–7. Cf. Hes. *Th.* 600–1 ὡς δ᾽ αὔτως ἄνδρεσσι κακὸν θνητοῖσι γυναῖκας | Ζεὺς ὑψιβρεμέτης θῆκεν. Semonides hammers home the point in 115–16.

102. Another line of Aeschylean generosity: cf. 40, 116, 118.

104. μοῖραν . . . χάριν: probably accusatives in apposition with

the whole ὅταν-clause: 'when a man thinks he is at his happiest in his home, thanks to God's dispensation or man's favour.' This use of χάριν was developed until it functioned as a preposition. The origin of the construction may be seen also in Il. 15.743–4 ὅς τις δὲ Τρώων κοίλης ἐπὶ νηυσὶ φέροιτο | σὺν πυρὶ κηλείῳ, χάριν Ἕκτορος ὀτρύναντος . . . For θεοῦ μοῖραν cf. Od. 11.292 θεοῦ . . . μοῖρα, and cf. Callin. 1.9n. Note synecphonesis of ἢ ἀνθρώπου.

107. προφρόνως δεχοίατο: cf. Il. 23.647 πρόφρων δέχομαι.

110. κεχηνότος: his dropped jaw probably denotes incredulity. Semonides draws the veil of silence over the wife's outrageous behaviour.

   οἱ δὲ γείτονες κτλ.: cf. Hes. Op. 701 μὴ γείτοσι χάρματα γήμῃς.

112. τὴν ἦν . . . γυναῖκα: 'his own wife' in contrast with τὴν . . . τοὐτέρου: cf. Il. 12.280 τὰ ἃ κῆλα, Od. 14.153 τὰ ἃ δώματα.

116. Cf. Il. 15.19–20 δεσμὸν . . . ἄρρηκτον, Il. 13.36–7 πέδας . . . ἀρρήκτους.

118. γυναικὸς . . . εἵνεκα: cf. Il. 2.161–2 Ἀργείην Ἑλένην, ἧς εἵνεκα πολλοὶ Ἀχαιῶν | ἐν Τροίῃ ἀπόλοντο, Od. 11.438, Hes. Op. 165–6. There is no good reason for suspecting that this is not the end of the poem: μέν in 117 may be simply emphatic, and we need not assume a δέ- clause which contained the fate of Agamemnon and others. ἀμφιδηριωμένους makes an impressive ending, like αἰκιζοίμεθα in 1.24.

SEMONIDES 29

From Stobaeus 4.34 (περὶ τοῦ βίου ὅτι βραχὺς κτλ.). 28: Σιμωνίδου. The Suda mentions Semonides' elegiacs, and the close resemblance of the thought with Semonides 1 suggests that Bergk was right in attributing the lines to him. Fränkel D.P. 237, n. 14 suggests that they are not earlier than the 5th century and may have formed part of an epitaph later ascribed to Simonides of Ceos.

1. Χῖος . . . ἀνήρ: Homer: cf. h. Ap. 172 τυφλὸς ἀνήρ, οἰκεῖ δὲ Χίῳ ἔνι παιπαλοέσσῃ, referred to by Th. 3.104.4–6; also Theoc. 7.47–8 Χῖον ἀοιδόν.

2. Il. 6.146, the line which formed the starting-point of Mimn. 2.

H

3. οὔασι δεξάμενοι: cf. *Il.* 12.442 οἱ δ᾽ οὔασι πάντες ἄκουον, where οὔασι is quite otiose.

4. στέρνοις ἐγκατέθεντο: cf. *Od.* 23.223 τὴν δ᾽ ἄτην οὐ πρόσθεν ἑῷ ἐγκάτθετο θυμῷ.

6. ἄνθος . . . πολυήρατον ἥβης: cf. *Il.* 13.484 ἔχει ἥβης ἄνθος, *Od.* 15.366 ἥβην πολυήρατον, *h. Ven.* 225, Hes. fr. 76.2 Rzach, and see Thgn. 1070n.

8–9. Cf. Odysseus' words on man's feebleness, *Od.* 18.132–3 οὐ μὲν γάρ ποτέ φησι κακὸν πείσεσθαι ὀπίσσω, | ὄφρ᾽ ἀρετὴν παρέχωσι θεοὶ καὶ γούνατ᾽ ὀρώρῃ.

9. καμάτου: 'sickness', the only early example of this meaning. Fränkel finds in the word an indication that the poem is 5th century or later.

10. νήπιοι: cf. Hes. *Op.* 40 νήπιοι, οὐδὲ ἴσασιν.

13. τῶν ἀγαθῶν: for gen. cf. *Od.* 1.140 χαριζομένη παρεόντων.

τλῆθι: 'hold out', i.e. accept the brevity of youth and life with resignation.

ALCMAN

Alcman is the earliest choral writer from whose work substantial fragments remain. Some 200 lines survive, half in brief quotations and half on papyrus, only a small portion of the six books mentioned in the *Suda*, but sufficient to allow a fascinating, if tantalising, glimpse of early Spartan choral poetry.

The chronology and birthplace of Alcman are disputed, but we can say with confidence that his work was written in Sparta in the middle or second half of the 7th century. The relevant entry in the *Suda* runs, 'he was alive in the 27th Olympiad (672–669), when Ardys, father of Sadyattes (MSS. Alyattes), was king of Lydia.' It looks as though Alcman referred somewhere in his poetry to Ardys, and Ardys' reign, according to the Assyrian records, began in 652. (The dates of his reign in Hdt. are 679–630.) Eusebius supplies two dates for Alcman, 659 and 609 (see Hieronymus, ed. Helm. 94, 98), not utterly incompatible with each other, since Alcman refers to his old age in fr. 26; but the second date is probably due to confusion of Alcman with Alcaeus. Another piece of evidence comes from *P. Oxy.* 2390 fr. 2 col. ii, 14 ff, which shows that Alcman mentioned Leotychidas, king of Sparta, and his son, Hippocratidas: their reigns must belong to the end of the 7th century, if not to the beginning of the 6th: see M. L. West, *C.Q.* n.s. 15 (1965), 188–94.

Ancient scholars debated whether Alcman was born in Sparta or Sardis, and if they could not solve the problem with much or all of his poetry before them, our chances of success are slim. *P. Oxy.* 2389 fr. 9 col. i = *P.M.G.* 13(a), part of a commentary on Alcman, cites an unidentified lyric fragment, ἀντίφαριν Λάκωνι τέ[κτονα or -ι πα]ρθενίων σοφῶν ’Αλκμᾶ[νι. The writer then says that Aristotle and (Crates?) reckoned Alcman to be Lydian, deceived by fr. 16 οὐκ ἦς ἀγρεῖος . . . ἀλλὰ Σαρδίων ἀπ’ ἀκρᾶν. These lines were never free from ambiguity (see notes there), or else there could have been no controversy. The *Suda* says Alcman was a Laconian from Messoa, and that Crates mistakenly made him a Lydian from Sardis; Alexander (?Aetolus) in *A.P.* 7.709, Velleius Paterculus 1.18.2 and Aelian (*V.H.* 12.50) sided with Crates, and the controversy is mentioned by Leonidas of Tarentum and Antipater of Thessalonica (*A.P.* 7.19 and 18) and in *P. Oxy.* 2389 fr. 6 col. i (*P.M.G.* p. 7) and *P. Oxy.* 2506 fr. 1 (= *P.M.G.* 7). Heraclides Ponticus (*Pol.* 2) said that Alcman was the slave of a Spartan named Agesidas, who set him free because he was εὐφυής, 'talented'. The *Suda* says curtly ἀπὸ οἰκετῶν δέ, 'of servile origin.' The evidence for his Lydian birth was inconclusive and remains inconclusive, but perhaps the reluctance of later Greeks to believe that Sparta could ever have produced her own native poets led them to scour his poetry over-zealously for signs of foreign extraction or servile background. Whatever his birthplace, all his work seems to have been composed for performance in Sparta, and it was in Sparta that he was buried (Paus. 3.15.2).

The bibliography of Alcman is confused. According to the *Suda* ἔγραψε βιβλία ἓξ μέλη καὶ κολυμβώσας: either six books, the contents of which were μέλη and the Κολυμβῶσαι, 'Swimming Women', whatever kind of composition that was, or five books of μέλη and a sixth, the Κολυμβῶσαι. Passages are cited from Books I, II, III and V, and we know of a commentary on Book IV, but the absence of any mention of Book VI may be only coincidental. The Louvre-Partheneion, fr. 1, probably belonged to Book I (see 1.1n.), and there may have been two books of partheneia (see fr. 16 introd.). We hear of hymns and wedding-songs, but most of the surviving fragments defy classification. 58 and 59(a) are examples of his love-poetry, a genre of which he was the εὑρετής, according to the *Suda*. Some of the poems were of considerable length: fr. 1 may have had 140 lines, fr. 3 had at least 126 lines.

The grace and gaiety of the scenes Alcman describes fit the picture of 7th century Sparta presented by archaeology and by Terpander's words (if they are his), ἔνθ' αἰχμά τε νέων θάλλει καὶ Μῶσα λίγεια. It was not until much later that Sparta became a forbidding, philistine city: nearly two centuries after Alcman Pindar could still say (fr. 238 Turyn) ἔνθα . . . καὶ χοροὶ καὶ Μοῖσα καὶ Ἀγλαΐα. Alcman's metres are jaunty and often, as far as we know, original, and his work is enlivened by simile and metaphor. But if the surviving fragments are typical, there was a strong provincial, almost parochial, element in his work: his audience may have known the women and the deities he mentions and understood his jokes, but he made no concessions to foreigners or posterity. No writer wrote less καθόλου, more for his own city. But he was fond too of references to obscure foreign tribes, real and fabulous, to the perplexity of scholars: τοσαῦτα καὶ τοιαῦτα ἔθνη καταλέγει ὥστ' ἔτι νῦν τοὺς ἀθλίους γραμματιστὰς ζητεῖν οὗ γῆς ταῦτ' εἶναι κτλ. (Aristides *Or.* 28.54, ii.159 Keil, and still relevant).

The surviving fragments are written for the most part in the Laconian vernacular, not, like most later choral poetry, in a literary language. The only borrowings are from Epic, preponderant in fr. 89, but found sporadically elsewhere, especially when a dactylic rhythm makes them welcome.

The following features of his language might cause difficulty:

α   for Attic ε: ἱαρός, ὄκα (ὅτε).

αι for ει: κυπαιρίσκω, αἴτις (εἴ τις).

η   for ει: γλυκῆα, κήνα (ἐκείνη), τίθη, σηραφόρῳ, and in infins. ἐσθίην.

ι   for ε before vowels: σιός (θεός), ἀργύριον, ὑμνιοισᾶν (ὑμνουσῶν).

οι for ου: φεροίσαις, ἔχοισα.
ω for ου: ὕπνω, ὠρανῶ, Μῶσα, τὼς ἀρίστως, τῶ κυπαιρίσκω.

σ for θ: σανάτω, σιός, παρσένος, ἔσηκε, σάλλει, πόσῳ, πάσον.
σδ for ζ: παίσδει, κιθαρίσδην.
νθ for λθ: ἐνθοῖσα (ἐλθοῦσα).
γλ for βλ: -γλεφάροι, -γλέποι.
σ for ν: παρήσομες (-μεν), ἦς.

Also καβαίνων (κατα-), ὤ (ὡς), ὥπερ (ὥσπερ), ὥτε (ὥστε), τως
(ὥς).

Note: this is an oversimplification, designed to give first aid. A
full account of the dialect may be found in Page, *Alcman: The
Partheneion*, 102–163.

The complete fragments of Alcman are edited with commentary
(in Italian) by A. Garzya, *Alcmane, I Frammenti*, Napoli 1954. For
fr. 1 see Denys L. Page, *Alcman: the Partheneion*, Oxford 1951,
J. A. Davison, *Hermes* 73 (1938), 440–51, M. L. West, 'Alcmanica',
C.Q. n.s. 15 (1965), 194–202. On Alcman's life and works see
J. A. Davison, 'Notes on Alcman', *Proceedings of the IX International
Congress of Papyrology* (Oslo 1958) 30–41.

ALCMAN I

The papyrus was discovered in 1855 at Saqqâra by the French
Egyptologist, Mariette, and is now in the Louvre. It was first
published by Egger in 1863. The handwriting has not been
precisely dated, but may belong to the middle of the 1st century
A.D. The text is in three columns, of which the first (lines 1–34)
has lost its left-hand half, the second (35–68) is in good condition,
the third (69–101) is rubbed away in places. A *coronis*, almost all
that remains of a fourth column, indicates that the poem ended
four lines after 101. How many stanzas are missing at the beginning we cannot say for certain, but it is noteworthy that another
column of 35 lines would bring the total to 140 lines, 10 stanzas of
14 verses each, of which the first 5 stanzas would be devoted to
the invocation and the telling of the legend, the second 5 to the
more light-hearted personal section. If the suggestion is correct,
we must conclude that Alcman spent little time on the legend, the

narration of which is complete (except for the catalogue of dead Hippocoontidae) by the beginning of our fragment.

The spaces above, below and between the columns contain 19 scholia written in two or three hands. These scholia refer to interpretations of the text by three Alexandrian scholars, Aristophanes, Aristarchus and Sosiphanes (if he is correctly identified as the Alexandrian tragedian), by Pamphilus, the glossographer of the 1st century A.D., and by an unknown Stasicles, proof of the attention given to the poem by the ancients. Alcman is not mentioned in the papyrus, but lines 6, 61 and 64–5 are elsewhere ascribed to him, so that the identification of the author is secure.

The occasion of the poem has been much discussed and even on the most important points there is little or no agreement among scholars. My view, explained in the notes, is briefly as follows: the lines are sung by a choir of ten girls (99), related to each other by family ties (52); they are competing with another choir called the Peleiades, either 'Doves' or 'Pleiads' (60), and success in the competition may have depended not only on music and dancing, but on good looks and grooming. The choir's hopes of victory are pinned on their leaders, Hagesichora and Agido, whose praises — Hagesichora's in particular — resound in each of the last five stanzas. The performance was at a festival (81) in honour of the goddess Ortheia (61n.), to whom a plough was offered (61), and of one or more other divinities (82); the festival began at night (62) and culminated at dawn (41–3). Hagesichora, the chorus-leader (44, 85), and Agido, perhaps her second-in-command and leader of a semi-chorus in the dancing, are twice described as occupied in ritual and prayers (41–3, 81–3). The second part of the poem (39–101), with its jocular bantering, is in contrast with the first part, in which the girls sang of the mythical Spartan king, Hippocoon, and his sons, slain for their *hybris* (15 ff, 34 ff). Alcman in his version of the myth seems to have made Castor and Polydeuces the killers, perhaps in collaboration with Heracles, whereas our first connected account of the story puts Heracles in this role.

Metre: The poem is written in 14-line stanzas in a predominantly trochaic rhythm, with dactyls in 13 and 14. Lines 2, 4, 6, 8, sometimes labelled 'enoplian', are aeolic: note the central choriamb and final bacchius. (The rhythm is used in *P.M.G.* 976 δέδυκε μὲν ἀ σελάννα.) The 'alcaic decasyllable' (the last line of *three* stanzas: lines 49, 63, 77), familiar as the last line of the 'alcaic stanza', is cognate: $-\cup\cup-\cup\cup-\overset{\cup\ \cup}{\vdots}\cup--$. The pattern ab ab ab ab cc dd ef is not incompatible with the supposition that the poem is in triadic structure, with strophe (1–4), antistrophe (5–8) and epode (9–14), but it does not prove triadic structure as the pattern abcd abcd eeffgh would. Note $\cup\cup$ for – in 2 ἀλέγω, 32 Ἀΐδας, 56 διαφαδαν, – for $\cup\cup$ in 6 Εὐτείχη, 77 Ἀγησιχορα, 90 Ἀγησιχορας 91 ἰρῆνας. There is synecphonesis at 50 ἦ οὐχ, synizesis at 69 ἰανογλεφάρων, 98 σιαί. Full metrical detail may be found in Page 23.

1. Πωλυδεύκης: who killed the sons of the Spartan king Hippocoon, ten of whom are listed in 3–11? Polydeuces (with Castor and their father Tyndareus) or Heracles or both? The mention of Polydeuces immediately before the catalogue of dead warriors suggests that it was the Tyndaridae who killed their cousins, the Hippocoontidae, but in later versions of the story (see below) it was Heracles who killed them to avenge his cousin Oeonus, whom they had murdered. Of Heracles there is no mention in what survives of Alcman's poem, but we can say with some certainty that he too figured in Alcman's version: Clement of Alexandria (*Protr.* 36) tells us that Sosibius, who wrote a commentary on Alcman, said Heracles was wounded in the hand by the Hippocoontidae, and the scholiast on the passage reports, 'Alcman mentions it in Book I' — most probably in this poem.

Tyndareus and his sons had good reason for fighting, since he had been exiled by Hippocoon when their father Oebalus died. On Apollo's throne at Amyclae, described by Pausanias (3.18.11), he was depicted fighting against Eurytus (mentioned by Alcman, 1.9); and after the battle Heracles made him king of Sparta in place of Hippocoon. A second reason is known for their quarrel: the Hippocoontidae were ἀντιμνηστῆρες, rival suitors, of the Tyndaridae (so Euphorion in his *Thrax*, according to the

scholiast on Clement): this explains why the moral of
Alcman's tale is that man must not fly to heaven nor try to
marry Aphrodite ... or a Porcid (15–19): the Tyndaridae,
sons of Zeus, might, but not the Hippocoontidae.

So both the Tyndaridae and Heracles fought in Alcman's
version, but whether he made them allies or made the
Tyndaridae the principal figures we cannot say. By introducing the Tyndaridae Alcman uses or invents a version
of the story in which Sparta emerges from the encounter
with more credit; the other version may have been
intended to strengthen the claim of Heracles' descendants
to the Spartan throne.

The myth is told in Diodorus Siculus 4.33 (the first connected account), Apollodorus 2.7.3, 3.10.4–5, Pausanias
3.15.3 ff. For full details of the sources see Davison 441–3.

2. οὐ μόνο]ν Λύκαισον: 'I sing not only Lycaethus among the
dead, but ...' Lycaethus was one of the Deritidae,
according to the scholiast here: he was therefore a distant
relative of the Hippocoontidae, since Derites was cousin to
Oebalus, the father of Hippocoon and Tyndareus (Paus.
3.1.3, 7.18.5). Apollodorus 3.10.5 names Lycaethus as one
of the sons of Hippocoon, perhaps confused by the present
passage. οὐ μόνον seems to have been in the scholiast's
text; the usual supplement, οὐκ ἐγών, is derived from the
scholiast on Pi. *O.* 11.15 ἀλέγων· ὑμνῶν. καὶ ’Αλκμάν (codd.
’Αλκαῖος)· οὐκ ἐγὼ Λύκον ἐν Μούσαις ἀλέγω, a garbled
version of our line. With οὐκ ἐγών tr. 'I pay no heed to L.
among the dead' rather than 'I do not number L. among
the dead': the scholium here is difficult to interpret, but it
seems to run, 'I do not number L. with the Hippocoontidae.'

καμοῦσιν 'the dead', as in *Il.* 3.278–9 καμόντας ἀνθρώπους,
23.72 εἴδωλα καμόντων (so *Od.* 11.476, 24.14).

3. ’Εναρσφόρον: Plutarch *Thes.* 31 says that Tyndareus entrusted
his baby daughter Helen to Theseus and Pirithous to protect her from E.'s violence. Cf. Hes. *Sc.* 192, where Ares is
ἐναρσφόρος, 'wearer of spoils'.

4. There is no certainty over the supplements of proper names

in 4, 5 and 9. In 4 Ἄλκιμον, Βώκολον and Ἱππόθων are possible, in 5 these three and perhaps Δορκέα, in 9 Σκαῖον and Δορκεα. The names are from Paus. 3.15.1 and Apollod. 3.10.5.

βιατάν: not in Homer; Pindar has it several times, e.g. *Pae.* 6.61 of Achilles.

5. κορυστάν: cf. *Il.* 13.201 δύω Αἴαντε κορυστά.

6. Quoted in *Anec. Ox.* Cramer I. 158.31 ff for the accentuation of Εὐτείχης: the adjective is εὐτειχής.

Ἀρήιον: the scholiast cites Pherecydes for the form Ἀρήιτος.

7. No available name fits the gap: the correct supplement will begin with a vowel (since the previous line ends with a consonant), end in -α, and provide a dactyl.

ἡμισίων: see Callin. 1.19n. With ἔξοχον cf. *Il.* 18.56 ἔξοχον ἡρώων.

8. We probably need a genitive plural before τὸν ἀγροτάν: cf. A. *Pers.* 1002 ἀγρόται στρατοῦ, Hsch. ἀγρέταν· ἡγεμόνα. But 8–9 may be supplemented in other ways.

9. Σκαῖον: mentioned by Hdt. 5.60 as well as by Apollodorus.

10. Perhaps 'amid the tumult of blind Ares', but the supplement is insecure. Ἄρεος will have to be scanned – ∪. With ἂν . . . κλόνον cf. *Il.* 16.331, 713 κατὰ κλόνον. πῶρος is explained by Hesychius as 'miserable' (= ταλαίπωρος), by *Suda* as 'blind': cf. S. fr. 754 N² τυφλὸς . . . Ἄρης.

11. Ἄλκωνα: the only available name which fits the metre.

12. παρήσομες: 'we shall pass over.'

13. Αἶσα: αἶσα is one's portion in life, and, personified, the goddess who allots it, like Μοῖρα. παντῶν: the accents here and throughout (e.g. 14 γεραιτάτοι) conform to the rules of Doric accentuation laid down by the ancient grammarians.

14. Πόρος: the scholiast's mention of Πόρος guarantees the restoration of his name to the text here or in the following line. When the scholiast identifies him with Hesiod's Χάος (*Th.* 116 ff), he may mean only that Πόρος and Αἶσα are 'the oldest gods' for Alcman, just as Chaos came first in Hesiod's cosmogony; but γεραιτάτοι may have meant simply 'most reverend': a fragmentary commentary on one of Alcman's poems (*P. Oxy.* 2390 fr. 2 col. iii = *P.M.G.* 5)

tells us that in his account of creation matter was first
organised by Thetis: only then did Πόρος appear 'like a
beginning', followed by Τέκμωρ, 'like an end'; there too
Πόρος seems to be described as πρέσγυς, and he was
probably thought of as 'the Contriver', 'the Way and
Means.' In the present passage he is linked with Αἶσα; his
name may have been connected with * πόρω (cf. πορεῖν,
'give'; πέπρωται, 'it is fated').

15. ἀπέδιλος ἀλκά: usually taken as a unit, 'valour is unshod',
but the explanations ('the power of Destiny is swift to
strike', 'the strength of man is without firm base', 'the
valour of the Hippocoontidae was without foundation')
illustrate the difficulty of the phrase. Page takes the words
with the following line: 'let not the bravery of man leave
the ground and soar to heaven': ἀπέδιλος, 'without
walking shoes' is linked with ποτήσθω, and ἀλκά has the
genitive it desiderates. ἀπέδιλος is found elsewhere only in
A. Pr. 135 σύθην δ' ἀπέδιλος ὄχῳ πτερωτῷ, where the shoe-
lessness is a sign of haste as it is at Theoc. 24.36.

17. Some such attempt 'to marry Aphrodite ... or a Porcid'
must have been made by the Hippocoontidae, since the
words are too specific to stand for a general reference to
hybris.

18. Page notes ἢ θιῶν as a possible alternative to Blass's
Κυπρίαν.

19. Another goddess must be named at the beginning of the line.
Πόρκω: Hesychius s.v. Νηρεύς says Alcman calls Nereus
Πόρκος. Page argues most convincingly that Porcus was a
primitive Laconian sea-god, and points to the word
πόρκος, explained as a fishing-net in Hesychius. Alcman
cannot have equated him with Nereus, however, since
Nereus' daughter Thetis was notoriously the bride of a
mortal. His reference to Porcus suggests that he did not
hesitate to mention a deity who was either obscure or
extremely provincial.

20. Χάριτες: Pausanias (3.14.6, 3.18.6) tells us that the Graces
were worshipped at Sparta, where they shared a temple
with the Dioscuri, and that Alcman called them Φαέννα

and *Κλήτα*. The sense here must be that the Graces protect the inhabitants of Zeus' house, and Page's suggestion *ἀμφιέπουσιν* fits nicely; but this function of the Graces is not known elsewhere, and Pi. *O.* 14.9–10 ἀλλὰ πάντων ταμίαι | ἔργων ἐν οὐρανῷ, which Page quotes, hardly shows the Graces as protectresses of the all-powerful Olympians from presumptuous mortals, but rather as 'stewards' of heavenly feasting and dancing. Indeed one might have expected the Graces, particularly if *ἐρογλεφάροι*, to make Aphrodite or a Porcid still more seductive.

21. *ἐρογλεφάροι*: 'whose eyes look love'; so Hes. *Th.* 910 τῶν (sc. Χαρίτων) καὶ ἀπὸ βλεφάρων ἔρος εἴβετο δερκομενάων.

22–34. Little can be made of these lines. They may have contained Alcman's conclusion of the story of the Hippocoontidae, driving home the moral of 16–21, or they may have provided a second example, treated less fully, of the punishment of *hybris*: Diels suggested that the Gods and Giants were the combatants.

31. *μαρμάρῳ μυλάκρῳ*: cf. the *μύλακες* used as missiles at *Il.* 12.161. Stones and arrows are mentioned together at *Il.* 3.80. A stone hurled by Patroclus in *Il.* 16.734–5 is described as *μάρμαρος*.

34–5. 'They suffered unforgettably, having devised evil.' The word-order suggests that *ἄλαστα . . . Ϝέργα* be taken together as object of *πάσον*: cf. *Il.* 18.77 παθέειν τ' ἀεκήλια ἔργα, but also *Od.* 24.199 κακὰ μήσατο ἔργα.

36. 'There is such a thing as the gods' vengeance.'

37–9. For the thought cf. Solon's answer to Croesus, who considered himself *ὀλβιώτατος* (Hdt. 1.30–32).

ὁ δ' ὄλβιος: cf. Pi. *O.* 7.10 ὁ δ' ὄλβιος, ὃν φᾶμαι κατέχοντ' ἀγαθαί, h. *Hom.* 25.4–5, 30.7–8.

εὔφρων: 'in wisdom' rather than 'happy'.

ἀμέραν διαπλέκει: 'weaves to the end the web of his life': the same metaphor in Pi. *N.* 7.98–100 βίοτον . . . διαπλέκοις | εὐδαίμον' ἐόντα, Hdt. 5.92. ζ. 1 διαπλέξαντος τὸν βίον εὖ: other examples in L.S.J. s.v. *διαπλέκω*. There seems to be no exact parallel for this use of *ἡμέρα*, although L.S.J.I. 2

gives examples with adjectives where ἡμέρα denotes a state
or time of life, e.g. S. *Tr.* 654 ἐπίπονος ἡμέρα.

ἄκλαυτος: 'unweeping', active as at *Od.* 4.494; 'unwept' e.g.
at *Il.* 22.386.

39–40. Alcman passes abruptly from the myth and the moralising
to the secular part of his poem. Note that the choir refer to
themselves sometimes in the singular (as here, ἐγών),
sometimes in the plural (as 41 ἅμιν).

40. τὸ φῶς: 'the brightness, radiance' of Agido. Cf. *Il.* 6.401 of
the baby Astyanax, ἀλίγκιον ἄστερι καλῷ, Alcm. 3.66–7 of
Astymeloisa, ὤ τις αἰγλάεντος ἀστήρ ὠρανῶ διαιπετής,
Sapph. 16.18 ἀμάρυχμα λάμπρον ἴδην προσώπω. The image
of light and the comparison to the sun in 41 are the more
striking for the contrast they make with the gloom of the myth.

41. F': i.e. Fε, 'her.'

ὤτε: Doric for ὥστε. 'I see her as the sun, which Agido asks
to shine on us as our witness.' We gather that the ceremony
took place just before sunrise. With μαρτύρεται cf. A. *Eum.*
643 ὑμᾶς δ' ἀκούειν ταῦτ' ἐγώ μαρτύρομαι.

42–3. οὔτ' ἐπαινῆν οὔτε μωμήσθαι: i.e. 'not to mention at all'. So
at *Il.* 10.249 μήτ' ἄρ με μάλ' αἴνεε μήτε τι νείκει.

ἁ κλεννὰ χοραγός: i.e. Hagesichora, called χοροστάτις at 84.
νιν is of course Agido. Hagesichora is the more important
figure: her praises are sung here and in each of the remaining stanzas (51 ff, 77 ff, 90 f and most probably
101 ff). Agido, commended again at 50 f and obliquely at
58 f and mentioned at 80 ff, seems to have been Hagesichora's assistant, and may have led one of the semi-
choruses in the dancing: an opaque marginal comment
opposite 48–9 seems to run αἱ π(ρὸς) τῇ(ς) Ἀγιδο(ῦς)
τοῦτ[ο . . . .] οτα αἱ π(ρὸς) τῇ(ς) Ἀγησιχό(οας) and to
indicate a division into semi-choruses.

45. δοκεῖ γὰρ ἤμεν κτλ.: 'for she herself appears supreme', rather
than the teasing 'she herself thinks she is supreme'. The
girls do not doubt her supremacy.

46. ἐκπρεπής: used by Homer in *Il.* 2.483 ἐκπρεπέ' ἐν πολλοῖσι
of Agamemnon, supreme as a bull among heifers. The
passage was doubtless in Alcman's mind.

τώς: the demonstrative adverb answered by ὥπερ, Doric for ὥσπερ.

47. βοτοῖς: 'grazing beasts', probably cattle and sheep.

48. Homeric reminiscence is strong in this dactylic sequence: cf. *Il.* 9.123-4 ἵππους | πηγοὺς ἀθλοφόρους, *Certamen* 100 καναχήποδες ἵπποι. The horse is the symbol of proud beauty in *Il.* 6.506 ff ὡς δ' ὅτε τις στατὸς ἵππος κτλ. of Paris. For women likened to horses see Semon. 7.57 ff, Ar. *Lys.* 1308 ff, Anacr. 417. Representations of horses are common among the votive offerings found on the site of the temple of Artemis Ortheia at Sparta: see Davison 455-6.

49. τῶν ... ὀνείρων: a quasi-partitive genitive, 'one of those dream-horses.' For visions larger or lovelier than life Page compares A. *Pers.* 183 ff, Ap. Rhod. 2.205 f, (Theocr.) 9.16 f.

ὑποπετριδίων: for ὑποπτεριδίων by metathesis, according to *Et. Mag.* 783.20. But the scholiast connects it with πέτρα and quotes *Od.* 24.11–12: the dreams are those of siestas taken under a shady rock.

50. ἦ οὐχ ὁρῇς; 'why, don't you see?'

ὁ μὲν κέλης κτλ.: 'the courser is Venetic, but the hair of my cousin H. has the bloom of pure gold.' The use of μέν ... δέ makes it clear that 'my cousin H.' is contrasted with 'the courser', who must therefore be Agido. That Agido is the courser when H. was the ἵππος in the lines immediately preceding is surprising, but the chorus may have used gestures to make the identification plain. Agido is metaphorically a horse in 58–9.

51. Ἐνητικός: two peoples called Ἐνετοί were known to the Greeks, those of Paphlagonia, known to Homer for their wild mules (*Il.* 2.851–2), and those of the northern Adriatic, whose horses were famous from the 5th century onwards. See R. L. Beaumont, *J.H.S.* 56 (1936), 191 ff. The form Ἐνητικός is warranted by the metre: for the long second syllable cf. Hesiod's Μακηδόνα for Μακεδόνα (fr. 5.2) and the Homeric τιθήμεναι for τιθέμεναι, obviating sequences of short syllables.

χαίτα: used by Homer for both a horse's mane and human hair.

52. ἀνεψιᾶς: the girls may all have been blood-relations; but ἀνεψιά may mean only a member of the same ἀγέλη or choir: cf. Hsch. κάσιοι· οἱ ἐκ τῆς αὐτῆς ἀγέλης ἀδελφοί τε καὶ ἀνεψιοί. καὶ ἐπὶ θηλειῶν οὕτως ἔλεγον Λάκωνες.

53. ἐπανθεῖ: cf. Alcm. 90.1 ὄρος ἀνθέον ὕλᾳ, and of hair Ar. Vesp. 1064–5, Eccles. 903. ἄνθος means basically 'that which rises to the surface': see 26.3. Here, however, ἐπανθεῖ must refer to the sheen of her hair.

54. χρυσὸς ... ἀκήρατος: so Archil. 51 (Mon. Par.) IA. 48–9, Simon. 592.

55. ἀργύριον: an unexpected epithet, used by Sappho 34 of the moon. Pindar called the Muses ἀργύρεαι, according to the Emperor Julian Ep. 18: but Julian's statement is probably based on Pi. P. 11. 41–2 μισθοῖο ... φωνὰν ὑπάργυρον and I. 2.8 ἀργυρωθεῖσαι πρόσωπα ... ἀοιδαί, where Pindar refers to poets' fees.

56. διαφάδαν: only here and Sol. 25.1 διαφάδην ὀνειδίσαι. There is probably aposiopesis after 55: instead of continuing the catalogue, the chorus cry, 'Why do I tell you in plain words? This is H.' Perhaps they point to her.

58. ἁ δὲ δευτέρα κτλ.: a vexed passage. I translate, 'but the second after Agido in beauty will run like a Colaxaean horse against an Ibenian': i.e. Agido and her superior H. far outstrip their rivals. γάρ in 60 explains the relevance of this remark: another choir, the Pleiads, is competing against them; and γάρ of 64 gives further explanation: the singers lack rich ornaments and do not count Nanno and others among their members: their hopes are pinned on H. (77). Of other interpretations those which equate ἁ ... δευτέρα with Hagesichora are ruled out by μέν ... δέ and by the whole tenor of the poem, which clearly makes H. superior to Agido, not second to her. An ancient commentary (P. Oxy. 2389. fr. 6.i.1 ff) tortured the Greek by taking Ἀγιδώ as nominative and πεδά as an adverb, 'Agido, in second place after.'

59. The provenance of the horses is uncertain, and was debated by the ancient commentators: Κολαξαῖος is probably

Scythian, since a king Colaxais of Scythia is mentioned by Hdt. 4.5–7: see G. Devereux, *C.Q.* 15 (1965), 176–84. For the Ibenians cf. Stephanus of Byzantium Ἰβαῖοι· οἱ καὶ Ἰβηνοί, ἔθνος Κελτικῆς. Ἰβηνοὶ δ'εἰσὶ καὶ Λυδιάς, οἱ καὶ Ἰαονῖται λέγονται. The commentator in *P. Oxy.* 2389, fr. 6.i.1 ff mentions the view that the Ibeni are a Lydian people and that this is evidence of Alcman's Lydian origin. Aristarchus, according to the same source, said that both breeds of horses were swift but the Ibenian the swifter.

δραμήται seems to govern the dative Ἰβηνῷ with the sense 'run against, compete with', by analogy with verbs like μάχεσθαι, ἀγωνίζεσθαι.

60. ταὶ Πεληάδες κτλ.: no part of the poem tells us more about the circumstances of its performance, and no part has been more diversely construed. I take it that the Pleiads, who 'fight against us', are a rival choir, and that the battle-metaphor of 65 ἀμύναι, 77 τηρεῖ and perhaps 91 ἰρήνας ἐρατᾶς ἐπέβαν begins, aptly enough, with μάχονται. Πεληάδες may mean either 'Doves' or 'Pleiads', but the comparison with Sirius (62–3) makes the latter more likely. The competition between the choirs will be won not only by singing and dancing, but by the appearance of the girls — their finery and their good looks (64–76); we need not suppose that the girls raced against each other too: Alcman's races are metaphorical only.

According to another interpretation of the passage, the actual Pleiads, the star-cluster, are the enemy of the chorus, in which case 64–76 will refer to magic used to avert their hostility. But it is difficult to see in what sense the Pleiads are hostile either to the choir or to the populace. Lastly, the scholiasts in the Louvre papyrus and in *P. Oxy.* 2389. fr. 6.ii took 'the doves' to be Hagesistrata and Agido; but ἀμιν . . . μάχονται is hardly explicable on this view.

61. Ὀρθρίᾳ: probably 'Dawn-goddess': cf. 87 Ἀώτι, which may mean something similar, even although ὄρθρος and ἕως are not identical (cf. X. *An.* 4.3.8–9). The identity of the

goddess is disclosed by the ancient comment in the Louvre
papyrus: 'Ορθία φᾶρος· Σωσιφάνης ἄροτρον, i.e. a φᾶρος
(explained by Sosiphanes as 'plough') for Ortheia. (The
form 'Ορθία is not known from inscriptions before Trajan's
reign, although it is regularly found in our MS. tradition.)
Ortheia's name may not however be imported into the text
in place of 'Ορθρία, since the second syllable of the trisyllabic forms of her name used in the 7th and 6th centuries is always long, αι or ει. (For details see Davison
457–8, Page 77–8.) Ortheia's name may well have been
mentioned at the beginning of the poem, or the commentator may have known 'Αῶτις as her cult-title.

Ortheia was a goddess of fertility and vegetation, in
whose worship girls played an important part; she was later
identified with Artemis, but the identification may not have
existed in the 7th century. Her shrine at Sparta was
excavated in 1906–1910 (see *Artemis Orthia, J.H.S. Suppl.* 5,
1929, ed. R. M. Dawkins), and the popularity of her cult
was demonstrated by the rich finds of votive offerings, e.g.
more than 15,000 lead figurines of the 7th century and
earlier. Why she should be the Dawn-Goddess is not clear,
however.

ορθρίαι (the form in which the word appears in our text)
may be taken as nominative plural with ταὶ Πεληάδες, but
it sits uneasily near νύκτα δι' ἀμβροσίαν; besides, the
dative 'Ορθρίᾳ fits more tidily into the unit ἆμιν 'Ορθρίᾳ
φᾶρος φεροίσαις.

φᾶρος: 'robe' or 'plough'? Robes are common offerings, e.g.
to Athena in Troy (*Il.* 6.302–3) and in Athens, and to Hera
at Olympia (Paus. 5.16.3). But the word ἄροτρον is written
over φᾶρος in our text, and Sosiphanes, according to the
scholiast, took it to mean 'plough', as in Antim. fr. 119
Wyss: cf. Call. fr. 287 Pfeiffer. The plough would be an
appropriate dedication to a goddess of vegetation, although
in fact no ploughs were found among the dedications to
Ortheia. Besides, Sosiphanes may have had knowledge of
the ceremony from another source: if he did not, it was
perverse of him to give the meaning 'plough'.

62. νύκτα δι' ἀμβροσίαν: another Homeric borrowing (cf. *Il.* 10.41 νύκτα δι' ἀμβροσίην) in the dactylic sequence: cf. 48n.

Σήριον ἄστρον: Σήριον is adj. as in Hes. *Op.* 417 Σείριος ἀστήρ. The rival choir has the brilliance of Sirius, the brightest star in the sky, and perhaps its menace too, since Sirius was regarded as baleful. For the heat of the 'dog days' (Sirius is Orion's dog, *Il.* 22.29) cf. Hes. *Op.* 582 ff, Alc. 347. The simile, 'rising like Sirius through the ambrosial night', may well have been suggested by the choir's name: it was unlikely to be used of the star-group itself, since the Pleiads were few and faint (Arat. *Phen.* 264 ὀλίγαι καὶ ἀφεγγέες). For the simile cf. 3.66–7.

63. ἀνηρομέναι: υ is substituted for Ϝ in the MS. tradition of Alcaeus and Sappho also. The meaning may be 'riding in the sky' rather than 'rising': cf. E. *Alc.* 450 ἀειρομένας παννύχου σελάνας. αἴρω is used of the sun rising in S. *Phil.* 1331.

μάχονται: the word is nowhere else used of competition which involves no form of fighting: it is used of a boxing-match at *Il.* 23.621 οὐ γὰρ πύξ γε μαχήσεαι or of the pancratium in Pi. *O.* 8.58. But the metaphorical use is not hard to accept here, if the two choirs were competing for the victor's prize. Cf. 60n.

64. οὔτε γάρ κτλ.: this stanza lists the assets which the singers do not themselves possess, and culminates in the last line, ἀλλ' Ἀγησιχόρα με τηρεῖ. For the negative phrases leading to ἀλλά cf. Alcm. 16. Here we might have expected a 1st pers. pronoun, 'We have neither sufficient purple to ward them off': the pronoun is delayed till 77.

65. κόρος: 'abundance' rather than 'surfeit': so at Hes. *Th.* 593, Heraclit. fr. 111 D.-K.

66. δράκων: probably a bracelet in snake form, ποικίλος as being enamelled or as having engraved patterns. For snakes in Ortheia's cult cf. the ivory plaque of the winged goddess with a snake hanging from her wrist (*Art. Orth.* 206, Pl. 92.2) and votive snakes in ivory (240, Pl. 170.2) and bone (242, Pl. 173.2).

67. οὐδέ after οὔτε gives the effect of climax, 'nor yet': Denniston *G.P.* 193.

μίτρα: a cap or head-band worn by women: cf. Sapph. 98(a).10–11 μιτράναν...ποικίλαν ἀπὺ Σαρδίων, 98(b)1–3, E. *Ba.* 833, *Hec.* 924. Pindar can use Λυδία μίτρα metaphorically of an epinician ode in Lydian mode (*N.* 8.15), since the μίτρα was worn by victors (e.g. *O.* 9.84).

68. Λυδία: Lydia was the centre of fashion for Sappho too: cf. ἀπὺ Σαρδίων in 67n. above, and Sapph. 39.2–3 ποίκιλος μάσλης ('shoe') ... Λύδιον κάλον ἔργον. Xenoph. 3.1 spoke of luxurious habits learned from the Lydians.

69. ἰανογλεφάρων: probably 'dark-eyed': cf. Hesiod in *Pap. Mich.* 11, 13 ἰάνοφρυς. Hesychius and the *Suda* connect ἰανοκρήδεμνος with ἴα, violets. See Taillardat, *Rev. Phil.* 27 (1953), 131–4. For the compound cf. 21 ἐρογλεφάροι.

ἄγαλμα: cf. Alc. 357.3–4 λόφοι ... κεφάλαισιν ἀνδρῶν ἀγάλματα.

70–6. The list continues with no interruption or change of construction, and we must assume that the girls mentioned here would be stalwart fighters, if only they were choir-members: but they are no more available than the sufficiency of purple, the golden snake or the Lydian headband. Other views are that the first four girls, Nanno, Areta, Sylacis, Cleësisera, are present (but not beautiful enough ὥστ' ἀμύναι), the other four, Astaphis, Philylla, Damareta, Vianthemis, absent; or that all eight girls are choir-members (but ineffectual in the fight) and together with Hagesichora and Agido make up the δεκάς (see 99n.).

71. ἀλλ' οὐδ': 'nor again': for the progressive use of ἀλλά see Denniston *G.P.* 21–2.

σιειδής: the Homeric θεοειδής.

73. ἐς Αἰνησιμβρότας: 'to A.'s house.' She may have been mother or trainer of the four girls named in 74–6.

φασεῖς: the future, like the optatives γένοιτο (74) and ποτιγλέποι (75), shows that the four girls are not part of the choir. The second person seems to generalise, though ἐνθοῖσα is feminine.

75. ποτιγλέποι: 'may she look upon me', perhaps as a protectress: but the precise sense is uncertain.

77. τηρεῖ: it is not clear whether the papyrus has τειρει or τηρει; the commentary on this passage in *P. Oxy.* 2389, 7(b) 3, 11 has τείρει. But τείρει makes no sense, and since in the old Laconian orthography *E* stood for *E*, *EI* and *H*, we must read τηρεῖ, which gives precisely the meaning the battle-metaphor requires.

78. καλλίσφυρος: a regular Homeric epithet, e.g. *Il.* 9.557, 560, *Od.* 5.333.

79. πάρ' = πάρεστι.
    αὐτεῖ: for αὐτοῦ, as the scholiast says.

80. ἴκταρ: only here with dative, if the supplement is correct, but ἐγγύς and πλησίον may have either genitive or dative.

81. θωστήρια: scholiast ἑορτ[ή: cf. Hsch. θωστήρια· εὐωχητήρια καὶ ὄνομα ⟨ἑορτῆς?⟩. Probably connected with θῶσθαι, 'to feast', θώς 'jackal', the devourer, θοίνη 'feast'. The religious ceremony must have included a banquet.
    ἅμ' (note ā) = ἡμέτερα.

82. τᾶν: i.e. Hagesichora and Agido, who are probably praying (and commending the festival to the gods, 81?) while the choir sings.
    σιοί: which deities? Ilithyia's temple was near Ortheia's, and objects bearing the name Ἐλευθία were found inside Ortheia's precinct, but the figures of unknown male deities also appear on the votive offerings. See Davison 455.

83. ἄνα = ἄνυσις, 'fulfilment'; elsewhere only in A. *Sept.* 713, Call. *Hymn. Jov.* 90 (with ἄ-).

84. τέλος: 'consummation': cf. Pi. *O.* 13.104–5 ἐν θεῷ γε μάν | τέλος, A. *Ag.* 973 Ζεῦ Ζεῦ τέλειε, τὰς ἐμὰς εὐχὰς τέλει, Sol. 1.58n.
    χοροστάτις: probably nominative used for vocative: see Kühner-Gerth i. p. 48. Hagesichora is meant: cf. 44 ἁ κλεννὰ χοραγός. χοροστάτις, fem. of χοροστάτης, occurs here only.

85. ἐγὼν μέν ... ἐγὼν δέ: the sense is 'I am only a poor singer, but such as I am I wish most to please Aotis'. For anaphora with μέν ... δέ see Denniston *G.P.* 370. But the true apodosis to ἐγὼν μὲν αὐτά is ἐξ Ἁγησιχόρας δέ, so that ἐγὼν δὲ ... ἔγεντο is parenthetic and μέν in τᾷ μὲν Ἀώτι

is *solitarium*. If the antithesis were between τᾷ μὲν ᾿Αώτι and ἐξ ῾Α. δέ, Alcman would imply that Hagesichora was the stronger.

86. θράνω: a roof-beam.

λέλακα: probably perfect tense with present meaning. λάσκω is used by Homer of the falcon (*Il.* 22.141) and Scylla (*Od.* 12.85), in *h. Merc.* 145 of dogs, and by Hesiod of the nightingale caught by the hawk (*Op.* 207). Semon. 7.15 uses it of the bitch-woman.

87. γλαῦξ: for the owl's unpleasant song cf. Ar. *Av.* 261 κικκαβαῦ, *Lys.* 760–1, Theoc. 1.136.

᾿Αώτι: 'Dawn-goddess' as ᾿Ορθρίᾳ: cf. 61n. The epithet may have a local sense, 'dwelling in the East', by analogy with Δερεᾶτις, Λιμνᾶτις, Καρυᾶτις, etc. It is found only here, and does not help to identify the goddess in whose honour the ceremony is held.

88. Ϝανδάνην: cf. Alcm. 45 Ϝάδοι Διὸς δόμῳ χορὸς ἁμὸς καὶ τοί, Ϝάναξ, 56.2 σιοῖσι Ϝάδη . . . ἑορτά.

πόνων κτλ.: 'for she has in the past been the healer of our troubles', probably troubles in general, rather than particular sufferings (e.g. in the second Messenian War). The πόνοι will hardly be the choir's labour of preparing for the ceremony, labour 'healed' by victories; and the victories are in any case due to Hagesichora (91n.), not to Aotis.

89. ἰάτωρ: only here. Homer and Pindar have ἰατήρ. For the gender cf. A. *Ag.* 111 χερὶ πράκτορι.

ἔγεντο: the aorist (by syncope for ἐγένετο: cf. Alcm. 139 κέντο for κένετο = κέλετο) as in 91 ἐπέβαν denotes what has often been observed to happen in the past.

90. ἐξ ῾Αγησιχόρας κτλ. 'thanks to H. girls have trodden upon the path of lovely peace.' This presumably means that H. has before now been χοραγός of winning choirs: the battle-metaphor which began in 63 μάχονται still persists, and it provides the last words of three consecutive stanzas, μάχονται, τηρεῖ, ἰρήνας ἐρατᾶς ἐπέβαν. It is strange, however, that Alcman spoke of 'peace' rather than of 'victory'.

ἐπέβᾱν: 3rd plur. 2 aor. act. of ἐπιβαίνω: cf. *Od.* 23.52 εὐφροσύνης ἐπιβῆτον.

92–101. The ink of the papyrus is badly faded in the middle of these lines, but they obviously explained why H. was so successful: as the trace-horse steers the chariot and the helmsman the ship, so H. steers the choir in its dancing. Homer uses the same images in *Il.* 23.316–18.

92. σηραφόρῳ: the trace-horses were the important ones in a four-horse chariot, and the right-hand horse especially required strength for the left-hand turns: cf. A. *Ag.* 842, 1640.

93. Supplement is quite uncertain. If αὐτῶς is correct, it may govern the dative τῷ σηραφόρῳ: Page suggests αὐτῶς ἐδάην στρέφεσθαι, 'for I have learnt to turn about just like my trace-horse (viz. Hagesichora).'

95. κἠν νᾱῒ gives good sense, but it is difficult to see the point of the scholiast's remark νᾱῒ νᾱι (i.e. νᾳ̂) ʼΑρι . . . , which implies that Aristophanes of Byzantium or perhaps Aristarchus took νᾶι as a monosyllable.

96. ἁ δέ: it is uncertain whether this is Hagesichora or the Chorus. Page makes it refer to the Chorus (παίδων δεκὰς ᾅδ' of 99), and treats 98–9 as a parenthesis, so that μέν (97) is answered by δέ (100), and ἁ δέ (101) introduces a new subject, as it ought — Hagesichora. He translates (p. 22), 'More tuneful than the Sirens (are we not) — for they are goddesses. and we but children ten, in place of eleven — yet we sing sweetly as a swan upon the streams of Xanthus: but she, with her lovely yellow tresses, (Hagesichora, . . .).' But, even if μέν and δεκάς are correct supplements, the explanation of ἁ δέ (96) can hardly be postponed till the appearance of δεκάς in 99, where in any case δεκάς is part of a parenthesis. I prefer to translate his text, 'And she (Hagesichora) is admittedly not more melodious than the Sirens, for they are goddesses; but this 'decade' sings as excellently as eleven girls: it sings like the swan on the waters of Xanthus; and she (Hagesichora) with her lovely yellow tresses (is a fitting leader of so fine a choir and will bring us victory.)' If the tone is less modest than at 85–7, this is not inappropriate at the end of the song; and the

choir at 85–7 were contrasting their individual feebleness
(αὐτά) with the prowess of Hagesichora.

Σηρηνίδων: probably used *metri gratia* for Σηρήνων, for which
cf. Alcm. 30 ἁ Μῶσα κέκλαγ' ἁ λίγηα Σηρήν. The singers of
Pindar's partheneion (fr. 106.7–8 Turyn) were more
confident: σειρῆνα δὲ κόμπον . . . μιμήσομ' ἀοιδαῖς.

97. ἀοιδοτέρα: ἀοιδός is probably adjectival also at 14(a).2.

98. ἀντὶ δ' ἔνδεκα: the fragmentary scholium says that the
chorus sometimes consisted of eleven girls, sometimes of
ten: so the scholiast probably took ἀντί to mean 'instead
of'. But ἀντί may have denoted equivalence, as in *Il.*
9.116–17 ἀντί νυ πολλῶν | λαῶν ἐστὶν ἀνήρ, *Od.* 8.546 ἀντί
κασιγνήτου ξεῖνος . . . τέτυκται, and the rival choir may
have had eleven singers. Indeed the idea of opposition may
also be present: the preposition ἀντί nowhere else means
'against', but cf. Homer's ἀντίβιος.

99. δεκάς: the papyrus has ἀεκ after παίδων, but the marginal
comment makes δεκ- certain, and if -ει is a verb-ending
δεκάς is secure.

100. δ' ἄρ': if correct, this is the only example of ἄρα in Alcman.
δ' ἄρα is common in Homer to express a lively feeling of
interest: see Denniston *G.P.* 33, 43.

   ἐπὶ Ξάνθω ῥοαῖσι: Xanthus is a river in Lycia (e.g. *Il.* 2.877,
5.479) or in the Troad (*Il.* 6.4 Ξάνθοιο ῥοάων; properly
called Scamander by men and Xanthus by the gods, *Il.*
20.74).

101. κύκνος: swans belonged to northern Greece and Thrace as
well as the rivers of Asia. Unless Hes. *Sc.* 316 is earlier,
this is the first reference to the song of swans; the belief
that swans sing before they die appears first in A. *Ag.*
1444; the present passage and others show that the song
was not necessarily mournful.

   ἐπιμέρῳ ξανθᾷ κομίσκᾳ: cf. 51–4, which makes the identi-
fication of ἁ δέ certain. Cf. Alcm. 3.9 κόμαν ξανθὰν τινάξω.
Was Alcman punning on Ξάνθω here? For ἐπιμέρῳ cf.
Archil. 18.3.

ALCMAN 3

P. Oxy. 2387, frr. 1 and 3, published in 1957. The attribution to Alcman is assured by the content, style, dialect and metre of the poem, all of which show close resemblance to the Louvre-Partheneion (=Alcm. 1). The papyrus belongs to the end of the 1st century B.C. or the beginning of the 1st century A.D. The poem had at least 126 lines, i.e. 14 stanzas. We cannot say with certainty on what occasion the song was performed: the ἀγών (8) might be a contest or no more than an assembly. The little we know of the πυλεών (65) suggests that the poem was composed for a festival in Hera's honour. The song has the grace and gaiety and also the allusiveness of the Louvre-Partheneion. Here too the singers are much occupied with the praises of another girl, Astymeloisa, who seems to lead their worship, but here they sing with a passion which was not to be found in the other poem.

Metre: the 9-line stanza has many of the components of Alcman 1. Lines 1, 7, 8 are dactylic, 2, 3, 4 trochaic, 5, 9 aeolic. Note synizesis in 5 ὑμνιοισᾶν, 65 πυλεῶν', synecphonesis in 69 ἦ ἁπαλόν.

Lobel's *editio princeps* in *P. Oxy.* vol. xxiv is reviewed by D. L. Page, *C.R.* n.s. 9 (1959), 16–18, W. S. Barrett, *Gnomon* 33 (1961), 683–5; see also W. Peek, 'Das neue Alkman-Parthenion', *Philologus* 104 (1960), 163–80.

1–5. Page (*P.M.G.* p. 13) suggests supplement on these lines: Μῶσαι 'Ολυμπιάδες, περί με φρένας | ἱμέρῳ νέας ἀοιδᾶς | πίμπλατ'. ἰθύω δ' ἀκούσαι | παρθενηίας ὀπός | πρὸς αἰθέρα καλὸν ὑμνιοισᾶν μέλος. Lines 9 and 81 ἱ]κέτις ... γενοίμαν show that the speaker is a girl or a girls' choir. The opening lines may be sung by a solo singer who introduces the song of the whole choir; or, less probably, the whole choir may look forward to hearing the song of other choirs at the ἀγών (8).

5. καλόν: ᾱ, though Alcman has κᾰλός elsewhere.

7. ὕπνον κτλ.: cf. S. *Tr.* 989 σκεδάσαι τῷδ' ἀπὸ κρατὸς βλεφάρων θ' ὕπνον. '(The song) will scatter sweet sleep from their (our?) eyelids.'

9. κόμαν ξανθάν: cf. 1.101.

11–60. Hardly anything remains except the adjective κρυερά,

extracted from a marginal comment. If the poem contained
a myth, it may have been told here. The gap is at least 50
lines long.

61. λυσιμελεῖ ... πόσῳ: cf. Hes. *Th.* 910–11 ἔρος ... λυσιμελής,
Archil. 118 λυσιμελὴς ... πόθος.

τακερώτερα κτλ.: 'She looks (at me) more softly than sleep
or death.' Cf. Ibyc. 287.2 of Eros, τακέρ' ὄμμασι δερκόμενος.

63. γλυκῆα κήνα alone fits space and metre, but the papyrus
seems to have had something else. 'Not at random is she
sweet' (Page); 'not at all in vain is she sweet' (Bowra). Peek
punctuates after μαψιδίως: 'and not by chance (am I in
love with her), for she is sweet.'

64. 'Αστυμέλοισα: she seems to have a position of importance not
unlike Hagesichora's in the Louvre-Partheneion. She
carries Hera's garland (65), and is spoken of with admiration (66 ff) and love (79 ff).

65. πυλεῶνα: probably a garland offered to Hera: so Pamphilus
in Ath. 15.678a πυλεών· οὕτως καλεῖται ὁ στέφανος ὃν τῇ
῞Ηρᾳ περιτιθέασιν Λάκωνες. Cf. Alcm. 60 καὶ τὶν εὔχομαι
φέροισα | τόνδ' ἑλιχρύσω πυλεῶνα | κήρατῶ κυπαίρω, 'this
garland of casidony and lovely galingale.'

66. αἰγλάεντος: cf. *Il.* 1.532 αἰγλήεντος 'Ολύμπου.
ἀστήρ: for the comparison cf. 1.41n., 1.62n. and *Il.* 4.75–7,
where Athena descends to earth like a meteor.

67. διαιπετής: 'flying through' the heavens; διαι-, found only
here in a compound, governs gen. ὠρανῶ.

68. ψίλον: Doric for πτίλον, 'feathers' (Paus. 3.19.6).

71. νοτία Κινύρα χάρις: 'the moist charm of Cinyras', an
elaborate periphrasis for Cyprian perfume or hair-oil. For
Cinyras, king of Cyprus, see Tyrt. 9.6n. Cyprus was
famous for its scents (Pliny *N.H.* 13.5).

72. παρσενικᾶν: an ink-mark over the final syllable may be a
correction of ν to ς: the sing. παρσενικᾶς (i.e. Astymeloisa)
is much more satisfactory. Page suggests καλλίκομος, ἤν,
ἦ μάν, ἔρχεται as the opening words of 71–4.

74. μέλημα δάμῳ: a punning reference to Astymeloisa's name.

75 ff. The text becomes more fragmentary. The sense of 79 ff

seems to be, 'If she took me by the soft hand, I should at once become her suppliant.'

ALCMAN 14(a)

Quoted from Alcman by Syrianus *in Hermog.* 1.61.14 Rabe (=Maximus Planudes in *Rhet. Gr.* 5.510 Walz) as an example of a complete strophe composed of dissimilar lines; cf. fr. 27. Other partial citations prove that the fragment belonged to Book I. It was clearly the first strophe of a partheneion, and Syrianus' remarks show that the poem was in triadic structure.

Metre: dactylic, with iambic admixture as in A. *Ag.* 140–59.

1. Μῶσ' ἄγε: so at 27.1, where ἄρχε again follows. Diodorus Siculus 4.7.1 says Alcman called the Muses daughters of Uranus and Ge, but there is no mention of this in the extant fragments: cf. 3.1n. and 27.1n. The Muses had a temple at Sparta (Paus. 3.17.5), and the Lacedaemonians sacrificed to them before battle (Plu. *Lyc.* 21, *Mor.* 221a).

λίγηα: cf. *Od.* 24.62 Μοῦσα λίγεια, Alcm. 30 ἁ Μῶσα κέκλαγ' ἁ λίγηα Σηρήν.

2. Bergk wrote αἰενάοιδε, but ἀοιδός is adj. at 1.97 ἀοιδοτέρα.

3. νεοχμόν: the Greeks loved novelty in song as in other spheres: cf. *Od.* 1.351–2 τὴν γὰρ ἀοιδὴν μᾶλλον ἐπικλείουσ' ἄνθρωποι, | ἥ τις ἀκουόντεσσι νεωτάτη ἀμφιπέληται, Pi. *O.* 3.4 μοι νεοσίγαλον εὑρόντι τρόπον, 9.48–9 αἴνει δὲ παλαιὸν μὲν οἶνον, ἄνθεα δ' ὕμνων | νεωτέρων, and many another.

ALCMAN 16

1–4 are quoted as Alcman's by Stephanus of Byzantium s.v. Ἐρυσίχη because of the difficulty over the accent of Ἐρυσιχαῖος: ἐρυσίχαιος, he says, would mean 'carrying a shepherd's staff (χαῖον)'. Stephanus says that the lines are ἐν ἀρχῇ τοῦ δευτέρου τῶν παρθενείων ᾀσμάτων, either 'at the beginning of the second poem of the book of partheneia' or, more probably, 'at the beginning of the second book of partheneia.' 4–5 in Strabo 10.2.22, 1–2 (σκαιός) in Chrysippus περὶ ἀποφατικῶν 21; a few references to the piece elsewhere.

This is the passage which was adduced as proof that Alcman

was Lydian: cf. the life of Alcman in *P. Oxy.* 2389 fr. 9 col. i.11 ff
=*P.M.G.* 13(a). ἧς in line 1 is probably 3rd person; but the
passage, even in its context, made no clear reference to Alcman,
or the dispute would never have arisen.

Metre: iambo-trochaic.

1. ἧς: Eustathius *Od.* 1892.44 quotes Heraclides as saying that
   Alcman wrote ἧς for the 3rd pers. ἧν; but ἧς may neverthe-
   less have been 1st pers. also, or it may have been mistaken
   for 1st pers. Stephanus has εἷς, 2nd pers.

   ἀγρεῖος: cf. Ar. *Nub.* 655 ἀγρεῖος εἶ καὶ σκαιός.

3. οὐδὲ παρὰ σοφοῖσιν: 'not even in the estimation of the wise
   (or of poets)', but this meaning of οὐδέ breaks the sequence
   of the repeated οὐδέ, and παρὰ σοφοῖσιν breaks the
   sequence of adjectives.

   Θεσσαλός: the Thessalians were cheats and gluttons (Weir
   Smyth), but boorishness is the point here.

4. Ἐρυσιχαῖος: i.e. rustic and outlandish. Erysiche was a hamlet
   in Acarnania (Strabo *loc. cit.*). Some editors prefer
   ἐρυσίχαιος, which fits ποιμήν nicely.

5. Σαρδίων: cf. 1.68n. Gyges' dedications at Delphi (Hdt. 1.14)
   displayed to the Greek world the prosperity and culture of
   Sardis.

ALCMAN 20

From Athenaeus 10.416d: 'in Book V Alcman reveals his
gluttony in these words.' Metre and content suggest a gay personal
poem.

Metre: iambic dimeter.

1. ὥρας . . . τρεῖς: Homer generally recognises three seasons,
   ἔαρ, θέρος, χεῖμα. At *Od.* 11.192 θέρος τεθαλυῖά τ' ὀπώρη
   there is no distinction between θέρος and ὀπώρη, but the
   two are distinct at *Od.* 12.76 οὔτ' ἐν θέρει οὔτ' ἐν ὀπώρῃ.
   Hesiod refers to three seasons only: the first clear appearance of four seasons is in Hippocrates *Aph.* 1.18, E.
   fr. 990N².

   ἔσηκε: sc. Zeus or perhaps Prometheus (cf. A. *Pr.* 454–8).

2. ὀπώρα: technically, from the end of July (Sirius' heliacal
   rising) to mid-September (Arcturus' heliacal rising). It was

the season of fruit and harvest: cf. 96.2 κηρίναν τ' ὀπώραν, 'the waxen harvest', of honey.

3. τέτρατον: spring is grudgingly introduced, as the season when stocks are low.

4. σάλλει: impersonal, 'things grow.'

ἐσθίην . . . ἄδαν: cf. *Il.* 5.203 ἔδμεναι ἄδην, 'to eat one's fill.' Cf. 17.4 ὁ παμφάγος 'Αλκμάν.

ALCMAN 26

Quoted from Alcman by Antigonus of Carystus, *Mir.* 23 (27): male halcyons, he says, are called κηρύλοι and in old age are carried on the wings of the female birds: so when Alcman declares that he is old and feeble and cannot join in the girls' song and dance he writes οὔ μ' ἔτι . . . ὄρνις. This travellers' tale, repeated in Aelian *N.H.* 7.17, *Suda* s.v. κηρύλος and elsewhere, gains no support from ἄμ' ἀλκυόνεσσι ποτῆται (3). Other writers quote parts of the passage, among them grammarians intrigued by the form βάλε. The passage is imitated in Ar. *Av.* 250–1 ὦντ' ἐπὶ πόντιον οἶδμα θαλάσσης | φῦλα μετ' ἀλκυόνεσσι ποτᾶται, Ap. Rhod. 4.363 κατὰ πόντον ἄμ' ἀλκυόνεσσι φορεῦμαι. (Plutarch) *Mus.* 4 says of Terpander that he wrote προοίμια κιθαρῳδικὰ ἐν ἔπεσιν, hexameter preludes for κιθάρα accompaniment: Alcman's lines may have been part of a prelude sung or recited by him before the performance of a partheneion.

Metre: lyric dactylic hexameters, with spondees only in the last foot and no hiatus at the ends of lines.

1. παρσενικαί: noun, as in Homer (*Il.* 18.567, *Od.* 11.39).

   μελιγάρυες: cf. *Od.* 12.187 μελίγηρυν . . . ὄπα of the Sirens.

   ἰαρόφωνοι: for Doric ἰαρός = ἱερός cf. line 4. The *Suda* and Photius seem to have read ἱεροφώνων for ἠεροφώνων in *Il.* 18.505, and explain it as 'loud-voiced'. The root of ἱερός may be that of ἴς (Fίς, Lat. *vis*), and the basic meaning, 'supernaturally strong', may underlie the Homeric ἱερὴ ἴς, ἱερὸν μένος. The context of Theognis 761 φόρμιγξ δ' αὖ φθέγγοιθ' ἱερὸν μέλος suggests that ἱερόν there = 'holy'. Barker emended to ἱμερόφωνοι, used by Sapph. 136 of the nightingale, Theoc. 28.7 of the Graces.

2. βάλε: Call. *Hec.* 254.2 has βάλε μοι βάλε τὸ τρίτον

εἴη. Elsewhere we find ἀβάλε, originally perhaps ἃ βάλε.

κηρύλος: a fabulous bird, often associated with the halcyon:
see Thompson, *Greek Birds* 139–40.

3. κύματος ἄνθος: possibly foam: cf. A. *Ag.* 659 ὁρῶμεν ἀνθοῦν
πέλαγος Αἰγαῖον νεκροῖς. κύματος ἄνθος was less startling
than 'the flower of the wave': see W. B. Stanford, *Greek
Metaphor* 111–14 and 1.53n.

ἀλκυόνεσσι: see Thompson, *Greek Birds* 46–51: 'a symbolic or
mystical bird, early identified with the kingfisher, *Alcedo
Ispida*.' The halcyon days, 14 calm days at the winter
solstice, when the halcyon lays and hatches her eggs, are
mentioned first by Simon. 508.

4. ἀλιπόρφυρος: in *Od.* 6.53, 306, 13.108 of purple wool and robes.

ἱαρός: 'strong' would be apt here, since Alcman has just
complained of his weakness. 'Holy' is apt enough too:
Simon. 508.4–6 called the halcyon days ὥραν . . . ἱεράν.

ὄρνις: the regular Doric form was ὄρνιξ.

ALCMAN 27

Quoted by Hephaestion 7.4 and Syrianus *in Hermog.* 1.61 as an
example of a strophe of Alcman consisting of three identical lines:
cf. fr. 14.

Metre: dactylic tetrameter.

1. Μῶσ' ἄγε: so at 14.1.

Καλλιόπα: Alcman, like Sappho, names no other Muse. She
was the chief Muse, according to Hes. *Th.* 79.

θύγατερ Διός: so in fr. 28 Μῶσα Διὸς θύγατερ.

2. ἐπί: with τίθη in tmesis: cf. *Il.* 1.509 ἐπὶ Τρώεσσι τίθει
κράτος. There is zeugma in 2–3: tr. 'set charm on our song
and make our dance graceful.' Otherwise we must assume
tmesis in ἐπί . . . ἵμερον (i.e. ἐπίμερον: cf. 1.101 ἐπιμέρῳ):
'make our chorus enchanting and delightful by its song.'

ALCMAN 41

From Plutarch, *Lycurgus* 21.6: Pindar and Terpander show that
the Spartans were both very musical and very warlike: ἕρπει . . .
κιθαρίσδην, 'as the Laconian poet has said.' Also in *de fort. Alex.* 2.2.

Metre: iambic dimeter + dactylic trimeter.

ἕρπει ... ἄντα: perhaps 'confronts', but Scaliger's ῥέπει is easier.

ALCMAN 56

Quoted in Athenaeus 11.498f from Alcman to illustrate the word σκύφος. The nocturnal celebration and above all the miracle of the milking of a lioness suggest the worship of Dionysus, so that the lines are addressed to a Bacchante. Cf. Virgil *Georg.* 2.487 *virginibus bacchata Lacaenis Taygeta*. Hermes, slayer of Argus (6), was often associated with Dionysus, notably in Praxiteles' statue of Hermes with the infant Dionysus in the Heraeum at Olympia; this theme occurred also in the throne of Apollo at Amyclae (Paus. 3.18.11). For Hermes and shepherds see Semonides 18.

Metre: dactylic, with spondaic clausulae in 2, 4, 5. Synizesis in σιοῖσι (2). The rhythm readily admits epic phrases.

1. κορυφαῖς ὀρέων: cf. 89.1 ὀρέων κορυφαί, *Od.* 9.121 κορυφὰς ὀρέων.
2. πολύφανος: 'with many torches' (φᾶνοί), here only.
3. σκύφον: Asclepiades (ap. Athen. *loc. cit.*) says the σκύφος was used by swineherds (e.g. Eumaeus in *Od.* 14.112), shepherds and rustics.
4. οἷά τε: for the change to plural cf. *Od.* 5.421–2 κῆτος ... οἷά τε πολλὰ τρέφει ... Ἀμφιτρίτη, 14.62–3.

   ποιμένες ἄνδρες: also in Sapph. 105(c).2, Semon. 18.2: cf. *Il.* 4.275 αἰπόλος ἀνήρ.

   ἔχοισιν: the Doric form was ἔχοντι, but cf. εὔδουσι in 89.1 and 6, where Homeric echoes are strong.
5. λεόντεον ... γάλα: Aristides *Or.* 41.7 says that according to 'a Laconian poet' Dionysus could milk lionesses. Dionysus may have milked the lioness and handed the milk to a Bacchante for her cheesemaking.
6. ἄτρυφον = ἄθρυπτον, 'unbreakable', not crumbly: cf. Hes. *Op.* 442 ἄρτον ... τετράτρυφον, a loaf breakable into four pieces.

ALCMAN 58

Quoted by Hephaestion 13.6 for Alcman's cretic rhythm, and by Apostolius 4.62b as proverbial. We cannot tell whether Alcman was speaking in his own person, but see on 59(a).

Metre: cretic hexameter catalectic.

1. μάργος: 'mad, wild, wanton': it is implied that Aphrodite
   brings tranquillity.
   οἷα παῖς: 'like a boy' or 'like the boy he is'. The boy Eros
   next appears in Anacreon.
2. καβαίνων: for καταβαίνων by apocope: Hesychius has κάβασι
   (= κατάβηθι), κάβλημα, 'coverlet', Καβάτας, a cult-title of
   Zeus, all Laconian. Late 6th century representations of
   Eros show him winged; the earliest certain literary
   reference to his wings is a verse in Plato Phaedr. 252b. But it
   is his gentle tread that Alcman alludes to: cf. Il. 20.227
   ἄκρον ἐπ' ἀνθερίκων καρπὸν θέον οὐδὲ κατέκλων of the
   horses of Erichthonius, and for Love's gentleness Plato
   Symp. 195e οὐ γὰρ ἐπὶ γῆς βαίνει οὐδ' ἐπὶ κρανίων, ἅ
   ἐστιν οὐ πάνυ μαλακά, ἀλλ' ἐν τοῖς μαλακωτάτοις τῶν ὄντων
   καὶ βαίνει καὶ οἰκεῖ.
   ἃ μή μοι θίγῃς: parenthetic, 'do not touch them, I pray.'
   For θίγῃς with acc. cf. Archil. 71n., S. Ant. 546-7 with
   Jebb's note.
   κυπαιρίσκω: dim. of κύπαιρος (Attic κύπειρος), a plant
   mentioned by Alcman in 60.3 as part of Hera's garland
   (πυλεών); it is 'galingale', a kind of sedge, mentioned in
   Od. 4.603 as a feature of the Spartan plain.

ALCMAN 59a

Athenaeus 13.600f quotes Chamaeleon as saying that Archytas
ὁ ἁρμονικός (presumably Plato's friend, the Tarentine mathe-
matician) maintained that Alcman was τῶν ἐρωτικῶν μελῶν
ἡγεμόνα, i.e. probably 'the first composer of amatory songs': this
fragment is quoted as an example. Athenaeus' text, corrupt at
this point, seems to say that Alcman had the attitude of a
libertine towards women and that he fell immoderately in love
with a seductive poetess called Megalostrate. So perhaps Alcman
does speak for himself here.

Metre: iambic trimeter catalectic.

1. Κύπριδος Fέκατι: 'at the command of the Cyprian (Aphrodite)':
   cf. Od. 20.42 Διός τε σέθεν τε ἕκητι, Archil. 104.2 θεῶν . . .
   ἕκητι.
2. κατείβων: intransitive, 'pouring down.'

καρδίαν ἰαίνει: 'warms my heart': cf. *Od.* 15.379 θυμὸν . . .
ἰαίνει, Archil. 41 καρδίην ἰαίνεται.

ALCMAN 89

Quoted by Apollonius the Sophist, *Homeric Lexicon*, s.v. κνώ-
δαλον, to show that Alcman used the word with the meaning 'sea-
monster'. The metre is uncertain, and we cannot say to what
extent the text should be emended; moreover the passage has so
many Homeric phrases that we cannot be sure how rigorously to
rewrite it in the Laconian dialect. The description of night may
have led to a contrast with the sleeplessness of some human
being(s) as in e.g. Theoc. 2.38 ff, Ap. Rhod. 3.744 ff, Virgil *Aen.*
4.522 ff and many others; or it may have set the scene for the
epiphany of a god: cf. E. *Ba.* 1084–5 with Dodds's note.

Metre: 2 trochaic, 4 iambo-trochaic, 5 iambic, 6 iambic +
hemiepes, 1, 3 aeolic lengths with iambic close. Note synizesis at 1
ὀρέων, 5 πορφυρέας.

See R. Pfeiffer, 'Vom Schlaf der Erde und der Tiere', *Hermes* 87
(1959), 1–6.

1. ὀρέων κορυφαί κτλ.: cf. *Il.* 12.282 ὑψηλῶν ὀρέων κορυφὰς καὶ
   πρώονας ἄκρους, Alcm. 56.1.

3. ἑρπετά: adj. here only, if our text is correct: cf. e.g. *Od.*
   4.417–18 ὅσσ' ἐπὶ γαῖαν | ἑρπετὰ γίγνονται. Pfeiffer's
   suggestion, ὗλα θ' ἑρπετά θ' ὅσσα, is attractive.
   τρέφει: cf. *Il.* 11.741 ὅσα τρέφει εὐρεῖα χθών.
   μέλαινα γαῖα: cf. Archil. 58.2n. μελαίνη . . . χθονί.

4. ὀρεσκῷοι: cf. *Il.* 1.268 φηρσὶν ὀρεσκῴοισι of the Centaurs.
   γένος μελισσᾶν: cf. *Il.* 2.87 ἔθνεα . . . μελισσάων, *Od.* 20.212, *h.
   Merc.* 309 βοῶν γένος, Mimn. 14 γένος ἵππων.

5. βένθεσσι: cf. *Il.* 1.358 ἐν βένθεσσιν ἁλός.
   πορφυρέας: cf. *Il.* 16.391 ἅλα πορφυρέην, Semon. 1.16 πορφυρῆς
   ἁλός.

6. εὕδουσι with neut. plur.: cf. *Il.* 2.87 ἔθνεα εἶσι μελισσάων:
   the noun is collective in both places.
   φῦλα: cf. *Il.* 19.30–1 ἄγρια φῦλα, | μυίας.
   τανυπτερύγων: cf. *Il.* 12.237 οἰωνοῖσι τανυπτερύγεσσι.

MIMNERMUS

Mimnermus was remembered as a gentle love-poet: *plus in amore valet Mimnermi versus Homero; | carmina mansuetus lenia quaerit Amor* (Propertius 1.9.9–10); but the fragments of his poetry and references by ancient authors show that he was more than a languid Ionian singing only of the pleasures of youth and the horrors of old age: mythological subjects, early history and, more remarkably, the fighting between Smyrna and the Lydians all figure in his poetry and suggest a sturdier character; in Stobaeus' anthology his poetry appears in the chapter on courage as well as in the chapters labelled Aphrodite, the brevity of life and complaints against old age.

Strabo (14.643) and Photius (*Bibl.* 319b.11) make Mimnermus a Colophonian, but the *Suda* (*s.v.* Mimnermus) lists three birthplaces — Colophon or Smyrna or the Dorian island of Astypalaea. The last is not explained, but the probability is that he belonged to Smyrna and was descended from the Colophonians who at some time before 800 settled in the Aeolic town of Smyrna (cf. Hdt. 1.149 f and for the dating J. M. Cook, 'Old Smyrna, 1948–1951', *A.B.S.A.* 53–54, 1–34, especially 13 and 27–8). Mimnermus identifies himself with those settlers in 12.3–6, especially 5–6 κεῖθεν (i.e. from Colophon) . . . ἀπορνύμενοι . . . Σμύρνην εἵλομεν Αἰολίδα. It may be that Smyrna's disappearance from Greek history for almost three centuries after 600 B.C. meant that the Colophonians' claim to Mimnermus, as indeed to Homer also, enjoyed better publicity, and that therefore there is significance in the fact that Smyrna's claim persisted for so long in the face of such competition. Mimnermus' connexion with Smyrna is also attested by the title of one of his works, the *Smyrneis*.

In fr. 13 Mimnermus commends the exploits of a warrior who fought against the Lydians in the plain of the Hermus and says that he heard of these exploits from his elders who were eyewitnesses. This reminiscence reads like a challenge to Mimnermus' contemporaries at a time of similar danger, and is almost certainly to be referred to the time of Alyattes' attack on Smyrna in the last decade of the 7th century, while the earlier fighting will belong to the time of Gyges' attack in the early years of the century. Pausanias 9.29.4 refers to Mimnermus' ἐλεγεῖα ἐς τὴν μάχην τὴν Σμυρναίων πρὸς Γύγην τε καὶ Λυδούς. We may guess that Mimnermus was born *c.* 670 and lived at least until Alyattes' sack of Smyrna *c.* 600. The *Suda* says that he was alive in the 37th Olympiad (632–629). Lines in which he expressed a wish for death at the age of 60 (fr. 6) were faulted by Solon, who corrected 60 to 80 (fr. 22); but this does nothing to establish his chronology more accurately.

Bibliographical details of Mimnermus' work are confused. Five of the fragments are cited from the *Nanno*, and according to the fourth-century elegiac poet, Hermesianax of Colophon, Nanno was a girl whom Mimnermus loved. Callimachus in the opening lines of his *Aἴτια* defends his preference for short poems by referring to Mimnermus: [τοῖν δὲ] δυοῖν Μίμνερμος ὅτι γλυκὺς α[ἱ κατὰ λεπτὸν | ῥήσιες,] ἡ μεγάλη δ' οὐκ ἐδίδαξε γυνή: Mimnermus' sweetness is shown by his short poems, not by 'the great lady', in other words, the long poem entitled 'Nanno' (so H. J. M. Milne in *C.R.* 43 (1929), 214, the most likely explanation). Porphyrio, commenting on Horace *Ep.* 2.2.101, has *Mimnermus duos libros †luculentibus† scripsit*. If there were in fact only two books, Callimachus' lines suggest that one of them was a collection of short love-poems, the other, the *Nanno*, a collection of poetry of a different kind. Our quotations from the *Nanno* are frr. 4 and 5, typical lines on old age and youth, 8 — 'let there be truth between us', 10 on the sun's unending toil and 12, the lines on Smyrna's early history: the *Nanno* was clearly a miscellany. But we hear also of the *Smyrneis* of Mimnermus: a couplet which speaks of the advance of the King's troops (fr. 12A) is cited from it by a scholiast on Antimachus (Wyss, *Antimachi Colophonii Reliquiae* 83). The title *Smyrneis* and the narrative content of our extract suggest that the *Smyrneis* had no connexion with the short love-poems. Can it have been another name for the *Nanno*, or was it part of the *Nanno*?

Propertius said that in love Mimnermus' poetry counted for more than Homer's; but even in his reflections on love, youth and age, Mimnermus' dependence on Homer is striking: it is amusing

I

to see him express such un-Homeric thoughts as those of fr. 1 in language which is almost entirely Homer's. Homer's vocabulary, line-endings, formulas, similes, all reappear, but from this material Mimnermus creates a quite distinctive poetry of easy grace and pleasing rhythm, and indeed the few occasions when he departs from Homeric vocabulary provide some of his finest lines: 2.3–4 τοῖς ἴκελοι πήχυιον ἐπὶ χρόνον ἄνθεσιν ἥβης | τερπόμεθα, 5.1–3 ἀλλ᾽ ὀλιγοχρόνιον γίγνεται ὥσπερ ὄναρ | ἥβη τιμήεσσα· τὸ δ᾽ ἀργαλέον καὶ ἄμορφον | γῆρας ὑπὲρ κεφαλῆς αὐτίχ᾽ ὑπερκρέμαται κτλ.

MIMNERMUS I

From Stobaeus 4.20 (περὶ Ἀφροδίτης). 16; attributed there to Mimnermus. Plutarch quotes a version of the first two lines as an example of licentious verse (virt. mor. 6.445f). Horace (Ep. 1.6.65 f) refers to the poem: si, Mimnermus uti censet, sine amore iocisque | nil est iucundum, vivas in amore iocisque.

Bowra notes the sensitive variation of rhythm in the lines: 'after the challenging, flaunting opening we are led through a swift account of youth, and then as we approach the horrors of old age, the verse becomes slower, the sentences shorter, the stops more emphatic, until the poet closes with a short, damning line of summary' (E.G.E. 19). The piece may be a complete poem — one of the short poems admired for their sweetness by Callimachus: see 1 n. Fr. 2 may be another.

1. δέ: no proof that this is not the beginning of the poem: see Archil. 1.1 n.

χρυσῆς Ἀφροδίτης: a Homeric line-ending (Il. 3.64, Od. 4.14 with the spelling χρυσέης). In early writers the epithet may have had a literal rather than a figurative meaning and be due to the rumour of a golden statue of Aphrodite in some Phoenician city: see H. L. Lorimer, 'Gold and Ivory in Greek Mythology', Greek Poetry and Life: Essays presented to Gilbert Murray, 14 ff. Pindar applies the epithet to the Muse (I. 8.5). Sophocles uses it of Athena (O.T. 188), and Aristophanes has the exclamation ὦ χρυσοῖ θεοί (Ran. 483), but by their time Pheidias' chryselephantine statue of Athena stood in the Parthenon.

2. μέλοι: optative by assimilation to τεθναίην, as in Od. 1.47

ὡς ἀπόλοιτο καὶ ἄλλος ὅτις τοιαῦτά γε ῥέζοι. Cf. Goodwin,
M.T. 177, 558.

3. The vocabulary is all Homeric: cf. *Il.* 6.161 κρυπταδίῃ
φιλότητι, h. *Hom.* 10.2 μείλιχα δῶρα, *Il.* 15.32 φιλότης τε
καὶ εὐνή.

4. ἥβης ἄνθεα: the metaphor, also at 2.3, is differently used in
Il. 13.484 καὶ δ' ἔχει ἥβης ἄνθος, ὅ τε κράτος ἐστὶ μέγιστον.
See Thgn. 1070n. Note that ἄνθεα scans as a spondee: for
the synizesis cf. 2.2. ἔαρος.

ἁρπαλέα: from the root of ἁρπάζω, 'to be seized', so 'attractive'. Homer has it of gain (κερδέων . . . ἁρπαλέων, *Od.*
8.164) and uses the adverb ἁρπαλέως, 'greedily', 'quickly'
(cf. Mimn. 10.8). See also Tyrt. 8.17n.

5. For ἐπεί with subjunctive cf. *Il.* 15.363. In 3.1 Mimnermus
has ἐπήν with subjunctive. For similar variations see
Callin. 1.13n.

6. 'old age which makes a man both ugly and base': cf. 5.3–4
γῆρας . . . , ὅ τ' ἄγνωστον τιθεῖ ἄνδρα. Homer uses αἰσχρός
only once of a man (as opposed to his actions): *Il.* 2.216
αἴσχιστος δὲ ἀνὴρ ὑπὸ Ἴλιον ἦλθεν — Thersites was the
ugliest man in the Greek army. So in h. *Ap.* 197–8 οὔτ'
αἰσχρὴ . . . οὔτ' ἐλάχεια, | ἀλλὰ μάλα μεγάλη τε ἰδεῖν καὶ
εἶδος ἀγητή. κακόν will here have its moral sense, since
otherwise ὁμῶς καί ('both . . . and') is pointless. The ᾰ of
MSS. καλόν can be paralleled in h. *Ven.* 29, Hes. *Op.* 63,
Th. 585, Sol. 1.21, Thgn. 17; but translations such as
'which puts the ugly and the handsome man in the same
condition' and 'which makes even a handsome man ugly
like the plain man' do violence to the meaning of the
common expression ὁμῶς καί.

τιθεῖ (=τίθησι), again at 5.4, occurs at *Il.* 13.732, Hdt.
1.113.2. It is usually called an Ionian form, but Chantraine,
G.H. i.298–9, argues that in Homer it is an archaic form,
not an Ionian contraction, and should be accented τίθει.

7. φρένας ἀμφί are to be taken together, as in Hes. *Th.* 554
χώσατο δὲ φρένας ἀμφί. Cf. too *Il.* 15.60–1 ὀδυνάων | αἳ
νῦν μιν τείρουσι κατὰ φρένας.

8. Cf. *Il.* 8.480–1 οὔτ' αὐγῆς Ὑπερίονος Ἠελίοιο | τέρποντ'. Even

in our few fragments we can see Mimnermus' fondness for both literal and symbolic mention of the sun; cf. 1.8, 2.2, 2.8, 11.5–7, 10, 13.11; according to Plutarch, *fac. lun.* 19, Mimnermus referred also to an eclipse of the sun. 'In the Sun's light and strength he found something which touched him deeply and resembled the glory which he found in the fleeting joys of youth' (Bowra, *E.G.E.* 35).

9. ἐχθρὸς μὲν παισίν: cf. Mimn. 3 τὸ πρὶν ἐὼν κάλλιστος, ἐπὴν παραμείψεται ὥρη, | οὐδὲ πατὴρ παισὶν τίμιος οὔτε φίλος. There παισίν = 'his sons', here 'boys'.

ἀτίμαστος: *hapax*: Homer has ἀτίμητος and ἄτιμος.

10. ἀργαλέον: a favourite adjective of Mimnermus: cf. 2.6, 5.2 of old age, 4.2 of death, 6.1 of cares, 9.2 of rumour, 12.4 of insolence.

θεός: cf. *Od.* 11.101 τὸν (sc. νόστον) δέ τοι ἀργαλέον θήσει θεός. In 2.16 and 4.1 Mimnermus refers the troubles of Tithonus and of all mankind to Zeus.

MIMNERMUS 2

From Stobaeus 4.34 (περὶ τοῦ βίου ὅτι βραχὺς καὶ εὐτελὴς καὶ φροντίδων ἀνάμεστος). 12; attributed by him to Mimnermus. This, like fr. 1, may be a complete poem.

1. The image of the leaves was used differently by Homer in *Il.* 6.146–9, where Glaucus says οἵη περ φύλλων γενεή, τοίη δὲ καὶ ἀνδρῶν. | φύλλα τὰ μέν τ' ἄνεμος χαμάδις χέει, ἄλλα δέ θ' ὕλη | τηλεθόωσα φύει, ἔαρος δ' ἐπιγίγνεται ὥρη· | ὡς ἀνδρῶν γενεὴ ἡ μὲν φύει, ἡ δ' ἀπολήγει. There the succession of one generation of mankind to another is likened to the seasonal changes of a tree, and the point is the transience of a man's life: here it is the brevity of youth that Mimnermus compares with the swift growth and decay of leaves.

2. ἔαρος: cf. 1.4n.
αὔξεται: φύλλα, which was object of φύει, has to be supplied as subject of αὔξεται.

3. πήχυιον ἐπὶ χρόνον: 'for a brief span.' πήχυιος, from πῆχυς, 'cubit', is used figuratively like δάκτυλος in Alcaeus' δάκτυλος ἀμέρα (346.1).

4. θεῶν: a monosyllable. Early elegiac writers allow it to be either monosyllabic or disyllabic. See 1.4n.

εἰδότες οὔτε κακόν κτλ.: Mimnermus must mean that since bliss is unmixed in our youth we do not distinguish then between good and bad fortune.

5. Κῆρες: spirits of death or fate in general, familiar from the *Iliad*. According to Thetis, Achilles had two κῆρες, the first to die young and famous at Troy, the second to return home and live a long but inglorious life (*Il.* 9.410–16). Cf. too Thgn. 767–8 τηλοῦ δὲ κακὰς ἀπὸ κῆρας ἀμῦναι | γήράς τ' οὐλόμενον καὶ θανάτοιο τέλος.

6. γήραος: genitive of equivalence or definition, as θανάτοιο (7): cf. τέκμωρ Ἰλίου (*Il.* 7.30–1), 'the goal of Troy.'

7. ἥβης καρπός: 'the harvest of youth', the imagery of the seasons again. Pindar uses the expression rather differently at *O.* 6.58, *P.* 9.109.

8. ὅσον τ' ἐπὶ γῆν κίδναται ἠέλιος: i.e. as brief as a sunrise. κίδναμαι and ἐπικίδναμαι are used by Homer as equivalents of σκεδάννυμαι for the 'spreading' of the sun's light over the earth, e.g. *Il.* 8.1 Ἠὼς μὲν κροκόπεπλος ἐκίδνατο πᾶσαν ἐπ' αἶαν. In *Il.* 7.451 τοῦ δ' ἦ τοι κλέος ἔσται, ὅσον τ' ἐπικίδναται ἠώς the sense is, 'Its fame will reach as far as the dawn's light spreads.' In the present passage μίνυνθα shows that ὅσον must have a temporal sense.

9. τοῦτο τέλος παραμείψεται ὥρης: the meaning must be the same as in 3.1 ἐπὴν παραμείψεται ὥρη, 'when youth passes.' τοῦτο τέλος seems to mean 'this degree of maturity, this time of life' (see L.S.J. s.v. II. 1), and ὥρης will be a defining genitive, 'this time of youth.' But although the context makes the sense clear, the choice of words is puzzling.

παραμείψεται is the short-vowel subjunctive familiar from Homer, e.g. ἴομεν, πειρήσεται (= Attic πειράσηται).

10. In 4.2 Mimnermus has γῆρας, ὃ καὶ θανάτου ῥίγιον ἀργαλέου.

11. ἄλλοτε: for the asyndeton at the beginning of an explanatory sentence see Callin. 1.14n.

οἶκος τρυχοῦται: 'his substance is consumed.' τρυχόω, elsewhere confined to prose writers, is another form of τρύχω

which Homer uses in this sense, e.g. *Od.* 1.248, 16.125
τρύχουσι δὲ οἶκον, Sol. 3.22.

12. πενίης . . . ἔργα: 'life of poverty'; so in Sol. 1.41. Homer has
similar periphrases, e.g. *Il.* 9.228 δαιτὸς . . . ἔργα. Solon
has ὕβριος ἔργα (1.16), ἔργα διχοστασίης (3.37).

14. εἰς ᾿Αίδην: cf. Tyrt. 9.38n.

15. νοῦσον . . . θυμοφθόρον: 'a fatal disease': cf. *Od.* 2.329
θυμοφθόρα φάρμακα. *Il.* 6.169 γράψας . . . θυμοφθόρα
πολλά. The adjective can also mean 'heart-breaking', e.g.
Od. 4.716 ἄχος . . . θυμοφθόρον, 10.363 κάματον θυμοφθόρον.
Hes. *Op.* 717 πενίην θυμοφθόρον.

16. διδοῖ: an Ionian contracted form =δίδωσι, found in Homer
(e.g. *Il.* 9.519). See Chantraine *G.H.* i.299.

MIMNERMUS 5

From Stobaeus 4.50 (περὶ γήρως· ψόγος γήρως). 69. Stobaeus
attributes the lines to Mimnermus' *Nanno.* 1–3 occur at Theognis
1020–2.

1. ὥσπερ ὄναρ: Theocritus uses Mimnermus' simile: τάχα γάρ σε
παρέρχεται ὡς ὄναρ ἥβη (27.8). Cf. Thgn. 985 αἶψα γὰρ
ὥστε νόημα παρέρχεται ἀγλαὸς ἥβη.

2. τιμήεσσα, 'precious': cf. 10.7 χρυσοῦ τιμήεντος.

4. ἄγνωστον: L.S.J. give 'unheard of, forgotten' as the meaning
here, but it is surely 'unrecognisable', as in *Od.* 13.191,
379 and probably *Od.* 2.175 (all of Odysseus on his home-
coming).

5. ἀμφιχυθέν: aor. pass. part. of ἀμφιχέω; cf. Sleep's words in
Il. 14.252–3 ἔθελξα Διὸς νόον . . . | ἥδυμος ἀμφιχυθείς,
Od. 4.716 τὴν δ' ἄχος ἀμφεχύθη.

MIMNERMUS 10

From Athenaeus 11.470a: 'Mimnermus says in the *Nanno* that
it is in a golden bed made for the purpose by Hephaestus that the
sun, while he is asleep, crosses to the east, with riddling reference
to the hollow of the cup. His words are as follows: ῾Ήέλιος μὲν γὰρ
κτλ.᾿ All extant references to the cup of the sun are in this chapter
of Athenaeus. The vessel is called δέπας by Peisander. Stesichorus
(fr. 185), Antimachus, Aeschylus (fr. 69N² ῾Ήφαιστοτυκὲς δέπας)

and Pherecydes; Panyassis calls it φιάλη, Theolytus λέβης. A cup in the Vatican (Gerhard, *Auserlesene Griechische Vasenbilder*, pl. 109; *Fifty Years of Classical Scholarship*, ed. M. Platnauer, pl. III, fig. 4) shows Heracles in the vessel.

Hudson-Williams calls attention to Pindar fr. 135 Turyn, which says of the underworld τοῖσι λάμπει μὲν μένος ἀελίου τὰν ἐνθάδε νύκτα κάτω, and notes that this was not Homer's view: cf. *Od.* 12.383.

1. μὲν γάρ: we are dealing with an excerpt from a long poem: μέν here and μέν in 5 are unanswered.

    πόνον ἔλλαχεν: Hudson-Williams keeps the MSS. ἔλαχεν πόνον, justifying γάρ by reference to *Il.* 2.39, 19.49. For the sun's toil cf. *Il.* 18.239 Ἥλιον δ᾽ ἀκάμαντα, Virgil, *Aen.* 1.742 *solis labores*.

    ἤματα πάντα: probably 'all his life', 'for ever', as often in Homer, though Mimnermus may intend a contrast with the sun's nightly rest.

2. ἄμπαυσις (= ἀνάπαυσις): 'respite', first here, then in P. *N.* 7.52. Hes. *Th.* 55 and Thgn. 343 have ἄμπαυμα.

5. πολυήρατος εὐνή: cf. *Od.* 23.354, Hes. *Th.* 404, πολυήρατον εὐνήν.

6. κοίλη: the form resembles Homer's γελοίιος and ὁμοίιος, for which see Chantraine, *G.H.* i.168. Hephaestus, κλυτοτέχνης, was metal-worker by appointment at the court of heaven. His work included the houses of the gods, and his masterpiece was the armour he made for Achilles to oblige Thetis (*Il.* 18.478 ff).

7. χρυσοῦ τιμήεντος: cf. *Il.* 18.475 χρυσὸν τιμῆντα. For the gen. of the material cf. *Il.* 18.574 of Achilles' shield: αἱ δὲ βόες χρυσοῖο τετεύχατο κασσιτέρου τε. See Chantraine, *G.H.* ii.57.

    ὑπόπτερος is used of a ship by Pindar *O.* 9.24. Cf. *Od.* 11.125 ἐρετμά, τά τε πτερὰ νηυσὶ πέλονται, 'oars, which are ships' wings.'

8. ἁρπαλέως: probably 'swiftly' with φέρει (5), with which the next words are also connected, rather than 'eagerly' with εὕδονθ᾽. The *Hesperides*, dwelling in the extreme west, appear first in Hes. *Th.* 215: the children of Night, they look after trees with golden apples beyond Ocean.

9. The *Ethiopians*, who live according to Mimnermus on the eastern edge of the world, appear several times in Homer. 'A visit to this remote people is Homer's regular way of motivating the absence of a god from Olympus' (Stanford on *Od.* 1.22, where Homer distinguishes between Ethiopians of the far east and those of the far west).

ἅρμα καὶ ἵπποι: Mimnermus does not tell us how they commuted from west to east. According to Pherecydes, whom Athenaeus cites, they travelled with the sun in his cup.

11. ἔνθ᾽: 'then' or 'there'.

ἐπεβήσεθ᾽ ἑῶν ὀχέων: cf. *Il.* 11.517 ὧν ὀχέων ἐπεβήσετο. Mimnermus' aorist must be classed as gnomic, expressing a habitual action, although such aorists belong rather to passages of moralising (γνῶμαι) than to descriptions of the regularities of the physical world.

Ὑπερίονος υἱός: i.e. the sun. In Homer the sun is commonly Ὑπερίων (twice in *Iliad*, frequently in *Odyssey*), but at *Od.* 12.176 we find Ἡελίου . . . Ὑπεριονίδαο, on which is based the Hesiodic version (*Th.* 371–4), followed here by Mimnermus as by most later poets, which makes Hyperion father of the sun.

MIMNERMUS 13

From Stobaeus 3.7 (περὶ ἀνδρείας). 11; attributed there to Mimnermus. It is most probably part of the poem in which he described Smyrna's exploits against Gyges and his Lydians: see 3n. The passage resembles Agamemnon's rebuke to Diomedes, son of Tydeus, in *Il.* 4.370 ff: cf. especially 372–4 οὐ μὲν Τυδέϊ γ᾽ ὧδε φίλον πτωσκαζέμεν ἦεν, | ἀλλὰ πολὺ πρὸ φίλων ἑτάρων δηΐοισι μάχεσθαι, | ὡς φάσαν οἵ μιν ἴδοντο πονεύμενον.

1. κείνου: we do not know who the warrior was.

μένος καὶ ἀγήνορα θυμόν: a line-ending at *Od.* 11.562.

2. ἐμεῦ προτέρων πεύθομαι: 'I learn from my elders.' For the gen. cf. *Od.* 10.537 πρὶν Τειρεσίαο πυθέσθαι.

3. Λυδῶν ἱππομάχων: Pausanias 9.29.4 refers to the elegiacs Mimnermus wrote on the Smyrnaeans' battle against Gyges and the Lydians. For the epithet cf. *Il.* 10.431 Φρύγες ἱππόμαχοι (so Aristarchus: MSS. ἱππόδαμοι).

κλονέοντα φάλαγγας: cf. *Il.* 5.96 θύνοντ' ἂμ πεδίον πρὸ ἕθεν
κλονέοντα φάλαγγας; cf. 93 πυκιναὶ . . . φάλαγγες.

4. φερεμμελίην: *hapax*, but ἐυμμελίης is common in Homer.

5. For Athene as judge of military prowess cf. *Il.* 13.128, 17.398.

8. βιαζόμενος: for the middle cf. *Il.* 22.229 σε βιάζετο ὠκὺς
'Αχιλλεύς, 'was pressing hard on you.' The meaning here
must be 'defying': cf. βίᾳ, 'in spite of' and *Il.* 11.558 ὡς δ'
ὅτ' ὄνος . . . ἐβιήσατο παῖδας.

9. ληῶν, if correct, is an Ionic gen. plur. of λαός: cf. Hippon. 88
(Bergk) ληὸν ἀθρήσας.

    ἀμεινότερος: this unusual comparative form is not Homeric,
    but Homer has λωΐτερον and χειρότερος as well as λώιον
    and χείρων.

11. εἴκελος: MSS. ὠκέος provides a hexameter-ending used by
    Mimnermus at 11.5, but can hardly stand here. Hudson-
    Williams and Diehl quote Hense, '*nullus illo melior dum
    vivebat*', but the use of the dative αὐγῆισιν for 'in the rays'
    and φέρετο for 'he lived, moved' is unparalleled and un-
    convincing. φέρετο = 'he rushed' (cf. φέρεται at *Il.* 20.172),
    and similes such as *Il.* 19.397–8 κορυσσάμενος βῆ 'Αχιλλεὺς |
    τεύχεσι παμφαίνων ὥς τ' ἠλέκτωρ 'Υπερίων, 17.87–8 βῆ
    δὲ διὰ προμάχων κεκορυθμένος αἴθοπι χαλκῷ | . . . φλογὶ
    εἴκελος 'Ηφαίστοιο, suggest that Meineke's εἴκελος is correct.

SOLON

Solon, the Athenian statesman, archon in 594/3, was also the
earliest figure in Athenian literary history and indeed the only
important Athenian poet before Aeschylus. He used verse both to
set out his political position and to express his thoughts on more
general topics — money-making, morality, man's life as a whole;
and it may have been his poetry no less than his politics which
gave him his place among the Seven Wise Men of the Greek
world.

In the early fr. 2, where he urges the Athenians to fight for Salamis, Solon refers to his use of poetry in preference to prose: αὐτὸς κῆρυξ ἦλθον ἀφ' ἱμερτῆς Σαλαμῖνος | κόσμον ἐπέων ᾠδὴν ἀντ' ἀγορῆς θέμενος (1–2). He must have realised that poetry is more easily remembered than prose, so that his audience would be more likely to mull over his words; and he had before him the example of Callinus and Tyrtaeus, who used elegiac couplets to urge their fellow-citizens to battle. Verbal echoes of Tyrtaeus are apparent not only in the political poems (cf. 4.6 οἳ πολλῶν ἀγαθῶν ἐς κόρον ἠλάσατε with Tyrt. 8.10) but in the reflective fr. 1 (cf. 1.32 with Tyrt. 9.30, 1.46 with Tyrt. 6.14 θνήσκωμεν ψυχέων μηκέτι φειδόμενοι). That Solon was *au fait* with contemporary poetry is shown by his exchange with Mimnermus (Sol. 22, Mimn. 6) and his enthusiasm for one of Sappho's poems (Stob. 3.29.58: asked why he wished to be taught it, he replied ἵνα μαθὼν αὐτὸ ἀποθάνω); but he shows close acquaintance too with Hesiod's poetry in the tone of his warnings to the Athenians, which recall Hesiod's words to his brother (cf. e.g. 1.7–10 with Hes. *Op.* 320), in his knowledge and use of Hesiod's *Theogony* (e.g. at 3.31–2), and in the techniques he employs when singing the praises of Eunomia (3.32 ff: cf. Hes. *Op.* 3–8, 225–37).

Solon leans much less heavily on Homer than do the earlier elegiac writers. There are fewer Homeric line-endings and epithets, and indeed Solon seems often deliberately to avoid the obvious Homeric expression (e.g. 1.49 πολυτέχνης for κλυτοτέχνης, 5.5 κρατερόν for στιβαρόν, 13.2 ἀγρευταί for θηρευταί). Words common in later Greek appear for the first time: ἁρπαγή, αὐξάνω, ἀφανής, δημόσιος, διπλάσιος, εὐθύνω, ἡσυχάζω, κίνδυνος, κλεινός, στάσις, σύνοδος, σύνοιδα, φλαῦρος, χάσκω, χαῦνος, all from Solon's elegiacs; and of course the trochaic and iambic lines, where Homeric influence has almost disappeared, show more: δουλεύω, ἐπισπάω, ἐπιτρίβω, μεταίχμιον, πολλαχῇ, συμμαρτυρέω, συναρμόζω, τυραννεύω. Homeric language occurs most thickly in three passages, one introductory (3.1–4) and two digressive (the simile at 1.18 ff and the catalogue of professions at 1.43 ff).

Solon's trochaic and iambic poetry, which forms only a small portion of his surviving work, deals almost exclusively with political matters, and the political pieces all belong to the years after his archonship when his measures and methods were under attack. The long iambic fr. 24 is written in polemic mood, and fr. 25 shows that Solon regarded iambics as the appropriate vehicle for ὄνειδος: δήμῳ μὲν εἰ χρὴ διαφάδην ὀνειδίσαι, | ἃ νῦν ἔχουσιν οὔποτ' ὀφθαλμοῖσιν ἂν | εὕδοντες εἶδον. His iambics and trochaics proceed at a vigorous pace and allow no digression or philosophical reflection such as we find in his elegiacs; and if the iambics have none of the virulence of Archilochus or Hipponax, this is no more than we should expect in a man whose self-restraint is always conspicuous. The trochaic lines at 23.1–7 reveal a sense of humour and a talent for characterisation which do not appear in the rest of his poetry.

It is easy to point to infelicities in his poems, and perhaps their unevenness is one of their main characteristics: note how in fr. 3 the fine lines on Justice (14–16) are followed by six clumsy lines, and these shortly after by the impassioned praise of Eunomia (32–9) to which Solon devoted especial care; fr. 1 also alternates between the impressive and the uncouth. His poems everywhere present a picture of an intelligent thinker, an ardent patriot, an enthusiastic but fair-minded reformer and a thoroughly honest man; and the influence on Herodotus and the tragedians of his moral thinking shows the high regard in which he was held in Greece.

SOLON 1

Quoted as Solon's by Stobaeus (3.9.23) under the heading περὶ δικαιοσύνης. Such a title is, however, too simple for so discursive a poem: there is no single subject but rather a series of reflections on several topics, one giving rise to another. R. Lattimore, 'The First Elegy of Solon', A.J.P. 68 (1947), 161–79, well describes the poem as 'a self-generating series of connected ideas: ... Solon is simply proceeding from thought to thought; talking to himself, that is, thinking, in such a way that we are not given the end-product, with reasons, but follow the train from its outset.'

A summary of the poem makes this clear:

1–6. Solon prays to the Muses for prosperity, a good reputation and the power to be loved and respected by his friends, hated and feared by his enemies.

7–32. The first of these prayers is modified: though Solon longs for wealth, he will not have it unjustly. Ill-gotten gains bring ruin, whether Zeus, who sees the end of all things, strikes early or late: sometimes it is the sinner's innocent descendants who have to pay the penalty.

33–42. Mortals, both good and evil, are (unlike Zeus, whose view is comprehensive) deluded by false beliefs and false hopes: e.g. the invalid, the coward, the ugly man, the pauper who expects to become wealthy one day.

43–62. Men seek wealth in various ways — trade, farming, craftsmanship, poetry, prophecy, medicine. (But in this catalogue the emphasis changes from methods of money-making to the uncertainty and lack of finality in human endeavours.)

63–70. The outcome of men's endeavours depends on the gods: success may come even to the man who sets about his business in the wrong way.

71–6. Worldly prosperity (the mention of 'success' in 70 may be the link here, but the transition is the most abrupt in the poem) causes greed, and greed brings ruin sooner or later.

The germ of the poem may have been the idea of wealth unjustly acquired, an idea which we find in other poems too — 3.5–6, 4.5–7, 5.9–10; but to call this Solon's subject *tout court* would be misleading.

The poem has not the melodious grace nor the meticulous finish of Mimnermus' lines. At its best, for example in the opening prayer or the simile of 17–25, it has a fine solemnity; but there is much that is harsh: ἰδεῖν ending lines 22 and 24 as well as 6; πάντως in 8, 28, 31, 42, 55 (see 8n.); πυθμήν pointlessly repeated, 10, 20; ἀργαλέος overworked, 37, 45, 61; τοῖσιν with ἄλλος as antecedent, 47–8.

See R. Lattimore l.c., F. Solmsen, *Hesiod and Aeschylus* 107–23, A. W. Allen, *T.A.P.A.* 80 (1949), 50–65.

1. Clement of Alexandria quotes this line as the beginning of the poem (*Strom.* 6.11.1). *Mnemosyne* (Memory) is mother of the Muses in *h. Merc.* 429–30 and Hes. *Th.* 52 ff, where we find also the canonical number and names of the Muses and their connexion with Pieria. Homer refers sometimes to a

single unspecified Muse, sometimes to an undefined number, e.g. *Il.* 2.491-2 'Ολυμπιάδες Μοῦσαι, Διὸς αἰγιόχοιο | θυγατέρες, but cf. *Od.* 24.60 Μοῦσαι . . . ἐννέα πᾶσαι with Stanford's note.

ἀγλαὰ τέκνα: a common line-ending in Homer; but except in the simile of 18–24 and the illustrative digression at 43-62 Solon borrows less from Homer than do earlier elegists: see 18n., 53n.

2. Μοῦσαι Πιερίδες: the epithet is in Hes. *Sc.* 206 but not in Homer: see Sapph. 55.2-3n.

3. πρὸς θεῶν: cf. *Od.* 11.302 τιμὴν πρὸς Ζηνὸς ἔχοντες. The Muses are not themselves asked to grant the blessings but may be imagined as putting the poet's request before the gods: 'give me prosperity from the immortal gods.' Note synizesis in θεῶν; also at 1.49 πολυτεχνέω, 51 Μουσέων, 72 ἡμέων, 3.2 θεῶν, 23.11 δοκέω; synecphonesis at 23.7 καὶ ἐπιτετρίφθαι.

4. δόξαν: first here in the sense of 'reputation'. Homer has the word only in the expression οὐδ' ἀπὸ δόξης 'and not other(wise) than one expects.'

ἔχειν: object of δότε, like ὄλβον.

5. ὧδε: 'in these (new) circumstances', i.e. blessed with prosperity and a good reputation, rather than 'as I now am'. For the prayer cf. Thgn. 869-72 and the particularly bloodthirsty 341-50. In *Od.* 6.184-5 Odysseus says that a happy marriage means πόλλ' ἄλγεα δυσμενέεσσι, | χάρματα δ' εὐμενέτῃσι, and Sappho's prayer for her brother is καὶ φίλοισ]ι Fοῖσι χάραν γένεσθαι | κωνίαν ἔ]χθροισι (5.6-7): cf. too Archil. 66n. The Cynic philosopher Crates in a parody of this poem wrote ὠφέλιμον δὲ φίλοις, μὴ γλυκερὸν τίθετε.

6. αἰδοῖον . . . δεινόν: Homer four times uses these adjectives together to describe one individual, e.g. *Il.* 3.172 (Helen to Agamemnon) αἰδοῖός τέ μοί ἐσσι . . . δεινός τε. Solon is probably giving a deliberate twist to the meaning of δεινός.

7. πεπᾶσθαι (=κεκτῆσθαι, ἔχειν), from *πάομαι. 'This word with its cognates is common in all dialects except Ionic-Attic' (Hudson-Williams); it is mainly poetic, though not Homeric. Theognis 145-6 has it in a passage similar to

Solon's: βούλεο δ' εὐσεβέων ὀλίγοις σὺν χρήμασιν οἰκεῖν | ἢ πλουτεῖν ἀδίκως χρήματα πασάμενος. For the idea cf. too E. fr. 362N².

8. πάντως: 'at all events', 'assuredly', a favourite word of Solon: cf. 28, 31, 42, 55; 3.16, 28. Defradas sees the repetition as deliberate and artistic: 'tout le développement est construit sur la reprise oratoire de πάντως, la conclusion se trouvant exprimée aux vers 31–32.' But πάντως recurs twice after this 'conclusion', and the repetition seems pointless rather, even slovenly. ἦλθε: the aorist is gnomic, as in 18, 22, 28, 29, 31, 38, 68.

9. πλοῦτος, subject of παραγίγνεται, has been attracted into the case of the relative pronoun: cf. S. O.T. 449 ff τὸν ἄνδρα τοῦτον, ὃν πάλαι | ζητεῖς . . . οὗτός ἐστιν ἐνθάδε and Jebb's note. δῶσι: for the absence of ἄν cf. Callin. 1.13n. and cf. 11, 29, 55. The same sentiment is in Hes. Op. 320 ff. χρήματα δ' οὐχ ἁρπακτά, θεόσδοτα πολλὸν ἀμείνω κτλ., Thgn. 197 ff, Pi. N. 8.17.

11. The imagery changes suddenly: wealth, a building or a tree or (Lattimore) standing grain in the last couplet, is now a disorderly follower.

12. ἔργμασι: not in Homer, though it occurs in the Homeric Hymns.

13. ἄτη: the idea of ἄτη, 'infatuation', is Homeric: cf. Il. 9.510–12: ὃς δέ κ' ἀνήνηται (i.e. rejects prayers) καί τε στερεῶς ἀποείπῃ, | λίσσονται δ' ἄρα ταί γε Δία Κρονίωνα κιοῦσαι | τῷ ἄτην ἅμ' ἕπεσθαι, ἵνα βλαφθεὶς ἀποτίσῃ. Solon's account, that ὕβρις brings ἄτη which brings the punishment of Zeus, became the canon for Herodotus (e.g. 1.34.1) and the tragedians, e.g. A. Pers. 821–2: ὕβρις γὰρ ἐξανθοῦσ' ἐκάρπωσε στάχυν | ἄτης ὅθεν πάγκλαυτον ἐξαμᾷ θέρος. Sol. 5.9–10 gives the first link in the chain: ὕβρις is bred by excessive wealth when the wealth is in the hands of irresponsible men.

14. ἀρχή: sc. ἄτης.

15. φλαύρη: the first occurrence of this favourite Attic adjective.

18 ff. Similes in elegiac writers are usually brief, like ὥστε πυρός in 14 above; but this poem moves at a leisurely pace, and

Solon now develops a simile with Homeric generosity. No closer parallel is cited from Homer than *Il.* 5.525–6 ζαχρηῶν ἀνέμων, οἵ τε νέφεα σκιόεντα | πνοιῇσιν λιγυρῇσι διασκιδνᾶσιν ἀέντες. But Homeric vocabulary is more evident in these lines than elsewhere in the poem except for 43–62: the epithets ἀτρυγέτοιο and πυροφόρον are familiar, and the *Iliad* has ἔργα . . . καλά (5.92), ἵκανε θεῶν ἕδος, αἰπὺν Ὄλυμπον (5.868), μένος ἠελίοιο (23.190), πίονα ἔργα (12.283). Yet Solon has his own ἠρινός (for Homer's εἰαρινός) and πολυκύμων (19).

25. ἐφ' ἑκάστῳ, 'at each thing', 'on each occasion.'

27. λέληθε: perfect tense with same meaning as present: cf. Semon. 7.9, Thgn. 121.

   διαμπερές with αἰεί, 'for ever, without a break': cf. *Il.* 15.70 αἰὲν . . . διαμπερές.

29 ff. For the idea of punishment delayed cf. *Il.* 4.160 ff. εἴ περ γάρ τε καὶ αὐτίκ' Ὀλύμπιος οὐκ ἐτέλεσσεν, | ἔκ τε καὶ ὀψὲ τελεῖ κτλ., Thgn. 203 ff. The construction of οἳ δὲ φύγωσιν is very free; ἐπ' αὐτούς can be supplied with ἤλυθε (31) to give an antecedent for οἵ.

30. θεῶν μοῖρα: cf. *Od.* 3.269, Callin. 1.9n.

31. τίνουσι: ι in epic, ῑ in Thgn. 740, Pi. *P.* 2.24 and in tragedy.

32. Cf. Tyrt. 9.30n.

34. The reading is much disputed; of the score of suggestions Ahrens' εὐθηνεῖν gives appropriate sense and acceptable Greek without departing too far from the MSS. ἐν δηνην: 'thus do we mortals reckon, both good and bad: each individual thinks he is prospering before something happens to him.'

37. νούσοισιν ὑπ' ἀργαλέῃσι: cf. *Il.* 13.667 νούσῳ ὑπ' ἀργαλέῃ, 61 below.

41. πενίης . . . ἔργα: for the periphrasis see Mimn. 2.12n. In 16 ὕβριος ἔργα may mean 'the products of ὕβρις'.

43. σπεύδει: sc. κτήσεσθαι; cf. 73 διπλασίως σπεύδουσι. Bacchylides 9.39–45 has a paraphrase of 43–54. ἀλᾶται: the verb is used of toiling sailors in *Od.* 2.370, 5.377, 9.254: cf. 3.73–4 (quoted in 46n. below).

45. Cf. *Od.* 9.82–3 φερόμην ὀλοοῖς ἀνέμοισι | πόντον ἐπ' ἰχθυόεντα.

Solon's placing of the word ἰχθυόεντα is startling, and reminds us that in Homer's view fish were grim creatures: cf. *Il.* 24.82 ἔρχεται ὠμηστῆσιν ἐπ' ἰχθύσι ('fish that eat raw flesh'), *Od.* 14.135 ἢ τόν γ' ἐν πόντῳ φάγον ἰχθύες, *Od.* 24.291. *Il.* 21.122–7. Hesiod too regarded sea-faring as a desperate way of making money (*Op.* 618 ff); cf. Tibullus 1.1.49–50.

46. Cf. Tyrt. 6.14 θνήσκωμεν ψυχέων μηκέτι φειδόμενοι, *Od.* 3.73–4 (of pirates) τοί τ' ἀλόωνται | ψυχὰς παρθέμενοι.

47. πολυδένδρεον: cf. *Od.* 23.139 ἀγρὸν ... πολυδένδρεον.

   εἰς ἐνιαυτόν: 'the whole year round': cf. *Il.* 21.444 θητεύσαμεν εἰς ἐνιαυτόν.

48. λατρεύει: 'works for hire.' The word and its cognates are not Homeric.

   τοῖσιν: relative pronoun with the singular ἄλλος as its antecedent, a harsh construction.

   καμπύλ' ἄροτρα: so *h. Cer.* 308.

49. Athena and Hephaestus (κλυτοτέχνης in Homer: cf. Mimn. 10.6n.) were patrons of craftsmen: cf. *Od.* 6.232–4 (=23.159–61) ἀνήρ | ἴδρις, ὃν Ἥφαιστος δέδαεν καὶ Παλλὰς Ἀθήνη | τέχνην παντοίην, χαρίεντα δὲ ἔργα τελείει, *h. Hom.* 20. They were worshipped in a common cult in Athens, where Athena was known as Ἐργάνη, the worker, and even as Ἡφαιστία.

51. Ὀλυμπιάδων Μουσέων: cf. 1n. above. For the gifts of the Muses see Archil. 1.2n.

   διδαχθείς: sc. ξυλλέγεται βίοτον. διδαχθείς answers χειροῖν in sense, but the participle δαείς in 50 makes the construction less harsh.

52. 'knowing the full measure of lovely skill'. σοφίη is used of musical skill in *h. Merc.* 483, 511: cf. Hes. fr. 306 M.-W. παντοίης σοφίης δεδαηκότα of Linus. Here it is used of the poet's skill as in later writers, Theognis and Pindar especially: see Thgn. 19n. For μέτρον cf. Hes. *Op.* 438, Thgn. 1119 μέτρον ἥβης, Sol. 16 γνωμοσύνης ... μέτρον (of god). In Thgn. 876 μέτρον ἔχων σοφίης means 'with due measure of wisdom'.

53. μάντιν: so *Od.* 15.252–3 Πολυφείδεα μάντιν Ἀπόλλων | θῆκε.

   ἄναξ ἑκάεργος Ἀπόλλων is a line-ending at *Il.* 15.253, 21.461,

Tyrt. 3a.1. Solon has more Homeric echoes in 43–62 than in any other part of the poem: cf. 1n., 18 ff n.

54· κακόν: gloom, absent from 49–52 alone, descends again on Solon's catalogue.

55· ᾧ συνομαρτήσωσι θεοί: the clause is conditional, 'if the gods are with him.' Attic prose would have ᾧ ἄν.

56· οἰωνός: cf. *Il.* 2.859 ἀλλ' οὐκ οἰωνοῖσιν ἐρύσσατο κῆρα μέλαιναν.

57· Παιῶνος πολυφαρμάκου: cf. *Il.* 16.28 ἰητροὶ πολυφάρμακοι. Homer uses the form Παιήων, e.g. *Il.* 5.401 ἐπὶ Παιήων ὀδυνήφατα φάρμακα πάσσων.

58· τέλος: 'finality', explained by 59–62: cf. Thgn. 660 θεοὶ ... οἷσιν ἔπεστι τέλος.

60. ἤπια φάρμακα: so in *Il.* 4.218 etc.

63· Μοῖρα: cf. Callin. 1.9n.

64· δῶρα δ' ἄφυκτα θεῶν: cf. *Il.* 3.65 οὔ τοι ἀπόβλητ' ἐστὶ θεῶν ἐρικυδέα δῶρα. There is nice irony in Solon's δῶρα δ' ἄφυκτα.

65–70. A version of these lines occurs in Thgn. 585–90, where the contrast is between ὁ μὲν εὐδοκιμεῖν πειρώμενος and τῷ δὲ καλῶς ποιεῦντι. With 65–6 cf. Thgn. 1075–8.

66. ᾗ μέλλει σχήσειν: 'where he will come ashore'. In Homer ἔχειν means 'to hold' a ship or a chariot in a certain direction, e.g. *Od.* 11.70 νῆσον ἐς Αἰαίην σχήσεις εὐεργέα νῆα. For the intransitive use cf. *Il.* 16.378 τῇ ῥ' ἔχε of Patroclus driving his chariot, and of ships coming ashore Hdt. 8.40.2 σχεῖν πρὸς τὴν Σαλαμῖνα, Ar. *Ran.* 188 ποῖ σχήσειν δοκεῖς.

67· εὖ ἔρδειν: 'to act in the right way', with reference to technical skill: ὁ κακῶς ἔρδων (69) sets about his business (e.g. healing the sick) in the wrong way, and his condition is ἀφροσύνη.

οὐ προνοήσας: 'unawares', with ἔπεσεν.

69. θεός: in 63 Solon had spoken of Μοῖρα and in 64 of δῶρα θεῶν; in 74 he uses ἀθάνατοι, in 75 Ζεύς. The expressions were clearly interchangeable for him.

70. ἔκλυσιν ἀφροσύνης: 'as an escape from his folly.'

71–6. Theognis has a version of these lines too (227–232), again

with the sense altered: χρήματά τοι θνητοῖς γίνεται
ἀφροσύνη, | ἄτη δ' ἐξ αὐτῆς ἀναφαίνεται . . .

71. Literally 'of wealth no limit is set up visible for men'.

73. διπλασίως σπεύδουσι: 'redouble their efforts.'

75. ἄτη: see 13n. above.

ἐξ αὐτῶν: i.e. from gain, κέρδεα. Cf. 5.9 τίκτει γὰρ κόρος
ὕβριν κτλ. There Solon makes explicit what he here leaves
implicit (in 72–3), that it is wealth in the hands of irresponsible men that brings ἄτη. In 76 ἄτην is to be supplied
as object of ἔχει.

SOLON 3

Quoted by Demosthenes, *De Falsa Legatione* 254 ff to convince
the jury that Solon hated the like of Aeschines. The poem has
much in common with fr. 1, but whereas there Solon simply gives
the substance of his reflections, here we find him giving explicit
warning and advice to his fellow-citizens: cf. 30 ταῦτα διδάξαι
θυμός 'Αθηναίους με κελεύει.

1. ἡμετέρα δὲ πόλις: this line is perhaps the best evidence
   that a poem might begin with a connective: see Archil.
   1.1n.

   κατὰ μὲν Διὸς . . . αἶσαν: cf. *Il.* 17.321 ὑπὲρ Διὸς αἶσαν,
   3.59 κατ' αἶσαν, 9.608 Διὸς αἴσῃ. The line-ending too is
   Homeric, e.g. at *Il.* 2.325; but there is less Homeric material
   after 1–4. For αἶσα see Alcm. 1.13n. Διὸς . . . αἶσα is 'the
   portion sent by Zeus', 'the dispensation of Zeus'.

2. μακάρων θεῶν . . . ἀθανάτων: cf. *Il.* 4.127–8 θεοὶ μάκαρες
   . . . ἀθάνατοι.

   φρένας: 'the purpose': cf. *Il.* 15.194 οὔ τι Διὸς βέομαι
   φρεσίν ('according to the will of Zeus I shall not live').

3. This passage is parodied in Ar. *Eq.* 1173–4 ὦ Δῆμ', ἐναργῶς ἡ
   θεός σ' ἐπισκοπεῖ, | καὶ νῦν ὑπερέχει σου χύτραν ζωμοῦ πλέαν
   ('a pot full of soup'): cf. 1178 ἡ δ' ὀβριμοπάτρα.

   ἐπίσκοπος is used of a protecting god for the first time here,
   though the gods are called ἐπίσκοποι ἁρμονιάων at *Il.*
   22.255, and Hector is ἐπίσκοπος of Troy, *Il.* 24.729. The
   rest of the couplet is thoroughly Homeric: cf. *Od.* 4.826–8
   τοίη γάρ οἱ πομπὸς ἅμ' ἔρχεται . . . | Παλλὰς 'Αθηναίη,

Od. 8.520, 13.121 μεγάθυμος and *Il.* 5.747 ὀβριμοπάτρη, both of Athena.

4. χεῖρας ὕπερθεν ἔχει: cf. *Il.* 9.419–20 Ζεὺς | χεῖρα ἑὴν ὑπερέσχε, sc. over Troy, 4.249, Thgn. 757–8 Ζεὺς μὲν τῆσδε πόληος ὑπειρέχοι ... | αἰεὶ δεξιτερὴν χεῖρ'. Defradas points out that Apollo on the west pediment of the temple of Zeus at Olympia holds his right arm outstretched.

5. αὐτοὶ κτλ.: Jaeger pointed out the similarity of the language with 8.1–4 (written when Peisistratus had seized power): εἰ δὲ πεπόνθατε λυγρὰ δι' ὑμετέρην κακότητα, | μὴ θεοῖσιν τούτων μοῖραν ἐπαμφέρετε· αὐτοὶ γὰρ τούτους ηὐξήσατε ..., and with *Od.* 1.32 ff where Zeus exclaims ὢ πόποι, οἷον δή νυ θεοὺς βροτοὶ αἰτιόωνται. | ἐξ ἡμέων γάρ φασι κάκ' ἔμμεναι· οἱ δὲ καὶ αὐτοὶ | σφῇσιν ἀτασθαλίῃσιν ὑπὲρ μόρον ἄλγε' ἔχουσιν.

ἀφραδίῃσι: a common Homeric line-ending, e.g. at *Od.* 10.27.

6. χρήμασι πειθόμενοι: 'putting their trust in money', rather than 'being bribed'; cf. 11 (also 1.12, Thgn. 380) ἀδίκοις ἔργμασι πειθόμενοι.

7. δήμου ... ἡγεμόνων: i.e. the nobles, the governing class.

ἑτοῖμον: 'certain': cf. *Il.* 18.96 αὐτίκα γάρ τοι ... πότμος ἑτοῖμος, Anacr. 395.11–12 ἑτοῖμον | καταβάντι μὴ ἀναβῆναι.

8. ἄλγεα πολλὰ παθεῖν: cf. *Od.* 9.53 ἄλγεα πολλὰ πάθομεν, 1.4 πολλὰ ... πάθεν ἄλγεα.

9. κόρον: 'their excessive wealth', or perhaps the result of it, 'insolence', as in 34 below, Pi. *O.* 2.95.

οὐδὲ παρούσας κτλ: literally, 'nor to conduct decently the present joys of their feasting in quietness'; this can hardly be interpreted metaphorically as e.g. Linforth would: the feasts are quite likely to be real, and Solon may be contrasting present pleasures with sorrows to come (ἄλγεα πολλά).

11. Hexameters have been lost before and after this pentameter. After 25 a pentameter is missing.

13. κλέπτουσι ἐφ' ἁρπαγῇ: ἐφ' ἁρπαγῇ should mean 'with an eye to plunder' as in 23.13 ἐφ' ἁρπαγαῖσιν ἦλθον, but it adds nothing to κλέπτουσιν. ἀφαρπαγῇ of the MSS. may conceal something quite different.

14. σεμνὰ Δίκης θέμεθλα: a fine phrase. The imagery is, as far as we can say, original, though θέμεθλα is a Homeric word. Δίκη is personified in Hes. *Th.* 902 (as child of Zeus and Themis and sister of Eunomia), *Op.* 256 ff: cf. V. Ehrenberg, *Aspects of the Ancient World,* 70 ff.

15. πρό τ' ἐόντα: cf. *Il.* 1.70 of Calchas, ὃς ᾔδη τά τ' ἐόντα τά τ' ἐσσόμενα πρό τ' ἐόντα.

16. ἦλθε: gnomic aorist, as in 20, 28, but probably not 18.

17–22. These lines are difficult. I take them as follows: 'this (i.e. the outrageous behaviour of the rich, 7–16) is now coming on the whole city (i.e. rich and poor alike) as an inescapable wound, and it (the city, but with reference to the poor) has swiftly come (aorist with perfect sense) to foul slavery, which rouses civil strife and war from sleep — war which destroys (gnomic aorist) the lovely youth of many; for at the hands of the enemy (i.e. the unruly rich of 7–16) swiftly the lovely city is being destroyed in associations dear to the unjust. These are the evils that are at large among the people.' The passage, in this interpretation as in others, has its infelicities: ἤλυθε (18), with perfect significance, between ἦλθε (16) and ὤλεσεν (20), gnomic aorists (but these are both in relative clauses; Schneidewin plausibly conjectured ἐπέγειρεν in 19, another gnomic aorist); the relative clause within a relative clause (19–20); ταχέως repeated (18, 21); δυσμενέων (21) used metaphorically without preparation, unless 19–20 on πόλεμος can be regarded as such; the harsh ἐν συνόδοις τοῖς ἀδικοῦσι φίλαις (22).

17. πάσῃ πόλει: 'the whole city' (as in Tyrt. 9.28), not only the sinners: cf. 26 δημόσιον κακόν.

19. στάσιν ἔμφυλον: cf. Alc. 70.11 ἐμφύλω . . . μάχας, Thgn. 51 στάσιές τε καὶ ἔμφυλοι φόνοι ἀνδρῶν, Hdt. 8.3.1 στάσις . . . ἔμφυλος.

πόλεμον θ' εὕδοντ' ἐπεγείρει: in *Iliad* Homer has ἐγείρειν with πόλεμον (20.31), μάχην (13.788), φύλοπιν (5.496 etc.), Ἄρηα (2.440 etc.). Solon's εὕδοντα makes the metaphor more telling.

21. ἐκ: cf. *Il.* 2.668–9 φίληθεν | ἐκ Διός ('they were loved by Zeus'). Sol. 10.3.

πολυήρατον ἄστυ: cf. *Od.* 11.275 Θήβη πολυηράτῳ.

22. συνόδοις: 'associations', almost certainly with reference to the political clubs (ἑταιρεῖαι) of Athens; the term is so used by Ar. *Eq.* 477, Th. 3.82.6, Pl. *Theaet.* 173d. Hdt. 5.71.1 speaks of the ἑταιρεία of Cylon (*c.* 630 B.C.).

23. στρέφεται: used of rampaging animals, *Il.* 12.41–2 ἔν τε κύνεσσι καὶ ἀνδράσι θηρευτῆισιν | κάπριος ἠὲ λέων στρέφεται, Sol. 24.27 ὡς ἐν κυσὶν πολλῆισιν ἐστράφην λύκος.

24. γαῖαν ἐς ἀλλοδαπήν: cf. *Od.* 9.36 γαίῃ ἐν ἀλλοδαπῇ.

25. πραθέντες: from πέρνημι; so in 24.9.

27. αὔλειοι . . . θύραι: cf. *Od.* 18.239 ἐπ᾽ αὐλείῃσι θύρῃσι, 'the courtyard door.'

ἔχειν οὐκ ἐθέλουσι: almost 'cannot keep it out'; cf. *Il.* 21.366 of the river Xanthus, οὐδ᾽ ἔθελε προρέειν, ἀλλ᾽ ἴσχετο. It is as though a failure of will-power brought total disability. For less clear examples see L.S.J. ἐθέλω I.2.

28. ὑπέρθορεν: cf. *Il.* 9.476 ὑπέρθορον ἑρκίον αὐλῆς.

29. For the sense cf. Callin. 1.15.

μυχῷ . . . θαλάμου: cf. *Il.* 17.36 μυχῷ θαλάμοιο, *Od.* 16.285 ἐς μυχὸν . . . θαλάμου.

30. θυμός . . . με κελεύει: cf. *Il.* 7.68 ὄφρ᾽ εἴπω τά με θυμὸς ἐνὶ στήθεσσι κελεύει.

31. Δυσνομίη and Εὐνομίη are personified in Hes. *Th.* 230, 902. In *Od.* 17.487 εὐνομίη is opposed to ὕβρις, and in Hesiod's account Eunomia is sister of Justice (Δίκη) and Peace (Εἰρήνη), children all of Zeus and Themis. One of Tyrtaeus' poems was entitled *Eunomia* by him or by later writers. Jaeger gave the same title to the present poem of Solon (*Solons Eunomie*, Sitzungsber. Preuss. Akad., 1926, 69 ff = *Scripta Minora* i.315). For a full account of Eunomia in Greek thought see V. Ehrenberg, *Aspects of the Ancient World* 70–93.

32 ff. Solon describes the blessings of Eunomia with the fervour of an Old Testament prophet. Jaeger (l.c.) draws attention to the techniques employed — antithesis (32–3), asyndeton and a double chiasmus (34), anaphora and the sequence of clauses begun by their verbs (35–8 αὐαίνει δ᾽ . . . εὐθύνει δέ . . . παύει δ᾽ . . . παύει δ᾽ . . . ἔστι δ᾽), homoeoteleuton

or rhyme (λειαίνει ... ἀναίνει, εὐθύνει ... πραΰνει), the
repetition of πάντα and ἄρτια (32, 39) to round off the
passage; he points out that the same devices were used by
Hesiod in his proem to *Works and Days* (3–8), and suggests
that Solon was borrowing devices of cult poetry to give his
work a religious solemnity. Jaeger also points out that
Solon's praise of Eunomia is written in the same spirit as
Hesiod's account of the blessings that befall just men (*Op.*
225–37).

ἄρτια: 'whole, sound', a favourite adjective of Solon: cf.
3.39, 4.8, 5.10.

35. This fine metaphor does not seem to be borrowed property.
Aeschylus may have had Solon's line in mind at *Pers.*
821–2 ὕβρις γὰρ ἐξανθοῦσ᾽ ἐκάρπωσεν στάχυν | ἄτης, ὅθεν
πάγκλαυτον ἐξαμᾷ θέρος, *Sept.* 601 ἄτης ἄρουρα θάνατον
ἐκκαρπίζεται.

36. εὐθύνει δὲ δίκας σκολιάς: cf. Hes. *Op.* 221 σκολιῆς ... δίκης,
250, 264; Pi. *P.* 4.153 εὔθυνε λαοῖς δίκας, Thgn. 40 εὐθυντῆρα
κακῆς ὕβριος ἡμετέρης.

37. ἔργα διχοστασίης: for the periphrasis cf. Mimn. 2.12n.
διχοστασίη appears first here: Thgn. 78 ends with διχοστασίη.

38. ἀργαλέης ἔριδος: cf. *Il.* 17.384–5 ἔριδος ... ἀργαλέης.

SOLON 5

These lines were written after Solon's legislation had been
passed. 1–6 and 7–10 are quoted separately by Aristotle *Ath. Pol.*
12.1 as evidence for his account of Solon's reforms and their
results. 1–6 were already known from Plutarch *Solon* 18.5, 7–8
from *Poplic.* 25.6. A version of 9–10 appears at Theognis 153–4.
11 is from *Solon* 25.

1. γέρας: cf. *Od.* 7.150 γέρας ... ὅ τι δῆμος ἔδωκεν, sc. to the
Phaeacian nobles; Thuc. 1.13 πρότερον δ᾽ ἦσαν ἐπὶ ῥητοῖς
γέρασι πατρικαὶ βασιλεῖαι.

2. ἐπορεξάμενος: 'giving in excess': τιμῆς is partitive gen. with
both participles. For ἐπορέγω (active) cf. *Il.* 5.224–5 εἴ περ
ἂν αὖτε | Ζεὺς ἐπὶ Τυδεΐδῃ Διομήδεϊ κῦδος ὀρέξῃ.

3. ἀγητοί: cf. Homer's εἶδος ἀγητοί.

4. ἐφρασάμην . . . ἔχειν: 'I saw to it that they should have'; for the infin. cf. *Il.* 9.347 φραζέσθω . . . ἀλεξέμεναι.

5. i.e. I gave my protection to both sides; but the metaphor, 'covering both sides with my stout shield', is not particularly happy. With ἀμφιβαλών cf. *Il.* 3.334–5 ἀμφὶ δ' ἄρ' ὤμοισιν βάλετο ξίφος . . . αὐτὰρ ἔπειτα σάκος.

7. σὺν ἡγεμόνεσσιν ἕποιτο: cf. Homer's line-ending ἅμ' ἡγεμόνεσσιν ἕποντο, *Il.* 12.87, 13.801. Theognis 41 has ἡγεμόνες of political leaders.

8. ἀνεθείς: aor. pass. part. of ἀνίημι, 'given the rein.' Cf. Plu. *Per.* 11 τῷ δήμῳ τὰς ἡνίας ἀνείς.

9–10. Cf. Pi. *O.* 1.55–7 of Tantalus: ἀλλὰ γὰρ καταπέψαι | μέγαν ὄλβον οὐκ ἐδυνάσθη, κόρῳ δ' ἕλεν | ἄταν ὑπέροπλον. Theognis' version of Solon's lines introduces a new idea: τίκτει τοι κόρος ὕβριν, ὅταν κακῷ ὄλβος ἔπηται | ἀνθρώπῳ καὶ ὅτῳ μὴ νόος ἄρτιος ᾖ. The parentage is reversed in Pi. *O.* 13.10 Ὕβριν, Κόρου ματέρα, and in an oracle at Hdt. 8.77.1 Κόρον, Ὕβριος υἱόν.

10. νόος ἄρτιος: see 3.32n. and cf. the Homeric ἀρτίφρων (*Od.* 24.261).

11. Cf. Thgn. 24 ἀστοῖσιν δ' οὔπω πᾶσιν ἀδεῖν δύναμαι.

SOLON 10

Quoted by Diodorus Siculus 9.20.2 with the words, 'Solon is said to have foretold the Athenians of the coming tyranny (i.e. the rule of Peisistratus) in elegiacs.' Diodorus 19.1.4 has 3–4, Diogenes Laertius 1.50 has 1–4, Plutarch *Solon* 3.6 has 1–2.

1. χιόνος μένος: for μένος of other natural forces cf. *Il.* 5.524 μένος Βορέαο, 6.182 πυρὸς μένος αἰθομένοιο, 12.18 ποταμῶν μένος, Sol. 1.23 ἠελίοιο μένος. The line recalls *Il.* 15.170 ὡς δ' ὅτ' ἂν ἐκ νεφέων πτῆται νιφὰς ἠὲ χάλαζα.

3. ἀνδρῶν δ' ἐκ μεγάλων: Solon links the couplets by a mere δέ, but it is clear that he regards political events as bound by laws similar to the laws of nature: as the cloud brings snow and hail, and lightning is followed by thunder, the emergence of 'great men' will lead to the destruction of the city. For ἐκ see 3.21n.

μονάρχου: the word occurs first here and in Thgn. 52 μούναρχοι. For the gen. with δουλοσύνην ('enslavement to') cf. Thuc. 1.8.2.

4. ἀϊδρείῃ as in *Od.* 12.41.

ἔπεσεν: gnomic aorist.

5. ἐξάραντ': better taken transitively, 'if you exalt a man too high it is not easy to keep him in check afterwards', than intransitively, 'when a man has risen too high': the blame for the exaltation of the men rests with the δῆμος; cf. 8.3 αὐτοὶ γὰρ τούτους ηὐξήσατε, Hdt. 6.126.1 Κλεισθένης μιν (sc. the family of Alcmaeon) . . . ἐξῆρε, ὥστε πολλῷ ὀνομαστοτέρην γενέσθαι.

6. τάδε is as likely a supplement as any: cf. *Od.* 2.122 τοῦτό γ' ἐναίσιμον οὐκ ἐνόησε.

SOLON 13

Quoted by Plato *Lysis* 212e without the poet's name; ascribed to Solon by the scholiast on *Phaedrus* 231e. For Theognis' version (1253–6) see 1n. and 2n. The lines remind us that Solon's family belonged to the hunting and shooting aristocracy.

1. Solon clearly meant 'Happy is he who has dear children, single-hoofed horses' etc. Theognis amusingly perverted the sense: after his version of the couplet he has ὅστις μὴ παῖδάς τε φιλεῖ καὶ μώνυχας ἵππους | καὶ κύνας, οὔποτε οἱ θυμὸς ἐν εὐφροσύνῃ. Of the epithets three are Homeric: cf. *Od.* 19.455 παῖδες φίλοι, *Il.* 11.708 καὶ μώνυχες ἵπποι (a line-ending), *Od.* 17.485 ξείνοισιν . . . ἀλλοδαποῖσι.

2. ἀγρευταί: first here. The Homeric word θηρευταί (cf. *Il.* 11.325, 12.41) is used in Theognis' version, θηρευταί τε κύνες καὶ ξένοι ἀλλοδαποί.

SOLON 19

Quoted as Solon's by Philo *De Opificio Mundi* 104, by Clement of Alexandria *Strom.* 6.144.3, and in *Anecdota Parisina* 1.46 Cramer, and referred to by various ancient writers. Solon's division of man's life into ten stages did not become canonical for later writers: Hudson-Williams 130–1 has an account of other divisions. Shakespeare's seven ages are found in Hippocrates

Hebd. 5 and Pollux 2.4. Solon's poem is graceless and has few striking turns of phrase such as Shakespeare introduced into his 'Seven Ages' (*As You Like It* 2.7); and, given the rigid format of the poem, only sharp characterisation of each age could have saved it from monotony. The ordinal numbers, omitted by Shakespeare, are intractable material, and the structure of the poem collapses when the seventh and eighth ages are combined in the seventh couplet.

1. ἔτι νήπιος must be taken with ἕρκος ὀδόντων φύσας, ἄνηβος ἐών with ἐκβάλλει. ἕρκος ὀδόντων in Homer always has the idea of a barrier, through which a man's words or dying breath (*Il.* 9.409) pass out or drugs in (*Od.* 10.328). For Solon the phrase is merely a convenient line-ending; one might regard its use as humorous if there were humour elsewhere in the poem.

2. φύσας: cf. Ar. *Ran.* 422 ὃς ἐπτέτης ὢν οὐκ ἔφυσε φράτερας (comically for φραστῆρας, his second teeth).

   πρῶτον: adverbially, 'for the first time.'

3. ἑτέρους: his 'second' seven years.

4. ἥβης: Heraclitus (fr. A 18 Diels-Kranz), Aristotle *Hist. Anim.* 581a and other ancient writers give fourteen as the age of puberty.

5. τῇ τριτάτῃ: sc. ἑβδομάδι (7).

   ἀεξομένων . . . γυίων: cf. Hes. *Th.* 492–3 γυῖα | ηὔξετο.

6. λαχνοῦται: cf. *Od.* 11.319–20 πρίν σφωῖν ὑπὸ κροτάφοισιν ἰούλους ('down') | ἀνθῆσαι πυκάσαι τε γένυς εὐανθέι λάχνῃ. χροιῆς ἄνθος ἀμειβομένης: copied by A. *P.V.* 23 χροιᾶς ἀμείψεις ἄνθος.

7. πᾶς τις: not Homeric, but at Thgn. 22, 621.

   μέγ' ἄριστος a Homeric line-ending, e.g. *Il.* 16.271. The lengthening of -ι before μέγ' is also epic: cf. *Il.* 6.91 ἐνὶ μεγάρῳ.

8. σήματα: for plural in apposition to singular (ἰσχύν, ἥν) cf. Hes. *Sc.* 312–13 τρίπος . . . | χρύσειος, κλυτὰ ἔργα . . . Ἡφαίστοιο.

   ἀρετῆς: 'excellence', in a general sense as in 16: cf. Tyrt. 8.13n. The word may be cognate with ἀνήρ, and 'manliness' would give the correct sense here.

9. ὤριον: neuter, 'it is the right time.' Cf. Hes. *Op.* 697 of marriage at thirty, γάμος δέ τοι ὥριος οὗτος. Plato agrees (*Resp.* 460e, *Leg.* 772e).

μεμνημένον εἶναι: Hesiod has μεμνημένος εἶναι twice as a line-ending (*Op.* 616, 641).

10. εἰσοπίσω: 'for the future', 'to come after him', as in *h. Ven.* 104 ποίει δ' εἰσοπίσω θαλερὸν γόνον. Cf. Tyrt. 9.30, Sol. 1.32 γένος ἐξοπίσω.

11. καταρτύεται: 'is disciplined', first here. Cf. S. *Ant.* 477–8 σμικρῷ χαλινῷ δ' οἶδα τοὺς θυμουμένους | ἵππους καταρτυθέντας, Pl. *Leg.* 808d ἔχει πηγὴν τοῦ φρονεῖν μήπω κατηρτυμένην.

12. ἀπάλαμνα: 'lawless' according to L.S.J.; but although it means 'lawless' in Thgn. 281 and Pi. *O.* 2.63, it seems to mean 'stupid' in Thgn. 481 and Alc. 360.2, and it may have that meaning here. It might equally well mean 'impossible': in *Il.* 5.597, Hes. *Op.* 20 and Simon. 542.34 it is used of 'shiftless' men (from ἀ- and παλάμη, cf. Scottish 'handless'), and like ἀμήχανος it may have been used also of impossible things (cf. Hsch. ἀπάλαμνος· ἀσθενής, ἀμήχανος).

13–14. ἑπτά . . . ὀκτώ τ': Solon abandons ordinal numbers, perhaps for variety, not because of the difficulty of introducing ἑβδόμη and ὀγδόη, since the Homeric ἑβδομάτη and ὀγδοάτη were available. μέγ' ἄριστος is repeated from 7 and ἀμφοτέρων τέσσαρα καὶ δέκ' ἔτη is mere padding. Solon may have found it difficult to distinguish satisfactorily between the 43–49 and 50–56 age-groups.

15. δύναται: i.e. 'he is still a forceful speaker and thinker', or perhaps 'he is still strong'.

μαλακώτερα: 'feebler': cf. Th. 2.18.3 ἐν τῇ ξυναγωγῇ τοῦ πολέμου μαλακός. In Homer it is used rather of 'soft, flattering' speech.

16. πρὸς μεγάλην ἀρέτην: probably 'in relation to great excellence', almost 'by the highest standards'.

17. κατὰ μέτρον ἵκοιτο = καθίκοιτο μέτρον, sc. τῆς δεκάτης, which some editors introduce into the text for τῇ δεκάτῃ, the reading of most MSS., 'if a man finally reached the full measure of the tenth age'; cf. *Il.* 11.225 ἥβης . . . ἵκετο μέτρον.

18. μοῖραν ἔχοι θανάτου: cf. Callin. 1.15n. Solon's view is expressed also in Herodotus' account of the discussion between Solon and Croesus (1.32.2): ἐς γὰρ ἑβδομήκοντα ἔτεα οὖρον τῆς ζοῆς ἀνθρώπῳ προτίθημι. But in 22.4 his prayer is ὀγδωκονταέτη μοῖρα κίχοι θανάτου.

SOLON 22

The three pieces need not belong to the same poem. 1–4 are quoted by Diogenes Laertius 1.60: 'They say that when Mimnermus wrote αἲ γὰρ ἄτερ νούσων τε καὶ ἀργαλέων μελεδωνῶν | ἑξηκονταέτη μοῖρα κίχοι θανάτου (fr. 6), Solon found fault with him and said, ἀλλ' εἴ μοι κτλ.' 5–6 are from Plutarch Poplic. 24.5 and Stobaeus 4.54 (περὶ πένθους). 3. 7 is from (Plato) Amatores 133c and was quoted by many other writers.

1. κἂν νῦν ἔτι: 'even at this late date.' κἂν may be taken with νῦν with the sense of καί, as in later Attic, e.g. Ar. Ach. 1021 κἂν πέντ' ἔτη. In this case εἰ . . . πείσεαι (fut. indic.) =εἰ ἐθέλεις πείθεσθαι. But εἴ (αἴ) κε with the fut. indic. is found in Homer, e.g. Il. 15.213–15 αἴ κεν ἄνευ ἐμέθεν . . . | Ἰλίου αἰπεινῆς πεφιδήσεται, οὐδ' ἐθελήσει | ἐκπέρσαι κτλ.. and this may be Solon's construction here.

τοῦτον: sc. τὸν στίχον or τὸν λόγον.

3. Λιγυαστάδη: Bergk corrected the text by reference to the Suda: Μίμνερμος Λιγυρτυάδου. . . . ἐκαλεῖτο δὲ καὶ Λιγυαστάδης (MSS. Λιγειαστάδης, Λιγιστιάδης) διὰ τὸ ἐμμελὲς καὶ λιγύ. The derivation from λιγύς and ἀστής ('singer', ᾄδω) is most likely.

4. ὀγδωκονταέτη: acc. sing., sc. με, object of κίχοι.

μοῖρα κίχοι θανάτου: cf. Callin. 1 introd. and 1.15n.

5. Cicero translated these lines (T.D. 1.49.117): mors mea ne careat lacrimis, linquamus amicis | maerorem, ut celebrent funera cum gemitu. There and in Cato Maior 20.73 he contrasted Solon's prayer with Ennius' nemo me lacrimis decoret, neque funera fletu | faxit, which he preferred.

6. καλλείποιμι: for καταλείποιμι by apocope.

ἄλγεα καὶ στοναχάς: cf. Homer's line-ending ἄλγεά τε στοναχάς τε (Il. 2.39, Od. 14.39).

7. διδασκόμενος: cf. A. *P.V.* 981 ἀλλ' ἐκδιδάσκει πάνθ' ὁ γηράσκων χρόνος. For the middle voice cf. Tyrt. 8.27n.

SOLON 23

Solon's version of the vulgar claptrap on his refusal to become tyrant; quoted by Plutarch *Solon* 14.8. The other dozen trochaic lines of Solon are similar in spirit to his elegiac verse, but these lines show a lively sense of humour and a gift for characterisation. 8–12 are from the same chapter of Plutarch, who says that the lines were addressed to one Phocus.

Metre: trochaic tetrameter catalectic.

1. βαθύφρων: elsewhere only in elevated surroundings, at Pi. *N.* 7.1 Ἐλείθυια, πάρεδρε Μοιρᾶν βαθυφρόνων.
   βουλήεις occurs nowhere else.

3. περιβαλών: so in Hdt. 1.141.2 λαβεῖν ἀμφίβληστρον καὶ περιβαλεῖν τε πλῆθος πολλὸν τῶν ἰχθύων καὶ ἐξειρύσαι.
   ἀγασθείς: 'in his amazement', aor. pass. part. of ἄγαμαι.
   ἐπέσπασεν: ἐπισπάω, 'pull to', is used of the tightening of a noose at Dem. 24.139 τέθνηκεν ἐπισπασθέντος τοῦ βρόχου.

4. ἁμαρτῇ: 'together, at one and the same time', the Homeric adverb.

5. ἤθελεν: Xylander, the 16th-century editor of Plutarch, emended the text to ἤθελον (1st pers. sing.), but ἤθελεν γάρ κεν comes aptly enough after lines 1 and 4: 'otherwise he would have been willing.'

6. τυραννεύσας: the verb is used for the first time here. For τυραννίς etc. see Archil. 22.3n. Euripides may have had this passage in mind when he wrote *Phoen.* 504–6.

7. A thoroughly Aristophanic line. ἀσκὸς ... δεδάρθαι: 'to be flayed as a wine-skin': cf. *Nub.* 440 ff τουτὶ τό γ' ἐμὸν σῶμ' αὐτοῖσιν | παρέχω ... ἀσκὸν δείρειν, *Eq.* 370 δερῶ σε θύλακον κλοπῆς, 'I'll flay you into a thief's purse.' ἐπιτρίβω is also a favourite verb of Aristophanes. The fate of Marsyas who was flayed alive may have been the source of the expression; cf. Hdt. 7.26.3 ὁ τοῦ Σιληνοῦ Μαρσύεω ἀσκός, Pl. *Euthyd.* 285c–d.
   γένος: probably acc. of respect, 'to have his posterity wiped out', rather than subject of ἐπιτετρῖφθαι.

SOLON 24

Aristotle *Ath. Pol.* 12 quotes these lines in connexion with Solon's cancellation of debts and the slaves freed by his σεισάχ-θεια. Most of the passage was quoted too by Aelius Aristides 28.138 ff, and a few of the lines are in Plutarch *Solon* 15.

Metre: iambic trimeter.

1. τῶν: relative pronoun with τούτων (2) as antecedent. τῶν μέν is echoed by ταῦτα μέν at 15 and answered by θεσμοὺς δ' at 18.

1–2. ξυνήγαγον δῆμον: variously interpreted as 'I united the people', i.e. in his capacity as arbiter between rich and poor (but Solon never claims elsewhere that the people were united in this sense as a result of his work: on the contrary, there were two sides, both dissatisfied); 'I formed the democratic party' (another unlikely claim); 'I called the people to an assembly': the last must be correct: ξυνάγειν is so used in Th. 1.120, 2.60.1, and Solon may refer to such a meeting in 23.18 ἃ μὲν γὰρ εἶπα, σὺν θεοῖσιν ἤνυσα. τί is object of τυχεῖν and τούτων is partitive gen., literally 'before achieving which of these things did I stop?' Solon claims to have achieved them all, as at 23.18.

3. ταῦτα: i.e. the whole situation, the truth of the matter.

ἐν δίκῃ χρόνου: 'in the court of Time'; this splendid phrase is bold, but emendation (such as Bergk's ἐν Δίκης θρόνῳ) is not needed. Pindar has ἀνδρῶν δικαίων χρόνος σωτὴρ ἄριστος (fr. 255 Turyn), Sophocles χρόνος δίκαιον ἄνδρα δείκνυσιν μόνος (*O.T.* 614).

4. μήτηρ ... δαιμόνων 'Ολυμπίων: according to Linforth, Earth is nowhere else referred to as the mother of the Olympians, although she is θεῶν μήτηρ in *h. Hom.* 30.17. Note that ἄριστα (5) is an adverb.

5. Γῆ μέλαινα: see Archil. 58.2n.

6. ὅρους: posts set up to record mortgaged land; see Plu. *Sol.* 15.5. For a full discussion see J. V. A. Fine, 'Horoi', *Hesperia, Supplem.* IX (1951), especially 181–3. Solon uses the word figuratively in other iambic lines (25.8–9): ἐγὼ δὲ τούτων (i.e. rich and poor) ὥσπερ ἐν μεταιχμίῳ ὅρος

κατέστην, 'I stood like a ὅρος in no-man's-land between them.'

8. θεόκτιτον: Homer has εὔκτιτος and θεόδμητος; cf. S. *El.* 707 Ἀθηνῶν τῶν θεοδμήτων. Solon's patriotism is never more in evidence than in this passage.

10–11. ἀναγκαίης ὑπὸ χρειοῦς: 'by dire necessity', like Homer's χρειοῖ ἀναγκαίῃ (*Il.* 8.57). Even in his iambics Solon occasionally uses the Homeric epithet: cf. Γῆ μέλαινα (5).

12. ὡς ἂν ... πλανωμένους: 'as one would expect in men who had been travelling far and wide.'

15–17. 'Now these things I did by force, linking together might and right.' Solon is contrasting his arbitrary measures with the θεσμοί which followed. It is as though he thought the term κράτει harsh, and modified it by line 16 — the same technique as in fr. 1. The London papyrus of *Ath. Pol.* has κρατεεινομου, which alone recommends the reading 'κράτει νόμου, 'by the force of law'; but Plutarch, who quotes line 16 by itself, begins it with ὁμοῦ, and, as Defradas says, the unusual combination of βίην τε καὶ δίκην is made more striking if it is flanked by ὁμοῦ ... συναρμόσας.

17. διῆλθον ὡς ὑπεσχόμην: so in his trochaics Solon said ἃ μὲν γὰρ εἶπα, σὺν θεοῖσιν ἤνυσα (23.18).

18. θεσμούς: Homer has the word once only, in *Od.* 23.296 λέκτροιο παλαιοῦ θεσμὸν ἵκοντο, where it probably shows its connexion with τίθημι and refers to the location of the bed; *h. Hom.* 8.16 εἰρήνης ... ἐν ἀπήμοσι θεσμοῖς refers to the ordered life of peacetime. The term is used by Solon here and in 28.2 (if the lines are genuinely his) of his laws; cf. too Plu. *Sol.* 19.3. It was the regular term for Draco's laws.

τῷ κακῷ τε κἀγαθῷ: a good example of the social and political use of the words.

19. εἰς ἕκαστον: 'for each man.'

20. ὡς ἐγώ: probably 'as I did'. The alternative is to take ἄλλος ὡς ἐγώ as 'another than I': see Xenoph. 3.4n.

21. κακοφραδής: 'unscrupulous', as in *Il.* 23.483.

22–4. ἤθελον has ἃ ... ἤνδανεν and ἃ ... φρασαίατο as its objects. τοῖς ἐναντίοισιν must be the opponents of the

δῆμος, so that τοῖσιν will also refer to the aristocrats and
οὕτεροι to the democrats. τότε presumably refers to the
time of the reforms, αὖθις to a later date. But the lines are
not pellucid.

25. ἐχηρώθη: Homer has Ἰλίου ἐξαλάπαξε πόλιν, χήρωσε δ᾽ ἀγυιάς
(*Il.* 5.642), and Herodotus echoes Solon: Ἄργος δὲ ἀνδρῶν
ἐχηρώθη (6.83.1).

26. ἀλκὴν πάντοθεν ποιεύμενος: probably 'displaying courage
everywhere'. In S. *O.C.* 459 ἀλκὴν ποιεῖσθαι means 'to
help'.

27. ἐστράφην: cf. Homer's simile of Hector's exploits against the
Greeks: ὡς δ᾽ ὅτ᾽ ἂν ἔν τε κύνεσσι καὶ ἀνδράσι θηρευτῇσιν |
κάπριος ἠὲ λέων στρέφεται (*Il.* 12.41–2).

STESICHORUS

Time has dealt more harshly with Stesichorus than with any
other major lyric poet. Ancient scholars were in no doubt of his
importance, and mention him in the company of Homer,
Simonides and Pindar; but no passage longer than six lines is
quoted from him, and papyrus finds have been meagre. For an
estimate of his poetry we depend almost wholly on hearsay.

He is the first great poet of the Greek west. He was probably
born in Mataurus in south Italy, but he was known as the
Himeraean and must have spent most of his life in Himera, the
Greek city on the north coast of Sicily, founded in 649 by Zancle
(Messana) with a mixed population of Ionian Chalcidians and
Dorian refugees from Syracuse; the city's dialect was a mixture of
Chalcidian and Doric (Th. 6.5.1; inscriptions show the characteristic Doric ᾱ). He is said to have died in Catana and been
buried there near the Stesichorean gate. His name, according to
the *Suda*, was originally Teisias, Stesichorus being a nickname for
'an organiser of choruses'. The dates given in the *Suda* for his
birth and death, Ol.37 (632–629) and Ol.56 (556–553), may well
be correct; he was contemporary with Sappho and Alcaeus, and

was said to have died in the year of Simonides' birth. Tradition
made him an opponent of the tyrant Phalaris of Acragas.

His work, according to the *Suda*, was collected in 26 books, but
it seems more likely that the 'books' were poems, since 26 books
seems an inordinately large number and quotations are given
from the poems by name. He wrote narrative poetry on epic
themes in metres predominantly dactylic and in the language of
Epic with an admixture of Doric features, notably the Doric *ā*;
one peculiarly Doric form, πέποσχα for πέπονθα, is cited (261).
We have the titles of a dozen poems: the *Helen*, *Oresteia* (in two
parts), *Sack of Troy* and *Homecomings* (Νόστοι) dealt with the
Trojan war and its aftermath, the *Funeral Games of Pelias* with the
Argonauts, the *Geryoneis*, *Cycnus*, *Cerberus* and perhaps *Scylla* with
Heracles' adventures, the *Eriphyle* and *Europeia* with Theban story,
the *Boar-hunters* with Meleager and the hunting of the Calydonian
boar. The details of his mythology were often interesting and
different from the versions of Homer and Hesiod: ἐκαινοποίησε
τὰς ἱστορίας (193.17–18). He is said to have been the first to tell
of the birth of the armed Athena from Zeus' head (233) and of
Electra's recognition of Orestes by a lock of hair (217).

Of his technique we can say little with certainty. The narration
of the myth must have occupied the greater part of each poem. He
began at least some of his poems by invoking the Muse, whom he
called ἀρχεσίμολπος, 'the beginner of song' (250): δεῦρ' ἄγε Καλ-
λιόπεια λίγεια was the first line of a poem (240; see also 210),
and his Palinodes began with the words δεῦρ' αὖτε θεὰ φιλόμολπε
and χρυσόπτερε παρθένε (193). He spoke once of 'seeking another
προοίμιον'. 'prelude' (241). References to his own life and work
found a place in his poetry: he sang the praises of Himera
(270), he found fault with Homer and Hesiod (193.1–7; for
another possible mention of Hesiod see 269), and he mentioned
an earlier lyric poet, Xanthus, whose *Oresteia* he was said to have
used (229: cf. 699, 700; we cannot tell if Xanthus too was a
western Greek). The number and excellence of his epithets are
mentioned by Hermogenes (*Id.* 3.322 Walz), and many rare or
unique epithets, a few of them also found in Ibycus, survive: see
223, and note also 184 ἀργυρορίζους of the waters of the Tartessus, 235 κοιλωνύχων ἵππων, 249 ἀνίψαλον παῖδα ('unharmed

child'), 250 ἀρχεσίμολπος, 251 ἄτερπνος, said to mean 'unsleeping', 253 ἐρίσφηλος, 'very strong', of Heracles, 254 ἠλίβατος of Tartarus, 256 λεύκιππος, 259 μεσόνυξ of a planet, 265 Τελχῖνες of the Κῆρες and σκοτώσεις, 'darkenings' ('killings'?), 266 ὑπερθυμέστατος, 268 πενταφύλακος of night. Stesichorus also enlivened his narrative with passages of direct speech (see 209, 228, 242; perhaps also 264). His powers of characterization were admired by Dionysius (*Imit.* 421).

The *Suda* (s.v. τρία Στησιχόρου) tells us that all the poetry of Stesichorus was epodic, i.e. written in the metrical pattern of strophe, antistrophe and epode. This would imply that it was all choral poetry, and when Athenaeus 13.601a tells us that Stesichorus (οὐ μετρίως ἐρωτικὸς γενόμενος of course) wrote love-poetry (παίδεια or παιδικά), the normal vehicle for which is the solo song, he may be referring to the love-interest of the *Rhadine* (278), a poem now regarded as spurious. Athenaeus 6.250b has a pleasant story of a party at the court of Dionysius II, at which ambassadors, joined by some of the crew who had brought them, sang 'paeans' of Phrynichus, Stesichorus and Pindar. Clement of Alexandria says Stesichorus invented 'the hymn' (*Strom.* 1.16.78 = *P.M.G.* 276c), but we cannot say what he meant by the term. His poetry was popular at parties (see *P.M.G.* 276b). When Socrates was in prison, he heard a man singing a song of Stesichorus and asked him to teach it to him, *ut aliquid sciens amplius e vita discedam* (Ammianus Marcellinus 38.4; a similar story was told of Solon and a poem of Sappho).

'Longinus' called him Ὁμηρικώτατος (13.3): Dionysius put him *longe proximus* after Homer, but made him (with Alcaeus) the finest of the lyric poets (*Comp.* 24). Horace spoke of his *graves Camenae* (*Od.* 4.9.8). Quintilian approved of his subject-matter: ... *maxima bella et clarissimos canentem duces et epici carminis onera lyra sustinentem. reddit enim personis in agendo simul loquendoque debitam dignitatem, ac si tenuisset modum, videtur aemulari proximus Homerum potuisse; sed redundat atque effunditur* (almost the only discordant note in the universal hymn of praise), *quod ut est reprehendendum, ita copiae vitium est* (10.1.62). Stesichorus provided inspiration for vase-painters and sculptors: see Bowra *G.L.P.* 119–26, Page *P.M.G.* 205 and pp. 95–6.

K

It was said of uneducated men that they did not know even
τρία τὰ Στησιχόρου, 'the three of Stesichorus'. The *Suda* explained this by reference to the triadic structure of his poetry, but
'the three' may have been the three famous lines of the Palinode
(192).

The only complete commentary is by J. Vürtheim, *Stesichoros'
Fragmente und Biographie*, Leiden, 1919. (See now *P. Oxy.* xxxii
(1967), Page, *L.G.S.* 263–4, M. L. West, 'Stesichorus', *C.Q.* n.s.
21 (1971) 302–14, and on the Palinode L. E. Woodbury, *Phoenix*
21 (1967) 157–76.)

STESICHORUS 185

Quoted from Stesichorus by Athenaeus 11.469e to illustrate
the sun's cup in which Heracles travelled: cf. Athenaeus 11.781d
and Eustathius *Od.* 1632.23. Athenaeus 470c gives further detail
from Pherecydes (*F.G.H.* 1.18 Jacoby): Heracles threatened to
shoot Helius, the Sun, but checked himself, and in gratitude the
Sun allowed him to travel to Erytheia in the golden cup in which
he used to cross Ocean by night with his chariot and horses on his
way to the East; on the journey Ocean rocked the cup to test his
spirit, but Heracles drew his bow on him too. See also Mimnermus 10 introd. Heracles was travelling to Erytheia to perform one
of his labours, the theft of Geryon's cattle. In the *Geryoneis*, from
which this fragment comes, Stesichorus placed Erytheia opposite the mouth of the river Tartessus, the Guadalquivir (184),
and described Geryon as six-handed, six-footed and winged
(186). The story of Geryon was told briefly by Hesiod (*Th.* 287–
94). (See now Page, *L.G.S.* 32, 263–4.)

Metre: 1–2 are dactylic, 3–6 may be regarded as dactylic, each
line introduced by ∪ ∪, or as anapaestic.

1. Ὑπεριονίδας: see Mimn. 10.11n.

   ἐσκατέβαινε: cf. ἐσκαταβαίνων, line-ending at *Od.* 24.222.
   Other epic words and phrases are 2 ὄφρα, δι' ὠκεανοῖο
   περάσας (cf. *Od.* 10.508 δι' ὠκεανοῖο περήσῃς, a line-
   ending), νυκτὸς ἐρεμνᾶς (cf. *Od.* 11.606 ἐρεμνῇ νυκτὶ
   ἐοικώς), possibly ἱαρᾶς . . . νυκτός, βένθεα, κουριδίαν τ'
   ἄλοχον, παῖδάς τε φίλους; see note on 5 κατάσκιον.

3. *ἱαρᾶς ποτὶ βένθεα νυκτὸς ἐρεμνᾶς*: 'to the depths of holy, dark night', but it is not clear where Stesichorus imagines the Sun's home to be. Mimnermus makes him journey from the country of the Hesperides to the land of the Ethiopians, where his chariot and horses stand, so that Dawn may come.

βένθεα: in Homer of the sea and once (*Od.* 17.316) of a wood.

ἱαρᾶς ... νυκτός: A. fr. 69 N² has *ἱερᾶς νυκτός* in his description of the cup of the Sun; cf. *Il.* 8.66 *ἱερὸν ἦμαρ*, 11.194 *κνέφας ἱερόν*.

4. *ματέρα*: Theia, according to Hes. *Th.* 371, Pi. *I.* 5.1.

ἄλοχον: Perseis, their children Circe and Aeetes (Hes. *Th.* 956–7); in later genealogies Phaethon was son of Helius and Clymene.

5. *ὁ δ'*: Heracles (*ὁ παῖς Διός*), who has now reached Erytheia.

κατάσκιον: the only non-Homeric word in the fragment; found in Hes. *Op.* 513: cf. Archil. 25.3–4.

6. *πόσι*: significant: he is on dry land again.

STESICHORUS 187

From Athenaeus 3.81d: 'Stesichorus mentions Cydonian apples in the *Helen* as follows.' The lines probably refer to the wedding of Helen and Menelaus, and are not unlike Sappho's description of the arrival of Hector and Andromache in Troy (44). It was doubtless in the *Helen* that Stesichorus mentioned the oath imposed by Tyndareus on Helen's suitors, that if her eventual husband were ever wronged on her account, they would all rally to his aid (190). The story that Iphigeneia was daughter of Helen and Theseus may also have been told here (191: see 192 introd.), and 223 too may have been part of the poem (see 223 introd.). For the Palinodes see 192 introd.

Metre: predominantly dactylic; if *μέν* in l. 1 is omitted (with Suchfort and Dobree), entirely dactylic. 2 and 3 repeat the rhythm of the end of 1.

1. *Κυδώνια μᾶλα*: quinces, mentioned also by Alcm. 99 and Ibyc. 286.1–2; cf. Pliny *N.H.* 15.11 *mala quae vocamus cotonea et Graeci Cydonia e Creta insula advecta.* Cydonia is in north-west Crete.

ποτερρίπτουν: cf. *Od.* 13.78 *ἀνερρίπτουν.*

ἄνακτι: presumably Menelaus.

3. ῥοδίνους στεφάνους: so Anacr. 434 στεφάνους ... ῥοδίνους.
κορωνίδας οὔλας: 'twined garlands'; for this unique sense of
κορωνίς cf. Lat. *corona* and Hsch. κορωνίδες· οἱ ἐκ τῶν ἴων
πεπλεγμένοι στέφανοι (similarly *Et. Mag.*), presumably
from the present passage.

STESICHORUS 192

From Plato *Phaedrus* 243a: 'for those who have sinned in their
treatment of myths there is an ancient purification, known not to
Homer but to Stesichorus, who when he was blinded because of
his slander of Helen was not unaware of the reason, like Homer,
but being μουσικός recognized the reason and forthwith wrote
οὐκ ἔστ᾽ ἔτυμος ... Τροίας; and having composed all the Palinode,
as it is called, he at once regained his sight.' Plato *Resp.* 586c says
that according to Stesichorus it was the phantom (εἴδωλον) of
Helen that was fought over by the warriors at Troy in ignorance
of the truth. Isocrates *Helen* 64 says that Stesichorus perpetrated
the blasphemy 'at the beginning of the poem', ἀρχόμενος τῆς
ᾠδῆς: the poem may have been the *Helen*, but the *Sack of Troy*
and *Oresteia* are other possibilities. Cf. also Hor. *Epod.* 17.42–4,
and for the many other references to the poem see *P.M.G.* 192.

All these references are to a single Palinode, but *P. Oxy.* 2506
fr. 26 col. i (=*P.M.G.* 193), part of a commentary on various
lyric writers, states that there were two Palinodes, the beginnings
of which were δεῦρ᾽ αὖτε, θεὰ φιλόμολπε and χρυσόπτερε παρθένε:
in the first Stesichorus found fault with Homer for placing Helen,
not her phantom, in Troy; in the other he faulted Hesiod — why,
we are not told, but it was not for the same offence, since Hesiod
was the first to speak of Helen's phantom (fr. 358 M.-W.). The
commentator quotes as his authority for the two Palinodes the
scholar Chamaeleon, who wrote a Περὶ Στησιχόρου (Ath.
14.620c); and he continues, 'Stesichorus himself says that the
phantom went to Troy while Helen remained with Proteus', i.e.
in Egypt. We can only guess at the relationship between the two
Palinodes, one of which was clearly much more famous than the
other. Perhaps it was a piece of pedantry on Chamaeleon's part to
call the second a Palinode. Only one Palinode was required by the

story of the blindness, however that arose. C. M. Bowra, 'The Two Palinodes of Stesichorus', *C.R.* n.s. 13 (1963), 245 ff, suggests that in the second Palinode Stesichorus blamed Hesiod for the story that Helen, τρίγαμος at 223.4, had an early affair with Theseus and was mother by him of Iphigeneia.

Metre: 1, 3 anapaestic 'paroemiacs', 2 trochaic.

1. οὗτος: presumably with backward reference: 'that story', 'the story which I told before.'

2–3. Stesichorus is probably making only one point, 'you did not sail to Troy', despite the οὐδέ . . . οὐδέ construction. There was a version of the story according to which she went by air to Egypt in Hermes' arms (E. *Hel.* 44 ff), but that is unlikely to be the point here.

οὐδ' ἔβας: Stesichorus now addresses Helen; in the first line of the poem he had addressed the Muse, δεῦρ' αὖτε, θεὰ φιλόμολπε.

STESICHORUS 219

Quoted by Plutarch *ser. num. vind.* 10 to show that Stesichorus' version of the dream of Clytemnestra was appropriate to the Orestes story: see 2n. The lines probably come from the *Oresteia*. It is possible that Stesichorus, the innovator, was the first to make Clytemnestra sole killer of Agamemnon; in the *Odyssey* she and Aegisthus shared the deed. The first clear testimony to her single-handed murder is a bronze shield-strap from Olympia dated *c.* 575–570.

Metre: dactylic; line 2 is an elegiac pentameter.

1. τᾷ δέ: i.e. Clytemnestra.

βεβροτωμένος: 'bloodstained': cf. *Od.* 11.41 βεβροτωμένα τεύχεα. No other part of βροτόω (from βρότος, 'gore') is found. κάρα . . . ἄκρον is acc. of respect.

2. In A. *Cho.* 527 τεκεῖν δράκοντ' ἔδοξεν, E. *Or.* 479 ὁ μητρο-φόντης . . . δράκων (cf. 1424), the snake is Orestes, but in Stesichorus the snake 'with bloody head' must be Agamem-non, and the Pleisthenid king, who grew out of the snake, will be Orestes. The point of the dream was that a Pleis-thenid, not a son of Aegisthus, must succeed Aegisthus on the throne.

Πλεισθενίδας: according to Hes. fr. 194 M.-W. Agamemnon was son of Pleisthenes. In A. *Ag.* 1598 ff Thyestes curses the whole race of Pleisthenes (cf. also 1569), but Aeschylus' genealogy is not clear. Cf. Ibyc. 282.21 Πλεισθενίδας βασιλεύς of Agamemnon, Stes. 209 col. ii. 4 Πλεισθενίδας probably of Menelaus, Bacch. 15.48 Πλεισθενίδας Μενέλαος.

STESICHORUS 223

The scholiast on Euripides *Orestes* 249 quotes the lines from Stesichorus. Hesiod fr. 176 M.-W. (from the same source) says that it was Aphrodite who brought ill-repute on Tyndareus' three daughters, Timandra, Clytemnestra and Helen. The passage may come from the *Helen*, the *Oresteia* or the *Sack of Troy*.

Metre: predominantly dactylic, with trochees in 3 and 4. Note synizesis at 3 Τυνδαρέου.

2. ῥέζων: 'sacrificing', absolutely as in *Il.* 2.400, etc.
   ἠπιοδώρου: in *Il.* 6.251 of Hecuba.

3. τριγάμους: Helen's partners were Theseus, Menelaus and Paris, Clytemnestra's Agamemnon and Aegisthus, Timandra's Echemus and Phyleus (Hes. l.c.). Cf. A. *Ag.* 62 πολυάνορος . . . γυναικός of Helen.

5. λιπεσάνορας: only here; Hesiod l.c. has Τιμάνδρη . . . "Εχεμον προλιποῦσ(α) and Κλυταιμήστρη προλιποῦσ' 'Αγαμέμνονα.

SAPPHO

Little is known for certain about Sappho's life. She was born at Mytilene or Eresus in Lesbos, perhaps *c.* 630 B.C.: the *Suda* reports γεγονυῖα κατὰ τὴν μβ' 'Ολυμπιάδα (i.e. 612–609) but we cannot say whether γεγονυῖα here means 'was born' or '*floruit*', which itself may mean either 'was famous' or only 'was alive'. Eusebius gives two dates for her *floruit*, 600/599 and 595/4. Strabo (13.617) says she was a contemporary of Alcaeus and the statesman Pittacus. She may refer to her own old age in fr. 58.13–17. We know the names of her father and mother, Scamandronymus and

Cleis; her brothers, Charaxus (for whose Egyptian adventures see fr. 5), Eurygyus or Erigyus, and Larichus, who poured wine in the town-hall of Mytilene and was commended by Sappho; her husband, the wealthy Cercolas of Andros: her daughter, Cleis; and little else. She was an orphan at the age of six, and she was short, dark and ugly. This unhelpful information was doubtless derived from her own poetry. The stormy politics of Lesbos, all-important to Alcaeus, find hardly any place in the shreds of her poetry, but fr. 98(b). 8 speaks of exile, and the Parian Marble tells us that she went to Sicily in her exile, probably at a date between 604/3 and 596/5 (see Page *S. & A.* 224–5). The fact of her exile suggests that her family or her husband's family led an active political life.

Of her own life we know little, perhaps because there was little to tell. Her interests, so far as they are revealed by her poetry, were her friendships and hatreds and her poetry itself. She seems to have presided over a literary coterie of women, bound together by the strongest ties of affection. Evidence for a formal appointment as teacher or as priestess is hard to find. She wrote wedding-songs, doubtless for real occasions, and there are traces of ceremonial song, but most of her poems are personal, intended in the first instance for the pleasure of her circle of friends.

Sappho's output was large: her lyric poems were edited by Alexandrian scholars in nine books, of which Book I, perhaps the largest, had 1320 lines, almost as many as the first two books of Horace's Odes. Book VIII, however, had only a tenth of that number. Her poems were arranged by their metres, Sapphic stanzas in Book I, 'dactylic pentameters' in Book II and so on; those Epithalamia which were excluded by their metre from the other eight books were gathered to form Book IX. We hear also of her elegiac poetry, but none survives.

We possess so little of her poetry — fr. 1 is our only complete poem — that generalisations are hazardous. We might guess from fr. 1 that she gave careful thought to the structure of her poems, but fr. 5, where most of the outline is clear, suggests that her transitions from one topic to another were not always adroitly managed. Clarity of language and simplicity of thought are everywhere evident in our fragments; wit and rhetoric, so common in English love-poetry and not quite absent from Catullus' love poems, are nowhere to be found. Her images are sharp — the sparrows that draw Aphrodite's chariot, the full moon in a starry sky, the solitary red apple at the tree-top — and she sometimes lingers over them to elaborate them for their own sake. She quotes the direct words of conversations real or imaginary and so gains immediacy. When her subject is the turbulence of her emotions, she displays a cool control in their expression. Above all, her words are chosen for their sheer melody: the skill with which she placed her vowels and consonants, admired by Dionysius of Halicarnassus, is evidenced by almost any stanza; the music to which she sang them has gone, but the spoken sounds may still enchant.

The definitive edition of Sappho's poems is that of Edgar Lobel and Denys Page, *Poetarum Lesbiorum Fragmenta*, Oxford, 1955, 1–110, with *Verborum Sapphicorum Index* 299–313. Max Treu, *Sappho*, Munich, 3rd ed. 1963, has a complete text, a commentary and a full bibliography. Denys Page, *Sappho and Alcaeus*, Oxford, 1955, 1–146, 318–329, has a commentary on the most important fragments, a study of the contents and character of her poetry, an appendix on metres and a note on the dialect. For detailed studies of her language and syntax see Lobel, Σάπφους Μέλη, Oxford, 1925, and Eva-Maria Hamm, *Grammatik zu Sappho und Alkaios*, Berlin, 1957.

The following features of the Lesbian dialect may cause difficulty; I have sometimes over-simplified, and refer the student to Page, *Sappho and Alcaeus* 327 ff, from which I have borrowed freely, for a fuller account. Attic equivalents are given where necessary in brackets.

1. *Breathings*: there are no initial aspirates: ἄρμα, ἴππος.
2. *Accents*: the accent goes as far back as it can, except in prepositions (περί etc.) and ἀλλά, οὐδέ, μηδέ, ἐπεί: so θέος (-ός), θέων (-ῶν), παῖδος (-ός), γυναίκων (-ῶν).
3. *Vowels*: original ᾱ is preserved: γᾶς μελαίνας (-ης).

    o = a, especially after ρ: βρόχυς (βραχύς), στρότος (στρατός); but elsewhere too: μόλθακος (μαλθακός), ὀνία (ἀνία), κόθαρος (καθαρός), τόμοντες (ταμόντες).

    ŭ = o, especially before labials: ὔμοι (ὁμοῦ); but elsewhere too: δεῦρυ, ὔσδος (ὄζος).

ε = ἄ: κρέτην (κρατεῖν).

ἄ = ε: ἄτερος (ἕτερος); and -τα = -τε: ὄτα (ὅτε), ποτά, ἄλλοτα, ὄππότα (ὁπότε), ἀτέρωτα (ἑτέρωτε).

οι = ου: πήλοι (τηλοῦ), ὔμοι (ὁμοῦ), ὔψοι (ὑψοῦ).

αις = original ανς: ἐλέφαις (ἐλέφας), ταίς (τάς), ζεύξαισα (-ασα), παῖς (πᾶς), φαῖσι (φασί).

οις = original ονς: λίποισα (λιποῦσα), Μοῖσα (Μοῦσα).

ο and ω = ου: ὄρανος, ὤρανος (οὐρανός).

η = ει: εὔρην (εὐρ.ίαν) and in infinitives ἔχην, πάθην.

αι = η: οἰνοχόαισον, ὀνέμαισε (ἀνέμηνσε), φώναισαι (φωνῆσαι), ἐπτόαισε, ἐξεπόναισαν, μαχαίτας (-ητής), Αἰολίδαις (-ης), Κρονίδαις (-ης), αἰμίονος (ἡμί-), αἰμίθεος (ἡμί-).

4. *Consonants*: σδ for ζ except initially: ἰσδάνει (ἱζάνει), ὑπασδεύξαισα (ὑποζεύξασα), εὐσδύγων.

   π = τ: πήλοι (τηλοῦ), πήλοθεν.

   νν for original σν: σελάννα (σελήνη): cf. also ὔμμες (ὑμεῖς), ἄμμες (ἡμεῖς), κρίννω (κρίνω), δίννημι (δινέω) and ἀέρρω (ἀείρω), χέρρες (χεῖρες).

5. *Conjugation of verbs*: note perf. inf. τεθνάκην (τεθνάναι), subjunctive of sigmatic aorists χαλάσσομεν (χαλάσωμεν).

6. *Contracted verbs*: pres. and imperf. of Attic contracted verbs in -άω, -έω, -όω have -μι conjugations (sometimes spelt -μμι): τίμαμι, φίλημι, δήλωμι, infin. τίμαν, φίλην, part. τίμαις (gen. -αντος), τίμαισα (gen. -αίσας), φίλεις (gen. -εντος), φίλεισα (gen. -είσας), τιμάμενος, φιλήμενος.

7. *Declension of nouns*: acc. plur., 1st and 2nd declension, has -αις and -οις, e.g. κόραις, ἵπποις; dat. plur. has -αισι and -οισι.

8. *Prepositions*: ὑπά (ὑπό), ὄν (ἀνά), sometimes ὄνν before vowels, ὀννέλην (ἀνελεῖν), ἀπύ (ἀπό), κάτ (κατά), πάρ (παρά), διά or ζά, πεδά (μετά), ἐν and ἐς before consonants, ἐνν and εἰς before vowels. ὑπέρ is not found: περί, πέρ, sometimes πέρρ before vowels, is used instead.

9. *Digamma*: Ϝ is found in 3rd pers. pron. Ϝε, Ϝέθεν, Ϝοι, adj. Ϝός; before initial ρ, where it is written as β: βρόδα (ῥόδα), βράδινος (ῥαδινός), βραΐδίως (ῥαδίως); between vowels, where it is represented by υ: αὔως (ἠώς), ναῦος (νηός).

10. *Miscellaneous*: note ἄγι (ἄγε), αἰ (εἰ, 'if'), ἄμμι (ἡμῖν), ὄππᾳ (ὄπη), πώνω (πίνω), τυίδε ('hither').

11. *Metric*: short vowels before mute + liquid (or nasal) are scanned long: see Sapph. 16.19n.

SAPPHO 1

Quoted by Dionysius of Halicarnassus, *Comp.* 173–9, as an example of the polished and exuberant style of composition (γλαφυρὰ καὶ ἀνθηρὰ σύνθεσις: the opposite was αὐστηρά) which he found also in Hesiod, Anacreon, Simonides, Euripides and Isocrates. He says that the euphony and charm of the piece lie in the cohesion and smoothness of its construction. *P. Oxy.* 2288 is a narrow strip with fragments of lines 1–21, nowhere more than nine letters wide. Hephaestion uses the poem to illustrate the Sapphic stanza, so that it may have been the first poem of Book I, all of which was in this metre.

Metre: Sapphic stanza. Sappho allows no elision between lines 1 and 2 or 2 and 3, and hiatus only when the last vowel of the line is long. Lines 3 and 4 form a unit: words spill over, e.g. at 1.11–12, and hiatus is not allowed. The 4th syllable of lines 1–3, long in Horace though not always long in Catullus, is long in only two-thirds of Sappho's lines; word-end after the 5th syllable, usual in Horace but observed in only two-thirds of Catullus' lines, occurs in less than half of Sappho's examples. Synecphonesis at 1.11 ὠράνω αἴθε-, 16.11 ἐμνάσθη ἀλλά.

(see G. L. Koniaris, *Philologus* 109 (1965) 30–38.)

1. **ποικιλόθρον'**: only here. Sappho pictures Aphrodite in her Olympian home: cf. the elaborate throne on which Charis, wife of the craftsman Hephaestus, seats Thetis, *Il.* 18.389–90 θρόνου ἀργυροήλου | καλοῦ δαιδαλέου, and the chair in Odysseus' house, *Od.* 1.132 κλισμὸν . . . ποικίλον. ποικίλος suggests woods of contrasting colours or a contrast of materials, e.g. wood and ivory.

   Ἀφρόδιτα: note the Aeolic vocative in -ᾰ.

2. **δολόπλοκε**: first here, but cf. Thgn. 1386 Κυπρογενὲς Κυθέρεια δολοπλόκε, Simon. 541.9–10 δολοπλόκου . . . Ἀφροδίτας, *P.M.G.* 949 (fr. adesp.) δολοπλόκου γὰρ Κυπρογενοῦς.

   λίσσομαί σε: the poem is cast in the form of a prayer: note the opening catalogue of epithets (1–2) and the formula, 'if

you ever helped before, help again now' (cf. e.g. *Il.*
5.116 ff, 16.233 ff, Pi. *I.* 6.42 ff, S. *O.T.* 163 ff, Ar. *Thesm.*
1156 ff). Sappho devotes most of her poem to a description
of the previous epiphany: the same emphasis on past
service appears in Diomedes' prayer, *Il.* 10.284 ff.

3. ἄσαισι: ἄσα, the verb ἀσάω and the adj. ἄσαρος are commoner in Sappho and Alcaeus than in other poets. They
refer to physical distress in the medical writers, but ἄσαισι
can hardly be distinguished from ὀνίαισι here. Page tr.
'heartache and anguish'. Cf. Alc. 335.2 προκόψομεν γὰρ
οὐδὲν ἀσάμενοι ('by distressing ourselves').

δάμνα: cf. Hes. *Th.* 122 of Eros, δάμναται ἐν στήθεσσι νόον.

5. ἀτέρωτα: 'on another occasion', like ἄλλοτα: cf. Alc. 38.11
αἴ ποτα κἀλλοτα.

6. ἀίοισα: 'having heard', whereas ἔκλυες = 'you paid attention'; so at Hes. *Op.* 9 κλῦθι ἰδὼν ἀίων τε. Both ἀίοισα and
ἔκλυες may be aorist.

8. χρύσιον: probably with δόμον, not ἄρμα; the papyrus fragment punctuates after χρύσιον. Cf. 127 δεῦρο δηὖτε
Μοῖσαι χρύσιον λίποισαι . . . The fourth line of Sappho's
stanza has closer connexion with the preceding line than
with the first line of the next stanza.

10. στροῦθοι: according to Ath. 9.391f Sappho made sparrows
draw Aphrodite's chariot since they are lubricious and pro-
lific: cf. Schol. B *Il.* 2.305 ἱερὰ μὲν Ἀφροδίτης ἡ στρουθός.

περὶ γᾶς μελαίνας: 'over the black earth': ὑπέρ is not found
in Lesbian. For μελαίνας cf. 16.2 ἐπὶ γᾶν μέλαιναν and
see Archil. 58.2n. There is strong epic influence in this
stanza and the next.

11. πύκνα δίννεντες πτέρα: cf. *Od.* 2.151 ἔνθ' ἐπιδινηθέντε τιναξάσθην
πτερὰ πυκνά.

13. αἶψα δ' ἐξίκοντο: cf. *Il.* 18.532 αἶψα δ' ἵκοντο.

14. μειδιαίσαισ(α) κτλ.: cf. *h. Hom.* 10.2–3 of Aphrodite, ἐφ'
ἱμερτῷ δὲ προσώπῳ | αἰεὶ μειδιάει, *Il.* 3.424, *h. Ven.* 49
φιλομμειδὴς Ἀφροδίτη. The smile here denotes good will
rather than amusement: Aphrodite could be πίκρα: cf.
15(b). 9. For ἀθανάτῳ προσώπῳ cf. e.g. *Il.* 1.530 κρατὸς ἀπ'
ἀθανάτοιο.

15. δηὖτε (=δὴ αὖτε): repeated in 16 and 18. It is often used of a renewed assault of love: cf. Alcm. 59(a). 1, Sapph. 22.11, 130.1, Anacr. 358.1, 376.1, 400.1, 413.1, 428.1. The repetition heightens the pathos; the tone is hardly one of reproof and impatience, as Page would suggest (S. & A. 12 ff).

17–18. 'And what in my maddened heart I most wish to happen for myself.' μαινόλᾳ is masc. and agrees with θύμῳ.

18–19. The actual words of Aphrodite are now quoted directly: 'Whom now am I to persuade to lead you back to her friendship?' ἄγην, 'to lead', is not entirely convincing, but is better than ἄγνην, inf. pass. of ἄγνυμι (the α is marked short in the papyrus), 'to be broken again to your (σὰν) friendship', or τάγην, 'to be ranked again in your (σὰν) friendship'.

20. Ψάπφ': i.e. voc. Ψάπφοι: so at 94.5.

21. ταχέως: 'soon', as in 23.

διώξει: we need not conclude that Sappho will be running away and that the tables will be turned: there is no suggestion in 22 that Sappho will reject the gifts she is given.

22. ἀλλὰ δώσει: 'she will actually give them instead'; for ἀλλά in the apodosis of a conditional sentence cf. 94.9 and see Denniston G.P. 11–12.

24. κωὐκ ἐθέλοισα: 'even against her will'. Aphrodite hints at her power. Note that the participle gives the only indication in this poem that Sappho's love is for one of her own sex. If the text is sound, this is the only certain example of ἐθέλω in Sappho and Alcaeus; they use θέλω often.

25. ἔλθε μοι καὶ νῦν: Aphrodite's speech and with it the description of the previous epiphany are ended, and Sappho concludes her prayer with an echo of 5 ἀλλὰ τυίδ' ἔλθ', 8 ἦλθες.

26–7. ὅσσα δέ μοι κτλ.: 'and all that my heart longs to have fulfilled for myself, fulfil.'

28. σύμμαχος ἔσσο: 'be my fellow-fighter.' σύμμαχος rarely occurs before Sappho (cf. Archil. 75 κλῦθ' ἄναξ Ἥφαιστε καί μοι σύμμαχος γουνουμένῳ | ἵλαος γένευ) and was used by no later melic poet except Pindar (only at I. 5.28).

SAPPHO 2

Written by an uncomprehending copyist on a potsherd of 3rd century B.C., published by Medea Norsa in 1937. 5–8 were known from Hermogenes *Id.* 2.4 (p. 331 Rabe), 13–16 from a version in Athenaeus 11.463e (ἔλθε Κύπρι ... οἰνοχοοῦσα: see 15–16n.). Before line 1 the potsherd has ρρανοθενκατιου[: if this was ὠράνοθεν κατίουσα (for -οισα), it is not the end of a Sapphic stanza. Turyn suggested καράνοθεν κατίουσα, 'coming down from the (Cretan?) mountain-top': cf. *Il.* 4.475 "Ιδηθεν. Line 1 can hardly be the beginning of the poem: mention of Aphrodite is needed earlier than 13 Κύπρι.

Sappho summons Aphrodite to a temple to join her and her companions in some festivity. The lines are among Sappho's most melodious.

1. ἐκ Κρήτας: Cretans claimed that Aphrodite was first worshipped on their island (Diod. Sic. 5.77.4–5); at Cnossus she was worshipped with the title "Ανθεια (Hsch. s.v. "Ανθεια).

2. τοι: pronoun: 'where your lovely grove is'.

3. μαλίαν: gen. pl. of μαλία (=μηλέα), 'apple-tree'. Adj. μάλινος (6). Ibycus uses μηλίδες (286.2).

4. λιβανώτῳ: our two earliest references to frankincense are here and at 44.30, where it is mentioned with cassia and myrrh. Homer never speaks of incense, which may have been introduced to Greece by Phoenician traders *c.* 700.

5. ἐν δέ: 'herein'.
   κελάδει δι' ὕσδων: presumably the sound is heard through branches (ὕσδων =ὄζων). Homer has κελάδω of water, *Il.* 18.576 πὰρ ποταμὸν κελάδοντα .

7. ἐσκίασται: cf. Semon. 7.66 of a woman's hair, ἀνθέμοισιν ἐσκιασμένην.
   αἰθυσσομένων: 'shimmering'; the first instance of this rare verb. See W. B. Stanford, *Ambiguity in Greek Literature* 132–6 for its use in poetry.

8. κῶμα: not simply 'sleep' or 'deep sleep' but sleep (or deep sleep) induced by enchantment or other special or supernatural means (Page: cf. *Il.* 14.358–9, *Od.* 18.201, Hes. *Th.*

798, Pi. *P.* 1.10–12), here by the babbling water and rustling leaves.

κααίρει: the reading is very uncertain. κααίρει comes closest to the reading of the potsherd: the verb, of which this would be the earliest example, is used especially of the descent of birds and bees: cf. Thgn. 238n.

9. ἱππόβοτος: Homeric, especially of Argos (e.g. *Il.* 2.287); Ithaca was not ἱππόβοτος, *Od.* 4.606. Sappho (except in 44) and Alcaeus use few of Homer's compound adjectives.

10. ἄηται: fem. also at Hes. *Op.* 645, 675; Homer has masc. ἀήτης.

13. σὺ . . . ἔλοισα: στέμ⟨ματ'⟩, the usual supplement, gives good sense but was probably not written on the potsherd.

14. ἄβρως = ἀβρῶς: 'gracefully.' ἀβρός, a favourite adj. of Sappho, is not Homeric; first in Hes. fr. 218 Rzach ἀβρὴ παρθένος.

15–16. 'Pour nectar that is mingled with our festivities'; but the phrase lacks Sappho's customary clarity. It appears that the poem did not end here, since the text of Athenaeus continues with the words τούτοισι τοῖς ἑταίροις ἐμοῖς γε καὶ σοῖς, probably a prose version of the beginning of another stanza.

SAPPHO 5

P. Oxy. 7 gives twenty lines of this poem, the last eight very gappy. *P. Oxy.* 2289.6 provides some six letters.

Herodotus 2.134–5 tells us that Sappho's brother Charaxus paid a large sum of money to buy the freedom of a notorious courtesan of Naucratis called Rhodopis: when he returned to Mytilene, Sappho ridiculed him in one of her poems. Strabo 17.808 says that Sappho called the woman Doricha (Athenaeus 13.596c rejects the identification) and that Charaxus was in Naucratis as a trader in Lesbian wines. The story is elaborated in Ovid *Her.* 15.63 ff. Our present poem can hardly be the one to which Herodotus refers: it was written before he returned home and in a spirit of sisterly affection, not ridicule.

1. Κύπρι: Aphrodite, born from the sea (Hes. *Th.* 190 ff), was worshipped as a goddess of the sea and seafaring with the titles Ποντία, Εὔπλοια, Γαληναία among others.

Νηρήιδες: there was a cult of these sea-goddesses on Lesbos.

3. The words recall 1.17–18, 26–7.

4. *τελέσθην*: aor. infin. pass.

5. *ὄσσα . . . ἄμβροτε*: 'his past sins, errors' (aor. of *ἀμαρτάνω*): Sappho refers to his Egyptian affair.

   λῦσαι: probably infin. after *δότε* with 'him' as subject: 'grant that he atone for . . .'

6–8. If the supplements *κωνίαν* (=*καὶ ὀνίαν*, i.e. *καὶ ἀνίαν*) and *πῆμ' ἔτι* are correct, Thgn. 871–2 is closely parallel: *εἰ μὴ ἐγὼ τοῖσιν μὲν ἐπαρκέσω οἵ με φιλεῦσιν, | τοῖς δ' ἐχθροῖς ἀνίη καὶ μέγα πῆμ' ἔσομαι*. But other supplements are possible in 8, e.g. *μηδάμα* (or *μηκέτι* or *μήποτα*) *μ]ηδ' εἷς*, 'may no-one ever be a grief to us': cf. Alc. 129.16 *μηδάμα μηδ' ἔνα*.

10. *ἔμμορον τίμας*: cf. *Od.* 8.480 *τιμῆς ἔμμοροί εἰσι*. Little more can be made of the poem; in 11 *τοῖσι* may be the relative pronoun; 13 has *εἰσαίω[ν] τὸ κέγχρω* ('millet-seed') or *τό κ' ἐν χρῷ*, 14 probably *ἐπαγορίᾳ πολίταν*, 'accusation of the citizens', 18 a mention of *Κύπρις*. 20 is perhaps the last line of the poem.

SAPPHO 15(b)

P. Oxy. 1231, fr. 1, col. i: nothing can be made of the scraps of the first eight lines. For Doricha see 5 introd.: Athenaeus (13.596 b–c) says she was reviled by Sappho.

9. *πικροτάταν*: *πικροτέραν* is usually preferred, but we have no information that either Charaxus or Doricha found Aphrodite harsh in the first instance.

   ἐπεύροι: the subject may be Charaxus or Doricha; Charaxus must be the subject of *ἦλθε* (12).

SAPPHO 16

P. Oxy. 1231, fr. 1, col. i: 2166(a)2 (in vol. XXI, p. 122) provides parts of 7–12. The echo of the first stanza at 19–20 suggests that the poem ended there.

1–3. The same technique of priamel is used by Tyrt. 9.1–14, Pi. *O.* 1.1–7, Plat. *Lysis* 211 d–e.

2. *ἐπὶ γᾶν μέλαιναν*: cf. 1.10 *περὶ γᾶς μελαίνας*, Archil. 58.2n.

3–4. κῆν’ ὅττω (=ἐκεῖνο ὅτου): 'that thing, whatever it be,
which one loves'; cf. 31.1–2 κῆνος . . . ὅττις and see note
there. Note the subjunctive ἔραται without κε: cf. 31.7
ὡς . . . ἴδω, 'whenever I look', 34.3 ὅπποτα . . . λάμπῃ,
98.3 αἴ τις ἔχῃ, and see Callin. 1.13n.

5. εὔμαρες: found first in Sappho and Alcaeus.

7. κάλλος: acc. of respect with περσκέθοισα, 'Helen, far
surpassing all mortals in beauty'. For περρέχω (=περιέχω)
cf. 96.9 πάντα περρέχοισ’ ἄστρα. The thought seems to be
that Helen, the most beautiful woman on earth, could have
had all she wanted, but left the noblest of the Greeks for the
man she loved.

8. πανάριστον: used by Hesiod, Op. 293; but μέγ’ ἄριστον is
just as likely here.

10. φίλων τοκήων: cf. Il. 3.139–40, where Iris fills Helen with a
sweet longing for her previous husband, her city and her
parents (τοκήων), 15.662–3. Alc. 283.7–8, also of Helen,
has παῖδά τ’ ἐν δόμοισι λίποισα . . . κἄνδρος εὔστρωτον
λέχος.

11. ἐμνάσθη ἀλλά: synecphonesis as at 1.11.

12–13. Page suggests something like αὔτικ’ ἴδοισαν (or οὐκ
ἀέκοισαν) | Κύπρις· εὔκαμπτον γὰρ . . .

15. The subject of ὀνέμαισε(ε) is lost, but was almost certainly the
pronoun ὅς or ἅ. Anactoria is probably the Milesian Ana-
gora mentioned in the Suda s.v. Σαπφώ.

17. ἔρατόν τε βᾶμα: 'her lovely walk'; so Catullus remembered
Lesbia's step, 68.70–2.

18. ἀμάρυχμα: 'the bright sparkle of her face': cf. Hes. fr. 73.3,
196.6 M.-W. Χαρίτων ἀμαρύγματ’ ἔχουσα(ν), h. Herm. 45 ἀπ’
ὀφθαλμῶν ἀμαρυγαί, 'twinklings'.

19. τὰ Λύδων ἄρματα: the Lydians used the old-fashioned war-
chariot as late as the 5th century: cf. A. Pers. 45 ff.

κἀν ὅπλοισι: the only example in Sappho and Alcaeus of a
vowel scanned short before mute and liquid (or nasal),
except in Sappho's dactylic verse. If we must emend,
Page's καὶ πανόπλοις is excellent. The chariots and in-
fantry recall the imagery of the first stanza. Lydians are
mentioned as a particularly powerful and splendid race:

cf. 132.3 ἀντὶ τᾶς ἐγωὖδὲ Λυδίαν παῖσαν . . . , 'in place of
her I (should not take) all Lydia.'

SAPPHO 31

Quoted and discussed by 'Longinus' 10.1–3 in his section on the
choice and arrangement of material. Sappho, he says, always uses
the feelings that accompany delirious passion in real life, and
displays her excellence in her skilful selection and unification of
the most important facts. After quoting the poem he notes the
objectivity of her description (πάνθ᾽ ὡς ἀλλότρια διοιχόμενα
ἐπιζητεῖ) and the way in which she experiences contradictory
sensations (hot and cold) and conditions (irrationality and
sanity). On the inadequacy of these criticisms see Page, S. & A. 27
and D. A. Russell's edition of 'Longinus', 102–3. Catullus 51 is a
free translation of the poem, and there are echoes in Theocritus
2.106 ff, Lucretius 3.152 ff (the symptoms of fear). The fashion of
calling the poem a wedding song is outmoded: Sappho sets out the
physical concomitants of her love when jealousy inflames it.

(See now G. Wills, G.R.B.S. 8 (1967) 167–97.)

1–2. κῆνος . . . ὄττις: cf. 16.3–4 κῆν᾽ ὄττω τις ἔραται, and see
   Page, S. & A. 20–1. The possible meanings are (1) 'that
   man has the luck of the gods, inasmuch as he sits . . .',
   (2) 'any man has the luck of the gods who sits . . .',
   (3) 'that man, whatever his name, who sits . . . , has the
   luck of the gods': the first is perhaps most likely; but we
   cannot say with certainty whether the reference is specific
   ('who is now sitting . . .') or general ('who often sits . . .':
   cf. Catullus 51.3 identidem): the latter is more probable.

   ἴσος θέοισιν: here 'as fortunate as the gods': cf. Homer's
   ἰσόθεος, θεοείκελος, θεοῖς ἐναλίγκιος, Sappho's θέᾳ σ᾽ ἰκέλαν
   (95.4), ἴκελοι θέοις (44.22), θεοεικέλοις (44.34).

4. ὑπακούει: 'listens': cf. Il. 8.4 θεοὶ δ᾽ ὑπὸ πάντες ἄκουον.

5. τό: the antecedent is probably the whole situation, the fact
   that the man enjoys the girl's company and attention.
   μ᾽ =μ(οι), dative.

6. καρδίαν ἐν στήθεσιν: cf. Od. 4.548–9 κραδίη καὶ θυμὸς . . . ἐνὶ
   στήθεσσι . . . ἰάνθη.

   ἐπτόαισεν (aor. of πτοέω): gnomic aorist ('has always set my heart trembling') if the reference is general, aorist of instant reaction (cf. ἤσθην) if Sappho is describing a specific occasion (see 1–2n.).

7 ὡς ... ἴδω: for the absence of κε see 16.4n.

βρόχε' (=βραχέα): 'briefly, for a moment', neut. plur. used adverbially. For ὡς ... ὡς, 'when ... then' cf. e.g. Il. 14.294 ὡς δ' ἴδεν, ὥς μιν ἔρως πυκινὰς φρένας ἀμφεκάλυψεν.

8. εἴκει: perhaps 'it is possible', like παρείκει, with infin. φώναισ(αι), although there is no other example of the impersonal use of εἴκει. Perhaps εἴκει stands for ἴκει, 'nothing comes to me to speak'.

9. ἄκαν: probably the Homeric adverb ἀκήν; but Hesychius gives the phrase ἀκὴν ἦγες, 'you kept quiet', and Sappho may have used some similar expression here.

γλῶσσα ἔαγε: the hiatus would be irregular, and the meaning, 'my tongue is broken', unsatisfactory, although Lucretius 3.155 in an echo of the present passage has *infringi linguam*. Cobet suggested πέπαγε, 'my tongue is fixed in silence (ἄκαν)', which is close to Catullus' *lingua sed torpet*.

11. ὀππάτεσσι: dat. plur. of ὄππα (=ὄμμα).

ἐπιρρόμβεισι δ'ἄκουαι: 'my ears hum': ἐπιρρομβέω occurs only here, and this is the first example of ἀκούη (=ἀκοή) ='ear'.

13. κὰδ ... ἔχει: tmesis, 'a cold sweat covers me.' The text of 'Longinus' is corrupt, and emendation jettisons either ψυχρός (which is referred to by 'Longinus', ἄμα ψύχεται καίεται) or κακχέεται. *An. Ox.* i.208 Cramer cites the passage as evidence for ἰδρώς as fem. in Aeolian (whence the emendation ἀ δέ μ' ἴδρως κακχέεται), but there is no other evidence for it.

14. ἄγρει: the Lesbian dialect regularly uses ἀγρέω for αἱρέω.

15–16. 'I seem to be little short of dying'; but the correct reading is doubtful. 'πιδεύσην in 'Longinus' is fut. infin. (of ἐπιδεύω), but there is no parallel for φαίνομαι with fut. infin.

16–17. After φαίνομαι 'Longinus' continues with ἀλλὰ πᾶν τόλματον, ἐπεὶ †καὶ πένητα†, 'but all must be endured (or dared), since ...', possibly the beginning of a fifth stanza; the new papyrus fragment completes 16 at last. The com-

mentary in 'Longinus' certainly begins after the word
πένητα: we cannot say why 'Longinus' broke off his quotation in the middle of a stanza. By a strange coincidence
Catullus' version of the poem is followed by the stanza
beginning *otium, Catulle, tibi molestum est*, which is hardly in
place there.

SAPPHO 34

Quoted by Eustathius, *Il.* 729.21 in his commentary on *Il.*
8.555 (see 1–2n.). Also in *Anecd. Paris.* (Cramer) iii 233.31. The
use of μέν (1) suggests that a δέ- clause followed, and the
analogy of 96.5 ff makes it likely that Sappho spoke here of a girl
who outshone her companions in beauty. According to Julian
Epist. 19 Sappho called the moon ἀργυρία in this poem. Cf. Ovid
Her. 18.71–3 *quantum, cum fulges radiis argentea puris, | concedunt
flammis sidera cuncta tuis, | tanto formosis formosior omnibus illa est.*

1–2. Contrast *Il.* 8.555–6 ὡς δ᾽ ὅτ᾽ ἐν οὐρανῷ ἄστρα φαεινὴν
    ἀμφὶ σελήνην | φαίνετ᾽ ἀριπρεπέα . . .

2. ἆψ ἀπυκρύπτοισι: perhaps 'hide back, hide away'.

3. ὅπποτα . . . λάμπῃ: for κε omitted see 16.3–4n. Since λάμπω
    is almost certainly intransitive, γᾶν ἐπὶ παῖσαν is a possible
    supplement.

SAPPHO 44

P. Oxy. 1232 fr. 1, coll. ii, iii, fr. 2, and 2076, col. ii, which
provides the beginnings of 23–34 and tells us that this was the last
poem of Book II. It is our only example of Sappho's narrative
poetry, and by far our longest example of her 'abnormal poetry',
Lobel's term for those poems in which Lesbian dialect and
metrical practice are contaminated by Epic usages. Sappho's
theme is an episode of the period of the Trojan War, Hector's
home-coming with his bride Andromache: this must explain her
Epic colouring, as it explains her choice of a predominantly
dactylic metre.

The following forms belong to Epic, not Lesbian: 6 ῑ̆έρας (for
ῐρας), 7 ἐνί (for ἐν or ἐνν), 11 ἀνόρουσε (pap. gives ὀν- in 24,
30, 33), 12 κατά (for κάτ), πτόλιν (for πόλιν), φίλοις and 21
θέοις dat. pl. (for -οισι), 13 εϋ-τροχοις (for εὐ-), 16 Περάμ-οιο

(for -ω), 23 and 26 ἐς before a vowel (for εἰς), 33 ὀνκαλέοντες
(for ὀνκάλεντες). The temporal augment, not omitted in Lesbian,
is omitted at 11 ἀνόρουσε, 26 ἵκανε, 31 ἐλέλυσδον, perhaps 23
ὄρματ' αἰ[. Vowels are scanned short before mute and liquid at 8
ἐλίγματα χρύσια, 14 ὄχλος, and there is epic correption at 5
συνέταιροι ἀγοισ'. There is hiatus between lines, although the
last syllable of the line is short, at 9 ἀθύρματα | ἀργυρα, 27 αἰθέρα |
ἄχω. None of this accords with Lesbian practice. Homeric
epithets are far commoner in this poem than elsewhere in Sappho.

The detail of the narrative, however, belongs to the Lesbos of
Sappho's time: myrrh, cassia and frankincense, the castanets, the
σατίναι in which the women drive, are all unknown to Homer. It
is suggested, but cannot be proved, that the poem was written for
performance at a real wedding.

Metre: glyconic with dactylic expansion: so 47, 49.

3. Ἴδαος: Idaeus was herald in Troy, e.g. *Il.* 3.248 κῆρυξ
Ἰδαῖος: at 24.577 he is called κήρυκα καλήτορα.

    τάχυς ἄγγελος: so at *Od.* 15.526: cf. *Il.* 24.292. After 3 the
omission of a line is noted in the papyrus.

4. κλέος ἄφθιτον: so at *Il.* 9.413.

5. συνέταιροι: a very rare word, used by Hdt. 7.193.2.

    ἐλικώπιδα: used in *Iliad* of young, lively people: e.g. 1.98
ἐλικώπιδα κούρην; cf. Hes. *Th.* 298 νύμφην ἑλικώπιδα.

6. Θήβας ἐξ ἱέρας: cf. *Il.* 1.366 Θήβην, ἱερὴν πόλιν Ἠετίωνος.

    Πλακίας: cf. *Il.* 6.395 ff Ἀνδρομάχη, θυγάτηρ μεγαλήτορος
Ἠετίωνος, | Ἠετίων, ὃς ἔναιεν ὑπὸ Πλάκῳ ὑληέσσῃ, | Θήβῃ
Ὑποπλακίῃ, Κιλίκεσσ' ἄνδρεσσιν ἀνάσσων. The line-ending
may be ἀπ' [ἀὶ]ν⟨ν⟩άω or ἀπ' [ἐυ]ν⟨ν⟩άω, Page.

7. ἄλμυρον: the conventional epithet appears also at 96.10
θάλασσαν ἐπ' ἀλμύραν, Alc. 334.2 ἄλμυρον . . . πόντον; cf.
Od. 4.511 ἁλμυρὸν ὕδωρ, Hes. *Th.* 964 ἁλμυρὸς . . . πόντος.

8. κἄμματα: καὶ ἔμματα (= εἵματα).

9. πορφύρα καταΰτ[. .]να: κὰτ αὔτμενα, 'with following wind',
can hardly be the correct supplement. Perhaps an unknown participle is hidden here and at 101.2, where the
text of Athenaeus has πορφύραι καταυταμενά-. Our text
gives πορφυρ[⁻]: Page explains πορφύρα as an Attic spelling

of the Epic πορφύρεα. (The Lesbian form is πορφύρια.) Cf. the Attic -εμίγνυντο in 24, though not in 30. So with 10 ἀργύρᾱ.

ἀθύρματα: cf. *Od.* 15.416 of Phoenicians, μυρί᾽ ἄγοντες ἀθύρματα νηῒ μελαίνῃ.

10. ἐλέφαις: nominative case, and so presumably all the neuter nouns in 8–10; but the case is unexplained. Perhaps line 9 is more corrupt than it appears to be. Ivory is mentioned twice in *Iliad*, but comparatively often in *Odyssey*: see H. L. Lorimer, *Homer and the Monuments* 507–8. Athenaeus quotes a garbled version of this line from Sappho Book II to illustrate the word ποτήριον (11.460d).

11. ὀτραλέως, ἀνόρουσε, πάτηρ φίλος: all Homeric and all here only in Sappho and Alcaeus.

12. πτόλιν εὐρύχορον: cf. *Od.* 24.468 πρὸ ἄστεος εὐρυχόροιο.

13. ᾽Ιλίαδαι: 'descendants of Ilos', i.e. Trojans; a very rare word, first here.

σατίναις: the σατίνη, a woman's carriage, is mentioned in *h. Ven.* 13, Anacr. 388.10 (where the effeminate Artemon drives in it), E. *Hel.* 1311, and nowhere else.

εὐτρόχοις: cf. *Il.* 24.189 ἄμαξαν εὔτροχον ἡμιονείην.

15. τε τανυσφύρων appears to be irreconcilable with the traces of the letters; τ᾽ ἀπαλοσφύρων (Pfeiffer) is too long and 'tender-ankled' an unacceptable epithet.

17. ἵπποις κτλ.: cf. *Il.* 24.279 ἵππους δὲ ... ὕπαγον ζυγόν.

18. μεγάλωστι: a Homeric word, not found elsewhere in Sappho and Alcaeus.

21. An unknown number of lines is missing after 20.
ἴκελοι θέοις: cf. 34 θεοεικέλοις and 31.1n.

25. κροτάλων: κρόταλα, 'castanets', are not mentioned by Homer: first here unless *h. Hom.* 14.3 is earlier. There is a clear illustration of κρόταλα in Max Wegner, *Musikgeschichte in Bildern*, Band II, Lief. 4, plate 25, p. 51.

ἄρα: once elsewhere in Sappho, nowhere in Alcaeus. The particle is not common in lyric writers, Pindar excepted: cf. Alcm. 1.100n.

26. ἵκανε δ᾽ ἐς αἴθερα κτλ.: cf. *Il.* 13.837 ἠχὴ δ᾽ ἀμφοτέρων ἵκετ᾽ αἴθέρα.

27. ἄχω θεσπεσία: cf. *Il.* 8.159 ἠχῇ θεσπεσίῃ, Alc. 130.34–5 ἄχω θεσπεσία γυναίκων | ἴρας ὀλολύγας ἐνιαυσίας.

30. Sappho is the earliest writer to mention myrrh, cassia and frankincense. Her use of μύρρα for σμύρνα 'in Book II' is noted in Antiattic. 108.22 (Bekker): Ath. 15.688c calls it Aeolic. λίβανος is the frankincense-tree, used for λιβανωτός: see 2.4n.

33. Πάονα . . . ἑκάβολον: ἑκηβόλος is Homer's epithet for Apollo (=Paeon).

εὐλύραν: first here; for Apollo's lyre see *Il.* 1.603.

34. ὕμνην: 3rd pers. plur. imperf. (=ὕμνουν).

θεοεικέλοις: another Homeric epithet.

SAPPHO 47

Lobel's reconstruction of the paraphrase in Maximus of Tyre xviii.9.i: τῇ δὲ (Σαπφοῖ) ὁ Ἔρως ἐτίναξεν τὰς φρένας, ὡς ἄνεμος κατ' ὄρος δρυσὶν ἐμπεσών. For the violence of love in Sappho cf. 130; for love as a wind, Ibycus 286.8–12.

Cf. Hes. *Op.* 509–11 πολλὰς δὲ δρῦς . . . | οὔρεος ἐν βήσσῃς πίλνᾳ χθονὶ . . . | ἐμπίπτων (sc. Boreas), *Od.* 5.368 ὡς δ' ἄνεμος . . . θημῶνα τινάξῃ.

SAPPHO 49

The first line is quoted by Hephaestion (*Ench.* vii.7) and his commentators as an example of Sappho's 'dactylic pentameter'. The second line is cited by Plutarch *Amat.* 5 and others for the sake of the term ἄχαρις. Terentianus Maurus (*de metr.* 2154–5) suggests by his version that the lines were consecutive; one would never have guessed as much. Atthis is mentioned several times in our fragments, e.g. at 96.16.

2. ἄχαρις: 'graceless', probably with the additional sense of 'immature', as Plutarch says (l.c.): cf. L.S.J. s.v. χάρις III.2. If the lines are not consecutive, σμίκρα and ἄχαρις may both be regarded as uncomplimentary.

SAPPHO 55

Quoted by Stobaeus 3.4 (περὶ ἀφροσύνης). 12 and labelled πρὸς ἀπαίδευτον γυναῖκα. Also in Plutarch *praec. coniug.* 4–8, where Sappho is said to have written it πρός τινα πλουσίαν, *quaest. conviv.* 3. 1. 2, πρός τινα τῶν ἀμούσων καὶ ἀμαθῶν γυναικῶν, and in Clement of Alexandria *Paed.* 2.8.72. The complete poem must have referred to the woman's wealth as well as to her lack of poetic talent. Aelius Aristides (*Or.* 28.51) probably has this poem in mind when he records Sappho's boast that the Muses have made her truly blessed and enviable, and that she will not be forgotten even after death.

Metre: greater Asclepiad, the metre of all the poems of Book III. The first two syllables (the Aeolic base) may be long or short. Note synecphonesis in 1 κείσῃ οὐδέ, 2 πόθα εἰς.

2–3. βρόδων τὼν ἐκ Πιερίας: Pieria is a mountainous district of Macedonia, north of Mt. Olympus (*Il.* 14.225 ff). Hesiod made it the birthplace of the Muses (*Th.* 53: but cf. 62): so *Op.* 1 Μοῦσαι Πιερίηθεν, *Sc.* 206 Μοῦσαι Πιερίδες, Sapph. 103.8 Πιερίδες τε Μοῖσαι. There are no other references in early poetry to the Muses' roses; Sappho's words suggest that the Muses give roses to their favourites.

3. ἀφάνης κτλ.: 'unseen in Hades' house too', as on earth.

4. ἀμαύρων νεκύων: cf. *Od.* 4.824 εἴδωλον ἀμαυρόν.
   ἐκπεποταμένα: 'flown from our midst' (Page): cf. *Od.* 11.222 ψυχὴ . . . ἀποπταμένη πεπότηται.

SAPPHO 81(b)

Quoted in connexion with garlands by Athenaeus 15.674e, who says that Sappho is advising people making sacrifice to wear garlands. *P. Oxy.* 1787. fr. 33 gives a few letters of three preceding lines.

Metre: Book IV of Sappho seems to have consisted wholly or mainly of poems in this metre, which resembles the greater Asclepiad (cf. fr. 55). It is an expansion of the line ∪ − ∪∪ − ∪ − − (e.g. δέδυκε μὲν ἀ σελάννα).

1. πέρθεσθ(αι): infin. for imperative.

2. ὄρπακας ἀνήτω συναέρραισ(α): 'binding together (συναείρω) stems of anise'. For garlands of ἄνητον (=ἄνηθον) cf. Alc. 362.1, Anacr. 496.
   ἀπάλαισι: a favourite adjective of Sappho; she usually applies it to girls or like Homer to parts of the body (cf.

94.16; Alc. 45.6 ἀπάλαισι χέρσι), but uses it of the plant chervil at 96.13 (cf. Alc. 117(b).9 of gourds).

3. εὐάνθεα κτλ.: no satisfactory emendation has been proposed. The sense seems to be, 'the Graces look rather on what is garlanded', if εὐάνθεα is neuter plural.

4. ἀστεφανώτοισι: the dative case is surprising.

SAPPHO 94

P. Berol. 9722 (*Berliner Klassikertexte* V.2, 1907, pp. 12–13) and Lobel Σαπφοῦς Μέλη p. 79. Fr. 96 and a few other scraps are from the same source, a 6th-century parchment. Sappho's theme is the departure of a friend, whom she reminds of happy days spent together.

Metre: two glyconics followed by a glyconic with dactylic expansion. Book V of Sappho probably contained poems written in various three-line stanzas. Note synecphonesis at 9 μή ἀλλά.

1–3. It is usually assumed that the words, 'Honestly I wish I were dead', are Sappho's expression of present grief uttered as she recalls the parting: 'she, weeping copiously (πόλλα), was leaving me behind, and said . . .' It is just as likely that it was the departing girl who said τεθνάκην . . . θέλω, and that πόλλα καὶ τόδ' ἔειπε means 'time and time again she said this too' or 'she said much and this in particular'; all the other stanzas end with at least a slight pause.

ἀδόλως: the word, common in treaties, may add solemnity, or it may be an everyday expression like Eng. 'honestly'. For the wish cf. 95.11–13 κατθάνην δ' ἴμερός τις [ἔχει με καὶ | λωτίνοις δροσόεντας ὄ- | χθοις ἴδην ᾿Αχερ[.

2. ψισδομένα: cf. Hsch. ψιζομένη· κλαίουσα.
κατελίμπανεν: like ἀπυλιμπάνω (5), a rare compound.

4. Perhaps no more than 'What bad luck has been ours!' Cf. 11 κάλ' ἐπάσχομεν and see note on 1 ἀδόλως.

6. ἀμειβόμαν: note ᾰ: perhaps Sappho's only example in a 'normal' poem of the omission of the temporal augment. Alcaeus has two: 255.5 ἔλε, 336 ἔλετο. But we need not emend to ἀμείβομαι (historic pres.).

7. χαίροισ' ἔρχεο: 'go and fare well.' Sappho alludes to the use

of χαῖρε in farewells. Cf. E. *Hipp.* 1440 χαίρουσα καὶ σὺ στεῖχε, and for 7–8 *Od.* 8.461–2 (Nausicaa to Odysseus) χαῖρε, ξεῖν᾽, ἵνα καί ποτ᾽ ἐὼν ἐν πατρίδι γαίῃ | μνήσῃ ἐμεῖ(ο).

8. μέμναισ(ο) = imper. μέμνησο.

πεδήπομεν = μεθείπομεν, 'we cared for you': cf. *Il.* 10.516 Ἀθηναίην μετὰ Τυδέος υἱὸν ἔπουσαν.

9. αἰ δὲ μή: i.e. if, through forgetfulness, you do not know.

ἀλλά: for ἀλλά in the apodosis of a conditional sentence cf. 1.22.

10. ὄμναισαι = ἀναμνῆσαι. The sense of 9–11 was doubtless 'I wish to remind you of the lovely times we had'.

13. κροκίων: κρόκιον, dim. of κρόκος, is nowhere vouched for, but fits well here.

14. περεθήκαο κτλ.: cf. 81(b). 1–2, Alc. 362.1–2 ἀλλ᾽ ἀνήτω μὲν περὶ ταῖς δέραισι | περθέτω πλέκταις ὑπαθύμιδάς τις, Anacr. 397 πλεκτὰς δ᾽ ὑποθυμίδας περὶ στήθεσι λωτίνας ἔθεντο.

18. μύρῳ: not a Homeric word, although perfumed oil was used by Hera at *Il.* 14.171–2: cf. *Od.* 18.192–4. μύρον occurs first in iambic lines of Archilochus (26.1, 27) and in Sappho and Alcaeus.

19. βρενθείῳ: elsewhere in literature only in Pherecrates fr. 101.2 Kock, where it is a noun. References in Hesychius and elsewhere to words beginning βρενθ- suggest that βρενθεῖος was used of a perfumed ointment made from some specific flower. Ath. 15.690c refers to this passage.

20. βασιληίῳ: i.e. 'fit for a queen', perhaps 'fit for the queen of Sardis'.

23. ἐξίης πόθον: 'you would satisfy your longing': cf. Homer's αὐτὰρ ἐπεὶ πόσιος καὶ ἐδητύος ἐξ ἔρον ἔντο (e.g. *Il.* 1.469).

24–7. The sense seems to have been, 'There was neither . . . nor shrine . . . from which we were absent, no grove . . . nor dance . . .'

SAPPHO 96

From the same parchment as fr. 94 (*BKT.* ibid. pp. 15 ff) + Lobel Σαπφοῦς Μέλη p. 80. Sappho comforts Atthis by assuring her that another girl, now in Lydia, has not forgotten her. Eight of the surviving lines (7–14) are occupied by a simile, which she develops for its own interest with Homeric generosity.

Metre: glyconic, preceded by cretic in l. 1, alone in l. 2, followed by bacchius in l. 3. Note 7 κεσσιν ὥς ποτ' ἀελίω, where – ∪ – ∪ – ∪ ∪ – corresponds to a glyconic (i.e. there is anaclasis of the 5th and 6th syllables): cf. Anacr. 357.5, Cor. 654.iii. There is frequent word-division between lines within stanzas.

1. A reference to Sardis seems certain: the absent girl is now in Lydia (6).

2. νῶν: i.e. νοῦν, but the sense of lines 1–3 is irretrievable.

4–5. σε at the beginning of 4 is probably the end of a verb, 'she honoured (regarded, considered) you like an easily-recognised goddess': cf. *Od.* 6.108 of Artemis (to whom Nausicaa is compared) ῥεῖά τ' ἀριγνώτη πέλεται.

7 ff. For the image cf. Sapph. 34, Bacchyl. ∗9.27 ff, Hor. *Od.* 1.12.46–8. The meaning of ποτ' is uncertain, and the metre is anomalous: perhaps the text is corrupt in this line as in the next.

8. ἀ βροδοδάκτυλος σελάννα: why our MS. should have the rare word μήνα (found nowhere else in Sappho and Alcaeus) for the metrically sound σελάννα is inexplicable. Beattie (*J.H.S.* 77 (1957), 320) suggests that it is the epithet βροδοδάκτυλος which is corrupt, but his βροδοδακτύληα μήνα, 'rosy-ringed moon' (with reference to a rosy halo) is unconvincing. If ἀ βροδοδάκτυλος σελάννα is correct, the epithet is hard to explain: βροδο- can be explained if we assume that the roses were white: this may be the meaning in Homer's ῥοδοδάκτυλος Ἠώς (most epithets for dawn refer to its whiteness) and in Sappho's βροδοπάχεες ... Χάριτες (53), βροδόπαχυν Αὔων (58.19) (hardly 'red-armed': cf. λευκώλενος) and 'Ροδῶπις (hardly 'red-faced'). But -δάκτυλος, though apt enough for the sun's rays at dawn, seems unsuitable for the moon's light. The use of the article accompanying adjective and noun is mentioned as a further difficulty by Lobel ('Αλκαίου Μέλη lxxvii) and Page (*S. & A.* 90); but Sappho and Alcaeus probably used the article more freely than they grant: see A. W. Gomme in *J.H.S.* 77 (1957), 265–6.

9. περρέχοισ(α) = ὑπερέχουσα, 'surpassing.'

ἐπίσχει: either transitive, 'the moon spreads her light' or intransitive, 'its light spreads' (cf. L.S.J. s.v. ἐπέχω V).

10. ἀλμύραν: see 44.7n.

11. πολυανθέμοις: first here and at Alc. 286(a).2. ἀνθεμώδης occurs first at 14.

12. κάλα: predicative: 'the dew is shed in beauty.'

τεθάλαισι = τεθήλασι, perfect tense with present sense.

15. ζαφοίταισ(α) = διαφοιτῶσα.

17. λέπταν ποι φρένα κτλ.: I follow Page's interpretation of this difficult line: 'her tender heart is consumed because of your fate.' The verb βορέομαι occurs only in Nicander (P. Oxy. 2221, col. ii. 29), where βορεῖται is 'feeds itself'. βοράω, 'eat', is known from E.M. 216.14, and βορά, 'food', is common enough. λέπταν. . . . φρένα is accus. of respect. After 17 our MS. gives fragments of another 19 lines, but the sense is seldom clear: 21–3 have 'it is not easy for us to rival goddesses in loveliness of form, but you . . .'; 26–8 'Aphrodite poured nectar from a golden . . .' (cf. 2.13–16); 29 'Persuasion'; 33 τὸ Γεραίστιον, probably the shrine of Poseidon at Geraestus in Euboea.

SAPPHO 102

Quoted from Sappho Book VII by the metrician Hephaestion *Ench.* X.5; l. 1 is quoted by dictionaries s.v. κερκίς. The lines are not far removed from folk-song, but πόθῳ δάμεισα seems sophisticated enough, and the adjective βραδίναν sets Sappho's mark on the poem. We cannot say whether Sappho is speaking in her own person or not.

Metre: two forms of the anacreontic: the shorter form, known from Anacreon 429 ὁ μὲν θέλων μάχεσθαι, combined with the commoner form used e.g. in Anacreon 395 πολιοὶ μὲν ἡμὶν ἤδη. Sappho used the metre in all or part of Book VII (Hephaestion l.c., but the text is corrupt).

2. πόθῳ δάμεισα: cf. Archil. 118 μ(ε) . . . δάμναται πόθος.

282   GREEK LYRIC POETRY

SAPPHO 104(a)

Quoted by Demetrius *Eloc.* 141, who says that the charm of the lines lies in the repetition of φέρεις; also in various dictionaries s.vv. Ἕσπερος, Αὔως, etc. and elsewhere. Catullus 62, a wedding-song, has such close similarity (note especially 20–37) that it may be an imitation. Sappho's lines too are often regarded as part of a wedding-song, in which case her continuation might have been either 'but Evening does not bring the bride back to her parents' home' or 'so Evening brings the bride to her husband's home'.

Metre: dactylic hexameter, but 2 is damaged beyond repair.

1. ὄσα: the Lesbian ὄσσα gives way to the Epic form (ὄσα) in hexameters; so probably ἐσκέδασ(ε) for ἐσκέδασσ(ε).
   φαίνολις . . . Αὔως: cf. *h. Cer.* 51 φαινολὶς ἠώς.
2. φέρεις ἄπυ (Bergk): 'you bring back', with anastrophe. Contrast Cat. 62.20–1 *Hespere . . . qui natam possis complexu avellere matris*, *32 Hesperus e nobis, aequales, abstulit unam.*

SAPPHO 105(a)

Quoted by Syrianus in his commentary on Hermogenes *Id.* 1. The scholiast on Theocritus 11.39 (γλυκύμαλον) refers to l. 1. Himerius *Or.* 1.16 says that Sappho compared the bride to an apple, the groom to Achilles; the lines, therefore, formed part of an epithalamium.

Metre: dactylic hexameter; whence the epic correction ἐρεύθεται ἄκρω ἐπ' and ο before mute + liquid in μαλοδροπηες, neither normal Lesbian practice.

2. ἄκρον ἐπ' ἀκροτάτῳ: cf. *Il.* 2.312 ὄζῳ ἐπ' ἀκροτάτῳ, Longus 3.33–4 καὶ ἓν μῆλον ἐπέττετο ἐπ' αὐτοῖς (sc. τοῖς κλάδοις) ἄκροις ἀκρότατον.
2–3. As in 96.7 ff the simile seems to be elaborated for its own sake; note however that Himerius l.c. says the girl had kept herself inaccessible like the apple.

SAPPHO 105(c)

Quoted without the author's name by Demetrius *Eloc.* 106, who says that the words χαμαὶ . . . ἄνθος are added for the sake

of adornment. The resemblance to 105(a) suggests that the lines
are part of an epithalamium; they are perhaps echoed, though
faintly, in Catullus 62.39–47.

   1. ὑάκινθον: masc. in *Il.* 14.348.

      ἐν ὤρεσι: ἐνν is used before vowels in Lesbian, and the
      Lesbian form is ὄρος (but cf. Alc. 181.3 ὤρεος); one would
      expect also πόσιν and κατ- in Lesbian: the Epic borrowings
      are probably due to the metre.

      ποίμενες ἄνδρες: so at Alcm. 56.4; cf. 111.3 τέκτονες ἄνδρες.

   2. δέ τε: this combination belongs to Epic rather than Lyric,
      but its use here is sufficiently explained by the metre.

SAPPHO 110(a)

   Quoted as an example of the 'Aeolic tetrameter catalectic' by
Hephaestion *Ench.* vii.6 and scholiasts on the passage. Demetrius
Eloc. 167 refers to the passage: 'different (from Sappho's poetry on
love, spring, the halcyon) is her mockery of the clumsy bridegroom and the doorkeeper at the wedding — cheap stuff, in the
language of prose, not poetry.' The banter resembles that of 111,
and makes sharp contrast with other snatches of epithalamia, e.g.
105(a), 115. Note that Sappho makes fun of the doorkeeper's big
feet as in 111 she alludes to the bridegroom's great height. Perhaps
she is mockingly making the conventional point that the bridegroom (together with his attendants?) is of epic stature, an
Achilles (cf. 105(a) introduction) or an Ares (cf. 111.4).

   Metre: pherecratean with dactylic expansion.

   1. θυρώρῳ: according to Hesychius and Pollux the 'doorkeeper'
      was the 'best man', a friend of the bridegroom who pre-
      vented the bride's attendants from coming to her rescue.

      ἐπτορόγυιοι: 'seven fathoms long', from ὀρόγυια =ὄργυια,
      the length of the outstretched arms (ὀρέγω).

   2. σάμβαλα = σάνδαλα.

      πεμπεβόηα =πεντα-βόεια, 'made of five ox-hides': cf. Homer's
      σάκος . . . ἑπταβόειον (e.g. *Il.* 7.222). For πεμπε- cf. Alc.
      350.7.

   3. πίσσυγγοι: 'cobblers', a rare word.

SAPPHO 111

Quoted by Demetrius *Eloc.* 148 for Sappho's graceful modification of her hyperbole (γάμβρος . . . "Αρευι) by the line ἄνδρος . . . μέζων. 1–5 are also in Hephaestion *Poem.* vii.1 for the refrain ὑμήναον and in Arsenius (p. 460 Walz) =Apostolius xvii.76a.

Metre: text and metre are uncertain. If Lobel's conjecture is accepted in l. 4, the six lines may be written as two stanzas, 1 ἴψοι δὴ τὸ μέλαθρον, 2 ὑμήναον, 3 ἀέρρετε τέκτονες ἄνδρες, 4 γάμβρος εἶσ' ἴσ' "Αρευι, 5 ὑμήναον, 6 ἄνδρος μεγάλω πόλυ μέζων. In this case 1 and 4 are pherecratean, 3 and 6 dactylic (∪ + hemiepes + −).

1. ἴψοι = ὑψοῦ: cf. *Il.* 10.465 ὑψόσ' ἀείρας.

   μέλαθρον: 'roof-tree, roof', as occasionally in Homer, e.g. *Od.* 8.279.

2. ὑμήναον: accusative, perhaps with ellipse of a verb such as μέλπετε.

3. τέκτονες ἄνδρες: cf. 105(c).1 ποίμενες ἄνδρες.

5. γάμβρος: 'bridegroom'; in Homer the word means 'son-in-law' or 'brother-in-law'.

6. G. S. Kirk, *C.Q.* n.s. 13 (1963), 51–2, suspects indecency in this line, but the fun may be childish as in 110(a).

SAPPHO 115

Quoted by Hephaestion *Ench.* vii.6 and by a scholiast on Hephaestion ix. The author's name is not given.

Metre: pherecratean with dactylic expansion.

1. τίῳ = Ionic τέῳ, Attic τίνι.

   εἰκάσδω: deliberative subj. Fraenkel on A. *Ag.* 1244 speaks of 'the well-known parlour-game τίνι σε μάλιστα εἰκάζω;'.

2. ὄρπακι: 'sapling': so ἔρνος of Achilles in *Il.* 18.56 ὁ δ' ἀνέδραμεν ἔρνεϊ ἴσσος, of Nausicaa in *Od.* 6.163 φοίνικος νέον ἔρνος.

SAPPHO 130

Also from Hephaestion *Ench.* vii.7 and the scholiast. The author's name is not given. Two more lines in the same metre (fr. 131) follow without a break and may be part of the same poem: "Ατθι, σοὶ δ' ἔμεθεν μὲν ἀπήχθετο | φροντίσδην, ἐπὶ δ' 'Ανδρομέδαν πόται.

1. δηῦτε: see 1.15n.
   λυσιμέλης: see Archil. 118n.
2. γλυκύπικρον: cf. Thgn. 1353 of love, πικρὸς καὶ γλυκύς
   ἐστι, Catullus 68.17–18 dea . . . / quae dulcem curis miscet
   amaritiem.
   ἀμάχανον: cf. h. Merc. 434 ἔρος . . . ἀμήχανος.

SAPPHO 132

Quoted by Hephaestion Ench. xv.18 without the author's name.
Metre: a variety of trochaic, according to Hephaestion, but text
and metre are both uncertain: see Page, S. & A. 131–2.
2. Κλέις: Cleis was also Sappho's mother's name: P. Oxy.
   1800.i.14.
   ἀγαπάτα =ἀ ἀγαπάτα: the contraction explains the long first
   syllable. Homer uses the adjective of only children: cf. Od.
   2.365 μοῦνος ἐὼν ἀγαπητός, Il. 6.401 Ἑκτορίδην ἀγαπητόν.

FRAG. ADESP. 976

Quoted for the metre by Hephaestion Ench. xi.5 and a scholiast
on the passage; also in Apostolius v.98c, where Arsenius attributes
it to Sappho. Arguments for and against this attribution are in
Page, S. & A. 128n.4, J.H.S. 77 (1957), 265–6, 78 (1958), 84–6; I
accept Gomme's arguments for Sappho's authorship and have
introduced Lesbian forms into the text.
Metre: the so-called 'enoplion'.
3. νύκτες: plural in Od. 12.286, Thgn. 460.

ALCAEUS

The stormy politics of Lesbos, little in evidence in Sappho's
fragments, provide the impulse for perhaps half of the surviving
poetry of her contemporary, Alcaeus. He seems to have been a
member of one of the noble families which competed for power
when the Penthilidae, descended from Orestes' son, Penthilus,
founder of the Aeolian settlement on Lesbos, were toppled for

their arrogance and cruelty. Of their successors in power we hear
of Melanchrus, Myrsilus and Pittacus. Melanchrus was over-
thrown by Pittacus and Alcaeus' brothers in the years 612–609,
when Alcaeus seems to have been too young to play his part
(75.7 ff). He was old enough to fight against the Athenians for
Sigeum at a date before 600 B.C., and like Archilochus before him
and Anacreon later he confessed to losing his weapons to the
enemy (Hdt. 5.95). Pittacus, the hero of the Mytileneans in the
Sigean war, seems next to have been allied with Alcaeus and
others against a new tyrant, Myrsilus; according to Alcaeus he
defected from the alliance (129.13 ff), and he seems to have
shared power with Myrsilus for a time (70.7). Myrsilus' death was
the occasion for an outburst of boisterous glee (332), but it was
followed in 590–580 B.C. by the rule of Pittacus, whom the people
chose as αἰσυμνήτης. Pittacus, for all the abuse that Alcaeus
might shower on him, was successful in bringing peace and
security to Mytilene and is said to have shown clemency to
Alcaeus himself. The other scraps of information that we have
about Alcaeus' life cannot be securely fitted into this framework;
he was in exile on Lesbos more than once, and is known also to
have gone to Egypt (Strabo 1.37).

The political poems are vigorous and passionate: 'often', says
Dionysius (Imit. 422), 'if you removed the metre you would find
political rhetoric;' political abuse also, he might have added,
since Alcaeus is always armed with some opprobrious epithet for
his opponent (see 129.21n.): he displays none of the Hesiodic
gravity which we find in the political writings of his contemporary,
Solon. His fondness for the allegory of the storm-tossed ship of
state (see 6 introd.) is the more striking because simile and
metaphor are rare in the rest of his work.

Politics, however, were not his only theme. He wrote hymns,
short poems composed in the spirit of the Homeric Hymns rather
for the pleasure of his friends than for the greater glory of the gods.
None survives complete, but we know enough about them to say
that Alcaeus showed originality in his handling of the myths, e.g.
in the Hymn to Apollo (307: the first poem of Book I in the
Alexandrian edition), and that he used the same metres for his
hymns as for his secular poetry, showing a preference for his

favourite Alcaic stanza. He turns to Homeric themes in several of his poems: he writes of Helen, Thetis, Achilles and others and in unhomeric fashion passes judgement on them: Helen's unfaithfulness brought destruction and disaster (42, 283); 'Thetis was not such a woman as that' (42.5).

One might guess that most of Alcaeus' poetry was written for performance among convivial friends. Much of it, at any rate, is concerned with drinking, and, as Athenaeus noted (see 332 introd.), any excuse for a party sufficed for him. Only once in our fragments does a Horatian melancholy intrude into the jollity: the message of 38 is that we should drink and enjoy ourselves in this world, since there is no returning to it from the next. Fr. 346 (πώνωμεν· τί τὰ λύχν' ὀμμένομεν; δάκτυλος ἀμέρα κτλ.) illustrates several of his characteristics: his directness and conciseness, his fondness for short sentences, his habit of beginning a poem with a verb (cf. 38, 326, 338, 347, 350, also 332, 335), his love of a proverbial expression (δάκτυλος ἀμέρα, unless he coined it himself: see 346.1n. and cf. 365 κεῖται πὲρ κεφάλας μέγας, ὦ Αἰσιμίδα, λίθος), his thought as clear and uncomplicated as Sappho's.

He wrote poetry of other kinds too. Fr. 10B is dramatic, in that it purports to be spoken by a girl in distress: ἔμε δείλαν, ἔμε παίσαν κακοτάτων πεδέχοισαν . . . That he wrote love-poetry we know from Horace's lines (Od. 1.32.9 ff) Veneremque et illi / semper haerentem puerum canebat / et Lycum nigris oculis nigroque / crine decorum and from Cicero Tusc. Disp. 4.71 and Quintilian 10.1.63 (see below). He addressed a poem to Sappho, in which, if our text is correct, he speaks of her in terms fit for a divinity: ἰόπλοκ' ἄγνα μελλιχόμειδε Σάπφοι (384). If we compare the two, we find that Alcaeus is versatile, Sappho narrow in her range; that his verse is less polished and less melodious than hers; and that the emotions which he chooses to display are less intense.

Alcaeus' songs were popular in 5th-century Athens: Athenaeus 15.694a quotes from the Banqueters of Aristophanes the line ᾆσον δή μοι σκόλιόν τι λαβὼν 'Αλκαίου κ'Ανακρέοντος. Horace owed more to him than to any other Greek poet; when he spoke of his success in naturalising Aeolian song in Italy (Od. 3.30.13–14), it was of Alcaeus rather than Sappho that he was speaking; cf. too

L

Od. 1.32.3 ff, 2.13.26 ff, and the schoolmasterish verdict of Quintilian 10.1.63 *Alcaeus in parte operis aureo plectro merito donatur, qua tyrannos insectatus multum etiam moribus confert; in eloquendo quoque brevis et magnificus et diligens, et plurimum oratori similis; sed in lusus et amores descendit, maioribus tamen aptior.*

Alcaeus' poems are edited by Edgar Lobel and Denys Page, *Poetarum Lesbiorum Fragmenta*, Oxford, 1955, 111–291; *Verborum Alcaicorum Index* at 314–35. Max Treu, *Alkaios*, Munich, 2nd ed. 1963, has a complete text, a commentary and a full bibliography. Denys Page, *Sappho and Alcaeus*, Oxford, 1955, 147–329, gives a commentary on the principal fragments and notes on metres and dialect. For detailed studies of language and syntax see Lobel, *Ἀλκαίου Μέλη*, Oxford, 1927, and Eva-Maria Hamm, *Grammatik zu Sappho und Alkaios*, Berlin, 1957. For the history of Lesbos in Alcaeus' times see Page, *S. & A.* 147 ff, A. Andrewes, *The Greek Tyrants* 92–9. (New fragment in Page, *L.G.S.* 75–7.)

ALCAEUS 6

The first three lines were known from Heraclitus, *All.* 5, who quotes them with 326 as an example of allegory. *P. Oxy.* 1789 has the centres of lines 1–4, the beginnings of 7–14 and scraps of 14 more lines; *P. Oxy.* 2166(e) 4 contributes parts of 17–24. Heraclitus' statement that the lines, like fr. 326, refer to a conspiracy of Myrsilus is supported by the occurrence of the word μοναρχίαν in l. 27 and the mention of Myrsilus in a marginal comment; by the tenses, which show that the 'storm' is in progress; and by the language of 9–14, which suggests a military harangue rather than exhortation to storm-tossed sailors. Horace *Od.* 1.14 has the same allegory.

Metre: Alcaic stanza, the commonest metrical scheme in Alcaeus' fragments. Diaeresis after the 5th syllable in lines 1 and 2, normal in Horace, occurs in two-thirds of our examples. Hiatus between lines 1 and 2 occurs once only (72.7–8 ἐπελάθετο | ὤνηρ), between 2 and 3 rarely and only when the final vowel is long, between 3 and 4 never. Horace's Alcaics are made weightier by his preference for a long first syllable and his invariable use of a long fifth syllable in the first three lines of the stanza.

1. τὼ προτέρω νέμω: so the MSS. of Heraclitus, except for O

whích has νόμω. The papyrus gives τωπ[ρ]οτερ[. Page's
suggestion νόμῳ, 'in the manner of the previous wave', is
the best of many, although there is no clear example of
νόμῳ in this sense; τὼν προτέρων ὄνω gives good sense, but
is less likely on palaeographic grounds.

3. νᾶος ἔμβα: it is not certain whether ἔμβᾳ governs the genitive.
Alcaeus may have written ἐμβαί- | νη: Heraclitus gives
ἐμβαίνει.

7. φαρξώμεθ(α): cf. Od. 5.256 φράξε δέ μιν (sc. the raft) ῥίπεσσι.

12. δόκιμος: from δέχομαι; the meaning is 'receiving (the
enemy's attack), standing firm in battle' rather than
'acceptable'.

14. The only significant words in the remaining scraps are 17 ἄπ
πατέρων (cf. 371 ἄπ πατέρων μάθος), 27 μοναρχίαν (see 326
introd.), and Μυρσίλου in the margin.

ALCAEUS 34(a)

From P. Oxy. 1233 fr. 4 with additions from 2166(b) 3, 9. There
were probably three more stanzas, of which a mere half-dozen
letters remain. We possess two other hymns to the Dioscuri,
Homeric Hymn 33 (which need not be earlier than Alcaeus'
poem) and Theocritus 22, 1–26, and many of the elements of
Alcaeus' poem are to be found in them. The poem is sometimes
thought to have been a prayer for a safe voyage, but it may have
been a prayer for Mytilene in distress, another example of the ship
of state metaphor.

Metre: Sapphic stanza, for which see note on Sappho 1. In
Alcaeus the fourth syllable of lines 1–3 is more often long than in
Sappho; diaeresis after the fifth syllable is commoner than in
Sappho. Note synizesis in 11 ἀργαλέᾳ.

1. δεῦτέ μοι: cf. Sapph. 128 δεῦτέ νυν ἄβραι Χάριτες.

    νᾶσον Πέλοπος: so Tyrt. 2.4 Πέλοπος νῆσον, Cypr. fr. 11, but
    cf. h. Ap. 250 Πελοπόννησον, Hes. fr. 189 M.-W. The
    Dioscuri were associated with Sparta: cf. Theocr. 22.5
    Λακεδαιμονίους δύ᾽ ἀδελφούς.

2. ἴφθιμοι: ἄλκιμοι is another possibility.

    ἠδέ: like 7 ῥήα Epic, not Lesbian. Note too the number of
    traditional epithets in the hymn: 5 εὔρηαν χθόνα, 6 ὠκυ-

πόδων ... ἵππων, 8 θανάτω ... ζακρυόεντος (see note there),
9 εὐσδύγων ... νάων, 12 ναῖ μελαίνα.

3. εὐνόῳ: cf. 129.9–10 εὔνοον | θῦμον σκέθοντες.

8. ζακρυόεντος (=δια-): a well-placed epithet. Homer applies
   the simple κρυόεις to φόβος and ἰωκή, Hesiod to πόλεμος.

9. ἐπ': ὂν (=ἀνά) is possible, but less likely if πρότον' ὀντρέχοντες is correct in the next line.

10. πήλοθεν λάμπροι: the reference here and in 11 φάος φέροντες
    is to St. Elmo's fire, the electrical discharge which creates a
    glow about the mast-head and rigging of ships: the glow
    was regarded as the epiphany of the Dioscuri. Xenophanes
    said that the phenomenon was caused by little clouds
    ignited by motion (Aetius II.18.1 =D.-K. A39).

    πρότον' ὀντρέχοντες: Bowra's brilliant supplement, 'running
    along the fore-stays'. πρότονοι is the Homeric form, but the
    neuter is known from Et. Gud. 483.13.

11. φάος: in its literal sense, no doubt, but Homer used it several
    times metaphorically for 'deliverance', e.g. Il. 17.615 καὶ
    τῷ μὲν φάος ἦλθεν.

12. μελαίνα: the conventional epithet may have some point
    here: the blackness of the ship is in contrast to the brilliance
    and light of the Dioscuri.

ALCAEUS 38A

From P. Oxy. 1233 fr. 1 ii 8–20, with additions in 2166(b) 1. A
drinking-song with a solemn warning of the finality of death. It is
possible that the poem ends at l. 12, in which case the warning is
central and flanked by adjurations to drink and (probably) be
merry.

Metre: glyconic with dactylic expansion, as in Book II of
Sappho.

1. Alcaeus addressed to Melanippus the poem in which he
   described the loss of his weapons in the Sigean War (Hdt.
   5.95.2).

2. If δυννάεντ' is correct, it can stand only as the beginning of the
   line, as in 8; but Alcaeus is hardly likely to have repeated
   the adjective. The sense is clear: 'why do you suppose that

having crossed (ζάβαις) Acheron you will see the sun's
pure light again?'

4. ὄψεσθ(αι): infinitive.

ἐπιβαλλέο: 'desire, aim at': cf. Sapph. 107 παρθενίας
ἐπιβάλλομαι.

5. *Sisyphus*: his exploits are related by Pherecydes 'the genea-
logist', fr. 119 Jacoby: when Zeus carried off Aegina,
Sisyphus informed her father Asopus: Zeus sent Death to
punish him, but Sisyphus enchained him, with the result
that no-one could die till Ares released Death and handed
Sisyphus over to him. Not yet outdone, Sisyphus told his
wife Merope to overlook his funeral rites, and was allowed
to return from the underworld to take her to task for the
omission. Once back, he stayed until he died of old age.
When he reached the underworld for the second time, he
was condemned to the eternal punishment of pushing a
boulder to the top of a hill from which it forthwith rolled
down again. Odysseus saw him pushing 'the shameless
stone' (*Od.* 11.593–600). In *Il.* 6.153–4 he is Σίσυφος
Αἰολίδης as here (cf. Horace *Od.* 2.14.20) and κέρδιστος
... ἀνδρῶν, and he is a type of the trickster in Hes. fr.
10.2 M.-W., Thgn. 701–3, Pi. *O.* 13.52.

7. ὑπὰ κᾶρι: 'at fate's command'.

9. Κρονίδαις βασίλευς: so at 296(a).3, 387 Κρονίδα βασίληος.

10. μελαίνας χθόνος: see Archil. 58.2n.

11. θᾶς τ᾽ ἀβάσομεν: 'while we are young'. Alc. has θᾶς at 70.8
(cf. 206.6) with the sense of ἔως. The form is unexplained;
Sappho uses ᾶς.

13. *Gr. Pap. Heidelb.* ed. Gerhard, pp. 17 f, contains fragments of
six lines of which the first is]ος βορίαις[. It may or may
not belong here.

ALCAEUS 42

P. Oxy. 1233 fr. 2 ii 1–16: the gaps in the text are extensive, but
the stories of Helen and Thetis are familiar and the supplements
are unlikely to mislead. Helen figured in other poems of the
period: in Alc. 283 her adultery and its consequences are the
subject of four stanzas of a longer poem, and there as here Alcaeus

speaks of her with clear disapproval. Stesichorus 192, the famous
Palinode, was his sequel to a poem in which he abused Helen.
But Sappho used Helen's story in fr. 16 as an illustration of the
power of love, and pronounced no judgement on her.

There are difficulties in the present poem. Why did Alcaeus
choose Thetis for his contrast with Helen? She was not a model
wife to Peleus, whom she seems to have abandoned after Achilles
was born; nor was she a happy mother: she grieved incessantly
for her doomed son (*Il.* 24.104–5). And why the emphasis on the
hardships of Troy, when the Greeks suffered too for ten years
on Helen's behalf? (See A. W. Gomme in *J.H.S.* 77 (1957),
257–8).

Metre: Sapphic stanza.

1. ὡς λόγος: for the ellipse of the verb cf. A. *Ag.* 264 ὥσπερ ἡ
   παροιμία with Fraenkel's note; ὡς λόγος in A. *Supp.* 230,
   E. *I.T.* 534, *Phoen.* 396.

2. Περράμῳ: Sappho has Περάμοιο at 44.16.
   ᾿Ωλεν᾿ = ὦ ῞Ελεν(α).

4. ῎Ιλιον: fem. also in Homer except *Il.* 15.71 ῎Ιλιον αἰπύ.

5. Αἰακίδαις: i.e. Peleus.

9. Χέρρωνος: Chiron, the kindly Centaur, friend of Peleus and
   tutor to Achilles.
   ἔλυσε ... ζῶμα: cf. *Od.* 11.245 λῦσε δὲ παρθενίην ζώνην.

10. φιλότας δ᾿ ἔθαλε: cf. *h. Hom.* 19.33 θάλε γὰρ πόθος, *Carm.
    Pop.* 873.2–3 ὁ λυσιμελὴς | ῎Ερως ... θάλλει.

12. ἐς δ᾿ ἐνίαυτον: 'within a year'; so at *Od.* 4.86 τελεσφόρον εἰς
    ἐνιαυτόν.

13. γέννατ(ο) = ἐγείνατο. Alcaeus regularly omits the syllabic
    augment in this word and once or twice elsewhere;
    see too Sapph. 94.6n.

ALCAEUS 45

From *P. Oxy.* 1233 fr. 9.9, 18 and 3.8–15, and 2166(b)2 (vol.
18) which gives the beginning of l. 8; the first two stanzas of a
hymn to the river Hebrus. Lesbos had two links with the river:
the town of Aenus (l. 1) was founded by Mytilene and Cyme; and
Orpheus' head was carried down the Hebrus and swept across the
sea to Lesbos, where it was buried at Antissa; indeed his head and

his lyre, preserved in a temple of Apollo, made Lesbos the musical
island that it was (Phanocles fr. 1.11 ff Powell).

Metre: Sapphic stanza.

1. "Έβρε: now the Maritza. Aenus at its mouth commanded the
   trade route up the Hebrus valley and over to the Black Sea.
   The scholiast on Theocr. 7.112 has 'Αλκαῖός φησιν ὅτι
   "Έβρος κάλλιστος ποταμῶν (-ός codd. boni), Διοκλῆς δὲ
   καταφέρεσθαι αὐτὸν ἀπὸ 'Ροδόπης καὶ ἐξερεύγεσθαι κατὰ πόλιν
   Αἶνον.

2. ἐξίησθ(α) =ἐξίης.
   πορφυρίαν θάλασσαν: 'the turbid sea'; so at *Il.* 16.391 ἅλα
   πορφυρέην of a place where torrents meet the sea.

3. ἐρευγόμενος: 'surging'; cf. Pi. *P.* 1.21–2 ἐρεύγονται . . .
   πυρὸς . . . παγαί of a volcano. Homer has ἐρευγομένης
   ἁλός (*Il.* 17.265) and κῦμα . . . ἐρευγόμενον (*Od.* 5.402–3),
   where ἐρεύγομαι may mean 'roar': see L.S.J.

4. Lobel notes Sipte or Sippe, a town near Aenus (Paus.
   5.27.12).

5. (ἐ)πέποισιν =ἐφέπουσιν, 'visit'.

6–7. The meaning seems to be that the girls pour the river-
   water over their thighs with their tender hands; but the
   text is baffling.
   θέλγονται: perhaps 'they are enchanted', if a participle (e.g.
   'handling') followed; but θέλγω may mean 'soothe' here
   and at Pi. *N.* 4.3.
   σόν: but σ seems not to be the reading of the papyrus.
   ἄλειπτα: an Aeolic word for 'unguent', known from *Et. Mag.*
   64.60.

8. θήϊον =θεῖον; for the scansion cf. Sapph. 94.20 βασιλήϊον.
   ὕδωρ: the υ is short elsewhere in Sappho and Alcaeus.

ALCAEUS 129

P. Oxy. 2165 fr. 1 col. i 1–32; a little information is added by
2166(c) 6. The fragment, one of our two longest pieces of Alcaeus,
is an example of his 'stasiotic' verse: in exile somewhere on Lesbos,
he cries to Zeus, Hera (?) and Dionysus for vengeance on Pittacus
the traitor.

Metre: Alcaic stanza.

1. τόδε: Alcaeus represents himself as speaking in the precinct: cf. 6 σέ, 8 τόνδε (if that is the correct reading).

2. εὔδειλον: only here for εὐδείελος, Homer's epithet for
   Ithaca (e.g. *Od.* 2.167 Ἰθάκην εὐδείελον), variously
   explained as 'clear, distinct' (cf. δῆλος), or 'fair, i.e. sunny,
   in the afternoon' (δείλη).

   τέμενος: the sanctuary may have been at Cape Phokas on the
   S. coast of the island: Jerome D. Quinn, *A.J.A.* 65 (1961),
   391–3, pl. 128–9; other sites are suggested by Louis Robert,
   R.E.A. 62 (1960), 285 ff and J. M. Cook, *C.A.H.* II (rev.
   ed. 1961), ch. 38, 7.

3. ξῦνον: 'common' either to the three divinities or to all
   Lesbians.

   κάτεσσαν = καθεῖσαν, aor. of καθίζω.

4. ἔθηκαν: a marginal note should probably be read as ζέθηκα,
   which suggests a variant reading ζέθηκα(ν) =διέθηκαν.

5. κἀπωνύμασσαν = καὶ ἐπωνόμασαν, 'they entitled Zeus "An-
   tiaeus".'

   ἀντίαον: ἀντίαος is Lesbian for ἀντίαιος, which presumably
   means the same as ἀνταῖος, 'invoked by suppliants.' A
   marginal note here seems to explain the adj. as ἱκέσιον.
   Cf. Sapph. 17.9 Δί' ἀντ[in a passage which refers to the
   same trinity, Hera, Zeus, Dionysus, as Alcaeus here.

6. Αἰολήαν: i.e. goddess of Aeolus, who gave his name to the
   Aeolians.

   θέον: the goddess is presumably Hera. We might not have
   guessed it from the present description alone, although
   Orph. Hymn 16.4 has παντογένεθλος of Hera; but Sappho
   17 says that the Atridae, returning home from Troy,
   invoked Hera, Zeus and Dionysus on Lesbos.

7. πάντων γενέθλαν: for γενέθλα, 'mother' instead of the usual
   'child, family', cf. *Il.* 2.857 ἀργύρου ... γενέθλη of a
   silvermine.

   τέρτον: Aeolic for τρίτον.

8. τόνδε κεμήλιον: cf. 1n. κεμήλιον, however, is unexplained,
   and Beattie's τὸν Σεμελήιον is attractive.

9. Ζόννυσσον = Διόνυσον.

   ὠμήσταν: 'eater of raw flesh'. ὠμοφαγία was the climax of the midwinter Dionysiac rite: see Dodds, *Bacchae*, 2nd ed., xvi–xx.

10. ἄρας: the term may include both the prayer of 11–12 and the imprecation of 13–14.

13. Ὕρραον = Ὑρραῖον and Ὕρραον ... παῖδα = 'son of Hyrrhas', i.e. Pittacus. The adj. is elsewhere always Ὑρράδιος.

14. κήνων Ἐρίννυς: 'their avenger': κήνων: presumably those who have lost their lives because of Pittacus' treachery. In *Il.* 19.259–60 the Erinyes are avengers of perjury: cf. Hes. *Op.* 803–4. For the genitive κήνων cf. *Od.* 11.280 μητρὸς Ἐρίννυες.

ὥς ποτ᾽ κτλ.: 'since once we swore'.

15. τόμοντες: Lobel suggested τόμοντες ἀμφ[εν] ἄρνος, 'slitting a lamb's throat': Page gives τόμοντες ἀμφ[αδ(α), sc. ὅρκια, 'taking public oaths', as another possibility. The line must also have contained an infinitive governed by ἀπώμνυμεν; the sense was probably 'we swore to betray none of our comrades', but the papyrus seems not to have had προδώσην.

17. γᾶν ἐπιέμμενοι (=Homeric ἐπιειμένοι): 'clad in earth': the same metaphor at Pi. *N.* 11.16 γᾶν ἐπιεσσόμενος and elsewhere.

18. ἐπικ .. ην: no known verb fits the traces.

19. ἤπειτα = ἢ ἔπειτα, 'or else', which in Homer normally introduces the less desirable alternative; cf. *Od.* 20.63 however.

21. φύσγων = φύσκων, 'pot-belly.' Diogenes Laertius 1.81 gives a list of epithets applied by Alcaeus to Pittacus: σαράπους and σάραπος (splay-footed), χειροπόδης (with chapped feet), γαύρηξ (boaster), φύσκων and γάστρων (big-belly), ζοφοδορπίδας (sup-by-night?), ἀγάσυρτος (dirty).

22. οὐ διελέξατο κτλ.: perhaps 'he did not discuss these things with his heart', i.e. 'he did not take them to heart'; the gen. κήνων must be explained by analogy with ἐνθυμεῖσθαι.

πόσιν κτλ.: oaths are similarly trampled underfoot at *Il.* 4.157 κατὰ δ᾽ ὅρκια πιστὰ πάτησαν, Archil. 79a.13 λὰξ δ᾽ ἐφ᾽ ὁρκίοις ἔβη.

23. δάπτει: 'devours', like a ravening animal: Homer has the

verb of a lion (*Il.* 11.481) and wolves (*Il.* 16.159); cf. *Il.* 23.183. Alc. 70.7 has δαπτέτω πόλιν of Pittacus.

24. Little can be gleaned from the scraps of 24–8. κὰν νόμον (25) = κατὰ νόμον. γλαύκας (26) might be followed by 'Α[θανάας (Diehl), or might qualify "Ηρας. Myrsilus seems to have been mentioned in 28. The coronis in the margin marks 32 as the last line of the poem.

ALCAEUS 130

From the same source as the last piece, *P. Oxy.* 2165, fr. 1, col. ii 9–28. Another poem written in exile, incomplete and difficult but full of interest.

Metre: an aeolic stanza. If lines 3 and 4 are considered as one, they give a glyconic + lesser asclepiad.

16. Since the metre of the previous lines, little of which survives, was almost certainly different, it is probable that a new poem begins at this point, although there is no coronis in the margin. But what the first words could have been is anyone's guess.

17. ἀγροϊωτίκαν: only here: Sapph. 57.1, 2 has ἀγροϊῶτις.

19. καρυζομένας = κηρυσσομένης, 'longing to hear the Assembly being summoned'.

    Ὠγεσιλαΐδα = ὦ 'Αγεσιλαΐδα; we do not know who Agesilaidas was.

20. βόλλας = βουλῆς.

21. The text is difficult. Lobel suggests that the pap. had κακγεγήρασ᾽ = καταγεγήρᾱσι, 'they have grown old', but γέγηρα is unknown, and -ᾱσι for Lesbian -αισι is unparalleled. Page's suggestion that the writer intended κἀπὶ γῆρας and that the verb, probably ἔξων, came at the beginning of 23 is more attractive, but it seems to be incompatible with the traces and ἔξων gives an anomalous contracted form for ἔξωον: no other verb fits the beginning of 23.

    τωνδέων: Aeolic gen. plur. of ὅδε with double flexion: cf. Homer's τοίσδεσι, τοίσδεσσι.

22. ἀλλαλοκάκων: 'hurting each other'.

24. ἐσχατίαισ᾽: 'in the outlying districts, at the back of beyond'; cf. 328 καί τις ἐπ᾽ ἐσχατίαισιν οἰκεῖς.

'Ονυμακλέης: Onomacles is unknown: presumably he was a recluse or exile.

25. λυκαιμίαις: only here, unless Hsch. λυκαιχλίας is a corruption of it. Page suggests a derivation from λύκος and αἱμός, 'thicket' (Hsch. αἱμοί· δρυμοί): λυκαιμίαις may be nom. sing. masc., 'I, a wolf-thicket man', or acc. plur., object of ἐοίκησα, 'I settled in the wolf-thickets.'

27. ὀννέλην = ἀνελεῖν: 'to get rid of, give up (?)' strife. But what precedes is quite uncertain, and ἄμεινον is unmetrical.

28. τέμενος θέων: probably the sanctuary of Zeus, Hera and Dionysus mentioned in 129.2 ff.

30. αὔταις: dat. pl., not acc. pl.: cf. 308(b).2 κορύφαισιν ἄγναις, Sapph. 160.

32. κριννόμεναι φύαν: Theophrastus ap. Ath. 13.610a mentions women's beauty competitions on Tenedos and Lesbos, Schol. A Hom. Il. 9.129 says that the competition on Lesbos, the καλλιστεῖα, was held ἐν τῷ τῆς Ἥρας τεμένει.

34. ἄχω θεσπεσία: so at Sapph. 44.27.

ALCAEUS 308(b)

The first stanza of a hymn to Hermes, quoted by Hephaestion *Ench.* xiv.1 and commentators on that passage, one of whom tells us that this was the second poem of Book I in the Alexandrian edition. Horace *Od.* 1.10, a hymn to Mercury in the same metre, owed much to Alcaeus' poem according to Porphyrion; in his third stanza Horace tells of Apollo's laughter when Hermes capped his theft of his cattle by stealing his quiver, and Porphyrion's comment here is *fabula haec autem ab Alcaeo ficta*: cf. Pausanias 7.20.4. Alcaeus' opening resembles the opening of the Homeric Hymn to Hermes, Ἑρμῆν ὕμνει, Μοῦσα, Διὸς καὶ Μαιάδος υἱόν, | Κυλλήνης μεδέοντα . . . ὃν τέκε Μαῖα | . . . Διὸς ἐν φιλότητι μιγεῖσα, but the resemblances, except for Κυλλήνης μεδέοντα (Alc. Κυλλάνας ὁ μέδεις), are not surprising, and in any case it is uncertain which poem is the earlier. It is noteworthy that the Homeric Hymn mentions the theft of the bow and arrows only in passing and in a different context (514–15). Alcaeus may have made the Charites midwives at Hermes' birth and the Horae his

nurses: see Philostratus Major, *Imag.* 1.25–6, Menander Rhetor
p. 39 Bursian.

Metre: Sapphic stanza. Hephaestion l.c. remarks that it is
uncertain whether Sappho or Alcaeus invented the stanza.

1. χαῖρε: the greeting is common at the *end* of the rhapsodic
   preludes, e.g. *h. Hom.* 6.19, and occurs too in the formula
   which ends some of the long hymns, *h. Ap.* 545, *h. Merc.*
   579, *h. Ven.* 292.

   Κυλλάνας: Mt. Cyllene in Arcadia, birth-place of Hermes.

   ὁ μέδεις: vocative; μέδεις is pres. part. = the Homeric
   μεδέων: cf. *h. Merc.* 2 Κυλλήνης μεδέοντα.

2. κορύφαισιν: presumably the peaks of Cyllene itself; but
   Philostratus, perhaps with ἄγναις or ἀγναῖς before him,
   said that Hermes was born and reared on Olympus.

4. παμβασίληι: not cited again before the Greek version of
   Ecclesiasticus, Lxx *Si.* 50.15(17), though Aristophanes has
   παμβασιλεία (*Nu.* 357, 1150).

ALCAEUS 326

Quoted like fr. 6.1–3 by Heraclitus, *All.* 5, as an example of
allegory: the first impression, that the lines describe an actual
storm at sea, is not to be trusted, he says: the poem is about
Myrsilus and his 'tyrannical' conspiracy against the Mytileneans.
Page (*S. & A.* 185–7) completes l. 9 with τὰ δ' ὀή[ἴα from a commentary on Alcaeus, *P. Oxy.* 2306 (= L.-P. 305), col. ii.20, and
adds to it another papyrus fragment, *P. Oxy.* 2297, fr. 5 (= L.-P.
208(a)).

Metre: Alcaic stanza.

1. ἀσυννέτημμι: an uncommon word; Hippocrates has ἀσυνετέω
   (*Fract.* 25).

   στάσιν: the word suggests both the direction from which the
   winds blow (cf. Hdt. 2.26) and their strife, and may also
   point forward to the allegory.

2. κῦμα κυλίνδεται: so at *Il.* 11.307. In 4 ναῖ ... μελαίνᾳ is
   also Homeric: cf. 34(a).12.

6. πὲρ ... ἔχει = ὑπερέχει, 'covers'; cf. Sapph. 16.6, 96.9.

7. ζάδηλον = διάδηλον, another uncommon word, here 'trans-

parent' (thanks to the great gaps in the sail); cf. Hor. *Od.* 1.14.9 *non tibi sunt integra lintea.*

9. χόλαισι = χαλῶσι, ἄγκοινναι = ἄγκοιναι, ropes of some kind.

ὀήϊα = Homer's οἰήϊα, 'rudders'.

If Page's reconstruction is correct, 12–14 give -τοι πόδες ἀμφότεροι μενο[| ἐν βιμβλίδεσσι· τοῦτό με καὶ σ[άοι | μόνον, 'both feet stay (entangled) in the sheets: it is this alone that saves me'; and 14–15 seem to say that the cargo is swept overboard. The description of the storm occupies at least the first four stanzas.

ALCAEUS 332

Quoted by Athenaeus 10.430c along with 335, 338 and 347 with the remark that Alcaeus is found drinking in all seasons and circumstances. Horace began his poem on the death of Cleopatra by alluding to Alcaeus' opening line (*Od.* 1.37.1 *nunc est bibendum*).

Metre: first two lines of Alcaic stanza.

1. τινα: subject of both μεθύσθην and πώνην.

πὲρ βίαν: 'with all one's might', lit. 'beyond one's strength'. πρὸς βίαν (cod.) means 'under compulsion', as in S. fr. 669 N² τὸ πρὸς βίαν | πίνειν ἴσον πέφυκε τῷ διψῆν κακόν, and would provide an anomaly in the short syllable before mute and liquid (τινᾰ προς).

ALCAEUS 333

From Tzetzes on Lycophron *Alex.* 212.

Metre: 3rd line of Alcaic stanza.

διόπτρον: only here; 'wine lets us see through, see through into, a man', rather than 'wine is the mirror (κάτοπτρον) of a man'. Cf. Thgn. 500 ἀνδρὸς δ' οἶνος ἔδειξε νόον, A. fr. 393 N² κάτοπτρον εἴδους χαλκός ἐστ', οἶνος δὲ νοῦ, and Alc. 366 οἶνος, ὦ φίλε παῖ, καὶ ἀλάθεα.

ALCAEUS 335

From Athenaeus 10.430bc: cf. 332 introd.

Metre: Alcaic stanza.

2. προκόψομεν . . . οὐδέν: 'we shall make no headway.'

ἀσάμενοι: Sapph. 1.3 has the noun ἄσαισι.

3. Βύκχι: mentioned elsewhere in our fragments (73.10) and
   commentaries.

   φαρμάκων: cf. Archil. 7.5–7.

4. ἐνεικαμένοις: aor. mid. part. of φέρω.

ALCAEUS 338

From Athenaeus 10.430ab: cf. 332 introd. P. Bouriant 8.20
supplies 3 ἔνθεν. Horace's Soracte ode (1.9) was probably
written with this poem in mind.

Metre: Alcaic stanza.

1. ὕει μὲν ὁ Ζεῦς: cf. *Il.* 12.25, *Od.* 14.457 ὗε δ᾽ ἄρα Ζεύς. The
   combination of rain and ice (l. 2) is noteworthy but credible enough: the rivers are solid, and it is raining now.

   ὀράνω: Alcaeus and Sappho used both ὀράνω and ὠράνω.

2. ὑδάτων: for plural cf. *Od.* 13.109 ἐν δ᾽ ὕδατ᾽ ἀενάοντα.

5. κάββαλλε = κατάβαλλε, but the precise meaning is uncertain;
   perhaps 'confound the storm'.

   ἐπὶ . . . τίθεις: tmesis, 'stoking up'.

6. κέρναις = κιρνάς (*Od.* 16.14), part. of κίρνημι.

7. μέλιχρον: 'sweet' or 'sweetened with honey': first here and
   Hippocrates *Morb.* 2.12.

   αὐτάρ: here only in Alcaeus and Sappho.

8. γνόφαλλον = κνέφαλλον, a cushion, pillow.

ALCAEUS 346

Quoted by Athenaeus 10.430d for the sake of 4 ἕνα καὶ δύο;
1–5 (πλήαις) also in 11.481a, 4 (ἔγχεε . . . δύο) in 10.430a.

Metre: greater Asclepiad.

1. ὀμμένομεν = ἀναμένομεν.

   δάκτυλος ἀμέρα: 'there is only an inch of daylight left', lit.
   'the day is a finger's breadth'; imitated in *A.P.* 12.50
   (Asclepiades) δάκτυλος ἀώς. The phrase was proverbial
   after Alcaeus if not before, and appears in various forms in
   the lexicographers and grammarians (see L.-P. 346 app.
   crit.).

2. κὰδ δ᾽ ἄερρε: probably = κατάειρε δή, since δέ seems inapt.

   κυλίχναις: the diminutive form has no force: the cups are
   large (μεγάλαις) and must be identical with the κύλικες

of l. 5. The MSS. readings point to ποικίλαις, 'decorated' cups, and Page's supplement αἴ ⟨πο⟩τα ποικίλαις accounts for the textual corruption, as αἶψ' ἀπὸ πασσάλων (Ahrens, Lobel) does not, although giving excellent sense and suiting κὰδ δ' ἄερρε well.

3. In Sapph. 17.10 Dionysus is son of Thyone, perhaps Semele under another name.

4. κέρναις: see 338.6n.

ἔνα καὶ δύο: when Hesiod (*Op.* 595) and Anacreon (356(a).3–5) mention the mixing of water and wine, they state the quantity of water first: see also Ath. 10.430de. If Alcaeus' mixture is one part water to two parts wine, his drink is unusually strong but not out of place in the kind of party he anticipates. Various proportions are given by ancient writers, from the weak 3:1 of Hesiod l.c. to the potent 1:2 of Alcaeus and Pherecrates ap. Ath. 10.430e. The Ismaric wine of *Od.* 9.209 required 20 parts of water to one of wine. Neat wine was used for libations and drunk in toasts, and could be taken for medicinal purposes, but it might cause paralysis (Ath. 2.36b); Pittacus' father or father-in-law drank it voraciously (Alc. 72.3–4), as did Heracles (E. *Alc.* 757).

5. πλήαις = πλείας, 'full'.

κὰκ κεφάλας: presumably 'from the brim down', i.e. 'up to the brim'.

6. ὠθήτω: 'let one cup jostle another.'

ALCAEUS 347

Proclus on Hesiod *Op.* 584 gives 1–3 (τέττιξ), with the omission of πάντα . . . καύματος, and 7–9, attributing the lines to Alcaeus. Athenaeus 1.22ef and 10.430b gives 1–2 in their entirety, and various other writers quote l. 1. 3–5 are in Demetrius *Eloc.* 142 without the author's name, but the lines clearly belong here. Pliny *N.H.* 22.86 refers to the passage. Alcaeus has recast the following lines of Hesiod (*Op.* 582–8) in Asclepiad metre and Lesbian dialect:

ἦμος δὲ σκόλυμός τ' ἀνθεῖ καὶ ἠχέτα τέττιξ | δενδρέῳ ἐφεζόμενος λιγυρὴν καταχεύετ' ἀοιδὴν | πυκνὸν ὑπὸ πτερύγων, θέρεος καματώδεος

ὤρῃ, | τῆμος πιόταταί τ᾽ αἶγες καὶ οἶνος ἄριστος, | μαχλόταται δὲ
γυναῖκες, ἀφαυρότατοι δέ τοι ἄνδρες | εἰσίν, ἐπεὶ κεφαλὴν καὶ γούνατα
Σείριος ἄζει, | αὐαλέος δέ τε χρὼς ὑπὸ καύματος.

Metre: greater Asclepiad.

1. τὸ ... ἄστρον: Sirius (l. 7), the dog-star, for which see Alcm.
1.62n. Cf. Alc. 352 πώνωμεν, τὸ γὰρ ἄστρον περιτέλλεται.

2. δίψαισ(ι): for the plural cf. *Od.* 17.594 πάντα μελόντων.

3. ἄχει = ἠχεῖ, ἄδεα = ἤδεα, neut. plur. as adverb.

4. κακχέει = καταχεῖ.

πύκνον: adverbial, as in Hesiod. ⟨θέρος⟩ ὅππποτα κτλ. will be
a paraphrase of Hesiod's θέρεος καματώδεος ὤρῃ, but the
correct reading is quite uncertain; πεπτάμενον, 'spread
abroad', is plausible.

7. μιαρώταται: perhaps a term of abuse, 'most pestilential, at
their worst'; Hesiod's μαχλόταται, 'most wanton', left less
to the imagination. But μιαρός may have meant 'lustful' at
S. *Ant.* 746: cf. μίασμα at E. *Hipp.* 946 (Lattimore, *A. J.
Phil.* 65 (1944), 174-5).

ALCAEUS 350

1-2 are from Hephaestion *Ench.* x 3 and Libanius *Or.* 13.5, the
rest composed by Ahrens, Hoffmann and O. Müller from Strabo's
paraphrase (13.617): τὸν ἀδελφὸν ᾽Αντιμενίδαν, ὅν φησιν ᾽Αλκαῖος
Βαβυλωνίοις συμμαχοῦντα τελέσαι μέγαν ἆθλον καὶ ἐκ πόνων
αὐτοὺς ῥύσασθαι κτείναντα ἄνδρα μαχαίταν βασιληῶν παλαιστάν,
ὥς φησιν, ἀπολείποντα μόνον μίαν παχέων ἀπὺ πέμπων. A
poem of welcome to Alcaeus' brother, Antimenidas, who seems to
have served as a mercenary in the Babylonian army; this may
have been during the series of Nebuchadrezzar's campaigns in
Palestine at the beginning of the 6th century (II *Kings* 24-5),
since another fragment of Alcaeus (48.10-11) mentions 'holy
Babylon' and Ascalon together.

Metre: lesser Asclepiad.

1. ἐκ περάτων γᾶς: so in Th. 1.69.5; cf. *Il.* 8.478-9 πείρατα ...
γαίης.

ἐλαφαντίναν κτλ.: 'with the ivory hilt of your sword bound
with gold'.

5. βασιληῖων κτλ.: 'lacking only one palm's breadth of five

royal cubits': the warrior stood about 8 ft. 4 in.; for the
royal cubit see Hdt. 1.178.3. Hdt.'s description of Ar-
tachaees, the tallest soldier in the Persian army, is close to
Alcaeus: ἀπὸ γὰρ πέντε πήχεων βασιληίων ἀπέλειπε τέσσαρας
δακτύλους.

ἴαν = μίαν.

πέμπων: note the declension of the numeral πέμπε.

ALCAEUS 357

Quoted by Athenaeus 14.627a with the remark, repeated by
Eustathius 1320.1–2, that Alcaeus for one who was μουσικώτατος
was warlike to an improper degree: the house should have been
full of musical instruments rather than armour. Scraps of the
poem survive on papyrus (P. Oxy. 2295 fr. 1, 2296 fr. 4).

Metre: two glyconics + iambic metron. The papyri, however,
show the poem in two-line stanzas with line-division after the
ninth syllable. Note 5 βέλεος with synizesis, 6 κοῖλαι.

2. μαρμαίρει: often of armour in the *Iliad*, e.g. 13.801 χαλκῷ
μαρμαίροντες of the Trojans.

μέγας δόμος: presumably the main room of a private house;
cf. Hdt. 1.34.3, where Croesus has the javelins and spears
removed from the men's rooms of his palace in case they
fall on his son. (Spears are conspicuously absent from
Alcaeus' catalogue).

ἄρ᾽ εδ: if Athenaeus' Ἄρῃ ('by' or 'for Ares') is kept, we have
an anomaly, since Alcaeus and Sappho elsewhere have
Ἄρευι (from Ἄρευς).

3. λάμπραισιν κυνίαισι: cf. *Il.* 17.269 λαμπρῇσιν κορύθεσσι.

κατέπερθεν = καθύπερθεν; cf. *Il.* 11.41–2 κυνέην ... | ἵππουριν·
δεινὸν δὲ λόφος καθύπερθεν ἔνευεν.

ἵππιοι λόφοι: cf. *Il.* 15.537 ἵππειον λόφον. The nodding
plumes mark the helmets as old-fashioned: the Corinthian
helmet worn by hoplites had a crest set in a ridge round the
top of the helmet or no crest at all: see Page *S. & A.* 212–13.

4. ἀγάλματα: cf. Alcm. 1.67–9 μίτρα Λυδία, νεανίδων ... ἄγαλμα.

5. ἔρκος ἰσχύρω βέλεος: cf. *Il.* 5.316 ἔρκος ... βελέων, 4.137
ἔρκος ἀκόντων. Homer does not use ἰσχυρός, but cf. *Il.*
5.104 κρατερὸν βέλος.

6. θόρρακες . . . λίνω: cf. *A.P.* 14.73.6 Ἀργεῖοι λινοθώρηκες in a Delphic oracle of perhaps the 7th century. Elsewhere the linen corslet, which must have been of little practical use unless it had a metal facing or attachments or was padded, is the dress of barbarians or an object suitable for a dedication: Homer uses λινοθώρηξ of Amphius, a Trojan ally (*Il.* 2.830), and of the Locrian Ajax (2.529), whose armament was unusual (13.712 ff). The Assyrians, Phoenicians and Syrians in Xerxes' expedition wore linen corslets (Hdt. 7.63, 89.1). For the dedication and gift of Amasis see Hdt. 2.182.1, 3.47.2, of Gelon, Paus. 6.19.7. Page *S. & A.* 215–16 has a full discussion.

κοῖλαι . . . ἄσπιδες: the epithet occurs in Tyrt. 1.50, Mimn. 12A.2 κοίλης ἀσπίσι; it does not help us to decide whether the shields were of hoplite pattern or not.

κὰτ . . . βεβλήμεναι: 'thrown down' on the floor.

7. πὰρ δέ: 'and beside them'.

Χαλκίδικαι σπάθαι: σπάθη, a rare word, almost confined to New Comedy, for the broad blade of a sword or the sword itself. Chalcis was famous for its copper and iron works: cf. A. *fr.* 356 Εὐβοικὸν ξίφος, and for Euboean swordsmen Archil. 3.3–5.

ζώματα: 'belts': cf. 42.10. In *Il.* 23.683 the ζῶμα is a boxer's loin-cloth, in *Il.* 4.187 it is worn under the ζωστήρ, itself probably a belt, in *Od.* 14.482 it may be a loin-cloth or a tunic.

κυπάσσιδες: 'tunics'.

8. τῶν οὐκ ἔστι λάθεσθ(αι) κτλ.: 'these we have been unable to forget, ever since we first undertook this task.'

ALCAEUS 362

1–2 are quoted for the sake of ὑπαθύμιδας by Athenaeus 15.674cd, 3–4 by Athenaeus 15.687d as an unwarlike extract from the warlike Alcaeus. Bergk united the fragments.

Metre: Sapphic stanza.

1. ἀνήτω: cf. Sapph. 81(b).2n.

2. πλέκταις ὑπαθύμιδας: cf. Sapph. 94.14–16 περεθήκαο | καὶ πόλλαις ὑπαθύμιδας | πλέκταις ἀμφ' ἀπάλᾳ δέρᾳ.

3. κὰδ δὲ χευάτω κτλ.: cf. 50.1–2 κὰτ τὰς πόλλα παθοίσας
κεφάλας κάκχεέ μοι μύρον | καὶ κὰτ τὼ πολίω στήθεος. For
μύρον see Sapph. 94.18n.

IBYCUS

Ibycus is the second great poet of Magna Graecia. He was born at
Rhegium in the 'toe' of Italy, but left the West for Samos, where
the wealthy tyrant Polycrates gave employment and encouragement to poets and other artists and craftsmen. His creative life
must belong to the second half of the 6th century: Eusebius says
he was famous (*agnoscitur*) in Ol.61 (536–3 B.C.), a date which fits
the period of Polycrates' reign (*c.* 535–*c.* 522); the *Suda* says that
he arrived in Samos in Ol.54 (564–1 B.C.) when Polycrates, the
father of the tyrant Polycrates, was on the throne, but this
contradicts Herodotus' account of Polycrates (3.39) at two points
— Polycrates' father was Aeaces, and Polycrates did not succeed
to his father in the tyranny but seized power by revolt — and the
date offered by the *Suda* is not usually accepted. We know little
else of his life: there was a story that he might have been tyrant in
Rhegium but left the city instead, whence the sayings ἀρχαιό-
τερος Ἰβύκου and ἀνοητότερος Ἰβύκου, 'more antiquated, more
stupid than Ibycus.' He was buried at Rhegium (*A.P.* 7.714).

He wrote poetry of two types, not quite distinct: narrative
poetry, so like that of Stesichorus that there was room for
doubt about which of the two wrote the *Funeral Games of Pelias*
(Athenaeus 4.172 d–f), and erotic poetry in praise of boys. We
have a score of references to his narrative poetry, in which he
handled the same themes as Stesichorus, the adventures of Heracles, Meleager and the Argonauts, and the Trojan war and
its sequel. He seems to have allowed himself the same freedom in
mythology as his predecessor, and more than once we are told
that he gave a unique account of some story (e.g. 299, 308, 324,
331). It is usual to assign the narrative poetry to the earlier part
of his life, when he lived in the West and followed in the footsteps

of Stesichorus, and to treat his love-poetry as the product of his life at the court of Polycrates. This is to oversimplify, however, since mythology played a part in his new poetry too: we hear of a poem addressed to one Gorgias, in which the rape of Ganymede by Zeus and of Tithonus by Dawn found a place, doubtless as illustrations of beauty loved and won (289); the handsome Endymion was mentioned in another poem (284), the love of Talos for Rhadamanthus in another (309). His poetry was arranged by his Alexandrian editor in 7 books, of which we have references to Books 1 and 5. The poem in which he told how Menelaus spared Helen's life in the temple of Aphrodite was called a dithyramb by the scholiast on Euripides (296). He wrote like Stesichorus in a literary language, largely Epic (note gen. in -οιο, the suffix -φι, omission of augment in verbs), but with some Doric features, notably the Doric ā, and a few Aeolisms (Μοίσαι, πέδα), introduced under the influence of the love-poetry of Sappho and Alcaeus. The rich language and vivid imagery of 286 and 287 set them among the finest examples of Greek poetry.

'The cranes of Ibycus' were proverbial. He was said to have been killed by robbers in an isolated place and to have cried out that the passing cranes would avenge him; afterwards the robbers, sitting in the theatre, jested when some cranes flew overhead: 'Look, the avengers of Ibycus!' They were overheard, tried and executed.

IBYCUS 282(a)

P. Oxy. 1790, with additional scraps in 2081(f). The dialect and metre, the triadic structure, the multitude of epithets and the promise of immortal fame to Polycrates (47) all point to the work of Ibycus, but the piece appears so insipid when set beside the other poems written at Samos (286, 287, 288) that we must either regard Ibycus as unhappy in his role of court flatterer or conclude that the work belongs to his school rather than to him. It must have been preserved under his name, or else it would hardly have survived to the 1st century B.C. The triadic structure implies that the poem is a choral song, unlike 286, 287, 288.

The first 35 lines of the fragment, which begins at the opening of an antistrophe, are occupied by a mention of the fall of Troy and a catalogue of Trojans and Greeks of whom the poet will not or cannot speak. The last strophe (36–9) is all but lost, but it must have continued the list of Greek warriors, one of whom, Zeuxippus, rivalled Troilus in beauty (40–5). The last three lines of the poem, the end of which is marked by a coronis at 48, may be taken in two ways: (1) 'among them for evermore, Polycrates, you too shall have fame for beauty everlasting, even as is my fame also in song' (Page: no punctuation after αἰέν, πέδα the preposition); the climax of the poem, the comparison of Zeuxippus and Troilus, leads to the compliment to Polycrates, who will be not the tyrant but his son, mentioned as ruler of Rhodes by Himerius (*Or.* 29.22 ff. Colonna); (2) 'they share in beauty for ever, and you too, Polycrates, shall have undying fame as song and my fame can give it' (πέδα = μέτεστι); in this interpretation, which gives point to the antithesis τοῖς μέν . . . καὶ σύ, Zeuxippus and Troilus are forever beautiful since the poets made them so, and likewise Polycrates, probably the tyrant himself, will be forever famous thanks to the present poem and the fame of the writer. 41–5 will be no more than a parenthesis at the end of the catalogue of Greeks, albeit a parenthesis fashioned to fit the predilections of Polycrates' court.

The poem is distinguished by its clusters of epithets (1–2, 20–2, 25–6, 34), almost all of them Homeric and none so striking as those of frr. 286, 287, 288; by its use of *praeteritio* (10, 15, 23), a device effective and amusing enough in oratory but alien to lyric poetry; and by its inept and slovenly language (16–19 ἡρώων . . . ἥρωας, 26–7 τὰ ἔκαστα . . . ναῶν, 27–8 ἀπ' Αὐλίδος . . . ἀπ' "Αργεος, 41–5, especially μάλ' εἴσκον ὅμοιον, 47–8 κλέος . . . κλέος and the prosaic ὡς κατά). The clear parts of the poem are dull, the few interesting parts unclear.

See D. L. Page, *Aegyptus* 31 (1951), 158–72; (J. P. Barron, *B.I.C.S.* 16 (1969), 119–49).

Metre: the structure is triadic, with four-line strophe and antistrophe, five-line epode. The rhythm is predominantly dactylic; the last syllable of lines 1–2 of str. and ant. is long at 24, where λόγῳ or λόγοις seems inevitable, and, unless epic correption is assumed, at 15 ἐπελεύσομαι (or ἐπανέρχομαι), 23 σεσοφισμέναι; the ending will be that of 'aeolic' dactyls as in Sapph.

44. Line 4 of epode is pherecratean with dactylic expansion; line 5 is also aeolic, beginning with two choriambs. Note 19 ἥρωας, 40 χρυσεο- or χρυσεο-.

1. Δαρδανίδα Πριάμοιο: cf. *Il.* 3.303 Δαρδανίδης Πρίαμος. Other epic borrowings are in 1–2 (cf. *Il.* 2.332 ἄστυ μέγα Πριάμοιο), 4 (*Il.* 12.235–6 Ζηνὸς ... βουλέων), 5–6 (*Od.* 24.515 ἀρετῆς πέρι δῆριν ἔχουσι), 7 (*Il.* 17.512 πόλεμον κατὰ δακρυόεντα), 8 (ταλαπείριος in *Odyssey* of people), 11 (*Od.* 22.392 τό μοι καταθύμιόν ἐστιν, Hes. fr. 94.23 τανισφύρου ... κούρης, *h. Cer.* 2 τανύ-), 14 (*Il.* 16.698 ὑψίπυλον Τροίην ἕλον), 17 (*Il.* 1.26 κοίλησιν ... νηυσί), 18 (Hes. *Op.* 660 νηῶν ... πολυγόμφων), 18–19 (*Il.* 13.453–4 νῆες ἔνεικαν, sc. Ἰδομενῆα, | σοί τε κακὸν καὶ πατρὶ καὶ ἄλλοισι Τρώεσσιν), 20 (*Il.* 1.130 κρείων Ἀγαμέμνων), 21 (*Il.* 4.519 ἀγὸς ἀνδρῶν), 25–6 (*Od.* 6.201 ἀνὴρ διερὸς βροτός), 26 (*Il.* 11.706 τὰ ἔκαστα διείπομεν), 30 (Hes. *Op.* 507 ἱπποτρόφος of Thrace), 32 (*Od.* 8.128 πάντων προφερέστατος ἦεν), 33 (*Il.* 1.58 πόδας ὠκὺς Ἀχιλλεύς), 34 (*Il.* 12.349 Τελαμώνιος ἄλκιμος Αἴας, 364 μέγας Τ. Αἴας), 47 (*Il.* 9.413 κλέος ἄφθιτον). The dactylic metre accommodates the formulas easily.

2. ἠνάρον: ἐναίρω usually of killing people, but cf. *Od.* 19.263 μηκέτι νῦν χρόα καλὸν ἐναίρεο, S. *O.C.* 842 πόλις ἐναίρεται.

9. χρυσοέθειραν: cf. Archil. 121 Bergk⁴ χρυσοέθειρ.

10. ξειναπάταν: first here. E. uses ξεναπάτης of Paris, *Tro.* 866.

11. τανίσφυρον: cf. Ibyc. 303(a). 1–2 γλαυκώπιδα Κασσάνδραν | ἐρασιπλόκαμον Πριάμοιο κόραν.

14–15. ἁλώσιμον ἆμαρ: 'the day of capture', a usage found in A. *Ag.* 10 ἁλώσιμον ... βάξιν, *Th.* 635 ἁλώσιμον παιῶνα.

ἀνώνυμον: used in its literal sense, 'nameless', at *Od.* 8.552. Here 'unspeakable'; cf. *Od.* 19.260, 597, 21.19 κακοΐλιον οὐκ ὀνομαστήν.

ἐπελεύσομαι: cf. E. *I.T.* 256 ἐκεῖσε δὴ 'πάνελθε, πῶς ...

17. ὑπεράφανον: 'splendid'; in this good sense nowhere else before Plato.

18. ἐλεύσαν: a Doric word (cf. *Leg. Gort.* 3.45 ἐπελεύθω),

apparently introduced by way of variation on Homer's
ἔνεικαν in *Il.* 13.453 (quoted above in 1n.).

21. Πλεισθενίδας: see Stesich. 219.2n.

22. ἐκ πατρός: cf. Homer's πατρόθεν (*Il.* 10.68). The expression
is inelegant and unnecessary.

23. σεσοφισμέναι: 'skilled': see Thgn. 19–20n.

25. θνατός κτλ.: cf. Tyrt. 8.15 οὐδεὶς ἄν ποτε ταῦτα λέγων
ἀνύσειεν ἕκαστα.

26. διερός: an obscure word, twice in Homer (*Od.* 6.201, quoted
in 1n., and 9.43 διερῷ ποδί), said to mean 'vigorous', and
derived from δίεμαι, 'speed', or διαίνω, 'moisten' (i.e.
with sap in one's limbs); after Homer the word nearly
always means 'wet, liquid'.

τὰ ἕκαστα: so in *Il.* 11.706 (see 1n. above), but the gen. ναῶν
is a harsh addition.

30. ἱπποτρόφον: cf. *Il.* 5.551 Ἴλιον εἰς εὔπωλον.

31. χαλκάσπιδες: not Homeric; next in Pi. *O.* 9.54, *I.* 7.25.

40. χρυσεόστροφος: 'golden-girdled', only here. S. *O.T.* 203–4
has χρυσοστρόφων ... ἀγκυλᾶν of bowstrings.

41. Ὕλλις: identified by J. P. Barron as mother of Zeuxippus,
king of Sicyon at the time of the Trojan war: cf. Paus. 2.6.7
and see *C.R.* n.s. 11 (1961), 185 ff.

Τρωίλον: Troilus was a son of Priam, mentioned as dead in
Il. 24.257; the tragedian Phrynichus wrote of him λάμπει
δ' ἐπὶ πορφυρέαις παρῇσι φῶς ἔρωτος (fr. 13 N²). Both
Zeuxippus and Troilus were said to have been sons of
Apollo (Paus. l.c., schol. Lyc. 307).

42. ὡσεὶ χρυσόν κτλ.: orichalc, brass, is coupled with gold at
h. Hom. 6.9, mentioned in Hes. *Sc.* 122 and cited from
Stesichorus (fr. 260) and Bacchylides (fr. 51). The point
seems to be that Zeuxippus and Troilus, like brass and
thrice-refined gold, were equally beautiful: μάλ' ἔϊσκον
ὅμοιον, a crude expression, must mean 'they found them
very much alike'. ἔϊσκον may come from ἴσκω or ἐΐσκω
(with augment and digamma neglected). ἐρόεσσαν μορφάν
is acc. of respect. With χρυσὸν ... τρὶς ἄπεφθον cf. Thgn.
449–50 ἄπεφθον χρυσόν with notes there and on 451,
Simon. 592 χρυσὸν ἐφθόν, Hdt. 1.50.2, 3 ἀπέφθου χρυσοῦ,

Th. 2.13.5 χρυσίου ἀπέφθου. ἄπεφθος is for ἄφεφθος, 'boiled down, refined', from ἀφέψω.

46. τοῖς· μὲν πέδα κτλ.: see introd.

47. κλέος ἄφθιτον ἑξεῖς: for immortality conferred by poetry cf. Sapph. 55, Thgn. 237 ff.

IBYCUS 286

Quoted by Athenaeus 13.601bc as an example of Ibycus' love-poetry.

Metre: the rhythm is mainly dactylic. 1, 2, 3, 8, 9 show an aeolic length known as the 'ibycean': so 317(a). 4. 7 and 12 give a recognisable clausula, used e.g. by Alcman 1.49 τῶν ὑποπετριδίων ὀνείρων and as the last line of the Alcaic stanza. Attempts to manipulate 8 ff so as to form a stanza corresponding to 1–7 are encouraged by the corruption of Athenaeus' text, but may be misguided. I have set out the poem as in Bowra *G.L.P.* 260.

1. ἦρι μέν: answered by 6 ἐμοὶ δ'. The contrast is between the seasonal regularity of nature and the ever-present love of Ibycus which knows no seasons; ἦρι is emphatic: 'it is in spring that. . . .' There is a clear contrast too between the tranquillity of nature and Ibycus' unresting love, harsh in its onslaught.

Κυδώνιαι: see Stesich. 187.1n.

2. μηλίδες: only here and Theoc. 8.79; for the usual form μηλέαι see Sapph. 2.6n.

ἀρδόμεναι ῥοᾶν: 'watered by streams'; ἄρδω has gen. in h. Hom. 9.3 ἵππους ἄρσασα . . . Μέλητος.

3. ἐκ ποταμῶν: the phrase has adjectival force. The apple-orchard is irrigated by river waters conducted in channels.

3. ἵνα Παρθένων κτλ.: 'where stands the inviolate garden of the Maidens'. The Maidens must be Nymphs, but the title occurs nowhere else; their garden may be the countryside with its orchards and vineyards, rather than a specific shrine.

4. οἰνανθίδες: here only, for οἰνάνθη, 'vine-blossom'.

7. κατάκοιτος: here only, 'in bed, at rest'.

8. ὑπὸ στεροπᾶς φλέγων: 'blazing with lightning'; ὑπό may denote the accompaniment as in ὑπ' αὐλοῦ, 'with pipe

accompaniment', or the agent, if the wind is regarded as
set on fire by the lightning.

9. Θρηίκιος Βορέας: so Hes. *Op.* 553 Θρηικίου Βορέω, Tyrt.
9.4n. For love as a wind cf. Sapph. 47.

10. παρὰ Κύπριδος: 'from Aphrodite's home'.

ἀζαλέαις: from ἄζω, 'parch'; in Homer with passive sense,
'parched'; here, as in Hes. *Sc.* 153 Σειρίου ἀζαλέοιο 'parching', in contrast with ἀρδόμεναι ῥοαῖ.

μανίαισι: the dative is probably to be associated with the
adjacent adjectives ἐρεμνὸς ἀθαμβής as well as with
τινάσσει: 'dark and shameless with parching fits of
madness.' The sentence has Aeschylean richness.

11. ἐρεμνός: cf. *Il.* 12.375, 20.51 ἐρεμνῇ λαίλαπι, 'a black
hurricane', Hor. *Od.* 1.5.7 nigris ... ventis, *Epod.* 10.5
niger Eurus, Virg. *G.* 3.278 nigerrimus Auster.

ἀθαμβής: a rare word, also at Bacch. 15.58 of Ὕβρις;
doubtless to be applied to ἔρος, but like ἐρεμνός applicable also to the wind: cf. Homer's λᾶας ἀναιδής (*Il.* 4.521,
Od. 11.598, also *Il.* 13.139).

12. πεδόθεν τινάσσει: cf. Hes. *Th.* 680 πεδόθεν δ' ἐτινάσσετο
μακρὸς Ὄλυμπος, Sapph. 47 Ἔρος δ' ἐτίναξέ μοι | φρένας, ὡς
ἄνεμος κτλ., a passage which gives strong support to Naeke's
τινάσσει. But Hermann's φλάσεν, 'crushes' (aor. of φλάω with
gnomic sense), is closer to the MSS. φυλάσσει, and preserves
the run of dactyls if 8 ff correspond metrically with 1–7.

IBYCUS 287

In Plato *Parmenides* 137a Parmenides paraphrases the lines to express his reluctance to embark on a lengthy exposition; the scholiast provides the passage of Ibycus, conceivably a complete poem.

Metre: the movement is dactylic.

1. Ἔρος αὖτέ με: cf. Sapph. 130.1 Ἔρος δηὖτέ μ' ὁ λυσιμέλης
δόνει. For αὖτε see Sapph. 1.15n.

κυανέοισιν ὑπὸ βλεφάροις: 'under dark eyelids': so Hes. *Sc.*
7 βλεφάρων ... κυανεάων, Alcm. 1.69 ἰανογλεφάρων. Cf.
Hesiod's description of the Graces: τῶν καὶ ἀπὸ βλεφάρων
ἔρος εἴβετο δερκομενάων | λυσιμελής· καλὸν δέ θ' ὑπ' ὀφρύσι
δερκιόωνται (*Th.* 910–11).

2. τακέρα ... δερκόμενος: τακέρα is adverbial; cf. Alcm.
3.61–2 τακερώτερα | δ᾽ ὕπνω καὶ σανάτω ποτιδέρκεται.
Anacreon 459 called Eros τακερός.

3–4. ἄπειρα δίκτυα: so A. Ag. 1382 ἄπειρον ἀμφίβληστρον of a
net from which there is no escape. Eros lures or drives the
prey into Aphrodite's net.

6. The dactyls give the impression of speed; note a similar effect
in Alcm. 1.48 (ἵππον) παγὸν ἀεθλοφόρον καναχάποδα.

For ἀεθλοφόρος see note there.

φερέζυγος: here only.

ποτὶ γήρᾳ: 'near old age'.

7. σὺν ὄχεσφι: cf. Il. 22.22 σευάμενος ὥς θ᾽ ἵππος ἀεθλοφόρος σὺν
ὄχεσφιν.

θοοῖς: cf. Il. 17.458, Mimn. 10.9 θοὸν ἅρμα.

ἔβα: aorist as in Homer's similes.

IBYCUS 288

From Athenaeus 13.564 f: lines of Philoxenus (fr. 821) are
called 'blind praise and nothing like this piece of Ibycus'.
Euryalus must be a young friend of Ibycus or Polycrates.

Metre: dactylic. Note 1 γλαυκέων.

1. γλαυκέων: 'blue-eyed', a meaning found elsewhere only in
prose authors. For the Graces' eyes cf. Hes. Th. 910–11,
quoted above (287.1n.).

Χαρίτων θάλος: cf. Ar. Ec. 974 Χαρίτων θρέμμα in lines very
similar to the present passage, Theoc. 28.7 Χαρίτων ἵερον
φύτον.

Ὡρᾶν: Page's supplement from Hes. Op. 73–5 Χάριτές τε
θεαὶ καὶ πότνια Πειθώ | ... ἀμφὶ δὲ τήν γε | Ὧραι καλλίκομοι
στέφον ἄνθεσιν.

2. μελέδημα: cf. Pi. fr. 110.3 Turyn σεμνᾶν Χαρίτων μέλημα
τερπνόν.

3. ἀγανοβλέφαρος: 'with soft eyelids', or perhaps 'gentle-eyed'.

Πειθώ: first in Hes. Op. 73. Sappho called her Aphrodite's
daughter (200): so A. Supp. 1040; Hes. Th. 349 made her
Ocean's daughter. Πειθώ is a cult-title of Aphrodite herself at Pharsalus and in Lesbos.

IBYCUS 317(a)

Quoted by Athenaeus 9.388e for the birds λαθιπορφυρίδες.

Metre: the movement is mainly dactylic, as in 287; trochaic metron in 2 as in Stesich. 187. 1.

2. αἰολόδειροι: 'dapple-necked', first here.

3. πανέλοπες: the πηνέλοψ was 'a kind of Wild Duck or Goose', D'A. W. Thompson, *A Glossary of Greek Birds* 248; mentioned also by Stesichorus (schol. Ar. *Av.* 1302 = Stesich. 262): cf. Alc. 345 ὄρνιθες ... πανέλοπες ποικιλόδειροι τανυσίπτεροι.

   λαθιπορφυρίδες: not identified (Thompson 46, 251). Cf. Ibyc. 317(b) αἰεί μ' ὦ φίλε θυμὲ τανύπτερος ὡς ὅκα πορφυρίς ...

4. ἀλκυόνες: see Alcm. 26.3n.

   τανυσίπτεροι: cf. *Od.* 5.65 ὄρνιθες τανυσίπτεροι, 22.468 κίχλαι τ., Alc. l.c.

ANACREON

Anacreon, the last great writer of solo song, was born in the Ionian city of Teos in Asia Minor. His father's name was variously given as Scythinus, Eumelus, Parthenius and Aristocritus (*Suda*). *Agnoscitur* in 531, according to Eusebius; he must have been born *c.* 575 and died *c.* 490: 'Lucian' *Macr.* 26 says he died at the age of 85, and he lived long enough to enjoy Aeschylus' lyrics (schol. A. *Pr.* 128). When Teos was attacked by Cyrus' general Harpagus *c.* 540, the Teians sailed to Abdera on the Thracian coast and settled there, Anacreon doubtless among them. His fame reached the court of Polycrates of Samos, who invited him to teach his son music and poetry (Himerius *Or.* 29.24 Colonna); his verses, according to Strabo 14.638, were full of references to Polycrates, and like Ibycus he seems to have provided love-poetry for the entertainment of the court. When Polycrates was murdered by the Persian satrap Oroetes *c.* 523, Hipparchus sent a warship to fetch

Anacreon to Athens, where like Simonides he added lustre and gave pleasure to the tyrants' court ('Plato' *Hipparch.* 228b). In Athens he sang the praise of Critias, grandfather of the politician (Plato *Charm.* 157e), perhaps associated with Xanthippus, father of Pericles (Himerius *Or.* 39.11 Colonna), and knew the poetry of the young Aeschylus. His statue stood on the Acropolis (Paus. 1.25.1). If frr. 107 and 108D., epigrams written for the Thessalian king Echecratidas and his wife, could be shown to be Anacreon's work, we might infer that he spent some part of his life at the Thessalian court.

His poetry was concerned with love and wine, love above all; Maximus of Tyre 37.5 summarised its content as 'the hair of Smerdies and Cleobulus, the flutes of Bathyllus, Ionian song': cf. Hor. *Epod.* 14.9–10 and *P.M.G.* 471. Asked why he wrote hymns not to the gods but to boys, he replied ὅτι οὗτοι ἡμῶν θεοί εἰσι, 'they are our gods.' Politics appear in 353, perhaps in 348 (see 348.4n.), and nowhere else. Most of his poems were short pieces in lyric metres, especially the slight and graceful anacreontics and glyconics linked with pherecrateans, but the *Suda* mentions also his elegiacs and iambics; a dozen elegiac pieces, not all authentic, are preserved under his name in the Palatine Anthology, and his iambics are represented by the poem on Artemon (388). He may also have written Partheneia (see *P.M.G.* 500, 501). He wrote in the Ionic dialect. The *Anacreontea*, a collection of dainty poems in Anacreon's metres, belong to the Hellenistic period and later. Anacreon's lyrics were edited by the great Alexandrian scholar, Aristarchus (Hephaestion p. 68.22, 74.11–14 Consbruch), probably in five books, since Crinagoras in *A.P.* 9.239 calls a birthday present of his works βίβλων ἡ γλυκερή λυρικῶν . . . πεντάς; we have references to Books 1, 2 and 3. The poems were probably arranged like Sappho's on metrical principles. Chamaeleon wrote a Περὶ Ἀνακρέοντος, and we hear of interpretative work by Zenodotus, Aristophanes of Byzantium and others. Of our fragments only two of any length survive on papyrus (346, 347). Aristophanes shows that the poems were popular at Athenian parties: ᾆσον δή μοι σκόλιόν τι λαβὼν Ἀλκαίου κ'Ἀνακρέοντος (*Banqueters*, ap. Ath. 15.694a).

Anacreon is perhaps the most meticulous craftsman of all the early lyric writers. He chooses his words carefully and positions them effectively, aiming always at neatness and symmetry: 358, 360, 395, 417, all of them perhaps complete poems, are the most striking examples of his art. He is also the wittiest of these writers, and makes his points concisely: note the compression of 358.5–8 or 360. His images are fresh and clearly expressed; it would be interesting to know whether he often kept the same metaphor throughout a poem as he does in 417; too often we have only an image out of context — the leap from the Leucadian rock (376), the flight to Olympus (378), Eros the sparring-partner (396), the dice-player (398), the smith (413), the charioteer (360, perhaps complete).

Posterity thought of him as a libertine and a drunkard: see *A.P.* 7.24, 25; Seneca mentions a thesis by the Alexandrian scholar Didymus which compared his prowess in these roles. The Acropolis statue represented him singing in a drunken state, and on another statue he was shown with one shoe missing, the other only just in place (*A.P.* 16.306): for the statues, vase-paintings, etc. see G. Richter, *The Portraits of the Greeks*, i. 75–8, figs. 271–98. The story went that he died when a grape pip lodged in his throat (Valerius Maximus 9.8).

The poems are edited by Bruno Gentili, *Anacreon*, Rome, 1958, with a full bibliography (xxxi–xli) and an Index Verborum (122–135). See also Page's review, *C.R.* n.s. 9 (1959), 234–7. The *Anacreontea* are in *Elegy and Iambus* ii, tr. J. M. Edmonds (Loeb).

ANACREON 348

Lines 1–3 are quoted by Hephaestion *de Poem.* iv.8 (p. 68 Consbruch) from 'the first song of Anacreon' and scholiast A provides the eight-line stanza (p. 172 Consbruch); parts of the stanza are quoted elsewhere, especially for the metre. Hephaestion says that in the 'present' edition (τὴν νῦν ἔκδοσιν, by which he means that of Aristarchus: cf. p. 74. 11 ff) the strophe or stanza has eight lines and the poem is monostrophic, but that it can also be grouped 3 + 5 with a pherecratean ending each group. So we have only the first stanza of a longer poem; Anacreon must have continued with the gist of his prayer to Artemis, which was

presumably not amatory like that to Dionysus (357), and may
have been political: see 4n.

Metre: glyconic (1–2, 4–7) and pherecratean (3, 8). Note 4
Λη̆θαίου.

1. γουνοῦμαί σ᾽: so at 357.6, *Il.* 21.74 γουνοῦμαί σ᾽, Ἀχιλεῦ,
  Od. 6.149 γουνοῦμαί σε, ἄνασσα.

  ἐλαφηβόλε: cf. *Il.* 18.319 ἐλαφηβόλος . . . ἀνήρ; of Artemis
  first in *h. Hom.* 27.2. For Artemis as huntress on mountains
  cf. *Od.* 6.102 ff, especially ἰοχέαιρα and τερπομένη . . .
  ἐλάφοισι.

3. δέσποιν᾽ . . . θηρῶν: cf. *Il.* 21.470–1 πότνια θηρῶν, | Ἄρτεμις
  ἀγροτέρη.

4. κου = που, 'somewhere' or 'perhaps', as in Alc. 325.1 ff
  ἄνασσ᾽ Ἀθανάα . . . | ἄ ποι Κορωνήας . . . Other Ionic forms
  in this poem are δίν-ησι, ἐσκατορᾷς (Attic -καθ-: noted as
  Ionic by Ap. Dysc. *Synt.* 1.92, ii.77 Uhlig), πολιήτας.

  Λη̆θαίου: a short river flowing south into the Maeander
  (Strabo 14.647). The city (ὁ πόλιν) on which Artemis
  looks down is Magnesia: her temple stood in the Lethaeus
  valley a mile or two from Magnesia; c. 399 the Spartan
  general Thibron persuaded the Magnesians to found a new
  Magnesia on higher ground in the area where the temple
  stood (Diod. Sic. 14.36.3). Artemis was worshipped as A.
  Leucophryene: Leucophrys may have been the name of
  the village or district where the temple was. Anacreon must
  have had reason for referring to this particular cult of
  Artemis. In Polycrates' day the Persian satrap of Sardis,
  Oroetes, had a residence at Magnesia, and it was there
  that he murdered Polycrates (Hdt. 3.122.1, 125.2).
  Anacreon seems to be saying that the city, though in
  barbarian hands, was none the less a Greek city. Bowra
  suggests that Polycrates planned to establish closer relations with the Magnesians (*G.L.P.* 274).

5. δίνησι: cf. *Il.* 21.353 κατὰ δίνας of a river.
  θρασυκαρδίων: Homeric: cf. *Il.* 10.41, 13.343.

6. ἐσκατορᾷς: from the temple or the hills nearby. The word
  occurs here only.

7. ἀνημέρους: first here and in Aeschylus. Note the metaphor in

ἀνημέρους ποιμαίνεις πολιήτας: Artemis, goddess of the uncultivated countryside and wild animals (ἀγρίων . . . θηρῶν), was also goddess of the civilised Magnesians.

ANACREON 356

Quoted as Anacreon's by Athenaeus 10.427ab: (a) illustrates the proportion of wine to water; 'further on (προελθών)', says Athenaeus, 'he calls the drinking of unmixed wine Scythian: ἄγε δηῦτε . . . ὕμνοις.' (b) then is from the same poem as (a), but probably not immediately consecutive, since Anacreon is unlikely to have used δηῦτε in adjacent lines; (a) need not be the beginning of the poem. Athenaeus 11.475c gives (a).1–5 (κυάθους) for the word κελέβη. The content of Horace Od. 1.27 is said by Porphyrion to be derived from Anacreon Book III, doubtless from the present poem.

Metre: anacreontics, with pure Ionics at (a) 5 and (b) 5 to give variety, as in 395. Note 3 ἐγχέας.

(a) 2. κελέβην: Ath. 11.475c–f gives information and examples of the use of the word. He calls it a drinking-cup, but Anacreon, like other writers, seems to mean rather a bowl: in 383 a girl pours wine from a τρικύαθον κελέβην, 'a bowl holding three ladlesful'; the present bowl holds at least 15 ladlesful. In 409 he talks of pouring 5 and 3 in a clean κελέβη.

ὅκως: Ionic for ὅπως.

ἄμυστιν προπίω: 'drink without stopping for breath' (ἀ- and μύω, 'close the mouth'). The word belongs mainly to comedy and satyr-plays, but Hippocrates uses the adverb ἀμυστί (Int. 12). Alc. 58.20 has ἀμύστιδος ἔργον εἴη. ἄμυστις can mean either a long draught or the appropriate vessel, a sconce. Here ἄμυστιν has the former sense, and is internal accusative: cf. Ar. Ach. 1229 ἄμυστιν ἐξέλαψα with Rennie's note, E. Cycl. 417 ἄμυστιν ἑλκύσας. προπίνω is 'drink up, drain dry'.

3–4. τὰ μέν . . . τὰ . . . δέ: with the meaning of μέν . . . δέ, probably first here. Homer has δοία ('in two ways')· τὸ μὲν πατέρ' ἐσθλὸν ἀπώλεσα, . . . νῦν δ' αὖ . . . (Od. 2.46–8).

δέκα . . . πέντε: Anacreon's mixture is not potent here or in

318 GREEK LYRIC POETRY

409 where he mentions 5:3. Alcaeus called for 1:2, a
mixture four times as strong: see Alc. 346.4n.

5. κυάθους: 'ladlesful'. The κύαθος as an Attic measure was
about $\frac{1}{18}$ of a pint.

ἀνυβριστί: 'decorously', Baxter's emendation, more probable palaeographically than Pauw's ἀνυβρίστως, which
however avoids hiatus at the end of the line. For ὕβρ cf.
346.3 καλλιπροσωπε, 357.3 Ἀφροδιτη. For the idea cf.
Xenoph. 1.17–18 οὐχ ὕβρις πίνειν ὁπόσον κεν ἔχων ἀφίκοιο |
οἴκαδ' κτλ.

6. ἀνὰ . . . βασσαρήσω: note tmesis. For the sense cf. ἀναβακχεύω
(E. Ba. 864). Βασσαρεύς, from βασσάρα, 'fox', a Cyrenaic
word according to Hsch., was a name of Bacchus: cf. Hor.
Od. 1.18.11 candide Bassareu. Anacr. 411(b) describes
Bacchanals as Διονύσου σαῦλαι Βασσαρίδες.

δηὖτε: a favourite word of Anacreon as of Sappho.

(b)1. μηκέτ' οὕτω κτλ: for similar observations on the conduct
of parties cf. Xenophan. 1.13 ff, Anacr. 96 Diehl; Anacr.
427 tells a friend not to chatter like the waves of the sea,
swilling his wine (καταχύδην πίνοντα).

3. Σκυθικὴν πόσιν: for Scythian drinking habits see especially
Hdt. 6.84, Pl. Leg. 637e; Hdt. mentions ἐπισκυθίζω,
'pour it out Scythian-style'. Cf. too Hor. Od. 1.27.1–2
scyphis / pugnare Thracum est, 1.36.14 Threicia . . . amystide,
after Callim. fr. 178.11 Pfeiffer Θρηϊκίην . . . ἄμυστιν.

5. ὑποπίνοντες: 'drinking in moderation': cf. Pl. Resp. 372d
μετρίως ὑποπίνοντες. The participle answers πατάγῳ τε
κἀλαλητῷ: the main verb, 'let us conduct our party', is
easily supplied. Meineke's suggestion that Anacreon continued after ὕμνοις with κλείσωμεν Διόνυσον is superfluous.

ἐν: perhaps 'to the accompaniment of', as in Pi. O. 5.19 ἀπύων
('speaking') ἐν αὐλοῖς: but 'between, amid' is more likely,
since the revellers presumably sang the hymns themselves.

ANACREON 357

Quoted by Dio Chrysostom Or. 2.62 to illustrate his point that
it would be inappropriate for a king to call on the gods in the

manner of Anacreon. The poem may not be complete, since its metrical pattern seems to be that of 348; Dio may have quoted only enough to make his point. The prayer has nothing to do with public cult, but is purely personal like Sappho's prayer to Aphrodite (Sapph. 1).

Metre: glyconic and pherecratean, as in 348. In line 5 $-\,-\,-\,\cup\,\cup\,-$ corresponds to a glyconic; cf. Sapph. 96.7, Cor. 654.iii. Note 4 ἐπιστρέφεαι, 5 ὀρέων, 9 Κλεοβούλῳ, γένεο, 11 Δεόνυσε.

1. ἄναξ: i.e. Dionysus (11); so in *h. Bacch.* 5.

   δαμάλης, 'subduer' (δαμάζω), here only in this sense. In later Greek the meaning is 'a young steer'; cf. δάμαλις, 'heifer'. But cf. Hsch. s.v. δαμάλην· τὸν Ἔρωτα. ἤτοι τὸν δαμάζοντα, ἢ ἀγέρωχον ('proud').

2. Νύμφαι: the nurses of Dionysus, often linked with him: cf. Scol. 887.2 βρομίαις . . . Νύμφαις, S. *O.T.* 1109 Νυμφᾶν Ἑλικωνίδων, αἷς πλεῖστα συμπαίζει (sc. Dionysus), doubtless an echo of Anacreon, Hor. *Od.* 2.19.1–3.

   κυανώπιδες: of Amphitrite in *Od.* 12.60.

3. πορφυρῆ: a unique epithet, noted by Aelian *H.A.* 4.2. The meaning may be 'radiant' rather than 'rosy': cf. 358.1n. Marzullo suggested that the word is an old cult-title with the sense '*marina*' (*Maia* 3(1950),132–6).

4. ἐπιστρέφεαι: 'haunt', with accus. as Hes. *Th.* 753, Thgn. 648 γαῖαν ἐπιστρέφεται. Note the Ionic ending -εαι (Attic -ει, -ῃ); other Ionic forms are 9 γένεο (Attic -ου), 11 Δεόνυσε (Attic Διό-).

5. ὑψηλὰς ὀρέων κορυφάς: cf. *Il.* 12.282, Ar. *Nub.* 279 ὑψηλῶν ὀρέων κορυφάς, Alcm. 56.1 κορυφαῖς ὀρέων, 89.1 ὀρέων κορυφαί, Alc. 304.i.6 ὀρέων κορύφαις ἔπι.

6. γουνοῦμαί σε: so at 348.1.

7. κεχαρισμένης: 'acceptable', as often in Homer, e.g. *Il.* 20.298–9 κεχαρισμένα . . . δῶρα θεοῖσι δίδωσι. Used proleptically here, it reinforces the verb ἐπακούειν: 'may my prayer be acceptable; I beg you, hear it.'

8. ἐπακούειν: infin. with imperatival force.

9. Κλεοβούλῳ: the boy is mentioned again in 359; Anacreon was always singing of his eyes (402).

10. σύμβουλος: doubtless with a pun on the boy's name.

M

ANACREON 358

Quoted by Athenaeus 13.599c *à propos* of the untenable view of
Hermesianax that Sappho and Anacreon were contemporaries:
'Chamaeleon in his Περὶ Σαπφοῦς declares that according to some
Sappho was the subject of Anacreon's lines σφαίρῃ . . . χάσκει.'
Athenaeus quotes a stanza alleged to have been written by
Sappho in reply, adding that it is clearly not by Sappho. The
poem, surely complete, was intended for performance among
friends who could identify 'the girl with the gay sandals', as they
could 'the girl with the lovely hair and the golden dress' (418
κλῦθί μεο γέροντος, εὐέθειρα χρυσόπεπλε κούρα) and perhaps also
'the Thracian filly' (417 πῶλε Θρηκίη).

See A. E. Harvey, 'Homeric epithets in Greek lyric poetry',
C.Q. n.s. 7 (1957), 213.

Metre: glyconic and pherecratean.

1. σφαίρῃ: Eros summons, perhaps rouses, Anacreon by throwing a ball at him. In later literature Eros is a ball-player:
   cf. *A.P.* 5.214 (Meleager) σφαιριστὰν τὸν Ἔρωτα τρέφω,
   Ap. Rhod. 3.132–41.

   πορφυρῇ: the colours of the first four lines, in which each noun
   has its colour-epithet, are in contrast with λευκή (7).
   Anacreon was fond of colour contrasts: cf. 357.2–3,
   379(a) ὑποπόλιον γένειον χρυσοφαέννων (Eros on golden
   wings flies past the greying Anacreon), 420 εὗτέ μοι
   λευκαὶ μελαίνης ἀναμεμείξονται τρίχες. Homer has σφαῖραν
   . . . πορφυρέην (*Od.* 8.372–3). We cannot say whether
   the adjective refers to a particular colour or to a quality
   in the colour — brilliance, richness, variety.

2. χρυσοκόμης: used by Hes. *Th.* 947 of Dionysus and by Tyrt.
   3a.2, Pi. *O.* 6.41, 7.32 of Apollo; cf. E. *I.A.* 548 Ἔρως ὁ
   χρυσοκόμας. Anacreon's own hair is white (7).

3. νήνὶ: for νήνυι by crasis, dat. of νῆνις =νεᾶνις, 'girl'.

   ποικιλοσαμβάλῳ: 'motley-slippered'; for σάμβαλα =σάνδαλα
   cf. Sapph. 110(a).2, Hippon. 24a.4 (σαμβαλίσκα). If the
   form is Aeolic (so L.S.J.), it is aptly used of the Lesbian girl.

4. συμπαίζειν: cf. 357.4; here the play is amorous, as in Theoc.
   11.77.

5. εὐκτίτου: of fine cities in *Il.* 2.592, *h. Ap.* 423, εὔκτιτον
Αἰπύ, Hes. fr. 81.5; but Anacreon must have in mind
Homer's ἐϋκτιμένῃ ἐνὶ Λέσβῳ (*Od.* 4.342, 17.133: so *Il.*
9.129, 271 Λέσβον ἐϋκτιμένην). The heroic over-tones give
a mock-solemnity to the poem: see Harvey.

8. She excuses herself by finding fault with Anacreon's white
hair; but the truth is that since she comes from Lesbos her
interest is in one of her own sex. The δέ-clause (8) carries
greater weight than the μέν-clause: cf. Denniston *G.P.* 370.
There is no need to explain ἄλλην τινά as 'some other
man's hair', if indeed the words could have that meaning;
and to alter ἄλλην to ἄλλον is irresponsible. Our poem
shows that the proclivities of Lesbian women had not
altered since Sappho's day, or at least that they were good
material for a joke. It is remarkable, however, that Catullus
did not hesitate to call his Clodia Lesbia.

χάσκει: 'gapes, gawks', her interest undivided; nowhere else in
an amatory context, unless the mating habits of partridges
are relevant (Ath. 9.389e: see J. A. Davison, *T.A.P.A.* 90
(1959), 44–5, M. Wigodsky, *Cl. Phil.* 57 (1962), 109).

ANACREON 359

Quoted as Anacreon's by ps.-Herodian, π. σχημ. *Rhet. Gr.*
viii.599–600 Walz to illustrate the figure called πολύπτωτον, the
repetition of a word in different cases; the writer quotes other
examples from the orator Cleochares and from Archilochus (fr.
70). Anacreon has anaphora in 396.1 and 402(c).2 χαρίεντα μὲν
γὰρ ᾄδω, χαρίεντα δ' οἶδα λέξαι.

Metre: glyconic and pherecratean. Note Κλεο-, ἐρέω, διοσκέω.

1. For Cleobulus see 357.9n.
   ἐρέω: Ionic for ἐράω, 'love', as in Archil. 22.3.

2. ἐπιμαίνομαι: with the same sense in *Il.* 6.160 τῷ δὲ γυνὴ
   Προίτου ἐπεμήνατο. Cf. 428 ἐρέω τε δηὖτε κοὐκ ἐρέω | καὶ
   μαίνομαι κοὐ μαίνομαι, 398.

3. διοσκέω: 'gaze at', cf. Hsch. διοσκεῖν· διαβλέπειν συνεχῶς τὴν
   ὅρασιν ⟨μὴ⟩ μεταβάλλοντα. τίθεται δὲ καὶ ἐπὶ τοῦ διαφορεῖσθαι
   τῷ σώματι καὶ τῇ ψυχῇ.

ANACREON 360

Quoted as Anacreon's by Athenaeus 13.564d as an illustration of the attention paid by lovers to the eyes of the beloved.

Metre: glyconic and pherecratean.

1. παρθένιον: neuter accus. of adj. used adverbially, 'with girlish glance': cf. 417.1 λοξὸν ... βλέπουσα, Ibyc. 287.2 τακέρα ... δερκόμενος. The boy may be Cleobulus: see 357.9n.

4. ἠνιοχεύεις: cf. *Il.* 11.103, 23.641, *Od.* 6.319; the impressive Epic verb with its unexpected metaphor is well-placed as the last word of the stanza. Hermesianax has the same metaphor, 3.84 Powell δεινὸν δ' ἦλθον ὑφ' ἡνίοχον, sc. Eros; cf. Pl. *Phdr.* 246a, Anacr. 417.

ANACREON 361

Quoted as Anacreon's by Strabo 3.2.14 in connexion with the prosperity and longevity of the Iberians. The gist of the lines seems to be μηδὲν ἄγαν, but we do not know their context.

Metre: glyconic and pherecratean. The first line begins with a short syllable. Note ἔτεα.

1. 'Ἀμαλθίης: Amalthea (usually 'Ἀμάλθεια: 'Ἀμαλθείης would be paralleled by 348.4 Ληθαίου) was the goat who nursed the baby Zeus; ambrosia flowed from one horn, nectar from the other (schol. Call. *Jov.* 49); one horn broke off and became the prototype of the *cornu copiae*, the horn of plenty: see Ov. *Fast.* 5.115 ff, where Amalthea is the nymph who owned the goat. The horn is mentioned first here and in Phoc. 7.2 ἀγρὸν γάρ τε λέγουσιν 'Ἀμαλθείης κέρας εἶναι.

4. Ταρτησσοῦ: district and city at the mouth of the Baetis (Guadalquivir), which Stesichorus calls the river Tartessus (184.2). Its trade with the Phoenicians and Carthaginians, Brittany and Cornwall, gave it its proverbial prosperity. Hdt. mentions Arganthonius, ruler of Tartessus for 80 of his 120 years (1.163.2); he was dead by the time of Harpagus' invasion of Ionia *c.* 540 (1.165.2). Anacreon's '150 years' is not intended as historical fact.

ANACREON 376

Quoted as Anacreon's by Hephaestion, *de poem.* 7.2 (p. 71 Consbruch) to illustrate the pro-ode (προῳδός), a short line followed by a longer line: Archilochus 88 illustrates the converse, the epode.

Metre: 1 glyconic, 2 an aeolic line, one syllable longer than the lines in Sappho Book IV: see Sapph. 81(b). The line may be regarded as a 'Hipponactean' ($--:-\cup\cup-:\cup--$) with choriambic expansion.

1. ἀρθείς: cf. *Il.* 13.63 of a hawk, ἀπ' αἰγίλιπος πέτρης περιμήκεος ἀρθείς, *Od.* 12.432 ὑψόσ' ἀερθείς, Thgn. 238 ἀειρόμενος.

   Λευκάδος πέτρης: for the island of Leucas, off the west coast of Greece opposite Acarnania, see Strabo 10.2.8–9: to leap from the high cliffs at the southern tip of the island was regarded as a cure for love. Sappho was said to have thrown herself off for love of Phaon (cf. Men. fr. 258, Ovid *Her.* 15.171–2). Cf. Servius ad V. *Aen.* 3.279. The expression is proverbial here as in E. *Cycl.* 166–7.

2. πολιόν: of the sea in *Il.* 4.248, 15.190.

   μεθύων ἔρωτι: a similar metaphor in 450 ἔρωτα πίνων and its imitations in *A.P.* 5.305, V. *Aen.* 1.749 *longumque bibebat amorem*.

ANACREON 388

From Athenaeus 12.533f–534b: 'Chamaeleon of Pontus in his Περὶ Ἀνακρέοντος quotes the lines ξανθῇ δ' Εὐρυπύλη μέλει | ὁ περιφόρητος Ἀρτέμων (*P.M.G.* 372), explaining that the luxurious Artemon was carried about in a litter. Indeed Anacreon says that he shot from poverty to luxury in the words πρὶν μὲν ... αὔτως.' Of this Artemon we know nothing else, except that two servants held a bronze shield over his head to ward off falling objects (Plut. *Per.* 27); but ὁ περιφόρητος Ἀρτέμων became a proverbial expression. Ar. *Ach.* 850 puns by crossing the words with ὁ πονηρὸς Ἀρτέμων (388.5) to produce ὁ περιπόνηρος Ἀρτέμων. A more distinguished Artemon, the engineer who helped Pericles in the siege of Samos (440/39), was nicknamed ὁ περιφόρητος Ἀρτέμων (Ephorus in Plut. *Per.* 27), supposedly because he was lame and 'carried about' on a stretcher. Indeed Chamaeleon's explanation of περιφόρητος need not be correct or complete: Anacreon may have meant simply 'notorious'. Our only other example of Anacreon's satire is also aimed at an effeminate: καὶ θάλαμος ἐν †ᾧ κεῖνος οὐκ ἔγημεν ἀλλ' ἐγήματο (424). The present passage has several rare or unique words; some are at home in comedy, and it seems fairly certain that the language is mostly or entirely colloquial, like that of the iambics of Hipponax. The poem may be complete.

Metre: choriambs and iambs; in 1, 2, 8, 10 two choriambs + ia. dim., in 4, 5, 7, 11 three choriambs + ia. metron. The short lines are ia. dim. Note 5 ὁμιλέων, 10 σατινέων, χρύσεα, φορέων.

1. βερβέριον: an obscure word. L.S.J. 'shabby garment', but it is probably a hat of some kind, since Anacreon goes on to describe Artemon's body-wrap in 2.4, and the apposition of βερβέριον καλύμματα is paralleled by ⟨δέρμα⟩ . . . εἴλυμα in 3–4.

καλύμματ' ἐσφηκώμενα: perhaps 'a hood tied tightly'; cf. *Il.* 17.52 πλοχμοί θ', οἳ χρυσῷ τε καὶ ἀργύρῳ ἐσφήκωντο of hair tightly bound. σφηκόω = 'make wasp-like'. For plural noun in apposition to singular cf. Hes. *Sc.* 312–13 τρίπος . . . κλυτὰ ἔργα, S. *Phil.* 35–6 ἔκπωμα . . . τεχνήματα, E. *Or.* 1053 μνῆμα . . . τεχνάσματα.

2. ἀστραγάλους: 'knuckle-bones, dice', here only as ear-rings.
ψιλόν: 'bare, worn smooth'.

3. Cf. Thgn. 55 ἀμφὶ πλευραῖσι δορὰς αἰγῶν κατέτριβον.

4. νήπλυτον: 'unwashed', here only. νη- is the negative prefix as in νηκερδής, νηλεής etc.
εἴλυμα: 'a wrapping'; cf. *Od.* 6.179 εἴλυμα σπείρων, 'a wrapping for clothes.'
ἀρτοπώλισιν: 'bread-women', whose language was notoriously bad (Ar. *Ran.* 858), like that of Billingsgate fishwives. Hermippus wrote a comedy called Ἀρτοπωλίδες about Hyperbolus and his mother.

6. κίβδηλον κτλ.: 'making a fraudulent living'; cf. Thgn. 965 κίβδηλον ἐπίκλοπον ἦθος ἔχοντες.

7. δουρί: 'stocks' (cf. Pollux 10.177), here only in this sense. The

τροχός, 'wheel', another instrument of torture, is mentioned several times in comedy and the orators.

8. θωμιχθείς: 'scourged', here only; Hdt. and Aes. use the noun
θῶμιγξ.

9. ἐκτετιλμένος: adulterers had their hair pulled out, Ar. *Nub.*
1083, *Plut.* 168.

10. σατινέων: a carriage used especially by women; see Sapph.
44.13n.

 κατέρματα: here only, but Homer has ἕρματα, 'ear-rings'
(*Il.* 14.182, *Od.* 18.297). Pliny *N.H.* 11.37.136 says that
Oriental men wear gold ear-rings.

11. σκιαδίσκην: here only, dim. of σκιάδειον, 'parasol', which
the comic writers use.

12. αὔτως: if Schoemann's emendation ἐμφερής is not accepted,
αὔτως probably takes dative case like ὁμοίως, 'like the
ladies'.

ANACREON 395

The only poem of Anacreon serious enough to find a place in
Stobaeus' anthology (4.51 περὶ θανάτου καὶ ὡς εἴη ἄφυκτος. 12).
The matter is solemn enough, but the metre is frivolous; contrast
the elegiacs of Mimnermus on the same topic.

Metre: anacreontic, varied by ionics in 5 and 11. There is the
same variation in 356(a) and (b), where the fifth lines are ionic.
Note synizesis at 4 γηραλέοι, 9 ᾿Αΐδεω, synecphonesis at 12
μὴ ἀναβῆναι.

1. πολιοί: cf. *Il.* 8.518 πολιοκροτάφους τε γέροντας, Bacch.
fr. 25.2–3 πολιοκρόταφον γῆρας, Theoc. 14.68–9 ἀπὸ
κροτάφων πελόμεσθα | πάντες γηραλέοι, *Il.* 22.74, 24.516
πολιόν τε κάρη, πολιόν τε γένειον.

3. χαρίεσσα . . . ἥβη: cf. *Il.* 24.348 τοῦ περ χαριεστάτη ἥβη, *Od.*
10.279.

4. πάρα = πάρεστι.

5. πολλός: Ionic = πολύς; note also gen. ᾿Αΐδ-εω.

7. ἀνασταλύζω: 'weep'; only here, unless ἀνηστάλυζον is correct
in *P. Strassb.* inv. gr. 1313 col. i. 16. Cf. Hsch. ἀσταλύζειν
(-χειν cod.)· ἀναβλύζειν, κλαίειν, and ἀσταλύζει· λυπεῖ(ται)
μετὰ κλαυθμοῦ.

8. θαμά: 'often', with ἀνασταλύζω.

10. μυχός: cf. Hes. *Th.* 119 Τάρταρά τ᾽ ἠερόεντα μυχῷ χθονός, A. *Pr.* 433 κελαινὸς ῞Αϊδος ... μυχὸς γᾶς, and elsewhere in tragedy.

11. καὶ γάρ: 'and further', a usage found in dialogue, but perhaps nowhere else in continuous speech: see Denniston *G.P.* 110 (no mention of this passage).

ἑτοῖμον: 'fixed, certain': cf. *Il.* 18.96 τοι ... πότμος ἑτοῖμος, Sol. 3.7. ἐστί is often omitted with ἑτοῖμος. For the thought that there is no return after death see among others *Il.* 9.408–9, Hes. *Th.* 770–3, A. *Pers.* 688–70, Theoc. 17.120, Philetas fr. 6 Powell, Catullus 3.11–12, V. *Aen.* 6.126–9, Hor. *Od.* 1.24.15–18.

ANACREON 396

Quoted by Athenaeus 11.782a from Anacreon as evidence that the ancients poured the water in the bowl before the wine. Demetrius *Eloc.* 5 says that the rhythm of the poem is exactly that of a drunk old man (μεθύοντος γὰρ ὁ ῥυθμὸς ἀτεχνῶς γέροντος); quoted for the metre also in P. *Oxy.* 220 col. vii 3–6, and by lexicographers for the verb πυκταλίζω.

Metre: anacreontic. Note ἀνθεμόεντας.

2. ἔνεικον: there is no distinction in sense here between aor. and pres. imper. (φέρε).

δή: in final clause to give added emphasis: cf. *Il.* 5.24 ὡς δή ... εἴη, and see Denniston *G.P.* 233.

πυκταλίζω: only here; πυκτεύω is the usual form. For the boxing match with Eros cf. S. *Trach.* 441–2 ῞Ερωτι μέν νυν ὅστις ἀντανίσταται | πύκτης ὅπως ἐς χεῖρας, οὐ καλῶς φρονεῖ, and perhaps Anacr. 346 fr. 4.1.

ANACREON 398

Quoted from Anacreon by Schol. A on *Il.* 23.88 ἀμφ᾽ ἀστραγά- λοισι χολωθείς: the fem. form -ησιν in the variant ἀμφ᾽ ἀστρα- γάλῃσιν ἐρίσσας (Bekker: MSS. ἐρύσας) is called 'more Ionic'.

Metre: a lengthened form of anacreontic followed by an anacreontic; so at 346 fr. 1. 7–8.

1. ἀστραγάλαι: masc. in 388.2, fem. also in Herodas 3.7, Ael.

Dion. fr. 359. In Ap. Rhod. 3.117 ff Eros and Ganymede play with golden dice; cf. *A.P.* 12.46 (Asclepiades).

2. μανίαι: see 359.2n., and cf. Thgn. 1231 σχέτλι' Ἔρως, μανίαι σε τιθηνήσαντο ('nursed') λαβοῦσαι, Pi. *N.* 11.48 ἀπροσίκτων δ' ἐρώτων ὀξύτεραι μανίαι.

κυδοιμοί: an epic word, 'din of battle, uproar'; cf. Hermesianax 7.83–4 Powell ἔρωτος ... κυδοιμὸν | μαινομένου. The mock-heroic touch is characteristic: see 358.5n., 417.2n.; combined with the frivolous imagery of the dice and the playful metre, it shows how far Anacreon was from taking love's anguish seriously.

ANACREON 408

Quoted as Anacreon's by Athenaeus 9.396d for the word γαλαθηνός, by Eustathius *Il.* 711.34 for νεβρός and by Aelian *N.A.* 7.39 and scholiast on Pindar *O.* 3.29 in connexion with antlered does. There was controversy in Alexandria over the lines: Zenodotus in the interests of zoological exactitude proposed ἐροέσσης ('lovely') for κεροέσσης (so Pindar's scholiast, but see G. M. Bolling in *T.A.P.A.* 71 (1940), 40–3) and was vigorously opposed by Aristophanes of Byzantium (so Aelian). The same mistake was made by Pindar (*l.c.*), Sophocles (fr. 86N²) and Euripides (*H.F.* 375, fr. 857N²). Anacreon may have had in mind Homer's simile of the fawns left in a lion's den by their mother (*Od.* 4.335 ff = 17.126 ff: see 1n.). Horace may echo Anacreon in *Od.* 1.23.1–4.

Metre: pure ionics combined with anacreontics. Note νεοθηλέα.

1. ἀγανῶς: 'gently, like a fawn ...' (note the accusative case). It is not easy to guess the occasion of the simile; perhaps 'I draw near you gently, as though you were a frightened fawn.'

νεβρὸν νεοθηλέα κτλ.: cf. *Od.* 4.336 (=17.127) νεβροὺς ... νεηγενέας γαλαθηνούς. Homer has νεοθηλέα ποίην ('grass') at *Il.* 14.347.

2. κεροέσσης: in fact reindeer are the only species of deer in which the females are antlered, but that is no reason for emending the text; as Pindar's scholiast says, the poets all give them horns.

3. ἀπολειφθεὶς ἀπὸ μητρός: 'left away from its mother'.
   ἐπτοήθη: aorist as in Homeric similes.

ANACREON 413

Quoted by Hephaestion 12.4 as an example of the brachy-catalectic Ionic *a minore* in which, he says, Anacreon composed whole poems. This is doubtless the beginning of a poem. The simile is more violent than Anacreon's others, and recalls Sappho 47 and Ibycus 286.

Metre: perhaps best regarded as an ionic metron followed by an expanded form of the anacreontic.

1. χαλκεύς: the smith hammers the piece of hot iron into shape, then plunges it into cold water to temper it: cf. *Od.* 9.391–2 ὡς δ' ὅτ' ἀνὴρ χαλκεὺς πέλεκυν μέγαν ἠὲ σκέπαρνον | εἰν ὕδατι ψυχρῷ βάπτῃ. The smith in Hdt. 1.68 was digging a well when he found Orestes' coffin. But perhaps the 'sousing in a wintry torrent' is a separate image as Bowra says (*G.L.P.* 290–1).

2. πελέκει: presumably a hammer rather than an axe: see E. Schwyzer, *Rh. Mus.* 79 (1930) 314.
   χειμερίη . . . χαράδρῃ: cf. Thgn. 347n.

ANACREON 417

Quoted by Heraclitus, *All.* 5, in company with Archilochus 56 and Alcaeus 326 and 6.1–3, as an example of allegory: 'Anacreon, abusing the meretricious spirit and arrogance of a haughty woman, used the allegory of a horse to describe her frisky disposition.' If Heraclitus has quoted the whole poem — it seems complete — we need not take such a solemn view of it; it has the air of a light-hearted poem, addressed perhaps to a Thracian girl known to his friends, and charming because of its imagery and its *risqué* metaphor.

Metre: trochaic. Note 5 βόσκεαι.

1. πῶλε Θρηκίη: if the poem was about a Thracian girl, this may explain Anacreon's choice of imagery: Thracian horses were famous from Homer's time onwards: cf. *Il.* 10.433 ff, 13.4, 14.227 ἱπποπόλων Θρῃκῶν, E. *Hec.* 428 φιλίπποις Θρῃξί, 1089–90 Θρήκης . . . εὔιππον . . . γένος.

For girls spoken of as horses cf. Alcm. 1.46–50, Thgn. 257–60, Lucil. 1041–2, Hor. *Od.* 3.11.9–12, Hsch. πῶλος· ἑταίρα. See also Hor. *Od.* 1.23, 2.5.

λοξὸν . . . βλέπουσα: i.e. looking out of the corner of your eye; of a shy glance also at Theocr. 20.13, Ap. Rhod. 3.445, of anger in Solon 23.17 λοξὸν ὀφθαλμοῖς ὁρῶσι. For the neuter adj. as adverb cf. 360.1 παρθένιον βλέπων.

2. νηλέως: 'stubbornly': cf. *Il.* 9.497 νηλεὲς ἦτορ, and see A. E. Harvey in *C.Q.* n.s. 7 (1957), 211–13: '(Anacreon) was deliberately introducing a heroic overtone into the banter of the poem. . . . The girl is stubborn with the epic stubbornness of an Achilles.' Other epic touches are οὐδὲν εἰδέναι σοφόν and ἀμφὶ τέρματα δρόμου.

μ(ε) . . . εἰδέναι: O.O. after δοκεῖς: 'you think I have no skill.'

3. τοι: first the particle, then the pronoun (with ἐμβάλοιμι). For χαλινὸν ἐμβάλοιμι cf. *Il.* 19.393–4 ἐν δὲ χαλινοὺς | . . . ἔβαλον.

4. ἀμφὶ τέρματα: cf. *Il.* 23.309 περὶ τέρμαθ', 462 περὶ τέρμα, S. *El.* 686 δρόμου . . . τὰ τέρματα.

5. βόσκεαι: transitive also in *h. Merc.* 27, 232, A. *Ag.* 119.

κοῦφα . . . σκιρτῶσα: for the neuter plural adj. used adverbially cf. Homer's μακρὰ βιβάς (e.g. *Il.* 7.213), Anacr. 369 ὑψηλὰ νεωμένος.

6. ἱπποπείρην: here only: Wilamowitz compares A. fr. 243N².3 θυμὸν ἱππογνώμονα.

ἐπεμβάτην: cf. E. *Ba.* 782 ἵππων . . . ἐπεμβάτας, Hes. *Sc.* 324 δίφρου ἐπεμβεβαώς.

ANACREON 419

Under Anacreon's name in the Palatine Anthology (13.4); that in itself is no guarantee of authenticity, but the lines have a strength and simplicity which suggest an early date. The couplet was probably composed not as an epitaph but for performance among friends.

Metre: trochaic tetrameter catalectic. Archilochus used it for solemn topics (see e.g. 58, 64, 65, 67); it may have been chosen here to accommodate the name Ἀριστοκλείδης.

1. ἀλκίμων ... φίλων: with πρῶτον, 'foremost among my brave friends'; the words are tellingly placed at the beginning and end of the line.

2. ὤλεσας δ' ἥβην: not in Homer, but common in elegiac epitaphs: *I.G. I*² 976 (=Friedländer 135: *c.* 550 B.C.) νεαρὰν ἥβην ὀλέσαντα, 943 ἀπώλεσαν ἀγλαὸν ἥβην, Simon. 87D.3 ἐρατὴν γὰρ ἀπωλέσαμεν νεότητα, 115D.1 ἀγλαὸν ὤλεσαν ἥβην. Note δέ=γάρ.

ἀμύνων: with acc. and gen. as in *Il.* 15.731 Τρῶας ἄμυνε νεῶν.

πατρίδος: Teos and Abdera are obvious possibilities, but the identification is unimportant. Cf. Simon. 119D.2 ἤρκεσαν ἀργαλέην πατρίδι δουλοσύνην.

ANACREON 96 DIEHL.

Quoted as Anacreon's by Athenaeus 11.463a together with Xenophanes 1 and Ion of Chios 2 for the correct conduct of a symposium. The thought that warlike subjects are unsuitable entertainment is expressed also by Xenoph. 1.21 ff: perhaps the two had Alcaeus' songs in mind. Cf. also Stesich. 210 Μοῖσα σὺ μὲν πολέμους ἀπωσαμένα κτλ., Phoc. 14, Thgn. 479 ff, 763.

Metre: elegiac couplet. Note synizesis in 1 φιλέω (so Archil. 60.1), 3 Μουσέων, and epic correption in 1 φιλέω ος and πλέω οιν-.

1. κρητῆρι παρὰ πλέῳ: cf. Thgn. 493 παρὰ κρητῆρι, 643 πὰρ κρητῆρι, *Od.* 21.145 παρὰ κρητῆρα.

οἰνοποτάζων: line-ending at *Il.* 20.84, *Od.* 20.262. The language is all Homeric except for μνήσκεται: note πόλεμον ... δακρυόεντα in *Iliad* (e.g. 5.737: cf. Thgn. 890), πόλεμος καὶ νεῖκος (*Il.* 12.361), ἀγλαὰ δῶρα passim, δῶρ' Ἀφροδίτης (line-ending at *Il.* 3.54: cf. Thgn. 250 ἀγλαὰ Μουσάων δῶρα).

3. Μουσέων ... δῶρα: cf. Archil. 1.2n.

4. συμμίσγων: an apt verb in this context.

εὐφροσύνης: see Xenoph. 1.4n.

The following are among the epigrams attributed to Anacreon in the *Palatine Anthology*:

101D.   καρτερὸς ἐν πολέμοις Τιμόκριτος, οὗ τόδε σᾶμα·
          Ἄρης δ' οὐκ ἀγαθῶν φείδεται, ἀλλὰ κακῶν.

This is almost certainly an epitaph (note τόδε σᾶμα), and if it were really Anacreon's it would be a unique example of an early epitaph whose author's name survived; but Simonides 83D., the epitaph on Megistias, has the strongest claim to be the first such epitaph (see notes there, and Friedländer 67–8). Note the Doric form σᾶμα, improbable in Anacreon.

102D. καὶ σέ, Κλεηνορίδη, πόθος ὤλεσε πατρίδος αἴης
      θαρσήσαντα νότου λαίλαπι χειμερίῃ·
    ὥρη γάρ σε πέδησεν ἀνέγγυος· ὑγρὰ δὲ τὴν σήν
      κύματ' ἀφ' ἱμερτὴν ἔκλυσεν ἡλικίην.

This is not an epitaph, but a commemorative elegy, and the attribution to Anacreon may be correct.

107D. σάν τε χάριν, Διόνυσε, καὶ ἀγλαὸν ἄστεϊ κόσμον
      Θεσσαλίας μ' ἀνέθηκ' ἀρχὸς Ἐχεκρατίδας.

108D. Πρηξιδίκη μὲν ἔρεξεν, ἐβούλευσεν δὲ Δύσηρις
      εἷμα τόδε· ξυνὴ δ' ἀμφοτέρων σοφίη.

These dedicatory epigrams were composed for Echecratidas, who ruled in Thessaly c. 500 B.C. or soon after, and for Dyseris, his wife. Chronology does not preclude their attribution to Anacreon.

XENOPHANES

Xenophanes was an Ionian, born in Colophon, but he spent most of his long life abroad. He tells us (fr. 7) that he travelled in the Greek world for sixty-seven years and that he was twenty-five when his travels began. If he left Colophon when it was captured by the Medes in 545, we can assign his birth to c. 570 and his death to c. 478 or a few years later if fr. 7 does not belong to the last year of his life. These dates are five years too early if 540 is the correct date for the capture of Colophon.

We know little else about him: Diogenes Laertius 9.18 says that he lived in Zancle and Catana, and that he used to give recitations of his poetry (ἐρραψῴδει τὰ ἑαυτοῦ). His words in fr. 7 suggest that he regarded his philosophising as the most important part of his life: 'sixty-seven years have kept my intellect (φροντίδα) tossing over the Greek world.' Late writers, e.g. Clement of Alexandria, regarded him as the founder of the Eleatic school of philosophy, but this is unlikely: he wrote a poem on the colonisation of Elea (Diog. Laert. 9.20) and may well have visited it or even lived there, since it was a colony from Zancle; but the story of his association with the Eleatic school may be due to mistaken inferences from Plato *Sph.* 242d τὸ δὲ παρ' ἡμῖν Ἐλεατικὸν ἔθνος, ἀπὸ Ξενοφάνους τε καὶ ἔτι πρόσθεν ἀρξάμενον . . . (note καὶ ἔτι πρόσθεν), and Aristotle *Met.* 986b ὁ γὰρ Παρμενίδης τούτου (sc. Ξενοφάνους) λέγεται γενέσθαι μαθητής, and from the similarity between Xenophanes' εἷς θεός (fr. 19) and the Parmenidean 'One'.

The nomenclature of Xenophanes' writings is unclear. We have two quotations from his Σίλλοι or 'Lampoons' (fr. 15, 17), both of which are usually emended to form hexameter lines, and we have a reference to the fifth book of the Σίλλοι. In addition fr. 18, also in hexameters, is quoted from his Παρῳδίαι (MSS. Παρῴδαι). Both titles are likely to be later than Xenophanes. Late sources refer to his Περὶ Φύσεως, but it is not certain that there was a poem or collection with this title. Diogenes Laertius 9.20 vouches for his 'Foundation of Colophon' and 'Colonisation of Elea in Italy', 2000 hexameters in all. His ἐλεγεῖα probably formed a separate collection. Diogenes lists three metres used by Xenophanes — hexameters, elegiac couplets and iambics. Our only iambic line is in fr. 12, and it is followed by a hexameter. For his philosophical writing he seems in general to have used hexameters, although he mocks Pythagoras in elegiacs (fr. 6). The other elegiac pieces contain his reflections on his own life, on the prizes deserved by poets but awarded to athletes, on the effete ways of the Colophonians; and his account of the preparations for a drinking-party, which turns into a series of rules for its proper conduct, is in elegiacs, although his advice on after-dinner fireside conversation is in hexameters (fr. 18).

Xenophanes, like Solon, has fewer Homeric echoes than the earliest elegiac writers, and his most notable borrowings are confined to fr. 2: see notes on lines 4, 5, 9, 20. In his description of the drinking-party, when he might have adhered to Homeric language, he avoids Homer's epithets for wine, honey and table, and uses arresting language of his own: κρατὴρ ... μεστὸς εὐφροσύνης (4), οἶνος ... ὃς οὔποτέ φησι προδώσειν (5), γεραρή ... τράπεζα (9). He puts epic language to humorous effect in his description of Pythagoras and the puppy (fr. 6). The short fragments are neatly composed, the longer pieces harsh and graceless.

Heraclitus said of Xenophanes among others that wide learning does not teach intelligence (fr. 40 πολυμαθίη νόον ἔχειν οὐ διδάσκει); but his intelligence and the independence of his thinking are amply attested by his attacks on the anthropomorphic view of the gods and by his deduction from fossils observed in Syracuse, Paros and Malta that everything was once covered with mud (Hippolytus *Haer.* 1.14). He seems to have been foremost a poet and a critic of morals and religion rather than a cosmologist like his Ionian predecessors, Thales, Anaximander and Anaximenes.

The testimonia to his life and works and his collected fragments are in Diels-Kranz, *Die Fragmente der Vorsokratiker* i.113–39. For a biography, an account of his philosophical views and an assessment of his importance see G. S. Kirk and J. E. Raven, *The Presocratic Philosophers* 163–81.

XENOPHANES I

Quoted by Athenaeus 11.462c with this introduction: 'So, since I see that your feast is in the words of Xenophanes of Colophon full of every happiness. . . .' Cleanliness and godliness are the marks of the symposium which he describes: in the first 12 lines we notice that the floor, the guests' hands and the cups are clean (καθαρόν, 1), as is the water (8), that the scent of frankincense is holy (ἁγνήν, 7), that the wine is loyal to its friends (5) and that even the table is reverend (γεραρή, 9); in the second half of the poem Xenophanes insists that the preparations be matched in beauty and order by the song and story to come: the god is to be hymned in stories that are reverent (εὐφήμοις) and words that are clean (καθαροῖσι again, 14); there is to be libation and a prayer for power to act justly; moderate drinking will betoken the absence of ὕβρις; lines 19–20 speak of good be-

haviour (ἐσθλὰ ... ἀναφαίνει) and ἀρετή; and the piece ends
with instructions to avoid tales of violence and 'stasis', since
there is nothing good in them, and to consider the gods at all
times.

Theognis wrote several poems giving instructions for drinking-
parties, notably 467–96, and in the 5th century Ion of Chios
(fr. 2) and Critias (fr. 4) continued the genre. Elegiac lines of
Anacreon (fr. 96 Diehl) give his views on the songs that should be
sung on such occasions. But the solemnity of Xenophanes' poem
distinguishes it from all these others (lines 17–18 alone are light-
hearted), and if there were good grounds for believing in Xenophanes as president of a philosophical school, Defradas' view that
this poem was written for a ritual meal of a Pythagorean-type
'thiasos' would be attractive ('Le Banquet de Xénophane',
Revue des Etudes grecques 75 (1962), 344–65).

On the poem see also C. M. Bowra, 'Xenophanes, Fragment 1',
Cl. Phil. 33 (1938), 353–67, republished with slight alterations in
Problems in Greek Poetry 1–14.

1. ζάπεδον: the only other example of ζάπεδον for δάπεδον,
'floor', is in a 6th-century Parian inscription in elegiac
couplets (*I.G.* XII(5). 215). It may be that popular
etymology changed δάπεδον to διάπεδον, which was then
Aeolized as ζάπεδον. See Hudson-Williams 31–2.

2. ἀμφιτιθεῖ: for the Ionic form for -τίθησι see Chantraine
G.H. i.298. With this verb ἄλλος or τις has to be supplied:
cf. *Il.* 22.157 τῇ ῥα παραδραμέτην, φεύγων, ὁ δ' ὄπισθε
διώκων, Pi. *N.* 8.37–8 χρυσὸν εὔχονται, πεδίον δ' ἕτεροι |
ἀπέραντον, and see Denniston *G.P.* 166.

3. μύρον: see Sapph. 94.18n.

4. εὐφροσύνης: 'merriment'. The word is associated with
feasting at *Od.* 9.6, Sol. 3.10 (cf. 'good cheer'), and when
the adjective occurs below (13 εὔφρονας ἄνδρας) there is
no need to translate 'of sound mind, reasonable' with
L.S.J. There too the word keeps the festive associations it
has in Homer, e.g. *Il.* 15.99 εἴ πέρ τις ἔτι νῦν δαίνυται
εὔφρων, *Od.* 17.531; *Il.* 3.246 οἶνον εὔφρονα. So in Pi. *N.*
5.38 εὔφρονες ἶλαι, 'festive bands'.

5. προδώσειν: 'to betray' by running short. Herodotus has the

same metaphor of rivers running dry: προδοῦναι τὰ ῥέεθρα
τῶν ποταμῶν ἔστι ὧν (7.187.1).

6. μείλιχος, 'gentle', continues the personification of the wine.
κεράμοις: 'wine-jars', as in *Il.* 9.469 πολλὸν δ᾽ ἐκ κεράμων
μέθυ πίνετο. For a wine's bouquet cf. *Od.* 9.210–11 ὀδμὴ δ᾽
ἡδεῖα ἀπὸ κρητῆρος ὀδώδει, | θεσπεσίη, Alcm. 92(b) ἄνθεος
ὄσδοντα.

7. λιβανωτός: see Sapph. 2.4n. Its scent is 'holy' since it is
associated with religious observances: so at the wedding of
Hector and Andromache (Sapph. 44.30), on Aphrodite's
altars (Sapph. 2.3–4), on the altar of Bel in Babylon (Hdt.
1.183.2), in Egyptian sacrifices (Hdt. 2.40.3), in the temple
of Aphrodite at Corinth (Pi. fr. 130.3 Turyn). Cf. Melanip-
pides *ap.* Ath. 14.651 f (= P.M.G. 757.5) ἱερόδακρυν λίβανον.

9. πάρκεινται: for παράκεινται by apocope.
   γεραρή: Homer has γεραρός only twice (*Il.* 3.170, 211), of
   'majestic', 'impressive' heroes, and in later writers it is
   used almost exclusively of men. Xenophanes personifies the
   table as he personified the wine.

10. ἀχθομένη: this literal sense of ἄχθομαι occurs at *Od.* 15.457
    κοίλη νηῦς ἤχθετο. The genitive is used by analogy with
    verbs and adjectives denoting fullness.

11. βωμός: the altar in Odysseus' house stood in the open court-
    yard (*Od.* 22.334, 379). This one was in the middle of the
    room (ἂν τὸ μέσον), and it was probably a small terracotta
    altar for burning incense (7 ἐν δὲ μέσοις). A few *arulae*
    of the 6th century B.C. are known from Magna Graecia
    and Greece proper: see C. G. Yavis, *Greek Altars* 137–8,
    171–3.

12. ἀμφὶς ἔχει has the meaning of ἀμπέχει: cf. *Od.* 8.340 δεσμοὶ . . .
    ἀμφὶς ἔχοιεν.

14. εὐφήμοις μύθοις: 'with reverent tales.' Pindar *P.* 10.35 uses
    εὐφαμίαι of worship; see L.S.J. s.v. εὔφημος II.

16. γὰρ ὦν: 'for indeed' in an explanatory parenthesis: cf.
    Denniston *G.P.* 447.
    προχειρότερον: perhaps 'this is the obvious prayer to make',
    sc. εὔξασθαι, but if this is Xenophanes' meaning, he would
    seem to be preaching to the converted, since a prayer 'to be

able to do what is just' was far from the obvious prayer for Greeks of his time.

17. οὐχ ὕβρις: cf. Anacr. 356(a).5–6.

18. μὴ πάνυ γηραλέος: the equivalent of a conditional clause.

19. αἰνεῖν: infin. with imperatival sense.

ὃς ἐσθλὰ ... ἀναφαίνει: 'whose performance (i.e. as story-teller or singer: lines 21–4, which follow with asyndeton, are explanatory) is honourable.' Cf. Thgn. 491–2 ἀνίκητος δέ τοι οὗτος, | ὃς πολλὰς πίνων μή τι μάταιον ἐρεῖ. The position of ἐσθλὰ is unexpected, but throws emphasis on the adjective: his performance is good, although he has been drinking.

20. The reading is uncertain. I keep Diehl-Beutler's text and translate 'as his memory and his enthusiasm for virtue enable him'. τόνος cannot be paralleled in this sense, but Pindar's ξυναῖσι δ' ἀμφ' ἀρεταῖς τέταμαι (P. 11.54, 'I am enthusiastic about virtues which help the community') is strikingly close.

21. διέπει: 'deals with, relates': Homer has it of Achilles' handling of the fighting (Il. 1.166) and of Odysseus' handling of the army (2.207). With Xenophanes' views expressed here cf. the elegiac lines of his contemporary Anacreon (96 D.).

22. πλάσματα τῶν προτέρων: 'the creations of our predecessors'. Xenophanes must have in mind Hesiod's Theogony (e.g. 629 ff) and similar works. We know Titanomachia and Gigantomachia as titles of epic poems. Od. 21.295–304 tells how one of the Centaurs was drunk and disorderly in Peirithous' palace. For the metaphorical uses of πλάσμα and πλάττω see L.S.J. We need not give a derogatory sense (e.g. 'fabrications') to πλάσματα here: that probably belongs only to later writers.

23. στάσιας σφεδανάς: 'violent factions'. Homer has σφεδανόν as an adverb. χρηστόν: found here first. It seems to have its 5th-century sense of 'useful (cf. χρῆσθαι) in relation to the community'. Xenophanes may have Alcaeus' political drinking-songs in mind.

24. θεῶν monosyllabic: cf. 2.11 ἐών.

προμηθείην: 'consideration', as in Hdt. 1.88.1 ἐν πολλῇ προμηθίῃ εἶχε (sc. αὐτόν), E. Alc. 1054 ἐγὼ δὲ σοῦ προμηθίαν ἔχω.

XENOPHANES 2

Athenaeus 10.413c–f, after quoting Euripides *Autolycus* (fr. 282 N²) to show that athletes are taught to eat heavy meals, says that Euripides took this from the elegiacs of Xenophanes of Colophon and quotes the present passage with the remark that Xenophanes made many other claims for his poetic art, attacking the uselessness of athletics. The uselessness, not the gluttony, of athletes is in fact the point made by both writers. Tyrtaeus 9.1–4 had set the prowess of the warrior above that of the athlete, and when Solon limited the civic rewards given to Olympic and Isthmian victors he said that it was boorish to add to their honours rather than to the honours of soldiers who died in battle (Diog. Laert. 1.55): boxers, sprinters and other athletes made no significant contribution to the safety of their states: only men of intelligence and virtue could protect their country in time of danger (Diod. 9.2.5).

On the poem see C. M. Bowra, 'Xenophanes and the Olympic Games', *A.J. Phil.* 59 (1938), 257 ff, republished in *Problems in Greek Poetry* 15 ff.

1. ἀλλ᾽: it is likely that this is the beginning of the poem: see Archil. 1.1n. Observe the echo of παρ Πίσαο ῥοῆς (3) in Πίσαο παρ᾽ ὄχθας (21).

   ταχυτῆτι ποδῶν κτλ.: the contests mentioned by Xenophanes are running, the pentathlon (i.e. running, jumping, throwing the discus, throwing the javelin and wrestling: see E. N. Gardiner (*Athletics of the Ancient World* 177), wrestling, boxing, the pancratium and chariot-racing. Bowra (*E.G.E.* 128) notes that there is no reference to the race in armour, which was first held at Olympia in 520 B.C., but Defradas points out that ταχυτῆτι ποδῶν may include all types of foot-racing.

3. Πίσαο: Pisa, the term often used as an equivalent for Olympia, was the name of a town near Olympia according to Paus. 6.22.1–4 and others, though Strabo 8.3.31 and Stephanus of Byzantium (Meineke p. 523) refer also to a spring of that name. But ῥοῆς (3) and ὄχθας (21) both suggest a river, and Πίσης (the masc. noun, not in L.S.J., which gives gen.

Πίσαο) is probably an equivalent for the Alpheus, 'the river of Pisa': see *R.E.* s.v. 'Pises'.

παλαίων: part. of παλαίω, 'wrestle'.

4. πυκτοσύνην ἀλγινόεσσαν: cf. *Il.* 23.653 πυγμαχίης ἀλεγεινῆς.

5. The use of τι and the Homeric echo in ὁ παγκράτιον καλέουσιν (cf. *Il.* 24.316 ὃν καὶ περκνὸν καλέουσιν, 18.487, 22.506, Xenoph. 28.1) are probably intended as sarcasm.

6. κυδρότερος: either more glorious than his fellows or more glorious than the poet.

7. προεδρίην . . . ἐν ἀγῶσιν: Herodotus tells us that the Spartans gave this privilege to their kings (6.57.2) and to their old allies, the Deceleans (9.73.3), and that Croesus enjoyed it at Delphi as recompense for his generosity (1.54.2). Cf. Ar. *Eq.* 575–6 ἐὰν μὴ προεδρίαν φέρωσι καὶ τὰ σιτία, | οὐ μαχεῖσθαί φασιν, Pl. *Leg.* 9.881b εἰς προεδρίαν τῶν ἀγώνων καλείσθω.

8. σῖτ(α) . . . δημοσίων κτεάνων: one of the earliest references to σίτησις ἐν Πρυτανείῳ, familiar from Aristophanes as a distinction conferred on deserving citizens. That noblemen of Mytilene drank wine in the Prytaneum we know from Athenaeus' report (10.425a) that Sappho's brother served it. In Athens σίτησις is said to have received Solon's attention: he restricted the number of meals given to any individual (Plu. *Sol.* 24) and replaced ἄρτος by the less attractive μᾶζα (Ath. 4.137e). Xenophanes' view that the wrong people were being given σίτησις is echoed by Socrates, who said that if a poor man does service to the city he, rather than an Olympic victor, should be given meals in the Prytaneum (Pl. *Apol.* 36d).

9. δῶρον, ὅ οἱ κειμήλιον εἴη: Xenophanes' most striking borrowing from Homer: cf. *Od.* 1.311–12 δῶρον . . . ὅ τοι κειμήλιον ἔσται.

10. ἵπποισιν: sc. νίκην τις ἄροιτο.

12. ἡμετέρη σοφίη: 'our poetic skill'; cf. Sol. 1.52n.

15. πύκτης ἀγαθός: ἀγαθός has to be supplied with the infinitive πενταθλεῖν, the accusative παλαισμοσύνην and the dative ταχυτῆτι.

18. ῥώμης ὅσσ' ἀνδρῶν ἔργα: with πρότιμον, 'most honoured of all men's deeds of strength'.

20. χάρμα: cf. *Il.* 24.706 μέγα χάρμα πόλει τ' ἦν παντί τε δήμῳ.

ἐπὶ τῷ: τῷ, which is explained by the next line, may be masculine or neuter.

21. νικῷ: optative: so *Od.* 20.12 ἐῷ from ἐάω. Tyrtaeus 9.4 has νικώῃ, the form familiar in Attic.

Πίσαο παρ' ὄχθας: cf. *Il.* 4.313 Ξάνθοιο παρ' ὄχθας.

22. 'For that does not enrich the city's chambers.' Xenophanes must mean not only that the city's finances are drained by athletes' rewards, but that poetic art brings glory to the city.

XENOPHANES 3

Quoted by Athenaeus 12.526a–b as evidence that the Colophonians foundered on the rocks of luxurious living when they formed an alliance with the Lydians. Athenaeus continues with words which may be a paraphrase of Xenophanes: οὕτω δ' ἐξελύθησαν διὰ τὴν ἄκαιρον μέθην ὥστε τινὲς αὐτῶν οὔτε ἀνατέλλοντα τὸν ἥλιον οὔτε δυόμενον ἑωράκασιν, 'they were so debauched by their untimely drinking that some of them saw neither sunrise nor sunset.' Lines 1–2 suggest that their subjection to the Medes was the consequence of their enervation, although Xenophanes is not so explicit as Theognis 1103–4 ὕβρις καὶ Μάγνητας ἀπώλεσε καὶ Κολοφῶνα | καὶ Σμύρνην.

See C. M. Bowra, *C.Q.* 35 (1941), 119–26.

3. ἀγορήν: presumably the citizen assembly in the agora.

4. οὐ μείους ὥσπερ χίλιοι: for ὥσπερ = ἤ ('than') cf. *Hist. Gr.* 2.3.16 and the same use of ὡς in Plato. See Kühner-Gerth II 540, Anm. 5.

5. ἀγαλλόμενοι εὐπρεπέεσσιν: for the violent synecphonesis cf. *Il.* 2.651 Ἐννυαλίῳ ἀνδρεϊφόντῃ.

ἀσκητοῖς: 'recherchés'. The epithet is used by Homer, e.g. of Odysseus' 'cunningly-made' bed (*Od.* 23.189). Here ὀδμήν is acc. of respect with ἀσκητοῖς.

XENOPHANES 6 (D.-K. 7)

Diogenes Laertius 8.36 in his life of Pythagoras says that Xenophanes in the elegy which begins νῦν αὖτ' ἄλλον κτλ. bears witness to Pythagoras' theory of reincarnation, and quotes καί

ποτέ μιν κτλ. (2–5). 2–5 occur also in *Anth. Pal.* 7.120 and *Suda*
s.v. Xenophanes, 2–4 in *Suda* s.v. στυφελίξαι. Pythagoras
claimed that he could remember his own four earlier incarnations
(Diog. Laert. 8.4–5): his psychic lineage was distinguished, since
in the first incarnation he was reckoned to be the son of Hermes.

2. στυφελιζομένου: an epic word of impressive bulk, used both
of striking in general and of the maltreatment of guests
(e.g. *Od.* 16.108, 18.416). Its associations, like those of
φθεγξαμένης (5), add to the humour of the piece.

4. ῥάπιζε: not an epic word. Also in Hippon. 56.2.

5. φθεγξαμένης: this seems to be the first use of the word for an
animal cry, though such usage became common (see
L.S.J. s.v. φθέγγομαι I.2). Theognis has it of the music of
pipes (532) and of lyre and pipe (761).

XENOPHANES 7 (D.-K.8)

Quoted by Diogenes Laertius 9.18–19 as evidence of Xenophanes' long life.

2. βληστρίζοντες ἐμὴν φροντίδα κτλ.: 'sending my wits tossing
over the land of Greece'. The verb is used by Hippocrates
(*Morb.* 3.7: cf. *Epid.* 1.26.β' πολὺς βληστρισμός) of an
invalid tossing on his bed, and elsewhere only by another
medical writer, Aretaeus. The words attributed to Xenophanes by the grammarian Erotian may be no more than
another version of our present passage: ἐγὼ δὲ ἐμαυτὸν
πόλιν ἐκ πόλεως φέρων ἐβλήστριζον (D.-.K.45). Instead
of the pronoun 'me' Xenophanes uses ἐμὴν φροντίδα,
perhaps to indicate his life of philosophical enquiry.

Ἑλλάδα: adjective as in Thgn. 247, Hdt. (e.g. 5.93.2 πόλιν
Ἑλλάδα) and the tragedians.

3. ἐκ γενετῆς: a line-beginning in *Il.* 24.535, *Od.* 18.6.

XENOPHANES 10 (D.-K.11)

From Sextus Empiricus *Adv. Math.* 9.193.

Heraclitus too spoke hard words of Homer: τόν τε ῞Ομηρον
ἔφασκεν ἄξιον ἐκ τῶν ἀγώνων ἐκβάλλεσθαι καὶ ῥαπίζεσθαι καὶ
Ἀρχίλοχον ὁμοίως (Diog. Laert. 9.1.1).

XENOPHANES 13 (D.-K.15)

Quoted by three writers on religion, Clement of Alexandria *Stromata* 5.109.3, Eusebius *Praepar. Evang.* 13.13.36, Theodoretus *Graec. Aff. Cur.* 3.72. The correct text is difficult to establish; I have followed Diehl and Diels-Kranz.

Two other fragments attack the anthropomorphic view of the gods: in fr. 12 Xenophanes says that men attribute to the gods their own clothes, speech and shape; fr. 14 goes further: the Ethiopians say that their gods are snub-nosed and black, the Thracians that theirs are blue-eyed and red-haired.

2. γράψαι: sc. ἔχον, 'were able to draw'.

ἔργα: works of art, statues.

XENOPHANES 18 (D.-K.22)

Athenaeus (epit.) 2.54e *à propos* of chick-peas quotes these lines from the Παρῳδίαι of Xenophanes.

1. πὰρ πυρί: a Homeric line-beginning, e.g. in *Od.* 7.154.

2. ἔμπλεον ὄντα: 'with a full stomach'.

3. ὑποτρώγοντ' ἐρεβίνθους: 'nibbling chick-peas'. Chick-peas were used to create or prolong a thirst, as we use salted nuts: cf. Ar. *Pax* 1136, Pl. *Resp.* 372c and the whole passage in Athenaeus. τρώγω with its compounds was the usual term for eating appetisers or dessert: cf. Hdt. 1.71.3 οὐ σῦκα δὲ ἔχουσι τρώγειν of the tough Cappadocians, Ar. *Pax* 1324 σῦκα . . . τρώγειν.

4. τίς πόθεν εἰς ἀνδρῶν; a greeting in Homeric style: cf. *Od.* 1.170 τίς πόθεν εἰς ἀνδρῶν; *Il.* 6.123 τίς δὲ σύ ἐσσι, φέριστε, καταθνητῶν ἀνθρώπων;

5. ὁ Μῆδος: Harpagus, whose attack on the Ionian cities *c.* 545 or 540 is described by Herodotus 1.162–9.

XENOPHANES 28 (D.-K.32)

From scholia BLT and Eustathius' commentary on *Il.* 11.27, where the snakes on Agamemnon's shield are said to resemble rainbows, ἴρισσιν ἐοικότες, ἅς τε Κρονίων | ἐν νέφεϊ στήριξε τέρας μερόπων ἀνθρώπων. Xenophanes was ready with a physical explanation for what the poets referred to as a divinity. Line 2 shows the cosmologist's theory embellished with the poet's artifice. *Il.* 17.547 has πορφυρέην ἶριν, where πορφυρέην may mean 'bright'.

PHOCYLIDES

Phocylides of Miletus probably belongs to the middle of the 6th century: the *Suda* makes him a contemporary of Theognis, dating both to Ol.59 = 544–1. Fr. 2 is fairly certainly based on Semon. 7. He wrote γνῶμαι, maxims, in short hexameter poems, and we have an elegiac couplet by him, a *jeu d'esprit* on one Procles (fr. 1).

PHOCYLIDES 1

Quoted by Strabo 10.5.12 in connexion with the island of Leros, and by Eustathius *ad Dionys. Perieg.* 530. *Anth. Pal.* 11.235 gives the same lines with Δημοδόκου for Φωκυλίδου and Χῖοι and δὲ Χῖος (unconvincingly) for Λέριοι and Λέριος. The joke might well have been made by a 19th- or 20th-century nonsense-writer.

1. καὶ τόδε Φωκυλίδου: his 'signature', mentioned by Cic. *Att.* 4.9.1. Cf. Demod. 1.1.

    Λέριοι: Leros, one of the Sporades, is not far from Miletus. See Demod. 1n.

PHOCYLIDES 3

From Stobaeus 4.29 (περὶ εὐγενείας). 28.

2. Cf. *Od.* 3.127 οὔτε ποτ' εἰν ἀγορῇ ... οὔτ' ἐνὶ βουλῇ.

PHOCYLIDES 4

From Dio Chrysostom 36.11–13, who gives it as an example of the brevity of Phocylides.

1. κατὰ κόσμον: a Homeric line-ending, e.g. *Il.* 10.472. The verb ἀφραίνω (l. 2) is also Homeric.

2. Νίνου: Nineveh, capital of Assyria, was destroyed by the Medes in 612. It stood on the edge of a fertile well-watered plain at the confluence of the Tigris and Khosr.

PHOCYLIDES 8

From Orion *Anth.* 1.22. Tzetzes on Ar. *Ran.* 962 cites l. 1. Attributed by both to Phocylides.

DEMODOCUS

Demodocus of Leros probably belongs like Phocylides to the 6th century, but we know nothing about his life and work. Only three lines can safely be called his: the elegiac couplet on the Milesians and a trochaic line which seems to refer to Bias of Priene.

DEMODOCUS 1

Quoted as τὸ Δημοδόκου by Arist. *E.N.* 7.9 p. 1151a, when he says that men with no self-control are not unjust but act unjustly. Could the couplet have been a Lerian answer to Phocylides' poem on Procles?

DEMODOCUS (4)

Attributed with three other pieces to Demod. in *Anth. Pal.* 11.237. The attribution of all four pieces is questionable, and this couplet like fr. (5) may have been directed at Joannes Cappadox, prefect of the praetorian guard under the Emperor Justinian.

THEOGNIS

Theognis is the only writer represented in this volume whose poetry has come down to us by a regular manuscript tradition. His works are to be found, in whole or in part, in more than forty

manuscripts, the oldest and best of which belongs to the early 10th
century. We have almost 1400 lines of elegiacs, which are
variously divided to form between 300 and 400 poems, most of
them single couplets, the longest two poems of 30 lines. At last,
the novice might think, the critic's task is straightforward: he is
dealing with complete poems instead of stray fragments and he
can ply his trade in peace. But alas! the field of Theognidean
studies is battle-scarred, strewn with theories dead or dying, the
scene of bitter passions and blind partisanship. Welcker in 1826
divided the poems into a small corpus of 'genuine Theognis' and a
large mass of poetry by other writers, earlier and later. Separatists
of various shades of opinion held the field till 1902, when Harrison
published a vigorous defence of the unity of the corpus, and since
then combat has been continuous, except for interruptions due to
real wars.

The separatist theory is based mainly on the presence in
Theognis of passages attributed on good authority to other
writers, e.g. Tyrtaeus, Mimnermus, Solon and Phocylides.
These the unitarian explains as deliberate borrowings and
alterations on Theognis' part, since in no case does his text
correspond precisely with the texts of the other writers. This is
clearly how Clement of Alexandria regarded one such case
(*Strom.* 6.2.8): Σόλωνος δὲ ποιήσαντος

τίκτει γὰρ κόρος ὕβριν ὅταν πόλυς ὄλβος ἔπηται (5.9)
ἄντικρυς ὁ Θέογνις γράφει

τίκτει τοι κόρος ὕβριν ὅταν κακῷ ὄλβος ἔπηται (153).

Solon had similarly given his revised version of a couplet of
Mimnermus (see Sol. 22), and Alcaeus 347 and other pieces make
it clear that it was common practice to take and remodel the
poetry of predecessors and contemporaries. No disrespect was
intended: if someone had pointed out to Theognis that such-and-
such a couplet resembled Mimnermus, he would have replied as
Brahms did when critics pointed to a resemblance between his
first symphony and Beethoven's last: 'any fool can see that.' In
some cases Theognis makes only slight changes in the lines he
takes over (e.g. 1020–2 from Mimn. 5.1–3); to some lines he gives
new life by placing them in a new context (e.g. 1253–4: see Sol.
13); sometimes he changes the force of a passage entirely (e.g.

585–90: see Sol. 1.65–70n.). Separatists claim that the differences between Theognis' text and the versions we find in other writers are due to textual corruption and the practice of quoting from memory.

A neighbouring skirmish is concerned with the repetition or near-repetition of passages within the corpus: the separatist sees this as further proof that our text is interpolated; the unitarian explains it by assuming that Theognis recast his own verses as he recast those of other poets, and that he often gave them new application by setting them in a new context (e.g. 509–10). Self-contradictions within the corpus are explicable if we grant that Theognis enjoyed three score years and ten and wrote both in his youth and in his old age, and if we remember that he was not setting out to compile a consistent set of rules for living but wrote as the mood seized him.

Even if we use all the corpus as evidence, we amass little information about his life. He was a citizen of Megara, the neighbour of Athens, and he visited Sparta, Euboea and Sicily. Plato called him a citizen of Sicilian Megara (*Leg.* 1.630a), and he may well have settled there at some time in his life, perhaps as an exile. The *Suda* records that he wrote an elegy εἰς τοὺς σωθέντας τῶν Συρακουσίων ἐν τῇ πολιορκίᾳ, but we cannot say which siege of Syracuse is meant.

Ancient authorities placed Theognis in the middle of the 6th century B.C., Eusebius and Cyril mentioning Ol.58 (548–5 B.C.), the *Suda* Ol.59 (544–1 B.C.), the *Chronicon Paschale* Ol.57 (552–49 B.C.). These authorities probably dated Theognis by reference to Harpagus' attack on the Greek cities of Asia Minor, since Theognis mentions the war of the Medes (764) and prays that Apollo will protect Megara from the wanton army of the Medes (773–82). But it is more likely that these lines refer to the invasion of Darius or even that of Xerxes, when there was a real threat to the cities of the Greek mainland. It is probable that the Simonides and Onomacritus to whom Theognis addresses some of his poems are the famous bearers of these names (see 667n. and 503n.) The politics of the poems fit the little certain knowledge we have of sixth-century Megara, where there was στάσις in the years between the fall of Theagenes *c.* 600 B.C. and the restoration of the

aristocracy c. 500. Theognis writes from the point of view of a
landed aristocrat appalled at the rise to power of the merchant
and peasant classes, indignant at the loss of his farmlands and
property. We may not be far wrong if we set Theognis' dates at
c. 550 to c. 480: it may be that there was a confusion over the
meaning of γεγονὼς ἐν τῇ νθ' 'Ολυμπιάδι, since the Suda uses
γεγονώς usually with reference to a datable event in a man's life,
but sometimes to denote the year of his birth. The only line in
Theognis which does not fit easily into such a scheme is 894, a
prayer for the destruction of the Κυψελιδῶν . . . γένος: the
Cypselids were the famous family of Corinthian tyrants, whose
last representative died c. 581 B.C., but it is possible that Theognis is alluding to the younger Miltiades, whose tyranny in the
Thracian Chersonese, inherited from his uncle, the elder Miltiades, may have given rise to a family nickname, the Cypselids,
since the father of the elder Miltiades was called Cypselus. The
younger Miltiades was sent to the Chersonese by the Peisistratids,
i.e. at some time between 527 and 510: cf. Hdt. 6.39.1.

Theognis' works are listed by the Suda as (1) the elegy on the
Syracusan siege, mentioned above, (2) γνῶμαι — 2800 lines of
elegiacs, (3) a γνωμολογία in elegiacs addressed to Cyrnus,
(4) other exhortations, (5) paederastic poetry, scattered throughout his exhortations. The connexion between this list and our
collection is not clear, although it is plain that we do not have
Theognis' total output as it was known, say, to the cataloguers of
the Alexandrian library. Much of the good advice to Cyrnus
occurs in lines 19–254, but not all of it: and paederastic pieces are
not scattered throughout the book but almost confined to 1231–
1389. Varying views on the transmission of our text in the 1400
years between Theognis' lifetime and the date of our earliest
manuscripts will be found in the writings of Harrison, Carrière,
Peretti and Young.

Theognis' poetry gives evidence of his close knowledge and
frequent imitation of Homer, Hesiod, Tyrtaeus, Solon and
Mimnermus. He was conservative in his writing as in his politics,
and worked unadventurously within the elegiac tradition. Of the
new words he used — new, so far as we can say — most are
compound words such as πολυκώκυτος, πολυπλοκία, ἀνακοινέω,

καταθηράω; some denote his political interests, e.g. δημοφάγος, κακεταιρίη, some his private pastime — οἰνοβαρέω, ἐπιοίνιος, μέθυσις, ὑπερβολάδην (how not to drink). His style is marked by brevity of expression and fondness for asyndeton: he is not always fastidious or even melodious, but he knows how to place his words to make the greatest effect. One forms a clear impression of his personality, sometimes high-spirited but more often despondent, and cynical even in his love poetry; a man of strong feelings and candid in their expression.

There are commentaries by T. Hudson-Williams, *The Elegies of Theognis*, London 1910 and (in Italian) by Antonio Garzya, *Teognide: Elegie*, Firenze 1958. The Teubner text edited by Douglas Young (1961) is indispensable for its preface on the manuscripts, its *apparatus criticus* and its *index verborum*. English readers will find the separatists' case in Bowra, *E.G.E.* 139 ff and Edmonds, *Elegy and Iambus* (Loeb) i.6 ff, the unitarian opposition in E. Harrison, *Studies in Theognis*, Cambridge 1902, T. W. Allen, 'Theognis', *Proceedings of the British Academy* 20 (1934) 71 ff, L. Woodbury, 'The Riddle of Theognis', *Phoenix* 5 (1951) 1 ff. Other important works of recent years are J. Carrière, *Théognis de Mégare*, Paris 1948 and *Théognis, poèmes élégiaques* (Budé), Paris 1948; A. Peretti, *Teognide nella tradizione gnomologica*, Pisa 1953, (B. A. van Groningen, *Théognis: Le premier livre*, 1966).

Of the manuscripts of Theognis A (early 10th century) is easily best: also important are O and X (early 14th century), Ur (*c.* 1430: contains lines 1–276 only) and I (*c.* 1450).

THEOGNIS 19–26

These lines follow four introductory poems (three if 1–4 and 5–10 are joined) addressed to Apollo, Artemis and the Muses and Graces. They form a preface into which the writer introduces his name, the name of his city and incidentally the names of the youth to whom many of the pieces are addressed.

19–20. A summary of the enormous literature on these lines may be found in Garzya 144–8 or L. Woodbury, 'The Seal of Theognis', *Phoenix* 6 (1952) (Studies in Honour of Gilbert Norwood) 20 ff. I translate, 'let me, a poet practising my craft, set a seal on these lines, and they will never be stolen unnoticed nor will anyone substitute a worse line for the good one that is there, but everyone will say, "They are the lines of Theognis the Megarian, and he is famous throughout the whole world." '

σοφίζομαι ='practise an art' in *I.G.* I².678, and the perf. part. in Hes. *Op.* 649 ναυτιλίης σεσοφισμένος, Ibyc. 282.23 Μοῖσαι σεσοφισμέναι, means 'practised, expert'. Theognis uses σοφίη of poetic and musical skill at 790, 942 and 995; cf. also 370 μιμεῖσθαι δ' οὐδεὶς τῶν ἀσόφων δύναται, and see Sol. 1.52n. σοφιστής is used of poets and musicians as early as Aeschylus (fr. 314 N²) and Pindar (*I.* 5.28). I have translated σοφιζομένῳ ... ἐμοί as a dative of the agent. Plato at any rate treated προσκεῖσθαι as passive when he wrote προσκείμενον ... ὑπὸ θεοῦ (*Apol.* 30e), and perhaps ἐπικεῖσθαι is nearly enough a perfect tense to have a dative of the agent; but even if we label σοφιζομένῳ ... ἐμοί as 'ethic dative' the general sense will be the same.

The σφρηγίς I take to be Theognis' name, introduced in this prefatory poem as proof of the collection's authenticity just as Herodotus and Thucydides introduced their names at the beginning of their histories, or Phocylides, Demodocus and Hipparchus theirs at the beginning of their poems. The seal, as Theognis himself makes clear, is intended as a precaution against the misappropriation of his poetry or the substitution of inferior work, and also as a means of identifying the author. The words πάντας δὲ κατ' ἀνθρώπους ὀνομαστός form part of the guarantee: any would-be pilferer will know better than to tamper with Theognis' lines, since his fame is so great that the theft would certainly be detected.

It is possible too that Theognis was referring to an actual seal. Diogenes Laertius 9.1.6 tells us that Heraclitus deposited a copy of his Περὶ φύσεως in the temple of Artemis at Ephesus, and Theognis may have put part of his writings (e.g. 1–254), sealed, in a temple at Megara. He appeals to two deities in the prefatory poems, Apollo, son of Leto (1,5), and Artemis (11), and Pausanias tells us (1.44.2) that he saw in the temple of Apollo Prostaterius at Megara statues of Apollo, Artemis and Leto, these three.

Of other views on the σφρηγίς only two need be mentioned: (1) that the seal is the word Κύρνε and that only poems which contain the word Κύρνε (or Πολυπαΐδη) have a claim to be considered genuine. This seal would hardly be more effective protection than the seal of Theognis' name — and the inefficiency of that precaution is a reason often given for rejecting that equation — since one need only exchange another metrically equivalent vocative for the tell-tale Κύρνε (or Πολυπαΐδη) to produce a new poem of one's own. But the main objection to the view is the difficulty of finding it in the Greek of line 19: to print Κύρνε in quotation marks is little short of cheating and leaves μέν in an intolerable position. It goes without saying that this view is incompatible with unitarianism; (2) that the seal is the excellence of the poetry, the genius of the poet. But these qualities are not external (note ἐπι-) like the seal of a letter or parcel, and they would make it easier, not more difficult, for a forger to substitute something worse.

Lastly, what answers μέν? The δέ of 20, of 22, of 24 or of 27 (which begins σοὶ δ' ἐγὼ εὖ φρονέων ὑποθήσομαι)? Or is it solitary? I take it with the δέ of 24, and think that Theognis used it to heighten the contrast between the proud words of 19–23 and the bitter realism of 24. Cf. 237–54 where σοὶ μὲν ἐγώ is answered 16 lines later by αὐτὰρ ἐγὼν ὀλίγης παρὰ σεῦ κτλ.: there too the confidence of the poet's boast is replaced by bitterness.

21. ἀλλάξει κάκιον τοὐσθλοῦ παρεόντος: usually translated 'take a worse thing when the better is at hand', τοὐσθλοῦ παρεόντος being regarded as gen. abs.. But the meaning of this is not clear. Others take κάκιον as predicative, 'make a change for the worse', but the gen. abs. has little point then. It seems better to translate 'substitute a worse line in place of the good one that is there', or, if we may not supply ἔπος, more generally 'substitute worse for the good that is there'. For the construction cf. A. Pr. 966–7 τῆς σῆς λατρείας τὴν ἐμὴν δυσπραξίαν | . . . οὐκ ἂν ἀλλάξαιμ' ἐγώ.

22. ὧδε δὲ πᾶς τις ἐρεῖ: cf. *Il.* 4.176 καί κέ τις ὧδ' ἐρέει. For πᾶς τις see Sol. 19.7n.

23. Note synizesis in Μεγαρέως: so at 46 κερδέων, 176 πετρέων, 188 ἀφνεόν, 343 μεριμνέων, 353 ἡμέων, 503 οἰνοβαρέω.

24. ἀστοῖσιν is in emphatic contrast to both σοφιζομένῳ μὲν ἐμοί and πάντας δὲ κατ' ἀνθρώπους. Theognis makes the same complaint at 367–70, and the more general one, 'No-one, not even Zeus, can please everyone', at 801–4. Cf. Sol. 5.11 πᾶσιν ἀδεῖν χαλεπόν.

26. ἀνέχων: intr., 'stopping': cf. X. *Hell.* 1.6.28 ἀνέσχεν (of a rainstorm).

THEOGNIS 39–52

The history of Megara at the time of the tyranny of Theagenes and after is not clear. Theagenes' tyranny is variously dated to *c.* 600 and to 640–620, but when Theognis wrote this poem the government was in the hands not of a single man but of 'the leaders' (ἡγεμόνες 41) who are identified with οἱ κακοί: in other words they were not aristocrats but the middle-classes; and what Theognis fears as the result of their κακότης (42), ὕβρις (44, explained in 45–6) and greed (50) is the emergence of another tyrant (cf. 39–40 and μούναρχοι 52): the memory of Theagenes' severity must have been vivid.

These lines have been divided so as to form two poems, 39–42 and 43–52, but it seems preferable to regard 43–52 as a generalisation prompted by the particular situation described in 39–42, and to take πόλει ... τῇδε (52) as rounding off the poem with an echo of πόλις ἥδε (39). A version of 39–42 occurs at 1081–2b, where however 1082 has ὑβριστήν, χαλεπῆς ἡγεμόνα στάσιος for 40 εὐθυντῆρα κακῆς ὕβριος ἡμετέρης.

The whole poem bears a close likeness to Sol. 3 (see notes on 40, 41, 50, 51) and Sol. 10 (see 52n.).

39. κύει: cf. the oracle in Hdt. 5.92β.2, Λάβδα κύει, τέξει δ' ὀλοοίτροχον ('a boulder')· ἐν δὲ πεσεῖται | ἀνδράσι μουν-άρχοισι. Note the alliteration in this couplet and in 42, 45, 46.

40. εὐθυντῆρα: 'a corrector': cf. A. *Suppl.* 717 οἴακος εὐθυντῆρος ὑστάτου νεώς, and Sol. 3.36n. εὐθύνει δὲ δίκας σκολιάς.

κακῆς: the keynote of the poem: cf. κακότητα (42), κακοῖσιν (44), κακοῖσι (49), κακῷ (50).

ὕβριος: cf. Hes. Op. 238, Sol. 3.8, Thgn. 603, 1103 for this civic ὕβρις.

ἡμετέρης: Theognis includes his fellow-aristocrats and himself among the guilty.

41. ἀστοὶ ... οἶδε: so at 61 and 283, 'the citizens of this city' (39 πόλις ἥδε).

σαόφρονες: σώφρων is opposed to ἄφρων at 431, 454 and 497, to νήπιος at 483.

ἡγεμόνες: cf. Sol. 3.7–8.

42. τετράφαται ... πεσεῖν: cf. Od. 4.260 μοι κραδίη τέτραπτο νέεσθαι, Od. 9.12–13 σοὶ ... θυμὸς ἐπετράπετο ... εἴρεσθαι, Th. 2.65.10 ἐτράποντο ... ἐνδιδόναι. τετράφαται here may denote the imminence of their fall.

45. δῆμον ... φθείρουσι: the expression probably refers to oppressive measures like usury, rather than to demagogic corruption of the masses.

δίκας ἀδίκοισι διδοῦσι: a puzzling expression. Hes. Op. 225–6 οἳ δὲ δίκας ξείνοισι καὶ ἐνδήμοισι διδοῦσιν | ἰθείας is similar, but there ἰθείας makes everything clear; so does εὐξυμβούλους in A. Suppl. 701–3 ξένοισί τ' εὐξυμβόλους ... δίκας ... διδοῖεν. The context demands that Theognis mean 'decide cases in favour of the unjust': clarity has been sacrificed in the juxtaposition of δίκας and ἀδίκοισι. For a similar juxtaposition cf. Hes. Op. 272 εἰ μείζω γε δίκην ἀδικώτερος ἕξει.

46. Some editors place a comma after κράτεος, making a parenthesis of 45–6, but it seems better to take 45–6 as a principal clause. The sentence beginning ἔλπεο μή ... gains force from the asyndeton.

47. For μή see Kühner-Gerth II. ii. § 512. I keep MSS. ἀτρεμέεσθαι. The middle of ἀτρεμέω is not found elsewhere, but Homer uses τρομέω intransitively in the middle at Il. 10.10. For the present tense, 'continue in a state of tranquillity', cf. E. Alc. 146 ἐλπὶς μὲν οὐκέτ' ἐστὶ σῴζεσθαι βίον; and Pl. Sph. 250e, and see Kühner-Gerth II.i. § 389 Anm. 7.

49. ταῦτα looks forward to κέρδεα: cf. Mimn. 1.2–3.

N

50. δημοσίῳ σὺν κακῷ ἐρχόμενα: cf. Sol. 3.26 δημόσιον κακὸν
ἔρχεται.

51. ἔμφυλοι φόνοι: see Sol. 3.19n.

52. μούναρχοί θ'· ἃ πόλει: I adopt Ahrens' emendation. A scribe
might well be puzzled by θα and make a change to δέ;
and the emendation gains support from Hdt. 3.82.3 ἐξ ὧν
στάσιες ἐγγίγνονται, ἐκ δὲ τῶν στασίων φόνος, ἐκ δὲ τοῦ φόνου
ἀπέβη ἐς μουναρχίην, which may well be a reminiscence of
Theognis. Cf. too Sol. 10.3–4. Young keeps μούναρχοι δὲ
. . . ᾄδοι of the best MSS., and defends it as an example of
Schema Pindaricum, but I can find no clear example of a
plural subject followed closely and for no good reason
by a singular verb.

THEOGNIS 53–68

Theognis' target here is the new class of citizens, whose fore-
bears were rustics and who now live in the city and claim
equality with the ἀγαθοί. This piece too has been treated as two
poems, 53–60 and 61–8; but Theognis first describes the situation
(53–60), then gives appropriate advice. 57–60 recur at 1109–14
with considerable alterations and a new couplet inserted.

54. οὔτε δίκας ᾔδεσαν: cf. *Od.* 9.215 (of the Cyclops) ἄγριον,
οὔτε δίκας εὖ εἰδότα οὔτε θέμιστας.

55. δορὰς αἰγῶν: so in Men. *Epitr.* 53 Körte δίκας λέγοντες
περιπατεῖτε διφθέρας | ἔχοντες. Cf. Anacr. 388.2–3 and for
other mentions of leather jackets Ar. *Nub.* 72, Men.
Dysc. 415, *Epitr.* 152, Ath. 14.657d (the uniform of the
helots).

56. ἐνέμοντο: a nicely ambivalent word, applicable equally to
men and deer.

πόλεος: disyllabic: cf. 776 πόλευς, 757 πόληος, 1043 πόλεως
A πόλευς *OXI*.

57. ἀγαθοί: 'noble men'; but the couplet defies translation.
Theognis uses ἐσθλός interchangeably with ἀγαθός at
189–90, δειλός with κακός at 101–2 and elsewhere; cf.
Hes. fr. 164 Rzach δειλῶν τε καὶ ἐσθλῶν.

58. ἀνέχοιτ' ἐσορῶν: cf. *Od.* 16.277 σὺ δ' εἰσορόων ἀνέχεσθαι.

59. ἐπ' ἀλλήλοισι γελῶντες: 'laughing at one other'; cf. the

Homeric line-ending ἐπ' αὐτῷ ἡδὺ γέλασσαν (*Il.* 2.270, *Od.* 20.358, 21.376).

60. γνώμας: γνώμη occurs only here in the plural in Theognis, and takes a genitive only at 832 γνώμη δ' ἀργαλέη γίνεται ἀμφοτέρων, 'the knowledge, realisation, of both these things distresses me'; but cf. also 717 γνώμην ταύτην, 'knowledge of this'. So, with some misgivings over the plural since Theognis has the singular μνήμην at 1114 in his other version of the passage, I translate 'having knowledge neither of bad things nor of good things', in other words, 'devoid of any moral sense'. Cf. Mimn. 2.4n. In other passages of Theognis (except for 1038, where the reading is uncertain) γνώμη can always be translated as 'good sense', 'reliable powers of judgement', but that cannot be the sense here. We need not have recourse to Arist. *Hist. Anim.* 576b.15, where he says that it is difficult to tell the age of a horse or mule when it has cast its teeth: λέγουσι γνώμην ('token') ἔχειν ὅταν ἄβολος ᾖ, ὅταν δὲ βεβληκώς, οὐκ ἔχειν: that use of γνώμη may have been confined to horse-breeders, and although Theognis shows interest in horse-breeding (183–4), he is unlikely to have used such a technical term without preparing the way for it.

61. Cf. 113 μήποτε τὸν κακὸν ἄνδρα φίλον ποιεῖσθαι ἑταῖρον.

62. ἐκ θυμοῦ: 'sincerely': cf. *Il.* 9.342–3 ἐγὼ τήν | ἐκ θυμοῦ φίλεον. χρείης: 'need.' This seems to be the first occurrence of the word.

63. ἀπὸ γλώσσης: cf. 979 μή μοι ἀνὴρ εἴη γλώσσῃ φίλος, ἀλλὰ καὶ ἔργῳ, S. *O.C.* 936 τῷ νῷ θ' ὁμοίως κἀπὸ τῆς γλώσσης λέγω. Theognis again advises duplicity at 213–18, 1071–4.

65. σπουδαῖον: well-placed here: 'no serious matter, at any rate'. Cf. *h. Merc.* 332 σπουδαῖον τόδε χρῆμα.
   ὀιζυρῶν, 'wretched, miserable', pejorative as in English: cf. Hes. *Op.* 639 ὀιζυρῇ ἐνὶ κώμῃ (of Ascra), Hdt. 9.82.3 δίαιταν . . . ὀιζυρήν, Ar. *Nub.* 655, *Av.* 1641 ὦζυρέ, Archil. 54 Πανελλήνων ὀιζύς.

66. ἔπι = ἔπεστι, with ἐπ' ἔργοισιν, 'there is in their deeds'.

67. πολυπλοκίας: only here, but cf. 215 πουλύπου . . . πολυπλόκου.
   ἐφίλησαν: aorist with perfect sense, 'they have come to love': cf. 189–90 ἔγημε . . . ἔμειξε, 675 ἔπαυσαν.

68. μηκέτι σῳζόμενοι: like Latin *perditi*, 'lost men'. Cf. 235–6, where ἀνδράσι σῳζομένοισι is contrasted with πόλει . . . ἁλωσομένῃ.

THEOGNIS 77–8

Quoted by Plato (*Leg.* 1.630a), Eusebius (*Praep. Evang.* 12.2.2), Theodoretus (*Graec. Aff. Cur.* 1.69).

77. ἀντερύσασθαι: L.S.J. cites only this passage and Nonnus for the word; but cf. *Il.* 22.351–2 (Achilles to Hector) οὐδ' εἴ κεν σ' αὐτὸν χρυσῷ ἐρύσασθαι ἀνώγοι | Δαρδανίδης Πρίαμος. There χρυσῷ is dat. of instrument, here the genitives depend on ἀντι- as in E. *Hec.* 57–8 ἀντισηκώσας . . . σε . . . τῆς πάροιθ' εὐπραξίας. For the metaphor cf. 157.

78. ἄξιος may preserve something of its basic meaning, 'counter-balancing': see L.S.J. s.v. It usually takes a passive infin., but cf. Th. 1.138.3 ἄξιος θαυμάσαι, and see Kühner-Gerth ii.15 Anm. 13.

διχοστασίη: cf. Sol. 3.37n.

THEOGNIS 87–92

87–90 are repeated with slight changes at 1082c–f, where they are followed by a different couplet. The poem is reminiscent of *Il.* 9.312–13 ἐχθρὸς γάρ μοι κεῖνος ὁμῶς 'Αΐδαο πύλῃσιν, | ὅς χ' ἕτερον μὲν κεύθῃ ἐνὶ φρεσίν, ἄλλο δὲ εἴπῃ.

87. ἔπεσιν: cf. 63 ἀπὸ γλώσσης.

στέργε: Theognis makes no distinction between στέργε and φίλει (89). Although the thought of the poem is clear, the expression is forced (στέργε . . . φιλεῖς . . . φίλει, νόον . . . νόος . . . νόον . . . νόον, μιῇ γλώσσῃ δίχ' ἔχει νόον).

ἔχε: either 'direct, turn' (Hudson-Williams) as *Il.* 3.263 πεδίονδ' ἔχον ὠκέας ἵππους, S. *Trach.* 272–3 ἄλλοσ' . . . ὄμμα, θατέρᾳ δὲ νοῦν | ἔχοντα, or 'keep'.

88. ἔνεστι νόος: a pentameter-ending at 622 and Sol. 8.6.

89. καθαρὸν θέμενος νόον: cf. Scol. 901.2 καθαρὸν θεμένη νόον. The expression was, as far as we can say, a striking one when Theognis used it. Homer used the adjective of 'clean' clothes (*Od.* 6.61: so Archil. 10.2) and 'clear' spaces (e.g. *Il.* 8.491), but also of a 'clean' death (death by the sword

as opposed to hanging, *Od.* 22.462: cf. Heraclitus 136
D.-K. ψυχαὶ ἀρηίφατοι καθερώτεραι ἢ ἐνὶ νούσοις). The
adverb appears in a religious context in Hesiod (*Op.* 337
ἀγνῶς καὶ καθαρῶς of sacrifice) and *h. Ap.* 121 (the same
phrase of the washing of Apollo). Theognis has both the
literal and the metaphorical uses: cf. 452 and 197–8
Διόθεν καὶ σὺν δίκῃ . . . | καὶ καθαρῶς. For θέμενος cf. A. *Pr.*
164 θέμενος ἄγναμπτον νόον.

ἀποειπών: 'refusing' or 'disowning me'? In Homer ἀποειπεῖν
is intransitive at *Il.* 1.515 and 9.675 and (unless we supply
κούρας) at 9.510. At *Il.* 19.35 μῆνιν ἀποειπών the object is
abstract, and Plato *Leg.* 11.928d τὸν υἱόν . . . ἀπειπεῖν
υἱὸν κατὰ νόμον μηκέτ᾽ εἶναι cannot justify the translation
'disown'. In Hdt. 1.59.2 τοῦτον (sc. παῖδα) ἀπείπασθαι the
middle is used. It seems prudent to regard ἀποειπών as
intransitive here ('refusing'), and to take μ᾽ as the object of
ἔχθαιρε: its position is due to the parallelism of ἤ με . . .
ἤ μ᾽.

91. μηῇ γλώσσῃ δίχ᾽ ἔχει νόον: a puzzling expression. I cannot
account for the dative, and the contrast between one tongue
(or one utterance) and double thoughts or duplicity is not
clearly expressed. Of the nearest parallels Homer's δίχα
θυμὸν ἔχοντες (*Il.* 20.32) refers to a difference of allegiance
and Theognis' δίχα θυμὸν ἔχω (910) to doubt, although
double-dealing is implied by the adjectives διχόνους (found
only in Philo) and διχόμυθος.

92. δεινός: 'grim', well-placed for emphasis.

THEOGNIS 113–14

For the advice cf. 61 ff.

113. ποιεῖσθαι: infinitive with imperatival force; so φεύγειν (114).
114. Theognis has nautical similes at 458–60, 576, 856, 970,
metaphors at 1273–4, 1361–2.

THEOGNIS 155–8

Stobaeus 4.32 (περὶ πενίας). 36 quotes these lines with
179–80 added, and attributes them to Theognis; Apostolius
(8.28a) quotes 157–8: cf. Basil *Lib. Gent.* 177d (Migne *P.G.* 31.

573a). The poem echoes Hesiod *Op.* 717–18 μηδέ ποτ' οὐλομένην
πενίην θυμοφθόρον ἀνδρὶ | τέτλαθ' ὀνειδίζειν, μακάρων δόσιν αἰὲν
ἐόντων.

155. πενίην θυμοφθόρον: cf. 1129 πενίης θυμοφθόρου, Hes. loc.
      cit., Mimn. 2.15n. For Theognis' own poverty cf. 1115
      χρήματ' ἔχων πενίην μ' ὠνείδισας.

      ἀνδρὶ χολωθείς: cf. the Homeric line-ending πατρὶ χολωθείς
      (e.g. *Il.* 2.629).

156. ἀχρημοσύνην: elsewhere only at *Od.* 17.502.

      οὐλομένην: cf. Hes. loc. cit.

      πρόφερε: cf. *Il.* 3.64 μή μοι δῶρ' ἐρατὰ πρόφερε χρυσῆς
      Ἀφροδίτης.

157. In the *Iliad* Zeus' scales are used always to decide the result
      of fighting (8.69 ff, 16.658, 19.223–4, 22.209 ff.: cf. too *Il.*
      14.99, A. *Pers.* 346). ἐπιρρέπειν is intransitive at *Il.*
      14.99, transitive here and (in the sense 'weigh out') at A.
      Ag. 250–1 Δίκα δὲ τοῖς μὲν παθοῦσιν μαθεῖν | ἐπιρρέπει,
      Eum. 888–9. Theognis uses the metaphor of scales at 77.

      ἄλλοτε ἄλλῳ: a line-ending at *Od.* 4.236.

158. For the use of the infinitive to express a result see Goodwin
      M.T. § 775.

THEOGNIS 173–82

These lines, usually divided to form three poems (173–8,
179–80, 181–2) or even four (173–4, 175–8, 179–80, 181–2), are
united by Young, who draws attention to the rhyme within each
pentameter, a sequence rivalled only by 133–42 where four
pentameters rhyme. (Note, however, that 132, also rhyming,
belongs to a separate poem.)

Stobaeus 4.32 (περὶ πενίας) quotes 175–6 (38), 177–8 (34, as
a continuation of 649–52) and 179–80 (36, as a continuation of
155–8), ascribing all the lines to Theognis. 175–6 and 177–8 are
quoted by a score of other writers. Note Plutarch *Stoic. rep.*
14.1039f: Chrysippus corrected χρὴ πενίην φεύγοντα to χρὴ
κακίαν φεύγοντα; and *poet. aud.* 4.22a: Bion's retort to 177–8 was
πῶς οὖν σὺ πένης ὢν φλυαρεῖς τοσαῦτα καὶ καταδολεσχεῖς ἡμῶν;

The variations found in the texts of Stobaeus and the others
at 175 and 177 must be due to a desire to form couplets which

would be intelligible in themselves. Euripides *Med.* 263 and *Heraclid.* 865 were similarly adjusted at Stobaeus 4.22(7). 143 and 4.41.26a.

173. ἄνδρ' ἀγαθόν: note ἀγαθόν: the advice is meant for fellow-aristocrats.

174. γήρως: sc. μᾶλλον, 'most of all things, and more than age or fever'.

πολιοῦ: so Pi. *I.* 6.15 γῆρας … πολιόν, Bacchyl. 3.88. Hudson-Williams compares *Od.* 11.43 χλωρὸν δέος, Hor. *Od.* 1.4.13 *pallida mors.*

ἠπιάλου: 'fever', usually explained as malaria.

175. βαθυκήτεα: ἅπ. λεγ., 'with deep gulfs'. μεγακήτεα πόντον is a line-ending at *Od.* 3.158, and Homer applies the adjective also to a dolphin and a ship: cf. κητώεις of Lacedaemon. But κῆτος is used also of large fish, and πολυκήτεα Νεῖλον (Theoc. 17.98) must refer to the fish of the Nile, if not to its crocodiles: see Gow's note.

176. ῥιπτεῖν: intransitive, 'to hurl oneself'.

πετρέων … ἠλιβάτων: the adjective, used only of rocks in Homer and Hesiod, is of doubtful etymology.

177. πενίη δεδμημένος: cf. *Od.* 14.318 καμάτῳ δεδμημένον.

178. Cf. 669–70 εἰμὶ δ' ἄφωνος | χρημοσύνη.

179. γάρ: not explanatory like γάρ of 177, but used to reinforce the idea of 175–6 that desperate measures are called for: this time, however, the measures are constructive, not evasive. With the rest of the line cf. Hes. *Th.* 762 γαῖάν τε καὶ εὐρέα νῶτα θαλάσσης, and the Homeric line-ending ἐπ' εὐρέα νῶτα θαλάσσης (e.g. *Il.* 2.159). Horace *Ep.* 1.1.45–6 may be a conscious echoing of this passage, and suggests that trading is meant: *impiger extremos curris mercator ad Indos, | per mare pauperiem fugiens, per saxa, per ignes.*

180. λύσιν πενίης: cf. *Od.* 9.421 θανάτου λύσιν.

182. χαλεπῇ τειρόμενον πενίῃ: cf. 684, 752 χαλεπῇ τειρόμενοι πενίῃ.

THEOGNIS 183–92

Lines 183–90 appear twice in Stobaeus: in 4.29 (περὶ εὐγενείας). 53 (Stobaeus¹) and 4.30 (περὶ δυσγενείας).11a (Stobaeus²); 183–6 also at 4.22 (περὶ γάμου).99 (Stobaeus³). Stobaeus¹ carries the heading Ξενοφῶντος ἐκ τοῦ Περὶ Θεόγνιδος: Xenophon's book is mentioned nowhere else, and the excerpt suggests indeed that there were other writings on Theognis (οἱ δὲ πολλοὶ ἐκ τούτων τῶν ἐπῶν οἴονται τὸν ποιητὴν κτλ.) of which we know nothing. The gist of Xenophon's words is that Theognis' poetry is about human goodness and badness, and that the starting-point (ἀρχή) of his work is τὸ εὖ γένεσθαι: no man, no thing can be good unless what produces it is good — witness animals; and here he quotes 183–90. Theognis' point, according to Xenophon, is that men are ignorant of the laws of eugenics.

The passage is echoed in ps.-Phoc. 199–206, E. *Androm.* 1279 ff, *El.* 1097–9 (probably an interpolation), fr. 95N², Arist. fr. 92 Rose, ps.-Plu. *nob.* 15 (Latin and Greek versions of the Xenophon passage).

183. κριούς: Megara's woollen goods were its staple product. Cf. Ar. *Ach.* 519 ἐσυκοφάντει Μεγαρέων τὰ χλανίσκια, X. *Mem* 2.7.6 Μεγαρέων δ' οἱ πλεῖστοι ἀπὸ ἐξωμιδοποιίας ('the manufacture of off-the-shoulder tunics') διατρέφονται. Paus. 1.44.3 mentions the shrine of Demeter μαλοφόρος at Nisaea, the harbour of Megara; and Diogenes the Cynic said he would rather be a Megarian's ram than his son (ἐβούλετο Μεγαρέως ἀνδρὸς κριὸς εἶναι μᾶλλον ἢ υἱός, ap. Ael. *V.H.* 12.56, cf. Plu. *de cup. div.* 7.526c). Note that the rams have been replaced by dogs in Stobaeus³, presumably to give the line wider application.

184. εὐγενέας: note the characteristic ambivalence of εὐγενής, ἀγαθός, κακός, ἐσθλός.

τις: 'everyone': cf. Callin. 1.5n.

ἐξ ἀγαθῶν βήσεσθαι: 'men want them — the rams etc. — to mate from good stock.' The expression is not lucid, and Garzya suggests that this may be intentional and due to the content. With βήσεσθαι cf. Themistius *Or.* 21.248b Hardouin τόν τε ἵππον ἐξετάζοντας τὸν βησόμενον (Themistius has the present passage of Theognis in mind, and mentions him shortly after), Hdt. 1.192.3 οἱ μὲν (sc. ἵπποι) ἀναβαίνοντες τὰς θηλέας . . . αἱ δὲ βαινόμεναι,

Pl. *Phaedr.* 250e τετράποδος νόμον βαίνειν ἐπιχειρεῖ καὶ παιδοσπορεῖν, etc.; cf. also βιβάζω. For ἐξ ἀγαθῶν cf. 189–90, 1112 μνηστεύει δ' ἐκ κακοῦ ἐσθλὸς ἀνήρ, Hdt. 6.130.2 ἐξ ἐμεῦ γῆμαι, 3.84.2, 5.92β.1. For the fut. infin. with βούλεσθαι cf. Hdt. 4.111.2 βουλόμενοι ἐξ αὐτέων παῖδας ἐκγενήσεσθαι, Th. 6.57.3 ἐβούλοντο ... προτιμωρήσεσθαι (M -ασθαι), and see Goodwin *M.T.* § 113. It is just possible that βήσεσθαι is present infinitive of a desiderative verb βήσομαι: cf. Chantraine *G.H.* i. 416–17.

185. γῆμαι ... οὐ μελεδαίνει: 'does not mind marrying': cf. 1129 πενίης ... οὐ μελεδαίνων.

187. Tr. 'nor does a woman refuse to be the wife of a base man, provided that he is wealthy.' Do not take γυνὴ κακοῦ ἀνδρός together.

ἀναίνεται: cf. *Il.* 18.450 ἠναίνετο ... ἀμῦναι, 1289 ἀναινομένην γάμον, 1294 καὶ μάλ' ἀναινομένη.

188. πλουσίου gains emphasis from its position.

ἀφνεόν: masculine, as ἀγαθοῦ.

189. χρήματα μὲν τιμῶσι: the burden of 699–718. μέν *solitarium* puts emphasis on χρήματα: cf. Denniston *G.P.* 359.

ἔγημε: aorist with perfect force: cf. 67 ἐφίλησαν. In 190 ἔμειξε also probably has perfect force, but it might be gnomic aorist.

191. οὕτω μὴ θαύμαζε: so at 1349. οὕτω = 'this being so'.

192. μαυροῦσθαι: 'to be blotted out, blurred': cf. A. *Ag.* 296 λαμπὰς δ' οὐδέπω μαυρουμένη, Hes. *Op.* 325 ῥεῖα δέ μιν μαυροῦσι θεοί, cf. 693.

σὺν γὰρ μίσγεται ἐσθλὰ κακοῖς: cf. Hes. *Op.* 179 μεμείξεται ἐσθλὰ κακοῖσιν. For the tmesis cf. 671, 680, 947.

THEOGNIS 213–18

213–14 have been regarded as a separate poem, but the asyndeton at 215 is characteristic of Theognis. 1071–4 give another version of 213–14, 217–18, addressed not to the poet's heart (θυμέ) but to Cyrnus: the octopus-couplet has disappeared, and the last line reads κρεῖσσόν τοι σοφίη καὶ μεγάλης ἀρετῆς. Harrison (138–9) (in my view, convincingly) explains the second piece as Theognis' conscious amendment of the first: for another view see F. R. Adrados, 'El poema del pulpo y los orígenes de la colección teognídea', *Emerita* 26 (1958) 1–10.

215–16 were much quoted and imitated, but they themselves probably derive from an epic couplet preserved in the company of 215–16 by Ath. 7.317a: πουλύποδός μοι, τέκνον, ἔχων νόον, Ἀμφίλοχ' ἥρως, | τοῖσιν ἐφαρμόζοι, τῶν κεν κατὰ δῆμον ἵκηαι. To this couplet Bergk added a line from Zenobius 1.24 and ps.-Diogenianus 1.23, ἄλλοτε δ' ἀλλοῖος τελέθειν καὶ χώρῃ ἔπεσθαι. These three hexameters contain the advice given by Amphiaraus to his son Amphilochus on Amphilochus' departure for Thebes. Pi. fr. 208 Turyn, S. fr. 286N² and Eupolis fr. 101 Kock may be echoes of the epic lines or Theognis or both. See also Powell, *Coll. Alex.* 246.

213. θυμέ: Theognis addresses himself thus at 695, 877, 1029, 1070a; cf. Archil. 67a.1n. I translate 'among all your friends — i.e. in your dealings with them — turn towards them a subtle disposition.'

κατά: cf. 23 πάντας δὲ κατ' ἀνθρώπους ὀνομαστός.

ἐπίστρεφε: cf. 1083 ἐπιστρέψαντα νόημα.

ποικίλον: skilfully used to convey the ideas of 'wily' (cf. Hes. *Th.* 510–11 Προμηθέα | ποικίλον) and 'many-coloured' in preparation for the mention of the octopus.

ἦθος: Homer has ἤθεα only of the 'haunts' of animals (*Il.* 6.511, *Od.* 14.411); Hesiod uses ἤθεα of 'customs' (*Th.* 66: cf. *Op.* 137) and ἦθος of 'character': cf. *Op.* 67, 78 ἐπίκλοπον ἦθος. Cf. S. *Ant.* 705 μή νυν ἓν ἦθος μοῦνον ἐν σαυτῷ φόρει. Note the alliteration in 213 and 215.

214. 'Mingling (with your ἦθος) the mood each friend has'.

ὀργὴν κτλ.: cf. 312 γινώσκων ὀργὴν ἥντιν' ἕκαστος ἔχει.

συμμίσγων: cf. 1162d θυμὸν ὁμῶς μίσγειν.

215. πουλύπου: Athenaeus 7.316a–318f gives much fascinating information about the octopus: cf. too *A.P.* 9.10. It figures in Mycenean and Minoan art, and appears in *Od.* 5.432, where Odysseus clings to a rock like an octopus (gen. πουλύποδος: cf. *h. Ap.* 77 πουλύποδες). L.S.J. quote ὀκτώπους of a sea-creature only from Cratinus 77, ὀκτάπους only from Alexander of Tralles (6th century A.D.): cf. Modern Greek 'κταπόδι.

215. πολυπλόκου: like ποικίλον, a well-chosen word, lit. 'of many convolutions', but met. 'wily': cf. Hsch. πολύπλοκος· πολύτροπος (the epithet of Odysseus above all), and Thgn. 67 πολυπλοκίας.

   ποτὶ πέτρῃ: line-ending at *Od.* 5.415. Theognis seems to have combined two ideas here, somewhat harshly: (1) the octopus is on a rock, (2) it resembles any rock to which it clings.

216. προσομιλήσῃ: usually of social converse, as 31–2 κακοῖσι δὲ μὴ προσομίλει | ἀνδράσιν, and so appropriate here.

   ἐφάνη: gnomic aorist.

217. τῇδ' ἐφέπου: a difficult expression, probably to be taken metaphorically, 'at one moment go along (with your companion) in one direction', and answered unexpectedly but intelligibly by 'at the next moment change the colour of your skin.' We find a similar unexpected answer at 1073 νῦν μὲν τῷδ' ἐφέπου (go along with this companion), τοτὲ δ' ἀλλοῖος πέλευ ὀργήν. The third epic line quoted above (introductory remarks on 213–18) has χώρῃ ἕπεσθαι, which is scarcely clear but does at least suggest movement.

218. κρέσσων: so at 618, 631, 996, κρείσσων at 1074, 1173.

   ἀτροπίης, 'inflexibility': a rare word, which caught the fancy of Apollonius Rhodius (e.g. 4.387, 1006, 1047). Cf. the name Atropos (one of the Fates), Pi. *N.* 7.103–4 ἀτρόποισι . . . ἔπεσι. Hdt. 2.121ε.3 has πολυτροπίη, 'versatility.' Theognis again chooses a word of both literal and metaphorical application.

THEOGNIS 237–54

This fine poem has been recast (247–50 before 239) and dismembered (237–46, 247–52, 253–4); its authenticity has been impugned because of its style, vocabulary and content; and it has been labelled pure and simple parody. To my mind it is among the best of Theognis, and the peevish complaint of 253–4, on which much suspicion has been cast, suits his cynicism nicely: cf. 24–6 after the proud 19–23. The connexion between σοὶ μὲν (237), reinforced by καί σε (241), and αὐτὰρ ἐγών (253) is as plain as a pikestaff, and a boy's ingratitude towards Theognis is the theme, much less elaborately treated, of 1263–6. The number of Homeric epithets and echoes suggests not 'un lyrisme un peu tapageur et étranger à l'inspiration habituelle de notre poète' (Carrière, *Théognis* 103) but Theognis' wish to remind his audience of Homer, who above all had conferred immortality on his heroes.

Sappho 55 speaks of a woman who will be forgotten after death since she does not share in the roses of Pieria: she may mean either that the woman is no poet or that her praises have been sung by no poet. Horace *Od.* 2.20, 3.30 and Ovid *Met.* 15.871–9 prophesy their own immortality. See Bowra *E.G.E.* 164–7.

237. σοὶ μέν: answered by αὐτὰρ ἐγών (253): cf. 19–24 σοφιζο-μένῳ μὲν ἐμοὶ ... ἀστοῖσιν δ'.

πτέρα: Pindar has the metaphor at *N.* 7.22 ποτανᾷ ... μαχανᾷ (of Homer's poetry), *P.* 8.33–4 τεὸν χρέος ... ἐμᾷ ποτανὸν ἀμφὶ μαχανᾷ, *I.* 1.64–5 εἴη νιν εὐφώνων πτερύγεσσιν ἀερθέντ' ἀγλααῖς | Πιερίδων, *I.* 5.70 πτερόεντα ... ὕμνον; so Pratinas 708.5 ποικιλόπτερον μέλος, B. fr. 20B.4 χρύσεον Μουσᾶν ... πτερόν.

ἔδωκα: aorist with perfect force, as at 67, 189–90.

σύν: instrumental: cf. *Il.* 8.530 σὺν τεύχεσι θωρηχθέντες and L.S.J. s.v. A4, 7.

ἐπ' ἀπείρονα πόντον: line-ending at *Il.* 1.350.

238. κατὰ γῆν πᾶσαν ἀειρόμενος: most editors accept Bergk's καὶ for κατά, joining πόντον and γῆν and taking ἀειρόμενος as 'soaring'. If we keep κατά we may take κατά ... ἀειρόμενος as an example of tmesis: καταίρω is used of birds landing in Ar. *Av.* 1288 κατῆραν ἐς τὰ βιβλία, and the words when taken in this sense lead easily to θοίνῃς ... παρέσσῃ ἐν πάσαις. Alternatively we may translate 'rising over the whole world': cf. καθ' Ἑλλάδα γῆν στρω-φώμενος, where the metaphor of flight still persists, as 249 shows.

239. θοίνῃς δὲ καὶ εἰλαπίνῃσι παρέσσῃ: cf. *Il.* 10.217 αἰεὶ δ' ἐν δαίτῃσι καὶ εἰλαπίνῃσι παρέσται. Neither noun occurs often before Theognis: θοίνη is a meal or dinner, εἰλαπίνη often a more elaborate and solemn feast (cf. Ath. 8.362e).

240. πολλῶν κείμενος ἐν στόμασιν: imitated at *A.P.* 9.62.6

πάντων δ' Ἑλλήνων κείσομαι ἐν στόμασιν. Cf. Ennius, *varia* 17.2 Vahlen³: *volito vivos per ora virum*, Virgil *G.* 3.9 *virum volitare per ora.*

241. σε . . . ᾄσονται: cf. *Il.* 1.1 μῆνιν ἄειδε.

σὺν αὐλίσκοισι: cf. 825 ὑπ' αὐλητῆρος ἀείδειν. αὐλίσκος, diminutive form of αὐλός, is very rare: of musical instruments only at Pi. *fr.* 106–8 Turyn αὐλίσκων ὑπὸ λωτίνων (pap. λαισκων), S. *fr.* 701.1N² οὐ σμικροῖσιν αὐλίσκοις, but cf. Hdt. 1.17.1 αὐλοῦ γυναικηΐου τε καὶ ἀνδρηΐου, two types of pipe used by Alyattes on the march: the first must have been 'treble' like the αὐλίσκος. The use of αὐλίσκοι suggests that the voices of the νέοι ἄνδρες . . . ἐρατοί were not yet broken. λιγύς and its compounds were often, but by no means exclusively, used of high-pitched notes: of the Sirens' song (*Od.* 12.44, 183, Alcm. 30) and the Muse (*Od.* 24.62, Alcm. 14(a).1), but also of Nestor (*Il.* 1.248, 4.293) and even of Thersites (*Il.* 2.246); λιγύφθογγος in Homer is used only of heralds, and 'penetrating' may be the basic meaning of λιγυ-.

242. ἐρατοί: used of persons by Hes. *Th.* 259, 355, Pi. *O.* 10.99.
λιγέα: cf. 939 λίγ' ἀειδέμεν, *Od.* 10.254 λίγ' ἄειδεν.

243. δνοφερῆς: cf. Hes. *Th.* 736 γῆς δνοφερῆς. Homer uses the adj. of water (*Il.* 9.15, 16.4) and night (*Od.* 13.269, 15.50).

ὑπὸ κεύθεσι γαίης: cf. *Il.* 22.482–3 Ἀΐδαο δόμους ὑπὸ κεύθεσι γαίης | ἔρχεαι; a line-ending also at Hes. *Th.* 300.

244. πολυκωκύτους: ἅπ. λεγ. Cf. S. *Ant.* 1316 ὀξυκώκυτος.

245. οὐδὲ θανὼν κτλ.: cf. *Od.* 24.93–4 ὡς σὺ μὲν οὐδὲ θανὼν ὄνομ' ὤλεσας, ἀλλά τοι αἰεί | πάντας ἐπ' ἀνθρώπους κλέος ἔσσεται ἐσθλόν, Ἀχιλλεῦ.

μελήσεις: cf. *Od.* 9.19–20 εἴμ' Ὀδυσεὺς Λαερτιάδης, ὃς πᾶσι δόλοισιν | ἀνθρώποισι μέλω, καί μευ κλέος οὐρανὸν ἵκει, 12.70 Ἀργὼ πᾶσι μέλουσα.

247. Ἑλλάδα: cf. Xenoph. 7.2n.

248. ἰχθυόεντα, ἀτρύγετον: epic epithets. For ἰχθυόεντα cf. Sol. 1.45n. πόντον ἐπ' ἀτρύγετον is a Homeric line-ending, e.g. *Od.* 2.370.

περῶν: cf. *Il.* 2.613 πέρααν ἐπὶ οἴνοπα πόντον.

249. οὐχ ἵππων νώτοισιν: contrast Alc. 34.5–6 (Castor and
     Pollux) οἳ κὰτ εὔρηαν χ[θόνα] καὶ θάλασσαν | παῖσαν ἔρχεσθ'
     ὠ[κυπό]δων ἐπ' ἵππων.

250. ἀγλαὰ . . . δῶρα: again Homeric (e.g. Il. 1.213). For the line-
     ending cf. 1304, 1332, 1383 Κυπρογενοῦς δῶρον ἰοστεφάνου.
     Μουσάων δῶρα: cf. Archil. 1.2, Sol. 1.51.

251. μέμηλε: sc. δῶρα rather than ἀοιδή. For the line-ending cf.
     Od. 8.580 ἵνα ᾖσι καὶ ἐσσομένοισιν ἀοιδή, Theoc. 12.11
     ἐπεσσομένοις δὲ γενοίμεθα πᾶσιν ἀοιδή.

252. ὁμῶς: with καὶ ἐσσομένοισιν, 'for all who are concerned
     . . . and for future generations alike'.
         ὄφρ' ἂν γῆ: the verb is omitted as at 859 ἦν δέ τί μοί ποθεν ἐσθλόν,
         864 ἦμος ἀλεκτρυόνων φθόγγος ἐγειρομένων.
         γῆ τε καὶ ἠέλιος: line-beginning at Il. 19.259.

253. οὐ τυγχάνω αἰδοῦς: cf. 1266 αἰδοῦς οὐδεμιῆς ἔτυχον.

THEOGNIS 341–50

Theognis' prayer for revenge on the men who had stolen his
property. For the behaviour of the Megarian revolutionaries cf.
Plutarch Quaest. Graec. 18.295d τά τ' ἄλλα τοῖς πλουσίοις ἀσελγῶς
προσεφέροντο, καὶ παριόντες εἰς τὰς οἰκίας αὐτῶν οἱ πένητες ἠξίουν
ἑστιᾶσθαι καὶ δειπνεῖν πολυτελῶς· εἰ δὲ μὴ τυγχάνοιεν, πρὸς βίαν καὶ
μεθ' ὕβρεως ἐχρῶντο πᾶσι.

341. ἀλλά: see Tyrt. 8.1n.
     καίριον: adj. with εὐχήν, 'the prayer which my circum-
         stances demand, my apt prayer', rather than 'in good
         time, before I die' or proleptically 'so that it may come
         true'. Cf. A. Sept. 1 χρὴ λέγειν τὰ καίρια, Hdt. 1.125.1
         εὑρίσκεται ταῦτα καιριώτατα εἶναι.

343. τεθναίην: cf. Mimn. 1.2.
     ἄμπαυμα = ἀνάπαυμα. Cf. Hes. Th. 55 ἄμπαυμά τε μερμηράων,
         Thgn. 1325 μερμήρας δ' ἀπόπαυε κακάς, Bacchyl. 5.6–7
         φρένα . . . ἀμπαύσας μεριμνᾶν.

345. αἶσα: 'my lot', i.e. κακά, μέριμναι, ἀνίαι. The Homeric
         κατ' αἶσαν ἔειπον (e.g. Il. 10.445) hardly justifies the
         translation, 'for that would be just, fitting': Lavagnini is
         wrong to say that αἶσα is a synonym of δίκη.
         φαίνεται: cf. Od. 10.79 οὐκέτι φαίνετο πομπή.

ἡμῖν: plural alternates with singular at 415–18, 504–5 γνώμης οὐκέτ' ἐγὼ ταμίης | ἡμετέρης, 649–50, 1101–2.

346. ἔχουσι: 'still have'. The emphatic position of συλήσαντες prevents us from translating 'they have stolen'.

347. κύων κτλ.: the resemblance to Aesop 186 Chambry (=233 Halm) κύων κρέας ἔχουσα ποταμὸν διέβαινε κτλ. suggests that another form of the fable, perhaps explaining πάντ' ἀποσεισάμενος, may be referred to here.

ἀποσεισάμενος: ἀποσείομαι is twice used by Hdt. (7.88.1, 9.22.1) of a horse throwing its rider. For the omission of ὡς or ὥστε with κύων cf. 1361 ναῦς πέτρῃ προσέκυρσας, Herodas 6.13–14 κἠγὼ . . . κύων ὑλακτέω.

χαράδρην: cf. Il. 4.454 χαράδρης after χείμαρροι ποταμοί at 452, 5.87–8 ποταμῷ . . . χειμάρρῳ, Anacr. 413.2 χειμερίῃ δ' ἔλουσεν ἐν χαράδρῃ.

349. εἴη: with infinitive also at 561, 1153, 1155.

μέλαν αἷμα πιεῖν: gruesome, but not more gruesome than Il. 4.34–6 (Zeus to Hera) εἰ δὲ σύ γ' . . . | ὠμὸν βεβρώθοις Πρίαμον Πριάμοιό τε παῖδας | ἄλλους τε Τρῶας, τότε κεν χόλον ἐξακέσαιο. Cf. 22.346–8, X. Anab. 4.8.14, Hell. 3.3, E. fr. 687N². μέλαν αἷμα, 'dark blood', frequently in Homer.

ἐπί . . . ὄροιτο: from ὄρομαι ('watch, guard') or ὄρνυμι (rise up')? At Od. 14.104 ἐπὶ δ' ἀνέρες ἐσθλοὶ ὄρονται and possibly 3.471, Il. 23.112 ἐπὶ δ' ἀνὴρ ἐσθλὸς ὀρώρει the sense seems to be 'guard'; but cf. Od. 19.201 χαλεπὸς δέ τις ὦρορε δαίμων, 'some unfriendly god raised (the storm).' 'Rise up' gives better sense here.

THEOGNIS 351–4

351. πενίη: for the personification cf. Πλοῦτος in Hippon. 29.

μένεις: there is no other example of μένω + infinitive = 'postpone', but the construction occurs at A. Eum. 677 μένω δ' ἀκοῦσαι, 'I wait to hear' (cf. Ag. 459).

352. For the ending cf. 1094 χαλεπὸν δ' οὐκ ἐθέλοντα φιλεῖν.

353. ἐποίχεο: simply 'go to', as at Il. 15.676 νηῶν ἴκρι' ἐπώχετο.

THEOGNIS 425–8

A poem much quoted, e.g. by Sextus Empiricus, *Pyrrh. hypot.*
3.231, Stobaeus 4.52 (περὶ ζωῆς). 30, and much imitated, notably
by Sophocles *O.C.* 1225 μὴ φῦναι τὸν ἅπαντα νικᾷ λόγον κτλ.,
Bacchyl. 5.160–2 θνατοῖσι μὴ φῦναι φέριστον | μηδ' ἀελίου
προσιδεῖν | φέγγος. The two hexameter lines occur in *Cert. Hom.
et Hes.* p. 37 Wil., and it looks as though Theognis added to them
two pentameters of his own. The view expressed in the poem is
said to have been expressed by Silenus to King Midas: see
Aristotle fr. 44 Rose, Cicero *T.D.* 1.48.114.

426. αὐγὰς ὀξέος ἠελίου: cf. *Il.* 17.371–2 αὐγή | ἠελίου ὀξεῖα,
Hes. *Op.* 414, *h. Ap.* 374 μένος ὀξέος Ἠελίοιο, *Il.* 14. 344–5,
Pi. *O.* 3.24.

427. Cf. *Il.* 23.71 θάπτε με ὅττι τάχιστα· πύλας Ἀίδαο περήσω,
5.646 πύλας Ἀίδαο περήσειν.

428. γῆν ἐπαμησάμενον: cf. Hdt. 8.24.1 γῆν ἐπαμησάμενος, of
Xerxes' arrangements for the burial of his dead at
Thermopylae; cf. Ap. Rhod. 1.1305–6 ἀμήσατο γαῖαν |
ἀμφ' αὐτοῖς, and *Od.* 5.482 εὐνὴν ἐπαμήσατο, of Odysseus
making a bed of leaves for himself.

THEOGNIS 447–52

447. πλύνειν: in Aristophanes (e.g. *Ach.* 381) and later writers
the verb means 'to abuse, insult', but the tone of the present poem is so elevated that such a slang usage is out of
place.

κεφαλῆς . . . ἀπ' ἄκρης: cf. *Il.* 8.83 ἄκρην κὰκ κορυφήν.

448. λευκὸν ὕδωρ: cf. *Il.* 23.282, *Od.* 5.70 ὕδατι λευκῷ.

449. ἄπεφθον: cf. 1105–6 εἰς βάσανον δ' ἐλθὼν παρατριβόμενός
τε μολύβδῳ | χρυσὸς ἄπεφθος ἐὼν καλὸς ἅπασιν ἔσῃ, 417–18,
499–500, and see Ibyc. 282(a).42n.

450. ἐρυθρόν: ἐρυθρός may refer to the darker shade or the glow
of pure gold. Cf. *Il.* 9.365 χαλκὸν ἐρυθρόν.

βασάνῳ: cf. Pi. *P.* 10.67–8 πειρῶντι δὲ καὶ χρυσὸς ἐν
βασάνῳ πρέπει | καὶ νόος ὀρθός, Bacchyl. fr. 14.1–2 Λυδία
μὲν γὰρ λίθος | μανύει χρυσόν. Theophrastus *De Lap.* 45
gives the two distinct methods of testing the purity of

gold, by fire and by the touchstone: see Eichholz ad loc.

451. χροιῆς: usually of human skin, aptly here of the surface of the gold; ἄνθος (452) too is used of the skin at Sol. 19.6 χροιῆς ἄνθος, A. *Pr.* 23 χροιᾶς ... ἄνθος. See W. B. Stanford, *Greek Metaphor* 111–14.

ἰός: rust or verdigris: cf. Sapph. 204 καίτοι καθαρεύειν γε τὸν χρυσὸν ἀπὸ τοῦ ἰοῦ ἥ τε ποιήτρια μάρτυς ἐστὶν ἡ Λεσβία καὶ αὐτὸς ὁ χρυσὸς ἐπιδείκνυσιν, Pi. fr. 261.1–2 Turyn Διὸς παῖς ὁ χρυσός· | κεῖνον οὐ σὴς οὐδὲ κὶς ('neither moth nor weevil') δάπτει.

THEOGNIS 503–10

503–8 are quoted by Stobaeus 3.18 (περὶ ἀκρασίας). 16, 509–10 by Stobaeus 3.18.11, Artemidorus *Onirocr.* 1.66, Galen *Script. Min.* II, p. 40 Müller, Clement of Alexandria *Strom.* 6.11.5. Not all the textual variants are noticed in the *apparatus*.

509–10 resemble 211–12, an independent couplet. Here Theognis belatedly recollects his own excellent advice. Onomacritus is most probably the Athenian oracle-monger known from Hdt. 7.6: he was expelled by Hipparchus (i.e. before 514 B.C.) for forging oracles, but went to Susa with the Peisistratids after the succession of Xerxes (i.e. after 485 B.C.).

503. οἰνοβαρέω: cf. *Od.* 9.374 οἰνοβαρείων, *Il.* 1.225 οἰνοβαρές, *Od.* 3.139 οἴνῳ βεβαρηότες.

βιᾶται: cf. 485–6, where the context is similar, μή σε βιάσθω | γαστήρ.

504. γνώμης ... ταμίης: 'master of my wits': cf. 1185 ἀμφοτέρων ταμίαι, sc. νοῦ καὶ γλώσσης, 1242 οὐκέτ' ἔσῃ ταμίης, sc. φιλότητος, Th. 6.78.2.

505. τὸ δὲ δῶμα περιτρέχει: cf. 843–4 ἀλλ' ὁπόταν καθύπερθεν ἐὼν ὑπένερθε γένηται, | τουτάκις οἴκαδ' ἵμεν παυσάμενοι πόσιος.

506. καὶ πόδας οἶνος ἔχει κτλ: 'the wine has hold both of my legs and of my wits.' Theognis has already said that the wine has gone to his head; now he tests his legs. Cf. Hes. fr. 121.3–4 Rzach σὺν δὲ πόδας χεῖράς τε δέει γλῶσσάν τε νόον τε | δεσμοῖς ἀφράστοισι.

507. καὶ νόον ἐν στήθεσσι: cf. line-beginning at *Od.* 20.366 καὶ νόος
ἐν στήθεσσι.

508. θωρηχθείς: 'drunk', a favourite usage of Theognis: cf. 413,
470, 842, 884, also Pi. fr. 84 Turyn and medical writers
from Hippocrates onwards. Aristophanes puns on the
word at *Ach.* 1132–5, *Pax* 1286.

μέγ' ὄνειδος: so at *h. Ven.* 247. Cf. Theognis' pentameter-
endings at 546 αἰσχρὸν ὄνειδος ἔχω, 1378 αἰσχρὸν ὄνειδος ἔχεις.

THEOGNIS 531–4

Usually regarded as two distinct couplets.

531. φίλον ἦτορ: so e.g. at *Od.* 1.60.

532. φθεγγομένων: cf. 761 φόρμιγξ δ' αὖ φθέγγοιθ' ἱερὸν μέλος ἠδὲ
καὶ αὐλός, Xenoph. 6.5n.

ἱμερόεσσαν ὄπα: cf. *Od.* 1.421 ἱμερόεσσαν ἀοιδήν, *Il.* 18.570
ἱμερόεν κιθάριζε, *h. Merc.* 452 ἱμερόεις βρόμος αὐλῶν.

533. ὑπ'... ἀκούων: tmesis. Cf. Sapph. 31.3–4 πλάσιον ἆδυ
φωνείσας ὑπακούει.

534. Cf. *Margites* 1.3 Allen φίλην ἔχων ἐν χερσὶν εὔφθογγον
λύραν, Aristonous 1.15 (Powell *Coll. Alex.* p. 163)
εὐφθόγγου τε λύρας.

THEOGNIS 567–70

Lines reminiscent of Mimnermus, as 1069–70b.

567. ἥβῃ τερπόμενος: cf. *Od.* 23.212 ἥβης (gen.) ταρπῆναι.

569. φάος ἠελίοιο: cf. Praxilla 747.1 κάλλιστον μὲν ἐγὼ λείπω φάος
ἠελίοιο, Pi. *O.* 10.75 σελάνας ἐρατὸν φάος.

570. ὄψομαι οὐδέν: Hudson-Williams recalls the popular derivation of 'Αίδης from ἀ + ἰδεῖν.

THEOGNIS 667–82

For the metaphor of the ship of state cf. Alcaeus 326n. The
picture drawn by Theognis is not always clear, perhaps because
he adds the scene of looting and insubordination to that of the
storm. The Simonides to whom the poem is addressed may well
be the famous poet.

667. οἷά περ ἤδη: to be taken with the following words, 'I should
not be distressed as I am now.'

668. ἀνιώμην: for ῑ cf. *Od.* 15.335.

669. 'Now (my) money recognises me but passes me by, cuts me':
we must supply χρήματα as subject of παρέρχεται. I have
translated γινώσκοντα as nomin. neut. plural, but it may
be acc. masc. sing. as at 419 πολλά με καὶ συνιέντα παρέρχεται. With παρέρχεται cf. 579 πάρειμι, 1285 παρελεύσεαι.
ἄφωνος: cf. 178–9.

670. γνοὺς ἄρ': 'although it appears after all that I have realised
better than most'.

671. οὔνεκα: used to introduce indirect speech, as with οἶδα, *Od.*
5.215–16, with ἔγνω, *h. Ap.* 375–6.
ἱστία λευκά: so e.g. at *Il.* 1.480, *Od.* 9.77.

672. Μηλίου ἐκ πόντου: presumably the open sea south of Melos.
Cf. Hdt. 6.96 ἐκ τοῦ Ἰκαρίου πελάγεος. For a specific
geographical reference in a nautical metaphor cf. Archil.
56.2.
νύκτα διὰ δνοφερήν: line-beginning at *Od.* 15.50.

673. ἀντλεῖν: cf. ἄντλος in Alcaeus' metaphor, 326.6.
οὐκ ἐθέλουσιν: sc. the crew.
ὑπερβάλλει: usually with acc., e.g. Hdt. 2.111.1 ὑπερέβαλε
τὰς ἀρούρας, but cf. E. *Ion* 1321 θριγκοῦ τοῦδ' ὑπερβάλλω
πόδα. Cf. too *Il.* 15.381–2 ὥς τε μέγα κῦμα θαλάσσης ... | νηὸς
ὑπὲρ τοίχων καταβήσεται, Theoc. 22.10 ff.

675. ἔρδουσιν: 'are acting'. Theognis uses the verb absolutely at
685, 741.
ἔπαυσαν: aorist with perfect sense: cf. 67n.

677. χρήματα: part of the metaphor, which continues till 680, so
presumably 'cargo'; but it clearly recalls χρήματα of 667.
κόσμος: 'order, discipline'.

678. δασμός: the sense is uncertain: perhaps 'division of power'
(cf. Hes. *Th.* 425, *h. Cer.* 86) or 'division of rations'. In *Il.*
1.166 it means 'division of spoils'.
ἐς τὸ μέσον: 'fairly', perhaps 'openly'. Cf. *Il.* 23.574 ἐς μέσον
ἀμφοτέροισι δικάσσατε.

679. φορτηγοί: the context suggests 'porters', the most menial
deckhands, though the word elsewhere means 'merchants'.

681. ἠνίχθω κεκρυμμένα: cf. Pi. *O.* 2.83 ff: Pindar has arrows
φωνᾶντα συνετοῖσιν· ἐς δὲ τὸ πᾶν ἑρμηνέων | χατίζει.

682. κακός: the reading of most editors. If κακόν is kept, it is difficult to make sense of καί.

THEOGNIS 783–8

783. Cf. 915 εἶδον μὲν γὰρ ἔγωγ'.

Σικελήν: an adj. also in *Od.* 24.211 γυνὴ Σικελή.

784. Εὐβοίης ἀμπελόεν πεδίον: cf. Pi. *I.* 8.49–50 ἀμπελόεν ... πεδίον. Both important plains of Euboea were famous for their vines: cf. 892 Ληλάντου δ' ἀγαθὸν ... οἰνόπεδον, *Il.* 2.537 πολυστάφυλόν θ' Ἱστίαιαν. Sophocles fr. 234N² speaks of a spectacular Euboean vine which produced flowers in the morning, grapes in the afternoon, wine in the evening.

785. Εὐρώτα ... ἄστυ: cf. Pi. *O.* 13.61 ἄστει Πειράνας of Corinth.

δονακοτρόφου: for the reeds of the Eurotas cf. E. *I.A.* 179 Εὐρώτα δονακοτρόφου, *Hel.* 210, 349, 493, *I.T.* 399, Corinna 684 Λάδοντος δονακοτρόφω.

786. ἐφίλευν: 'entertained, treated hospitably': cf. *Od.* 1.123–4 χαῖρε, ξεῖνε· παρ' ἄμμι φιλήσεαι· αὐτὰρ ἔπειτα | δείπνου πασσάμενος μυθήσεαι κτλ., Pi.*P.* 2.16 προφρόνως ἐφίλασε, 10.66.

787. τέρψις ... ἐκείνων: cf. Hes. *Th.* 917 τέρψις ἀοιδῆς, Pi. *P.* 9.19 δείπνων ... τέρψιας.

788. Cf. Odysseus on the attempts of Calypso and Circe to detain him, ὣς οὐδὲν γλύκιον ἧς πατρίδος οὐδὲ τοκήων | γίγνεται κτλ., *Od.* 9.34 ff, E. fr. 6N² τί γὰρ πατρῴας ἀνδρὶ φίλτερον χθονός;

THEOGNIS 1069–70b

Often taken as two separate couplets. 1070a–b occur, with ἥβα μοι for τέρπεό μοι, at 877–8, where they probably form the beginning of an eight-line poem. The lines have the melancholy of Mimnermus: cf. 567–70.

1069. ἄφρονες ἄνθρωποι καὶ νήπιοι: so at 1039.

1070. ἥβης ἄνθος ἀπολλύμενον: cf. 1131 ἀλλ' ἥβην ἐρατὴν ὀλοφύρομαι, ἥ μ' ἐπιλείπει. 'The flower of youth', found at *Il.* 13.484 καὶ δ' ἔχει ἥβης ἄνθος, ὅ τε κράτος ἐστὶ μέγιστον, is a favourite expression of Theognis: cf. 1007–8 ἥβης | ἀγλαὸν

ἄνθος ἔχων, 1018 ἄνθος ὁμηλικίης, 1305 παιδείας πολυηράτου
ἄνθος, 1348 παιδείης ἄνθος ἔχοντ' ἐρατόν, 994 παῖς καλὸν
ἄνθος ἔχων, and in earlier elegiacs Tyrt. 7.28 ἐρατῆς ἥβης
ἀγλαὸν ἄνθος ἔχῃ, Sol. 12.1 ἥβης ἐρατοῖσιν ἐπ' ἄνθεσι.
Mimnermus 1.4, 2.3 has a similar but different metaphor. J. M. Aitchison, 'Homeric ἄνθος', Glotta XLI
(1963) 271–8, suggests that in Homer ἥβης ἄνθος may
refer to the growing beard, and show an original
meaning of ἄνθος, 'growth'. But the sequel at Il. 13.484
shows that ἥβης ἄνθος is merely a periphrasis for ἥβη,
'youth', and at Od. 11.319–20 down is explicitly men-
tioned: πρίν σφωϊν ὑπὸ κροτάφοισιν ἰούλους | ἀνθῆσαι.
If the original sense was 'growth', it was lost early:
h. Cer. 108 has κουρήϊον ἄνθος ἔχουσαι of girls, and
Tyrtaeus was not thinking of the sprouting beard when
he wrote ἥβης ἀγλαὸν ἄνθος. See also 1200n. and W. B.
Stanford, Greek Metaphor 111–14.

1070a. μοι: 'ethic' dative, 'I say'.

   φίλε θυμέ: cf. 213n.

1070b. ἄνδρες: the emphatic position makes it clear that ἄνδρες
   is predicative and so parallel to γαῖα μέλαινα. On γαῖα
   μέλαινα see Archil. 58.2n.

THEOGNIS 1101–4

Harrison joined these couplets: if they are not linked, the first
is a piece of flotsam and we must posit a lacuna after it. 1101–2
recur in exactly the same words at 1278a–b: there too they are
probably to be joined with the following couplet.

1103. ὕβρις: cf. 541 δειμαίνω μὴ τήνδε πόλιν . . . ὕβρις (sc. ὀλέσῃ).

   Μάγνητας κτλ.: Colophon was captured by Gyges in the
   early years of his reign, i.e. at the beginning of the 7th
   century (Hdt. 1.14.4); Magnesia too fell to Gyges (Nic.
   Dam. fr. 62) and in the middle of the century to the
   Cimmerians (cf. Archil. 19 τὰ Μαγνήτων κακά, Thgn.
   603–4 τοιάδε καὶ Μάγνητας ἀπώλεσεν ἔργα καὶ ὕβρις | οἷα
   τὰ νῦν ἱερὴν τήνδε πόλιν κατέχει); Smyrna fell to Alyattes'
   attack at the very end of the century (Hdt. 1.16.2:
   cf. introduction to Mimnermus).

1104. πάντως: cf. Sol. 1.8n.

   ὔμμε: you and your new-found friend.

THEOGNIS 1197–1202

   Hesiod *Op.* 448–51 was doubtless in Theognis' mind: φράζεσθαι
δ', εὖτ' ἂν γεράνου (crane) φωνὴν ἐπακούσῃς | ὑψόθεν ἐκ νεφέων
ἐνιαύσια κεκληγυίης· | ἥτ' ἀρότοιό τε σῆμα φέρει καὶ χείματος ὤρην |
δεικνύει ὀμβρηροῦ· κραδίην δ' ἔδακ' ἀνδρὸς ἀβούτεω (without oxen).
But Theognis' poem springs from his own unhappy experience,
and shows how a poet might use the work of a predecessor and
produce something fresh and individual from it: cf. Alcaeus 347
for a similar lyrical handling of a passage from Hesiod *Op.*

1197. ὄρνιθος: the crane: cf. Hes. *Op.* 448, Ar. *Av.* 710 σπείρειν
      μέν, ὅταν γέρανος κρώζουσ' ἐς τὴν Λιβύην μεταχωρῇ,
      Theoc. 10.30–1 ὁ λύκος τὰν αἶγα διώκει, | ἁ γέρανος
      τὤροτρον. The crane's autumn migration to Africa (ἐς
      τὴν Λιβύην) is meant.

      ὀξὺ βοώσης: cf. *Il.* 17.89 ὀξὺ βοήσας, a line-ending.

1198. ἀρότου | ὡραίου: cf. Hes. *Op.* 616–17 ἀρότου . . . | ὡραίου.

1199. κραδίην . . . μέλαιναν: cf. *Il.* 1.103 φρένες ἀμφὶ μέλαιναι,
      where as here anger is the dominant emotion. Fear and
      distress may also be denoted: cf. A. *Pers.* 115, *Cho.* 413,
      Suppl. 785. At Pi. fr. 131.4 Turyn μέλαιναν καρδίαν is
      rather an 'insensitive' heart.

      ἐπάταξε: intrans. at *Il.* 13.282 ἐν δέ τε οἱ κραδίη μεγάλα
      στέρνοισι πατάσσει.

1200. εὐανθεῖς . . . ἀγρούς: 'fields rich in flowers', when
      ploughing is in Theognis' mind? εὐανθής may show an
      older meaning of ἄνθος, 'growth', as at *Od.* 11.320
      πυκάσαι . . . γένυς εὐανθέϊ λάχνῃ, 14.353 πολυανθέος ὕλης:
      see J. M. Aitchison, 'Homeric ἄνθος', *Glotta* XLI
      (1963), 271–8. On the other hand Theognis' epithet may
      be purely decorative, or it may be an echo of Homer's
      λειμῶν' ἀνθεμόεντα (*Od.* 12.159: cf. *Il.* 2.467).

1201. κυφόν: 'curving'. -ον is lengthened in arsis at the caesura.

1202. *locus nondum sanatus.* ναυτιλίης may well be Theognis'
      journey into exile, but there are poor grounds for taking
      ἄλλης as 'bad', though μνηστῆς, 'memorable', is sup-

ported by ἀείμνηστον in A. *Pers.* 760 of a catastrophe
never to be forgotten, *Ag.* 1459 πολύμναστον ... αἷμα.
For the fem. termination cf. *Od.* 4.770 πολυμνήστη,
'much-wooed', Empedocles 3.3 D.-K. πολυμνήστη ...
Μοῦσα.

HIPPONAX

The entry in the *Suda* (Adler ii. p. 665) runs: 'Hipponax, son of
Pythes and Protis, of Ephesus, iambic writer. He lived in
Clazomenae, after being driven out by the tyrants Athenagoras
and Comas. In his writings he attacks the sculptors Bupalus and
Athenis, because they made insulting statues of him.' Pliny (*N.H.*
36.5) tells us that Bupalus and Athenis were sons of a Chian
sculptor, Achermus, and gives the story of their caricature of
Hipponax (for whom he gives the date Ol. 60 = 540–37), together
with the report that Hipponax' attacks drove them to suicide.
(The same efficacy was credited to Archilochus' iambics.) Pliny's
date, given also by the Parian Marble, is confirmed by the
inscription of the name Achermus on a base from Delos which is
dated *c.* 550. We may safely place Hipponax' work in the second
half of the 6th century.

The remains of his poetry tantalize either by their brevity or by
their gappiness. The longest piece, one of a dozen Oxyrhynchus
papyrus fragments published in 1941, has parts of over 50
choliambics. His language is Ionian with a small admixture of
Lydian and Phrygian words which may have been current in the
Ionian cities where he lived. Most of his fragments are in the
choliambic metre, but he wrote epodes of mixed rhythms (even if
the Strasbourg epodes are not his: see Archilochus 79a), and we
have a few hexameters and tetrameters.

Almost all his poetry, so far as we can say, dealt with affairs of
his private life — his enmities above all, his amatory adventures,
his poverty. Politics are absent; epic themes are rare and usually
treated in burlesque style, γνῶμαι rarer still. He seems deliberately

to have lowered the tone of poetry: his use of colloquial Ionian language with its admixture of oriental words, his fondness for choliambic metres, which dislocate iambic or trochaic lines with a jarring syncopation, and his avoidance of epic and political themes in favour of everyday affairs, often sleazy or disreputable, all point to a new conception of the poet's function.

Although Bupalus was not his only target, it was invectives against him that particularly impressed antiquity: cf. Callimachus *Iamb*. I.191.3–4 Pfeiffer μάχην . . . τὴν Βουπάλειον, Horace *Epod.* 6.14 *acer hostis Bupalo*. The offending statues may have been representations of 'the type of an ugly man' rather than realistic portraiture, since caricature at so early a date is improbable: see G. M. Richter, *Portraits of the Greeks* i.30–1. Our fragments suggest that jealousy over Bupalus' girl-friend Arete accounted to some extent for Hipponax' hostility.

Hipponax was a favourite of the Alexandrians, who edited his works in two or perhaps three books. Callimachus and Herodas used the choliambic metre, Lycophron helped himself to the rare words.

Hipponax is edited by A. D. Knox in the Loeb Classical Library (in the same volume as *The Characters of Theophrastus*). There are good editions by Olivier Masson, *Les fragments du poète Hipponax*, Paris, 1962 and W. de S. Medeiros, *Hipónax de Éfeso*, I, *Fragmentos dos Iambos*, Coimbra, 1961. There is a study of his language in Joshua Whatmough, *Poetic, Scientific and Other Forms of Discourse*, Berkeley and Los Angeles, 1956, pp. 69–82.

HIPPONAX 24a and 24b

Tzetzes on Lycophron 855 quotes 24a.1 and 3–5 together with fr. 25 to illustrate the word ἀσκέραι. 24a.1–2 are used by Heliodorus in Priscian III p. 428 Keil as evidence that Hipponax mixed pure iambics with his choliambics. 24b.1–2 are from Plutarch, *absurd. Stoic. opin.* 6 p. 1058e, 24b.1 also at p. 523e and p. 1068b. 24a, 24b, 25 and 29 may all have belonged to the same poem.

Metre: choliambic (or scazon: the limping iambic), an iambic trimeter in which the second-last syllable is long. 24a.1 is a pure iambic line.

24a.1. Μαιαδεῦ: the form occurs only here and perhaps at IV.14 Μαια]δεύς. Hermes' mother was Maia.

Κυλλήνιε: a pure iambic line in a choliambic sequence occurs also at 29.4 φρένας, 39.1, IX.11 ῥύδην.

3–4. κυπασσίσκον, σαμβαλίσκα, ἀσκερίσκα are diminutives, colloquially or perhaps here depreciatingly used, of κύπασσις ('tunic'), σάμβαλα ('sandals'), ἀσκέραι ('winter shoes'). All three words may be oriental.

5. τουτέρου τοίχου: a puzzling expression; perhaps 'belonging to the other, i.e. the lucky, side'. There may be a naval metaphor, τοῖχος being the side of the ship: cf. Ar. Ran. 536 μετακυλίνδειν αὑτὸν ἀεὶ πρὸς τὸν εὖ πράττοντα τοῖχον, E. fr. 89N² ἐς τὸν εὐτυχῆ | χωροῦντα τοῖχον.

24b.2. βαμβαλύζω: cf. Hsch. βαμβαλύζει· τρέμει. τοὺς ὀδόντας συγκρούει. ῥιγοῖ σφόδρα. Homer has βαμβαίνω in the same sense (Il. 10.375). Cf. P. Oxy. 2317.4 (probably by Archilochus)]εβαμβάλυζε.

HIPPONAX 25

Quoted by Tzetzes: see note on 24a and 24b.

Metre: choliambic.

4. χίμετλα: 'chilblains.' Probably cognate with χεῖμα, 'wintry weather'.

HIPPONAX 29

Quoted by Tzetzes on Ar. Pl. 90 with the comment that Ar. got the idea of Plutus' blindness from Hipponax.

Metre: choliambic.

4. δείλαιος γὰρ τὰς φρένας: he is feeble-minded. If the reading is correct, we have αι in δείλαιος and a pure iambic among choliambics: see 24a.1n.

HIPPONAX 70

The lines are cited separately, the first by the Suda s.vv. Βούπαλος and κόπτω, the second for the sake of the word ἀμφιδέξιος by Erotianus p. 15 Nachmanson and Galen Hipp. Aphor. p. 148 Kuhn and Glossar. Hippocr. p. 430. Bergk united them. Ar. alludes to the lines in Lys. 360–1.

376 GREEK LYRIC POETRY

Metre: trochaic tetrameter catalectic scazon, i.e. troch. tetr. cat. with the second-last syllable long.

HIPPONAX 77

Ath. 15. 698b–c: 'Polemo *contra Timaeum* XII on the subject of parody writes as follows: Hipponax, the iambic writer, must be declared the inventor of the genre, for he says in his hexameters Μοῦσά μοι . . . ἀτρυγέτοιο.'

Metre: dactylic hexameter. Note Εὐρυμεδοντιάδεα, -εα scanned long.

1–3. Hippon. uses *Od.* 1.1 ἄνδρα μοι ἔννεπε, Μοῦσα and *Il.* 1.1 with its patronymic Πηληιάδεω.

1. We cannot identify 'the child of Eurymedon'.

   ποντοχάρυβδιν: presumably 'the sea-swallower', who could drain the sea dry: cf. Ar. *Eq.* 248 Χάρυβδιν ἁρπαγῆς.

2. ἐγγαστριμάχαιραν: 'belly-knife': perhaps the knife in his belly accelerates the digestive processes. Neither of the comic compounds has the happiness of Aristophanes' creations.

   οὐ κατὰ κόσμον: line-ending at *Od.* 20.181. All four of Hippon.'s endings can be paralleled in Homer: *Od.* 12.113 Χάρυβδιν, *Il.* 3.417 κακὸν οἶτον ὄληαι, *Il.* 1.316 παρὰ θῖν' ἁλὸς ἀτρυγέτοιο.

3. ψηφῖδι: by stoning, as a φαρμακός or scapegoat. φαρμακοί are mentioned several times in Hippon.: see frr. 6–11.

   ὄληται has the force of a future indicative. οἶτον is internal accus. with ὄληται.

HIPPONAX [81]

This iambic piece is attributed to Hipponax by Stobaeus 4.22 (περὶ γάμου). 123, but belongs almost certainly to the 5th or 4th century, perhaps to New Comedy: cf. e.g. Men. *Mon.* 148 Jäkel γυναικὶ κόσμος ὁ τρόπος, οὐ τὰ χρυσία. The two other pieces credited to Hipponax by Stobaeus are also of uncertain authorship; one is the couplet which follows.

4. †τρυφῶς†: unless a compliment is concealed by the corruption in the text, we must posit a lacuna after this line. Knox suggests ἀτρύφερον, 'plain'.

Fragmentum Choliambicum Adespoton 1

Like the last piece, this is attributed to Hipponax by Stobaeus 4.22 (περὶ γάμου). 35. The lines occur also in a Berlin anthology (*P. Berol.* 9773), which gives the author's name as [. . .]λυ[. .]ς.

SIMONIDES

Although Simonides was an internationally famous figure and his long life extended well into the 5th century, his biography can be given only tentatively and in barest outline. He was born in 556 in Iulis, the main town of the Ionian island of Ceos, which lies some fifteen miles to the south-east of Attica. The date of his birth is established by fr. 77D., a dedicatory epigram, which, whether authentic or not, shows that he was 80 in the archonship of Adeimantus, 477/6 B.C.: the *Suda* gives Ol.56 (556–3) for the date of his birth, the Parian Marble implies 558.

Ceos was famous for its boys' choirs which sang hymns in Apollo's honour on Ceos and Delos, and it is likely that Simonides' interest in choral singing was due to these festivals. He must already have made his mark as a composer when, like Anacreon, he was summoned to Athens by the tyrant Hipparchus (527–514) and persuaded to remain at his court by generous fees and gifts ('Plato' *Hipparchus* 228c). If there is any substance in Aristophanes' joke at *Vesp.* 1410–12, he defeated Lasus of Hermione in the contest for dithyrambs: the victory must belong to this period of his life. (Lasus's comment was ὀλίγον μοι μέλει.)

Simonides spent some part of his life with the Aleuadae and Scopadae, the royal families of Thessaly, and it is usual and convenient to date this episode between the death of Hipparchus and the Persian Wars; for information about these rulers of Thessaly see Gow on Theocritus 16.34 ff, J. S. Morrison, *C.Q.* 36 (1942), 59–61. That Simonides commemorated their victories in the games is shown by Theocritus l.c.; the famous poem on excellence (542) was addressed to Scopas, and he also wrote a dirge (528) on the death of Antiochus, son of the Echecratidas and

Dyseris for whom Anacreon wrote epigrams (107, 108D.). When the banquet-hall of the Scopadae collapsed and killed the entire household, Simonides was saved, so the story went, only by the agency of the Dioscuri; the story is told with amusing elaboration by Cicero *de orat.* 2.86, Quintilian *Inst. Or.* 11.2.11 (*P.M.G.* 510: see introd. to 521). Simonides wrote a dirge on the catastrophe. His epinician ode or odes in honour of Eualcidas, the Eretrian commander killed by the Persians in the Ionian Revolt, must have been written before 499 (Hdt. 5.102.3).

Simonides was probably in Athens at the time of the Persian Wars. The story goes that after the battle of Marathon he and Aeschylus submitted epitaphs for the Athenian dead and his was preferred (*Vit. Aes.* 8), and it has been claimed that fragments of both epitaphs survive on the base of a stele found in the agora of Athens (James H. Oliver, *Hesperia* 2 (1933), 480–94, *A.J.P.* 56 (1935), 193–201). But the account of the competition between the two poets should surely be dismissed, if not as an old wives' tale, at least as the fabrication of comedy — Aeschylus, the story continues (*Vit. Aes.* 8), went off to Sicily in a fit of the sulks; for a different view of the inscription see F. Jacoby, *Hesperia* 14 (1945), 161–85. After Xerxes' invasion Simonides was invited to compose poems in honour of those who died at Thermopylae, Artemisium, Salamis and Plataea: epitaphs for Athenians, Spartans and Corinthians, poems on Artemisium and Salamis, a commemorative song for Leonidas and his Spartans and a dedicatory epigram for the Spartan king Pausanias are all known. In Athens Simonides was the friend of the great Themistocles (whose recorded remarks on him are not without asperity: Plu. *Them.* 5), of Megacles and Callias (see 84D.) and of Theognis (see Thgn. 667–82n.).

The last years of his life were spent in Sicily, where he was the friend of Hiero, tyrant of Syracuse. He is said to have prevented war between Hiero and Thero of Acragas. Simonides' nephew, Bacchylides, and Pindar were also in Sicily at this time, and Pindar's reference to the pair of fools chattering ineffectually like ravens against the holy bird of Zeus — himself — can only be intended as an insult to his rivals, Simonides and Bacchylides (*O.* 2.83–9 and schol.). Simonides died in 468 and was buried in Acragas.

He wrote a wide range of choral and elegiac poetry, the former in Ionic with Doric flavouring, the latter in Ionic. Almost all of it was for public performance or public inscription, very little for the entertainment of his own circle of intimates. 'With Simonides the age of individualism in lyric poetry has passed' (Weir Smyth 301).

He was perhaps the first to write epinician odes, and the Alexandrians arranged these according to the events in which the victories were won, not, as in Pindar's case, according to the venue. We know of poems for winners in sprinting, wrestling, the pentathlon, boxing, riding, chariot-racing and mule-racing. The surviving scraps give little idea of his methods of composition: of the boxer Glaucus of Carystus he wrote οὐδὲ Πολυδεύκεος βία | χεῖρας ἀντείναιτό κ' ἐναντίον αὐτῷ, | οὐδὲ σιδάρεον 'Αλκμάνας τέκος, 'neither the mighty Polydeuces nor Alcmene's iron son would have raised his hands to fight him' (509). Indeed it was said of one of his poems on victorious boxers that he had so much to say of the Dioscuri that Scopas, who commissioned the poem, cut the fee by half: Castor and Polydeuces, he said, would pay the rest. (They did so by saving his life when the palace roof collapsed.) Mules he dignified in the line χαίρετ' ἀελλοπόδων θύγατρες ἵππων (515), but only after his reluctance to sing the praises of a mule-race-winner had been overcome by an increase in his fee. His avarice was the subject of many anecdotes, doubtless because he was the first poet to charge fees for his services; he was generous enough to pay for the inscription of his friend Megistias' epitaph (83D.).

His θρῆνοι, 'dirges', are known to us from several short fragments, notably 520 and 521, and we hear also of his paeans (519 fr. 35), prayers (κατευχαί; perhaps 'curses'; the nature of the work is obscure: 537, 538), and lyric poems on the battles of Artemisium (532–535) and Salamis (536: this may however have been in elegiacs). His dithyrambs were particularly successful: fr. 79D. records fifty-six victories in dithyrambic contests. Strabo 15.3.2 (=P.M.G. 539) mentions a dithyramb Memnon, in which Simonides set Memnon's burial-place in Syria: this suggests that he did not deal exclusively with legends of Dionysus in his dithyrambs, but used other heroic material (see A. W. Pickard-

Cambridge, *D.T.C.* 15–17 and for the dirges, paeans and dithyrambs A. E. Harvey, *C.Q.* n.s. 5 (1955), 168–74). The *Suda*
mentions that he wrote tragedies also (so schol. Ar. *Vesp.* 1410),
but we know nothing of them. In his fragments there are references to the Argonauts, Meleager and other heroes of epic, but
we cannot say to which genre of lyric they belong.

It is seldom possible to distinguish the authentic from the
spurious among the many short poems in elegiac couplets which
have been handed down under his name. He was known as the
writer of epitaphs on those who died in the Persian Wars, and
consequently many others were attributed to him, as wise saws to
Confucius or musical anecdotes to Beecham. But the author's
name was not added to epitaphs or dedications until the late 5th
century — the first known example is the name of Ion of Samos
on a stone of 404 B.C. — and unless there is good external
authority, as in the case of the epitaph for Megistias (83D.),
ascription of the 'Simonidean' epigrams must always be insecure.
Besides, it goes without saying that Simonides was not the only
writer of epigrams: the epitaph for the Thespians who died in the
Persian Wars was the work of one Philiadas of Megara (Steph.
Byz. s.v. Θέσπεια), and there must have been others whose names
are lost. We must remember too that Simonides was in no sense
the earliest writer of fine sepulchral epigrams: excellent examples
are known from the mid-6th century and perhaps even earlier
times, e.g. Friedländer *Epigrammata* 135, set up in Attica *c.* 550
B.C.:

> [εἴτ' ἀστό]ς τις ἀνὴρ εἴτε ξένος ἄλ(λ)οθεν ἐλθών
> Τέτ(τ)ιχον οἰκτίρας ἄνδρ' ἀγαθὸν παρίτω
> ἐν πολέμωι φθίμενον, νεαρὰν ἥβην ὀλέσαντα·
> ταῦτ' ἀποδυράμενοι νεῖσθε ἐπὶ πρᾶγμ' ἀγαθόν.

The sayings attributed to Simonides in later times are as
apocryphal as the elegiac poems. The most famous are πόλις
ἄνδρα διδάσκει (53D.), 'painting is silent poetry, poetry painting
that speaks' (τὴν μὲν ζωγραφίαν ποίησιν σιωπῶσαν προσαγορεύει,
τὴν δὲ ποίησιν ζωγραφίαν λαλοῦσαν, Plu. *Glor. Ath.* 3) and 'the
word is image of the thing' (ὁ λόγος τῶν πραγμάτων εἰκών ἐστιν,

Mich. Psell., 821 Migne). Simonides was accredited with the invention of the letters η, ω, ξ and ψ, and with a system of mnemonics based on the correct ordering of concepts and the association of the unfamiliar with the familiar; on which Themistocles observed that an Art of Forgetfulness would have been better, 'for I remember what I would rather not remember, and cannot forget what I would rather forget' (Cic. *de Fin.* 2.32).

Ancient critics, doubtless with the dirges and epitaphs in mind, noted the pathos of Simonides' poetry: he had 'the simplicity needed to arouse sympathy', ἡ περὶ τὸ συμπαθὲς λεπτότης, which Aeschylus' elegiacs lacked (*Vit. Aes.* 5); Dionysius of Halicarnassus (*Vet. Script.* 420 Reiske) considered that he excelled Pindar in the expression of pity, since he did not write grandiloquently like Pindar but rather stirred the emotions (μὴ μεγαλοπρεπῶς ... ἀλλὰ παθητικῶς); so Quintilian 10.1.64 finds his special virtue *in commovenda miseratione*. Both writers mention his skilful choice of words, and Quintilian reluctantly grants him also 'a certain sweetness' (*Simonides, tenuis alioqui, sermone proprio et iucunditate quadam commendari potest*). Catullus asked a friend for a scrap of sympathy 'sadder than the tears of Simonides' (38.8 *maestius lacrimis Simonideis*); Horace described solemn themes as *Ceae ... munera neniae* (*Od.* 2.1.38).

Simonides displays great clarity and simplicity in expression. He makes telling use of short clauses, notably in 520, 531, 542 (26, 29–30, 37–8), 581, sometimes balancing them by the use of μέν ... δέ (520, 531). He has none of Pindar's splendid imagery or allusive style, but relies rather on straightforward statement. His narrative poetry, however, if 543 is typical, was written in richer language and more elaborate style than the rest. Analysis of 581, which is almost certainly complete, shows a most satisfying structure: the erroneous view of Cleobulus is stated in one long sentence, modelled on Cleobulus' lines, while the truth of the matter, as Simonides sees it, is expressed in three short staccato sentences. It is noteworthy that although so little of his lyric poetry survives, we should be able to point to several occasions on which he mentions his predecessors, either to disagree with them, as with Cleobulus in 581, Pittacus in 542, or to agree, as with Homer and Stesichorus in 564 (4 οὕτω γὰρ Ὅμηρος ἠδὲ Στασίχορος ἄεισε λαοῖς); in 579 he elaborates a passage of Hesiod (*Op.* 289 ff).

See Wilamowitz, *Sappho und Simonides* (1913); M. Boas, *De Epigrammatis Simonideis* (1905); Paul Friedländer with Herbert B. Hoffleit, *Epigrammata*: Greek Inscriptions in Verse from the Beginnings to the Persian Wars (1948); Werner Peek, *Griechische Vers-Inschriften*, Band I, Grab-Epigramme (1955); H. T. Wade-Gery, 'Classical Epigrams and Epitaphs', *J.H.S.* 53 (1933), 71–104; F. Jacoby, 'Some Athenian Epigrams from the Persian Wars', *Hesperia* 14 (1945), 157–211, W. J. H. F. Kegel, *Simonides* (1962).

SIMONIDES 520

From Plutarch, *consol. Apoll.* 11: 'death is better than life: ὁ γοῦν Σιμωνίδης ἀνθρώπων, φησίν, ὀλίγον ... κακός.' The lines almost certainly belong to a dirge. Simonides writes with the pessimism of Semonides or Mimnermus.

Metre: difficult to classify: 2 and 3 are clearly dactylo-epitrite (e–D), 4 and 5 just recognisable as dactylo-epitrite. Maas' notation does not cover 1, a 'pherecratean'.

2. ἄπρακτοι δὲ μεληδόνες: 'their sorrows are incurable' or, more probably, 'their aims are unattainable.'

3. αἰῶνι δ' ἐν παύρῳ: 'within their brief lifetime'.

πόνος ἀμφὶ πόνῳ: 'toil upon toil', a unique sense for ἀμφί. Cf. S. *Aj.* 866 πόνος πόνῳ πόνον φέρει. Semon. 3.2 makes the same point: ζῶμεν δ' ἀριθμῷ παῦρα ⟨παγ⟩κάκως ἔτεα.

4. ὁμῶς ἐπικρέμαται: i.e. hangs over all alike: cf. *Il.* 9.319–20 ἐν δὲ ἰῇ τιμῇ ἠμὲν κακὸς ἠδὲ καὶ ἐσθλός· | κάτθαν' ὁμῶς ὅ τ' ἀεργὸς ἀνὴρ ὅ τε πολλὰ ἐοργώς. Simonides expresses the same thought in 522 πάντα γὰρ μίαν ἱκνεῖται δασπλῆτα Χάρυβδιν, | αἱ μεγάλαι τ' ἀρεταὶ καὶ ὁ πλοῦτος and in 524 ὁ δ' αὖ θάνατος κίχε καὶ τὸν φυγόμαχον, both possibly extracts from dirges. For the metaphor in ἐπικρέμαται cf. Thgn. 206 ἄτην ... παισὶν ἐπεκρέμασεν, Mimn. 5.3 γῆρας ὑπὲρ κεφαλῆς ... ὑπερκρέμαται.

SIMONIDES 521

From Stobaeus 4.41 (ὅτι ἀβέβαιος ἡ τῶν ἀνθρώπων εὐπραξία μεταπιπτούσης ῥᾳδίως τῆς τύχης). 9, with the heading Σιμωνίδου

Θρήνων. Lines 1–2 recur in the same chapter (4.41.62) with
Favorinus' comment, which begins, 'Not even a house (will last):
for example, the poet tells of the utter destruction of the Scopads.'
We cannot say whether Favorinus is referring to the present
poem. 3 is quoted in *P. Oxy.* 1087 col. i 30 in a commentary on
Homer. Horace *Od.* 1.9.13 alludes to line 1: *quid sit futurum cras
fuge quaerere.*

Metre: a free aeolic rhythm with prominent choriambs and
choriambs with dactylic expansion giving – ∪ ∪ – ∪ ∪ – (hemiepes)
and – ∪ ∪ – ∪ ∪ – ∪ ∪ –. See A. M. Dale, *C.Q.* n.s. 1 (1951), 121.

1. ὅ τι γίνεται αὔριον: 'what is destined to happen tomorrow';
   γίνεται resembles the oracular present, for which see
   Kühner-Gerth i.138. In some other passage Simon. called
   Αὔριον a god, according to the orator Menander (see
   P.M.G. 615).

3. τανυπτερύγου: also at Alcm. 89.6.

4. μετάστασις: 'even a long-winged fly does not change its
   position so swiftly' as the circumstances of the prosperous
   man change. The noun fits both the movement of the
   dragonfly and the change from prosperity to adversity.
   The meaning 'death' (cf. L.S.J. s.v.) is less probable here.
   Simon. expresses the same idea in 527 οὐκ ἔστιν κακὸν |
   ἀνεπιδόκητον ἀνθρώποις· ὀλίγῳ δὲ χρόνῳ | πάντα μεταρρίπτει
   θεός.

SIMONIDES 531

Quoted by Diodorus 11.11.6 and Arsenius p. 342 Walz.
Diodorus calls it an 'encomium' written by Simonides for those
who died at Thermopylae, but he can hardly be using the term
in its technical sense. It is probably a hymn sung at a Spartan
ceremony in honour of the dead. Pausanias 3.14.1 says that at the
tombs of Pausanias, the general at Plataea, and Leonidas, whose
bones were taken from Thermopylae to Sparta in 440, speeches
were delivered and contests held annually; he mentions also a
shrine of Maron and Alpheus, whose bravery at Thermopylae
was second only to that of Leonidas (3.12.9: cf. Hdt. 7.227). The
present poem suggests a commemoration of all the dead in a
sacred place (6 ὅδε σηκός) with an altar (3 βωμός).

o

384 GREEK LYRIC POETRY

Metre: perhaps best regarded as aeolic. For a detailed analysis see A. M. Dale, *C.Q.* n.s. 1 (1951), 119–20.

1. ἐν Θερμοπύλαις: the words show that the poem is being performed not at Thermopylae but at Sparta.

2–3. Note the short clauses, the extreme compression and the variation in the order of subject and predicate — the predicate comes first thrice, then second twice.

τύχα: not the same as πότμος ('doom', i.e. death), but 'the chance' that was theirs at Thermopylae to win κλέος.

βωμός κτλ.: 'for tomb they have an altar . . . for pity, praise.'
πρό: 'instead of' (= ἀντί), a very unusual meaning.

4. ἐντάφιον δὲ τοιοῦτον: ἐντάφιον, found here first, is used in the plural of funeral offerings at S. *El.* 326 and elsewhere, and the meaning 'such an offering (to the dead)' fits the present passage well. In later Greek it is used of winding-sheets (*A.P.* 11.125, anon.) or funeral expenses (Plu. *Arist.* 27). The singular occurs only in contexts like the present: Isoc. 6.44 καλὸν ἐντάφιον ἡ τυραννίς, 'it is a fine thing to die a tyrant', Plb. 15.10.3 κάλλιστον ἐντάφιον ἕξουσι τὸν ὑπὲρ τῆς πατρίδος θάνατον, Plu. *an seni resp. ger.* 1, where Plutarch quotes Simonides immediately afterwards (see *P.M.G.* 594), *A.P.* 9.294.

5. πανδαμάτωρ: in Homer of sleep (*Il.* 24.5, *Od.* 9.373); of time also in Bacchyl. 13.205.

6. οἰκέταν: a dweller, inhabitant: the shrine's inhabitant is the glory of Greece. For the formation of the word from οἰκέω see Buck and Petersen, *Reverse Index* 545. In Sparta the word had religious associations, Οἰκέτης being in particular a cult title of Apollo; a priest and priestess of Carnean Oecetes are known from inscriptions of imperial date (Καρνείου Βοικέτα, *I.G.* 5(1). 497, 589, 608), and Pausanias 3.13.4 says that the cult went back to pre-Dorian times.

7–9. The fact that Leonidas enjoys so fine a reputation is claimed as proof that the glory of Greece is the holy inmate of the shrine. Cf. Pi. *O.* 9.98–9 σύνδικος δ' αὐτῷ Ἰολάου | τύμβος . . . ἀγλαΐαισιν, 13.108 μαρτυρήσει Λυκαίου βωμὸς ἄναξ.
ἀέναόν τε κλέος: so Heraclitus fr. 29 D.-K. κλέος ἀέναον θνητῶν.

SIMONIDES 542

The poem is discussed in Plato *Protagoras* 339a–347a; it is not quoted in full, since Socrates assures Protagoras that there is no need: he knows and admires the poem and has studied it carefully. Only those portions of the poem are quoted which are considered relevant to the discussion; some passages are given only in paraphrase. The correct sequence of the extracts has been much discussed but is no longer in dispute, and the number of lines completely omitted is small. The poem is monostrophic and consists of four stanzas. Simonides addressed it to Scopas, son of Creon, the Thessalian (*Prot.* 339a); it may have been an encomium, but only lines 4–10 could make this clear. Much of the discussion in the *Protagoras* is of more value to the student of Plato than to the commentator on Simonides, and the unhelpful and frivolous interpretations are not reproduced here.

Parts of the poem are quoted by later writers (e.g. Diogenes Laertius 1.76), especially 3 τετράγωνον ἄνευ ψόγου τετυγμένον (e.g. Ar. *Eth. Nic.* 1.11.1100b.20, *Rhet.* 3.11.1411b.26) and 29–30 ἀνάγκᾳ δ᾽ οὐδὲ θεοὶ μάχονται (e.g. Pl. *Leg.* 7.818b); all these later quotations are probably taken from Plato's text and not directly from Simonides' collected works (Wilamowitz, *S.S.* 159 with n.2).

Simonides considers whether true goodness is possible: his answer is that man cannot be truly good since, unlike the gods, he is at the mercy of circumstances; Simonides reserves his praise and love for the man of his own will does nothing base, is not κακός and not too shiftless, and — the only positive standard among virtues of omission — observes the laws of the city, is a sound citizen. His sights are not set on the Homeric and aristocratic ideal: something more modest and attainable is adequate.

Metre: many of the features belong to aeolic verse: e.g. l. 5 of the stanza is glyconic and glyconics may be discerned in 2–4; 9 is pherecratean, and 1, 6, 7 also show choriambs. For detailed analysis see P. Maas, *Greek Metre*, tr. H. Lloyd-Jones, § 70, p. 50, D. L. Page, *J.H.S.* 71 (1951), 140. Note synizesis in 23 βαλέω, 24 εὐρυδέος, 30 θεοί, synecphonesis in 15 μὴ οὐ.

See Leonard Woodbury, 'Simonides on 'Ἀρετή', *T.A.P.A.* 84

(1953), 135–63, A. W. H. Adkins, *Merit and Responsibility* 165–8, 196–7, 355–9, (W. Donlan, *T.A.P.A.* 100 (1969), 71–95).

1–3. ἄνδρ' ἀγαθὸν μὲν κτλ.: 'it is hard for a man to become truly good, foursquare in hands, feet and mind, fashioned without blemish.' This is, of course, Simonides' own view, not advance notice of the dictum of Pittacus with which he disagrees: see 13n. μέν may have had an answering δέ in the lost lines 4–10: Simonides perhaps made a complimentary reference to the success Scopas had achieved in life.

χερσίν κτλ.: cf. *Il.* 15.641–3 υἱός ἀμείνων | παντοίας ἀρετάς, ἠμὲν πόδας ἠδὲ μάχεσθαι, | καὶ νόον ἐν πρώτοισι Μυκηναίων ἐτέτυκτο, Pi. *P.* 1.42 σοφοὶ καὶ χερσὶ βιαταὶ περίγλωσσοί τε, 10.23 χερσὶν ἢ ποδῶν ἀρετᾷ, *O.* 4.28–9 οὗτος ἐγὼ ταχυτᾶτι· | χεῖρες δὲ καὶ ἦτορ ἴσον, *I.* 8.41.

τετράγωνον: a Pythagorean usage: for the Pythagoreans the square was the image of divine being (Proclus on Euclid *Elem.* 48g) and their symbol for justice. Aristotle notes the metaphor: both the good man and the square are complete (τέλεια) (*Rhet.* 3.11.1411b.26: cf. *Eth. Nic.* 1.11.1100b.20).

ἄνευ ψόγου: like πανάμωμον (24) and Homer's ἀμύμων; cf. Semon. 4 πάμπαν δ' ἄμωμος οὔτις.

4–10. It is likely that only seven lines are omitted here: cf. *Prot.* 339d ὀλίγον δὲ τοῦ ποιήματος εἰς τὸ πρόσθεν προελθών, 344b ὀλίγα διελθών. The lines must have contained the address to Scopas, son of Creon, and were not mentioned in the *Protagoras* because their content was of no relevance.

11–12. οὐδέ μοι ἐμμελέως κτλ.: well paraphrased by Woodbury 140 n. 9, 'the maxim of Pittacus, although current coin, does not ring true in my ear.' With νέμεται cf. νομίζεται in its earliest sense, 'is observed as a custom, is current usage'. μοι goes with οὐδέ . . . ἐμμελέως, 'not harmoniously, in my view'. For Pittacus, ruler of Lesbos and one of the Seven Sages, see introd. to Alcaeus.

καίτοι: with the sense and construction of καίπερ: see Denniston *G.P.* 559.

13. χαλεπὸν φάτ' ἐσθλὸν ἔμμεναι: Protagoras caused a sensation by alleging that Simonides is inconsistent in that he now faults a saying of Pittacus when he had a moment earlier

said the same thing himself. The supposed inconsistency
has been disposed of in several ways, two of which deserve
mention: (1) Simonides begins his poem by quoting the
text of Pittacus (1–3) and refers it to its author only when
he reverts to it in 11–13 (see e.g. Bowra *G.L.P.* 327–8); but
neither Protagoras nor Socrates suggested that the words
could be taken in this way, although neither displayed any
lack of ingenuity in his exegesis of the text, and besides the
language of 11–12 strongly suggests that the saying of
Pittacus is here advanced for the first time: οὐδέ seems to
introduce a new point. (2) ἔμμεναι does not mean the
same thing as γενέσθαι. This must be the correct explanation: Simonides says that it is difficult for a man to *become*
truly ἀγαθός, i.e. by his own exertions, although he might
be ἀγαθός if his circumstances were favourable (17 πράξας
εὖ); the best are those whom the gods love (19–20).
'Becoming', not 'being', is within a man's capabilities, and
so only 'becoming' deserves praise or blame: when
Pittacus said, 'It is difficult for a man to *be* ἐσθλός', he
used the wrong verb in Simonides' view, since it is neither
difficult nor easy: it does not depend on the man's efforts
at all, but on the gods' will. Man *is* ἀγαθός or κακός if god
makes him so (14–18).

  If 541, a papyrus fragment, is correctly ascribed to
Simonides and correctly supplemented, Simonides there
says οὐ γὰρ ἐλαφρὸν ἐσθλ[ὸν ἔμμεναι (7). Our present
poem may have been written later, when Simonides had
decided to refine his terminology.

15. μὴ οὐ: after οὐκ ἔστι, 'it is impossible for a man not to be
    κακός.'

17. πράξας . . . εὖ: 'if he fares well', i.e. if the gods are good to him.

18–20. Simonides may have written something like καὶ | τοὐπὶ
    πλεῖστον ἄριστοι | τούς κε θεοὶ φιλέωσι. Cf. 526.1–2 οὔτις
    ἄνευ θεῶν | ἀρετὰν λάβεν, οὐ πόλις, οὐ βροτός.
    ἐπὶ πλεῖστον: 'for the most part'.

21. γενέσθαι: placed at the end of the line, it recalls the first line
    of the poem at the moment when the second half of the
    poem begins.

22. κενεάν: probably with ἐλπίδα rather than μοῖραν.

    ἄπρακτον: cf. 520.2 ἄπρακτοι δὲ μεληδόνες.

23. μοῖραν αἰῶνος: 'my allotted span': cf. Pi. *O.* 7.94 ἐν δὲ μιᾷ μοίρᾳ χρόνου, S. *Ant.* 896 μοῖραν . . . βίου.

24–5. εὐρυεδέος ὅσοι κτλ.: 'among all of us mortals who win the fruit of the broad-based earth': cf. *Il.* 6.142 εἰ δέ τίς ἐσσι βροτῶν οἳ ἀρούρης καρπὸν ἔδουσιν, *Od.* 8.222. The epic reminiscence may tinge the passage with sadness, or may prepare for the gentle mockery of the next line. εὐρυεδής is not found elsewhere: Homer has χθονὸς εὐρυοδείης (e.g. *Il.* 16.635), 'the earth of the broad ways'.

26. ὑμῖν: with general reference.

27. ἐπαίνημι: Socrates suggested that the Lesbian form in -ημι was directed at Pittacus (346d); but Hesiod used αἴνημι (*Op.* 683), and Pindar has αἴτημι (fr. 150 Turyn).

28. ἑκών: the distinction between voluntary and involuntary had been drawn in Draco's legislation: cf. Tod *G.H.I.* 87 ἐὰμ μὴ 'κ προνοίας κτείνῃ τίς τινα (l. 10) . . . , κτείνῃ δὲ ἄκων (l. 17). Examples of compulsion are given in 541.8–11 ἢ γ]ὰρ ἀέκοντά νιν βιᾶται | κέρ]δος ἀμάχητον ἢ δολοπλ[όκου | με]γασθενὴς οἶστρος Ἀφροδίτ[ας | ἀρτι]θαλοί τε φιλονικίαι. Cf. too A. *Pr.* 266 ἑκὼν ἑκὼν ἥμαρτον, *Ag.* 1613 σὺ δ' ἄνδρα τόνδε φὴς ἑκὼν κατακτανεῖν.

31 ff. The sense of 31–2 is lost; 32–4, paraphrased in Plato, may be reconstructed as οὔκ | εἰμ' ἐγὼ φιλόμωμος, ἐξαρκεῖ δ' ἔμοιγ' | ὃς ἂν ᾖ κακὸς μηδ' ἄγαν κτλ. (Page).

34. ἀπάλαμνος: 'helpless', 'shiftless', here: see Sol. 19.12n.

    εἰδώς: another epic touch; cf. *Od.* 20.287 ἀνὴρ ἀθεμίστια εἰδώς.

35. ὀνησίπολιν δίκαν: cf. S. *Ant.* 368–70 νόμους περαίνων χθονὸς | θεῶν τ' ἔνορκον δίκαν, | ὑψίπολις.

36. ὑγιής: 'sound': cf. A. *Eum.* 534–5 ὑγιείας φρενῶν, and similar metaphorical uses of σαθρός and νόσος. If Bergk's supplement is correct, this may be the earliest example of οὐ μή with fut. indic.

37–8. 'The generation of fools is numberless.' Cf. *Il.* 24.776 δῆμος ἀπείρων.

40. τε: the gnomic use.

SIMONIDES 543

Quoted from Simonides by Dionysius of Halicarnassus, *Comp.*
26; Athenæus 9.396e gives the beginning of Danae's speech (ὦ
τέκος ... κνώσσεις). Dionysius uses the passage to show that if a
piece of lyric poetry is written out as prose, it will be impossible to
grasp the rhythm or distinguish strophe, antistrophe and epode.
In the previous chapter he had pointed out the resemblance
between rhythmical prose and poetry, and in the earlier part of
ch. 26 he quoted *Od.* 14.1–7 and iambic lines from the *Telephus* of
Euripides (fr. 696N²) to show how close they are to prose. When
in the case of the quotation from Simonides he talks of strophe,
antistrophe and epode, he must mean that at least parts of all
three are given; his aim was not to hoax scholars, and his contemporaries could consult the complete poem if in difficulty.
Posterity, less fortunate, has butchered the quotation in quest of
the true articulation; but it seems that Dionysius, no more honest
than he had to be, quoted in such a way that there was only
the slightest corresponsion to be found, 1–3 (from the middle
of the antistrophe) answering 25–7 (from the middle of the
following strophe): what we have is the second part of an antistrophe (1–7), a whole epode (8–20), and the first part of a strophe
(21–7).

The fragment, which may be part of a dithyramb, a dirge or an
epinician, is our only example of Simonides' narrative style. It
tells the story of Danae and her infant son Perseus, put to sea in
a chest by her father Acrisius because of a prophecy that his
grandson would kill him. Danae's lament begins with short
clauses in antithesis (7–8 οἷον ἔχω πόνον· σὺ δ' ἀωτεῖς), such as we
find elsewhere in Simonides (e.g. 520, 531); but the style becomes
more elaborate with accumulated adjectives (10–11), unusual
epithets (5 ἀδιάντοισι, 8 γαλαθηνῷ, 11 νυκτιλαμπεῖ, 17 πρόσωπον
καλόν, 22 ἄμετρον), other rare words (8 ἀωτεῖς, 9 κνοώσσεις,
23 μεταβουλία), and anaphora (21–2 εὗδε ... εὑδέτω ... εὑδέτω),
none of them features of our other fragments. The passage shows
that the pathos of Simonides was displayed not only in his
epitaphs and commemorative verse. Much of the text and metrical
pattern is uncertain.

Metre: free dactylo-epitrite, as in 542, but in the absence of responsion line-division and even stanza-division are insecure. There is an analysis by D. L. Page in *J.H.S.* 71 (1951), 140. There may be synizesis in 13 τεᾶν.

See J. A. Davison, *C.Q.* 29 (1935), 85–95, D. L. Page, *J.H.S.* 71 (1951), 133–40, G. Perrotta, *Maia* 4 (1951), 81–117.

1. λάρνακι: used especially of an ark in which children were exposed: cf. Hsch. ἐκ λάρνακος· νόθος.

5. ἔρειπεν: 'cast her down with fear', but the text of 3–5 is uncertain.

   οὐκ ἀδιάντοισι παρειαῖς: 'with streaming eyes', litotes as in Homer's τὼ δ' οὐκ ἀέκοντε πετέσθην (*Il.* 5.366, *Od.* 3.484).

6. ἀμφί ... χέρα: cf. *Od.* 21.433 ἀμφὶ δὲ χεῖρα φίλην βάλεν ἔγχεϊ, although φίλαν here has more force.

8. ἀωτεῖς: Homer uses the verb with ὕπνον, *Il.* 10.159 τί πάννυχον ὕπνον ἀωτεῖς; *Od.* 10.548 ἀωτεῖτε γλυκὺν ὕπνον. The word occurs elsewhere only in the lexicographers.

   γαλαθηνῷ: elsewhere only in a literal sense, 'sucking', as in 553.2 γαλαθηνὸν τέκος, Anacr. 408.2.

9. κνοώσσεις: cf. *Od.* 4.809 ἡδὺ μάλα κνώσσουσ' ἐν ὀνειρείῃσι πύλῃσιν, Pi. *O.* 13.71 and Theoc. 21.65 (also of dreamers), Pi. *P.* 1.8 (of Zeus' eagle, lulled by music).

10. χαλκεογόμφῳ: here only; cf. Hes. *Op.* 660 νεῶν ... πολυγόμφων, Ibyc. 282(a).18 νᾶες] πολυγόμφοι, A. *Supp.* 846 γομφοδέτῳ δόρει. For δόρυ = 'ship' cf. Pi. *P.* 4.27, 38, Bacchyl. 17.90 and the tragedians.

11. νυκτιλαμπεῖ: 'shining in the night', a remarkable epithet, whether it be applied to the chest or to the dark gloom — and the listener could hardly have told which Simonides meant. Euripides' μελαμφαὲς ... ἔρεβος (*Hel.* 518) and Aristophanes' κελαινοφαὴς ὄρφνα (*Ran.* 1331 in parody of Euripides) point to the second interpretation.

12. ταθείς: 'stretched out' (τείνω).

14. βαθεῖαν: with ἅλμαν, as the accent shows; cf. Pi. *N.* 4.36 βαθεῖα ποντιὰς ἅλμα.

15. οὐκ ἀλέγεις: cf. *Il.* 16.388 θεῶν ὄπιν οὐκ ἀλέγοντες, Alcm. 1.2 οὐ μόνο]ν Λύκαισον ... ἀλέγω.

17. πρόσωπον καλόν: 'lying, a lovely face, in your purple mantle':

only the baby's face appears from his χλανίς. Editors who find the construction too harsh prefer Ahrens' conjecture πρόσωπον καλὸν προφαίνων, based on πρόσωπον καλὸν πρόσωπον in one MS. (see J. A. Davison, *J.H.S.* 72 (1952), 120).

18. 'If to you the danger were danger'.

19. καί: for its use in the apodosis see Denniston *G.P.* 308. καί κεν occurs in *Il.* 5.898, *Od.* 11.111.

20. λεπτὸν . . . οὖας: 'your small ear': so often in Hdt., e.g. 8.137.2 τὰ λεπτὰ τῶν προβάτων. There is pathos also in Sappho's use at 96.17 λέπταν ποι φρένα . . . βόρηται, 'her tender heart'. οὖας for οὖς here only, but Homer uses οὔατος, οὔατα, οὔασι. ὑπεῖχες οὖας takes the genitive as the equivalent of a verb of hearing.

22. εὑδέτω δὲ πόντος: cf. Alcm. 89, A. *Ag.* 565–6 εὖτε πόντος ἐν μεσημβριναῖς | κοίταις . . . εὕδοι πεσών, Theoc. 24.7.
ἄμετρον: 'measureless', first here.

23. μεταβουλία: here only, but cf. *Od.* 5.286–7 μετεβούλευσαν θεοὶ ἄλλως | ἀμφ' Ὀδυσῆϊ.

25. ὅττι δὲ θαρσαλέον κτλ.: i.e. 'if there be any bold or unjust word in my prayer, pardon me.' Dionysius probably ended his quotation with the end of Danae's speech.

SIMONIDES 567

Quoted from Simonides by Tzetzes, *Hist. var. chil.* 1.309 f in connexion with Orpheus. The lines show the vividness and economy of his writing.

Metre: dactylo-epitrite.

1. τοῦ: i.e. Orpheus.

3–5. ἀνὰ . . . ἄλλοντο: tmesis.

5. καλᾷ σὺν ἀοιδᾷ: 'to his fair song': for σύν of accompanying sounds cf. Pi. *N.* 5.38 σὺν καλάμοιο βοᾷ, fr. 91.19 Turyn σὺν αὐλοῖς.

SIMONIDES 579

Quoted from Simonides by Clement of Alexandria, *Strom.* 4.7.48; Theodoretus *Gr. aff. cur.* 12.46 has l. 2. Simonides has recast a passage of Hesiod (*Op.* 289–92):

τῆς δ' ἀρετῆς ἱδρῶτα θεοὶ προπάροιθεν ἔθηκαν
ἀθάνατοι· μακρὸς δὲ καὶ ὄρθιος οἶμος ἐς αὐτὴν
καὶ τρηχὺς τὸ πρῶτον· ἐπὴν δ' εἰς ἄκρον ἵκηται,
ῥηιδίη δὴ ἔπειτα πέλει, χαλεπή περ ἐοῦσα.

Tyrtaeus had spoken of reaching 'the peak of excellence' (9.43):
ἀρετῆς εἰς ἄκρον ἱκέσθαι: cf. Pi. N. 6.23–4 πρὸς ἄκρον ἀρετᾶς | ἦλθον.
For the thought that excellence is difficult to achieve cf. 526.1–2
οὔτις ἄνευ θεῶν | ἀρετὰν λάβεν, οὐ πόλις, οὐ βροτός.

Metre: 1, 3, 6, 7 are single-short, mainly trochaic in flavour;
2, 4, 5 combine double- and single-short movement, 2 as in
dactylo-epitrite, 4 and 5 as in aeolic rhythm.

1. ἐστί τις λόγος: so Pi. N. 9.6 ἔστι δέ τις λόγος ἀνθρώπων, Alc. 42.1.

2. δυσαμβάτοις: here only. Th. 4.10.3 has δυσέμβατος.

3. Text uncertain: Arete (μιν) is said 'to tend' (perhaps 'to
   dwell in' or 'to control') 'the holy place': cf. Pi. P. 5.68–9
   of Apollo, μυχόν τ' ἀμφέπει μαντήϊον, Cor. 654.iii.40.

5. ἔσοπτος: another rare formation, found elsewhere only in
   Hdt. 2.138.2.

   ᾧ μή κτλ.: i.e. she is not to be looked on 'by the man to
   whom . . .'.

   δακέθυμος ἱδρώς: the epithet, found also in S. *Phil.* 705, is
   less startling than the English 'heart-biting': see L.S.J.
   s.v. δάκνω III.

6. μόλῃ: for the omission of ἄν see Callin. 1.13n.

7. ἵκῃ: the subject ὅς is supplied from ᾧ (5). The pronoun is
   regularly omitted in these circumstances: cf. e.g. *Od.* 2.54
   δοίη δ' ᾧ κ' ἐθέλοι καί οἱ κεχαρισμένος ἔλθοι.

   ἀνδρείας: 'comes to the peak of manliness', but this blurs
   the picture of the steep crags on which Arete dwells.
   Hesiod has simply εἰς ἄκρον ἵκηται, and ἀνδρείᾳ 'by his
   manliness', may well be correct. ἀνδρεία occurs first here.

SIMONIDES 581

Quoted from Simonides by Diogenes Laertius 1.90 as evidence that Cleobulus, not Homer, wrote the epitaph of Midas
(W. Peek, *Griechische Vers-Inschriften* 1171, Friedländer, *Epigrammata*
p. 131, Entretiens Hardt xiv, 12f, 34f):

χαλκῆ παρθένος εἰμί, Μίδεω δ' ἐπὶ σήματι κεῖμαι.
ἔστ' ἂν ὕδωρ τε νάῃ καὶ δένδρεα μακρὰ τεθήλῃ,
ἠελιός τ' ἀνιὼν λάμπῃ λαμπρά τε σελήνη,
καὶ ποταμοί γε ῥέωσιν ἀνακλύζῃ τε θάλασσα,
αὐτοῦ τῇδε μένουσα πολυκλαύτου ἐπὶ τύμβου
ἀγγελέω παριοῦσι Μίδης ὅτι τῇδε τέθαπται.

Simonides' poem is of the same length as Cleobulus' epitaph and must surely be complete. The presentation is direct and arresting: note especially the emphasis which ἀντιθέντα μένος στάλας derives from its long postponement by the series of datives and from the long syllables -νος στάλας, the balance within 2 and 3, echoing the balanced lines of Cleobulus (2–4), and the contrast between the long opening question and the short statements, the more forceful for their conciseness.

Metre: almost strict dactylo-epitrite. In 3 χρυσέας may be – ∪ – or with synizesis – –. For detailed analysis see A. M. Dale, *C.Q.* n.s. 1 (1951), 119.

1. τίς κεν αἰνήσειε . . . Κλεόβουλον: reminiscent of Archil. 88.1–2 πάτερ Λυκάμβα, ποῖον ἐφράσω τόδε; | τίς σὰς παρήειρε φρένας; but not so violent; Cleobulus was long dead when Simonides wrote.

νόῳ πίσυνος: cf. *Il.* 11.9 ἠνορέῃ πίσυνοι καὶ κάρτεϊ χειρῶν. The epic colouring may be used in mockery as in 4 μένος στάλας.

ναέταν: first here.

Κλεόβουλον: tyrant of Lindus in Rhodes *c.* 600 B.C. Some made him one of the Seven Sages, but see Plu. *de EI* 3. Diogenes tells us (1.89) that he wrote songs and riddles, 3000 hexameters in all.

2. ἀεναοῖς ποταμοῖς: so A. *Suppl.* 553 ποταμοὺς ἀενάους, E. *Ion* 1083.

ἄνθεσι τ' εἰαρινοῖς: cf. *Il.* 2.89 ἄνθεσιν εἰαρινοῖσιν.

3. Closely modelled on Cleobulus. Cf. A. *Pr.* 22 ἡλίου φοίβῃ φλογί, E. *I.T.* 1207.

4. θαλασσαίαισι: here and at Pi. *P.* 2.50.

μένος στάλας: the phrase recalls the epic μένος ἠελίοιο (*Od.* 10.160), πυρὸς μένος (*Il.* 6.182) etc. (see Sol. 10.1n.), but

Simonides means 'the strength of a mere gravestone', not 'a strong gravestone'.

5. λίθον: 'stone' in general: Midas' tomb must have had the bronze figure of a girl set on a stone base.

6. βρότεοι: the Homeric form (Attic βρότειοι).

θραύοντι = θραύουσι. The Doric form -οντι, found only here in Simonides, may be part of the mockery of the Rhodian.

μωροῦ κτλ.: the final sentence gains by the asyndeton.

SIMONIDES 595

Quoted from Simonides by Plutarch *Quaest. conviv.* 8.3.4 as evidence that sounds carry better when there is no wind.

Metre: mostly dactylic.

1. ἐννοσίφυλλος: Homer has εἰνοσίφυλλος of mountains, e.g. *Il.* 2.632. Cf. ἐννοσίγαιος, ἐνοσίχθων of Poseidon.

ἀήτα: cf. *Il.* 15.626 ἀνέμοιο . . . ἀήτη.

4. ἀραρεῖν κτλ.: 'from fastening on the ears of mortals'.

SIMONIDES 76D.

Quoted from the epigrams of Simonides by Hephaestion 4.6 (p. 15.3 Consbruch) and Eustathius *Il.* 984.8 for its faulty structure; but, as Hephaestion says, drastic measures are necessary if the name Ἀριστογείτων is to be included in elegiacs. A fragment of a base found in the agora at Athens provides what must be the end of our couplet together with the end of a second couplet:

] Ἁρμόδιος
] πατρίδα γῆν ἐθέτην.

A bronze group of Harmodius and Aristogeiton was set up in 510 B.C. to commemorate their murder of Hipparchus. It was removed during the Persian occupation in 480/79, and replaced in 477/6 by a similar group. We cannot tell whether both couplets, the first only or neither appeared on the original monument of 510. The attribution to Simonides is in any case implausible, since he had enjoyed the hospitality of Hipparchus (see also 85D. introd.). The tyrannicides figured in several scolia (893, 894, 895, 896).

See Benjamin D. Meritt, *Hesperia* 5 (1936), 355–8, Friedländer
Epigrammata 150 (pp. 141–2), Entretiens Hardt xiv, 89.

1. ἦ: as in Homer, e.g. *Il.* 21.54 ἦ μέγα θαῦμα τόδ(ε), and an
early 5th-century epitaph ἦ καλὸν τὸ μνῆμα κτλ. (Friedländer 60).

φόως: common in Homer as a metaphor for deliverance, e.g.
Il. 11.797 αἴ κέν τι φόως Δαναοῖσι γένηαι. Friedländer
(p. 142) notes that the fact that they 'slew Hipparchus' is
subordinated in a non-Homeric manner to the affirmation
'the light came', which is the permanent meaning of the
historical event.

SIMONIDES 83D.

Quoted by Herodotus 7.228.3 after the two other epitaphs on
those who died at Thermopylae (91, 92D.); also in *Anth. Pal.*
7.677. Hdt. says that the Amphictyons set up the other two
pillars with their inscriptions, but that Simonides set up Megistias'
inscription for friendship's sake; we cannot doubt that he composed it himself, and it is very probable that he composed the
other two also. Megistias was the seer from Acarnania who on the
day before the battle warned the Greeks of their approaching
death: Leonidas gave him permission to leave, but he chose to stay
and die, and sent away his only son instead (Hdt. 7.219.1, 221).

1. μνῆμα τόδε κλεινοῖο Μεγιστία: cf. the opening of Friedländer 8 (from Piraeus, *c.* 500 B.C.) μνῆμα τόδ᾽ Αἰνείου
σοφίας and many others. κλεινός is not Homeric, but
common in Alcman, Pindar and tragedy.

ποτ᾽: used also in 90D., 91D., 97D. (τούσδε ποτ᾽ ἐκ Σπάρτας).
Wade-Gery 72–3 points out that after Thermopylae the
Greeks did not regain possession of the site for some
eighteen months, by which time the events of the battle had
already fallen into perspective. It is likelier, however, that
ποτέ was used with posterity in mind: future generations
would read, 'Once upon a time Megistias was slain by the
Medes.' Cf. the use of ποτέ in *Il.* 7.89–90.

2. Σπερχειόν: the river of south Thessaly which flows into the
gulf of Malis a few miles from Thermopylae; cf. A. *Pers.*
487, Hdt. 7.198.2.

3. *Κῆρας*: see Mimn. 2.5n., Sim. 533(b) ἀποτρέπουσι κῆρας.

4. οὐκ ἔτλη: 'could not bear to'.

SIMONIDES 84D.

Quoted under Simonides' name in *Anth. Pal.* 7.511. The couplet is not an epitaph, although it begins with a formula common in epitaphs (e.g. Friedländer 80 σῆμα Φρασικλείας); it is rather a commemorative poem written to console Callias. The extreme simplicity of thought and language are notable, but Friedländer (pp. 69–70) rightly points to the grandeur of the two names centrally placed and the shift from the tomb and the deceased to 'I' and 'you'. Callias and Megacles cannot be certainly identified, but we know of famous Athenians of those names: Megacles, an Alcmaeonid, uncle of Pericles, who was ostracized in 486 (see Tod *G.H.I.* 15) and won the chariot-race at the Pythian games in his exile (Pi. *P.* 7), and Callias who won Olympic victories in the chariot-race in 496, 492 and 488, distinguished himself at Marathon, and concluded the Peace of Callias with Persia in 449. We know nothing, however, of their personal relationship.

1. καταφθιμένοιο: cf. the line-beginning at *Il.* 22.288 σεῖο καταφθιμένοιο, also οἴδε νόμοι περὶ τῶν καταφθιμένων as the heading of an inscription from Iulis, birthplace of Simonides (*I.G.* 12(5). 593).

SIMONIDES 85D.

Thucydides 6.59.3 says that Hippias married his daughter Archedice to Aeantides, son of the tyrant of Lampsacus, because the tyrant had influence with Darius; her tomb in Lampsacus, he says, bears this inscription: ἀνδρὸς . . . ἀτασθαλίην. Thucydides does not mention Simonides, but Aristotle *Rhet.* 1367b.19 quotes l. 3 and names Simonides as author. Isidore of Pelusium quotes 3–4 (Migne *Gr.* 78). Note the structural resemblance to 83D.: in each a relative clause forms the second couplet, and each clause uses a concessive participle followed by a negated verb (εἰδὼς οὐκ ἔτλη, οὖσα . . . οὐκ ἤρθη); this of course does not prove Simonidean authorship. The high praise of Hippias reminds us that Simonides enjoyed the hospitality of the tyrants' court in Athens, but hardly suits Simonides the patriot and laureate of

Marathon and the other victories of the democracy. We should confess doubt about the authorship rather than pass judgement on Simonides' character. See Friedländer 138 (pp. 127–8), C. M. Bowra, *Cl. Phil.* 29 (1934), 231.

1. ἀριστεύσαντος: Homeric, e.g. at *Il.* 6.208 αἰὲν ἀριστεύειν.
2. ἥδε κέκευθε κόνις: so in 'Simon.' 116.14 and other examples in Friedländer; cf. Pi. *O.* 8.79–80 κατακρύπτει δ' οὐ κόνις . . . χάριν.
3. ἤρθη: perhaps the earliest example of this metaphorical use of ἀείρω.

   ἀτασθαλίην: often in Homer (in plural), 'presumptuousness, reckless sin', not unlike ὕβρις.

SIMONIDES 87D.

In *Anth. Plan.* 26 under Simonides' name, but the occasion, date and authorship of the poem are in dispute. The lines are generally taken to refer to the victory of the infant democracy of Athens over her neighbours the Boeotians and Chalcidians *c.* 506 B.C. and to be the epitaph for the fallen Athenians. Herodotus 5.77 quotes the epigram for the *quadriga* which was dedicated on the Acropolis to mark the victory, but not this epitaph. Friedländer doubts the connexion with 506 and suggests, unconvincingly, that ἐδμήθημεν and the last line speak of the vanquished rather than of the conquerors (p. 5, n. 6). Suspicion has been cast on the second couplet, which is grammatically dispensable (Bowra, *E.G.E.* 190, Jacoby, *Hesperia* 14 (1945), 159–60), but in 83D., 85D. and other early inscriptions, as here, the second couplet gives the particular distinction of the dead or expresses the poignancy of their death. There seems no good reason for doubting that the lines were for the dead Athenians of 506; we cannot say if Simonides, who may then have been in Thessaly, was the author.

1. Δίρφυος: Dirphys is the highest peak of Euboea, in the central range north-east of Chalcis.

   ὑπὸ πτυχί: cf. *h. Ap.* 269 ὑπὸ πτυχὶ Παρνησοῖο, *Il.* 20.22 πτυχὶ Οὐλύμποιο.

2. δημοσίᾳ: 'at public expense', first here.

   κέχυται: so in Homer, e.g. *Il.* 24.799 σῆμ' ἔχεαν, Friedländer 29.2 τοῦτο δ' ἑταῖροι σᾶμα χέαν.

3. οὐκ ἀδίκως: so in a 4th-century epitaph (Kaibel, *Epigr. Gr.* 38), but that does not prove late authorship here.

ἐρατὴν κτλ.: cf. Anacr. 90D.2n., Simon. 130.2 ἐρατῇ ... νεότητι, *Od.* 15.366 ἥβην πολυήρατον.

4. 'When we had awaited the harsh (lit. jagged) cloud of war', a bold piece of writing with no close parallel.

SIMONIDES 90D.

The lines, together with a second couplet

> ἐνθάδε Φοινίσσας νῆας καὶ Πέρσας ἑλόντες
> καὶ Μήδους ἱερὰν Ἑλλάδα ῥυόμεθα,

were known from Plutarch *de mal. Herod.* 39, p. 870e and Favorinus (or Dio Chrysostom) 37.18 (II.21 Arn.), who calls them Simonides' epitaph for the Corinthians buried at Salamis. Fragments of the first couplet only, written in Corinthian alphabet and dialect, have been found on a marble slab on Salamis:

> ὄν ποκ' ἐναίομες ἄστυ ᾳορίνθο
> ντος   ει Σ

The second couplet can never have been on the stone, and must have been added when taste 'demanded something more coloured and more emphatic' (Bowra *E.G.E.* 189).

See Tod *G.H.I.* 16.

1. ὦ ξεῖν': so in 92D.
   εὔυδρον: first here. It is the harbours of Corinth that the dead sailors recall.
2. ἀμ(έ) = ἡμᾶς.
   Αἴαντος νᾶσος: Ajax was son of Telamon, king of Salamis, and commanded the Salaminian ships at Troy (*Il.* 2.557).

SIMONIDES 91D.

From Herodotus 7.228.1: those who died at Thermopylae were buried there, and this is the epitaph of the whole army. It is almost certainly the work of Simonides: see 83D. introd. In *Anth. Pal.* 7.248 it is attributed to him; it is quoted also by Diodorus 11.33.2 and Aristides 28.65.

1. μυριάσιν κτλ.: Hdt.'s figures are 3,100 Peloponnesians (see

7.202; perhaps the figure of 4,000 was made up by
Perioeci) and 2,641,610 Persian fighting men, servants and
camp followers excluded (7.185.3), an impossible number:
for modern estimates see C. Hignett, *Xerxes' Invasion of
Greece*, Appendix I.

2. τέτορες: note the Doric form, protected by metre: MSS. of
Hdt. vary between -νάσου and -νήσου, and Schneidewin
may have been right in reading τᾷδε τρια-.

SIMONIDES 92 D.

The epitaph for the 300 Spartans led by king Leonidas: Hdt.
7.228.2, *Anth. Pal.* 7.249 under Simonides' name, *Suda* s.v.
Λεωνίδης. The version in the orator Lycurgus, *Leocr.* 109,
Diodorus 11.33.2 and Strabo 9.4.16 (p. 429) has πειθόμενοι
νομίμοις for ῥήμασι πειθόμενοι. The couplet is rightly admired
for its dignity and reticence: there is no mention of numbers
(although τριηκόσιοι was at hand) or even of valour, only of
obedience. There is little doubt that Simonides wrote it: see 83D.
introd.

1. ὦ ξεῖν': so in 90D.1. For appeals to the wayfarer in early
epitaphs see Friedländer 82 and the remarkable 83
(ἄνθρωπε, ὃς στείχεις καθ᾽ ὁδὸν φρασὶν ἄλλα μενοινῶν, | στῆθι
καὶ οἴκτιρον σῆμα Θράσωνος ἰδών).

ἀγγέλλειν: the infin. for imper. is thought by some scholars
to have a military ring, but the examples in Kühner-Gerth
§ 474 give little support to this view.

2. ῥήμασι πειθόμενοι: 'obedient to their words' (as in Thgn.
1152, 1262 ῥήμασι πειθόμενος), i.e. to such precepts as
'return with your shield or on it'. There is no evidence for
ῥήμασι as an equivalent of ῥήτραις 'ordinances, decrees'
(used by Tyrt. 3b.6). In Lycurgus' version νομίμοις may
mean either 'established customs' or 'laws' (which suits
πειθόμενοι better); Cicero's translation was

> dic, hospes, Spartae nos te hic vidisse iacentes
> dum sanctis patriae legibus obsequimur.

The Herodotean version has greater euphony and vigour
than the other; but Strabo (l.c.) seems to say that the

inscription could still be seen in his day at Thermopylae, and our texts of Strabo give πειθόμενοι νομίμοις.

SIMONIDES 97D.

Attributed to Simonides in *Anth. Pal.*, where it is given after 7.650; *A.P.* 7.270 attributes the following version to Simonides: τούσδε ποτ' ἐκ Σπάρτας ἀκροθίνια Φοίβῳ ἄγοντας | ἐν πέλαγος, μία νύξ, ἓν σκάφος ἐκτέρισεν. In 474 Hiero of Syracuse defeated the Etruscans in a naval battle off Cyme, and the poem may have been composed for the cenotaph of Syracusans drowned while taking spoils to Delphi: Simonides in that case may well have written the couplet. For Hiero's dedication of a helmet at Olympia see Tod *G.H.I.* 22. The version which records a victory over Sparta is almost certainly later, whether we regard it as an actual epitaph modelled on the other or as an imperfect recollection with the familiar Spartans substituted for the Etruscans.

1. ἀκροθίνια: spoils offered to a god in thanksgiving: first in an inscription found at the Athenian Treasury at Delphi: Ἀθηναῖοι τῷ Ἀπόλλων[ι ἀπὸ Μήδ]ων ἀκροθίνια τῆς Μαραθῶνι μ[άχης (Tod *G.H.I.* 14). Pindar described the Olympic Games as ἀκροθίνια πολέμου, referring to the spoils taken by Heracles from Augeas (*O.* 2.4).

2. μία ναῦς, εἷς τάφος: the version at *Anth. Pal.* 7.270 has μία νύξ, ἓν σκάφος, which is more imaginative but not necessarily the earlier version (*pace* Wilamowitz *S.S.* 213 n. 2, who accepts only μία νὺξ, εἷς τάφος).

SIMONIDES 99D.

Quoted as Timocreon's epitaph by Athenaeus 10.415f; also in *Anth. Pal.* 7.348 with an amusing ascription, 'Simonides on Timocreon of Rhodes, whose inclinations and habits were those of my uncle.' For Timocreon see p. 406. As far as chronology goes, the couplet may have been by Simonides, and unfriendliness between the writers is suggested also by the juxtaposition in *Anth. Pal.* 13.30 and 31 of couplets attributed to Simonides and Timocreon: Timocreon's couplet speaks of Κηΐα ... φλυαρία, 'balderdash from Ceos'. But we cannot be certain about the authorship of these couplets or of the 'epitaph', which in any case was doubtless written in jest in Timocreon's lifetime.

1. πολλὰ κάκ' εἰπών: for example Timocreon 727, the attack on Themistocles.

2. κεῖμαι: regularly of the dead in epitaphs, e.g. Friedländer 76.

SIMONIDES 121D.

From *Anth. Pal.* 7.251, under the heading Σιμωνίδου· εἰς τοὺς αὐτοὺς μετὰ Λεωνίδου πεσόντας. Bergk referred the lines not to Thermopylae but to Plataea, suggesting that they were the epitaph of the Spartans who died there and that *Anth. Pal.* 7.253 (= 118D.) was the corresponding Athenian epitaph (so Edmonds, Bowra); but 118D. belongs almost certainly to the 4th century, and the rhetoric of οὐδὲ τεθνᾶσι θανόντες in the present poem, though undoubtedly impressive, suggests the 4th century rather than the early 5th.

1. ἄσβεστον κλέος: line-beginning at *Od.* 7.333 (cf. *Od.* 4.584).
   περὶ . . . θέντες: as a garland. Note tmesis.

2. κυάνεον . . . νέφος: cf. *Il.* 23.188 κυάνεον νέφος, *Il.* 20.417–18 of a dying warrior, νεφέλη δέ μιν ἀμφεκάλυψε | κυανέη.

4. 'Αΐδεω· note synizesis (εω).

SIMONIDES 122D.

Anth. Pal. 7.512, attributed to Simonides. The occasion may have been the Tegean battle against Sparta *c.* 473 (Hdt. 9.35.2), although earlier Tegean battles are known (Hdt. 9.26.7). But the lines are sometimes referred to 362 B.C., the year of the battle of Mantinea.

1–2. Cf. *Il.* 18.207 ὡς δ' ὅτε καπνὸς ἰὼν ἐξ ἄστεος αἰθέρ' ἵκηται.
   εὐρυχόρου: Tegea lies in one of the eastern plains of Arcadia.

4. ἐν προμάχοισι θανεῖν: cf. Tyrt. 9.23.

SIMONIDES 130D.

Anth. Pal. 7.515, under Simonides' name. The poem is not an epitaph but a commemorative piece like 84D. and less restrained than early epitaphs. The poignancy of a young person's death before marriage is expressed in the 6th-century epitaph of Phrasycleia (Friedländer 80):

σῆμα Φρασικλείας· κούρη κεκλήσομαι αἰεί
ἀντὶ γάμου παρὰ θεῶν τοῦτο λαχοῦσ' ὄνομα.

2. ἐρατῇ . . . νεότητι: cf. 87D.3.

3. γλυκερῆς αἰῶνος ἀμέρσας: cf. Hes. Sc. 331 εὖτ' ἂν δὴ Κύκνον
γλυκερῆς αἰῶνος ἀμέρσῃς, Il. 22.58 αἰῶνος ἀμερθῇς.

SIMONIDES 135D.

Anth. Pal. 7.510, attributed to Simonides. Ostensibly written
for a Chian cenotaph, it gains its effect from its extreme simplicity,
its Homeric vocabulary (ἀλλοδαπή, πλαζόμενον, μελίφρονος, ἀμφιρύτην: see also 3n.) and its rhythmic interest.

1. κεύθει κόνις: cf. 85D.2 ἥδε κέκευθε κόνις.

2. μοῖρ' ἔκιχεν θανάτου: cf. Callin. 1.15n. Similar phrases occur in
    epitaphs from the 6th century onwards, e.g. Friedländer
    77 (from Eretria, 6th century), 90 (from Thasos, *c.* 500).

3. γλυκεροῦ . . . νόστου: so *Od.* 22.323 νόστοιο . . . γλυκεροῖο,
    Archil. 12.2 γλυκερὸν νόστον.

4. Χῖον: the noun has ῐ (e.g. *Od.* 3.170), but Χῖος is found in
    I.G. 2.3412.

SIMONIDES 138D.

Anth. Pal. 7.254b, under Simonides' name. But the humour of
the second line points away from Simonides, perhaps even away
from true epitaph, unless we regard it as naïve and pathetic.
Peek (no. 349) suggests that the couplet was part of Meleager's
anthology.

SIMONIDES 142D.

An epitaph for a hound, quoted as Simonides' by Pollux 5.47;
also in *Anth. Plan.* 130. The Thessalian background suits the
ascription to Simonides well enough.

2. ἴσκω: 'I fancy': cf. *Od.* 22.31 ἴσκεν ἕκαστος ἀνήρ, 'each man
    was guessing'.
    ἄγρωσσα: here only.

4. Cithaeron, which stands between Attica and Boeotia, seems
    out of place here.
    οἰονόμοι: 'with lonely pastures', first here: cf. Homer's οἰοπόλος.

PRATINAS

The entry in the *Suda* gives us almost all our information about Pratinas. He belonged to Phlius in the Peloponnese, and was the first to write satyr-plays: of the fifty plays he staged thirty-two were satyric, and he won one victory. He competed against Aeschylus and Choerilus in Ol.70 (500–497 B.C.). Arg. A. *Sept.* tells us that when Aeschylus won in 467 B.C., the second prize went to Aristias for a tetralogy of which at least the satyr-play was written by his father Pratinas; this may indicate that Pratinas was dead by 467. He had an important place in the history of music as lyre-player and composer (see e.g. ps.-Plu. *de Mus.* 1146b).

PRATINAS 708

This, our only extensive fragment, is quoted by Athenaeus 14. 617b–f: 'when hired aulos-players and dancers occupied the orchestras, Pratinas of Phlius was angry because the aulos-players did not accompany the choruses in the traditional way, but the choruses sang an accompaniment to the aulos-players; so he displayed his animus against the offenders in this hyporcheme: τίς ὁ θόρυβος κτλ.' What Athenaeus meant by hyporcheme is unclear: if this was a choral song, it is surprising to find the chorus (or poet) singing, 'It is for me to shout and make the din, rushing over the mountains with the Naiads, singing . . .' (3–5). This language, like the cult-cries at 15, comes more appropriately from satyrs, and Athenaeus may mean that this was a hyporcheme from a satyr-play; the prominence of the dance-element in 14 may have prompted his use of the word; for hyporchemes see A. M. Dale, *Eranos* 48 (1950), 14–20. The protest of Pratinas was probably directed against Lasus of Hermione, who increased the importance of auloi in his dithyrambs (ps.-Plu. *de Mus.* 1141b–c); in this case it will have been written not long after 500 B.C.

Metre: it is easier to sense the moods of the poem than to affix labels: the extended runs of short syllables convey excited indignation in 1–4, stopping when song is first mentioned (5);

they recur when the abuse of the aulos reaches its greatest vehe-
mence (11–12). The central passage of the poem, where the poet's
view of the matter is given, is calm (6–9), as is the prayer to
Dionysus (15–16). Lines 1–4 are anapaestic with much resolution, 5–10 mainly iambic, trochaic and cretic, 11–16 mainly
iambic with resolution in 11–12 and a run of cretics in 14.

See Pickard–Cambridge *D.T.C.* 17–20, H. W. Garrod, *C.R.* 34
(1920), 129–36.

1. τίς ὁ θόρυβος ὅδε; one might guess that the song was preceded
   by a dance with noisy aulos accompaniment in parody
   of Lasus or some other. Note the alliteration of *t* and *d*.

2. Διονυσιάδα πολυπάταγα θυμέλαν: with Διονυσιάς cf. Βορεάς
   in Bacchyl. 17.91. θυμέλη is commonly used of the altar of
   Dionysus in the orchestra. πολύπαταξ probably refers to the
   din made by the aulos: the chorus claim that it is for them to
   make the din (3 παταγεῖν), but on the mountains. For
   παταγεῖν cf. Fr. Adesp. 1030 *P.M.G.* Γάλλαι μητρὸς ὀρείης
   φιλόθυρσοι δρομάδες | αἷς ἔντεα παταγεῖται καὶ χάλκεα κρόταλα.

4. The line recalls Alcm. 56.

5. οἷά τε: so at *Od.* 3.73.
   κύκνον: for swan songs see Alcm. 1.101n.
   ἄγοντα: the verb is unexpected. Hsch. ἄγω· μέλπω, ᾄδω may be
   derived from this passage.
   ποικιλόπτερον μέλος: 'a song with varicoloured wings': for
   the wings of song see Thgn. 237n. In the present passage
   κύκνον dictated the choice of the adjective, although the
   swan could not itself be called ποικιλόπτερος. For ποικίλος
   of song cf. Pi. *O.* 6.87 ποικίλον ὕμνον, *N.* 4.14 ποικίλον
   κιθαρίζων, and see 10 below.

6. Πιερίς: i.e. the Muse.

7. καὶ γάρ: livelier than the simple γάρ: 'why, he's only the
   servant!'

8. κώμῳ: for the αὐλός in revelry cf. Thgn. 1065 ἔστι δὲ
   κωμάζοντα μετ' αὐλητῆρος ἀείδειν, 940–1, Bacchyl. fr. 4.30
   αὐλῶν τε καὶ κώμων.

9. στρατηλάτας: note the echo of 7 ὑπηρέτας: the servant is com-
   manding officer, but only of drunken revellers.

10. φρυνεοῦ: the toad, with whose croak the din of the αὐλός

might be compared: see Ar. *Ran.* 212–13 ξύναυλον ὕμνων βοὰν | φθεγξώμεθ(α); but there is probably a reference to the tragic poet Phrynichus, and if the reference is admitted, we have another indication that the song is dramatic. The toad, perhaps his song also, might be called ποικίλος; see 5n. Note the alliteration of *p* in this line.

11. ὀλεσι-σιαλο-κάλαμον: 'made of spittle-wasting reed'. The compounds are worthy of Aristophanes. A. M. Webster, *Words, Music and Dance* (1960) suggests ὀλοο-σιαλο-κάλαμον, -σιαλο- from the bird σιαλίς: cf. Ath. 9.392f.

12. λαλο-βαρύ-οπα: βαρύς may suggest both low pitch, as at Ar. *Nub.* 313 Μοῦσα βαρύβρομος αὐλῶν, E. *Hel.* 1351 βαρύβρομον αὐλόν, and the distress caused by the noise.
παρα-μελο-ρυθμο-βάταν: 'striding across melody and rhythm'.

13. ὑπαὶ τρυπάνῳ κτλ.: 'its shape fashioned under the auger', δέμας being acc. of respect. The vituperation seems to end tamely, unless the line can bear an indecent interpretation also: see Garrod 135.

14. The chorus probably give another example of a dance, with arms and legs akimbo. The ethic dative σοι complements ἢν ἰδού: they may be addressed to the αὐλός or to Dionysus. ἢν ἰδού, 'here you are', is at home in comedy, e.g. Ar. *Ran.* 1390; once in tragedy, E. *H.F.* 867.

15. θρίαμβε διθύραμβε: first here as epithets of Dionysus: διθύραμβος was used for the song by Archil. 77.2, and θρίαμβος has the same meaning in Cratinas 36 Kock. The words are now explained as meaning 'three-step and four-step' (with ἴαμβος as 'one-' or 'two-step'): see Pickard–Cambridge *D.T.C.* 7–9. Popular etymology made διθύραμβος refer to the double birth of Dionysus — the doors (θύραι) opened twice (δίς).
κισσόχαιτ(ε): cf. E. *Ba.* 81–2 κισσῷ τε στεφανωθείς | Διόνυσον θεραπεύει, also 177. For the importance of ivy in Dionysiac ritual see Dodds on *Ba.* 81.

16. Δώριον: fem. The αὐλός was often called Phrygian (e.g. E. *Ba.* 127); 'Dorian dance-song' may refer to the Dorian mode of the music, or to Pratinas' own Dorian origin.

TIMOCREON

Timocreon was a Rhodian from Ialysus (727.7). His plight after
the Persian Wars, in which he medized (729.1–2 οὐκ ἄρα Τιμο-
κρέων μόνος | Μήδοισιν ὁρκιατομεῖ), is the background of fr. 727,
a lampoon against Themistocles, probably written in 479 or 478
B.C.; frr. 728, 729 and 730 continue the invective after Themistocles' ostracism. At some time he was at the Persian court (Ath.
10.415f). For his unfriendly relations with Simonides see Simon.
99D. He had a reputation as a pentathlete and a great eater
and drinker (Ath. l.c., Simon. l.c.). His poems were probably
convivial songs; fr. 731 is referred to as a σκόλιον. He wrote
in the language of choral lyric, but introduced some Rhodian
features.

TIMOCREON 727

Quoted by Plutarch, *Them*. 21 in his account of Themistocles'
opportunism in the Aegean after Salamis. Herodotus, whom
Plutarch cites, tells us that Themistocles went off with a fleet to
extort cash payments from the islanders who had medized:
Carystus in Euboea and Paros submitted, Andros refused to pay
and was blockaded (8.111–12). Herodotus, like other writers,
comments on Themistocles' greed (112.1 οὐ γὰρ ἐπαύετο πλεον-
εκτέων), and notes that his actions took place without the
knowledge of the other commanders (112.3). Timocreon seems
to have been a victim of his venality (note 6 ἀργυρίοισι,
8 ἀργυρίου, 10 ἀργυρίων) and bad faith: he had handed over
three talents on the understanding that Themistocles would
take him home to Rhodes — he may have been on one of
the Cyclades — but some rogue countered with a second bribe,
so that Timocreon lost his money and his chance of returning
home.

Metre: dactylo-epitrite, used unexpectedly in what is clearly
not a choral song but a solo: 1 – D – E ⌣ 2 D ⌣ E – 3 D –
4 ⌣ D ⌣ E –. In 12 Timocreon seems to have regarded – E – E –
as a valid variation in his last line. Note the frequent

synizesis: 2 ἐπαινέω, 5 Τιμοκρέοντα, ἐόντα, 8 πλέων, 10 ὑπόπλεως, 12 Θεμιστοκλέος.

1. ἀλλ(ά): for its use at the beginning of a poem see Tyrt. 8.1n.

   τύ γε: the repetition is vivacious. The men named distinguished themselves in the Persian War of 480–79 B.C., Pausanias and Aristides at Plataea, Xanthippus and Leotychidas at Mycale, Themistocles at Salamis. Mention of Pausanias suggests that he had not yet fallen into disgrace: he was recalled to Sparta in the winter of 478–7 for his tyrannical behaviour.

2. ἐγὼ δ': for δέ in the apodosis see Denniston *G.P.* 181.

4. ἕνα λῷστον: for the intensifying use of εἷς with superlative, common in tragedy, see Kühner-Gerth i.28 and Jebb on S. *O.T.* 1380.

   ἤχθαρε Λατώ: why Leto displayed hatred is not clear. Her connexion with Delos suggests an incident involving the Delian League, but that was not formed till the spring of 477. Leto, however, was linked also with the battle of Salamis: cf. Simon. 108D. ταῦτ' ἀπὸ δυσμενέων Μήδων ναῦται Διοδώρου | ὅπλ' ἀνέθεν Λατοῖ μνάματα ναυμαχίας: Diodorus was the Corinthian commander, but we know nothing of a temple of Leto in Corinth, and his dedication may have been elsewhere. If Leto had something to do with the Greek victory at Salamis, Themistocles' failure to win the prize for excellence after Salamis (see 10n.) could be put down to her hatred.

6. κοβαλικοῖσι: *hapax*, but κόβαλος, 'rascal', belongs to comedy.

7. πατρίδ' Ἰαλυσὸν εἴσω: Page compares *Il.* 1.71 ἡγήσατο . . . Ἴλιον εἴσω.

8. ἔβα πλέων εἰς ὄλεθρον: 'sailed off to the devil': cf. Oedipus' imprecation on Teiresias in S. *O.T.* 430 οὐκ εἰς ὄλεθρον;

10–11. Ἰσθμοῖ γελοίως πανδόκευε: the ludicrous inn-keeping at the Isthmus is probably to be connected with the meeting of the Greek commanders there to award the ἀριστήια for distinguished service: each commander, with due sense of his own worth, gave his first vote for himself, but the second votes nearly all went to Themistocles (Hdt. 8.123–4). Perhaps Themistocles had spent part of his fortune on a

vote-catching dinner for the others; but no award was
made — his party was 'a frost'. For ψυχρός, 'ineffectual',
cf. Hdt. 6.108.2, Ar. *Th.* 848 of a play that flopped, etc.

κρεῖα: probably = κρέα. *Il.* 9.206 has κρεῖον, 'a meat-block'
for chopping and carving, but the word is unsuitable here
unless it could also mean 'meat-plate' or 'helping of meat'.

12. μὴ ὥραν Θ. γενέσθαι: prayed 'that no attention be paid to
Themistocles'; cf. Tyrt. 6.11–12 ἀνδρός τοι ἀλωμένου
οὐδεμί' ὥρη | γίγνεται.

TIMOCREON 731

A scolion, quoted by the scholiast on Ar. *Ach.* 532, the Aldine
scholiast on *Ran.* 1302 and the *Suda* s.v. σκόλιον. St. Isidore of
Pelusium *Ep.* 2.146 (7th century A.D.) refers to it. The parody in
the *Acharnians* refers to the Megarian decrees of Pericles: ἐτίθει
νόμους ὥσπερ σκόλια γεγραμμένους, | ὡς χρὴ Μεγαρέας μήτε γῇ μήτ'
ἐν ἀγορᾷ | μήτ' ἐν θαλάττῃ μήτ' ἐν ἠπείρῳ μένειν (532–4).

Metre: trochaic: five dimeters followed by a catalectic dimeter.

1. ὤφελεν: impersonally with acc. and inf., as at Pi. *N.* 2.6–10
ὀφείλει … δρέπεσθαι … Τιμονόου παῖδ(α).
τυφλὲ Πλοῦτε: cf. Hippon. 29.1.

3. ἐν ἠπείρῳ: In Asia. Timocreon spent some time with the
king of Persia (Ath. 10.415f), and it was his medizing that
cost him three talents (727.8).

CORINNA

Corinna belonged to the Boeotian town of Tanagra or, less
probably, to Thebes (cf. Paus. 9. 22, *Suda*, Cor. 655. 1–5). Her
date is much debated: the orthography of our papyrus fragments,
which belong to the first and second centuries A.D., proves that
our text was written c. 200 B.C. But she was probably an elder
contemporary of Pindar; at any rate, her relationships with him
formed the basis of several anecdotes of later times.

Corinna is mentioned by no writer earlier than Propertius

(2.3.21 *antiquae . . . Corinnae*) and Antipater of Thessalonica (*A.P.* 9.26); she was not edited by Alexandrian scholars, and was not included in their canon of nine lyric poets, although in later times she was sometimes added as a tenth. The *Suda* has the following notice: 'Corinna, daughter of Acheloodorus and Procatia, of Thebes or Tanagra, pupil of Myrtis, nicknamed Μυῖα, "Fly", lyric poetess; defeated Pindar five times, so the story goes; wrote five books and epigrams and lyric nomes.' Her connexion with Myrtis is almost certainly deduced from 664(a), in which she blames Myrtis for competing, albeit a woman, with Pindar; and the five victories over Pindar are derived from a foolish story in Aelian, *V.H.* 13.25: when Pindar had been defeated five times by Corinna because the judges were stupid Thebans, he exposed the judges' boorishness by calling Corinna a sow. The source of this tale must be *O.* 6.90 Βοιωτίαν ὗν: but 'Boeotian sow' is what other Greeks called the Boeotians, and even the keen-scented scholiasts found no allusion to Corinna here. Note however the five defeats: one defeat would have sufficed to explain Pindar's alleged rudeness, and Paus. 9.22 speaks of only one: did Aelian get his figure from a reputable source or invent it for the sake of artistic verisimilitude? Corinna is linked with Pindar in another story (Plu. *glor. Ath.* 4.347f): she criticised him in his youth for not using myths in his poetry, and when he countered with a poem beginning Ἰσμηνὸν ἢ χρυσαλάκατον Μελίαν | ἢ Κάδμον ἢ σπαρτῶν ἱερὸν γένος ἀνδρῶν (fr. 19 Turyn), with eight myths mentioned in six lines, Corinna laughed and said he should sow with the hand and not the whole sack. If Corinna really was a contemporary of Pindar, we must assume that her work was lost soon after it was written, and rediscovered only in the late 3rd century. Metrical evidence gives little assistance: choriambic dimeters like those of iii.12 ff are not found before the *Antigone* of Sophocles and are common only in Euripides; but Sappho and Anacreon sometimes substituted choriambic dimeters for glyconics (see metrical note on iii.12–51), and Corinna may have decided to use them systematically. When so much early lyric is lost, we need not conclude that she copied Euripides.

The little we have of her work is derived almost wholly from papyrus. Her subjects are exclusively the legends of her native

Boeotia, unless the fragment *Orestes* (*P.S.I.* 1174 = *P.M.G.* 690) is hers. Her style is clear, straightforward and unsubtle, with few graces other than an occasional interesting epithet, e.g. i.21 κάλπιδας ἐν χρουσοφαῖς; her clauses are short and simply linked. She writes in the language of Epic poetry, now and again using features of the Boeotian vernacular as it is known from inscriptions; the unfamiliar appearance of her language is due to the Boeotian spelling.

See D. L. Page, *Corinna*, Society for the Promotion of Hellenic Studies, Suppl. Paper no. 6 (1953), with text and commentary and sections on the dialect and orthography, the metres and the date of Corinna.

The following features of her orthography might perplex:

ει for Attic η: Κώρειτες, εἴρισε (= ἤρεισε).

η for αι: μάκηρα, Μώση (= Μοῦσαι), πῆς, πήδων, κή, ἐλέσθη, τή (= ταί, 'they'), ὁμήμων, δημόν-, μέμφομη, φωνή (= φωνᾷ).

ἰ for ε before a vowel: θιᾶς, δάθιον (= ζάθεον), πλίονας, ἀνεκόσμιον, τιώς (= τεούς, 'your'), ἰῶν ('his').

ῑ for ει: γεγάθι (= γεγήθει), εἴρισε (= ἤρεισε), τρῖς, ἔχι, δουῖν (= δυεῖν, δυοῖν), κρατούνι (= κρατύνει), ἔπιτα, Fῖκε (= εἶκε).

οι for ῳ: ἄντροι, πράτοι (= πρώτῳ).

ου for υ, scanned as short when it represents ŭ: ἔκρουψαν, χρουσο-, ἀούσας, λούπησι, οὐψόθεν, δουῖν, τού (= τύ, 'you'), νου (= νυ), δάκρου, φοῦσα(ς).

ῡ for οι: τύ (= τοί, 'they'), στεφάνυσιν, ὐκτρῶς, λάυς, ἀθανάτυς.

ω for ου: Κώρειτες, Κρόνω, τιώς, δόμως, ὠρανόν, though not in οὔταν (= ταύτην).

δ for initial ζ: δάθιον, Δεύς.

ττ for σσ: λιττάδα.

μ for ν before μ: ἔμελψεμ· μάκαρας, ἐμ μουριάδεσσι.

ἐς for ἐκ, ἐσς for ἐξ, ἐν for εἰς.

ἀγείρω = ἀγήραοι, 'ageless'; βανά = γυνή; ἴαν = μίαν; ἰώνγα = ἔγωγε; ὄκταλλος = ὀφθαλμός; περάγείς = περιαγής; -νθη = -νθαι for -νται in verbs (κάσσονθη = καὶ ἔσονται), -νθι for -ντι (ἐσγεννάσονθ' = ἐκγεννήσουσι).

CORINNA 654

From the Berlin Papyrus (*P. Berol.* 284), first edited in 1907 by Wilamowitz, *Berliner Klassikertexte* V.2.

col. i. 12–34. Corinna is describing a singing-match between the Boeotian mountains Helicon and Cithaeron. 12–18 give the end of one of the songs, 19–34 tell how the gods voted Cithaeron the winner to the chagrin of Helicon; the scraps of the remaining thirty lines of the poem tell us nothing. Other sources speak of a battle between the mountains, but we do not find their literary contest elsewhere.

Metre: ionic, with a clausula ∪∪ – – ∪∪ – ∪ – –. Note synizesis at 13 θιᾶς, 27 ἀνεκόσμιον.

14. βρέφος: the baby Zeus, protected by his mother Rhea from his father Cronus; Corinna seems to have Hes. *Th.* 468 ff in mind.

ληθράδαν: *hapax*, with the sense and construction of λάθρᾳ; κρουφάδαν at iii.20 is also unique.

ἀγκουλομείταο Κρόνω: Homer's Κρόνου . . . ἀγκυλομήτεω (e.g. *Il.* 2.205).

18. ἕλε: the subject might be Zeus or, more probably, Rhea.

19 ff. The details of the voting are amusing: it is secret, pebbles are dropped in urns, decision is reached by simple majority, and a herald proclaims the verdict — all very democratic.

21. χρουσοφαῖς: seemingly the Boeotian spelling of Attic χρυσοφαεῖς, but why Corinna used an Attic form is not clear.

31. λιττάδα πέτραν: so A. *Supp.* 794 λισσὰς . . . πέτρα.

34. μουριάδεσσι λάυς: the reading is uncertain: cf. E. *Rhes.* 913 μυριάδας πόλεις for μυριάς as an adj., but πόλεις, unlike λάυς, is fem.

col. iii. 12–51. From the fragments of the first 50 lines of this poem little of value can be expiscated: 12–46 come from the revelation of the prophet Acraephen, whom Asopus has consulted about the disappearance of nine daughters: they have become the brides of Zeus (3), Poseidon (3), Apollo (2) and Hermes (1), and are assured of a glorious future. Acraephen gives his credentials and the history of his office in 27–46. After 51 we have the beginnings

of 52 more lines, from which we gather only that Asopus
was pleased with the news and promised dowries. As in the
last poem, the protagonists belong to Boeotian topography:
Asopus is the river-god, Acraephen the eponymous hero of the
town Acraephia, near which stood the sanctuary of Apollo Ptoios.

Metre: polyschematist choriambic dimeters with pherecratean
clausula. In the choriambic dimeters the choriamb $-\cup\cup-$ is
preceded by a variety of four-element bases (whence the lable
'polyschematist'):⁀usually by $-\cup--$ or $----$, but also by
$---\cup$, $\cup---$, $-\cup-\cup$, or, with resolution of the first syllable,
$\cup\cup\cup-\cup$ (44, cf. 27: elsewhere only in tragedy). By way of variation a glyconic may take the place of the choriambic dimeter: so
at 19, 29, 30, 40. It may begin $--$, $-\cup$ or $\cup-$. In Sapph. 96.7
$-\cup-\cup-\cup\cup-$ corresponds to a glyconic, in Anacr. 357.5
$---\cup-\cup\cup-$. In the pherecratean, with which the stanza ends,
the base is usually $--$, but may be $-\cup$ (46?) or $\cup\cup\cup$ (26). The
stanza-form resembles that of Anacr. 348, 357 etc. Note synizesis
at 38 'Ωαρίων.

12. The daughters were named some six stanzas earlier: for an
    attempt to recover the names see C. M. Bowra, *Problems in
    Greek Poetry* 54–65. Corcyra is there and probably Sinope,
    perhaps also Thespia and Aegina; Salamis and Euboea can
    be fitted into the gaps. Corinna called Tanagra a daughter
    of Asopus (Paus. 9.20.2).

23 εἰμιθίων: see Callin. 1.19n.

24. κάσσονθη: καί + ε might have been expected to result in κη-
    in Boeotian spelling: see Page *Corinna* 58–9.
    πολουσπερίες: cf. *Il.* 2.804 πολυσπερέων ἀνθρώπων, Hes. *Th.*
    365 πολυσπερέες of the daughters of Ocean.

25–6. The meaning seems to be: 'so I was taught by the oracular
    tripod.' ὧτ' [ἐδιδάχθειν] is too long: there is room for no
    more than eight letters.

27 ff. Presumably 'This privilege I alone of fifty strong brothers
    obtained'.

29. πέροχος: for περίοχος, πέρροχος in Sapph. 106; so 47 περάγείς
    for περιαγής.

33. Euonymus was son of Cephisus and father of Aulis (Steph.
    Byz. s.v. Εὐωνυμία).

35. Hyrieus, son of Poseidon (37) and Alcyone, was father of Orion (38).

38. Orion held office, 'having regained his own land': this story is not known. When Artemis killed him (*Od.* 5.121–4), he became the constellation (40). See Rose's article in *O.C.D.* and references there.

ἀππασάμενος: Attic ἀνα-πασάμενος, from ἀνα-πάομαι.

46. δημόνεσσ᾽ ἐκουρεύων: 'being father-in-law to gods': the verb is found here only, but a marginal comment referring to marriage suggests that the supplement is correct. If it is, Corinna neglects F in Fεκ-.

CORINNA 664(a)

Quoted by Apollonius Dyscolus, *Pron.* 64b for the form ἰώνγα. Herodian π.μ.λ. 1.18.25 comments on Corinna's use of βανά for γυνή. We know almost nothing of Myrtis who competed with Pindar: the *Suda* s.vv. Corinna and Pindar makes the two her pupils; Plutarch *quaest. graec.* 40 calls her Myrtis of Anthedon (a town of Boeotia), and paraphrases one of her poems, a tale of unrequited love, false accusation, murder and suicide (*P.M.G.*716).

Metre: as in 654.iii. 1 and 3 are choriambic dimeters, 2 probably glyconic with synizesis in ἰώνγ᾽, but it is doubtful if βανά can be scanned – ∪.

2. ἰώνγα: the form ἰώγα is used by the Boeotian in Ar. *Ach.* 898.

βανά: here only, but Hsch. has βανῆκας.

BACCHYLIDES

Bacchylides like his uncle Simonides was born in Iulis on the island of Ceos. His grand-father, Bacchylides, was a famous athlete, his father, Meidylus (*Et. Mag.* 582.20) or Meidon (*Suda*), married Simonides' sister. His chronology is disputed. Severyns (*Bacchylide* 15–30) dates his birth to 518 or 517, in which case he is an exact contemporary of Pindar, Bowra (*O.C.D.*) to c. 524–1; but an ancient tradition preserved in Eustathius (*prooem. ad Pind.*

25) made Pindar the older of the two, and Jebb put Bacchylides' birth *c.* 507. Eusebius has three relevant entries: 467 B.C. *Bacchylides et Diagoras . . . celebrantur*, 451 B.C. *Crates . . . et Telesilla ac Bacchylides lyricus clari habentur*, 431 B.C. *Bacchylides carminum scriptor agnoscitur*; in addition *Chron. Pasch.* 162b has 480 B.C. Βακχυλίδης ἤκμαζεν, Georgius Syncellus 257c offers 428–5 B.C. Βακχυλίδης μελοποιὸς ἐγνωρίζετο. Bacchylides could have been alive at the beginning of the Peloponnesian War, but the use of *agnoscitur* and ἐγνωρίζετο, which should refer to the poet's *début*, suggests that an error has been made. His ode for Pytheas of Aegina (13) is dated tentatively to 485, and fr. 20B, the encomium for Alexander of Macedon, may be earlier. The last datable poems, 6 and 7, belong to 452 B.C.

Fortunately the chronology of Bacchylides' relations with Hiero of Syracuse is secure. Ode 5, which like Pindar's first *Olympian* celebrates Hiero's Olympic victory in the horse-race, belongs to 476 B.C., and in it Bacchylides describes Hiero as his ξένος (11): Bacchylides must have visited Syracuse before 476, probably in the company of his uncle. In 470 he wrote the short ode 4 for Hiero's Pythian victory in the chariot-race; Pindar on this occasion wrote the splendid first *Pythian*. Two years later Bacchylides celebrated Hiero's victory in the four-horse chariot-race at Olympia in ode 3, but Pindar for some reason wrote no work for this, the most splendid of Hiero's triumphs, unless the second *Pythian* celebrates it. That Pindar was on bad terms with his rivals Simonides and Bacchylides seems proven by his allusion to the pair of chattering crows in *O.* 2.86–8 (written in 476 B.C.), and the scholiasts found uncomplimentary reference to Bacchylides in *N.* 3.80 ff (especially κραγέται δὲ κολοιοὶ ταπεινὰ νέμονται, 'shrieking jackdaws inhabit low levels' — lower than the Pindaric eagle), *P.* 2.52–3, 72–3 (καλός τοι πίθων παρὰ παισίν, αἰεὶ | καλός: 'the monkey is pretty in the eyes of children', but the passage need not refer to Bacchylides).

Of the rest of his life we know little. He was exiled from Ceos for a time, and lived in the Peloponnese (Plu. *de exil.* 14.605c). He wrote epinician odes for patrons in Aegina, Phlius, Athens, Thessaly and Metapontium (in S. Italy), as well as four for victors from Ceos itself and the three for Hiero.

Only some 100 lines were known from quotation when a remarkable papyrus find in Egypt restored portions of fourteen epinician odes and six dithyrambs. The papyrus fragments reached the British Museum in 1896, and the *editio princeps* by F. G. Kenyon appeared in the following year.

Bacchylides' reputation has always suffered from the urge of critics to compare him with his rival, Pindar: (Longinus) *de Sublim.* 33 exclaims τί δ' ἐν μέλεσι μᾶλλον ἂν εἶναι Βακχυλίδης ἕλοιο ἢ Πίνδαρος . . .; The most notable feature of his writing is his clarity: his thought is simple, its expression pellucid; not for him Pindar's mixed images and overloaded aphorisms, which have perplexed ancient and modern commentators: there is hardly a sentence which is not clear at first glance. One can understand why Hiero preferred him to Pindar (schol. Pi. *P.* 2.91; his less severe moralising may also have pleased the tyrant). But in his simplicity he loses as much as he gains: the elusiveness and subtlety which make Pindar so interesting and rewarding are absent. When he modelled 3.85 ff on the opening of Pindar's first *Olympian*, a foolhardy undertaking, he botched the job. Only once, in 5.16 ff, did he succeed in sustaining the lofty Pindaric style. His virtues lie elsewhere: his narrative is gripping, often exciting; he is fond of direct speech for its immediacy, and it is no surprise to find a dithyramb written in the form of a dialogue (18). He is adventurous in his coining of compound adjectives, a few of them memorable (e.g. 5.1–2 Συρακοσίων ἱπποδινήτων), most of them forgettable (5.6 φρένα . . . εὐθύδικον), one or two better forgotten (5.40 χρυσόπαχυς Ἀώς); his aim in using them is clearly to recapture in lyric the atmosphere of epic. His language is Ionic with many Doric and a few Aeolic forms, the Dorisms being less common than in Pindar. Most of his poems are dactylo-epitrite, but he uses Aeolic rhythms also (e.g. in 18), and in 17 he experiments with iambics and cretics as Pindar did in his second *Olympian.*

His works were collected in nine books: dithyrambs, paeans, hymns, prosodia, partheneia and hyporchemata, all in honour of deities, and epinicians, erotica and encomia in honour of men. The Alexandrians thought highly enough of him to include him in the Nine Lyric Poets, and Ptolemaeus (2nd century B.C.) and

P

Didymus (1st century B.C.) wrote commentaries on his poems. The papyrus finds demonstrate his popularity in the first three centuries A.D.

The best text is *Bacchylidis Carmina cum Fragmentis*[10], ed. Snell–Maehler, 1970 (Teubner). The commentary by R. C. Jebb (1905) is indispensable. For interpretation see A. Severyns, *Bacchylide* (1933), A. W. Pickard-Cambridge, D.T.C. 25–30, D. C. Carne-Ross, *Arion* 1.3 (1962), 65–88, G. M. Kirkwood in *The Classical Tradition: Studies . . . H. Caplan* (1966), 98–114. Note that Jebb's numbering of the poems (used also in L.S.J.) differs from Snell's (=Kenyon's) from poem 8 onwards (Snell 9 = Jebb 8 and so on).

BACCHYLIDES 3

An ode for Hiero of Syracuse on the occasion of his greatest athletic triumph — victory in the chariot-race at the Olympic Games of 468 B.C. The poem was Bacchylides' most important commission, and is the finest display of his talents, a vivid, exciting work, only half as long as his epinician for Hiero's victory in the Olympic horse-race of 476 (no. 5), but no less impressive for its briefer compass.

The myth, which Bacchylides ties firmly to its context both at its beginning and at its end (17 ff, 58 ff), is the story of Croesus, who for his generosity to Apollo in Delphi was miraculously preserved on his pyre by Zeus and transported by Apollo to live among the Hyperboreans. Pindar in his first *Pythian*, written for Hiero two years earlier, took Croesus as an illustration of piety rewarded (*P.* 1.94 οὐ φθίνει Κροίσου φιλόφρων ἀρετά), and Bacchylides may have found there the idea of telling the story in detail. His account differs from that given later by Herodotus (1.86 ff): in Herodotus Croesus is put on the pyre by Cyrus' orders; he appeals to Apollo, not Zeus; and after his rescue he lives on at Cyrus' court (3.36). Bacchylides, however, did not invent the story of Croesus' self-immolation: a red-figured amphora dated *c.* 500 B.C. shows Croesus seated on the pyre and calmly making libation, while a 'kindly' attendant, labelled Εὔθυμος, busies himself with the pyre (illustrated in *J.H.S.* 18 (1898), 268, *Fifty Years of Classical Scholarship*, Oxford, 1954, pl. IV, fig. 6: see Beazley *A.R.V.*² 238, no. 1). It is remarkable that Croesus should have joined the ranks of mythological figures so soon after his death (546 B.C.).

Metre: the epode is in dactylo-epitrites, the metre used for all the long epinician odes: $\cup$ D – | E | E | – E | E $\cup$ e | E; but here, uniquely, a different rhythm, iambic and aeolic, is used for strophe and antistrophe; the two rhythms, however, are not widely different in character: line 4 of the epode can be regarded as iambic, and lines 2 and 3 of strophe and antistrophe have dactylic sequences like the first line of the epode. The fourth line of strophe and antistrophe is the hendeca-syllabic line of the Sapphic stanza. Note $\cup\cup$ for – at 40 Ἀλυάττα, 83 ὅσια; synizesis in 7 Ἀλφεόν, Δεινομένεος, 79 ὄψεαι, 81 ἔτεα; and a harsh synecphonesis at 22 ἀγλαΐζέτω· ὁ.

1. ἀριστοκάρπου κτλ.: Bacchylides begins impressively with the two goddesses closely associated with Sicily; Hiero was their hereditary priest (see Hdt. 7.153.2), and his brother Gelo had built them temples in Syracuse.

   ἀριστοκάρπου: *hapax*. Bacchylides was fond of compound adjectives: new creations (so far as our evidence goes) are 3 γλυκύδωρος (already at 5.4, also 11.1), Ὀλυμπιοδρόμος, 6 εὐρυδίνας (already at 5.38), 10 τρισευδαίμων, 12 πλείσταρχος, 13 μελαμφαρής, 18 ὑψιδαίδαλτος, 32 χαλκοτειχής, 44 χρυσοδίνας (?), 55 μελαγκευθής (?), 64 μεγαίνητος (also at 1.154) 82 βαθύπλουτος; none of them is particularly adventurous, but they give an epic richness. Sicily was famous for its corn-lands: cf. Pi. *N.* 1.14–15 ἀριστεύοισαν εὐκάρπου χθονὸς | Σικελίαν, fr. 121.12–13 Turyn ἀγλαοκάρπου Σικελίας, A. *Pr.* 369 τῆς καλλικάρπου Σικελίας.

2. ἰοστέφανον: used of festal divinities — Aphrodite, the Muses (e.g. 5.3), the Graces — and heroines of romance, e.g. Eurydice. Pindar had used it of Athens in his famous dithyramb (fr. 92 Turyn).

3. ὑμνεῖ: Clio's song is to be of Demeter, Persephone and — Hiero's race-horses; Calliope's at 5.178 ff moves less abruptly from the divine to the secular.

   Κλεοῖ: Bacchylides invokes Clio also at 12.2, 13.9, 228:

Calliope at 5.176, 19.13; he is 'servant of Urania' at 5.13–14, and Urania inspires him at 4.8, 6.11, 16.3. The Muses did not obtain their special provinces in literature until Hellenistic times: Bacchylides, like Pindar, appeals to them indiscriminately. Clio's name is usually Κλειώ, but cf. Pi. *N.* 3.83 Κλεοῦς.

θοάς: mares were generally used in racing.

5. Νίκα: personified several times, e.g. 5.33, 12.5 πότνια Νίκα, but Ἀγλαΐα here only in Bacchylides; Pindar has νικαφόρον ἀγλαΐαν (*O.* 13.14).

6. εὐρυδίναν: so at 5.38; Pindar has Ἀλφεὸν εὐρὺ ῥέοντα (*O.* 5.18). Cf. 5.181 ἀκαμαντορόας, 8.26 ἀργυ]ροδίνας, 11.26 καλλιρόας, of the Alpheus, the river of Olympia.

7. Deinomenes was father of Gelo and Hiero.

9. The correct supplement is probably the Homeric ἀπείρων: cf. *Il.* 24.776 ἐπὶ δ᾽ ἔστενε δῆμος ἀπείρων. Bacchylides 9.30 has Ἑλλάνων ... ἀπ[εί]ρονα κύκλον of the crowd at the Nemean Games.

10–14. The figurative language suggests that this is the exclamation of the poet rather than the crowd's cry of admiration.

12. πλείσταρχον Ἑλλάνων γέρας: i.e. the privilege of ruling more Greeks than any other. This may have been literally true of the ruler of Syracuse: cf. Hdt. 7.157.2.

13. οἶδε κτλ.: 'knows how not to hide his towering wealth in black-cloaked darkness'. For the metaphor in πυργωθέντα πλοῦτον cf. Sol. 1.9–10. Pindar had commended the display of wealth: οὐκ ἔραμαι πολὺν ἐν μεγάρῳ πλοῦτον κατακρύψαις ἔχειν (*N.* 1.31: cf. *I.* 1.67). So the victory must not be kept silent (94–6: cf. Pi. *I.* 2.43–5).

15. βρύει: with dative, but βρύουσι (16) has genitive.

16. βρύουσι: the omission of δέ in the anaphora βρύει μὲν ... βρύουσι is rare: cf. *Orph. Hymn* 22.7 and see Denniston *G.P.* 376–7.

φιλοξενίας: Bacchylides may have been present in Syracuse: see 5.11n., and cf. Pi. *N.* 1.19–20 ἔσταν ('I stand') δ᾽ ἐπ᾽ αὐλείαις θύραις | ἀνδρὸς φιλοξείνου καλὰ μελπόμενος.

17. λάμπει κτλ.: the transition from Syracuse to Delphi, necessary for the introduction of the Croesus story, is unexpected.

ὑπὸ μαρμαρυγαῖς: for ὑπό with dat. of attendant circumstances see L.S.J. s.v. B II 4.

18. ὑψιδαιδάλτων: i.e. high and elaborate; in other compounds ὑψι- means 'on high'.

τριπόδων: Gelo gave a tripod in thanks for his victory over Carthage in 480, Hiero for his defeat of the Etruscan fleet at Cyme in 474. The bases on which these tripods stood have been found at Delphi: see Tod *G.H.I.* 17 (also 22).

21-22. θεὸν . . . ἀγλαϊζέτω: 'let god be honoured', i.e. with gifts. The repeated θεόν sounds like a cult-cry: cf. Diagoras, *P.M.G.* 738.1 θεὸς θεός, Hor. *Epod.* 14.6 *deus, deus.*

22. ὁ γὰρ ἄριστος ὄλβων: 'for that is the best of prosperities': i.e. the prosperous man who gives gifts to god is the best prosperous man. Cf. 83-4 τοῦτο γὰρ | κερδέων ὑπέρτατον. The repetitions (cf. 6 Ἀγλαΐᾳ, 1 ἄριστο-, 8 ὄλβιον) help to round off the introductory part of the poem, and the maxim introduces the story of Croesus.

23. ἐπεί ποτε: 'for once upon a time'. Croesus is linked to Hiero by his wealth, his generosity to Apollo at Delphi, and his horses (δαμασίππου | Λυδίας ἀρχαγέταν: cf. 69 φίλιππον ἄνδρ(α) of Hiero).

δαμασίππου: for Lydian cavalry and the warlike character of the Lydians of Croesus' day see Hdt. 1.79.3 and cf. Mimn. 13.3 Λυδῶν ἱππομάχων, Alcm. 1.59n., Sapph. 16.19 τὰ Λύδων ἄρματα.

25-6. 'Zeus having brought about the fated issue'.

28. χρυσάορος: of Apollo in *Il.* 5.509, 15.256.

29. ἄελπτον ἆμαρ: i.e. the day on which Cyrus captured Sardis.

30. οὐκ ἔμελλε: 'did not intend'.

31. ἔτι: 'in addition' to defeat.

32. χαλκοτειχέος . . . αὐλᾶς: the adjective probably refers to bronze plates fastened to the walls: cf. *Od.* 7.86 of Alcinous' palace: χάλκεοι μὲν γὰρ τοῖχοι ἐληλέατ' ἔνθα καὶ ἔνθα.

33. νάησατ' = ἐνήήσατο, from νηέω (=νέω), 'he had a pyre built': cf. Hdt. 1.50.1 νήσας πυρήν.

34-5. ἄλαστον . . . δυρομέναις: so *Od.* 14.174 ἄλαστον ὀδύρομαι.

36. αἰπύν: in Homer of Troy and of hills: first here of the sky.

σφετέρας: 'his'. In Homer as in prose σφέτερος is a plural

possessive adjective, 'their', but Hesiod, Pindar and Aeschylus use it for the singular.

37. γέγωνεν: imperf. from γεγώνω: cf. *Il.* 14.469 ἐγέγωνεν.

ὑπέρβιε δαῖμον: Zeus. ὑπέρβιος is pejorative in Homer, but Pindar had used it of Heracles in its favourable sense (*O.* 10.15).

38. θεῶν ... χάρις: in Hdt. 1.90.4 Croesus, saved from the pyre, sent a message to Delphi to ask εἰ ἀχαρίστοισι νόμος εἶναι τοῖσι Ἑλληνικοῖσι θεοῖσι, 'if the Greek gods were habitually ungrateful'.

39. Λατοίδας: trisyllabic as in Pi. *P.* 1.12; elsewhere Λητοΐδης.

40. Ἀλυάττα: gen. of Ἀλυάττης: father of Croesus, and king of Lydia *c.* 610–560. In 41–3 the sense may have been 'Apollo shows no gratitude for my countless (μυρίων) gifts: the Persians are sacking my city.'

44–5. χρυσοδίνας Πακτωλός: Sardis stood on the Pactolus, a tributary of the Hermus, famous for the gold-dust it brought down from Mount Tmolus: cf. e.g. V. *Aen.* 10.142, Hor. *Epod.* 15.20.

46. ἐϋκτίτων: cf. Anacr. 358.5n.

47. Note the abruptness of the asyndeta. θανεῖν particularises τὰ πρόσθεν ἐχθρά.

48. ἀβροβάταν: Aeschylus had used the word at the end of his *Persae* (1073) γοᾶσθ' ἀβροβάται, where it may be a noun, as here, or an adjective. Leumann says ἀβροβάτας, 'softly-stepping', is a piece of popular etymology, and that the word is in fact the Persian *awra-pāta, *a(h)ura-pāta, 'protected by Ahura (Mazda)', i.e. a Persian; see Snell's *app. crit.*

49. ξύλινον δόμον: 'the wooden structure', i.e. the pyre: so Pi. *P.* 3.38 τείχει ... ξυλίνῳ of a pyre.

50–1. ἀνὰ ... ἔβαλλον: tmesis, 'threw up' their hands to their mother.

51. ὁ ... προφανής: i.e. the φόνος ('violent death') that is foreseen.

53–4. πυρός ... μένος: so *Il.* 6.182 πυρὸς μένος; see Sol. 10.1n.

55. μελαγκευθές: the supplement is from fr. 29, where μελαγκευθὲς εἴδωλον may be the correct reading.

57. ἄπιστον οὐδέν κτλ.: cf. 17.117–18. Pindar had written ἐμοὶ

δὲ θαυμάσαι | θεῶν τελεσάντων οὐδέν ποτε φαίνεται | ἔμμεν
ἄπιστον (P. 10.48–50): cf. too Archil. 74.5. Here the maxim
refers to what follows, the translation of Croesus.

58. Δαλογενής: so at 11.15, Adesp. P.M.G. 950(a).

59. Ὑπερβορέους: the Hyperboreans, a legendary race of the far
    north, are not mentioned by Homer, but appear first in
    Hesiod fr. 150.21 M.-W., Epigoni fr. 3 Kinkel and h. Hom.
    7.29. Pindar had sung of them in P. 10.29–44 as a happy,
    musical race, immune from sickness, age and strife, the
    favourites of Apollo; in O. 3.16 he called them 'Apollo's
    servants'. Cf. Alc. 307 with Page S. & A. 244–52, J. D. P.
    Bolton, Aristeas of Proconnesus, passim. Hdt. 4.32 ff tells of the
    offerings they sent to Apollo at Delos.

60. κατένασσε: from κατανaίω, 'settled, gave a home to', as in
    Hes. Op. 168.

62. ἀγαθέαν = ἠγαθέην, used of Pytho by Hes. Th. 499, Pi. P. 9.71.

63. γε μέν: 'however', like γε μήν: so at 90 below; used also by
    Homer, Pindar and others: see Denniston G.P. 386–7.

64. μεγαίνητε Ἱέρων: note the hiatus and the lengthened ε
    before it: cf. 92 τρέφει. Ἱέρων, where the hiatus is made less
    harsh by the full stop. Bacchylides may have supposed,
    wrongly, that Ἱέρων originally began with F: he made a
    similar mistake at 5.75, 17.131.

65. φάμεν: the Aeolic infinitive, used also by Pindar.

68. φθόνῳ: Bacchylides speaks elsewhere of the envy aroused by
    successful men: cf. 5.188–9, 13.199–202 εἰ μή τινα
    θερσιεπὴς | φθόνος βιᾶται, | αἰνείτω σοφὸν ἄνδρα | σὺν δίκᾳ;
    also Pi. fr. 105.8–9 Turyn παντὶ δ' ἐπὶ φθόνος ἀνδρὶ κεῖται |
    ἀρετᾶς.

    πιαίνεται: Pindar had spoken of Archilochus ἔχθεσιν πιαινόμενον
    (P. 2.55–6).

71. ἰοπλόκων ... Μουσᾶν: at 5.3 the Muses are ἰοστεφάνων, at
    Pi. P. 1.1, Adesp. P.M.G. 1001 ἰοπλοκάμων. Sappho spoke
    of their roses (55.2).

72–4. Supplement is uncertain, but there may be a contrast
    between Hiero's earlier military life (δειμαλέᾳ ... or
    ῥωμαλέᾳ ... χειρί) and the quiet life he is now forced to
    lead. He had been ill for several years (cf. Pi. P. 3, written

perhaps in 474), and died in the year after the present ode was written.

75. Jebb supplied ὑπὸ κέαρ δέδυκεν, 'Hope has crept into the hearts of men.'

77. Φέρητος υἱ̇: Admetus, king of Pherae in Thessaly. Zeus made Apollo the servant of Admetus for killing the Cyclopes (E. *Alc.* 1–9).

78. ἀέξειν: 'to cherish': cf. *Od.* 17.489 μέγα πένθος ἄεξε.

79 ff. Epicharmus has the same idea (fr. 267 Kaibel): ὡς πολὺν ζήσων χρόνον χὡς ὀλίγον, οὕτω διανοοῦ.

80. μοῦνον: with αὔριον, 'tomorrow only'.

82. 'Thou wilt live out thy life in ample wealth' (Jebb).

85. 'I speak what the wise may understand': an imitation of Pindar's 'arrows that speak to the wise', βέλη . . . φωνάεντα συνετοῖσιν (*O.* 2.83–5, written in 476 B.C.). Note that the Pindaric passage is that in which Pindar contrasts himself with the pair of chattering crows (Simonides and Bacchylides?).

βαθὺς μὲν κτλ.: in this passage too there is unmistakable imitation, this time of *O.* 1.1 ff, composed for Hiero in 476. Pindar's splendid lines move from the images of water, gold and the sun to the Olympic Games; Bacchylides, copying the abrupt, paratactic style, moves from air, sea and gold to the irretrievability of man's youth, and then from bodily decay to immortality conferred by the Muse; but his grip of the Pindaric manner is insecure: whereas Pindar startled by his hint that water, gold and the sun are *not* more splendid than the Games, Bacchylides blurs his point: air and sea (and gold?) do not decay; *but* youth cannot be regained (i.e. man decays): yet man's ἀρετή is saved from decay by the Muse. The weakness of εὐφροσύνα δ' ὁ χρυσός, where the sense required is 'gold is indestructible', shows that Bacchylides was distressed in this rare atmosphere: *ceratis ope Daedalea | nititur pennis.*

86. ἀμίαντος: of light in Pi. fr. 117.5 Turyn; in A. *Pers.* 578 ἡ ἀμίαντος is used of the sea; cf. too Thgn. 447.

87. εὐφροσύνα δ' ὁ χρυσός: 'gold is a joy', but the sentiment is not apt here.

88. παρέντα: perhaps 'omitting, by-passing', rather than 'having passed through' as at S. *O.C.* 1229, Pl. *Resp.* 460e.

90. γε μέν: see 63n.

μινύθει: with ῦ as at 5.151.

92–4. For δέ postponed when the sentence begins with a vocative see Denniston *G.P.* 189. The usage belongs to serious poetry.

ὄλβου . . . ἄνθεα: Pindar had written πλοῦτον ἀνθεῖν (*P.* 10.18).

94. πράξαντι δ' εὖ κτλ.: cf. 5.187–90, Pi. *I.* 2.44 μήτ' ἀρετάν ποτε σιγάτω πατρῴαν.

96–8. 'Together with true glories (i.e. the glories of Hiero) men will praise also the charm of the melodious Cean nightingale.' So Pindar ended *O.* 1 with a prayer for Hiero's prosperity and his own success: cf. also Ibyc. 282.47–8. In 10.10 Bacchylides is 'the clear-voiced island bee', in 5.16 ff the eagle. ἀλαθείᾳ καλῶν must mean 'the reality of glories': cf. Th. 6.33.1 τοῦ ἐπίπλου τῆς ἀληθείας. ὑμνεῖν is the first and last verb of the poem.

BACCHYLIDES 5

Composed like Pindar's first *Olympian* for Hiero's Olympic victory with the race-horse Pherenicus in 476 B.C. It may have been the poet's first commission from Hiero, whose hospitality he had already enjoyed (see 11n.); the poem is sent from Ceos.

The myth cannot be easily applied to Hiero's life as can the Croesus story in the third ode, and its profound sadness is hardly attuned to a song of celebration. Bacchylides moves from Hiero's victory and prosperity to the thought that no man is blessed in all respects, and he illustrates this text by the story of Heracles' encounter with the spirit of Meleager in the underworld. If the myth does have any relevance to Hiero, it must be found in the illness from which he suffered; we know from Pindar *Pythian 3* that he was ill at least as early as 474 B.C. In the myth it is Heracles who provides the example of one blessed in most respects but not in all: the wording of 56 ff and the emphasis on Heracles' tears at 155 ff both suggest this, and the hint at his terrible death in the last words of the myth (172–5) is conclusive. The tale of Meleager provides a second example of unhappiness, this time unrelieved — the tale of his struggle with the boar, of his

battle against his relatives, and of his murder by his mother. The
last lines of the myth seem at first an anticlimax: Heracles asks
Meleager if he left at home any sisters as handsome as he; but
Bacchylides introduces Deianeira to leave his listeners with
thoughts of a third instance of male destroyed by female: as
Artemis ruined Oeneus and his family and Althaea killed
Meleager, so Deianeira with the magic robe (note Κύπριδος
θελξιμβρότου at 175) was to bring about Heracles' death.

The poem contains much of Bacchylides' finest work, and the
description of the eagle's flight (16–30) is the most impressive
passage in his extant poetry. Several lines were known before the
papyrus discovery: 26–7 are in schol. Hes. *Th.* 116, 37–40 in schol.
Pi. *O.* 1 *argum.*, 50–5 in Stobaeus 4.39 (περὶ εὐδαιμονίας). 2 (cf.
4.34.25), 160–2 in Stobaeus 4.34 (περὶ τοῦ βίου κτλ.). 26.

(See Mary R. Lefkowitz, *H.S.Ph.* 73 (1969), 45–96.)

Metre: dactylo-epitrite: str. – D | E – | – D | – D ⌣ e | D | – D |
E – | E | – D – e – | D | – D | E | – D – | D | E; ep. – d¹ E ⌣ | D |
– D ⌣ e – | E – | D | – E ⌣ e | – D ⌣ | E ⌣ | D | E ⌣ e –. The first triad
was composed less strictly than the rest of the poem: note 8 (ee),
11, 26 (– D –), 14, 29 (D ⌣); short *anceps* is commoner there than
later in the poem. There is synizesis at 15 στηθέων, 50 θεός, 53
ἀφνεόν, 95 θεῶν, 118 ἀδελφεῶν, 120 Οἰνέος, 157 ταλαπενθέος, 181
Ἀλφεόν, 196 εὐκλέα. Note 189 ἀπωσάμενον.

1. εὔμοιρε: as in poem 3 Bacchylides clusters new adjectives at
   the beginning: cf. 2 ἱπποδίνητος, 4 γλυκύδωρος (also at
   3.3, 11.1), 6 εὐθύδικος, 19 εὐρύαναξ, 33 κυανοπλόκαμος
   (also at 9.53, 11.83), 34 χαλκεόστερνος, 38 εὐρυδίνας (also
   at 3.7), 39 ἀελλοδρόμας, 40 χρυσόπαχυς, 48 νεόκροτος, 52
   ἐπίζηλος, 56 ἐρευψιπύλας, 73 λιγυκλαγγής (also at 14.14),
   74 χαλκεόκρανος, 98 καλυκοστέφανος (also at 11.108), 102
   φοινικόνωτος, 105 ἀναιδομάχας, 120 περικλειτός (also at
   9.8, 10.19, 11.81), 138 κακόποτμος, 139 ἀτάρβακτος, 155
   ἀδεισιβόας (also at 11.61), 175 θελξίμβροτος(?), 180 ἀκαμαντορόας, 199 μεγιστοπάτωρ. New verbs are 44 καταχραίνω,
   49 the active τιτύσκω, 80 γελανόω, 136 ἐπιλέγομαι, 152
   ὀλιγοσθενέω, and 110 εἰσάνταν is *hapax*.

2. γνώσῃ: with ὀρθῶς, long postponed: 'you will judge rightly.'
   Pindar too in his poem on Hiero's victory says that Hiero

has no peer as a literary critic (*O.* 1.103 ff): the compliments found their recompense in later commissions. Hiero is said to have had no interest in music and the arts until his illness forced him to lead a more sedentary life (Aelian *V.H.* 4.15).

3. *ἰοστεφάνων*: of the Muses at Thgn. 250: cf. 3.2 and 3.71 *ἰοπλόκων Μουσᾶν*.

4. *Μοισᾶν γλυκύδωρον ἄγαλμα*: i.e. the sweet gift of the Muses sent to honour you: -*δωρον* may refer both to the gift given by the Muses and to the gift sent to Hiero: for *ἄγαλμα* cf. 10.11 *ἀθάνατον Μουσᾶν ἄγαλμα*, Pi. *N.* 3.13 *χώρας ἄγαλμα*, 8.16 *Νεμεαῖον ἄγαλμα*. Note the Aeolic form *Μοῖσα* which Pindar always uses; elsewhere Bacchylides has *Μοῦσα*, except at fr. 55.2 if that is his.

τῶν γε νῦν κτλ.: 'you, if any mortal now alive': cf. 18.12–14.

6. *εὐθύδικον*: *εὐθυδίκαν* may be correct: cf. Pi. *P.* 11.9 *ὀρθοδίκαν*.

7. *ἀτρέμ(α)*: proleptic, 'so that it may enjoy repose'.
ἀμπαύσας = *ἀναπαύσας* by apocope.

8. *ἄθρησον*: cf. Pi. *P.* 2.69–70 τὸ *Καστόρειον* ('hymn to Castor') . . . *θέλων ἄθρησον*.

9. *βαθυζώνοις*: of the Graces also at Pi. *P.* 9.2, of the Muses at *I.* 6.74. The Graces are asked to inspire Bacchylides at 9.1, and are inspirers of song at 19.5.

ὑφάνας: of poetic composition also at 19.8; cf. Pindar's bolder *ὑφαίνω δ' Ἀμυθαονίδαις ποικίλον ἄνδημα* (fr. 207 Turyn).

11. *ξένος*: Bacchylides must have been Hiero's guest in Syracuse; cf. 49 *φιλοξείνῳ*, 3.16 *φιλοξενίας*. Pindar calls Hiero *ξένον* in *O.* 1.103, and in *P.* 3.71 says of him *ξείνοις δὲ θαυμαστὸς πατήρ*.

ὑμετέραν: plural, of Hiero and his brothers: cf. 31–6.

12. *κλεεννάν*: the Aeolic form, followed at once by *κλεινός*; a very fastidious writer might have avoided the change of dialect, although the repetition of the word is forceful enough.

13. *χρυσάμπυκος*: in Hes. *Th.* 916, Pi. *P.* 3.89 of the Muses. On individual Muses see 3.3n.

14. *θεράπων*: the metaphor is common: cf. Archil. 1.2n.

16. αἰνεῖν Ἱέρωνα: the words are well placed here. Strophe,
antistrophe and epode all begin with Hiero's praises.

βαθὺν κτλ.: Hiero's achievements give wide scope to the poet
as the heavens to the eagle: cf. 31–4.

17. ξουθαῖσι: the meaning may be 'nimble', as most probably
in *h. Hom.* 33.13 ξουθῆισι πτερύγεσσι δι' αἰθέρος ἀΐξαντες
of the Dioscuri, in which case ταχείαις adds little, or
'yellow, tawny' of the golden eagle; used of the nightingale
at A. *Ag.* 1142, where 'tawny' and 'trilling' are both
possible meanings.

19. αἰετός: Pindar had used the image of the eagle as poet in
N. 5.20–1, and in *O.* 2.87–8, written for the same victory as
the present poem, he contrasted the pair of chattering
crows (Simonides and Bacchylides?) with himself, the
divine bird of Zeus. It is possible that Bacchylides wrote the
present passage as a retort to Pindar: Snell considers for
metrical reasons that the first triad was written later than
the others or at least revised (introd. p. 41). Pindar used
the image again in *N.* 3.80 ff, and in *P.* 1.6 ff his picture of
the sleeping eagle has some slight resemblances with the
present passage.

20. ἐρισφαράγου: of Poseidon in *h. Merc.* 187; of Zeus also in Pi.
fr. 303 Turyn.

22. ἰσχύϊ: the dative may be taken with θαρσεῖ (cf. Anacr.
102.2D.) or with πίσυνος (cf. Simon. 581.1) or jointly.

πτάσσοντι: B. uses the Doric -οντι for -ουσι after σ (or ξ):
cf. 13.231 καρύξοντι, Simon. 581.6. For πτάσσω cf. the
Lesbian fragment ἔπταζον ὡς ὄρνιθες ὦκυν | αἴετον ἐξαπίνας
φάνεντα (*Incert.* 10 L.-P.).

24. νιν ... ἴσχουσι: 'bar his way'.

26. δυσπαίπαλα: excitingly used of the waves; Archil. 116 used it
of 'rough and steep' glens.

νωμᾶται: with ἔθειραν. The middle is unexpected (elsewhere only in Quint. Smyrn. 3.439), and the papyrus
seems to offer νωμᾷ as a correction.

27. ἀτρύτῳ: 'limitless', properly 'unwearied': cf. 9.80 ἄτρυτον
χρόνον.

χάει: 'the air', a meaning noted by schol. Hes. *Th.* 116; cf.

Ar. *Av.* 192, where the scholiast quotes ποτᾶται δ' ἐν ἀλλοτρίῳ χάει from Ibycus in imperfect recollection of the present passage.

28. λεπτότριχα: of the eagle's 'fine' plumage (ἔθειραν).

31. ἐμοὶ μυρία πάντᾳ κέλευθος: cf. Pi. *I.* 4.1 (=3.19: variously dated to 478, 476 and after 474) ἔστι μοι θεῶν ἔκατι μυρία παντᾷ κέλευθος, followed at l. 3 by ὑμετέρας ἀρετὰς ὕμνῳ διώκειν. There is no closer imitation: but who was the imitator? For the metaphor cf. 19.1–2 πάρεστι μυρία κέλευθος . . . μελέων, 9.47–8, Pi. *N.* 6.47–8 (461 B.C.?), and οἴμη and οἶμος in Homer.

33. κυανοπλοκάμου: of Thebe at 9.53, of the daughters of Proetus at 11.83; cf. Pi. fr. 46.61 Turyn κυανόπλοκος of Thetis.

34. χαλκεοστέρνου: cf. χαλκοθώραξ in Homer. The reference is to the battle of Himera (480 B.C.), when Gelo and his brothers defeated the Carthaginians; cf. Simon. 106a.1–3D. φημὶ Γέλων', Ἱέρωνα, Πολύζηλον, Θρασύβουλον, | παῖδας Δεινομένευς, τοὺς τρίποδας θέμεναι | βάρβαρα νικήσαντας ἔθνη.

37. ξανθότριχα: cf. *Il.* 11.680 ἵππους δὲ ξανθάς.

39. πῶλον: here = ἵππον: only in 384 B.C. were special races for πῶλοι, 'colts', established.

   ἀελλοδρόμαν: *hapax*, but Homer has ἀελλόπος of Iris, and cf. Simon. 515, Pi. *N.* 1.6 ἀελλοπόδων . . . ἵππων. The idea of of ἀελλο- is repeated at 46 ῥιπᾷ . . . Βορέα.

40. χρυσόπαχυς: *hapax*. Cf. Homer's ῥοδοδάκτυλος ἠώς, S. *Ant.* 103–4 ὦ χρυσέας | ἁμέρας βλέφαρον. Horseraces must have been run early, like chariot-races (cf. S. *El.* 699).

41. Pherenicus had won at Delphi in 478 and may have been Hiero's winner in 482 also: cf. Pi. *P.* 3.73–4 (474 B.C.?) στεφάνοις | τοὺς ἀριστεύων Φερένικος ἕλεν Κίρρᾳ ποτέ (i.e. at the Pythian Games), where στεφάνοις may refer to a single victory.

42. γᾷ δ' ἐπισκήπτων: explained by the fuller version at 8.19–20 γᾷ δ' ἐπισκήπτων χέρα | κομπάσομαι: one rested one's hand on the ground while calling earth or the chthonian gods to witness something; cf. *Il.* 9.568, 14.272, *h. Apoll.* 333.

43. προτέρων: the local sense is rare.

46. ῥιπᾷ . . . Βορέα: cf. *Il.* 15.171, 19.358 ὑπὸ ῥίπης . . . Βορέαο.

47. κυβερνήταν: perhaps not elsewhere of a jockey.

    φυλάσσων: not simply 'keeping him safe' but also 'obeying him'.

48. ἵεται: historic present, rare in Bacchylides, not used at all by Pindar.

    νεόκροτον: 'greeted with fresh applause'.

50. ὄλβιος κτλ.: cf. fr. 11.1–3 εἰς ὄρος, μία βροτοῖσίν ἐστιν εὐτυχίας ὁδός, | θυμὸν εἴ τις ἔχων ἀπενθῆ δύναται | διατελεῖν βίον, Alcm. 1.37–9.

53–5. The general truth that no mortal is prosperous in all respects introduces the myth: cf. 3.21–2. The reference may be to Hiero's illness; so Pindar in *P.* 3.81–2 (474 B.C.?) alludes to Hiero's ill-health, and reminds him that the gods give mortals two hardships for every blessing: 'not even Peleus or Cadmus had a life free from reverses' (86–8).

56. καὶ γάρ ποτ': so at Pi. *O.* 7.27, *N.* 6.35 at the beginning of a mythical allusion.

    ἐρειψιπύλαν: cf. ἐρειψίτοιχος at A. *Th.* 881, perhaps at Bacchyl. 13.167. Heracles had captured Troy, Oechalia and Pylus; the journey to Hades was his greatest labour (*Od.* 11.623–4).

60. καρχαρόδοντα: of dogs in *Il.* 10.360, 13.198.

    κύν' ἄξοντ(α): so at *Od.* 11.623.

62. υἱὸν . . . Ἐχίδνας: Cerberus was son of Typhaon and Echidna according to Hes. *Th.* 310 (cf. S. *Tr.* 1099), but of Tartarus and Ge in S. *O.C.* 1574.

64. ἐδάη: 'became acquainted with' (aor. of *δάω, 'learn').

    Κωκυτοῦ: the water of wailing (κωκύω); cf. *Od.* 10.514.

65. οἷά τε κτλ.: 'like the leaves buffeted by the wind over the headlands of Ida'. V. *Aen.* 6.309–10 has the same simile of the spirits of the dead; cf. also Ap. Rhod. 4.216 ff.

66. μηλοβότους: Pindar had used the adj. of Acragas (*P.* 12.2).

67. ἀργηστάς: with πρῶνας, 'clear'. Homer has ἀργεστής of a 'clearing' wind. Cf. S. *O.C.* 670 ἀργῆτα Κολωνόν, where the adj. probably refers to light-coloured soil.

69. θρασυμέμνονος: Homer uses the epithet of Heracles, *Il.* 5.639, *Od.* 11.267.

    ἐγχεσπάλου: at *Il.* 2.131 etc.

70. Πορθανίδα: Meleager was son of Oeneus, who was son of Porthaon, king of Pleuron and Calydon. Πορθᾱνίδης is from Πορθάν: cf. Ἀλκμάν for Ἀλκμάων in Pi. P. 8.46 and in the poet's name.

71. Ἀλκμήνιος: Alcmena's son, Heracles.

73. ἐπέβασε: transitive aorist of ἐπιβαίνω, 'put the string on the bowtip': bows were usually carried unstrung.

   λιγυκλαγγῆ: 'shrill.' When Odysseus tested his bowstring, it sang like a swallow (Od. 21.411).

75. εἵλετο ἰόν: but ἰός, 'arrow', did not have Ϝ: cf. Il. 4.116 αὐτὰρ ὁ σύλα πῶμα φαρέτρης, ἐκ δ' ἕλετ' ἰόν. ἰός, 'poison' (cf. Lat. virus), and ἰόν (Lat. viola) both had Ϝ. Bacchylides makes the same mistake at 17.131 φρένα ἰανθείς.

78. εἰδώς: masculine after ψυχά, constructio ad sensum exactly as at Od. 11.90–1.

80. ἐν χώρᾳ: i.e. 'where you are'.

   γελανώσας: 'cheering', hapax; Pindar uses the adj. γελανής (O. 5.2, P. 4.181).

81–2. ταῦσιον . . . ὀϊστόν: cf. Od. 3.316 τηϋσίην ὁδὸν ἔλθῃς.

84. οὔ τοι δέος: 'you have nothing to fear'; cf. Il. 1.515 οὔ τοι ἔπι δέος, 12.246 σοὶ δ' οὐ δέος ἔστ' ἀπολέσθαι.

85. For the long word see Callin. 1.2n.

87. ἔρνος: in Homer a young man or woman may be compared to a sapling: see Sapph. 115.2n. Pindar uses ἔρνος for 'offspring' at N. 6.38 ἔρνεσι Λατοῦς: cf. I. 3.62–3.

90–1. κεῖνον: the masculine comes naturally from the questioner, but the killer was no man. Jebb notes the same device at S. Ant. 248 τίς ἀνδρῶν ἦν ὁ τολμήσας τάδε;

   ἐφ' ἁμετέρᾳ . . . κεφαλᾷ: i.e. 'to take my life'. Hera plagued Heracles as the illegitimate son of her husband; it was because of her jealous hatred that he underwent his twelve labours. Pallas Athene (91–2) was Heracles' protecting deity: cf. Il. 8.363, Od. 11.626 and many vase-paintings.

92. ξανθᾷ: so Pi. N. 10.7 ξανθᾷ . . . Γλαυκῶπις.

97. καὶ γὰρ κτλ.: 'for otherwise Oeneus would have checked. . . .'

   πλάξιππος: in Homer of heroes. Homer has ἱππηλάτα Οἰνεύς (Il. 9.581), ἱππότα Οἰνεύς (Il. 14.117).

100. πολέων: gen. plur. of πολύς, trisyllabic as perhaps at Il.5.691.

102. βοῶν φοινικονώτων: cf. 11.104–5 βοῦς ... φοινικότριχας, Pi. P. 4.205 φοίνισσα ... ἀγέλα ταύρων.

104. ἔσχεν: 'kept' her anger unallayed, or 'had conceived' anger that could not be overcome (Jebb). She was angry because Oeneus had neglected her in his harvest thanksgiving to the gods (Il. 9.534–5).

ἔσσευε: Epic aor. of σεύω, as in Il. 5.208.

106. Calydon stood in a plain near the Aetolian coast not far from the entrance to the Gulf of Corinth: cf. Il. 9.577 πιότατον πεδίον Καλυδῶνος ἐραννῆς.

107. πλημύρων σθένει: 'overflowing with strength', a striking and perhaps original expression: the boar damaged the coastal plain of Calydon as a flood-tide might.

110. εἰσάνταν: hapax, =Homer's εἰσάντα. ἄντην is common in Homer.

111. στυγεράν: of war in Il. 4.240.

112. στασάμεθ(α): cf. Il. 18.533 στησάμενοι δ' ἐμάχοντο μάχην, Od. 11.314 φυλόπιδα στήσειν, Il. 17.158 ἀνδράσι δυσμενέεσσι ... δῆριν ἔθεντο.

ἐνδυκέως: 'steadfastly', 'strenuously', 'stubbornly': the word has various shades of meaning; repeated in 125.

113. συνεχέως: with ῡ also in Hes. Th. 636; so Homer has σῠνεχές. κάρτος: 'victory', as in Homer.

Αἰτωλοῖς: i.e. to Meleager and his companions.

116. ἐριβρύχας: 'squealing'; elsewhere 'roaring', as in Hes. Th. 832, of a bull.

117. Ancaeus, a prince of Arcadia (Il. 2.609) and one of the Argonauts. He was represented in the sculpture of the Calydonian boar-hunt on the pediment of the temple of Athena Alea in his native Tegea (Paus. 8.45.6).

120. Althaea, important in the sequel, is introduced here. It would be interesting to know whether the missing word was an adj. describing her (e.g. θοῦρις, Schwartz) or a dull word like πατρός (Kenyon) or παῖδας (Schadewaldt): according to Snell, only παῖδας fits the space.

121–2. σὺν δ' ὤ]λεσε μοῖρ' ὀλοὰ | πλεῦνα]ς (Edmonds and Housman) gives good sense. For μοῖρ' ὀλοή cf. Il. 16.849 etc.

δαΐφρων: 'warlike', as in the *Iliad*; but in the *Odyssey* δαΐφρων is 'wise', e.g. of Penelope.

123. ἀγροτέρα: so Ἄρτεμις ἀγροτέρη in *Il.* 21.471.

124. αἴθων: 'reddish-brown, tawny': so *Il.* 2.839 of horses, *Il.* 15.690 of an eagle.

125. These Curetes are not of course the genial deities who nursed Zeus but an Aetolian clan from Pleuron (151) to which Meleager's mother's family belonged (129): cf. *Il.* 9.529.

127. πολλοῖς σὺν ἄλλοις: i.e. he killed many others.

129. μάτρωας: i.e. Althaea's brothers.

132. τυφλά: predicative: 'weapons go blindly.' Cf. S. fr. 754 N² τυφλὸς ... Ἄρης.

140–1. δαιδαλέας ... λάρνακος: so in Simon. 543.1–2.

ὠκύμορον: 'swift-dying' or perhaps 'bringing swift death' (to Meleager).

142. φιτρόν: the story of the log is not in Homer; Phrynichus mentioned it in his play *Pleuroniae* (fr. 6 N²), which may have been earlier than the present poem.

†ἐγκλαύσασα: 'weeping over it'? cf. Ov. *Met.* 8.470 *inveniebantur lacrimae tamen*. But ἐκ λάρνακος needs a participle such as ἐξαύσασα (Wackernagel): cf. Hsch. ἐξαῦσαι· ἐξελεῖν. The rare word might easily be corrupted.

143. μοῖρ' ἐπέκλωσεν: cf. Callin. 1.9n. 'Fate decreed that it should then be the limit of my life': τότε refers to the day on which Althaea took the log from the box rather than the day, the seventh after Meleager's birth (Apollodorus 1.8.1), when the prediction was made.

144. τύχον μέν: the μέν clause merely gives the circumstances in which the events of the δέ clause (151–2) take place.

147. ἀμώμητον: see Archil. 6.2n.

148. πύργων: of Pleuron (151).

152. ὀλιγοσθενέων: *hapax*; cf. Homer's ὀλιγοδρανέων, ὀλιγηπελέων.

154. ἀγλαὰν ἥβαν: so Thgn. 985 ἀγλαὸς ἥβη, Simon. 115.1D. ἀγλαὸν ὤλεσαν ἥβην.

160. ταδ(ε): perhaps for τῇδε, 'thus'; so at 191. Cf. 10.47 πᾷ for πῇ.

θνατοῖσι κτλ.: for this famous maxim see Thgn. 425–8n. It comes with a special poignancy from the mouth of the invincible (57) Heracles. He tactfully omits the other half of the saying, that an early death is next best.

162. ἀλλ' οὐ γάρ κτλ.: cf. *Od.* 10.202, 568 ἀλλ' οὐ γάρ τις πρῆξις ἐγίγνετο μυρομένοισιν, *Il.* 24.524 οὐ γάρ τις πρῆξις πέλεται . . . γόοιο. For ἀλλά . . . γάρ cf. Tyrt. 8.1 and see Denniston *G.P.* 101: the particles mark the contrast between what is irrelevant or subsidiary and what is vital, primary or decisive.

164. ὅτι καὶ μέλλει τελεῖν 'that which is in fact likely to be effective'; but Jebb supplies τις, 'that which he can hope to accomplish'.

165. ἦρα = ἦ ἄρα, interrogative as at *Il.* 5.421. In Pindar (schol. *Il.* 21.194) Meleager asked Heracles to marry Deianeira to protect her from her suitor Achelous.

167. ἀδμήτα: cf. *Od.* 6.109 παρθένος ἀδμής.

169. λιπαρὰν . . . ἄκοιτιν: 'my radiant wife'; perhaps of a bride prepared for her wedding: cf. Hes. *Th.* 901 ἠγάγετο λιπαρὴν Θέμιν.

172. χλωραύχενα: with the bloom of youth on her neck. Simon. 586.2 used the adjective of nightingales, either 'green-necked' (cf. *Od.* 19.518) or 'fresh-throated'.

174. νῆϊν: cf. *Od.* 8.179 οὐ νῆΐς ἀέθλων.
χρυσέας: of Aphrodite, see Mimn. 1.1n. Note ῠ as in Pindar and the lyrics of tragedy.

175. θελξιμβρότου: cf. *Il.* 14.215 of Aphrodite's girdle, ἔνθα τέ οἱ θελκτήρια πάντα τέτυκτο. The reference to Love's magic is sinister: when Deianeira resorted to magic to regain Heracles' love, she killed him.

176. Καλλιόπα: see 3.3n.

177. στᾶσον εὐποίητον ἅρμα: Pindar has similar metaphors, e.g. *P.* 10.51 κώπαν σχάσον (at the end of the myth), *N.* 5.16 στάσομαι: cf. *P.* 4.247–8. Bacchylides apologises for his digression at 10.51–2 τί μακρὰν γλῶσσαν ἰθύσας ἐλαύνω ἐκτὸς ὁδοῦ; εὐποίητον as in *h. Apoll.* 265 ἅρματά τ' εὐποίητα. In Pi. *O.* 9.81 the poet rides ἐν Μοισᾶν δίφρῳ: cf. *I.* 2.2, *P.* 10.65, *I.* 8.61–2.

178. ἀρχαγόν: not in Homer. Simon. 105.1D. has Ἑλλήνων ἀρχηγός of Pausanias. Zeus and Hera were the deities of Olympia.

181. Pelops defeated Oenomaus, king of Pisa, who had imposed a chariot-race on all his daughter's suitors, and could be styled the first Olympic victor; his grave stood near the altis, and sacrifices were offered to him.

184. Συρακόσσας: the Doric form.

186. εὐδαιμονίας πέταλον: of the victor's wreath: cf. 3.92 ff ὄλβου . . . ἄνθεα.

188. αἰνεῖν: the object is the successful man of 190 (εἴ τις κτλ.). φθόνον: see 3.68n.

190. πράσσοι: one might have expected pres. indic. (or ἐάν with subjunctive), but cf. Pi. P. 8.13–14 κέρδος δὲ φίλτατον, | ἑκόντος εἴ τις ἐκ δόμων φέροι, Od. 14.56–7, S. Ant. 666, and see Goodwin M.T. § 555.

191. τάδε: see 160n. The passage (fr. 202 Rzach) does not occur in Hesiod's extant works. Thgn. 169 is close: ὃν δὲ θεοὶ τιμῶσιν, ὁ καὶ μωμεύμενος αἰνεῖ.

192. πρόπολος: in h. Cer. 440 too as a 'minister' of gods.

196. εὐκλέα . . . γλῶσσαν: i.e. speech which glorifies: Pindar has εὐκλέης thus at O. 2.90, N. 6.30. The gen. κελεύθου suggests some such supplement as οὐκ ἐκτὸς προείς (Jurenka: cf. 10.51–2 τί . . . ἐλαύνω | ἐκτὸς ὁδοῦ;) or οὐ πλανώμενος (Bucherer).

197. τόθεν: with reference to εὐκλέα . . . γλῶσσαν.

198. πυθμένες θάλλουσιν ἐσθλῶν: 'happy fortunes, once firmly planted, flourish' (Jebb), literally 'the stocks of blessings (ἐσθλῶν is neuter) flourish.' Pindar uses the image in N. 8.40 ff.

199. μεγιστοπάτωρ: so 19.21–2 μεγιστοάνασσα . . . Ἥρα.

BACCHYLIDES 17

This poem, entitled Ἠΐθεοι ἢ Θησεύς in the papyrus, is a dithyramb only in the Alexandrian sense of the word — a choral song with mythological subject-matter: it is more likely to be a paean, sung in honour of Apollo at Delos by a choir from Ceos (see 128–32: but Pickard-Cambridge D.T.C. 26 says it may have

been a dithyramb, sung at Delos by a circular chorus). Its subject
is the quarrel between Theseus and Minos on board the ship
which carried the fourteen Athenian victims to the Minotaur in
Crete: Theseus' boast that he is Poseidon's son is answered by
Minos' claim that *his* father is Zeus himself; he makes good his
claim, and challenges Theseus to do the same; Theseus is equally
successful. The poem has no preliminaries and ends abruptly with
a brief prayer to Apollo; in its economy and concentration, as in
the prominence of direct speech, it resembles the Alexandrian
epyllion. The cult of Theseus flourished in Athens in the 470^s and
460^s: a Theseum was built, and Cimon brought the bones of
Theseus from Scyros to Athens. His adventures are the subject of
poem 18. He was connected also with Delos, where he inaugurated
the Delian *geranos*-dance on his journey home from Crete to
Athens (Plu. *Thes.* 21: see Lillian B. Lawler, *The Dance in Ancient
Greece* 46–8). Severyns (56–9) argued that a poem written for
Delos and glorifying the 'patron saint' of Athens belongs to the
early years of the Delian Confederacy, say 478–470. Simonides 550
told the story of the voyage to Crete; for illustration on vases see
A. H. Smith, 'Illustrations to Bacchylides', *J.H.S.* 18 (1898),
276 ff with pl. XIV. Servius refers to the poem in his commentary
on V. *Aen.* 6.21 ('*Bacchylides in dithyrambis*': see 2n.) *P. Oxy.* 1091
(O) contains lines 47–78 and 91–2.

Metre: the scheme is complex and resembles that of Pi. *O.* 2
(476 B.C.). The rhythm is basically 'single-short' (i.e. trochaic,
iambic or cretic), but there are many sequences with three short
syllables, and two consecutive lines (str. 10–11) show 'double-
short'. The rushes of short syllables generate excitement. Note
anceps at the beginnings of lines, so that 41, 43, 86 begin with short
syllables, 74 and perhaps 90 with long. 87 begins with ∪ – for ∪ ∪,
110 with – –. 118 may begin with an extra short syllable, but the
text is uncertain. Note – or ∪ ∪ for ∪ at the beginning of an iamb
at 35 πλαθεῖσα, 40 κέλομαι, 83 πάκτων, 101 μεγάρον. Long
syllables are resolved at 72 χέρα, 112 αιονα, 116 δόλιος, 130
Δαλιε χόροισι, 132 θεόποτμον; conversely – for ∪ ∪ at 94 θορεν
ποντονδε. Note – ∪ ∪ for ∪ ∪ – at 103 κόρας απο, 109 πατρος

ἄλοχον. The fourth syllable of 102 is regarded as *anceps* in the proper name Νηρηος. Note short αι at 92 Ἀθαναίων, 128 παιάνιξαν, and synizesis at 39 Κνωσίων, 43, 93 ἠϊθέων, 66 μεδέων, 96 χέον, 112 πορφυρέαν, 128 ἠΐθεοι.

1. κυανόπρωρα: Homeric epithet of ships; bows might be painted dark-blue, crimson or vermilion.

μέν: no δέ follows, but 8 κνίσεν τε κτλ. provides an answer of sorts.

μενέκτυπον: *hapax*, like the Homeric μενεπτόλεμος of 73, μενεχάρμης, μενεδήϊος etc. Other words found first or solely in this poem are 7 πελέμαιγις, 9 ἱμεράμπυξ, 23 μεγαλοῦχος, 24 παγκρατής(?) (also at 11.44, fr. 14.4), 31 ἐρατώνυμος, 47 ἀρέταιχμος, 56 πυριέθειρα, 66 ἀναξιβρέντας, 70 πανδερκής, 71 θυμάρμενος, 82 ἀνακάμπτω, 85 θελημός, 88 εὐδαίδαλος (also at fr. 15.3), 90 ὠκύπομπος, σοέω, 97 ἁλιναιέτας, 106 χρυσεόπλοκος, 118 φρενοάρας, 119 λεπτόπρυμνος, 121 στραταγέτας (also at 18.7), 124 ἀγλαόθρονος(?), 126 νεόκτιτος, 132 θεόπομπος(?). Bacchylides' new compound adjectives belong equally to his epinicians and to his dithyrambs.

2. δὶς ἑπτά: i.e. seven boys and seven girls, as in Sapph. 206, E. *H.F.* 1326–7 and Pl. *Phaedo* 58a, who perhaps alludes to the present passage: Θησεύς ποτε εἰς Κρήτην τοὺς δὶς ἑπτὰ ἐκείνους ᾤχετο ἄγων. Servius refers to these writers and to this passage in his commentary on V. *Aen.* 6.21.

ἀγλαούς: of young people, as in Pi. *I.* 6.62 ἀγλαοὶ παῖδες: cf. 5.154 ἀγλαὰν ἥβαν and ἀγλαῶν . . . γυίων at 103–4 below.

3. Ἰαόνων: i.e. Athenians, as in 18.2; they were travelling to the Dorian island of Crete. For the form cf. *Il.* 13.685.

5. τηλαυγεῖ: it was black, according to the legend: Aegeus gave the helmsman a white sail (red, in Simon. 550) to be hoisted if Theseus returned safely.

7. πελεμαίγιδος: 'wielding the aegis' (πελεμίζω, shake): cf. αἰγίοχος and Hes. *Sc.* 344 αἰγίδ' ἀνασσείσασα of Athena. But the correct reading may be πολεμαίγιδος. On the Louvre *kylix* of Euphronius (*c.* 500–490) Athena stands in the background while Amphitrite greets Theseus in her submarine home (see *J.H.S.* 18 (1898), pl. XIV).

8. κνίσεν: Pindar had written ἔρως ὑπέκνισε φρένας (P. 10. 60).

9. ἱμεράμπυκος: hapax: cf. 5.13 χρυσάμπυκος Οὐρανίας, Pi. N. 7.15 Μναμοσύνας . . . λιπαράμπυκος.

10. Κύπριδος . . . δῶρα: i.e. the attractions of one of the girls. Either αἰνά or ἁγνά (the likelier reading, according to Snell) is suitable: see Douglas E. Gerber, Phoenix 19 (1965), 212–13.

14. βόασε: transitive as in Pi. P. 6.36 βόασε παῖδα ὅν.

15. Pandion was father of Aegeus and grandfather of Theseus.

16. μέλαν: either simply of colour or of 'black looks'.

18. δίνασεν: hyperdorism. We should have expected δίνησεν from δινέω: cf. 107 δίνηντο, 5.2 ἱπποδινήτων, 5.191 φώνησεν from φωνέω.

19. ἄμυξεν: cf. 18.11 and Il. 1.243–4 θυμὸν ἀμύξεις | χωόμενος.

20. εἶρεν: so at 74. Homer has εἴρω, 'I say', in the Odyssey. Bacchylides uses εἶπεν at 47, 52, 81 and needed variety.

22. κυβερνᾷς: for the metaphor cf. Pi. fr. 256.3 Turyn ἐλπίς, ἃ μάλιστα θνατῶν πολύστροφον γνώμαν κυβερνᾷ. A. Pers. 767 φρένες γὰρ αὐτοῦ θυμὸν ᾠακοστρόφουν.

23. μεγαλοῦχον: hapax, 'haughty': cf. Hsch. μεγαλουχία· μεγαλαυχία, ὑψηλοφροσύνη.

24. ὅ τι μὲν ἐκ θεῶν κτλ.: 'whatever the all-powerful fate sent from the gods has decreed for us — and the scale of Justice falls that way — we shall fulfil as our allotted portion when it comes.' For ἐκ θεῶν μοῖρα cf. Od. 11.292 θεοῦ . . . μοῖρα, 22.413 μοῖρ(α) . . . θεῶν, A. Pers. 93 θεόθεν . . . μοῖρα, and see Callin. 1.9n.

   ῥέπει: probably intransitive here, but the passive at A. Suppl. 405 shows that a transitive use (as with ἐπιρρέπω, καταρρέπω) is possible. The image of the balance is found notably at Il. 22.210 ff: see Thgn. 157n.

28. βαρεῖαν κτλ.: 'check your disastrous intention'; cf. 40–1.

30. κρόταφον Ἴδας: cf. A. Pr. 721 κροτάφων ἀπ' αὐτῶν of a mountain. Ida is the Cretan mountain.

31. Φοίνικος: Phoenix was father of Europa.

33. ἀλλά: for the use in the apodosis see Sapph. 1.22n.

34. Πιτθέος θυγάτηρ: Pittheus was father of Aethra (59). He was son of Pelops and king of Troezen.

38. The papyrus reading is one syllable short; no convincing emendation has been made. In the papyrus the line-division is ἰόπλοκοι | κάλυμμα.

41. ἐρύκεν: Doric infin., as 88 ἴσχεν.

43. ἠϊθέων . . . ἀέκοντα: with reference to both boys and girls.

44. δαμάσειας: optative as in a conditional sentence: cf. Il. 13.343–4 μάλα κεν θρασυκάρδιος εἴη, | ὃς τότε γηθήσειεν, and see Goodwin, M.T. § 531.

47. ἀρέταιχμος: hapax, compounded unusually from two nouns, ἀρετή and αἰχμή. πολέμαιγις (see 7n.) would be another example.

50. 'Αλίου . . . γαμβρῷ: Minos' wife was Pasiphae, daughter of Helius, the Sun.

χόλωσεν: transitive: Theseus angered Minos' heart.

51. ὕφαινε: of scheming in Od. 4.678 et al.

53–4. νύμφα Φοίνισσα: i.e. daughter of Phoenix (31).

55. νῦν πρόπεμπ(ε) κτλ.: so Odysseus' prayer for a sign from Zeus was answered by a thunderclap from a cloudless sky (Od. 20.98 ff).

56. πυριέθειραν ἀστραπάν: equally picturesque is A. Ag. 306 φλογὸς πώγωνα of the beacon.

57–8. εἰ δὲ καὶ σέ: 'and if you for your part'. καί has the force of αὖ: see Denniston G.P. 305.

59. φύτευσεν: rare of the mother (cf. E. Med. 834), but τέκεν has been hard-worked (30, 35, 54). φύτευσε again at 68.

61–2. χειρὸς ἀγλαὸν . . . κόσμον: i.e. Minos' ring, which he now throws overboard. The ring is not mentioned again; this is of course a blemish, but the important point was established, that Theseus could survive under water; he did bring back other tokens (124). Jebb points out that Bacchylides is unlikely to have invented the ring motive which he treats so carelessly; it is not known elsewhere, except from Pausanias' description of Micon's mural in the Theseum (1.17.3), and it is almost certainly not used by vase painters.

63. δικών: 'throwing', participle of δικεῖν.

66. ἀναξιβρέντας: Bacchylides also created ἀναξίαλος, ἀναξίμολπος and ἀναξίππος, and may have used ἀναξιφόρμιγξ (cf. Pi. *O.* 2.1) at 4.7.

67. ἄμεμπτον: 'blameless' in the view of Zeus.

68. Μίνοϊ: the required scansion is – ∪ – unless the last syllable is *anceps*, – ∪ ⌣. Wilamowitz wrote Μινόϊ: for the final ῐ cf. Homer's Ἀχιλλῆϊ at *Il.* 1.283. At 8 Μίνωϊ gives – – ∪.

φύτευσε: cf. Pi. *P.* 4.69 τιμαὶ φύτευθεν ('were created').

70. πανδερκέα: with reference to τιμάν, 'wishing to make it conspicuous for his son'.

71. θυμάρμενον: cf. Homer's θυμαρής.

77. Κρονίδας: both Poseidon and Zeus were sons of Cronus.

84–5. πόντιον . . . ἄλσος: so at A. *Pers.* 103. ἄλσος means simply 'a sacred precinct'.

87. κέλευσε κτλ.: this instruction makes the miracle still more remarkable. Minos clearly hoped that Theseus would drown — but fate willed otherwise (89).

89. ἑτέραν . . . ὁδόν: 'a different course', but ὁδόν refers also to the voyage.

90. ἵετο: – ∪ ∪ for ∪ ∪ ∪, unless Bacchylides scanned with ῑ.

δόρυ: 'ship': see Simon. 543.10n.

σόει: imperf. of σοέω, which is found only here and in Hsch. ἐσσοημένον. For δόρῠ σόει cf. the adj. δορυσσόος and *Il.* 17.463 ὅτε σεύαιτο.

91. βορεάς: fem. adj. with ἄητα: cf. A. fr. 195 N² βορεάδας . . . πνοάς.

ἄητα: this form is not certainly attested, and one might have expected it to be masc. (=ἀήτης). If ἀήτα, the Doric form of ἀήτη, is read here as at Simon. 595.1, the final syllable of the line will be *anceps*: it is short in the corresponding lines 2, 25, 68.

94. πόντονδε: as in *Od.* 10.48. -δε only here in Bacchylides.

95. λειρίων . . . ὀμμάτων: 'tender eyes': cf. *Suda* λειρόφθαλμος· ὁ προσηνεῖς ('gentle') ἔχων τοὺς ὀφθαλμούς, *Il.* 13.830 χρόα λειριόεντα, Pi. *N.* 7.79 λείριον ἄνθεμον, 'lily'.

96. ἐπιδέγμενοι: 'expecting': cf. *Il.* 9.191 δέγμενος, 'waiting for'.

99. ἱππίου: Poseidon created the horse: so Stesich. 235 calls him κοιλωνύχων ἵππων πρύτανιν, Pi. *P.* 4.45 ἱππάρχου. See also S. *O.C.* 55, 711 ff.

100. δόμον· ἔμολεν: for -ον lengthened cf. 5.189.

105. ὧτε: Doric form for ὥστε, common in Pindar; also at Alcm. 1.41, 100.

πυρός: cf. *Il.* 19.366 λαμπέσθην ὡς εἴ τε πυρὸς σέλας of Achilles' eyes.

107. δίνηντο: probably for pluperf. ἐδεδίνηντο.

108. ὑγροῖσι ποσσίν: 'with supple feet' (cf. Pi. *P.* 1.9 ὑγρὸν νῶτον), but the adjective is quaintly used of sea-nymphs.

112. ἀΐόνα: a linen garment: see K. Latte, *Philol.* 87 (1932), 271. Hsch. has ἔλυμα· καὶ ἡ ἀιών.

116. δόλιος Ἀφροδίτα: cf. Sapph. 1.2 δολόπλοκε, Simon. 575.1 δολομήδεος Ἀφροδίτας.

117. ἄπιστον...φρενοάραις βροτοῖς: 'beyond the belief of sane men'. See 3.57n. φρενοάρας = φρενήρης.

119. φεῦ: of surprise.

121. ἔσχασεν: 'checked, interrupted' (σχάζω): cf. Pi. *P.* 10.51 κώπαν σχάσον, 'stop the oar.' Minos thought that he had seen the last of Theseus: Theseus 'checked' him in these thoughts.

122. ἀδίαντος: at Simon. 543.5; Pi. *N.* 7.73 has σθένος ἀδίαντον, 'unsweating'.

124–5. ἀγλαόθρονοι ... κοῦραι: i.e. the Nereids. Pindar uses the adj. of the Muses (*O.* 13.96) and the Danaids (*N.* 10.1).

128. ἐγγύθεν: near Theseus, who was now by the ship: the Nereids had cheered from the depths of the sea.

129. παιάνιξαν: the mention of their thanksgiving song prepares the way for the prayer to Apollo.

131. φρένα ἰανθείς: as at 5.75 εἵλετο ἰόν, Bacchylides has wrongly assumed a digamma: cf. *Il.* 19.174 φρεσὶ σῇσιν ἰανθῇς. The digamma correctly excuses hiatus two lines earlier: ἐρατᾷ (F)οπί.

132. ἐσθλῶν τύχαν: a fortune consisting of blessings: so μοῖραν ἐσθλῶν at the end of the fourth ode (4.20), πυθμένες ... ἐσθλῶν at the end of the fifth (5.198).

BACCHYLIDES 18

This poem, entitled the *Theseus* in the papyrus, is our only example of a lyric dialogue in dramatic form. Aegeus answers a questioner who is (like Aegeus) unnamed in the papyrus, but is clearly a chorus or chorus-leader. Question and answer are of equal length and in the same metrical pattern, with the result that the questions are diffuse, the answers closely-packed: symmetry was the author's main consideration. Aristotle 1449a.10 found the origin of tragedy in the early dithyramb, but we cannot assume that early dithyramb had much in common with the *Theseus*. Brevity and an abrupt ending are the striking features here as in poem 17: Bacchylides high-lights one moment in a saga, Theseus' approach to Athens, and omits earlier events, such as Theseus' discovery of Aegeus' sword and sandals, and later events, in particular Aegeus' recognition of his son by these tokens. He chooses a moment of excitement and suspense, and uses the dramatic structure to represent it with immediacy. His fondness for direct speech was noted in 17 (which of course need not be earlier). The compliment to Athens with which the work ends suggests that it was written to be performed there. Jebb notes that Theseus was said to have inaugurated the expiatory rites of the Thargelia, so that the poem would have been suitable for performance at that festival.

Metre: based on a free version of the glyconic, in which the characteristic choriamb is preceded by $\cup\!\!\!\cup \underset{\smile}{}$, so that the glyconic may begin 1 $\cup \cup - 3 \cup \cup \cup 5 \underset{\smile}{\cup\!\!\!\cup} \underset{\smile}{} 8$, 15 $- - 9 - \cup$ 11, 13 $- \underset{\smile}{}$. It is combined with bacchius, lecythion and iambic metron. Run together, the lines give 1 gl. gl. ba. 3 gl. gl. ba. 5 gl. gl. lec. 8 gl. gl. gl. 11 gl. gl. ia. 13 gl. 14 lec. 15 gl. ba. Note synizesis at 52 πορφύρεον.

2. ἁβροβίων: cf. Th. 1.6.3, where he speaks of luxurious living (τὸ ἁβροδίαιτον) as characteristic of the rich Athenians of his father's generation, giving their long tunics and grasshopper-hairclips as examples. The epithet is found first here: other new words are 3 χαλκοκώδων, 21 Λυταῖος, 23 ἀνδροκτόνος, 37 ἀλλοδαμία, 51 πυρσόχαιτος, 53 οὔλιος, 57 πρώθηβος, 59 χαλκεόκτυπος.

'Ιώνων: Athenians, as in 17.3.

3. νέον: 'just now', as at 16.

ἔκλαγε χαλκοκώδων: note alliteration, perhaps illustrative of the trumpet's harshness: κώδων is the mouth of the trumpet, as at S. *Aj.* 17 χαλκοστόμου κώδωνος.

4. ἀοιδάν: no parallel is adduced for the 'song' of such an instrument.

6. ὅρι' ἀμφιβάλλει: 'oversteps the boundaries'.

8. ff. Cf. *Od.* 9.405 ἦ μή τίς σευ μῆλα βροτῶν ἀέκοντος ἐλαύνει;

10. σεύοντ(ι): for σεύουσι since elision is required, unless it stands for σεύονται; so with fr. 4.39 βρίθοντ'.

11. ἀμύσσει: see 17.19n.

15. Elsewhere Creusa is wife of Xuthus and mother of Ion, and Aegeus' mother is Pylia, daughter of Pylas.

16–17. δολιχὰν ἀμείψας . . . 'Ισθμίαν κέλευθον: 'having completed the long journey from the Isthmus', some 45 miles. For ἀμείψας cf. A. *Pers.* 69 πορθμὸν ἀμείψας, 'having crossed the Hellespont'.

18. ἔργα: the five encounters listed here are given together with a sixth, the killing of Periphetes the Clubman at Epidaurus, in Diodorus 4.59 and Plu. *Thes.* 8–11. Plu. 9 says Theseus wanted to rival Heracles; their legends are certainly alike.

20. Sinis, known as πιτυοκάμπτης, Pine-bender, tied his victims' arms to two bent pines, which he then released (Diodorus). He operated at the Isthmus.

21. Λυταίου: Poseidon the Loosener, supposedly because he opened up the vale of Tempe to let the river Peneius through. Λυταί is a place in Thessaly, which itself could be called Λυταίη (Hsch.).

23. σῦν: the man-eating sow of Cremmyon was called Phaea. Cremmyon or Crommyon was roughly midway between Corinth and Megara.

25. Sciron was a robber who made travellers wash his feet and kicked them over the Scironian Rocks as they did so. Hdt. 8.71.2 mentions τὴν Σκιρωνίδα ὁδόν, Strabo 9.1.4 Σκιρωνίδες πέτραι. In Megarian legend he was a fine, brave man (Plu.).

26. Cercyon wrestled with passers-by and killed the losers. As

Bacchylides picturesquely puts it, Theseus put an end to his wrestling-school.

27–9. 'Procoptes has dropped Polypemon's mighty hammer': Procoptes (Cutter) is elsewhere called Procrustes (Crusher: Προκρούστης); in Bacchylides' version he seems to be son or at any rate successor to Polypemon, but Paus. 1.38.5 identifies the pair. Procrustes fitted his victims to his bed by cutting off overlapping limbs of the larger ones and hammering out the legs of the shorter. Ancient writers sited his exploits in various parts of Attica.

30. ὅπα τελεῖται: literally 'how they will end'. Fut. middle of τελεῖν is used as passive as in *Od.* 23.284.

36. ἔμπορον . . . ἀλάταν: ἔμπορος must mean 'traveller' as in the tragedians, rather than 'merchant'.

42. μήσεται: fut. indic. of μήδομαι, 'contrive'. For fut. indic. after ὄφρα cf. *Il.* 16.242–3 ὄφρα καὶ Ἕκτωρ | εἴσεται, and see Goodwin *M.T.* § 324.

44. αἰὲν ἔρδοντα: 'being always active': cf. Pi. *N.* 4.32 ῥέζοντά τι καὶ παθεῖν ἔοικεν.

45. τελεῖται: an echo of τελεῖται at the end of the previous strophe (30).

46. δύο . . . φῶτε μόνους: probably two attendants (ὀπάονες: cf. 35). Theseus was usually represented as making the journey alone, e.g. in the sculptures of the Theseum; but on a vase in Munich (Beazley, *A.R.V.²* 889. no. 169, Penthesilea Painter) he kills Sinis and Procrustes with the help of two companions.

ἁμαρτεῖν=ὁμαρτεῖν, 'to accompany': cf. Homer's ἁμαρτῇ, 'together'.

48. ἐλεφαντόκωπον: in Ovid's version of the story the ivory hilt of Theseus' sword led to his recognition by Aegeus (*Met.* 7.422–3 *cum pater in capulo gladii cognovit eburno | signa sui generis*). Cf. Alc. 350.1–2 ἐλεφαντίναν | λάβαν τῶ ξίφεος χρυσοδέταν ἔχων.

50. εὔτυκτον κυνέαν: so *Il.* 3.336 κυνέην εὔτυκτον.

53. τ(ε): unusually placed after the third word.

οὔλιον: οὔλιος elsewhere = 'destructive', here 'woolly, thick' (= οὖλος).

54. χλαμύδ(a): a cloak worn by young men (cf. 57 πρώθηβον) at
 Athens. Jebb quotes the 4th-century comic writer Antidotus
 fr. 2.1 Kock πρὶν ἐγγραφῆναι (i.e. before being enrolled in
 the deme register) καὶ λαβεῖν τὸ χλαμύδιον.

55. Λαμνίαν: cf. Ar. Lys. 299 κάστιν γε Λήμνιον τὸ πῦρ, Hsch.
 Λήμνιον βλέπειν. The island of Lemnos once had an
 active volcano, Mosychlus.

56. φοίνισσαν φλόγα: so Pi. P. 1.24 φοίνισσα . . . φλόξ of Mt.
 Etna's eruption.

57. πρώθηβον: Homer has πρωθήβης and (at Od. 1.431) a fem.
 πρωθήβη.

57. ἀρηΐων . . . ἀθυρμάτων: 'the toys, delights of Ares': cf. epigr.
 1.3 ἀθύρμασι Μουσᾶν, 9.87 Μουσ[ᾶν . . . ἄθ]υρμα, Pi. P.
 5.23 Ἀπολλώνιον ἄθυρμα.

58. μεμνᾶσθαι: 'to be intent on'.

60. φιλαγλάους: Pindar had used the adj. of the protecting
 goddess of Acragas (P. 12.1).

BACCHYLIDES FR. 4 SNELL

 This catalogue of the blessings of peace is quoted by Stobaeus
4.14 (περὶ εἰρήνης). 3 with the heading Βακχυλίδου Παιάνων;
Plutarch Numa 20.6 has lines 31–7 without the author's name.
P. Oxy. 426 is a long, narrow strip with the middle of lines 1–32: it
is too fragmentary to set 23–40 firmly in their context, but it
speaks of Apollo and an altar and τέμενος set up to him by the
seer Melampus.

 Metre: dactylo-epitrite. Note synizesis at 27 θεοῖσιν, 33 ἔγχεα,
ξίφεα.

 (On context and metre see W. S. Barrett, Hermes 82 (1954),
421–44.)

23. τε: introducing the gnomic passage. The combination δέ τε,
 also at 13.129, belongs to epic rather than lyric: cf. Sapph.
 105(c).2n.

24. μεγαλάνορα πλοῦτον: 'noble wealth'. Pi. fr. 120 Turyn has μεγαλ-
 άνορος Ἡσυχίας, 'Peace', and calls faction πενίας δότειραν. Cf.
 too O. 1.2 μεγάνορος . . . πλούτου, P. 10.18 ἀγάνορα πλοῦτον.

25. μελιγλώσσων: of Bacchylides himself at 3.97. For 'flowers of
 songs' cf. Pi. O. 9.48–9 ἄνθεα δ' ὕμνων | νεωτέρων.

27 ff. *αἴθεσθαι* . . . *μηρί(α)* and *μέλειν* are objects of *τίκτει*.

28. *εὐτρίχων*: Homer has *εὔθριξ* of horses (*Il.* 23.13, 301).

29. *γυμνασίων*: cf. Pi. fr. 135.4–5 Turyn in his picture of a blissful
      life after death: *καὶ τοὶ μὲν ἵπποισί τε γυμνασίοις τε* . . .
      τέρπονται.

30. *αὐλῶν τε καὶ κώμων*: for the *αὐλός* in revelry see Pratin. 708.8n.

31. *σιδαροδέτοις πόρπαξιν*: the *πόρπαξ* was the leather thong
      running round the inside edge of the shield, gripped by the
      soldier's left hand. It was fastened in loops by *πόρπαι*,
      'pins', whence *σιδαροδέτοις*. Cf. Ar. *Pax* 662 *ὦ γυναικῶν*
      μισοπορπακιστάτη to Peace. *σιδηρόδετος* is new, like 33
      λογχωτός.

      αἰθᾶν: from *αἰθός*, 'burnt', 'reddish-brown': cf. *αἴθων* of the
      boar's hide at 5.124.

33. *ἔγχεα* . . . *λογχωτά*: 'sharp-pointed spears'.

34. *ἀμφάκεα*: cf. *Od.* 16.80 *ξίφος ἄμφηκες*.

      δάμναται: apt, since often found in the context of war; so 36
      συλᾶται.

35. *χαλκεᾶν* . . . *σαλπίγγων*: cf. 18.3–4.

36. *μελίφρων*: so *Il.* 2.34 *μελίφρων ὕπνος*.

38. *ἀῷος*: cf. Pi. *P.* 9.23–5 *τὸν δὲ σύγκοιτον γλυκὺν* . . . *ὕπνον* . . .
      ῥέποντα πρὸς ἀῶ.

      θάλπει κέαρ: cf. fr. 20B.7 *θάλπησι θυμόν*.

39. *βρίθοντ' ἀγυιαί*: cf. 3.16 and for the Doric *-οντ(ι)* see 18.10n.

40. *παιδικοί* . . . *ὕμνοι*: either songs addressed to boys, as Pi.
      I. 2.3 *παιδείους* . . . *ὕμνους*, or songs or hymns sung by boys.

      φλέγονται: so Pi. *O.* 9.21–2 *πόλιν* | *μαλεραῖς ἐπιφλέγων ἀοιδαῖς*.

BACCHYLIDES FR. 20B SNELL

Athenaeus *epitom.* 2.10 p. 39e has lines 6–16 (*γλυκεῖ' ἀνάγκα*ͺ
. . . *κέαρ*). *P. Oxy.* 1361, which contains fragments of encomia,
provided the beginning of the poem and fragments of the following stanzas, in which Alexander is advised to enjoy himself since
prosperity is fleeting. There may have been eight stanzas in all.
Alexander, son of Amyntas, was king of Macedon from 498 to 454,
and since the subject-matter suggests that Bacchylides and
Alexander were both young, the poem may have been written
before 490. Its theme closely resembles that of an encomium

written c. 490 by Pindar for Thrasybulus of Acragas (fr. 127 Turyn): note especially 5–9 ἁνίκ' ἀνθρώπων καματώδεες οἴχονται μέριμναι | στηθέων ἔξω, πελάγει δ' ἐν πολυχρύσοιο πλούτου | πάντες ἴσᾳ νέομεν ψευδῆ πρὸς ἀκτάν· | ὃς μὲν ἀχρήμων, ἀφνεὸς τότε, τοὶ δ' αὖ πλουτέοντες | . . . ἀέξονται φρένας ἀμπελίνοις τόξοις δαμέντες. It may well be that on this occasion it is Pindar who is the debtor: in either case Bacchylides' lighter touch and gayer metre fit the subject better than Pindar's harsh splendour.

See C. M. Bowra *Pindar* 232–5.

Metre: dactylo-epitrite.

1. πάσσαλον φυλάσσων: 'clinging to your peg': cf. *Od.* 8.67 ἐκ πασσαλόφι κρέμασεν φόρμιγγα, Pi. *O.* 1.17–18 ἀπὸ φόρμιγγα πασσάλου | λάμβαν(ε). For φυλάσσων cf. *Od.* 5.208 τόδε δῶμα φυλάσσοις.

2. ἑπτάτονον: seven was the canonic number of strings from 7th century.

   κάππαυε = κατάπαυε by apocope; so 9 ἀμμειγνυμένα = ἀναμειγ.

4. χρύσεον Μουσᾶν . . . πτερόν: 'a golden wing of the Muses' — opulent language for Bacchylides: cf. Stes. 193.11 χρυσόπτερε παρθένε of the Muse. For winged song see Thgn. 237n.

5. συμποσίαισιν: the fem. form συμποσία occurs at Alc. 368.2, Pi. *P.* 4.294, but need not be correct here.

   ἐν εἰκάδεσσιν: perhaps 'in the twenties' (i.e. at the end of the month): cf. Diog. Laert. 10.18 ἑκάστου μηνὸς ταῖς εἰκάσι, Plu. *Mor.* 1089c ἀναλέγεσθαι . . . ποίας εἰκάδος ἐδείπνησαν πολυτελέστατα.

6. ἁπαλὸν . . . θυμόν: so Archil. 112.3 ἁπαλὰς φρένας.

8. αἰθύσσῃ φρένας: 'flutters the heart': cf. Sapph. 2.7 αἰθυσσομένων δὲ φύλλων.

10. ὑψοτάτω: *hapax*, superlative of ὑψοῦ: 'sends their thoughts soaring'.

11. κράδεμνα λύει: cf. *Il.* 16.100 Τροίης ἱερὰ κρήδεμνα λύωμεν. The epic reminiscence is apt. λύω usually has ῠ in Homer, but ῡ at *Il.* 23.513, *Od.* 7.74 as in Attic.

12. μοναρχήσειν: first here? Also at Pi. *P.* 4.165, fr. 44.24 Turyn (with dative Ἄργει).

14. πυροφόροι: 'wheat-bearing', of fields and plains in Homer.

PRAXILLA

Praxilla belonged to Sicyon, and according to Eusebius 'was well-known' in Ol.82.2 (451 B.C.). We know of her hymns, her dithyramb *Achilles* and her drinking-songs (παροίνια); σκόλια were attributed to her: cf. Scol. 903. Fr. 747 caused amusement, and 'sillier than Praxilla's Adonis' became proverbial. Cf. Tatian, *Or. Gr.* 33: 'a bronze statue of her was made by Lysippus, although she said nothing worth-while in her poetry.'

PRAXILLA 747

Quoted by Zenobius 4.21 in his explanation of the proverb ἠλιθιώτερος τοῦ Πραξίλλης ᾿Αδώνιδος: 'Praxilla in her hymns makes Adonis, when asked by those below what was the most beautiful thing he had left behind, give this answer: κάλλιστον μὲν κτλ.' For the form of Adonis' reply cf. Scol. 890.

Metre: dactylic hexameter.

1. Cf. Teiresias' question to Odysseus in Hades (*Od.* 11.93–4): τίπτ᾿ αὖτ᾿, ὦ δύστηνε, λιπὼν φάος ἠελίοιο | ἤλυθες;

2. Cf. *Il.* 8.555 ἄστρα φαεινὴν ἀμφὶ σελήνην, Sapph. 34.1–2. S. fr. 787.6 N² speaks of the moon's πρόσωπα.

3. σικύους: hinting at Sicyon? σικυών = cucumber-bed.

CARM. POP. 848

The Rhodian swallow-song (Mod. Gk. χελιδόνισμα), cited from the Rhodian historian Theognis by Athenaeus 8.360b. We need not believe Athenaeus (or Theognis) when he says that Cleobulus of Lindos (see Simon. 581.1) introduced the begging-song 'when a collection of money was needed'. Eustathius *Od.* 1914.45 gives an abbreviated version of the song. For modern examples see A. Passow, *Pop. Carm. Graec. Rec.* 306–8, C. A. Trypanis, *Mediaeval and Modern Greek Poetry* 107. Halloween customs provide the nearest northern analogy: the north American 'trick or treat' is the equivalent of 12 πότερ' ἀπίωμες ἢ λαβώμεθα; and 13 εἰ δὲ μή, οὐκ ἐάσομες, and the removal of gates, ploughs and wagons, if not wives, has been known in country districts of Scotland, Ireland and the U.S.A.

Metre: 1–10 are in the short Aeolic scheme ⏓⏓ : – ⏑ ⏑ – : – ('Reizianum'), 11 is an Adonean or headless Reizianum. 13–19 are slightly irregular iambic trimeters. 12, where the rhythm changes, is troch. tetr. cat. as it stands, but the iambics may be regarded as beginning after οὐκ ἀπω-. It is unlikely that 17 is other than iambic, but Page suggests anapaests: ἂν δή τι φέρῃς, μέγα δή τι φέροις. Note the use of rhyme and assonance in 4–5, 8–9, 10–11, 13 ἐάσομες . . . 16 οἴσομες, and repetitions and anaphora in 1, 2–3, 4–5, 14–15, 17, 18. There is synecphonesis at 13 μή, οὐκ.

1. Cf. Ar. *Eq.* 419 σκέψασθε, παῖδες· οὐχ ὁρᾶθ'; ὥρα νέα, χελιδών, perhaps an echo of a swallow-song, and a red-figured pelike, formerly attributed to Euphronius (Leningrad 615: Beazley *A.R.V.*² 1594. no. 48) on which a young man cries ἰδοὺ χελιδών, a man νὴ τὸν Ἡρακλέα, a boy αὑτηΐ: ἔαρ ἤδη is written to one side: see P. Kretschmer, *Die Griechischen Vaseninschriften* 66 (p. 91).

2. καλὰς ὥρας ἄγουσα: note the Doric -ᾱς. For ὥρας see Alcm. 20.1n. The Greeks had a proverb μία χελιδὼν ἔαρ οὐ ποιεῖ (Cratin. 33 Kock, Arist. *E.N.* 1098a.18).

3. ἐνιαυτούς: perhaps with something of its original sense of 'anniversary' (the moment when things are 'as they were', ἐνὶ αὐτῷ).

4. For ἐπί cf. *Il.* 2.308 δράκων ἐπὶ νῶτα δαφοινός.

6. παλάθαν: used of various kinds of cake.

πρόκυκλει: 'roll out', *hapax*; presumably the παλάθα was round.

7. ἐκ πίονος οἴκου: digamma is neglected: contrast *Od.* 9.35 πίονα οἶκον.

10. πύρνα: 'wheaten loaves', humble fare in *Od.* 15.312, 17.362.

11. λεκιθίταν: Ath. 3.114b mentions ἄρτος λεκιθίτης, 'pulse bread': cf. λέκιθος, pease-pudding. Eustathius, probably wrongly, connects the word with ᾠοῦ λέκιθος, yolk of egg.

12. ἀπίωμες: note Doric -μες for -μεν in 12–16.

13. εἰ μέν τι δώσεις: 'if you mean to give us something, well and good', but the apodosis is left to the imagination.
   οὐκ ἐάσομες: 'we shall not leave you in peace.'
14. φέρωμες: subjunctive, indistinguishable in sense from the future, as often in Homer: see Goodwin *M.T.* § 284.
17. Cf. Herodas 7.47 φέρ' εἰ φέρεις τι. For the use of δή to stress the indefinite τι see Denniston *G.P.* 212.

CARM. POP. 853

Quoted in Athenaeus 15.697b as an example of a risqué Locrian song. It is addressed by a married woman to her lover.
   Metre: trochaic and iambic. Note synecphonesis at 5 καὶ ἤδη, 6 διὰ monosyllabic.
1. τί πάσχεις: 'what is the matter with you?'
2. κεῖνον: the husband.
4. ἁμέρα καὶ ἤδη: 'why, it's daylight already!' For Bergk's καὶ δή see Denniston *G.P.* 250–1.

CARM. POP. 869

Quoted by Plutarch *sept. sav. conv.* 14, where the following words are attributed to Thales: 'when I was in Eresos I heard my hostess singing to her handmill ἄλει ... βασιλευών'; the attribution may not be accurate.
   Metre: if 1 is written ἄλει μύλ' ἄλει, the characteristic aeolic choriamb may be seen in each line. The scansion of 2 ἄλει depends on whether it is pres. or imperf.
2. For Pittacus, tyrant of Mytilene, see introd. to Alcaeus. If Thales, his contemporary, really spoke the words, ἄλει will be present tense; otherwise imperfect is likely. Ancient writers (Aelian, Diogenes Laertius, Clement of Alexandria, St. Isidore of Pelusium) took ἄλει literally, explaining the

milling as Pittacus' daily dozen. But it may be metaphorical, either with the meaning 'oppress' or with obscene
reference.

SCOLIA

We owe our collection of scolia or drinking-songs to Athenaeus
(15.693f–695f), who gives general information about them and
quotes twenty-five examples, the choice of his deipnosophists. He
mentions Alcaeus and Anacreon as notable composers of scolia,
citing Aristophanes *Banqueters* (fr. 223 Kock) ᾆσον δή μοι σκόλιόν
τι λαβὼν Ἀλκαίου κ' Ἀνακρέοντος, and adds that Praxilla was
admired for hers. Quoting Artemon of Casandreia as his authority,
he says that they might be sung in chorus by all the guests, or in
succession round the table, or by the best singers present, this last
type giving rise to their name σκόλια, 'crooked songs', from their
zig-zag course among the guests; he notes their moral or practical
content. Other authorities mention the sprig of myrtle passed from
one singer to the next, and suggest more fanciful explanations of
the name (see L.S.J. s.v.). In Ar. *Vesp.* 1216 ff Bdelycleon tests his
father's ability to take up scolia from his fellow-guests (1222 τὰ
σκόλι' ὅπως δέξει καλῶς), but when he begins οὐδεὶς πώποτ' ἀνὴρ
ἔγεντ' Ἀθήναις, which he calls Harmodius' song, his father goes
on οὐχ οὕτω γε πανοῦργος ⟨ὡς σὺ⟩ κλέπτης. This may be only a
comic interruption, or it may suggest a different sense in which
one performer took up the song from another. Whatever the
origin of the scolia, it was in Athens of the 5th and late 6th centuries that they were sung: the political allusions are to the end of
tyranny in Athens, and the songs were known as Ἀττικὰ σκόλια
(e.g. Ath. 693f). It seems that the tunes were traditional and that
new scolia were fitted to the existing musical and metrical frame-
works.

884.

Metre: the rhythm is aeolic: each line shows the characteristic
choriamb. The first two lines are in the 'phalaecian' hendeca-

syllabic metre familiar from Catullus (*passer, deliciae meae puellae*);
the 3rd line may be a resolved form of the 'polyschematist'
choriambic dimeter $--\cup-\mid-\cup\cup-$.

1. Τριτογένεια: the derivation and meaning are uncertain; if
   from a root *trit*, 'water' (cf. Τριτωνίς, a lake in Libya,
   Τρίτων, a stream in Boeotia, Τρίτων and ᾿Αμφιτρίτη, marine
   deities), we have a hint of a myth different from that in
   which she springs fully-armed from the head of Zeus.
   L.S.J. give other derivations.
   ᾿Αθηνᾶ: the contracted form of ᾿Αθηναία, adjectival in origin.
2. ὄρθου: cf. Pi. *I.* 5.48 πόλις Αἴαντος ὀρθωθεῖσα ναύταις.
3. ἀλγέων: cf. A. *Suppl.* 1043–4 κακά τ᾿ ἄλγη | πολέμους θ᾿
   αἱματόεντας.

887.

Pan cheered the 'Marathon' runner, Philippides, on his way
from Athens to Sparta; after the battle the Athenians built a
shrine for him under the Acropolis and instituted annual sacrifices
and a torch-race in his honour (Hdt. 6.105). One of Pindar's
Partheneia begins ὦ Πάν, ᾿Αρκαδίας μεδέων, | καὶ σεμνῶν ἀδύτων
φύλαξ, and ends Ματρὸς μεγάλας ὀπαδέ, σεμνᾶν Χαρίτων μέλημα
τερπνόν (fr. 110 Turyn).

Note synizesis in 1 μεδέων.

2. ὀρχηστά: cf. A. *Pers.* 448–9 ὁ φιλόχορος | Πάν, Pi. fr. 114
   Turyn.
   βρομίαις ... Νύμφαις: cf. Anacr. 357.2 for the association of
   the Nymphs and Dionysus, *h. Hom.* 19.2, Ar. *Thesm.* 977 ff
   for Pan and Nymphs.

889.

Eustathius (*Od.* 1574.16) quotes the scolion and mentions a
fable of Aesop in which Momus ('Blame') faulted Prometheus for
not making a door (πύλαι) in man's breast. Ar. *Eccl.* 938–41 has a
very funny parody: εἴθ᾿ ἐξῆν παρὰ τῇ νέᾳ καθεύδειν κτλ.

1. ὁποῖος: scanned $\cup\cup-$.
   ἦν: ἐστίν has been attracted into the imperfect by ἐξῆν: see
   Goodwin *M.T.* § 559.
4. ἀδόλῳ φρενί: 'by reason of his guileless heart'.

890.

Variously attributed to Simonides and the comic poet Epicharmus by the ancients. Plato alludes to it several times, e.g. *Leg.* 631c, *Gorg.* 451e.

Note 1 ὑγι-, ∪∪ for –, unless the iota was regarded as a consonant.

892.

Metre: 1, 3, 4 glyconic, 2 telesillean; if δέ is excised, 1 becomes telesillean.

1. For the use of δέ see Archil. 1.1n.
3. The point is revealed by Aesop's fable (211 Hausrath): when the crab kills the snake for his treachery, he says οὕτως ἔδει καὶ πρόσθεν εὐθὺν καὶ ἁπλοῦν εἶναι· οὐδὲ γὰρ ἂν ταύτην τὴν δίκην ἔτισας. 'The only straight snake is a dead snake' (Bowra *G.L.P.* 385): they stiffen out when they die.
4. σκολιὰ φρονεῖν: contrast *Il.* 12.124 ἰθὺς φρονέων.

893–6.

Four versions of the 'Harmodius' song; a fifth is implied by Ar. *Vesp.* 1225–6 ᾄδω δὲ πρῶτος 'Αρμοδίου· δέξαι δὲ σύ· | 'οὐδεὶς πώποτ' ἀνὴρ ἔγεντ' 'Αθήναις . . .', and there were doubtless others. Aristophanes mentions it also in *Ach.* 980 τὸν 'Αρμόδιον ᾄσεται (where schol. gives 894.1 as the beginning of the song): cf. *Lys.* 632. Hesychius says that it was composed by Callistratus, of whom we know nothing. For the murder of Hipparchus (514 B.C.) see Hdt. 5.55, 6.123.2, Th. 1.20.2, 6.54–9, and for the honours paid to the tyrannicides see Simon. 76D. introd.

893.

1. ἐν μύρτου κλαδί: the pair seem to have hidden their swords in myrtle-branches, which might well have been carried at a festival (the Panathenaea: cf. 895.3).
4. ἰσονόμους: ἰσονομία became one of the catchwords of the democracy; first in Hdt. 3.80.6.

894.

1. οὔ τί που τέθνηκας: 'surely you cannot be dead': οὔ τί που in questions is common in Euripides and Aristophanes, but unparalleled in a statement: see Denniston *G.P.* 492.

2. νήσοις δ' ἐν μακάρων: cf. Hes. *Op.* 170–2 καὶ τοὶ μὲν ναίουσιν ἀκηδέα θυμὸν ἔχοντες | ἐν μακάρων νήσοισι παρ' Ὠκεανὸν βαθυδίνην, | ὄλβιοι ἥρωες.

3. Various accounts were given of Achilles' after-life: in *Od.* 11.488 ff he speaks sadly of his life in Hades; but Ibycus 291 and Simonides 558 set him in the Elysian fields, where he married Medea. In Pi. *N.* 4.49–50 he lives on the island of Leuce at the mouth of the Danube, but in *O.* 2.79 he is on the islands of the blessed.

4. Athena made Diomedes immortal: cf. Pi. *N.* 10.7.

896.

1. ἔσσεται and αἶαν belong to epic.

2. Ἁρμόδιε: the *ε̄* may be explained by the urge not to alter the form of the line more than was necessary; but φίλταθ' Ἁρμόδιος κ' Ἀριστογείτων (Ilgen) would be paralleled by *Il.* 4.189 φίλος ὦ Μενέλαε.

900–1.

Dio Chrysostom *de regno* 2.63 quotes both poems as examples of prayers not fit for a king.

Metre: aeolic rhythms, the second line an expansion of the first.

900.

2. Διονύσιον ἐς χορόν: the reference may be to a dithyrambic performance: dithyrambs were sometimes sung by choirs of fifty boys.

901.

2. This line may refer to the Panathenaic procession, in which virgins of noble birth and good character (καθαρὸν θεμένη νόον) carried vessels of gold and silver.

902.

Reminiscent of Anacreon; cf. also Thgn. 313–14 ἐν μὲν μαινο-
μένοις μάλα μαίνομαι, ἐν δὲ δικαίοις | πάντων ἀνθρώπων εἰμὶ δικαιό-
τατος, and the proverbial μαινομένοις ἀναγκασθέντες συμμανῆναι.

Metre: greater Asclepiad.

903.

Cf. Ar. *Thesm.* 528–30 τὴν παροιμίαν δ᾽ ἐπαινῶ | τὴν παλαιάν·
ὑπὸ λίθῳ γὰρ | παντί που χρὴ | μὴ δάκῃ ῥήτωρ ἀθρεῖν, where the
scholiast refers to the line attributed to Praxilla, ὑπὸ παντὶ λίθῳ
σκορπίον ὦ ἑταῖρε φυλάσσεο (*P.M.G.* 750). The proverbial
'scorpion under the rock' was used also by S. fr. 34N² ἐν παντὶ γάρ
τοι σκορπίος φρουρεῖ λίθῳ.

Note synecphonesis in 1 ὦ ἑταιρ᾽.

904.

Note the change from the Doric of line 1 (in a maxim?) to
Attic in line 2; ἁ ὖς may be the Atticized ἁ σῦς (in which there is
no hiatus)

907.

Quoted also by Arist. *Ath. Pol.* 19.3, and by the *Etymologica,* the
Suda, etc. After Hipparchus' murder in 514 the Alcmaeonidae
fortified Leipsydrion on Mount Parnes in an unsuccessful attempt
to expel Hippias from Athens (Hdt. 5.62.2, Arist. l.c.). The song
must have been sung first in Alcmaeonid circles.

3. εὐπατρίδας: 'nobly-born', first here: κακοπατρίδας in Alc.,
e.g. 348.1, fem. κακόπατρις in Thgn. 193.

Appendix on Metre

THE following summary is intended as a guide only. For detailed analysis and comment see P. Maas, *Greek Metre* (tr. H. Lloyd-Jones, Oxford, 1962), A. M. Dale, *The Lyric Metres of Greek Drama*[2] (Cambridge, 1968), 'The Metrical Units of Greek Lyric Verse', *C.Q.* 44 (1950), 138–48, n.s. 1 (1951), 20–30, 119–29. D. S. Raven, *Greek Metre* (London, 1962) is a valuable introduction to the subject.

GLOSSARY OF TERMS

Anaclasis: the inversion of syllables: e.g. the ionic
dimeter ∪ ∪ − − | ∪ ∪ − − produces the anacreontic
∪ ∪ − ∪ − ∪ − − by anaclasis of the 4th and 5th
syllables.

Anceps: a syllable which may be long or short, e.g. the
first syllable of an iambic metron ⏒ − ∪ − .

Arsis: the heavy beat (down-beat) of a rhythm: e.g.
the first syllable of each foot in a dactylic hexameter is said to be in arsis.

Caesura: a break between words in the middle of a foot
or metron.

Catalectic: incomplete, abbreviated (καταλήγω, 'stop').
The catalectic form of trochaic dimeter
− ∪ − ⏒ | − ∪ − ⏒ is − ∪ − ⏒ | − ∪ − .

Clausula: a metrical unit which may form the end of a stanza or period.

Contraction: the use of a long syllable in place of two short syllables.

Correption: 'epic' correption is the shortening of a long final vowel or diphthong before a following vowel,

e.g. ἐρεύθεται ἄκρῳ ἐπ' ὕσδῳ. In 'Attic' correption a naturally short vowel remains short before

the combination of mute + liquid, e.g. κύμασι πλαζόμενος.

Epode: (1) see triadic structure; (2) a two-line stanza in which a short line follows a longer line.

Hiatus: a final vowel is in hiatus when it is left unelided before another vowel, e.g. εἵλετο ἰόν.

Metron: the basic unit of a line, e.g. – ∪ ∪ in dactyls, ∪ – ∪ – in iambics.

Resolution: the breaking of a long syllable into two short syllables.

Responsion: the metrical correspondence between strophe and antistrophe.

Strophe: a stanza. See also triadic structure.

Syncopation: the suppression of a short syllable: ∪ – – is a syncopated iambic metron (∪ – ∪ –), – ∪ – a syncopated trochaic metron (– ∪ – ∪).

Synecphonesis: the running together of a final vowel with a following vowel, e.g. μὴ ἀλλά.

Synizesis: the running together of two vowels within a word, e.g. θεός, a monosyllable.

Triadic structure: structure based on three stanzas, strophe, antistrophe, epode, strophe and antistrophe having the same metrical pattern. The resultant scheme aab may be repeated ad lib.

The following are the main classes of verse. A broken line ⋮ is used only to aid recognition of units. An unbroken line | marks the division of metra. A double line ‖ marks the caesura.

DACTYLIC

Dactylic hexameter

$$- \overline{\smile\smile} \mid - \overline{\smile\smile} \mid - \overline{\smile\smile} \mid - \overline{\smile\smile} \mid - \overline{\smile\smile} \mid - -$$

Caesura occurs either $- \overline{\smile\smile} \mid - \overline{\smile\smile} \mid - \parallel \overline{\smile\smile} \mid$ etc.

or $- \overline{\smile\smile} \mid - \overline{\smile\smile} \mid - \overline{\smile\smile} \mid - \parallel \overline{\smile\smile}$ etc.

Hemiepes

$$- \smile\smile \mid - \smile\smile \mid -$$

Adonean

$$- \smile\smile \mid - -$$

Elegiac couplet: a dactylic hexameter followed by a so-called pentameter, in fact a repeated hemiepes:

$$- \overline{\smile\smile} \mid - \overline{\smile\smile} \mid - \parallel - \smile\smile \mid - \smile\smile \mid -$$

ANAPAESTIC

The anapaestic metron has two anapaests $\smile\smile - \smile\smile -$. A long syllable may be resolved or two short syllables contracted, so that spondee ($- -$) and dactyl ($- \smile\smile$) may stand in place of anapaest ($\smile\smile -$).

Paroemiac: a catalectic anapaestic dimeter

$$\smile\smile - \smile\smile - \mid \smile\smile - -$$

IAMBIC

Iambic trimeter

$$\underline{\smile} - \smile - \mid \underline{\smile} - \smile - \mid \underline{\smile} - \smile -$$

Caesura occurs either ⏓ – ⏑ – | ⏓ ‖ – ⏑ – | etc.

   or   ⏓ – ⏑ – | ⏓ – ⏑ ‖ – | etc.

In the early iambographers it is unusual for long syllables to resolve, but Archilochus has – ⏑ ⏑ ⏑ – in the first metron of 18.4, – – ⏑ ⏑ ⏑ in 22.3. The first syllable of each metron is *anceps* and may not normally resolve.

Choliambic or *Scazon*

   ⏓ – ⏑ – | ⏓ – ⏑ – | ⏑ – – –

TROCHAIC

Trochaic tetrameter catalectic

   – ⏑ – ⏓ | – ⏑ – ⏓ ‖ – ⏑ – ⏓ | – ⏑ –

Resolution of long syllables is rare in early verse: Solon 23.3 begins ⏑ ⏑ ⏑ – ⏑.

Scazon

   – ⏑ – ⏓ | – ⏑ – ⏓ ‖ – ⏑ – ⏑ | – – –

Lecythion

   – ⏑ – ⏑ – ⏑ –

and

Ithyphallic

   – ⏑ – ⏑ – –

may be regarded as iambic or trochaic.

CRETIC

The unit is – ⏑ –. Long syllables may resolve to produce – ⏑ ⏑ ⏑ or ⏑ ⏑ ⏑ –, called *paeonic*.

Allied to cretic is *bacchius* (⏑ – –).

IONIC

Ionic dimeter

   ⏑ ⏑ – – | ⏑ ⏑ – –

Anacreontic

$$\cup \cup - \cup - \cup - -$$

(an anaclastic ionic dimeter). The name is applied also to the shorter form

$$\cup - \cup - \cup - -$$

AEOLIC

These metres, first found in Sappho and Alcaeus, contain as a nucleus the *choriamb* ($- \cup \cup -$). The choriamb may be placed at the beginning, middle or end of a line; in the two latter cases the syllables, up to five in number, which precede the choriamb are variable in quantity, and form the 'aeolic base' (e.g. $\underset{\smile}{} \underset{\smile}{}$ at the beginning of the pherecratean and glyconic). The lines vary in length from five syllables upwards. The commonest are

Adonean

$$- \cup \cup - \vdots \, -$$

Reizianum

$$\underset{\smile}{} \vdots \, - \cup \cup - \vdots \, -$$

($- \cup \cup - \vdots \, \cup -$ in scolia, e.g. 884.4, 900.1, is nameless.)

Pherecratean

$$\underset{\smile}{} \, \underset{\smile}{} \vdots \, - \cup \cup - \vdots \, -$$

Telesillean

$$\underset{\smile}{} \vdots \, - \cup \cup - \vdots \, \cup -$$

Aristophanean

$$- \cup \cup - \vdots \, \cup - -$$

($\underset{\smile}{} \vdots \, - \cup \cup - \vdots \, \cup - -$ in Sappho, *P.M.G.* 976, is sometimes called '*enoplian*'.)

Glyconic

$$\underset{\smile}{-} \underset{\smile}{-} \mid - \cup \cup - \mid \cup -$$

Choriambic dimeter

$$- \cup \cup - \mid \underset{\smile}{-} - \underset{\smile}{-}$$
$$\text{or} \quad \underset{\smile}{-} \overset{\frown}{\cup} \underset{\smile}{-} \overset{\frown}{\cup} \mid - \cup \cup -$$

Hipponactean

$$\underset{\smile}{-} \underset{\smile}{-} \mid - \cup \cup - \mid \cup - -$$

Phalaecian

$$\underset{\smile}{-} \underset{\smile}{-} \mid - \cup \cup - \mid \cup - \cup - -$$

in scolia (e.g. 884.1), Catullus' hendecasyllable.

In these lines the nucleus can be expanded (*a*) by choriambs, (*b*) by dactyls:

(*a*) choriambic expansion of the glyconic gives

Lesser Asclepiad

$$\underset{\smile}{-} \underset{\smile}{-} \mid - \cup \cup - \mid - \cup \cup - \mid \cup -$$

Greater Asclepiad

$$\underset{\smile}{-} \underset{\smile}{-} \mid - \cup \cup - \mid - \cup \cup - \mid - \cup \cup - \mid \cup -$$

(*b*) dactylic expansion of pherecratean gives

$$\underset{\smile}{-} \underset{\smile}{-} \mid - \cup \cup - \cup \cup - \mid -$$
$$\text{or} \quad \underset{\smile}{-} \underset{\smile}{-} \mid - \cup \cup - \cup \cup - \cup \cup - \mid -$$

Expanded glyconic is

$$\underset{\smile}{-} \underset{\smile}{-} \mid - \cup \cup - \cup \cup - \mid \cup -$$
$$\text{or} \quad \underset{\smile}{-} \underset{\smile}{-} \mid - \cup \cup - \cup \cup - \cup \cup - \mid \cup -,$$

sometimes called 'aeolic dactyls'.

Sapphic stanza

Three hendecasyllabic lines

$$- \cup - \underset{\smile}{-} \mid - \cup \cup - \mid \cup - -$$

followed by an Adonean.

Alcaic stanza

Two hendecasyllabic lines

$$\smile - \smile - \underline{\smile} \mid\mid - \smile\smile - \vdots \smile -$$

followed by $\quad \underline{\smile} - \smile - \underline{\smile} \vdots - \smile - -$

$$- \smile\smile - \smile\smile - \vdots \smile - -$$

DACTYLO-EPITRITE

In this metre, as in aeolic metres, both single-short and double-short occur. The units are

$$- \smile\smile - \smile\smile - \quad \text{(dactylic hemiepes)}$$

and $- \smile -$ (cretic: epitrite is the name given to $- \smile - -$). The units may be preceded, separated or followed by an *anceps* (usually long). Great variety is possible in the length and pattern of lines: a common example is

$$- \smile - \vdots \underline{\smile} \vdots - \smile\smile - \smile\smile - \vdots \underline{\smile},$$

i.e. cretic + link *anceps* + hemiepes + final *anceps*.

The notation adopted in this book is that of Maas, who represented the units as follows:

$- \smile\smile - \smile\smile -$	D
$- \smile -$	e
$- \smile\smile -$	d¹
$\smile\smile -$	d²
$- \smile - \underline{\smile} - \smile -$	E

Thus $- \smile - \underline{\smile} - \smile\smile - \smile\smile - -$ is shown as e $\underline{\smile}$ D $-$ and $- \smile - - - \smile - - - \smile -$ as E $-$ e.

Index

ἁβρός 268
ἀγαθός 386
Αἶσα 164, 199, 364
ἀλλά 140, 171, 266
ἄνθος 204, 218, 225, 370
ἁπαλός 277–8
ἄρα 212, 275
ἀρετή 173, 177–8, 247
ἁρπαλέος 173, 225
ἄτη 236
βωμός 335
δέ 140
ἐντάφιον 384
ἕτοιμος 326
Εὐνομία 243
ἡμίθεος 166–7
ἱαρός 217, 218
καθαρός 354
κῆρ 227
κόρος 245
κῶμα 267
λιβανωτός 267, 276, 335
μέλας 151

μένος 245
μέτρον 238, 248
μοῖρα 164, 191; μοῖρα . . .
   θανάτου 162, 166
Μοῦσαι 141, 215, 218,
   234–5, 254, 277, 417–18
μύρον 279
νέοι 163
οἰκέτης 384
Πιερία 277
πόλεμος 165
Πόρος 199
προεδρία 338
ῥοδοδάκτυλος 280
σατίνη 275
σίτησις 338
σοφία 238, 348
σοφίζομαι 348
τέλος 209
τις 164
Τριτογένεια 450
ὕβρις 245